Parties and Elections in America
The Electoral Process

Stephen J. Wayne
George Washington University
Consulting Editor

PARTIES AND ELECTIONS IN AMERICA
THE ELECTORAL PROCESS

Second Edition

L. SANDY MAISEL
Colby College

McGraw-Hill, Inc.

New York   St. Louis   San Francisco   Auckland   Bogotá   Caracas
Lisbon   London   Madrid   Mexico   Milan   Montreal   New Delhi   Paris
San Juan   Singapore   Sydney   Tokyo   Toronto

PARTIES AND ELECTIONS IN AMERICA
The Electoral Process

1 2 3 4 5 6 7 8 9 0 DOC DOC 9 0 9 8 7 6 5 4 3 2

ISBN 0–07–039738–4

This book was set in Plantin by Arcata Graphics/Kingsport.
The editors were Peter Labella and Fred H. Burns;
the production supervisor was Denise L. Puryear.
The cover was designed by Rafael Hernandez.
R. R. Donnelley & Sons Company was printer and binder.

Library of Congress Cataloging-in-Publication Data

Maisel, Louis Sandy, (date).
    Parties and elections in America: the electoral process / L.
Sandy Maisel.—2nd ed.
      p.   cm.
    Includes bibliographical references and index.
    ISBN 0–07–039738–4
    1. Elections—United States.   2. Electioneering—United States.
3. Political parties—United States.   I. Title.°
JK1965.M35   1993
324.973—dc20
                                        92–37941

Permissions Acknowledgments

Permission to reprint the following material is gratefully acknowledged:

Table 1.3: From *Congress and the Nation,* vol. 7, 1985–1988, and annual Congressional Quarterly editions. Used by permission of Congressional Quarterly, Inc.

Table 3.1: Reprinted by permission of the publishers from *Party Campaigning in the 1980s* by Paul S. Herrnson, Cambridge, Mass.: Harvard University Press, Copyright © 1988 by the President and Fellows of Harvard College.

Table 3.2: Used by permission of Herbert E. Alexander, Citizen Research Foundation, University of Southern California.

Table 4.2: Miller, Warren E., and the National Election Studies, *American National Election Studies Cumulative Data File, 1952–1990* (computer file). 6th release. Ann Arbor, MI: University of Michigan, Center for Political Studies (producer), 1991. Ann Arbor, MI: Inter-university Consortium for Political and Social Research (distributor), 1991.

Tables 4.3 and 4.4: Reproduced by permission of the publisher, F. E. Peacock Publishers, Inc., Itasca, Illinois. From Michael M. Gant & Norman L. Luttbeg, *American Electoral Behavior,* 1991 © copyright, page 69.

Table 4.6: Reprinted by permission of the publishers from *The Responsible Electorate* by V. O. Key, Cambridge, Mass.: The Belknap Press of Harvard University Press, Copyright © 1966 by the President and Fellows of Harvard College.

Table 4.7: Reprinted by permission of the publishers from *American National Election Studies Data Sourcebook, 1952–1978,* by Warren E. Miller and Santa A. Traugott, Cambridge, Mass.: Harvard University Press, Copyright © 1989 by the President and Fellows of Harvard College. Miller, Warren E., and National Election Studies/Center for Political Studies. *American National Election Study, 1980* (computer file). Conducted by University of Michigan, Center for Political Studies, ICPSR ed. Ann Arbor, MI: Inter-university Consortium for Political and Social Research (producer and distributor, 1982). Miller, Warren E., and the National Election Studies/Center for Political Studies. *American National Election Study, 1984* (computer file). Conducted by University of Michigan, Center for Political Studies, 2nd ICPSR ed. Ann Arbor, MI: Inter-university Consortium for Political and Social Research (producer and distributor), 1989. Miller, Warren E., and the National Election Studies. *American National Election Study, 1988: Pre- and Post-Election Survey* (computer file). Conducted by University of Michigan, Center for Political Studies, 2nd ICPSR ed. Ann Arbor, MI: Inter-university Consortium for Political and Social Research (producer and distributor), 1989.

About the Author

L. Sandy Maisel is the Charles A. Dana Professor of American Democratic Institutions at Colby College, where he has taught for more than two decades. He received his Ph.D. degree from Columbia University. Professor Maisel, an active politician as well as a scholar, ran unsuccessfully for Congress in 1978 and has consulted on many campaigns. More recently, he chaired the platform committee for the 1992 Maine State Democratic Convention and served on the platform committee for the 1992 Democratic National Convention. He is the author of *From Obscurity to Oblivion: Running in the Congressional Primary* and a large number of articles. In addition, he has edited six books including *The Parties Respond: Changes in the American Party System.* Professor Maisel also served as general editor of *Political Parties and Elections in the United States: An Encyclopedia,* a two-volume, 1200-entry reference work published in 1991.

To my students at Colby College

Contents

5   Organized Groups in the Political Process   121

6   State and Local Nominations   147

7   State and Local Elections   175

8   Presidential Nominations   215

9   Presidential Elections   256

Preface to the
Second Edition

It snowed in Maine last night. Thank goodness. It is not that I need a white Christmas. It is not that the Maine landscape is desolate without the blanket of white. What I am concerned about is political imagery. How can candidates for their parties' presidential nomination "troop through the snows of New Hampshire" if there is no snow? Now the image is fulfilled.

And this preface is written as yet another presidential campaign heats up. My last task before sending this book to the publisher is to write this preface—and just before writing this, I reread the preface to the first edition. Well, my motivation for writing this book remains the same. But now it is after twenty-one years, not fifteen, that I still feel the need to reach out to students, to bridge that same gap between political science and practical politics, to generate the excitement that those of us who love politics feel as each new campaign begins.

But this book has had the benefit of more than my own experience as a teacher. I have also had the opportunity to reflect on comments from those who used the first edition, to see how that volume worked in my own classroom, to edit an anthology for a course on parties and elections (Maisel, 1990c) and to confer with the other authors on that book on an appropriate structure, to compile an encyclopedia on parties and elections (Maisel, 1991) and to discuss topics appropriate for inclusion with a wide range of scholars in political science and closely related fields, to interact with another generation of college students (into whose ranks two of my own children have ascended), and to rethink my own political involvement. Each of these experiences has had an impact—hopefully a positive impact—on this second edition.

Let me start with my political involvement and that of my students. In 1978 I ran for Congress. That campaign was for me what the parlance of the day is now calling a "defining" moment. It ended my dream of serving in elective office—and cemented my desire to teach about politics. That campaign also led me to begin a slow withdrawal from active involvement in politics. The personal commitment was one I very much believed in, but was no longer willing to make (see Maisel, 1986, for my account of that campaign). When I wrote the first edition of this book, I was out of active politics. I did not mention my campaign in that book—and have, in fact, been criticized for that.

Situations change with time. Two changes have affected me. First, more and more citizens have become disillusioned with politics and with politicians.

Poll after poll shows that citizens do not trust politicians, do not think elected leaders are working for their best interest, would not want their children to go into politics. Those views have been reflected by my students, and I find that distressing. At the same time, students have become more and more involved in the wider community. Volunteerism is on the rise. And some students are beginning to see that involvement in politics has the potential to lead to solutions to some of the societal problems with which they are concerned. I agree with that assessment; after all, the real reason to be involved in active politics, the real reason to care about the political process, is because governmental decisions affect all of us—for good or ill. I believe I have a responsibility to help my students see that involvement in government, volunteering and working for those running for office or for those concerned with particular issues, is a way to move the country in the direction they desire. I also believe that modeling behavior is a way to do that. Thus, I am back in active politics, not as a candidate, but as a worker on a campaign and as chair of the platform committee for my party's state convention. I hope that the lessons learned from my personal involvement are reflected in this text in ways that benefit the students who read it.

The other experiences I noted above have all had more direct impact on the organization of material in this book. First, I believe more strongly than ever that discussing political parties not in the context of elections is a mistake. Surely one can do so in a theoretical way, but it is difficult to see how students will be engaged if the two topics are not melded. In the first edition, I did not have a chapter on party organization (though much of the discussion of party as organization was found in various places throughout the text). Many who used that edition found the omission an error; so too did my colleagues with whom I compiled *The Parties Respond*. In fact, though party organization per se is not inherently of interest to many students, important changes are taking place; these must be understood. Of course, if one is to discuss party as organization in a text on parties and elections, the chapter must be near the front of the book. It makes little sense to talk about how parties are organized after one talks about all that they do.

Similarly, the first edition did not have a chapter on party in government. The reason was simple. My course does not have a week devoted to party in government. I cover that material in other courses. However, many of my colleagues reach different pedagogical decisions. Furthermore, as I worked on a book of readings and on an encyclopedia, I was struck over and over by how much important work has been done on the evolving role of political parties in the governing process. So a new chapter has been added, placed after the chapters on various aspects of elections, because the parties affect the government after the electoral process has ended (for one cycle). Those two changes alter slightly, but not fundamentally, the basic framework of the book.

Chapter 1 is a conceptual introduction to the study of political parties and elections. Parties are defined, and their role in the electoral process is made clear. The issues raised in that introductory chapter go far toward structuring the rest of this book. The electoral process is the phenomenon under examination, an electoral process that is not a simple phenomenon but a multidimensional one. All those dimensions are examined in turn.

Chapter 2 recognizes that parties do play a key role in the electoral process. Modern political parties are a distinctly American invention, and yet our politicians have had an ambivalent view of parties, playing a role in their development while often bemoaning their existence. This chapter examines the development of American political parties in two ways. First, the history of parties as a history of distinct party systems is outlined. In addition, the chapter focuses on the development of the institutions and structures of political parties as organizations, a development that sometimes has, sometimes has not, run parallel to transformations in party alignment. Like every chapter (but the last), Chapter 2 ends with an assessment of how politicians view the topic under discussion, in this case the current structure and strength of party organization.

Chapter 3 then details how political parties are organized throughout the nation. The chapter makes clear that party as organization has evolved in important ways in recent years, responding to challenges to the roles that parties have traditionally played. This chapter also notes the significant role played by organizations at the county and state as well as national levels.

Chapters 4 and 5 focus on different aspects of individuals' political activities. In the first of these chapters, the emphasis will be on different levels of activity—who votes and who does not vote, who participates in political party activities, who participates in other political activities. While the numbers of participants in each category are important, Chapter 4 also probes motives and incentives of political participants and assesses the pleasures and the pains derived from political involvement.

No text on the electoral process would be complete, furthermore, without a clear and careful review of the voluminous professional literature on voting behavior. Students should understand the early community-based voting studies, the model of the classic *American Voter,* and the progression through *The Changing American Voter* and more recent studies. Students not only should be familiar with these empirical studies of voting behavior, but also should place these studies in historical and political context. What concept of party membership is implied in the National Election Studies question on party loyalty? Is there any connection between that definition and the (implied) one used by politicians as they set election strategies? Would the definitions differ if elections for the Senate, Congress, or statewide or local offices were under examination? Chapter 4 also addresses all these questions.

Political observers from Tocqueville to V. O. Key have commented that Americans congenitally tend to join groups and to act as members of these groups. Individual voters often perceive themselves and relate to the electoral process as members of groups. In addition, organized group behavior has long had an impact on American politics. This phenomenon is perhaps more important today than at any other time in our history. It could even be argued that some interest groups fit our definition of political party almost as well as the Democratic and Republican parties do, indeed better than some minor parties do. The only difference is that "they don't quack like a duck." Chapter 5 examines the behavior and influence of organized groups in American politics. The electoral activities of these groups and the extent to which they attempt to influence and succeed in influencing the voting behavior of their members are stressed.

Chapters 6, 7, 8, and 9 examine nominations and election campaigns in the United States. The first two of these chapters deal with gubernatorial, senatorial, congressional, and state and local elections; the latter two with the presidential election. Chapter 6 begins with a discussion of common views on the nominating process and then examines how reality differs from these views. The development of the direct primary as a means of securing partisan nominations, the variety of primaries that exists in various jurisdictions, and the politics of securing party nominations are all explored at some length.

Chapter 7 examines general election campaigns below the presidential level. The conventional wisdom holds that politics has changed dramatically as the age of television and computers has evolved. The argument presented in this chapter is that "new politics" is very much in evidence in some campaigns, but the "old politics," the politics of personal contact, of detailed organization, remains essential for many local politicians. In addition, the important question of whether or not general election campaigns make a difference in who is elected is explored in some detail.

The presidential election process is so complex and so important in the American system of government that it is dealt with as a separate topic. Despite the prominent attention they receive in the national media, few truly understand presidential nominations. In Chapter 8 the nominating process is explored, beginning with a review of recent changes and continuing with a review of recent nominating contests and the strategic considerations that determine how they were fought. National party conventions, the ultimate spectacle in American politics, are discussed in light of current criticism that they represent useless vestiges from a bygone era, no longer worthy of serious consideration, and in light of contrary opinions that conventions remain an important element of the electoral process.

When many Americans think of election campaigns, they focus on the general election of the president. Chapter 9 looks at how such an election is organized, at recent strategies and tactics for implementing those strategies, and at the impact of the campaigns. While the topic would seem to be a familiar one, many of the nuances of presidential campaigns are obscure except to the most practiced observer.

Throughout the chapters on nominations and elections, the importance of money in electoral politics is stressed. Campaign financing is such an important topic that an entire chapter has been devoted to exploring the current situation. Chapter 10 examines the campaign financing reforms of the 1970s and the current climate for further changes. Data are presented that summarize the costs of maintaining our democracy. In addition, the sources to which politicians turn for campaign funding are examined, with particular emphasis placed on political action committees. In this chapter, to an even greater extent than in some of the earlier ones, views of politicians are seen as going a long way toward determining how the process will function.

As noted above, the role of party in government has received considerable attention in the professional literature. In Chapter 11 this text turns to that topic. Ours is not a parliamentary system in which decisions by party members as party members directly impact on governmental policy. However, our governing institutions are structured by political parties; appointments tend to be made with due recognition given to party affiliation. In short, despite the fact that parties are organized to help candidates win election, they play a vital role in governing as well. That role is outlined, and recent changes in it are explored, in this chapter.

The concluding chapter returns to the themes raised in the introductory chapter. How well does the electoral process function? What roles do parties play? How are those roles different from the role as traditionally viewed? What institutions have replaced parties in functional terms? What are the consequences for our political system of candidate-oriented campaigns? Of increased PAC influence? Of public financing? What does this view of the electoral process imply about the link between parties as the organizing structure of an election and parties as the organizing structure of our governmental institutions? Can and should this process be reformed?

The chapters that follow are meant to instruct, to tell the reader how the process works, to explore its complexity. But these chapters are also meant to cause the reader to empathize, to understand what it feels like to be part of this process, to share the perspective of politicians and political activists, to become part of the system that affects all our lives. This text can be deemed to be a success or a failure according to whether or not the reader gains an understanding of the American electoral process in not only an analytical but also a pragmatic and emotional way.

ACKNOWLEDGMENTS

A textbook is by definition a book written for students. This book is dedicated to my students at Colby College. A local real estate firm purchases a newspaper advertisement each year in which it simply fills a page with the names of people who have been its clients. I am sorely tempted merely to fill page after page with my students' names, as my way of saying "Thank you." I will resist that temptation.

But I am grateful to generation after generation of Colby students—and to those students I have taught at the University of Melbourne, at Monash University, and at Harvard. One of the real joys of teaching is to have the opportunity to test one's ideas on the palette of relatively unpainted young minds and to learn from the ways in which the colors are reflected. For more than two decades I have tested my ideas about elections and politics on Colby students. Their insights have helped me to shape and refine those ideas; their reactions have led me to a better understanding of what works and what does not work in a teaching environment, of how complex ideas can be effectively communicated, of how concern and enthusiasm can be transmitted to those who will carry the political banners in the years ahead. In a very real sense this book is written for my students and because of my students; any success it enjoys as a teaching tool is a direct result of what I have learned from them.

Of course, some students stand out. I could go back over twenty years of rosters and name student after student who has had a direct impact on the concepts developed in this book; but I fear if I did so I would miss some people. The students with whom I have worked most closely know who they are and know how much I value the times we have spent together. In recent years Colby has developed a work-study program that allows those of us on the faculty to hire undergraduate students as research assistants, a liberal arts college equivalent of graduate assistants. My work on the first edition of this book was immensely aided by the work of my first student assistants: John Ayer, John Kramer, Becky Hart, David Scannell, and, most especially, John Beaudoin. Another generation of students has helped as I have updated the data in this edition: Gretchen Anglund, Ashley Cornell, Julie Daniele, Suzanne LaPrade, Chuck Thompson, and, most especially, Heather Hartshorn; Josh Maisel spent part of one summer massaging the last of the tables. I am most grateful to each of these friends—the next generation of teacher-scholar-activists, I hope. I also want to thank the students in my most recent class on parties and elections in America. They read drafts of these chapters and suggested important improvements.

I also want to thank my colleagues who have generously given their advice as I have worked on this text. Steve Wayne has served as political science consulting editor for McGraw-Hill as I have worked on this revision; his prodding and thoughtful comments have been most helpful. I also want to express my appreciation to my editors at McGraw-Hill—Peter Labella and his predecessor Bert Lummus, and Fred Burns, senior editing supervisor—and others who have worked on this book. Paul Herrnson, Bob Huckshorn, Mac Jewell, and Dave Rohde have all commented on the new material in this book in ways that have improved it significantly. The reviewers for McGraw-Hill—Lisa Langenbach, Lafayette College; Jan P. Vermeer, Nebraska Wesleyan University; and David Woodard, Clemson University—and those who sent comments on the first edition also have played a key role in aiding my work on this revision. While the text is clearly improved by the efforts of all these colleagues, it goes without saying that they bear none of the blame for any errors that remain.

As one finishes work on a text, one almost automatically thinks back to those who have influenced the book's development in less specific ways. I feel fortunate to be a member of two very special communities. First, I am part of the community of scholars, in this case the specific community of scholars of American politics. My work has been influenced over the years by conversations with and encouragement from literally scores of fellow political scientists. I cannot help mentioning my close friends and colleagues who have been important influences in my professional development—Dave Brady, Chuck Bullock, Joe Cooper, Linda Fowler, Chuck Jones, Ruth Jones, Warren Miller, Ron

Rapoport, and Walt Stone among others—and those who have led and contributed to three groups in which I have been active and from which I have gained a great deal: the Legislative Studies, Political Organizations and Parties, and Presidency Research Groups of the American Political Science Association. Much of the material in this book is derived from the ideas and research of the colleagues and friends who have seen the importance of sharing ideas, working together, and growing as a cooperating community of scholars. I feel fortunate to work in a profession that so clearly sees growth as a community to be a critical common goal.

Second, I am part of a uniquely American phenomenon, the community of a small liberal arts college. And what a wonderful community that is in which to live and grow. Colby College as an institution has been enormously supportive of my work. I specially want to acknowledge financial support from the college through the Social Science Grants Committee and the Committee on Research, Travel, and Sabbatical Leaves.

Throughout the years I have benefited from discussions with my colleagues Al Mavrinac, Guenter Weissberg, Chip Hauss, Roger Bowen, Pam Blake, Bev Hawk, Ken Rodman, and Guilain Denoeux. I have team-taught a large number of courses with Tony Corrado, Cal Mackenzie, and Charles Bassett. Their influence on my thinking and my writing—especially Bassett's on the quality of my writing—is inestimable; I hope they are aware of how much I appreciate their efforts, support, and friendship.

And finally, everyone who knows me knows what an important part Patricia Kick plays in the Colby community. It would be insulting merely to thank her for typing and retyping draft after draft of this manuscript. It would be insulting merely to cite her as our efficient departmental secretary. But she has processed revision after revision; she does keep our entire department on its toes. Most important, however, Patricia Kick gives of herself so that all of us can be the best we can; she cares and is concerned and for twenty years has played a most important part in the lives of all of us in the Government Department at Colby. Saying "Thanks" is hardly sufficient, but it carries special feelings, as I hope she knows.

Finally, to my family and friends who support me in all that I do—as an activist, as a teacher, as a political scientist, as a parent—thanks is never enough. Their support and love is what everything else one does is all about. I know they are all aware of how much I cherish that.

L. Sandy Maisel

Preface to the First Edition

I do not remember when I was not interested in politics. My earliest political memory is of my father's excitement when he was invited to a campaign breakfast with the President. I remember fighting with my first grade friends over our choices in the 1952 election. My enthusiasm grew as my knowledge and level of political sophistication grew. Those who knew me during my youth in Buffalo or during my college days could not have been surprised that I have become both a political scientist and a political activist. I am one of those fortunate few who can merge vocation and avocation.

For fifteen years I have taught courses about various aspects of the electoral process in America to students at Colby College. Each time I plan a new syllabus, the challenge is renewed. How do I excite a new generation of students in the subject matter that consumes my interest? How can I communicate the reasons for my excitement to a generation seemingly turned off to politics?

More specifically, how can I demonstrate the nexus between important issues of the day, news media personalities, and practical politics on one hand, and a rich body of analytical literature on the other? Political parties seem irrelevant to many students; the various theories of voting behavior and the means used to study that subject are often difficult for students to grasp; the rules of the political game seem mysterious. Undergraduates who are interested in politics acquire their interest because they (and/or their families) favor one particular candidate or another. Their arguments are often highly emotional; their factual understanding of how the political process functions is often flawed. A huge information gap needs to be bridged.

This book represents my attempt to bridge that gap. The book is about elections and political parties. In the chapters that follow, readers will learn about the electoral process in America. They will learn not only the mechanics of how the system works and how it has worked in the past, but they will also learn about the impact of the way it works, and why it has come to work in that way. The book is written from the perspective of a political scientist, but this political scientist has run for office and has been actively involved in politics for more than two decades. I have been chastened by criticism from politicians who claim that most political scientists know nothing about how politics really work. That criticism has not fallen on deaf ears. This book is about the political process, as it is analyzed by political scientists and as it is experienced by politicians.

My teaching experience has proven that that mix of perspectives is a happy one. Enthusiasm for the study of politics follows from a concern about the political world we are all experiencing. A glance at New England politics today, in the fall of 1986, demonstrates this point.

The political landscape is as rich as the fall foliage. Tip O'Neill is retiring; to many this symbolizes the end of an era of old-style politics. The Democratic nominee to replace him is Joe Kennedy, who, with his sister, a congressional candidate in Maryland, represents the newest political generation of a family that has played an important role in moving American politics into the age of television. In Maine, two independent candidates are mounting serious challenges in the gubernatorial election. These candidates have obvious implications for the two-party system. In New Hampshire and Vermont, debates over nuclear power separate political candidates.

And hanging over all of this is the World Series. Which campaign dominated the news? The campaign of the Red Sox against the Mets. And how do politicians relate to this? They go to the ball games to be seen; they tell their workers not to bother voters while the games are in progress. They understand where they fall on the pecking order of voter interest.

These are all important phenomena to understand; it is important for students of American politics to think about the passing of political generations, the appeal of charismatic candidates, the decline in party identification and the attempts to rejuvenate parties, the prominence of highly emotional issues, the difficulty politicians face in convincing voters of the importance of their messages. How we elect those who govern us is of undeniable importance to every citizen; yet many disdain the political process. The goal of this book is to inform students about the electoral process and to stimulate their interest in politics. I strive to do so by presenting the electoral process as the glorious array that those of us who study and teach about politics as a vocation and who are involved in politics as an avocation see it to be, an array of intriguing complexities, of analytical insights, of important values, of fascinating personalities. If the goal is met, in the end the readers of this book will not disdain politics, but rather they will become part of the informed and knowledgeable citizenry participating in and analyzing the political arena.

L. Sandy Maisel

Parties and Elections in America
The Electoral Process

Elections and Political Parties

On November 2, 1982, Congressman Phil Gramm (D., Tex.) won reelection to the House of Representatives. Gramm polled more than 91,000 votes, approximately 94.5 percent of those cast; the Republican party did not field a candidate, Gramm's token opposition coming from a candidate of the Libertarian party.

On January 5, 1983, after House Democrats denied him reappointment to the Budget Committee in retribution for his collusion with the Reagan White House on budgetary matters during the Ninety-Seventh Congress, Gramm resigned from Congress, vowing he would seek reelection as a Republican. Five weeks later the citizens of Texas's Sixth Congressional District reelected Phil Gramm, now a Republican, to Congress. He received more than 55 percent of the votes in the special election, even though he faced *ten* challengers. Gramm's victory was the first for a Republican in Texas's Sixth District's history. After he was "resworn in," on February 22, the House Republicans immediately appointed Gramm to the Budget Committee.

Phil Gramm's passage from Democrat to Republican and from the Ninety-Seventh Congress to the Ninety-Eighth is an instructive place to begin an examination of elections and political parties in the United States. Under the American system of government, elections are used to assure popular support and legitimacy for those who make governmental decisions. In his classic study *The Theory and Practice of Modern Government*, Herman Finer (1949) summarized this connection between democracy and elections:

> The real question . . . is not whether the government designs to take notice of popular criticisms and votes, but whether it can be voted out of office or forced by some machinery or procedures to change its policy, above all against its own will. (p. 219)

I. AN EXAMINATION OF ELECTIONS IN THE UNITED STATES

The contest for office is the machinery used by Americans to change policy, to change, often against their will, those who govern. And the American electoral process is clearly different from that in other countries. A number of aspects distinguish how we use this machinery from how other countries do so. *First, Americans are*

1

TABLE 1-1. Example of Elections Held, Selected Municipalities

Boca Raton, Florida

Odd year	
March	Municipal election
September	Initiative
Even year	
March	Presidential primary
	Municipal election
September	Federal, state, and county primaries
October	Runoff primary
November	General election for federal, state, and county offices

Waterville, Maine

Odd year	
September	Initiative
November	Municipal and state elections*
Even year	
March	Caucuses for presidential delegate selection
May	State conventions for presidential delegate selection
June	Primaries for federal, state, and county offices
November	General elections for federal, state, and county offices
	Referenda†

San Diego, California

Odd year	
September	Primary for municipal, county, and some school district elections
November	Municipal, some county, and some school district elections (initiative and referenda)
Even year	
June	Primary for presidential, some state, some municipal, some county, and some school district elections
November	Presidential, some state, some municipal, some county, and some school district elections‡
	Initiatives and referenda

Whitefish Bay, Wisconsin

Odd year	
February	Nonpartisan primary for judicial offices
	Party primaries for municipal and county offices
April	Nonpartisan judicial election
	Municipal and county elections
	Constitutional amendments
July	Approval of school budget
Even year	Nonpartisan primary for judicial offices
	Primary for municipal and county offices

expected to go to the polls more frequently and to vote for more officeholders than are citizens of any other country. Table 1-1 shows the elections in which citizens of four different cities had to vote in the eighteen months before the 1984 presidential elections.

TABLE 1–1. Example of Elections Held, Selected Municipalities (*cont.*)

Whitefish Bay, Wisconsin

April	Nonbinding Democratic and Republican primary for presidential delegates
	Nonpartisan judicial election
	Partisan municipal and county election
	Referenda on constitutional questions
April	Democratic caucuses§
July	Approval of school budget
September	Primary for federal, state, and county offices
November	General election for federal, state, and county officials

* Two elections, one week apart, were held in November.
† Referenda by state law limited to regular elections after four special referenda elections held in 1980.
‡ County and school district terms are staggered; some elections are held each year.
§ Democratic party had a nonbinding primary and later binding caucuses to send delegates to the national convention.

Source: Robert Huckshorn, Gary Jacobson, John Bibby, and John Kramer were kind enough to provide the data for this table.

Second, our elections are held at regular intervals, regardless of the flow of world events. President Bush does not have the luxury, which, say, Prime Minister John Major of England has, to call for an election at a time when his popularity is high or to postpone the election if his popularity is low. Our presidential elections are held on the first Tuesday after the first Monday in November of every fourth year. Period! No exception! For example, President Franklin D. Roosevelt won reelection twice during World War II, once on the eve of our entry into the war and once as the push to victory neared completion; the dates of American elections are never changed because of particular national crises.

Third, the regular intervals between elections for different offices are not necessarily coterminous. All the members of the House of Representatives are up for election every two years; only one-third of the Senate seats (plus special elections to fill vacancies) are contested in any one national election. The president, on the other hand, is elected for a four-year term, as are most governors. Some, however, are elected for two-year terms, and most of the four-year gubernatorial terms do not end at the same time as does the president's. The complexity is accentuated by the state legislatures and local offices. Table 1-2 summarizes the terms of office and election cycles for major offices by state

Fourth, the rules in different states and for different offices vary significantly. For example, in some states it is possible to run for more than one office in the same election. Lloyd Bentsen (D.) was reelected to the Senate from Texas on the same day in 1988 that he lost the election to be vice president of the United States under Michael Dukakis (D., Mass.).[1] In Pennsylvania, one can run for the party nomination for more than one office on the same day. At the opposite extreme in Hawaii a state officeholder must resign if he or she seeks another

[1] This "double election" was permissible only because of the precedent set when Lyndon Johnson ran for vice president under John F. Kennedy in 1960 at the same time he sought reelection to the Senate. The Texas legislature passed a special law in 1960 to permit Johnson to seek both offices.

TABLE 1-2. Terms of Office and Election Cycles

State	Governor Term—Ends	Senator Term	Representative Term
	Election Cycles		
AL	4—1/96	4	4
AK	4—12/94	4	2
AZ	4—1/95	2	2
AR	2—1/93	4	2
CA	4—1/95	4	2
CO	4—1/95	2	2
CT	4—1/95	4	2
DE	4—1/95	2	2
FL	4—1/95	2	2
GA	4—1/95	4	2
HI	4—12/94	4	2
ID	4—1/95	4	2
IL	4—1/95	4[a]	2
IN	4—1/95	4	2
IA	4—1/95	4	2
KS	4—1/95	4	2
KY	4—12/95	4[b]	2
LA	4—3/96	4[b]	4
ME	4—1/95	2	2
MD	4—1/95	4	4
MA	4—1/95	2	2
MI	4—1/95	4	2
MN	4—1/95	4	2
MS	4—1/96	4[b]	4
MO	4—1/93	4	2
MT	4—1/93	4[c]	2
NE	4—1/95	4	unicameral
NV	4—1/95	4	2
NH	2—1/93	2	2
NJ	4—1/94	4[bd]	2
NM	4—1/95	4	2
NY	4—1/95	2	2
NC	4—1/93	2	2
ND	4—1/93	4	2
OH	4—1/95	4	2
OK	4—1/95	4	2
OR	4—1/95	4	2
PA	4—1/95	2	2
RI	2—1/93	2	2
SC	4—1/95	4	2
SD	4—1/95	2	2
TN	4—1/95	4	2

office. Vacancies in some offices are filled through an automatic succession: nationally, the vice president becomes president upon the death, resignation, or declared disability of the president. Other vacancies are filled by appointment; governors appoint senators to fill vacant seats until the next general election.

TABLE 1-2. Terms of Office and Election Cycles (*cont.*)

State	Governor Term—Ends	Senator Term	Representative Term
		Election Cycles	
TX	4—1/95	4	2
UT	4—1/95	4	2
VT	2—1/93	2[b]	2
VA	4—1/94	4	2
WA	4—1/93	4	2
WV	4—1/93	4	2
WI	4—1/95	4	2
WY	4—1/95	4	2

Note: Table reflects the legislatures as of January 1, 1993, except for Kentucky, New Jersey, and Virginia; jurisdiction information as of January 1, 1992.

[a] Illinois: All senators ran for election in 1972, and all will run every ten years thereafter. Senate districts are divided into thirds. One group elects senators for terms of four years, and two years; the second group for terms of four years, two years, and four years; the third group for terms of two years, four years, and four years.
[b] Kentucky, Louisiana, Mississippi, New Jersey, Virginia: statewide elections are held in odd-numbered years.
[c] Montana, Louisiana, Mississippi, New Jersey, Virginia: statewide elections will be for four-year terms.
New Jersey: Senate terms beginning in January of the second year following the U.S. decennial census are for two years only.

Source: *Congress and the Nation.*

Still other vacancies are filled by special elections, as, for example, in the House of Representatives.

Despite these wide variations in American elections, some constant factors predominate. This text examines partisan elections in the United States. While political parties structure these contests for office, this text is not meant to be a detailed examination of political parties per se. Rather, we will be studying American *elections,* in all their variety and complexity. This study, however, does start with the explicit assumption that political parties play a major role in structuring most contests for office, but it will constantly reassess that assumption. It also assumes that the electoral contest does provide a mechanism for expressing popular support—or disapproval—and for granting legitimacy, as Finer posited; it will also reassess that assumption.

Remember Phil Gramm. In the 1982 election he was virtually unopposed. How, then, could political parties structure that contest for office? What possible interpretation could be given to Gramm's mandate to continue or change his role in the budget process in the House? Or in any of the other political decisions he made?

In 1982, fifty-six incumbent members of the House of Representatives faced no major party opposition in the November general election; by 1990, this number rose to eighty-three.[2] What kind of popular control was expressed in these "contests" for office?

[2] These numbers includes the eight Louisiana members of Congress who faced reelection in that state's unique nonpartisan primary held in September.

Reprinted courtesy of David Horsey and the Seattle *Post-Intelligencer.*

After the Democrats punished Gramm for his disloyalty during the Ninety-Seventh Congress, he merely quit that party and ran successfully in a special election as a Republican, raising $600,000 for a five-week-long campaign, using the same organization of "Democrats" he had used in the past. What does Gramm's experience say about the role of party in elections themselves? While party switching is not commonplace, four members of the House did indeed "cross the aisle" during the Ninety-Seventh Congress, two current senators—Thurmond (R., S.C.) and Riegle (D., Mich.)—were originally elected as members of the other party, and even President Reagan was himself originally not only a Democrat but an active member of the quintessentially liberal Americans for Democratic Action. Thus, ample evidence exists for the proposition that the most basic assumptions about the role of party and even the role of elections themselves require careful study.

While our goal is to examine the process through which partisan elections are contested in the United States,[3] and while certain basic assumptions about the role of political parties have been called into question, it would be naïve to ignore the role that parties historically have played in American elections and that they continue to play.

Despite appearances, this statement does not contradict the argument made earlier. Partisan elections are, by definition, elections contested by nomi-

---

[3] Most of the prominent elections in the United States are partisan elections, that is, contests between nominees of political parties. However, when one considers all the contests for offices—including local contests for such positions as member of the city council, selectman, and less prominent positions, e.g., trustee of the local library—nonpartisan elections outnumber those in which parties are involved. This text will deal only with partisan elections, though elections for a wide variety of offices will be considered.

nees of political parties. For much of our nation's history, the parties dominated the contest for office. Citizens typically supported candidates of one party or the other with great loyalty. In order to understand elections in the contemporary contexts, it is essential to understand this background.

Thus, this text will look at the history and development of the role played by parties in structuring American elections. It will look at the current role of parties in the contest for office, exploring ways in which other groups may now be playing the role that parties once played and, if so, with what impact.

Nevertheless, the clear theme of this book is that the contest for office is the most crucial element to be examined. Political parties play an important role in that process, but that role is only one aspect of the phenomenon under study.

II. THE ROLE OF ELECTIONS IN DEMOCRATIC THEORY

Scholars are fond of pointing out that modern political parties are an American invention even though they are never mentioned in the Constitution. In *Federalist X* (1787) Madison warns of the mischief of faction, reasoning that many groups must be allowed to flourish so that no one group becomes too powerful. Such was the concept of "party" at the time the Constitution was drafted.

The Founding Fathers, moreover, defined democracy in a somewhat limited way: the masses were not to be trusted with political power. Thus, while the House of Representatives was to be popularly elected—certainly a necessity, given the history of our Revolution—the Senate was indirectly elected by state legislatures, and the president was even more indirectly elected through the cumbersome mechanism of the Electoral College.

What general principles guided these rules for contesting offices? For direct representation in the House of Representatives, two were primary—small units and frequent elections. The Founding Fathers would have been appalled by twentieth-century recommendations to extend congressional terms to four years. They envisioned an intimate connection between a congressman and his constituents. He would be one of them, one who was just like his neighbors and thus best suited to serve them. He would do his duty and return home to be replaced by another. If he became too headstrong in support of his own alien ideas, frequent elections would guarantee that the violation of trust would not go on too long.

The other elected officials of the federal government were chosen through a filtering process. Only the "best of the best" were supposed to make the grade and be chosen to represent the interest of the people. Only those who really understood what was best for the masses would be chosen to serve in the Senate. Further, the elaborate mechanism for choosing the president can be understood best if one realizes that all those at the Constitutional Convention assumed that the towering Washington would be the first president. The mechanism was designed to pick the "right" leader, i.e., someone like Washington.

However, this system of elected representatives—or any other system yet devised—faces an inherent conflict. On one hand, elected representatives should accurately represent the views of the people who choose them. On the other hand, they must have enough freedom to act on what they determine to be in the best interest of the people. One need not long debate the merits of the two theories of representation implied by these statements to see that a conflict exists. The American solution to this problem has been to give representatives a good deal of freedom to act, but to hold elections frequently in order to assure that these same representatives be accountable for their actions. One of the basic questions raised in this text is, how does that system work.

Democratic theory also requires that the citizenry have the ability to convert its views on the issues of the day—certainly the pressing, salient issues—into public policy. Frequent elections do not serve their intended purpose if the electorate is not given a choice, nor if, after that choice is expressed, public policy does not reflect that preference.

The role that political parties have traditionally played in this context has been to structure the contest for office so that elections can perform their role most effectively. One of the key questions facing the American polity concerns how effectively that role is played (Brady, Bullock, & Maisel, 1988; Brady & Stewart, 1986). Pomper (1972) and Fishel (1977), among others, have demonstrated that the Republican and Democratic parties differ from each other on major policy questions.

But the links among differing party platforms, elections, and subsequent public policies are not so clear in the American system as they are in parliamentary democracies. V. O. Key, Jr. (1964), highlighted the important distinctions among party in the electorate, party organization, and party in government. While this text deals mainly with the first two of these, the context cannot be ignored. We elect congressmen in individual districts and stress their electoral independence, but we cannot forget that party unity scores among Republicans (as computed by *Congressional Quarterly*) have topped 70 percent for all but one session of Congress in the last decade, and similar scores even among the frequently divided Democrats have exceeded the same levels during the Reagan administration.

Similarly, the extent to which the Reagan administration imposed partisan tests on its appointees is without recent precedent (Mackenzie, 1991). Reagan loyalists claimed that the 1980 and 1984 presidential elections called for a profound change in the direction our government was taking, a change to be implemented by Republicans, not Democrats. The Reagan "revolution" has not been so complete as its perpetrators would have hoped, but it is not without significance. For our purposes, that significance involves the ways in which and the extent to which partisan elections affect subsequent governmental actions.

The function for political parties of serving as the linkage mechanism between the electorate and governing officials was not envisioned by the Founding Fathers and, in fact, evolved quite slowly (see Chapter 2). Historically, it has not been a role that parties have played to universal acclaim, nor is it a role that has remained constant in the face of a changing political environment. Before proceeding further and in order to understand this role, we must more carefully define what is meant by "political party" in the American political context.

III. DEFINITIONS OF "POLITICAL PARTY" AND "PARTY SYSTEMS"

The French political scientist Maurice Duverger, in a classic study entitled *Political Parties,* drew an important sociological distinction between "cadre" parties and "mass membership" parties (1951, pp. 62 ff). Duverger starts with a definition of party member in the European setting, one that most Americans would find restrictive. For Duverger "the concept 'member' of a party coincides with that of adherent. . . . The latter is distinguished from the 'supporter,' who declares his agreement with the doctrines of the party and sometimes lends it his support but who remains outside its organization and the community it forms" (1951, p. 62). Cadre parties, then, have relatively few *members;* mass membership parties tend to have a large number of dues-paying supporters.

However, Duverger's distinction is broader than that. *Cadre parties,* into which category Duverger places American as well as most moderate and conservative European parties, *are organizations whose primary goal is to obtain electoral success.* They are subordinate to leaders in government and are basically inactive between elections. Not only are there not many members, but the staffs of these organizations are also small.

Mass membership parties, at the opposite extreme, *are ideological and educational organizations.* Their goal is to convince the working class of the desirability of their point of view and thus to change the system radically. To succeed, they must maintain a large, permanent, continuously active professional organization. When mass membership parties gain control over the government, the party organization maintains an influence unimagined in the case of cadre parties. Socialist parties in Europe meet most of Duverger's criteria for mass membership parties.

Duverger's definition is really a distinction among types of political parties. He never does arrive at a concise definition of what constitutes a political party, though he identifies a number of important considerations—membership, level of activity, type of activity, type of leadership, relationship to the government. On the other hand, several scholars studying American parties have attempted to define exactly what constitutes a political party:

We may define "political party" generally as the articulate organization of society's active political agents, those who are concerned with the control of governmental power and who compete for popular support with another group or groups holding divergent views. (Sigmund Neumann, 1956, p. 396)

A political party is a team of men [*sic*] seeking to control the governing apparatus by gaining office in a duly constituted election. (Anthony Downs, 1957, p. 25)

Pat definitions may simplify discussion but they do not necessarily promote understanding. A search for the fundamental nature of party is complicated by the fact that "party" is a work of many meanings. . . . The nature of parties must be sought through an appreciation of their role in the process of governance. (V. O. Key, Jr., 1964, p. 200)

Any group, however loosely organized, seeking to elect governmental office-holders under a given label. (Leon D. Epstein, 1967, p. 9)

The major American political parties exist, as do other political organizations, to organize large numbers of individuals behind attempts to influence the selection of public officials and the decisions these officials subsequently make in office. . . . The differences between parties and other political organizations are often slender. (Frank J. Sorauf, 1980, p. 17)

A Party is any political group that presents at elections, and is capable of placing through elections, candidates for public office. (Giovanni Sartori, 1976, p. 64)

A number of themes emerge from this group of definitions. *First, as Sartori claims, a minimal definition of contesting for office emerges. Second, as Neumann, Downs, and Epstein state, some type of organization is assumed. Third, as Key and Sorauf imply, "party" is a multidimensional term.* If one defines "party" too narrowly, one excludes organizations that ought to be included. If one defines "party" too broadly, one takes in organizations that would be excluded by general consensus. The student almost has to fall back on the classic "if it looks like a duck, swims like a duck, flies like a duck, and quacks like a duck. . . ." Thus, the Republican party is a party; the AFL-CIO, despite the fact that it does many of the same things, is not.

For most purposes this definition is sufficient, but for others, often very important ones, it is not. For instance, the Federal Election Commission (FEC) had to rule on whether John Anderson's "party" in the 1980 presidential election constituted a party in any meaningful sense. The FEC ruled that it did, thus making Anderson eligible for federal campaign financing in 1984.[4] What definition is appropriate in that context?

For the purposes of this text, we will adopt a fairly restrictive definition of political parties. *Political parties are organizations, however loosely organized, that have, for a period of time, run candidates for public office, that have earned the support of a significant following in the electorate for those candidates because of their allegiance to the organization, and that must be taken into account by other similar competing organizations.* Did Anderson's party meet this definition? It did not, because it did not meet the test of time.

This definition also implies acceptance of the concept of party *systems,* at least in its simplified form.[5] In democracies, if parties are to contest for public office, they must take into account others who are also competing for office. William N. Chambers (1975) defines a party system as:

a pattern of interaction in which two or more political parties compete for office or power in government and for the support of the electorate, and must therefore

---

[4] Anderson later decided he would not run in 1984, preferring to concentrate on building the organizational base of his "party."

[5] Party systems are described, classified, and criticized in many scholars' works, for example, Chambers and Burnham (1975, chap. 1), Sartori (1976), and Sundquist (1983).

United States Senator Warren Rudman (R., N.H., 1981–1993) was one of many legislators who did not seek reelection in 1992, citing frustration with accomplishing legislative goals because of divided government. (Jon Pierre Lasseigne /AP/ Wide World Photos)

take one another into account in their behavior in government and in election contests. (p. 6)

Party systems are characterized on two different axes. First, they are distinguished by the number of parties competing. Second, they are distinguished by the intensity of competition. The American national party system is generally classified as a competitive two-party system. The Democratic and Republican parties compete with each other for national offices; each has a chance of winning. Minor parties may be on the ballot from time to time, but they neither persist nor have a chance of winning. Our national system has been a competitive two-party system since the election of 1828, though the parties have changed during that period.[6]

Table 1-3 shows a number of different measures of national electoral competition in this century. The pattern is clear; Democrats compete with Republicans for control of our national government. Other parties may contest for some offices (more than thirty did so in the 1990 congressional election), but real competition is restricted to two parties. It is in this sense of structuring the contest for national power that the role of parties in the electoral process must be evaluated.

[6] Silbey (1991) applies a very different definition of party system, emphasizing the centrality of parties to the electoral process. See Chapter 2.

For all that, it is very misleading to look only at national politics; American politics is perhaps most notably characterized by its decentralization. An observer cannot stop after saying that the American party system is a competitive two-party system. At the very least, one must look at the fifty separate state party systems. Presidential politics may be very close at the national level, but Alabama has not had a Republican governor since David P. Lewis was elected in 1872; Kansas has had two Republican senators in every Congress since 1939. Thus the domination of a single party within certain states is veiled by a claim that we have a competitive two-party system nationally.

Austin Ranney, perhaps the dean of this generation's scholars of American politics, has attempted to categorize American state party systems according to level of competition. Ranney has constructed an index of state party competitiveness consisting of four criteria: popular vote for Democratic candidates for governor; percentage of the seats in the state senate held by Democrats; percentage of the seats in the state house of representatives held by Democrats; and terms for governor, Senate, and House in which the Democrats held control (Ranney in Jacob & Vines, 1971, pp. 85–86). State rankings, using the Ranney index of competitiveness, are presented in Table 1-4. Two time periods are shown.

TABLE 1-3. National Electoral Competition

A. Results of Presidential Elections, 1900–1988*

Year	Percentage of Popular Vote	
	Democratic, %	Republican, %
1900	45.5	51.7
1904	37.6	56.4
1908	43.0	51.6
1912	41.8	23.2
1916	49.2	46.1
1920	34.2	60.3
1924	28.8	54.1
1928	40.8	58.2
1932	57.4	39.6
1936	60.8	36.5
1940	54.7	44.8
1944	53.4	45.9
1948	49.5	45.1
1952	44.4	55.1
1956	42.0	57.4
1960	49.8	49.5
1964	61.0	38.5
1968	42.7	43.2
1972	37.5	60.7
1976	50.1	48.0
1980	41.0	50.7
1984	40.6	58.8
1988	45.6	53.4

TABLE 1-3. National Electoral Competition (*cont.*)

B. Number of Seats Occupied by Party in the Senate†

Year	Congress	Democratic	Republican	Other
1899–1901	56th	26	53	8
1901–1903	57th	31	55	—
1903–1905	58th	33	57	—
1905–1907	59th	33	57	—
1907–1909	60th	31	61	—
1909–1911	61st	32	61	—
1911–1913	62d	41	51	—
1913–1915	63d	51	44	1
1915–1917	64th	56	40	—
1917–1919	65th	53	42	—
1919–1921	66th	47	49	—
1921–1923	67th	37	59	2
1923–1925	68th	43	51	1
1925–1927	69th	39	56	—
1927–1929	70th	46	49	1
1929–1931	71st	39	56	1
1931–1933	72d	47	48	1
1933–1935	73d	60	35	2
1935–1937	74th	69	25	4
1937–1939	75th	76	16	4
1939–1941	76th	69	23	2
1941–1943	77th	66	28	1
1943–1945	78th	58	37	1
1945–1947	79th	56	38	—
1947–1949	80th	45	15	—
1949–1951	81st	54	42	—
1951–1953	82d	49	47	1
1953–1955	83d	47	48	1
1955–1957	84th	48	47	—
1957–1959	85th	49	47	—
1959–1961	86th	64	34	—
1961–1963	87th	65	35	—
1963–1965	88th	67	33	—
1965–1967	89th	68	32	—
1967–1969	90th	64	36	—
1969–1971	91st	57	43	—
1971–1973	92d	54	44	2
1973–1975	93d	56	42	2
1975–1977	94th	60	37	2
1977–1979	95th	61	38	1
1979–1981	96th	58	41	1
1981–1983	97th	46	53	1
1983–1985	98th	45	55	—
1985–1987	99th	47	53	—
1987–1989	100th	55	45	—
1989–1991	101st	55	45	—
1991–1993	102d	56	44	—

TABLE 1-3. National Electoral Competition (*cont.*)

C. Number of Seats Occupied by Party in the House of Representatives†

Year	Congress	Democratic	Republican	Other
1899–1901	56th	163	185	9
1901–1903	57th	151	197	9
1903–1905	58th	178	208	—
1905–1907	59th	136	250	—
1907–1909	60th	164	222	—
1909–1911	61st	172	219	—
1911–1913	62d	228	161	1
1913–1915	63d	291	127	17
1915–1917	64th	230	196	9
1917–1919	65th	216	210	6
1919–1921	66th	190	240	3
1921–1923	67th	131	301	1
1923–1925	68th	205	225	5
1925–1927	69th	183	247	4
1927–1929	70th	195	237	3
1929–1931	71st	167	267	1
1931–1933	72d	220	214	1
1933–1935	73d	310	117	5
1935–1937	74th	319	103	10
1937–1939	75th	331	89	13
1939–1941	76th	261	164	4
1941–1943	77th	268	162	5
1943–1945	78th	218	208	4
1945–1947	79th	242	190	2
1947–1949	80th	188	245	1
1949–1951	81st	263	171	1
1951–1953	82d	234	199	1
1953–1955	83d	211	221	1
1955–1957	84th	232	203	—
1957–1959	85th	233	200	—
1959–1961	86th	283	153	—
1961–1963	87th	263	174	—
1963–1965	88th	258	177	—
1965–1967	89th	295	140	—
1967–1969	90th	247	187	—
1969–1971	91st	243	192	1
1971–1973	92d	254	180	—
1973–1975	93d	239	192	—
1975–1977	94th	291	144	—
1977–1979	95th	292	143	—
1979–1981	96th	273	159	—
1981–1983	97th	243	192	—
1983–1985	98th	267	168	—
1985–1987	99th	252	182	—
1987–1989	100th	258	177	—
1989–1991	101st	259	174	—
1991–1993	102d	267	167	1

* Data from *Congress and the Nation,* vol. VII, 1985–1988.
† Data from *Congress and the Nation,* vol. VII, 1985–1988, and annual *Congressional Quarterly* editions.

A number of interpretations should be noted. First, his criteria have allowed Ranney to divide the states into five possible categories, ranging from one-party Democratic, through competitive two-party systems, to one-party Republican. However, the one-party Republican cell was empty for the entire period covered; the modified one-party Republican grouping had shrunk to one state by the second period. Second, Ranney's categories, or any similar groupings, are time-bound. One need only look at Republican gains in the south or Democratic gains in states like Maine and New Hampshire to see that movement is not only possible, but likely (see also Sundquist, 1983, Chapters 11 and 12). Third, and perhaps most important, Ranney's rankings depend upon a number of research decisions that he made. He is concentrating only on state offices. His judgment in so choosing cannot be questioned, but one must recognize that in restricting himself in this way, he did not take into account two sets of variables: (1) the distorting idiosyncrasies of "unusual" presidential candidacies such as Goldwater's (R., Ariz., 1953–1965, 1969–1987) in 1964, Wallace's (D., Ala.) in 1968, and McGovern's (D., S.D., 1957–1961, 1963–1981) in 1972 and (2) the sometimes wide variation within state party systems. To demonstrate how different research decisions lead to different interpretations—and also to show changes over time—Table 1-4 also includes two other means of characterizing state systems, one relying on governorships and state congressional delegations (Jewell & Olson, 1988, pp. 26–27) and one relying on party

New York State Governor Mario Cuomo (left) and New York City Mayor David Dinkins (right), here shown with State Budget Director Dall Forsythe, frequently work together to make the best case for New York City's needs. (Richard Drew /AP/ Wide World Photos)

identification as provided by respondents to surveys (G. Wright, Erikson, & McIver, 1985, pp. 476–477)

If the concept of party system is a valid one, the most crucial research decision involves defining the boundaries of that system. Pat answers will not suffice. Surely we can look at our national system and draw conclusions about par-

TABLE 1-4. Measures of State Party Competition

1956–1970*	1974–1980†	1965–1988‡	Party Identification§
	One-Party Democratic		
Louisiana	Alabama	Mississippi	Louisiana
Alabama	Georgia	Georgia	Georgia
Mississippi	Louisiana	Alabama	Arkansas
South Carolina	Mississippi	Louisiana	Alabama
Texas	Arkansas	Arkansas	Mississippi
Georgia	North Carolina		Maryland
Arkansas	Maryland		Kentucky
	Rhode Island		Oklahoma
			Texas
			North Carolina
	Modified Democratic		
North Carolina	South Carolina	Hawaii	West Virginia
Virginia	West Virginia	Maryland	New Mexico
Florida	Texas	South Carolina	Massachusetts
Tennessee	Massachusetts	Texas	Minnesota
Maryland	Kentucky	Kentucky	South Carolina
Oklahoma	Oklahoma	Florida	Tennessee
Missouri	Nevada	New Mexico	Rhode Island
Kentucky	Hawaii	North Carolina	Florida
West Virginia	Florida	Oklahoma	Nevada
New Mexico	Connecticut	Rhode Island	Missouri
	New Jersey		Wyoming
	Virginia		
	New Mexico		
	California		
	Oregon		
	Missouri		
	Minnesota		
	Tennessee		
	Wisconsin		
	Rhode Island		
	Two-Party		
Alaska	Montana	Massachusetts	Virginia
California	Michigan	West Virginia	Washington
Nebraska	Ohio	Missouri	California
Washington	Washington	Tennessee	Oregon
Minnesota	Alaska	Virginia	New Jersey
Nevada	Pennsylvania	Minnesota	Wisconsin

ties and elections at that level. But even casual observers of politics will see that concentration on the *national* scene masks important differences at the *state* level that must be understood if one is to understand how American politics really works.

Similarly, viewing state party systems is useful—and the data are easily obtained—but this perception also obscures important distinctions for the purpose of simplicity. For example, what purpose is served by trying to understand Illi-

TABLE 1-4. Measures of State Party Competition (*cont.*)

1956–1970*	1974–1980†	1965–1988‡	Party Identification§
		Two-Party	
Connecticut	Delaware	California	Delaware
Delaware	New York	Nevada	South Dakota
Arizona	Illinois	Washington	New York
Montana	Nebraska	Michigan	Arizona
Oregon	Maine	Oregon	Connecticut
New Jersey	Kansas	Connecticut	Illinois
Pennsylvania	Utah	New York	Pennsylvania
Colorado	Iowa	Arizona	Ohio
Michigan	Arizona	Utah	Montana
Utah	Colorado	Alaska	Michigan
Indiana	Indiana	Wisconsin	Indiana
Illinois	New Hampshire	New Jersey	Maine
Wisconsin	Idaho	Montana	Colorado
Idaho	Wyoming	Maine	North Dakota
Iowa	Vermont	Delaware	Vermont
Ohio	South Dakota	Pennsylvania	Iowa
New York		Ohio	Kansas
Maine		Iowa	New
HampshireWyoming		Illinois	
		North Dakota	
		Indiana	
		Idaho	
		Kansas	
		Colorado	
		Vermont	
		Wyoming	
		Modified Republican	
North Dakota	North Dakota	South Dakota	Nebraska
Kansas		New Hampshire	Utah
New Hampshire			Idaho
South Dakota			
Vermont			

Note: There are no one-party Republican states in this period.
* Measure taken from Ranney in Jacob & Vines, 1971, p. 87.
† Measure taken from Bibby, Cotter, Gibson, & Huckshorn, 1983, p. 66.
‡ Measure taken from Jewell & Olson, 1988, pp. 26–27.
§ Measure taken from G. Wright, Erikson, & McIver, 1985, pp. 469–489.

nois as a competitive two-party state without noting the differences among Cook County, the Chicago suburbs, and downstate Illinois? The same can be said of northern and southern California; New York City, the immediate suburbs, and upstate New York: and less well-known variation in states as widely separated as Massachusetts, Virginia, and Texas. In evaluating the role that party plays in structuring the contest for office, the careful student must draw these distinctions appropriately. What is the *dimension* of the party system that is under examination?

IV. POLITICIANS VIEW THE PARTY SYSTEM

This text is not intended as a workbook. However, if one homework exercise were to be assigned, it would be to have each reader call his or her state representative and ask, "What is the dimension of the party system that I should examine in order to understand the role that party plays in structuring your own electoral contest?" Merely posing the question should be sufficient to demonstrate how ludicrous it is. While it is important to understand "the role of party," "structuring the contest for office," and "party systems" in order to analyze elections in America, these abstract terms are not in the working vocabulary of most politicians. Throughout this text, constant efforts will be made to step back from the analytical world of the student of politics to the practical world of the politician.

In that regard, it is important to understand that politicians only rarely look beyond the next election. Elections serve as their link to the people in a very concrete way. If the people vote for them, they are in office; if the people vote for someone else, they are out. The questions that politicians ask relate to what they must do in order to assure their continuation in office or advancement to the next office that they decide to seek.

Important questions immediately arise. Are elections in America an effective way for the citizenry to control politicians? That is, do politicians lose because of the dissatisfaction of their constituents? This question can be answered empirically by looking at incumbent losses and the reasons for them, at the knowledge that constituents have of their officeholders' position, and at major swings in the fortunes of the two parties (see Jacobson, 1980; Maisel & Cooper, 1981; Stokes & Miller, 1962; Sundquist, 1983).

However, equally important is how politicians think the electoral process works. Do politicians change their positions because they fear electoral reprisals? The late Senator Henry Jackson (D., Wash., 1952–1983), sometimes referred to as the senator from Boeing—an aircraft manufacturer located in Washington state—early in his Senate career explained the apparent contradiction between his "liberal" views on social and economic policies and his "conservative" views of defense matters. Resolving a "contradiction" in the 1960s that has become an accepted pattern in the 1980s, Jackson contended, "I have to be a senator before I can be a statesman." His winning percentages in four reelection campaigns for the Senate were 72 percent, 82 percent, 72 percent, and 69 percent; consequently, his fear of electoral reprisal might have been slightly exaggerated. But it was real nonetheless.

Anyone who has worked closely with an elected officeholder facing another election knows that nearly all such officeholders consider public opinion to be very important.[7] Politicians panic if their margin of victory goes down from one election to the next; they fret over the effects on their popularity of votes on controversial, salient issues. Thus, regardless of the often proved fact that few incumbents are thrown out by constituents because of their stands on public policy issues, elections do work as a means of public control because politicians act as if they *might* be thrown out by the voters if perceived voter opinion is not heeded. In this case, a politician's perception of reality is more important than reality itself.

Similarly, just as it is important to understand how politicians view elections, it is important to know how they view party. In this case, the answer is very simple. It all depends.

Politicians may not understand the abstract notions of party system and electoral environment, but they certainly do understand what the party—whether it is defined as the label or the formal organization—means for their election or reelection chances. In all but a very few cases, office seekers need a major-party nomination in order to get on the ballot and stand any chance for success. However, that is perhaps the only generalization that one can make.[8]

Beyond a means of access to the ballot and perhaps some legitimacy in the eyes of the voter, major-party designation means different things to different politicians. The key variables are the office being sought and the strength of the party, in terms of both organizational resources and voter identification, in the particular district.

Thus, as a candidate for mayor in Philadelphia in 1983, W. Wilson Goode realized that beating former Mayor Frank Rizzo in the Democratic primary was tantamount to election. On the other hand, in many other cities, candidates know that their nomination is no guarantee of election. Furthermore, the help that the candidates can expect from party organization varies widely.

Similarly, campaigns for state legislature vary widely from area to area. In Florida in the 1990 elections for representative to the state house of representatives, Democratic candidates ran unopposed by Republican opponents in 37 of 120 races. Republican candidates faced no major-party opposition in 20 races. In Maine organized parties rarely have enough strength to help state legislative candidates significantly; however, in states such as Minnesota—or in some areas in other states, such as Cook County in Illinois—party organizations practically run the campaign for candidates.

Congressional elections engender another set of problems. Congressional

---

[7] Richard Fenno (1978, chap. 1) writes at length of how politicians judge public opinion and about the ways in which they reach their judgments. Jacobson (1980, p. 108) suggests that this process might well be a natural act, even for seemingly safe incumbents.

[8] And even the necessity of party nomination does not apply in some states for some offices. While Nebraska's state legislature is the only such body with nonpartisan elections, Louisiana has a "nonpartisan" primary for Congress and statewide offices. See Chapter 5.

districts only occasionally share boundaries with other political units. Most American political organizations are based on the county as the organizing unit. In some states congressional districts span more than one county—some of those counties may have strong parties, some weak; some may be heavily Republican, some competitive, some heavily Democratic—while in other states or areas within states, several congressional districts may be found in the same county. Only rarely is a U.S. congressman a key figure as a party leader; Henry Waxman (D., Calif.) distinguishes himself as one example. Similarly, party leaders do not play key roles in many congressional campaigns. But one cannot overgeneralize; certainly members of Congress as different as Henry Nowak (D., N.Y.), Mel Levine (D., Calif.), John Myers (R., Ind.), and Barbara Kennelly (D., Conn.) would never deny the importance that party organization has played in their electoral careers.

Statewide elections differ widely as well. Party nomination is often decisive in strong one-party or modified one-party states. However, some of the strongest one-party states have the weakest party organizations. Thus, candidates must form their own organization and draw on their own resources in order to capture first the party nomination and subsequently the office they seek. On the other hand, party nomination guarantees considerable support in some of the more competitive states.

Finally, in the battle for the White House, only the two major-party candidates really have a chance to win. Merely winning the nomination guarantees them access to the ballot in nearly every state[9] and financial support through federal funding. However, access to additional resources for the party nominee varies significantly from state to state. Further, whether party organization is of any help to a candidate before the nominating convention varies with incumbency and intraparty competition.

What role do politicians see party playing in the elections? Again, it all depends. The biggest mistake a political analyst can make in writing about elections is to overgeneralize. We must distinguish election from election by constituency and by geography. Campaigns for local office are, for example, different from those for congressional or statewide offices. And no other election compares to a race for the presidency.

Those who are tremendously successful at one level often find that they fail miserably at another. Consider the experiences of Democrat Wilbur Mills (Ark., 1939–1977), the once-powerful chairman of the House Ways and Means Committee, whose presidential campaign in 1972 was all but ignored by the voters; of Republican (but former Democrat) John Connally, a former governor of Texas and secretary of the treasury, who spent more money to win fewer delegates to a nominating convention than anyone would have thought possible; or

---

[9] Some state party organizations have on occasion been so opposed to the national candidate that they have denied him a place on the ballot. This happened throughout the south to Harry Truman in 1948 and in two states to John Kennedy in 1960. State party organizations placed the names of Strom Thurmond (1948) and Harry Byrd (1960) on the ballot instead of those of the national standard-bearers. On the other hand, the problems of ballot access for even these nominees pales in comparison to those faced by "independent" candidates like George Wallace in 1968 or John Anderson and Barry Commoner in 1980.

of former Republican Senator Howard Baker of Tennessee, who felt that a leadership position in the Senate would aid a bid for the Republican presidential nomination. Baker discovered that his duties in Washington left him too little time to campaign and that the voters were not in the least interested in the important role he played in senatorial debates, only in whether he cared enough to trudge through the snows of New Hampshire in that state's media-dominated primary election. Demonstrating the lesson he learned, Baker declined to seek reelection to the Senate in 1984 in order to run for the presidency in 1988, a race he eventually passed up when he was asked to serve as White House Chief of Staff under Ronald Reagan.

The list of congressmen seeking to move to the Senate or of state legislators seeking to move to the House and failing repeatedly would fill volumes. Likewise, no modern mayor of the City of New York has ever successfully sought higher office.

In much the same way, campaigns in the east are different from those in the midwest, and each of these is different from campaigns in the south or the far west. Significant variations exist among geographic areas within these regions. The history of a particular area—particularly its political history—must always be taken into account. Perhaps the single most salient feature of the American political system is its decentralized nature. Unfortunately for the social scientist, much more is lost in accumulating what should be kept separate than is gained by trying to generalize about a series of diverse experiences.

For a political analyst to state at the outset of a text that generalizations about the electoral process might prove imprecise seems blasphemous, but the key point is that practicing politicians do not base their judgments on such academic generalizations. They base judgments on instincts, often faulty instincts, about individual situations in particular circumstances. One might argue that politicians are foolish to do so, but that does not change the reality. If we are to examine the electoral process and to be mindful of the views of politicians, we cannot forget that politicians and political scientists too often seem to be operating in different worlds.

2

The History of American Political Parties

Modern political parties are a distinctly American invention. They did not emerge fully formed; rather, they evolved slowly, the product of experimentation and innovation by the leaders of the nation's new form of government, at the end of the eighteenth and beginning of the nineteenth centuries. And what was the identity of these leaders who concocted this new form of political activity?

The Federalist party was shaped during the administration of George Washington, largely by his secretary of the treasury, Alexander Hamilton. This same Alexander Hamilton is most often credited with drafting Washington's Farewell Address, the theme of which was to warn of the dangers of party.

> In contemplating the causes which may disturb our Union, it occurs as a matter of serious concern, that any ground should have been furnished for characterizing party by *geographical discriminations*. . . . To the efficacy and permanency of your Union, a Government of the whole is indispensable. . . . Let me now take a more comprehensive view, and warn you in the most solemn manner against the baneful effects of the spirit of party, generally. (Sparks, 1840, pp. 221–224)

The opposition party was organized both by James Madison and by Thomas Jefferson, who served as secretary of state in Washington's first administration. Madison, in *Federalist X*, wrote in some detail of the evils of citizens forming factions which by their very nature are "adverse to the rights of other citizens, and to the permanent and aggregate interest of the community." Madison pressured Jefferson into forming a political opposition; Jefferson himself was so wary of splitting the nation that he stayed in the Washington cabinet until 1793. In 1796, Jefferson had to be persuaded to oppose John Adams, despite his significant policy disagreements with Washington's Federalist successor.

Why did these early political leaders, virtually all of whom took pride in their stands against the evil of party, play such critical roles in shaping modern political parties? Certainly part of the answer is found in the notion that the "parties" against which the founders railed were not the same as the "parties" we know today. Parties in the 1990s are descendants, but distant descendants in important ways.

This chapter deals with the history of American political parties. For many decades parties played a central role in the electoral process in America. Despite the fact that their role has been diminished in recent years, their history cannot be ignored. Thus, this historical analysis is important background for what follows.

The first section of this chapter traces the transition from "faction" to "party," from the evil that the early leaders reviled to the uniquely American institution that they invented. Subsequent sections describe how this institution has evolved over nearly two hundred years, how individual parties have come and gone, how the role that the parties have played in the American system has changed as the country has changed.

I.   FROM FACTION TO PARTY

Giovanni Sartori (1976, pp. 3–4) discusses the transition from faction to party in a detailed introduction to his study of party systems. *He concludes that "party" came into use as a word less derogatory than "faction."* According to Voltaire, "The term *party* is not in itself loathsome; the term *faction* always is" (Sartori, 1976, p. 3).

"Faction" comes from the Latin *facere,* meaning "to act," and was used by conservative Latin writers to refer to political groups bent on acting in a harmful fashion. "Party" also comes from the Latin, *partire,* "to divide"; however, the term has taken on another connotation, "to share or partake." Thus semantically "party" seems less a negative term than "faction" (Sartori, 1976, p. 4).

The discussion of "party" by political philosophers dates back to the English democratic conservative, Lord Bolingbroke, in 1732. Bolingbroke and those who wrote after him in the eighteenth century had difficulty distinguishing party from faction, or party in a negative sense from party in an acceptable sense. Bolingbroke concluded, for instance, "Governing by party . . . must always end in government of a faction. . . . Party is a political evil, and faction is the worst of all parties" (Bolingbroke, 1976, p. 401; Sartori, 1976, pp. 6, 30).

David Hume, another British political philosopher of the eighteenth century, was not so antiparty as Bolingbroke, though on factions he was very hard. "Factions subvert government, render laws impotent, and beget the fiercest animosities among men of the same nation" (Hume, 1976, p. 58; Sartori, 1976, pp. 7, 31). Hume concluded that parties, as coalitions, formed naturally in free governments; he accepted them, even if he did not favor them.

The British statesman Edmund Burke learned from Hume and Bolingbroke, but chose a different direction. In 1770 he defined party as "a body of men united, for promoting by their joint endeavors the national interest, upon some particular principle in which they are all agreed" (1976, pp. 425–426). Note that by now the divisive nature of party has disappeared; parties advance the national interest. They are *for* the common good, not for subversion of it. In essence, Burke proposed that parties play a role in doing the work of governing within an established set of rules for governing. Burke's definition of party was unique largely because he was describing a political entity that could in fact exist, but that did not exist until that time (Sartori, 1976, p. 10).

Background information like this would be totally useless if one were seeking to explain the behavior of mid- and late-twentieth-century politicians. Which of the modern presidents—Eisenhower, Kennedy, Johnson, Nixon, Ford, Carter, Reagan, or Bush—has read and followed philosophical debates in Europe? Which of today's politicians deal in theoretical abstractions about political science? Forms of government? Economic theory? Would any contemporary politician be considered among the leading minds of the late twentieth century?

A comparison of the writing and thinking of today's politicians with those of two centuries ago is not edifying. President Kennedy's oft-quoted toast to the group of Nobel laureates he had asked to dinner—"I think this is the most extraordinary collection of talent, of human knowledge, that has ever been gathered together at the White House—with the possible exception of when Thomas Jefferson dined alone" (Adler, 1964, p. 73)—holds more truth than many of us would like to admit. By contrast, the nation's founders, our early politicians, were an extraordinary group of political intellectuals and intellectual politicians. Their education and their activism merged.

During their younger years—and it must be remembered that these leaders were relatively young men at the time of the nation's founding—these men read and thought about revolution, about rights, and about justice. Jefferson's Declaration of Independence marks the end of this phase. Next they fought the Revolutionary War together and won their cherished rights.

The period under the Articles of Confederation can be viewed as one of experimenting with forms of government and noting that their experiment failed. The Constitutional Convention took note of this failure and sought to correct the major flaws that had been revealed. The resulting mixed form of government stands as testimony to the continuing influence of European experience and of European thinkers—of Montesquieu, Hobbes, Locke, and their contemporaries.

Knowledge of these philosophers and their views contributed to the skepticism of the founders about factions, the only types of parties they knew. This skepticism was equally strong among the leaders of the French Revolution. Factions and parties divided the citizenry, formed on the basis of economic self-interest, were opposed to the common good. They were to be prevented, or failing that, their influence was to be controlled. Thus, Washington, Hamilton, Jefferson, and Madison all followed Bolingbroke and Hume in denouncing parties.

But these American politicians were also practical men (see Roche, 1961). For example, the Constitution was written because the Articles of Confederation did not work. And Hamilton was a democrat only so long as the popular opinion coincided with his own; when it did not, he sided with the elite. None of these men remained consistent in their views throughout their careers. How could they be expected to? Too much was changing; they had a new country to run.

II.   THE FIRST AMERICAN PARTIES

In the early years under the new Constitution, most political leaders did reverse their opinions of parties (see Beeman, 1991). While they were loathe to endorse the concept of political parties—because the concept they endorsed had yet to be devised—*they did perceive the need to organize those who shared their views in order to succeed with this new form of government they had established.* In their efforts to make our democracy work, they invented the political institution that suited their needs. But this gestation had difficulty coming to term; the birth was dangerous.

One commonly held view about the founding of American political parties is that the first parties grew out of the fight over the ratification of the Constitution. While surely that fight did divide the new nation, once Washington's government took office, nearly all those involved worked for its success. As Washington said in addressing the First Congress, "The fight over the Constitution is over."

But other battles were to be fought, even among those who had previously sided together to gain ratification. The first session of the First Congress went smoothly as the mechanics of governing were worked out. By the time that Alexander Hamilton presented his economic program to the second session of that Congress, however, President Washington's "honeymoon" period had ended.

A.   Funding and Assumption

The keystone of Hamilton's program, which Washington adopted, was funding of the federal debt and assumption of the various state debts by the federal gov-

Hamilton (left), Madison (center), and Jefferson (right), despite their protestations against parties, were among the organizers of the first true political parties in the United States. (Left and center, Library of Congress; right, Thomas Jefferson Memorial Foundation)

ernment. Hamilton felt that the strength of the new government would depend on its ability to demonstrate economic stability. Thus he favored full funding of the entire federal debt and the assumption of all the state debts by the national government.

Others disagreed. On the question of funding, Madison and his followers felt that only notes held by original lenders, the true patriots, should be fully paid off. Those notes held by speculators should only be repaid in part so that individuals did not profit from the war effort.

How one stood on the question of assumption of the state debts came down to which states stood to gain and which states to lose, coterminous with the political and theoretical question of how one stood on the necessity of expansion of the central government.

These two issues—funding and assumption—led to new lines of division. The fight over the Constitution pitted large states against small states. Economic issues presented to Congress in 1790 likewise divided the nation on sectional lines. Broadly speaking, the north was for Hamilton's funding plan; the south opposed it. Similarly, the north was for assumption, but the southern states opposed it. According to political historian Joseph Charles (1956):

> There were two votes against Assumption from New Hampshire but none from the other New England States. There were three against it from New York, none against it from New Jersey, and four against it from Pennsylvania. Thus from the Northern states there were nine votes against the measure, while there were twenty-four in favor of it. In the South . . . a total of ten [were] for the bill, while eighteen were against it, but we should remember that the four votes from Maryland and Virginia had to be arranged. (p. 23)

B. Continuing New Divisions

Certainly parties in the sense of permanent entities with well-developed organizational bases had not formed, but funding and assumption marked the start of enduring new divisions. The other major issues of Hamilton's economic program—the charter of the Bank of the United States and the imposition of an excise tax—crystallized and invigorated public opinion and hardened the lines that had been drawn over funding and assumption.

Leaders in Washington's administration were uncertain about how to deal with these political differences. The overriding factor for most was success of the new government. A close second was personal loyalty to Washington, who, it is said, reigned more than he ruled. The first president gave a considerable amount of autonomy to his cabinet secretaries, intervening only when they disagreed. Hamilton aggressively took the initiative and gained Washington's support for his program of economic growth. Adams, who personally disliked Hamilton and who also opposed some of his programs (feeling, for instance, that banks helped only the moneyed class), went along for the good of the nation. Jefferson also felt that his hands were tied; despite his strong objection to Hamilton's program, he remained in the cabinet until 1793, demonstrating his intense loyalty to Washington.

These divisions carried over into Congress, reaching new heights with the debate over ratification of the Jay Treaty with Great Britain. Hamilton, the Anglophile, led the Federalist party in support of the treaty that Ambassador Jay had consummated, a treaty that those who would become the Jeffersonian Republicans denounced as a complete concession to the British. While the Senate ratified the treaty before the opposition had time to focus its efforts, the battle carried over into the House's consideration of appropriations to implement Jay's economic compromise with Great Britain. This battle marked the first—and perhaps only—time in our history in which the issue dividing our political parties involved foreign policy. Those politicians, headed by Madison and Jefferson, who also opposed the administration realized that they had to organize their supporters if their vision of a new American society was to be fulfilled.

In his own way each of the earlier political leaders contributed to the development of political parties. Alexander Hamilton developed an unpopular program, but he linked it to George Washington, who was too popular to oppose. John Adams stuck with that program out of loyalty to Washington, but he provided a target for the opposition. James Madison voiced the early opposition in Congress and corresponded with others who shared his views, but he felt he was too young to lead the opposition. Finally, Thomas Jefferson, overcoming his sense of loyalty to Washington and fear of dividing the nation, assumed the leadership of the opposition, presenting an alternative vision of how American society should evolve.

C.   Organizing to Gain Supporters

But how could this alternative be established? The target was the policy of the administration. Jefferson hoped that Washington and his associates would see that their policies were unpopular and change; had they done so, no parties would have been necessary. In any event, because the policies did not change, it was necessary to change the officials who implemented them. Who knew enough about these policies and cared enough to take action? Only those involved closely with the national government, for the government was still small and remote from the people. Information could not be disseminated easily to voters. Thus, it was largely the legislative leaders who met together, planned strategy, and sought and decided upon candidates.

How were these leaders to act? They had to discuss the matters among themselves, form groups of like-minded individuals, and then try to affect the next election by taking the word back to their local constituents. Who were their local constituents? Their friends, those who had served with them in the Revolutionary War, the local politicians. These leaders, in Camden, New Jersey, or Portsmouth, New Hampshire, or Savannah, Georgia, had to take action in turn to elect a president and a Congress responsive to the people's wishes. But suffrage was limited; presidents and senators were not popularly elected; progress had to be slow.

From the perspective of the late twentieth century, this process all seems simple enough. But one must recall the times. The "loyal opposition" were not professional politicians; Jefferson was perfectly happy, even eager, to return to Monticello when he left Washington's cabinet in 1793. He did not need to spend his life solving these problems. But he and his cohort were also concerned men, and so they fought on.

D.   The Elections of 1796 and 1800

Two elections were critically important for our nation's development. In 1796 George Washington stepped down, declining to seek a third term, thus establishing the important two-term precedent, violated only once in our history and now written into the Constitution. Washington's action provided for orderly succession in a way virtually unknown until that time.

In 1796 John Adams defeated Thomas Jefferson. While partisan ties were strong enough to carry the day for Adams, the votes for vice president were widely scattered. Thus Jefferson finished second and, by virtue of the electoral system in place at that time, became vice president. Jefferson agreed to serve under Adams, who thus accepted the legitimacy of his political opposition.

In 1800 the Federalists chose President Adams to seek reelection against the Republican's choice, Vice President Jefferson. By this time, partisan allegiance was much more firmly established. Jefferson and his running mate, Aaron Burr of New York, each received seventy-three electoral votes. Adams and his vice presidential nominee, Charles Cotesworth Pinckney of South Carolina, received sixty-five and sixty-four votes, respectively. Because Jefferson's copartisans each cast their two electoral votes for both of the party's candidates, the election ended in a tie and went to the House of Representatives, to the Federalist-controlled House. Rumors of possible Federalist action to prevent Jefferson's election were rife. Federalist Hamilton devised a strategy to secure concessions from Jefferson; Adams met with Jefferson for the same purpose. The House meanwhile cast thirty-five inconclusive ballots. Finally, after several desperate Federalist caucuses, Jefferson was elected (see Chambers, 1963, pp. 162–169, for a discussion of this infighting).

The new governmental system had thus demonstrated remarkable stability; the House had ratified as the new president the man the nation had elected, despite the fact that he epitomized the political opposition. The peaceful transfer of power from Adams to Jefferson marked a most critical step in legitimating our new system of government and the role of opposition parties within that government.

The election of 1800 marked the high point of partisan conflict during these early years. The Federalist party soon became largely a New England sectional party. The Republicans dominated the political scene for twenty-four years without serious opposition during the administrations of Jefferson, Madison, and Monroe. Recall William N. Chambers's (1975) definition of a competitive party system:

> A pattern of interaction in which two or more political parties compete for office or power in government and for the support of the electorate, and must therefore

take one another into account in their behavior in government and in election contests. (p. 6)

With the advent of the "era of good feeling," with the virtual collapse of the Federalist party, the first American party system collapsed.

E. Contributions of the First Party System

However, many significant advances in building our nation's political system can be traced to this period. *The most important contribution of the first party system was the provision of an orderly means of settling political disputes and legitimating the victory of the winner.* The election of 1800 was critically important in this regard.

Second, modern political parties, distinctly different from any known before, were invented during this period. The American parties became an important part of the government; they were not antigovernment. Parties were the mechanism through which it became possible legitimately to oppose the policies of the government and the leaders of the government without seeming to be opposed to the form of government itself. They were, in fact, the kind of parties that Burke had hypothesized as possible some thirty years earlier.

Third, the leaders of these new parties, or at least of the Republican party, in order to be successful became extraordinarily sensitive to the will of the people in this broadening democracy. They realized that new situations required new responses, that competing demands had to be accommodated, that the American polity was changing, and that they had to respond specifically to the changing social situation.

Fourth, parties as political institutions developed as enduring organizations during this period. The first party system grew from the center out, the parties at first being elite associations without grass-roots support. The Republican party began with an opposition to administration policy; then legislators realized that they had to find a means to induce the election of like-minded colleagues if their policy preferences were to be adopted. *Voilà,* a functioning political party. (See Cunningham, 1957; for other interpretations of this period on the history of American political parties, see Binkley, 1963.)

The congressional caucus as a means of nominating candidates was unique to this early party system. It suited politicians and their needs particularly well. In addition these leaders developed means of gaining support for their candidates, through letters of correspondence, drawing on friendships and alliances formed during the colonial and Revolutionary years.

Fifth, the two parties in this period also developed clearly distinguishable national ideologies. As early as 1792, a noticeably partisan James Madison wrote of these differences in the Philadelphia *National Gazette.*

> One of the divisions consists of those, who from particular interest, from natural temper, or from the habits of life, are more partial to the opulent than to the other classes of society; and having debauched themselves into a persuasion that mankind are incapable of governing themselves, it follows with them, of course,

that government can be carried on only by the pageantry of rank, the influence of money and emoluments, and the terror of military force. Men of those sentiments must naturally wish to point the measures of government less to the interest of the many than of a few. . . .

The other division consists of those believing in the doctrine that mankind are capable of governing themselves, and hating hereditary power as an insult to the reason and an outrage to the rights of man, are naturally offended at any public measure that does not appeal to the understanding and to the general interest of the community, or that is not strictly conformable to the principles, and conducive to the preservation of republican government. (Cunningham, 1965, p. 11)

Not only were the ideologies clear, but politicians were already beginning to bring the American art form of rhetorical overstatement into the public eye.

The development of parties in this early period went further. The Republicans began to develop a party structure, based on the congressional caucus, and to recruit candidates for all offices. State legislators had to be recruited to elect senators; congressional candidates were also needed, in addition to presidential candidates. In order to secure the election of these candidates, the parties had to develop popular followings. And to attract a popular following, they had to enlist party workers, adherents who would carry their cause to the voters. The first quarter of the nineteenth century was not a period when the franchise was extended, but, among other priorities, the parties had to convince eligible voters that participation was worthwhile. *In short, American politics was born at this time. During this relatively short period was laid the groundwork on which subsequent politicians were to build.*

F. The Collapse of the First Party System

The Republicans learned the lessons of cohesive politics in this early period. The first system collapsed because the Federalists never really learned those lessons; they split internally over matters of policy and personality. More than that, the Federalists never realized that their policy preferences were too conservative and appealed to too few people to be successful electorally. Never able to develop the national following that the Republicans enjoyed, they quickly became politically irrelevant.

Why did this happen? Why did a ruling party's leaders allow their organization to collapse so completely, so quickly? While such a collapse may seem incredible from today's perspective, we must remember that parties were weak and fragile in the early years of the nineteenth century. Partisan loyalties were not well established; political leaders themselves shifted frequently. Even in Jefferson's administration, few legislators identified themselves according to party. James Young's renowned study of early American party politics (1966) demonstrates that boardinghouse ties were as strong as party, that President Jefferson's personal appeals through carefully planned dinners were necessary to gain supporters of his legislation. These coalitions were built from the center out, not from the grass roots into the political arena. Consequently, when the Federalists adopted unpopular policies, they did not respond to popular protest and quickly lost support. No stable organization saved them from their decline.

Finally, the patrician politicians of the Federalist party had few incentives to save their party. They viewed themselves as political amateurs, happy to return to their prosperous farms and businesses once their service was over. The first "professional" politicians did emerge in this era—lawyers like Aaron Burr and the first clerk of the House, John Beckley—but these men were thought to be morally inferior to such "true" leaders as Washington, Adams, and Hamilton.

Parties thrive on tension and conflict; they cannot grow if they are electorally irrelevant. Thus, the Federalists faded, and the Republicans had no competition by the 1820s. The first competitive party system ended, but competition was soon to be restored.

III.   THE SECOND PARTY SYSTEM

A.   The Election of 1824 and Its Aftermath

Today's political analysts complain about the length of presidential campaigns, but long campaigns are not a strictly modern phenomenon. Campaigning for the 1824 presidential election began shortly after Monroe's reelection in 1820. John C. Calhoun, the secretary of war, declared himself a candidate in 1821. Within the next two years the names of Secretary of State John Quincy Adams, Secretary of the Treasury William H. Crawford, Speaker of the House Henry Clay, and the hero of the battle of New Orleans, General Andrew Jackson, had all been put forward by their supporters.

Crawford might well have been the front-runner, but he suffered a paralyzing stroke in the fall of 1823 and had to stop campaigning. Calhoun withdrew when he was promised the vice presidential nomination by both Adams and Jackson. In the election itself, Jackson led both the popular vote (in the eighteen states in which electors were chosen by popular vote) and the electoral vote, but he lacked the majority of the electoral vote needed to gain election. Once again, as was the case in 1800, the election was thrown to the House of Representatives, where each state's delegation cast one vote.

The House had to choose among the top three finishers—Jackson with ninety-nine electoral votes, Adams with eighty-four, and Crawford with forty-one. Clay, whose power came from the House, had been eliminated by finishing fourth with thirty-seven electoral votes, but his allies in the House guaranteed him influence. After careful consideration, Clay threw his support behind Adams, who was then chosen. When the new president subsequently made Clay his secretary of state, cries of "corrupt bargain" were heard throughout the land. No clear evidence of such a trade-off exists, but the "coincidence" of events permanently scarred Clay's reputation. The results also angered Jackson, who felt he had been deprived of what was rightly his.

John Quincy Adams (left) and Henry Clay (center) were accused of entering into a "corrupt bargain" that denied the 1824 presidential election victory of the popular and electoral vote leader Andrew Jackson (right). (Left, The Museum of Fine Arts, Boston, bequest of Charles Francis Adams; center, Brady Collection, National Archives; right, The Metropolitan Museum of Art, Harris Brisbane Dick Fund)

The election of 1824 created a violent split in the Jeffersonian Republican party between the backers of Adams (the National Republicans) and those of Jackson (the Democratic Republicans). Jackson's men organized furiously, and the personal competition increased national interest in politics. By 1828 all but two of the twenty-four states selected their electors by popular vote. The popular vote in 1828 more than tripled that of 1824, and Andrew Jackson had his revenge. He defeated King Caucus (selection by legislators) and elite rule with a populist "revolution." More importantly, Jackson's election marked the beginning of a series of maneuvers that were to solidify the shape of American politics from that date onward.

B. Electoral Phases in the Second Party Period

The so-called second party period can be broken down into different eras. *The first phase, of critical importance for the future shape of American politics, was a period of intense grass-roots organization by Jackson's supporters.* It culminated in Jackson's victory in 1828. *The second phase, corresponding roughly to Jackson's presidency, was a time during which both parties worked diligently to mobilize the voters.* As the Jacksonian Democrats continued to build support, a new opposition party, the Whigs, was formed to oppose Jackson. The national convention as a means of nominating presidential candidates destroyed the power of Congress over this important part of the process. King Caucus was dead for good. Finally, new sectional voting patterns began to emerge.

By the election of 1836, competition between the Democrats and the Whigs was intense, and this level of competition lasted into the 1850s. The Democrats originally had been a coalition of southern agrarians and egalitarian New York City residents, but during this period their adherents seemed to live everywhere in the nation. For as long as possible they managed skillfully to skirt the slavery issue in favor of other, less divisive domestic issues. Democrats were nationalistic, insular, antielitist.

It is less easy to characterize the Whigs. While the traditional view is that they represented the more prosperous classes or that the split echoed ethnic heritage, these easy answers do not explain why New Hampshire was heavily Democratic and Vermont was heavily Whig, or why adjacent areas in New York State often differed in partisan allegiance. The simple truth is that the Whigs united those who opposed Jackson. Old Hickory had honed the spoils system to a fine point, rewarding legions of friends who helped him politically. Those who lost jobs, or who sought and did not get jobs, became his enemies and organized as the political opposition.

C.   Innovations of the Second Party Period

The second party system was a period of true innovation in terms of party mechanisms and processes. As mentioned earlier, national conventions replaced the legislative caucus as the means of doing party business. *But perhaps the key innovation of this period was the development of an elaborate, complex, and decentralized party organization.* Parties began to organize followers and workers at the local, grass-roots level.[1]

Why did they organize at this level? Because, unlike the first party system in which policy differences were critical, *the electoral aspects of party were critical in this second party system.* And the local level is where the voters are. Parties established autonomous local units, again decentralized, to see to the business of elections. National conventions drew on these local units, again emphasizing citizen participation. By the 1830s, politics involved true two-party competition in every region, in fact in every state except perhaps South Carolina.

Politicians sought votes as best they could. One means was to make politics fun for the people. Mid-nineteenth-century politicians raised the practice of their profession to an art. Political rhetoric incited the people; parades stoked their emotions; military heroes sought their allegiance; catchy slogans simplified their views. "Tippecanoe and Tyler Too" had a lot less to do with governing than had the earlier political debate over the Jay Treaty, but it was a lot easier for the average voter to relate to. Politics emerged as the true national pastime.

The changing attitude toward politics was accompanied by equally significant changes in the law, changes that encouraged the spread of popular participation. Presidential electors came to be chosen by popular vote, with a whole slate of electors running at large in each state. The Constitution leaves the method of choosing electors to the states (Article II, Section 1). State politicians soon realized that their state's strength would be maximized if the winner received all the electoral votes, not just a share. Thus, the "winner-take-all" system, still in

---

[1] The best description of the history of party organization, per se, in America is found in Mayhew (1986).

IN MEMORIAM—OUR CIVIL SERVICE AS IT WAS.

North Wind Picture Archives

place in every state except for Maine and Nebraska today, was born in order to magnify political advantage, not to serve some higher principle.

On the other hand, the laws in many states were rewritten so as to mandate the election of congressmen by district, rather than at large. Because the presidency is a singular office, states wanted to increase their influence on the presidential selection process. However, because each state numbered its congressmen in proportion to its size and because each was an autonomous actor, politicians deemed it important to elect congressmen by district, supposedly in order to keep them closer to the people who chose them. Election of congressmen by district was written into law as part of the reapportionment legislation following the Census Act of 1840[2]; the Constitution only requires that members of Congress reside in the state from which they are elected. But the need for a close link between a representative in Washington and the people who elected him was recognized and actuated by district elections as early as the Jacksonian period.

Similarly, the populace began to participate in other elections during this time. More and more governors came to be popularly elected, whereas they had once been selected by state legislatures. Many local officials, heretofore appointed, had to stand for election. And these elections were conducted according to new democratic rules designed to encourage increased participation. Some of these election procedures were basic, like the provision of printed ballots by the state. Some seem only logical, like drawing small voting districts to decrease unneeded, difficult travel or holding all elections on the same day. All these regularized procedures taken together had an enormous impact. Change came slowly during the second party period, but these changes were profound. *By 1850, the basic features of the American political system were not very different from those in place today.*

IV. THE COLLAPSE OF THE SECOND PARTY SYSTEM: REALIGNMENT

Why then did this highly developed, highly competitive party system collapse? One answer to this question is probably too simple: the party system failed to respond to the stress on the American polity caused by the slavery issue. A longer answer is that this change is a perfect example of how political realignments occur in the American system and of how that system adapts to significant change. We will view the collapse of the second party system in these terms.

A party realignment may be defined as a lasting change in established patterns of political behavior. A grossly elementary picture of any party system (Figure 2-1) shows the electorate as split by one major issue and voting accordingly (see Sundquist, 1983, chaps. 1 and 2).[3] This picture can apply just as easily to a college campus (where the line of cleavage might be on a profraternity or antifraternity split) as to a national or state party system. A system is said to change fundamentally with a relocation of the line of cleavage, and hence a resplitting of the electorate (see Figure 2-2).

Systems can change in less dramatic ways: for example, when the voting age is changed and the electorate either expands or contracts, or simply when individuals change their views.

James Sundquist (1983, pp. 41–47) maintains that the interaction of five

[2] I am indebted to David Brady for pointing out this piece of electoral trivia to me.
[3] Much of this and the following sections draw heavily on Sundquist (1983). I unapologetically offer this statement as acknowledgment of the debt that all of us owe to Sundquist's impressive scholarship.

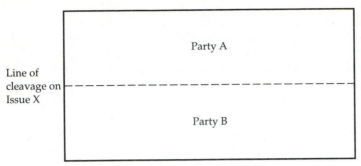

FIGURE 2-1 Hypothetical representation of any party system.

variables determines when and in what ways established patterns of political behavior will change. The five variables are:

1. The breadth and depth of the underlying grievance which is affecting the
   system.
2. The capacity of those supporting the status quo to resist change.
3. The skill of the political leaders.
4. The pattern of division of the polar forces on the new issue between the existing parties; i.e., does the new cleavage cut across existing differences or
   mirror them?
5. The strength of existing party attachments.

With these factors in mind, it is possible to examine American politics in the
1850s.
    Slavery was the issue that raised the passion of the country. In the pre-
alignment period, as depicted in Figure 2-3, the parties did not divide on this
issue. Rather, in order to avoid making enemies and losing elections, they
skirted the most important issue of the day. Issues in Congress which made the
slavery issue become the most important item on the political agenda included
the matter of whether or not to accept petitions (the gag rule), the abolition of
slavery in the District of Columbia, the admission of Texas as a free or slave

FIGURE 2-2 New line of cleavage relocates party division.

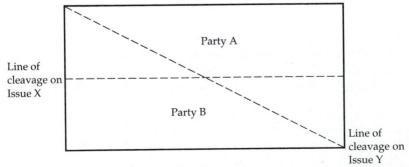

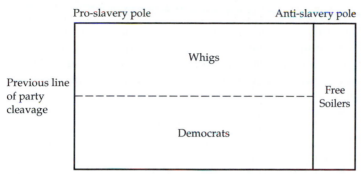

FIGURE 2-3 Party division prior to realignment on slavery issue.

state, the prosecution of the Mexican war, the Wilmot Proviso, and the Compromise of 1850. While the major parties tried to skirt the most crucial question of the 1850s, others were willing to stand or fall on that issue alone. New parties—first the Liberty party and then the Free Soil party—brought the slavery issue to the political forefront. Each of these antislavery factions drew significant numbers of votes in presidential elections and elected their supporters to Congress and the state legislatures. The shape of the political system was changing (Figure 2-4).

The major parties tried to compromise on these slavery-oriented issues but could not. According to Sundquist, five responses to such stress were possible. The easiest solution would be for the issue to disappear. In this case no realignment would have occurred and the previous line of cleavage would have divided the electorate again. Slavery and the abolition movement refused to vanish, however.

Second, the two parties could have realigned along the new line, the slavery dimension. One party could have become the proslavery party, the other antislavery. Again, no such rearrangement took place because the leaders of each existing party tried to straddle an issue that cut squarely across existing party lines.

FIGURE 2-4 Stress on party system caused by slavery issue.

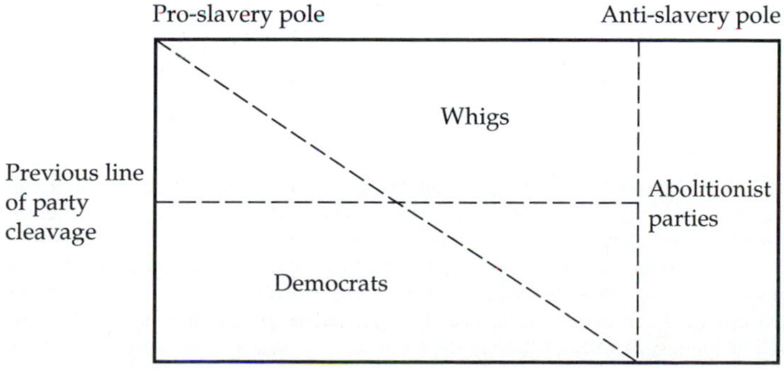

Pro-slavery pole   Anti-slavery pole

Whigs

Previous line
of party   Abolitionist
cleavage   parties

Democrats

A third response would be for a third party to form and then be taken over by one of the existing parties, moving that party to take a stand on the new issue. Such ingestion was possible, but again existing party leadership did not move in that direction, each party's leaders hoping that passions aroused by the issue that brought the Liberty party and the Free Soil party into existence would eventually cool.

The fourth response would be for a third party to form and to replace one of the existing parties. This "small fish eats big fish" scenario did not happen with the Liberty party or with the Free Soilers, but the Republican party did absorb the Whig party, which had lost its appeal by the 1852 election, receiving a majority of the votes in only one state.

In 1856 the new Republican party held its first national nominating convention. The nominee, General John C. Fremont, called for the admission of Kansas to the Union as a free state and advocated a policy that upheld congressional authority over slavery in the territories. The Republican party was a sectional party from the start. Drawing on "conscience Whigs," antislavery Democrats, and old Free Soilers, Fremont got nearly 40 percent of the vote in 1856 (a majority in the north); but he was not even on the ballot in most of the southern states. The Whigs were gone, replaced by a new party that served virtually no "apprenticeship" as a third party but rather immediately achieved major-party status. Figure 2-5 depicts the realignment at the time of the Civil War.[4]

The Civil War, of course, meant much more than a change in party system. Our entire political system was threatened and nearly collapsed. What emerged was a badly torn nation, divided on the issue of slavery, an issue that

FIGURE 2-5 Party system after realignment.

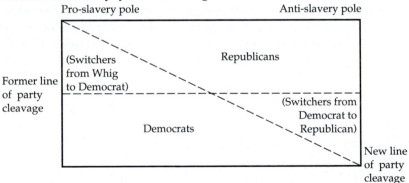

---

[4]William E. Gienapp (1987, 1991) provides a detailed analysis of the formation of the Republican party. His account makes note of the importance of temperance and of nativism as well as of the antislavery movement in describing the demise of the Whigs and their replacement by the Republicans—as opposed to other anti-Democratic parties. While his discussion of realignment and the decomposition of the Whig coalition is consistent with that provided here, he gives a much more detailed, state-by-state account of the strategies followed by Republican politicians and of the role of pragmatic politics as well as ideology in the decisions they made.

was resolved by bloodshed, not political debate. The politics of the post–Civil War period reflected the split of the nation and a whole new way of resolving debates.[5]

V. THE THIRD PARTY SYSTEM: INDUSTRIALIZATION OVER POLITICS

Politicians who could not adapt to change failed to settle the conflict caused by the issue of slavery; they also did not regain their former prominence after the great battle that resolved that issue. The political system that emerged after the Civil War, while still characterized as a competitive two-party system, was vastly different from the one that preceded it.

The Republican party became the majority party during almost all of the third party period. But the leaders of American society during the last third of the nineteenth century were industrialists, not politicians, who once again were largely retired military leaders. America was dominated by men like Andrew Carnegie, Marshall Field, J. Pierpont Morgan, John D. Rockefeller, Leland Stanford, Cornelius Vanderbilt, and Aaron Montgomery Ward. No one doubts the importance of their reputations and accomplishments, particularly in comparison to those of politicians like Ulysses S. Grant, James Garfield, Chester Arthur, or Benjamin Harrison. Both national parties were captured by the industrialists, but it was the Republicans who dominated, sponsoring governmental programs favoring industrial growth and westward expansion.

The partisan split in this period was largely sectional. The Republicans dominated the east and the west. The Democrats, after Reconstruction, made political gains in the south, where resentment by whites toward Republican domination of their region after the Civil War was high. Southern blacks, moreover, were prohibited from active participation in politics by notorious Jim Crow laws.

While the nation as a whole was very competitive, rare was the state that was not dominated by one party or the other. For example, when Garfield won the election of 1880 or Cleveland the election of 1884, in each case with a popular plurality of less than 1 percent, the winning candidate had a 10 percent or larger margin in over half of the states. The Republicans would have dominated this period more convincingly had not a series of seemingly unrelated events hurt Republican political fortunes—a bad depression in 1873, the scandals of the Grant administration, a decline in agricultural production in 1884, and an economic downturn in 1890. Democrats may have gained some white votes by intimidating blacks in the south, but such action also served to characterize a party that had been on the losing side of a great struggle. The Democrats won some political skirmishes, but the Republicans were the well-financed and powerful party of the captains of American capitalism.

---

[5] The fifth possible response to stress was for both parties to be replaced by new major parties. This response did not eventuate, as the Democrats survived by embracing the southern cause.

In addition to being a time of rapid industrialization, the last quarter of the nineteenth century was also a period of significant immigration. The newly arrived immigrants came to play an important role in the development of the most significant political innovation of this period, the urban political machine.[6] In many ways it is logical that political machines grew up during an era dominated by business growth. As Banfield and Wilson argue, the party organization of this period was essentially "a business organization in a particular field of business—getting votes and winning elections" (1963, p. 115). How was the politician to get what was desired in this context? Put simply, in business terms, American machine bosses bought the product needed. More precisely, they bought what was needed from whomever would sell the product most cheaply. For political leaders in an age of large-scale immigration, this formula implied giving material incentives to immigrant groups in exchange for their votes.

This formula was not as evil as it is often depicted. The political system was an effective means for immigrants to assimilate themselves into American society. The political machine provided jobs, lodging, extra groceries, and a means of socialization for new groups of citizens. In exchange, the immigrant groups provided votes for the machine. The bosses dominated politics; the industrialists dominated society. As immigrants found jobs in the expanding factories, their employment symbolized a period of transition in American life from an agricultural economy to an urban, industrial economy. The political system reflected this shift.

But not everyone was satisfied. With the rapid industrialization of the country and the domination of politics and government by the business community, the farmers of the midwest soon discovered that they were the consistent losers. As neither major party took up their cause, they soon set out on their own, forming a series of organizations to challenge the existing power structure. The Granger movement spread rapidly in the 1870s and 1880s; the Farmers' Alliance was politically active during much of this time as well; and finally, the Populists raised concerns that threatened the continuation of the existing two-party system. These groups signaled splits that were to lead to a significant change in the context of American partisan politics.

VI.   THE CRITICAL ELECTION OF 1896 AND REPUBLICAN DOMINATION

America entered the last decade of the nineteenth century with a competitive two-party system at the national level. The election of 1876 had to be decided by a special commission, settling disputes over contested electoral votes and at the same time setting the course for the nation's industrial growth. Grover Cleveland won the elections of 1884 and 1892 by extremely close popular pluralities; he lost in the electoral college in 1888, despite his popular plurality of

---

[6] Mayhew's (1986) discussion of traditional party organizations is particularly important on this point.

Few, if any, American politicians have ever matched the rhetorical skills of three-time Democratic presidential nominee William Jennings Bryan. (Library of Congress)

less than 1 percent. The Democrats won congressional majorities in 1890 and 1892. The country seemed to be turning away from the "bloody shirt"-waving Republican politics of the post-Civil War era.

All of that was to change quickly. The panic of 1893, during a Democratic administration, led to a huge Republican landslide in the congressional election of 1894; the Republicans gained 132 seats and completely controlled 24 state delegations. The debacle for the Democrats was a precursor of Republican William McKinley's defeat of the quasi-Populist Democrat, William Jennings Bryan, in 1896, an election that determined a new course for American politics, setting a pattern that would see the Democrats as the minority party for years to come.

A.   The Critical Election of 1896

Political scientists refer to the election of 1896 as a realigning election that marks the beginning of the fourth party system. The major parties did not change in 1896; Republicans still competed with Democrats. But the issues that separated the parties and the allegiances of large groups of voters did change.[7]

Before 1896 both parties favored industrialization; both parties sought to appeal to urban populations. In 1896 not only did the Democratic party have to carry the burden of the 1893 economic downturn, but it also became associated with a charismatic leader who attacked the business interests, called for softer

[7] Pomper (1973, p. 104) describes the 1896 election as a "converting," not a realigning, election, because the same party maintained majority status though the electoral coalition changed.

money and a silver standard, and appealed to the farmers of the nation in a way that alienated urban workers. None could deny the power of Bryan's rhetoric:

> The humblest citizen of all the land, when clad in the armor of a righteous cause, is stronger than all the hosts of Error. . . . You shall not press down upon the brow of labor this crown of thorns. You shall not crucify mankind upon a cross of gold.

But many doubted the economic effectiveness of the cause. McKinley's campaign, led by perhaps the first modern campaign manager, Marcus A. Hanna, and financed by the nation's industrial leaders, was efficient and effective. Bryan was portrayed as a radical enemy of urban workers. Virtually all the cities came into the Republican fold. The new issue that divided the nation, the silver standard versus the gold standard, caused new regional splits, west versus east, rural areas versus urban, and the Democrats had defined for themselves a losing coalition.

The election of 1896 illustrates another important concept in the analysis of American electoral history, the *critical election* (Key, 1955, pp. 3–18). In a seminal article in 1959, V. O. Key maintained that some elections were more significant in electoral history than were others. Key defined a critical election as "a type of election in which there occurs a sharp and durable electoral cleavage between the parties" (1959, pp. 198–210). That is, critical elections mark changes in party *systems* as we have defined them. These changes occur because of shifts, either temporary or permanent, in the line of cleavage. Key claimed that critical elections were marked by high levels of electoral involvement by the populace, depth of concern about the election's outcome by the voters, and profound readjustments in the power relationships within a community.

Key (1959, pp. 198 ff) also qualified this theory with the concept of *secular realignment* (which he defined as gradual, rather than sudden and sharp), a long-term redistribution of party strength. He claimed that movement to a new party alignment might happen at different times in different regions and thus, when viewed nationally, appear almost imperceptible.

B.   The Classification of Presidential Elections

Using Key's concepts, political scientists have been able to refine their classifications of various presidential elections. Angus Campbell and his associates classified elections according to whether or not the majority party won the election and whether or not the existing line of cleavage prevailed or was changed (Campbell, Converse, Miller, & Stokes, 1960, pp. 531–538). They identified three types of elections—maintaining, deviating, and realigning. Seeing a logical gap in this reasoning and referring particularly to the election of 1896, Gerald Pomper (1973, p. 104) added a fourth category, the converting election. These concepts are shown in Figure 2-6.

According to this theory, one party system ends and another begins when the line of cleavage changes. Thus, 1860 (Lincoln-Douglas-Breckinridge-Bell) was a realigning election, ushering in the third party system. In the election of 1896,

MAJORITY PARTY

	Same	Different
Same	Maintaining election (e.g., 1904, 1940)	Deviating election (e.g., 1912, 1952)
Different	Converting election (e.g., 1896)	Realigning election (e.g., 1860, 1932)

LINE OF CLEAVAGE

FIGURE 2-6 Classification of presidential elections.

however, the majority party from the previous electoral era remained the same. The election was a converting election, shifting the line of cleavage from old Civil War allegiances, which had weakened and led to more intense competition by the 1890s, to economic issues of gold versus silver. Geographically, urban and northern areas were aligned against rural, southern, and western areas. Even though the majority party remained the same, a new party system was in place.

The Republicans dominated the fourth party system, holding the White House for sixteen consecutive years and for twenty-eight of the next thirty-six years. The elections of 1912 and 1916 are, on the other hand, deviating elections. The electoral coalitions did not change; the Republicans remained the majority party. Woodrow Wilson won the 1912 election because Teddy Roosevelt split the Republican vote, running on his own Bull Moose ticket. Wilson barely won again in 1916 as many old progressives marched back to the Republican party. By 1920 the Republican coalition had regained prominence.

C. The Progressive Era: A Systemic Change

One can question whether the change in 1896 was as significant as others that were taking place during this period. By 1896 the issue that had divided the electorate before 1860, slavery, was resolved. After all, voters who were forty years old in 1896, men who had been voting for almost twenty years, had been only nine years old at the time of Lincoln's assassination. The issues of gold and silver and of the pace and cost of industrialization obviously were important to those interested in politics. But the techniques of politics were not changing; the party structure did not change in 1896; which parties had to be taken into account and how they interacted—the definition of a political system—did not change. Machines flourished; Mark Hanna transformed the role of a political boss into the ultimate, logical extension of the spoils system, the type of political organizations perfected by the Jacksonian Democrats.

More fundamental changes in terms of how the political battle was fought occurred during the so-called Progressive Era. These changes did not result in an electoral realignment, because progressives belonged to both the Republican and the Democratic party. But the reforms associated with the progressives caused fundamental changes in the ways the parties interacted, thus altering our entire political system in ways surely as profound as any electoral realignment.

The progressive era had an impact on all aspects of American government. It was symbolized by the "sociological" briefs presented to the Supreme Court by Boston attorney (and later Associate Justice) Louis Brandeis, by the revolt against the dictatorial powers of the Speaker of the House exercised by "Uncle Joe" Cannon in the House of Representatives, by the "stewardship theory" under which Theodore Roosevelt expanded the powers of the presidency, and by the "New Freedom" of Woodrow Wilson.

In electoral terms, the rules of the game were dramatically changed. The first of these changes has been traced to Charles J. Guiteau, the deranged, disappointed office seeker who shot President Garfield and indirectly created the Civil Service System. *The demise of the spoils system was the first step in the decline of the urban machines, a disintegrative process that went on for many years through the New Deal to modern reform clubs.*

Other progressive changes had more immediate impacts. *The invention of direct primary elections as a means to win party nominations took away from parties one key to their power—control over access to the ballot.* No change could have had greater impact on the strength of parties. *In 1913 the Seventeenth Amendment called for the direct election of United States senators.* In this case one of the important stakes in the political game was changed. Again, party strength was weakened. *When women won the right to vote in 1920, the political electorate was doubled.* While participation by women was not at the same level as men's, parties still had to contend with a whole new body of voters. *Finally, to rid themselves of the evils of party bosses and machine corruption, many cities introduced nonpartisan elections.* Once again the electoral system was greatly altered.

These innovations in the first decades of the twentieth century revised the shape of American politics most significantly. Although they are not associated with a new "party system" as traditionally defined by social scientists, the modifications represent changes as significant as those between the first and second party systems, changes much more fundamental than mere realignments. These shifts, when combined with the technological advancement that allowed for instantaneous political communication through radio, determined the parameters of political contests for more than four decades.

VII.   THE NEW DEAL COALITION

The line drawn between the Democrats and Republicans in 1896 remained in place for over thirty years. The context of electoral battles shifted during the progressive era, but the line of cleavage dividing the American electorate did not. However, the great depression broke traditional allegiances and recast the shape of electoral coalitions. While some observers feel that a secular realignment may have been under way as early as the 1920s, virtually all analysts agree that 1932 was a critical election that defined a new line of cleavage that became dominant in American elections.

In simplest terms, the American public blamed the great depression on Herbert Hoover and the Republican party. Franklin Roosevelt gave millions who had been hurt by the depression hope; they responded by giving their allegiance to the Democratic party.

A.   Defining the New Deal Coalition

The New Deal coalition has been defined in many ways (see, for example, Erikson, Lancaster, & Romero, 1989; Ladd & Hadley, 1975; Stanley, Bianco, & Niemi, 1986). Journalists would say that the New Deal coalition included urban workers, ethnic Americans, blacks, the academic elite, and the traditionally Democratic south. Political scientist Robert Axelrod (1972) has defined this coalition more carefully. Axelrod maintains that a group's contribution to a political coalition is a product of three factors: the size of the group, the percentage of the group that turns out to vote, and the loyalty of the group's members to a political party (1972, pp. 11–12). The interplay of these factors is crucial. For instance, blacks were very loyal to the Democratic party during the New Deal (and remain so). But because they represented a small percentage of the population (approximately 10 percent) and because many blacks either chose not to vote or were prevented from doing so (average turnout of under 25 percent), they did not make up a very large portion of the New Deal coalition.[8] According to Axelrod, those groups contributing most to the New Deal coalition were Roman Catholics and union members and their families (each accounting for approximately two in five Democratic voters). Significant, but smaller, contributions to the New Deal coalition were made by (1) the poor (defined as those with annual incomes under $3000 at the time), (2) the residents of the twelve largest metropolitan areas, (3) southerners, and (4) blacks (Axelrod, 1972, p. 14).[9] With the exceptions of the poor and the large-city residents, each of these groups was significantly more loyal to the Democratic party during the New Deal than was the country as a whole.

On the other hand, while Axelrod was able to sort out members of a Republican coalition—nonunion members, nonpoor, whites, Protestants, residents of smaller cities and rural areas—significantly, none of these groups was much more loyal to the Republican party than was the nation as a whole (Axelrod, 1972, p. 18). That is, the Republicans attracted voters disaffected by the Democratic party, but these disaffected were so few as to constitute only a losing coalition during the period of the New Deal and its immediate aftermath.

The division as outlined above defined the cleavage in the American polit-

[8] Others would argue that Axelrod's analysis was flawed in that it fails to incorporate geography. That is, as an example, blacks might not have made as significant a contribution to the New Deal coalition nationally as they did in some specific and important geographic areas.
[9] It should be noted that membership in these groups is overlapping. Thus, Catholic union members who live in one of the twelve largest metropolitan areas would be counted in all three groups.

ical system for an unprecedented period of time. Most analysts feel that a description of electoral coalitions which was accurate in the mid-1930s would
have been similarly accurate into the 1960s. Even though the Republicans won
Congress in 1946, and despite President Eisenhower's defeats of Democrat Adlai Stevenson in 1952 and 1956, these elections were seen as deviations. The
majority of Americans still owed allegiance to the Democratic party. The issues
dividing the electorate were still the New Deal issues: whether the government
had a responsibility to serve as the employer of last resort, to intervene actively
in the economy, to help those who were unable to help themselves. For more
than three decades these issues defined the political agenda. For most of that
time, the American public agreed with the Democrats' approach to the nation's
problems.

   Less consensus exists about whether the New Deal coalitions survived the
turbulent sixties and seventies. A good deal of evidence suggests that the tie of
parties is less strong and that the issues that are important to the electorate have
changed. Wattenberg (1989, 1990a, 1991), for instance, points to issues such as
women's rights, the environment, or the impact of drugs on American society
which concern citizens today much more than they did two decades ago. How
these issues relate to the traditional appeal of the New Deal coalition is not
clear (see Norputh, 1987; Petrocik, 1987a; Stanley et al., 1986).

B.   Changing Campaign Technology

While the line of cleavage defining the fifth party system has remained remarkably constant, the political system as a whole has once again undergone changes
that are as significant as those of the progressive era or the Jacksonian era. This
time the changes have not involved the rules of the political game, though party
rules have changed and the electorate has expanded again with the granting of
the franchise to eighteen-to-twenty-one-year-olds and the reinfranchisement of
blacks and other minorities with the Voting Rights Act of 1965 and its exten-
sions. The important change in most recent years has involved rapidly changing
campaign technology.

   Earlier the impact of radio was briefly noted. Radio gave politicians the
ability to communicate instantly and personally with large numbers of citizens.
This advance, however, pales in comparison with the change in the ways politicians communicate with the electorate through television. Campaign technology has changed rapidly and frequently during the fifth party period. The direction of all the changes has been away from party-centered campaigns toward
candidate-centered ones. This movement has gone further with computer technology, sophisticated direct-mail solicitations, and scientific analysis of voter
opinion. It will continue as television moves into the age of cable. These innovations go far to shape the context of the current political system.

C.   The Erosion of the New Deal Coalition

The New Deal coalition has eroded since the mid-1960s. Note that the word
"eroded" was carefully chosen. Political journalists and political scientists have

spent a substantial amount of time and effort defining whether the fifth party system came to an end (see, for example, Aldrich & Niemi, 1990). The best answer seems to be that no such point can be isolated. The American political system has recently been undergoing a gradual transformation, not a radical realignment (Ladd, 1978, pp. 81–91; Ladd & Hadley, 1975).

What is significant to note about the current coalition in American politics is that it seems to be quite different from the coalition of two or three decades ago, not necessarily in terms of partisan alignment but in terms of the meaning of partisanship to the voters. A clue to this change can be found in voter attitudes toward the role of parties in American politics. Whereas once citizens voted for candidates *whom they viewed as candidates of political parties,* today the norm is to vote for the candidate, not the party. Larry Sabato (1988, p. 133) has noted that 92 percent of Americans agree with the statement "I always vote for the person who I think is best, regardless of what party they belong to," while only 14 percent claim they "always support the candidate of just one party."

Evidence of this change can be seen in a number of different ways. Voters are reflecting these attitudes at the polling place. Fewer and fewer are casting straight party votes. More and more are splitting their tickets, voting Democratic for Congress and Republican for president; Republican for Congress and Democratic for Senate; for one party for national office and the other for local office (see Wattenberg, 1989, p. 23; 1990b, pp. 162–166; 1991). Furthermore, fewer and fewer voters claim strong allegiance to one party or the other. The point is not that voters are alienated from the two parties, but rather that they are ambivalent toward the parties. Martin Wattenberg believes we are seeing a "dealignment" in American politics, a time in which citizen attachment to party is declining and the relevance of party for the vote has been greatly reduced (Wattenberg, 1990a, 1991).[10]

It should be noted, however, that the consensus with which political scientists and journalists described the New Deal coalition of the 1930s through the 1950s has not been matched in descriptions of the electorate in recent decades. Warren Miller (1990), for instance, argues persuasively that partisanship is still very strong among *voters,* and that the trend toward dealignment appears most strongly among those who opt not to vote. A large number of analyses, again by both political scientists and journalists, have discussed a Reagan-led realignment, focusing at times on national trends and at other times on geographic and/or demographic trends (Edsall, 1988; MacKuen, Erikson, & Stimson, 1989; Norpoth, 1987; Petrocik, 1987, 1989; Petrocik & Steeper, 1987; Schneider, 1988). In subsequent chapters we will discuss the current configuration of the American political system as well as the role that changing technology has played in determining the shape of that system.

---

[10] Wattenberg (1991) notes that the concept of "dealignment" was first raised by Inglehart and Hochstein (1972), but that their discussion was preceded by two years by Walter Dean Burnham's (1970) discussion of "electoral disaggregation" and the "onward march of party decomposition." The term "dealignment," in the sense described first by Burnham, has become more commonly used.

VIII.   A POLITICIAN'S VIEW OF POLITICAL HISTORY

Two seemingly distinct strands have been interwoven in this brief history of American political parties. One strand has been the traditional outline of American party systems. These are summarized in Table 2-1. These party systems are defined by the lines of cleavage, the "issue clusters," which divide the political parties. Politicians understand these lines of division. They "cause" them by responding to problems facing the government in one way or another. They "respond" to them—often in their younger years—by joining one coalition or another. But they do not spend much time thinking about them. Does anyone think that many United States senators really care when our last realigning election was? How many congressmen are concerned over why the second party system collapsed, or even whether the fifth party system is still intact? These concepts are important from an analytical point of view—and they do have practical consequences—but surely they are not the stuff of which politics is made.

The second strand running through this history has signaled systemic changes in a broader sense. What rules structure the political contest? How are political campaigns run? How do these areas relate to political parties? At times such changes have occurred at the same time as electoral coalitions have changed. Thus, the second party system was different from the first both in terms of electoral coalitions and in terms of how political contests were fought. At other times systemic changes have taken place while electoral coalitions have remained intact; this was the case of the reformers of the progressive era.

Practical politicians are aware of and very concerned about this aspect of electoral history. Even senators who neither knew nor cared about our last realigning election are all aware of the changes in campaign techniques, of what worked and what did not in the last election, *and of the impact these changes are having on political parties.* Congressmen who could never define the fifth party

TABLE 2-1. Realigning Elections

	1860	1896	1932
Original parties	Whigs v Democrats	Republicans v Democrats	Republicans v Democrats
Issues	Slavery	Gold standard (economic)	Government involvement in domestic economic affairs
Third parties	Liberty party Free Soilers Conscience Whigs Cotton Whigs Barnburners Hunkers	Populists Greenbacks	League for Independent Political Actions
Resulting parties	Republicans v Democrats	Republicans v Democrats	Republicans v Democrats

system all know about the Republican advantage over the Democrats in the use of computerized mail for fund-raising; they also know that donations to both parties' congressional committees were down in 1990. These are not abstract questions to them. Vic Fazio (D., Calif.) wants to know how fast the Democratic Congressional Campaign Committee (DCCC), which he chairs, can catch up to the Republicans. He wants to know how to get "ahead of the curve," to set new strategies for using new techniques, not to respond to them. Vic Fazio was reticent to take over the DCCC, not because the committee lacks political ambition, but because he feared that trends in raising money for political parties will continue downward and thus the ability to use new techniques to aid colleagues seeking to defend their seats after the redistricting (which followed the 1990 census) will be restricted.

Joel Silbey (1990, 1991) has analyzed the history of American political parties in terms different from those discussed above. Silbey claims that American political history can be divided into four periods, distinguished by the importance of the role of political parties.

> The justification for arranging American political history in this way grows out of the different kinds of political institutions, norms, and behavior which have *predominated* in each era. Thus, although two parties have always been on the scene, only once—from 1838 to 1893—did parties totally dominate the American political landscape. (Silbey, 1990, p. 4)

The period from the 1790s until the 1830s was a period of party development, but parties really did not predominate in electoral politics; in fact, they were resisted by many in politics. This was the preparty period (Formisano, 1974). The period from the 1830s until the 1890s was one in which parties did dominate American politics (Silbey, 1991). From the 1890s until the 1950s, parties were on the decline; this was the postparty period. And, according to Silbey, the most recent decades have been marked by candidate-centered politics; this is the nonparty period.

The intertwining of the strands discussed above and the separate analysis by Silbey is crucial. One learns from history. How politicians respond to systemic changes will determine the shape of politics in the years ahead. Those responses will determine whether we are indeed entering an era of politics without parties, as Silbey believes; whether the fifth party system will revive; or whether we will enter a sixth party system, and, if so, what its new shape might be. Throughout the rest of the book these questions will recur. How is the American political system responding to the changes it is undergoing? (See Herrnson, 1988; Maisel, 1990c; Sabato, 1988.)

Politicians are fond of recalling the names of the heroes from their party's past. "The party of Lincoln" does not forget its first successful presidential candidate—although Republicans rarely evoke the memory of Harding, Hoover, or Nixon. The names of Franklin D. Roosevelt, Harry Truman, and John Kennedy roll off Democratic politicians' tongues like marbles from a table—although Lyndon Johnson is mentioned somewhat less frequently. But these evocations of the political past are purely rhetorical, and they should be treated as such. The true importance of the history of the great American political parties relates to the roles they have played in shaping electoral contests, in defining issues, in gaining voter allegiance, in governing—and in whether or not they can adapt to new political techniques, to a changing political system, and can continue to do so.

chapter

3

Party Organization

What do you think of when you think of a "party organization"? Political bosses? City machines? Politicians? Are they all alike? Is the picture one of strength or of weakness? Is it of a modern office or a smoke-filled, dank, and dark back room? Or is there no picture?

These images are a metaphor for the problem involved in discussing party organization. We are tempted to ignore the subject; no one likes to discuss party organization. After all, the "real" party organizations—at least for those who conjure up images of big-city machines, local clubhouses as a hub of social life, and the like—went out of existence years ago. But modern party organizations exist, and they play an important and evolving role in the political process.

Recall the definition of political party developed in Chapter 1. It said, in part, that "political parties are organizations, however loosely organized, . . ." The goal of this chapter is to describe the organizational aspects of political parties. We will begin with a road map, looking at different kinds of organizations and the formal relationships among them. Then we will turn to separate examinations of various types of organizations.

I. THE ORGANIZATIONAL FRAMEWORK

In the simplest terms, the organizational framework for political parties mirrors the geographic organization of the United States. That is, parties begin at the very local level and eventually emerge at the national level. However, specifying that structure says nothing about the relationships among the various parts. Party organization becomes clearer if one recalls that these organizations came into existence in order to help with election campaigns. Therefore, the organizational charts essentially parallel the ways in which elected offices are distributed across the country. It is interesting to note that some elected officials represent areas for which there is no preexisting governmental unit; e.g., congressional districts often cross city or even county lines.

Political organization begins in the neighborhood. Generally, people who live in the same neighborhood vote in the same place. These polling places define *precincts*, the most local organizational level in American politics. In rural areas, frequently all the people in a town vote in one place; the town then is the

functional equivalent of the precinct. Towns or precincts are politically organized as town or precinct committees, with chairs and other officers. Theoretically, each political party will have a committee at this level. But do not try to
look your local precinct committee up in the telephone book. Don't try to find
its office. Throughout most of America, precinct or town committees "work"
out of the kitchen of the committee's leader. One person—or sometimes a couple of people—has an interest in organizing the area for the political party he or
she favors. That person then becomes the foundation of an organization; he or
she attracts friends; the committee members communicate with other organizations; they work with candidates and help on campaigns. These people are not
"politicians" in any meaningful sense of the word. They are citizens interested
in politics.

It was not always that way—and it is not the same in every neighborhood.
In the days of the classic political machine, precinct leaders were men (almost
never women) deeply involved in politics. They frequently held patronage jobs,
jobs that depended on their delivering votes. Precinct committees were active
and vibrant; the clubhouse was a social center for the lives of many in the neighborhood. Politics was a critically important part of the lives of those who
worked for the government—because their livelihood depended on the outcome
of elections. While that is rarely the case today, in some urban centers with

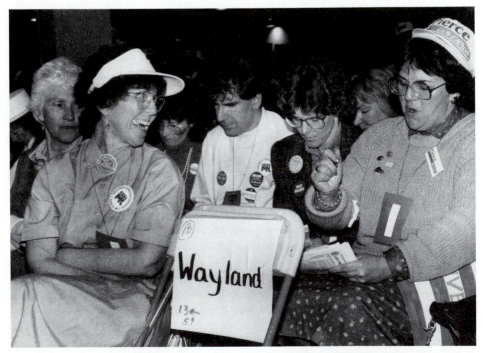

Delegates at the Massachusetts Republican Convention show support for their favorite
candidates as they discuss party business. (Lora B. Askinazi/The Picture Cube)

stronger organizations, in areas in which patronage still is available to elected leaders, precinct leaders, often called precinct captains, remain active and committed. (See Banfield & Wilson, 1963; Gosnell, 1939; Tolchin & Tolchin, 1971.)

In larger urban areas, members of precinct committees elect representatives to serve on *ward* committees. Wards are simply groupings of precincts. Often city councillors are elected by ward. Thus, an obvious connection exists between the governmental organizational unit and the political unit. Ward organizations are more active in those areas in which the political stakes are higher, e.g., those in which politicians elected at the ward level have favors to confer.

While the most local level of political organization is the precinct, most observers agree that the *county* is the more important level of party organization. Again, this significance follows from the fact that the county is the organizing unit for most governmental offices. Counties, of course, elect their own governments—and these governments often control jobs. State legislative districts often fall within county lines. Furthermore, counties tend to be large enough that a "critical mass" of active politicians can form. Thus, county committees, typically formed by elections from precinct, town, or ward committees, are often much more politically active than are more local units. County chairs are often important political leaders, men (again, infrequently women) of influence with politicians in an area.

Party organization at the *state* level parallels that at the county level. Each of the major political parties has a central committee in each of the fifty states. Committee members are typically chosen by delegates to county (or sometimes congressional district) conventions. In some states, state committee members are elected in primary elections. Each state committee has a slate of officers. State chairs tend to be significant political figures in their states, and on occasion at the national level.

At the pinnacle of the party organizational hierarchy are the two *national committees* and the two national chairs. The compositions of the two national committees do not directly parallel each other (see Section IV below); however, in each case representatives to the national committee come from the state committees and from others in the states. The national chairs are chosen by the committees, often with direct input from presidential candidates, particularly successful candidates. Party chairs whose party controls the White House, usually referred to as "in-party" chairs, serve as the president's spokesperson on party matters; "out-party" chairs tend to play a more independent role. While politicians and political analysts would agree that the chairs of the two national committees are important political figures, few of us would recognize Richard Bond or Ronald Brown, respectively the chairs of the Republican and Democratic National Committees in 1992, if they stood in front of us in a line. Their influence is with other politicians and perhaps as spokespersons for their parties, but not as politicians who command the public's attention.

While technically the national committees are at the pinnacle of the party organizational hierarchy, that status does not reflect relationships among these

Democratic party precinct leaders discuss strategy at local meetings such as this one in a South Texas Hispanic-American community. (Michael D. Sullivan/TexaStock)

organizational units. Writing almost three decades ago, Samuel Eldersveld (1964) described party organization as a *stratarchy,* implying that each organizational level occupied a separate strata, distinct from the others. Connections across the various strata existed; but the organizations really *co*existed under a code of "mutual deference." While Eldersveld's conclusions were based on a study of political organization in the Detroit area in the 1960s, many felt it possible to generalize from this picture of the relationship among political organizational units.

The picture seems less accurate in the 1990s. Many observers have noted the "nationalization" of party organizations—that is, more influence from the national level, less local color painting the organizational picture. Variations exist within that pattern. Democratic party reforms in the presidential nominating process have nationalized party rules to a great extent (see Chapter 8). The Republicans have not followed this pattern and allow much more local autonomy; in fact they favor autonomous local organizations as a matter of principle. However, for some time the Republicans have funded many of their state and local efforts with funds raised at the national level. The Democrats have emulated this pattern, but they have been much less successful than the Republicans. Raising funds in Washington for state and local use is another type of nationalization. A central feature of American political life has always involved decentralization. The sections below describe the various types of party organizations and the patterns that exist in the relationships among them.

II. LOCAL AND COUNTY ORGANIZATIONS

The heyday of strong party organizations, roughly the period from the 1870s until the end of World War II, was largely the heyday of strong local or county party organizations. Most frequently when muckrakers berated the political machines and the corrupt political bosses, they were criticizing local party organizations. And those bosses and their machines were legendary—Boss William Marcy Tweed of New York City's Tammany Hall, depicted as the very stereotype of a corrupt political boss in Thomas Nast's famous cartoons in *Harper's Weekly* in the 1870s; Frank Hague of Jersey City, New Jersey, and the four O'Connell brothers of Albany, New York, dominant bosses in their homes for most of the first half of this century; James Michael Curley of Boston, the engaging rogue on whom Edwin O'Connor patterned *The Last Hurrah;* Tom Pendergast of Kansas City, Missouri, a local boss who started the career of President Harry Truman; Ed Crump of Memphis, Tennessee; Anton Cermak, Pat Nash, and Richard Daley of Chicago, Illinois. . . . The list goes on and on. Their stories are the stuff of legend. (See Mayhew, 1986; Steinberg, 1972).

The picture of these *political machines* is clear. Each had a dominant leader, the *political boss.* Each was organized as a structured hierarchy, with ward leaders beholden to the boss, precinct leaders beholden to their ward leader, and those who worked the streets beholden to those organizing the precinct. The glue that held these machines together was material incentives. Patronage jobs were the reward for electoral success. Aid to the newly arrived immigrant, the unemployed or underemployed, ensured loyalty to the machine. The machines were also important socializing elements, helping immigrants adjust to American society; interpersonal ties added to the binding of followers to their party leaders. The names given to the organization leaders spoke wonders—the boss, the ward heeler, the precinct captain. Friends were rewarded; enemies were punished. Winners advanced; losers fell by the wayside. Results were what mattered, and methods were rarely questioned. The machine era was marked by charges of corruption and attempts at reform. The charges were not without foundation in many cases; the reformers succeeded only when party organizations strayed too far from accepted norms. These seventy-five years marked a time of colorful, if corrupt, politics in America (Banfield & Wilson, 1963; Bridges, 1984; Erie, 1988; Rakove, 1975; Riordan, 1963; Tolchin & Tolchin, 1971; J. Wilson, 1973).

But a word of caution is in order. Even at their height, organized machine politics did not dominate all of American politics. About two-thirds of the largest American cities had some sort of political machine during at least part of this period; but they were not all in existence at the same time, and they did not all maintain the same level of dominance. And many areas of the country were never under machine dominance. As David Mayhew (1986) has observed, machine politics was much more likely to exist in those states that had been settled by the beginning of the second party system, the Jacksonian party system. The spoils system established a base and gave rise to a political culture that persisted for some time. But other areas never followed suit. And surely, by the last quarter of the twentieth century, traditional political machines had been changed not only by new moralities, but also by new styles of politics and political communications.

What then is the nature of political organization in the roughly 190,000 precincts in the 3000 counties in the United States? A terrific variety exists. At the precinct or town level, organization is minimal. Each party would like to have a functioning organization in each local precinct. But in actuality, if the parties can have a name on paper—a possible contact person who is interested—that is often a bonus. In urban areas with larger precincts (sometimes as many as 2000 voters) one party or the other might be organized; but only rarely are competing organizations in place. In smaller communities, combining several of these local units is often necessary before enough activists come together to form an organization.

On the other hand, each party *is* organized, at least at some level, in most counties. County organizations tend to have formal rules and officers. One of the jobs of these officers is to find leaders for precinct politics, and part of their success is measured by their ability to appoint leaders. County committees and county chairs are usually elected by meetings of the party faithful; in large part they are self-selected, with real competition a rarity. County leaders are mostly volunteers; few officers are paid. Only the very wealthiest county organizations maintain a paid staff or a permanent headquarters.

Voter registration drives like this one are one of the most important tasks performed by party organizations. (Bob Daemmrich/The Image Works)

County organizations are most active during the campaign season. The most active and "professional" county organizations work year-round, building local organizations, recruiting desirable (or discouraging undesirable) candidates, raising money. But during campaign season, activity heats up for all these organizations. They help to register voters, work on get-out-the-vote drives, and coordinate the field campaigns for all the candidates running within their jurisdiction. County committees focus their activities on candidates for local office or on local candidates for state office. These men and women are known commodities; many of the volunteer activists are involved because of their connections with these candidates. Many of the candidates are themselves active in the organization. This is the politics of the *grass roots,* the bread and butter of local politics. These party volunteers make it possible for local candidates to run credible campaigns, to distribute literature, to woo voters.

How important are these activities in the age of modern campaigns, with polling, television, computers, and relatively little grass-roots campaigning (see Chapter 7)? Two answers seem apparent. First, many races are far from "new-style" campaigns. Often local candidates cannot afford the cost of modern campaigning, and their campaigns remain labor-intensive efforts. They still rely heavily on the foot soldiers of American politics, the organizational volunteers at the precinct and county level.

But, second, a good deal of evidence points to the conclusion that strong party organizations do indeed contribute to larger numbers of votes for the party (Frendeis, Gibson, & Vertz, 1990; Gibson, 1991). Party organizations help coordinate the various campaigns in an area. In addition, by pooling resources, they allow some local candidates who could not otherwise afford to do so to make use of some of the modern campaign technology, thus improving their campaigns. More important in this context is the role that party organizations play even before the campaign begins. Stronger party organizations are clearly better at recruiting candidates. Frendeis et al. (1990) demonstrate that slates of candidates are more likely to be full in those counties with actively functioning party organizations. If slates are not full, obviously voters cannot express support for that party's candidates. When this recruitment function is added to the more traditional grass-roots roles that party organization plays, the total impact of a strong organization on vote totals—while not overwhelming—is still significant.

For local party organization to be successful, first, the organization must have a solid base. Grass-roots politics is about people, and people need incentives to participate. Without the material incentives most often connected with patronage jobs, fewer and fewer people are becoming involved in local politics. The primary goal for those interested in maintaining organizational strength then involves energizing the activists, recruiting the volunteers.

Second, organizations need resources to do the jobs of politics: money remains high on the list of needed resources. The national parties seem to be recognizing this need. In the last two presidential campaigns they have each invested hundreds of thousands of dollars in local and county organizations. The Republicans particularly have set a real goal of building organization at the local level. As state organizations grow and the national organizations invest more in local and county party committees, these local units will continue to seek a new role in an emerging political reality.

III. STATE PARTY ORGANIZATIONS

Most casual observers cannot distinguish one level of political organization from another. And they don't spend much time thinking about any level of organization. Who is the chair of the Democratic State Committee in your home state? Of the Republican State Committee? Can you name any state committee members? What do they do? Where do they meet? What difference would it make if they did not exist?

A. The Age of Strong State Party Organizations

Such cloudiness was not always so. In the early years of the twentieth century, state party organizations mattered. Generally the organization of the dominant party in a state was headed by one of its two United States senators. Why would a senator care about party organization? You must remember the political context of the time. First, senatorial courtesy gave majority-party senators control of most federal patronage in their states at the time. Thus, the material incentives to cement a party organization, at least those that emanated from Washington, were controlled by this particular senator. Second, United States senators were appointed by state legislatures, not elected by the people, until the passage of the Seventeenth Amendment to the Constitution, part of the progressive agenda, which was passed in 1912 and ratified in 1913. Thus, senators were motivated to involve themselves with state legislative politics, at the very least to assure their party the majority status that would lead to their own re-election.

Some of these senator-bosses were as powerful and almost as legendary as the urban machine leaders mentioned above—Republicans Simon Cameron, Matthew Quay, and Boies Penrose of Pennsylvania, Thomas Platt of New York, and Stephen B. Elkins of West Virginia; Democrats Arthur Pue Gorman of Maryland and Thomas Martin of Virginia. While the power of state organizations seemed to wane after World War I, some notable exceptions persisted— the Democratic machine begun by Huey Long and continued by his heirs in Louisiana, Eugene Talmadge's Democratic organization in Georgia,[1] and the Republican organization headed by J. Henry Roraback and the Democratic organization controlled by John M. Bailey, both of Connecticut.[2]

---

[1] It should be noted that all "machines" are not necessarily alike. The southern Democratic machines of Long and Talmadge are clear examples of very personal organizations, which emerged largely because of the powerful demagogic appeals of their leaders. See Steinberg (1972) and Williams (1969).

[2] Roraback was the most powerful figure in Connecticut politics from the early 1910s until the New Deal; he remained the most important Republican in the state until his death in 1937. The Democrats took over the state in the 1930s; Bailey took over leadership of the state committee in 1946 and built a powerful organization that persisted until his death in 1975.

In the 1930s, Louisiana's powerful Democratic boss Huey P. Long frequently took to the stump to urge support from his followers. (UPI/Bettmann Newsphotos)

For a period of time, however, state party organizations seemed ready to disappear not only from public view but also from any place of significance in the political process (Key, 1956). Party committees were largely shadow organizations, with their only possible function being to serve the will and the cause of a few elected politicians. In the last quarter century, however, in terms of their role in the political system and the interest of political analysts, state-level organizations have made a remarkable comeback (Cotter, Gibson, Bibby, & Huckshorn, 1984, 1989; Huckshorn 1976).[3]

B. The Structure of State Committees

State party central committees operate for both parties in each of the fifty states, where generally the means of choosing state party committee members is set by state law. In twenty-seven states, state committee members are chosen by other activists—by committee members at more local levels or delegates to state, congressional district, or county conventions. In fourteen other states, party rules determine the manner of selection, and again election by other party activists is the norm. Voters in primary elections choose state committee members in the remaining nine states. All of these means of selection are significant. Those who favor strong party organizations—such as the bipartisan Committee for Party Renewal (L. Epstein, 1991; Mileur, 1991)—feel that the state should interfere as little as possible with the internal workings of political parties. Furthermore, party activists can, of course, have more to say about the direction toward which they chart organizational activity if they themselves select their leaders. That is, the further that selection of state committee members is removed from the public—though not from public view or accountability—the more likely it is that party leaders will maintain a firm hold on state committee priorities.

State committees vary in size from relatively few to several hundred members. Some operate as committees of the whole; others have strong executive committees. Some meet with relative frequency; others only a few times a year, especially in nonelection years. State committees usually have the *formal* responsibility for calling party conventions, and they often choose some members of the state's delegation to national nominating conventions as well. These committees are consistently engaged in fund-raising efforts for the support of party candidates throughout the state.

All these formal duties were in place during the period of state party organization decline; they have not changed in the ascendancy. But two other factors have changed: the role of the state party chair and the role of the state party headquarters. In a very real sense the most important function of the state committee has become to elect the state party chair and then—as individual members who are themselves influential political figures in their home communities,

---

[3] To a large extent what the political science community knows about state-level organizations—and what the remainder of this section draws on—comes from the Party Transformation Study conducted by Cornelius P. Cotter, James L. Gibson, John F. Bibby, and Robert J. Huckshorn about a decade ago, and by a subsequent confirming study conducted by the Advisory Commission on Intergovernmental Relations. Those interested in pursuing this topic further are directed to Bibby (1990); Bibby et al. (1983); Conlan, Martino, and Dilger (1984) for the Advisory Commission Study; Cotter & Bibby (1980); Cotter et al. (1984, 1989); Gibson, Cotter, Bibby, & Huckshorn (1983, 1985); Huckshorn (1991); and Huckshorn, Gibson, Cotter, & Bibby (1986).

not so much as a committee—to support the state chair and the headquarters staff in the initiatives that they put forth.

C.   The Role of the State Party Chair

Robert Huckshorn (1976, chap. 4) has developed a now familiar categorization of the types of party leadership exercised by party chairs. His categorization relates to the role played by the state chair, regardless of the formal means by which that leader was selected. About three-quarters of the state chairs are chosen by the committees they lead; the remainder are elected at state conventions. But the choice and the role played are reflections of political realities well beyond the means of selection.

An *out-party independent* is a state party chair whose party does not control the governorship. Frequently these men (again infrequently women) are important politicians in their own right, elected from their own political base and serving as spokespersons and leaders for a party with few comparably placed politicians in the state.

Most of the state party chairs serving while their party is in control of the governorship are classified as *political agents* of the governor. Many of these state chairs have had political careers tied closely to the incumbent chief executive; they have managed his or her campaign or have served the governor or with the governor in another capacity. The state chair is frequently the governor's choice for that position. Power and influence flow to the state chair as a result of ties to the governor; the role of the state chair is to mold the party machinery to meet the governor's best interest. Some political agent–state chairs are highly visible and reputedly powerful political figures; others are more obscure party technicians. But their goal remains the same: to serve the governor.

The third leadership style for state party chairs is the *in-party independent*. These leaders come to office in a variety of ways. Depending on the timing of the selection of the state party chair, they may well be in office before the governor is elected, perhaps even as a supporter of someone who has opposed the winning governor for nomination. Party rules do not require state chairs to resign if the candidate they support loses; norms for remaining in this position vary from state to state. More frequently in this age of personalized campaigning, governors have shown little interest in the state party chair (thus permitting state committees to select their own leaders) because the governor has his or her own, totally independent, campaign organization. In still other cases state party chairs serve for longer periods of time, remaining in office even though the governorship changes hands and, more seriously, the other party takes control. In any of these instances the state party chair and the committee work separately from the governor. The strength of the leader depends on his or her ability to run an organization that has a significant impact on the electoral process.

No matter how they are chosen, state party chairs must fulfill certain responsibilities. They must lead the state committee that they head, developing a relationship with its members, defining tasks that they can accomplish, setting goals toward which they can strive. The chairs must also be a link to the grass roots, to the county and local organizations. Effective chairs know that coordinated organizational effort results in more support for party candidates. But coordination among individuals, each with his or her own stake and priority, is not easy to achieve. State party leaders spend a good deal of time mending fences and stroking individuals with easily bruised egos. The third responsibility for the state chairs—and the one that has led to their increasingly important role in the electoral process—is to maintain and direct increasingly complex and involved state headquarters. It is the state headquarters and the staff of the state headquarters, whose roles nominally are to support the state committee but who in fact are the engine that drives whatever gets done, that define the success or failure, the power or impotency, of state organization.

D.   The Ascendancy of the State Party Headquarters

Data on the state party headquarters size and staff are difficult to come by for all but the most recent years. Surely state party machines of the pre-World War I period had headquarters and workers on a payroll. But for many years, from roughly the Franklin Roosevelt through the Eisenhower administrations, little was heard from and little is known about what went on in state headquarters.

The rejuvenation of state headquarters seems to have begun in the early 1960s. At that time only a few state chairs occupied full-time paid positions; as many as half of the state committees—far more for the Republicans than the Democrats—employed full-time professional staff members. By 1990, however, approximately 30 percent of the state chairs were paid for working full-time for the party; nearly every state party was administered by either a full-time paid chair or a full-time paid executive director or both. Whereas once the headquarters of the state committee "traveled" from city to city as the hometown of the state chair changed, now virtually all state committees are housed in permanent headquarters, almost always in the state capital. Some of the headquarters contain the most up-to-date campaign technology, allowing for sophisticated campaigning for candidates for state and local office (Bibby, 1990; Sabato, 1988).

Concomitant with this increased presence has come a sizable increase in the budgets for state headquarters. Again, data are difficult to come by. However, the Party Transformation Study revealed that the average budget for state parties rose nearly *five times* (to nearly $300,000 annually) between 1961 and 1979. By 1984, the average had risen to nearly $350,000, with the largest state budgets reaching $2.5 million and with only one-quarter of the party committees operating with budgets of less than $100,000. Jumps in the ensuing decade apparently have been even larger, with Florida's Republican state party having a reported budget of $6 million in 1988 (Bibby, 1990, p. 28).

Professional staffs, permanent headquarters, and increased budgets are taken as measures of enhanced and reputedly more significant electoral activity. Huckshorn (1991, pp. 1061–1063) has outlined ten separate kinds of activities carried on by various state party committees. Observers note, of course, that all state committees do not engage in all these activities. Variety among the political experiences in the American states is still one of the defining characteristics of our body politic. In the more heavily one-party states (recall Table 1-4), mi-nority-party organization is not very well developed. The Republicans in strongly Democratic Mississippi, for example, are involved in relatively few of these activities. Still, the list is instructive to demonstrate the kinds of activities that organizations carry on when they are functioning effectively.

Five of the activities deal with supporting the development of the party it-self. Thus, state parties are involved in significant *fund-raising* activities to sup-port the budgets referred to above. Moreover, professionally generated fund-raising is not cost-free: donor lists have to be developed, computers maintained, telephone campaigns managed, large contributors involved, and the like. A number of state party organizations maintain full-time, paid fund-raising staffs to support these activities.

Second, parties are involved in various efforts to *mobilize their electorate.* This mobilization is a traditional party activity, but state headquarters are in-volved in more and more sophisticated ways of identifying potential voters, of registering new voters, of maintaining lists of party supporters, and of getting out the vote on election day. Whereas once the files for local communities were kept on three-by-five cards in a precinct leader's kitchen drawer, now state headquarters maintain, update, and distribute computer-generated lists of po-tential supporters in every community in a state.

State headquarters with larger budgets are also involved in *public opinion polling* for the entire state party ticket. These activities are particularly impor-tant to candidates for local office who cannot afford polling themselves. While data provided by these polls are often not specific about how one particular candidate or another is doing, or how one campaign technique or another is working, they do give general information about the mood of the electorate, re-actions to statewide or national events, and the like. Similarly, a number of state committees make an ongoing effort to be involved in *issue development.* State party platforms are normally written at state conventions, but throughout the political cycle issues change and new issues emerge. State party headquarters try to keep abreast of these developments, to monitor how the party is doing on its platform pledges, and to react to changing situations. Once again, individual state and local candidates and officeholders do not have the sophistication to keep up with all emerging issues. The coordinated efforts of a state headquar-ters can be very helpful in this regard.

The final activity relating to support of party development is the publica-tion of a *newsletter* or the development of other means of assuring communica-tion throughout the party. Most party committees do publish newsletters that provide a good forum for the party chair and a means for party members to know what others are thinking.

The other state party activities outlined by Huckshorn relate more directly to candidates for office. For instance, many parties are involved in the *recruit-ment* of candidates to run for office. One test of the strength of a state party or-ganization is the extent to which it is able to fill the slate of candidates running for state legislature and other state offices. Massachusetts Republicans point with pride, for instance, to the fact that they competed for over three-quarters of the seats in the lower house of the state legislature and all but two state senate seats in 1990. Only four years earlier, 103 (of 160) Democratic candidates for state representative and 25 (of 42) Democratic candidates for state senate had faced no Republican opposition. (See Chapter 6, Table 6-1, to see variation across states and within states over a period of years.)

Not only do state parties recruit some candidates for office, but in roughly half of the states, state party officials are involved in *endorsing candidates* before primary elections are held (see Chapter 6). At times endorsement is a *derecruitment* function, convincing prospective candidates for a nomination that they are likely to lose because the party will support someone else. State party officials involve themselves this way when they believe that one candidate would clearly be stronger in the general election or when they believe that a primary would so divide the party as to make the one who received the party endorsement a weaker candidate in the general election. At other times, parties use a formal or informal mechanism for stating their preference among candidates competing in a primary. Endorsement by a strong and effective party organization can have a great deal of impact because primaries are typically characterized by low voter turnout.[4]

Closely related to this endorsement function is the role that state parties play in *selecting delegates to national nominating conventions.* Democratic state party chairs (and the highest-ranking officer of the opposite gender) are automatically members of the Democratic National Committee and delegates to the national convention. While Republican rules are not so formal, party leaders play an equally important role. In some states, in both parties, state committees select other delegates to national conventions. And in all states, in both parties, state leaders to various degrees are able to influence how the other delegates are chosen and which individuals are selected.

The final two activities are more directly related to candidate campaigning in the general election. State parties make *financial contributions* to individual candidates, and they provide a range of *services for campaigns.* Again, the variety of experiences among the states is wide. State party financial contributions are probably least significant for candidates running for statewide office, because of the relatively small proportion of the large campaign budgets that state parties can give to candidates for statewide posts. They are most significant for campaigns with smaller campaign expenditures, e.g., campaigns for state representative. Depending on the sophistication of the state headquarters, the state party can supply a whole range of services for the party's candidates. Frequently because of economies of scale, because of their ability to piggyback with statewide campaigns, and because of their willingness to coordinate messages for all of a party's candidates, state headquarters can provide candidates with assistance in dealing with the media, designing paid advertising, complying with financial disclosure regulations, polling, developing issue positions, telephoning,

---

[4] I am indebted to Paul Herrnson for reminding me that party endorsement can be the"kiss of death" in some states and in areas of other states. Democrats in Massachusetts and New York have been made painfully aware of this in recent years.

distributing literature, identifying and turning out voters, and conducting other common campaign activities.

State party organizations have grown and developed in recent decades, in part at least because of an infusion of funds and influence from the national level. At the same time, state organizations stand as a cogent reminder of an organization's ability to adapt to a changing environment. Three decades ago candidates could safely ignore most state party organizations if they were interested in running for office. Analysts could be ignorant of the functioning of the state party and miss little of what was important in a state's politics. Neither is true today. More and more, state party organizations are vibrant and growing, commanding increased attention by those running for office and those analyzing their campaigns.

IV. PARTY ORGANIZATION AT THE NATIONAL LEVEL

In 1964 Cotter and Hennessey called their important study of the two national committees *Politics without Power.* Their title aptly caught the significance of what went on at the two national committee offices. Politics was everywhere; politicians were everywhere; intrigue was everywhere. But no one cared. The national committees had no resources, they had no influence, and they had no power.

Nearly three decades later Paul Herrnson (1990b, p. 41) wrote that "national party organizations in the United States are now financially secure, institutionally stable, and highly influential. . . ." And he too aptly captured the aspect of politics he was observing. Virtually *every* aspect of party organization has been transformed in recent years, but in no case is this change more apparent than in the national party organizations.

A. The Structure of National Party Organizations

Cotter and Hennessey's book dealt with the two national committees. When analysts discuss the federal nature of the American party system, they are naturally led to the national committees; for these committees stand atop the organizational pyramid whose base is the precinct worker.[5] In the politics of the 1990s, however, party organization at the national level must involve the so-called Hill committees, the congressional and senatorial campaign committees of the two parties as well.

1. The National Committees The Democratic National Committee has existed continuously since 1848; the Republican National Committee since 1856. Each was structured as a means of coordinating national election campaigns.

---

[5] To be technically accurate, the national conventions stand atop the pyramid. However, the conventions come together only once every four years, and the national committees are the ongoing symbols of the national party organizations.

(For an exhaustive history of the national committees and their chairs in addition to Cotter and Hennessey, 1964, see R. Goldman, 1990.) Formation of the national committees was an important step in changing the parties from loose and totally autonomous confederations of state party activists to more federalized organizations with a unified purpose (Herrnson, 1990b, pp. 41–42). For the first century of their existence, the two national committees were involved principally with presidential elections. Only in recent decades has their role expanded.

Membership The two national committees have some similarities and some differences. As an example, each party is composed of representatives from the various states. However, the Republican National Committee (RNC) has normally followed a principle of equality among the states. Thus, the RNC is now composed of three representatives from each state: a national committeeman, a national committeewoman, and the state party chair.[6]

On the other hand, the Democratic National Committee (DNC) begins with state representation—a national committeeman and national committeewoman, the state chair, and the highest-ranking officer of the opposite gender from each state—and expands from there. Two hundred additional members are apportioned among the states according to a formula weighing population and Democratic vote in the last presidential election. Others are added ex officio because of positions they hold—the officers of the DNC (who need not otherwise qualify as members); three governors including the chair of the Democratic Governors' Association; the party leaders in the House and Senate and an additional member of each body; representatives of the Young Democrats, the National Federation of Democratic Women, and Democratic mayors, county officials, and state legislators; and up to twenty other at-large members to accommodate groups still underrepresented.[7] The total membership of the DNC in 1990 had reached over four hundred members.

Executive Committees Obviously each committee is too large and unwieldy to work as an efficiently functioning body. Each meets only twice a year but has an executive committee that meets between full committee meetings and is, in actuality, the decision-making organization. The RNC's Executive Council comprises eleven members, three appointed by the chair and eight elected from regional caucuses; in addition it has a number of ex officio members—the RNC officers and chairs of the various committees.[8] The DNC's Ex-

[6] The addition of representatives from American Samoa, the District of Columbia, Guam, Puerto Rico, and the Virgin Islands brings the total membership of the RNC to 165. For a period of time, from 1952 to 1968, the RNC membership reflected Republican voting strength in the most recent elections; this scheme was abandoned with a return to the principle of state equality after the 1968 election.

[7] These at-large members and two additional vice chairs were added to the DNC in 1988, primarily to include the followers of unsuccessful presidential candidate Jesse Jackson.

[8] The RNC also has an Executive Committee that includes the Executive Council and the officers of auxiliary organizations, e.g., the Young Republican National Federation, the National Republican Heritage Council (ethnics), the Republican Labor Council, and Republican elected officials' organizations and others whose activities the RNC is trying to coordinate with its own. The Executive Committee is advisory to the chair and has no formal powers within the party.

ecutive Committee is chosen in such a way as to reflect the constituent groups that constitute the full committee.

Chairs Obviously the most visible members of the two national committees are their chairs. Each chair and the other officers of the national committees are formally elected by the committee members. For the Republicans the chairman (and the cochairman who must be of the opposite gender) is elected by the full committee in January of each odd-numbered year for a two-year term.[9] The chairman and cochairman must be full-time paid employees of the RNC, according to committee rules. In most recent years they have been "nominated" by Republican presidents and anointed by the RNC. When the Republicans last did not control the White House, the RNC chose as its chair William Brock, a former United States senator from Tennessee, who was defeated in his bid for reelection in 1976.

Typically less precise, the Democratic party rules call for a chairperson, five vice chairpersons, a secretary, a treasurer, and "other appropriate officers." The DNC officers have traditionally been chosen at a committee meeting on the day following the adjournment of the national convention. When tradition was followed, the chair, who served for the length of the campaign, was the choice of the presidential nominee. However, in 1984, candidate Walter Mondale wanted to select Bert Lance, the chair of the Georgia State Democratic Party and an early and influential Mondale backer. Many committee members objected, however, citing Lance's forced resignation as budget director in the Carter administration. Mondale was forced to back down and go with the DNC's preference, incumbent chair Charles Manatt, who had played a key role in rebuilding the national headquarters during his term of office. In January after a presidential election, Democrats choose their leader again. Again the "old tradition" allows for the successful presidential candidate to name his party leader; but competition is more open if the Republicans have prevailed in gaining the White House. As the Democrats have not won a presidential election since the revolt against Bert Lance, no one knows if the old tradition will operate in the future.

2. The "Hill Committees" The National Republican Congressional Committee (NRCC) and the Democratic Congressional Campaign Committee (DCCC, or D triple C) have been in existence since the end of the Civil War, growing out of incumbents' typical insecurity concerning their parties' electoral chances. The National Republican Senatorial Committee (NRSC) and the Democratic Senatorial Campaign Committee (DSCC) were created by party leaders in the Senate after the passage of the Seventeenth Amendment. During most of their existence, however, these committees, composed of incumbent representatives and senators, have been of little consequence.

These Hill committees tried to aid their party candidates. However, in an age when strong party allegiance dominated voting patterns, the Hill commit-

---

[9] Usage here follows the *Rules of the Republican Party,* adopted by the Republican National Convention in New Orleans, August 16, 1988.

tees had little impact. The situation changed, ironically, when candidate-centered campaigns became the norm. As candidates began to run their own personalized campaigns, the most important resource was money—and the role of the Hill committees followed logically, and the role of the national party organizations changed.

B.   The Enhanced Role of the National Party Organizations

Just as the two national committees differ in their composition—reflecting a philosophical difference between a Republican party that reflects geographic constituencies and a Democratic one that reflects both demographic and geographic constituencies—so too does the functioning of the national organizations of the two parties reflect broader party differences.

Political parties as significant contributors to electoral politics were "threatened" by changes in how campaigns worked. Once campaigns were labor-intensive, relying heavily on grass-roots efforts and established party loyalty to draw voters. In the most recent years, however, campaigns have become more candidate- rather than party-centered; they have relied on the "wholesale" technique of reaching the voters—radio, television, computer-generated mailings—rather than the "retail" techniques involving personal relationships and loyalty. The role of party organization, for the Democrats and the Republicans, appeared to be becoming obsolete. But the parties did respond, looking for a new role to play in an evolving new political reality.

The parties' first responses were very different. The Democrats undertook a period of intense *party reform* after the 1968 party convention. (This aspect of changes in the Democratic national party organization is described in detail in Chapter 8.) The goal of the reforms was to make the party more open, more representative, more democratic. The means to achieve this goal was a series of changes in party rules and the imposition of those rules on state and local parties by the national organization. The party thus became more centralized, with reform commissions operating out of national headquarters stipulating rules that governed state and local party procedures.

The Republicans were satisfied with their rules—and philosophically did not believe in the national organization working its will on state and local party units. Except for those situations in which state law required party rule change, the Republicans were firm in their belief that a decentralized federation of state parties best reflected their view of how a national organization should be governed.

But after Watergate, the disastrous congressional elections in 1974, and the defeat of Gerald Ford by Jimmy Carter in the 1976 presidential election, the Republicans became dissatisfied with the outcome of electoral competition. As noted before, former Tennessee Senator William Brock, an advocate of *party renewal*, won the election to head the Republican National Committee in 1977. At approximately the same time two other strong party men—Congressman Guy Vander Jagt of Michigan and Senator Robert Packwood of Oregon—were chosen to head the NRCC and the NRSC. These three leaders saw it as their mission to build their organizations into effective campaign support for Republican candidates. They did so through a rigorous program of building the party's financial base, of developing the party's organizational structure, and of hiring a sophisticated staff to serve the campaign needs of Republicans throughout the nation.

Table 3-1 shows the dramatic increase in the Republican party's financial base after Brock, Vander Jagt, and Packwood took command. You will note that there is a slight lag before anyone could realize the fruits of their efforts. Fundraising is a slow process. The figures in Table 3-2 show how much money must be spent in order to undertake a major and continuing fund-raising effort.

And what was done with this money? The Republicans moved all their national organizations into a party-owned national headquarters. They hired a large number of staff members. They worked with the states and with regions, appointing political directors, organizational consultants, and fund-raising directors who fanned out across the nation. They made computer services available for all party candidates, assisting, for instance, with fund-raising, compliance with campaign finance regulations, research on public opinion, compilation of voting lists, and analyses of opponents' records. They established local liaisons to help recruit strong candidates and to train and assist local candidates and campaign managers. In short, they provided a full-service campaign consulting organization for Republican candidates. (See Bibby, 1981.)

The Republicans did not stop there. The RNC and the two Hill committees developed truly awesome fund-raising capabilities so that they could support Republican candidates for federal office to the full extent permitted by the law. In fact, the NRCC and the NSCC entered into "agency agreements" with state party organizations, empowering the national offices to pay the state parties' share of campaign contributions and coordinated expenditures in House and Senate races (Herrnson, 1988, 1990b; Jacobson, 1985a).

In the starkest terms, the Democrats were caught napping—and they fell far behind. While their party's reforms may have conformed to a philosophical

TABLE 3-1. National Party Receipts, 1976–1990 (in millions)

Party	1976	1978	1980	1982	1984	1986	1988	1990
Democrats								
DNC	$13.1	$11.3	$15.4	$16.5	$46.6	$17.2	$52.3	$14.4
DCCC	.9	2.8	2.9	6.5	10.4	12.3	12.5	9.1
DSCC	1.0	.3	1.7	5.6	8.9	13.4	16.3	17.5
Total	$15.0	$14.4	$20.0	$28.6	$64.9	$42.9	$81.1	$41.0
Republicans								
RNC	$29.1	$34.2	$77.8	$84.1	$105.9	$83.8	$91.0	$68.7
NRCC	12.2	14.1	20.3	58.0	58.3	39.8	34.5	33.8
NRSC	1.8	10.9	22.3	48.9	81.7	86.1	65.9	65.1
Total	$43.1	$59.2	$120.4	$191.0	$245.9	$209.7	$191.4	$167.6

Source: For 1976–1988, Herrnson, 1990b, p. 49; for 1990, FEC Press Release, March 15, 1991.

TABLE 3-2. National Committee Receipts and Expenditures, 1981

A. Republican National Committee

Receipts		
Direct response	$26,710,400	
Major contributors	5,651,800	
Miscellaneous	1,149,000	
Total receipts		$33,511,200
Expenditures		
Chair's office	347,100	
Cochair's office	218,200	
Deputy chair—liaison	331,600	
Deputy chair—political	271,000	
Fund-raising	8,845,000	
Political	5,979,700	
Administration	1,959,000	
Communications	2,488,900	
Redistricting	1,318,700	
Media	1,401,000	
White House support	1,898,700	
RNC meetings	160,500	
Polling	880,300	
1980 obligations	1,492,800	
Total expenditures		$27,592,500

B.   Democratic National Committee

Receipts		
Direct mail	$1,722,423	
Prospect mail	1,001,349	
Major contributor and fund-raising events	1,919,724	
Joint fund-raising contributions	32,275	
Contributions for payment of pre-1975 indebtedness	220,222	
Nonfederal contributions	1,093,389	
Other	118,930*	
Total receipts		$6,108,090
Fund-raising expenses		
Direct mail	820,812	
Prospect mail	1,277,811	
Major contributor and fund-raising events	1,080,486	
Total fund-raising expenses	3,179,109	
General and administrative expenses		
Payroll and related expenses	1,407,776	
Office and equipment rental	312,300	
Telephone and telegraph	168,565	
Professional services	407,907	
Travel	299,877	
Printing and office supplies	124,878	
Postage	72,158	
Depreciation, repairs, maintenance	20,846	
Interest, insurance, other taxes	38,135	
Other	82,034	
Total general and administrative expenses	2,934,480	

TABLE 3-2. National Committee Receipts and Expenditures, 1981 (*cont.*)

B. Democratic National Committee	
Political projects and constituency building	
Transfers for voter registration	15,000
Contributions and campaign support	273,214
Total political projects and constituency building	296,647
Total expenditures	$6,410,236

*DNC officials determined that a reserve for possible vendor claims arising out of previous national conventions was excessive and recorded the balance of $68,000 as other income.

Source: Data provided to Citizens' Research Foundations by national committees.

need to democratize the party, party renewal was necessary before the DNC and the Democratic Hill committees could begin to aid their party's candidates in ways even remotely similar to those that the Republicans were using. The Democrats' effort began after their massive defeat in the 1980 election—an election that saw President Carter's landslide loss to Ronald Reagan, the loss of the Democratic majority in the Senate for the first time since 1954, and the loss of thirty-four House seats, half of the margin they held before the election.

Charles Manatt, a long-time Democratic activist and fund-raiser, was elected chair of the DNC after the 1980 debacle. At the same time, the enter-prising and ambitious Representative Tony Coelho of California took over the DCCC (Herrnson, 1988; B. Jackson, 1988). And in rapid succession, two sena-tors committed to party building—Lloyd Bentsen of Texas and George Mitchell

Reprinted with permission of Auth/Universal Press Syndicate

of Maine—were elected to chair the DSCC. Tables 3-1 and 3-2 demonstrate how far behind the Republicans the Democrats really were. But by the 1986 election, party efforts finally began to pay off. New DNC Chair Paul Kirk established task forces of consultants to aid Democrats in about a third of the states with the same kinds of services the Republicans were supplying throughout the nation. By 1988 they had doubled these efforts. The Democrats too have moved all their organizations into a new party-owned building, complete with an impressive media studio. But catch-up is a difficult game to play. Even though Republican fund-raising has slowed in the most recent electoral cycles, the Democrats still cannot match Republican efforts in terms either of supplying services or of helping candidates and parties with significant infusions of funds (Herrnson, 1990b).

The national organizations of both parties then have made major efforts to modernize and to professionalize their operations. To paraphrase George Washington Plunkett of Tammany Hall, the Republicans saw their opportunities first and they took them. The Democrats have been swimming upstream ever since, but the distances seem to be narrowing in the 1990s.

Both parties have used the knowledge and experience gained at the national level to improve state and local organization. While the national Democratic party has imposed rules on its local party units, "sticks" to compel action, the Republicans have refused to do so. On the other hand, the Republican party has used money and services as financial inducements to entice its state and local units to professionalize their operations, "carrots" also used by the Democrats but in much smaller amounts. Thus, though in different ways, the "nationalization" of party organization goes on in both parties, affected more by the recognition of the sources of funds and of expertise than by philosophical concerns. The parties have adjusted to new situations, realizing that they are primarily electoral institutions and that they have had to find a means to make their contribution significant to those running for office.

V.   POLITICIANS VIEW PARTY ORGANIZATION

John S. Trinsey, Jr., a Pennsylvania real estate developer, has a very clear view of party organization. He does not like it. Trinsey, a Republican, wants to be a United States senator. When Pennsylvania Republican U.S. Senator John Heinz was killed in a tragic airplane-helicopter accident on April 4, 1991, Trinsey wanted to run to succeed Heinz. The laws of the commonwealth of Pennsylvania call for the major parties to nominate candidates for office by primary elections, except in the case of special elections (to fill unexpectedly vacated seats). In those cases commonwealth law permits the state party committee to make the nomination.

The Republican State Party Committee in Pennsylvania was prepared to nominate former governor and current United States Attorney General Richard Thornburgh as the party's candidate to succeed Heinz. Trinsey, bitter in his disappointment, interceded with a lawsuit, claiming that nomination by party organization violated the Seventeenth Amendment to the United States Constitution, which called for the direct election of senators. United States District Court Judge Edward N. Cahn ruled in favor of Trinsey in early June, causing Thornburgh to delay the announcement of his candidacy and his resignation from the Bush cabinet, and throwing the election into disarray.[10] Finally in early August a three-judge panel of the United States court of appeals overruled Judge Cahn and allowed the nominations and special election to proceed. John Trinsey had lost; party organization had won.

The Pennsylvania case is probably unique. But the point is illustrative. When party organization is strong, or state laws favor strong parties (as do those that allow nomination by caucus or formal endorsements before primaries; see Chapter 6), politicians care a great deal about those organizations. The most important traditional tool available to party organization was control over nominations. When that power was given to the ordinary voters by the spread of direct primary elections during the progressive era, party organizations suffered (Key, 1956). Those party organizations that rapidly adapted or those favored by state law retain power and remain important to the politicians in their areas.

In recent years, however, smart politicians have taken note of the increased importance of the role of party. The debate over reform of the federal campaign finance laws during the 102d Congress has largely been a debate over two ingredients: the role of political action committees and the role of political parties. The Republican party has a much stronger financial base than does the Democratic party. Democrats in Congress are certainly not going to permit any change that deprives them of their base of campaign support but leaves the Republicans in an advantageous position. Candidates for office know that the new role for political parties is an important one, one that can powerfully affect their careers.

Similarly, the 1988 presidential candidates considered the role of grassroots organizations as crucial to their efforts. Both the Bush and the Dukakis campaigns turned their impressive fund-raising efforts toward raising money for state and local organizations' campaigns after their own nominations were secure. In large part this strategy was a recognition of the campaign finance laws, which permitted money in excess of the federal grant to presidential campaigns to be spent in this way. But the two candidates also recognized that their support for strong local efforts would result in higher vote totals for themselves (see Chapter 9).

Thus, from the politicians' point of view, party organization is far from inconsequential. While party machines no longer exist, while elected politicians no longer pay undying homage to the political boss, today's candidates for office have taken cognizance of a new reality—the redefined and enhanced role that party organization is playing in the electoral process.

---

[10] Pennsylvania's Democratic Governor Robert P. Casey, after some delay, appointed Harris Wofford to replace Heinz until the time of the special election. The Democratic State Committee nominated Wofford as its candidate in that special election, by acclamation, on June 1, before Judge Cahn's ruling. The relatively unknown Wofford was considered an underdog to Thornburgh. Any delay in the special election was to Wofford's advantage, as it gave him more time to spread his name throughout the state.

chapter

4

Political Participation
and Voting Behavior

The question of political participation is answered in either of two ways. Some contend that America is a democracy; everyone should vote. Citizens who don't vote can't complain. The system is clearly in trouble, then, if nearly half of the eligible voters stay home.

Others feel that those who really care enough *do* vote. We don't want those who must be dragged to the polls, who vote for the candidate who looks best on television, to determine who will govern us. If citizens don't like what the government is doing, they will vote; low turnout shows satisfaction, not dissatisfaction. (For a discussion of this debate in the political science literature, see, as examples, Bennett & Resnick, 1990; Gant & Luttbeg, 1991, chap. 3; Piven & Cloward, 1988.)

In the eyes of politicians, who votes is more than a theoretically interesting question. It is a matter of the most significant political consequence.

In Florida, in 1988, two incumbent members of Congress squared off in the Senate race, to fill the seat vacated by Democrat Lawton Chiles, who retired. Republican Connie Mack III defeated Democrat Buddy MacKay by fewer than 35,000 votes out of the more than 4 million votes cast. For MacKay it was a race of "what ifs?" Democratic presidential candidate Michael Dukakis had pulled out of Florida weeks before the campaign ended, knowing that the state was lost and reallocating his disappearing resources elsewhere. MacKay wonders if more Democrats would have turned out to vote—and would have voted for him—had Dukakis not closed camp. Mack thought he had lost when the votes were counted on election night, awakening to find himself a winner because a vast majority of those who voted absentee favored him. MacKay wonders what would have happened if he had invested more of his resources into gathering absentee ballots. Who turned out to vote—and who did not turn out to vote—determined Florida's newest senator.

Four years earlier, the congressional race in Indiana's Eighth District between incumbent Democrat Frank McCloskey and Republican challenger Richard McIntyre was determined by four votes out of nearly a quarter of a million cast. Because of a number of irregularities in counting the vote, the election was disputed and eventually decided on a party-line vote in the House. But if either candidate had convinced more of his potential supporters to turn out to vote, the dispute might have been avoided. Much the same can be said for the New Hampshire Senate race between Democrat John Durkin (1975–1981) and Republican Louis Wyman (1963–1975) a decade earlier. That race was so close that after seven months of hearings and debate the full Senate refused to declare a winner and ordered a reelection. Each election year finds a number of close races throughout the nation, for offices great and small. Politicians thus expend a high percentage of their resources convincing those who support their candidates to turn out to vote on election day.

Voting is only one aspect of political participation, albeit the only type of activity engaged in by most citizens. This chapter will begin with an examination of voting, exploring the expansion of the franchise and the exercise of the right to vote. It will then look at other forms of political participation, activities that require more commitment by citizens and are therefore the choice of fewer Americans.

While many citizens vote because of a feeling of civic responsibility, many others expend what political energy they have out of loyalty to a political party, concern about a particular issue, or belief in a specific candidate. Politicians want citizens to go to the polls, but they also want them to pull the "right" levers. This chapter will then turn to the question of how individual citizens decide for whom they will vote. The rich political science literature on this subject will be reviewed before the entire subject is viewed from the perspective of practicing politicians.

I.   WHO VOTES; WHO DOESN'T

The discussion of voting in America can be broken down into two separate topics: who is eligible to vote and who exercises the franchise.

A.   Expansion of the Franchise

In 1789, generally only white males who owned property were eligible to vote. According to Hugh Bone and Austin Ranney (1976, p. 35), the electorate was composed of only one in thirty Americans. Today, legal limitations keep very few citizens from voting. The history of this aspect of electoral reform in America has been one of continuous expansion of the franchise. This history has had four separate phases—increase in white male eligibility, enfranchisement of black citizens, enfranchisement of women, and enfranchisement of those between the ages of eighteen and twenty-one. Additional recent steps—and proposed reforms—seek to make voting easier for all potential voters.

1. Property Requirements   In colonial times only those who owned land were empowered to vote. The first step in expanding the franchise involved eliminating the property requirement for white males, often replacing it with the requirement that only taxpayers could vote. This reform happened on a state-by-state basis, starting even before the ratification of the Constitution, when Vermont granted universal male suffrage in 1777 and South Carolina substituted a taxpayer requirement for a property-holding requirement in 1778. The property qualification finally disappeared when Virginia eliminated it in 1850. A taxpayer requirement persisted for some years, often being fulfilled with the payment of a nominal poll tax. The poll tax was employed mainly in the south to keep blacks from voting; poor whites were also affected. By the 1960s all but five states had eliminated even nominal poll taxes. Those remaining taxes were rendered void for national elections with the ratification of the Twenty-Fourth Amendment in 1964; two years later, the Supreme Court held poll taxes to be unconstitutional in *any* election in the case of *Harper v. Virginia State Board of Elections,* 383 US 663 (1966).

2. Black Suffrage The extension of the franchise to black males was not so unidirectional as it was for white males. The Fifteenth Amendment to the Constitution, ratified in 1870, was the culmination of a number of post-Civil War steps toward granting black males the right to vote. That amendment forbade states from denying or abridging the right to vote based on "race, color, or previous condition of servitude."

However, that seemingly broad prohibition did not end the problem of racial discrimination in voting. Post-Reconstruction southern legislators were extremely inventive in creating ways to prevent or at least discourage blacks from voting. These legal limitations included literacy tests, tests on interpreting the Constitution, "white only" primaries, poll taxes, and residency requirements. Administrative decisions—such as placement of polling places in remote areas or in areas that had been the sites of black lynchings—and social and economic pressures further restricted black voting. The result was that the black vote was more apparent than real in most southern states during the first half of the twentieth century.

The first important attack on southern restrictions of black voting was the landmark Supreme Court decision in *Smith v. Allwright,* 321 US 649 (1944). Southern states had attempted to establish in law that political parties were private organizations and that party primary elections were therefore private matters not regulated by state law. Since the Republican party was very weak throughout the south, the Democratic party nomination in the primary was frequently tantamount to election. By setting party rules that limited the Democratic party primary to whites only, southern states effectively eliminated blacks from the political process. In *Smith v. Allwright* the Court ruled that the primaries were part of one electoral process and that, consequently, exclusion of blacks violated the Fifteenth Amendment. The "whites only" primary was thus ruled unconstitutional.

Black enfranchisement was an important goal of the civil rights movement of the 1950s and 1960s. The Civil Rights Act of 1957 created the Civil Rights Commission and empowered that commission to investigate voting rights violations and to suggest appropriate legal remedies to those violations. The 1957 act also gave the attorney general the power to seek court relief from voting rights violations through the injunction process. The follow-up 1960 Civil Rights Act empowered the federal courts to appoint referees to help blacks to register in areas where discrimination had been found.

Thus, the federal government was interceding to change the situation, but as Table 4-1 shows, such efforts had little effect on black suffrage in many states until a full century after the passage of the Fifteenth Amendment.

Many states used literacy tests or tests on the Constitution to keep blacks from the polls. Local officials exercised a good deal of leeway in administering these tests. In the Voting Rights Act of 1965 Congress suspended the use of such literacy tests. This suspension, renewed with the Voting Rights Act in 1970, was upheld by the Supreme Court in *Oregon v. Mitchell,* 400 US 112 (1970). In that important 1965 act, federal registrars were empowered to replace local or state officials in those areas which had used literacy tests in the 1964 election and in which fewer than half of those eligible had registered and voted in 1964 (in a total of seven states). That act, which was renewed and expanded not only in 1970, but also in 1975 and 1982,[1] has been credited with causing the dramatic impact on black registration that is shown in Table 4-1.

The 1970 extension of the Voting Rights Act also dealt with the question of residency requirements. Local officials have long asserted that they have a legitimate need for some residency requirements so that they can maintain accurate voting lists, preventing vote fraud by people casting ballots in more than one locality. However, in many areas, local officials used residency requirements as a means to keep mobile populations—often blacks in the south, but certainly others such as young people, as well—from voting. The 1970 Voting Rights Act set thirty days as the maximum residency requirement permissible for presidential elections. In *Dunn v. Blumstein,* 405 US 330 (1972), the Supreme Court ruled that the thirty-day residency limit should be used for all elections.

Legal restrictions to black voting have been all but eliminated through a long series of constitutional amendments, congressional actions, and Supreme Court decisions. The path to this goal has been long, but *legal* limitations on black suffrage no longer keep black Americans out of polling places in the south or anywhere else in this country.

3. Woman Suffrage While pages of many history books are devoted to a discussion of the civil rights movement and the struggle for black suffrage, relatively little coverage is generally afforded to the equally important and instructive battle for female suffrage.

In the early years of the abolition movement, the call for woman suffrage was closely linked to the cries for black freedom and eventually black voting rights. However, male leaders of the abolition movement soon found it in their interest to separate the two causes (for a full history of the struggle for woman suffrage see Catt & Shuler, 1969). While not abandoning their participation in

---

[1] Arguments over the extension of the Voting Rights Act were effectively ended on June 23, 1982, when the Voting Rights Act was extended an additional twenty-five years.

TABLE 4-1. Black Voter Registration in Southern States*

State	1960	1964	1969	1970	1971	1976	1980	1982	1984	1986
Ala.	13.7	19.3	61.3	66.0	54.7	58.4	55.8	69.7	71.4	68.9
Ark.	38.0	40.4	77.9	82.3	80.9	94.0	57.2	63.9	71.2	57.9
Fla.	39.4	51.2	67.0	55.3	53.2	61.1	58.3	59.7	57.3	58.2
Ga.	29.3	27.4	60.4	57.2	64.2	74.8	48.6	50.4	58.0	52.8
La.	31.1	31.6	60.8	57.4	58.9	63.0	60.7	61.1	74.8	60.6
Miss.	5.2	6.7	66.5	71.0	59.4	60.7	62.3	64.2	85.6	70.8
N.C.	39.1	46.8	53.7	51.3	49.8	54.8	51.3	50.9	59.5	58.4
S.C.	13.7	37.3	54.6	56.1	49.2	56.5	53.7	53.9	62.2	52.5
Tenn.	59.1	69.5	92.1	71.6	65.6	66.4	64.0	66.1	78.5	65.3
Tex.	35.5	—	73.1	72.6	68.2	65.0	56.0	49.5	65.3	68.0
Va.	23.1	35.5	64.8	57.0	52.0	54.7	53.2	49.5	62.1	56.2
Total	29.1	35.5	64.8	62.0	58.6	54.7	53.2	49.5	66.3	60.8

* All figures are percentages of the eligible, voting-age population. Florida, Louisiana, North Carolina, South Carolina, and Georgia since 1980 keep records of voter registration by race. The other states' figures are based on estimates by state officials.

Source: U.S. Bureau of the Census, *Statistical Abstract of the United States: 1982–1983*. Data for 1984 taken from "Population Characteristics," *Current Population Reports*, series P-20, no. 397, issued January 1985. Note that the figures for 1964 and 1969 are based on the recorded voting-age population for 1960. All other data collected by Voter Education Project, Inc., Atlanta, Ga.

The fight for woman suffrage was carried out on a state-by-state, as well as a national, basis. (Culver Pictures)

the movement to free those who were enslaved, women came together in the famous conference at Seneca Falls, New York, in 1848 to assert their own rights. From that point until the successful adoption of the Nineteenth Amendment in 1920, women suffragists waged a valiant, prolonged, often brilliant, frequently frustrating battle to win the right to vote.

The arguments against woman suffrage were, in their own way, as illogical and immoral as the arguments favoring slavery. According to Georgia Senator Joseph E. Brown, "The Creator intended that the sphere of the males and females of our race be different." Men, he claimed, "were qualified for those duties which required strength and the ability to combat with the sterner realities and difficulties of life." Thus, governing was "a laborious task, for which the male sex is infinitely better fitted than the female sex. . . . On the other hand, the Creator has assigned to women very laborious and responsible duties. . . . When the husband returns weary and worn in discharge of the difficult and laborious tasks assigned to him, he finds in the good wife solace and consolation which is nowhere else afforded." If woman were to engage in the affairs of state, "Who is to care for and train the children while she is absent in the discharge of these masculine duties?" (This argument is quoted from Key, 1964, p. 613; Key, in turn, cites Porter, 1918, p. 141, and Anthony & Harper, 1902, vol. IV, pp. 93–100.)

Women fought back against these arguments as best they could, starting at the local and state levels. First women were given the right to vote on school questions, presumably because these matters were closely related to "female" duties. By 1890 women could vote on educational matters in frontier states and territories (Key, 1964, p. 614). Wyoming had granted women the right to vote on all matters in 1869, while still a territory. In applying for admission to the Union, Wyoming included women suffrage in its constitution. When Congress first rejected this expansion of the franchise, Wyoming insisted on woman suffrage. Congress ultimately had to relent, admitting Wyoming as the first state with universal female suffrage in 1890. Other western states followed Wyoming's lead, in at least partial recognition of the important and equal role women played in the settlement of the frontier. But the progress was slow and often frustrating.

The suffrage movement had to fight on a state-by-state basis while still pursuing a national strategy. Campaign after campaign was fought on the state level; meanwhile, pressure was brought upon Congress. A variety of tactics were used. In those states in which women had the right to vote, they pressured congressmen and senators to push for a national amendment. When the Democratic party proved recalcitrant, women organized a campaign against all Democratic congressmen in suffrage states, to demonstrate their power. More than half of the Democratic candidates in the new suffrage states lost in the 1884 election; suffragists were credited with influencing this outcome.

Faced with this power, the parties began to listen. By 1916 woman suffrage was in both of the parties' platforms, though the suffragists still wanted state action. In 1917 the women turned to more militant actions, picketing the White House and delivering petitions to the president. Some were jailed; others replaced them. Those in jail demonstrated for the cause of prison reform; some engaged in hunger strikes. When female prisoners were force-fed, the press had a field day. More women came to Washington, and the jails became increasingly crowded. The effect of the pressure was telling.

The woman suffrage amendment passed the House in the second session of the Sixty-Fifth Congress, but it failed to achieve the two-thirds vote necessary in the Senate. More women came to Washington; more picketed; more were jailed; more hunger strikes ensued. Finally, President Wilson was won over to the cause. When the Republican-controlled House repassed the measure in 1919, Wilson pressured his fellow Democrats in the Senate to enact woman suffrage. At long last, in August 1920, the Nineteenth Amendment was ratified by the requisite number of states, and women won the right to vote in all elections. No further *legal* barriers could be used to impede women from voting.

This abbreviated discussion of the battle for woman suffrage points to a number of important conclusions. First, the tactics of the suffragists deserve much more attention than they are traditionally given. The suffragists' ability to gain their end, without the stimulus of a cataclysmic event like the Civil War or the benefit of the threat of electoral reprisal in most states, is a tribute to the skills of the women as politicians, skills seldom recognized by American scholars.

Second, political participation is most often defined as voting (or perhaps voting and other activities connected with the electoral process). The suffragists demonstrated that less traditional political participation (e.g., the hunger strike) can be equally effective in the American polity.

Third, the contrast with black suffrage is instructive. Black men won the right to vote through a constitutional amendment that forbade certain disenfranchisements by the states. Many found ways around that amendment for nearly a century before black voting was successfully in place in states that resisted that movement, most notably southern states. Women won their right to vote first on a state-by-state basis, and only after decades of struggle at the national level. Yet once that battle was won, no further legal impediments stood in women's way. The south, for example, did not try to discourage women from voting; there was never an "all-male" primary there. However, as will be discussed below, social pressures did keep women from voting in numbers equal to men for many years; the difference between legal eligibility and actual voting requires further examination.

4. Lowering the Voting Age For much of American history, twenty-one was the traditional age at which one might begin to vote. During World War II, when eighteen-year-olds were conscripted into military service, many people felt that the voting age should be lowered to eighteen. In 1943 Georgia did lower its voting age to eighteen, but no other state followed suit. President Eisenhower expressed support for eighteen-year-old voters during his first term (1953–1957), but only Kentucky amended its constitution to effect that change. When Alaska and Hawaii were admitted to the Union in the late fifties, their constitutions called for voting ages of nineteen and twenty, respectively.

No further changes ensued until the United States became embroiled in the Vietnam War. Once again, cries of "Old men send young men to die in foreign wars" and "Old enough to die but not old enough to vote" were heard. In response to this agitation and to the general public dissatisfaction with the war in Vietnam, Congress enacted the Voting Rights Act of 1970, one provision of which made eighteen-year-olds eligible to vote in all national, state, and local elections. In *Oregon v. Mitchell,* however, the Supreme Court struck down this provision, asserting that Congress could not constitutionally take such actions for state and local elections. As a response to this ruling, Congress passed—and the requisite number of states ratified—the Twenty-Sixth Amendment to the Constitution, making eighteen the minimum voting age for all elections, expanding the electorate in one step by more than it had been expanded by any action other than the Nineteenth Amendment.

5. Additional Regulations: Residency and Registration With few exceptions,[2] the potential voting population in the United States today includes all citizens over eighteen years of age. Even those citizens who had been prevented

---

[2] Currently, one must be a resident for thirty days within a state to be eligible to vote in a presidential election. About half of the states have month-long residency requirements for state and local elections; Arizona and Tennessee have fifty-day requirements; the rest have none. Additionally, "virtually all the states restrict the suffrage for reasons of crime or mental incompetence." For further information see Sorauf and Beck (1988, pp. 213–218).

from voting because of their inability to read and understand English can now vote; the 1975 extension of the Voting Rights Act requires bilingual ballots in areas of the country with large non-English-speaking populations. An American Indian tribe with no written language is even permitted to vote orally.

The other major barrier to voting involves the mobility of the American electorate. The 1970 Voting Rights Act extension established a maximum of thirty days for a residency requirement; it also established uniform state standards for absentee voting.

Some feel these standards and requirements are still too strict. Four states—Maine, Minnesota, Oregon, and Wisconsin—allow so-called instant registration; citizens may register to vote up to and on the day of an election. While some feel this procedure could lead to voter fraud, no evidence of efforts to subvert the system has been uncovered in states where it has been used. In any case, voter registration has increased in each such state.

A similar debate surrounds the question of the ease of voter registration. Robert Erikson (1981) has demonstrated that the biggest reason citizens do not vote is that they are not registered. A number of studies have examined the relationship between registration laws and the number of people registered (Powell, 1986; Rosenstone & Wolfinger, 1978; Squire, Wolfinger, & Glass, 1987; Wolfinger & Rosenstone, 1980). In the 101st Congress, the Democrats proposed legislation that would link voter registration to motor vehicle registration. The bill (HR 2190, S 874) passed the House in February 1990; but it died when efforts to break a Republican filibuster in the Senate were unsuccessful as the session drew to a close in the fall of that year. Similar legislation passed in the 102nd Congress in 1992 but failed to become law because of a veto by President Bush.

The debate on voter registration laws continues today. On the one hand, the question is a normative question about public policy: Shouldn't a democracy encourage its citizens to vote? Shouldn't all restrictions to voting be eliminated? On the other hand, the question is a pragmatic one: Is there evidence that restrictive voter registration laws impact significantly on participation? Would those whose names were added to the rolls by eased registration requirements necessarily turn out to vote? (See Bennett, 1990; Bennett & Resnick, 1990; Cassel & Luskin, 1988; C. Gans, 1990; Jackman, 1987; Piven & Cloward, 1988, 1989, 1990; Powell, 1986; Rosenstone & Wolfinger, 1978; Squire et al., 1987; Texeira, 1987; Wolfinger & Rosenstone 1980).[3] And further, the question is a political one. Surely Republicans and Democrats did not split on the motor vehicle registration bill because of differing views on the questions raised above. And surely the question of the cost of this procedure for registering voters was not enough to cause such a complete partisan division. The crucial question was the political one: if people were encouraged to regis-

---

[3] This debate also points to the cumulative way in which a discipline informs itself. A careful review of this literature reveals concern with normative questions, with pragmatic consequences of those normative questions, and with methodological controversies over how to answer the important questions posed.

ter, and they turned out to vote, for whom would they cast their ballots? Democrats and Republicans alike believed that more of these newly registered voters would vote Democratic; thus they split on this seemingly innocuous change in electoral law.

Regardless of how one feels about the impact of changes in registration laws, it is clear that instant registration and even the thirty-day limit, and certainly registration tied to motor vehicle registration, cause problems for communities with large, transient student populations. Permanent residents of relatively small communities with large residential universities fear, with some cause, that students will dominate local governmental elections. This issue continues to spark controversy whenever a college student is elected to a city council; to date it is more a problem in theory than in practice.

B.   Decline in Voter Participation

Let us recall the Florida Senate campaign in 1988, in which a lack of effort by the Democratic presidential campaign might have resulted in a low turnout among likely supporters of the Democratic candidate for the Senate. The non-voters were not kept from the polls by legal restrictions.[4] They simply were not motivated to exercise their right to vote.

Figure 4-1 shows that relatively low voter turnout is common in the United States. Turnout has actually been declining, in recent years, with turnout for presidential elections reaching a high point in 1960. Since then the decline has not been precipitous, but it has become a cause for concern among many political observers (Gant & Luttbeg, 1991, pp. 86–87).

1. Voting by Blacks Some aspects of this decline can be easily observed. For example, despite intense registration efforts by federal officials, particularly in certain southern states, and despite the success of these efforts depicted in Table 4-1, turnout rates for black voters have actually fallen since 1966, and the difference between turnout for blacks and whites has not varied significantly since 1968. (See Figure 4-2.)

These data make the registration efforts of the Reverend Jesse Jackson and Operation PUSH all the more important, particularly if new registrants turn out to vote. If Jackson's efforts can increase the black percentage of the vote, as they appear to have in 1984, blacks can have a major impact on national elections. The 1988 experience does little to confirm or refute this trend.

2. Voting by Young Voters Furthermore, for many years political scientists have known that the youngest voters vote in the smallest proportion (A. Camp-

---

[4] The Florida Senate race also illustrates the difficulty in providing simple explanations for complex phenomena. Supporters of the Democrat MacKay also claim that the form of the ballot used in this particular race might well have resulted in some of their potential supporters leaving the Senate election blank on their ballots. While the Democrats did not complain about the ballot form before the fact, this post hoc explanation of the high "drop-off," i.e., people who voted in the presidential election at the top of the ballot but not the senatorial election further on down, demonstrates how difficult it is to determine the exact cause of failure to vote.

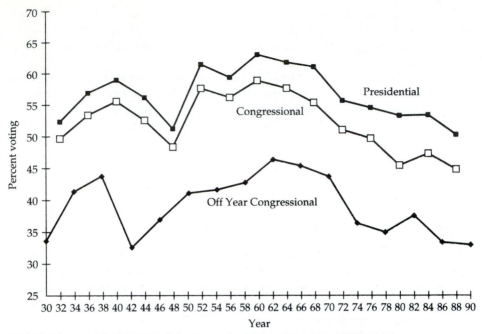

FIGURE 4-1   Presidential and congressional voter turnout, 1930–1990.

Source: *Congressional Quarterly's Guide to U.S. Elections,* 2d ed. Washington, D.C.: Congressional Quarterly, Inc. 1985, p. 320; for 1986–1990, see Ornstein, Mann, & Malbin, 1992, p. 48.

bell et al., 1960; Converse & Niemi, 1971). (See Figure 4-3.) Since the passage of the Twenty-sixth Amendment, the young have constituted an increased portion of the total electorate; therefore, their unwillingness to vote contributes increasingly to the overall decline in voter turnout.

Recent evidence suggests that most recent young voters have come of political age in an era during which political activity was not an expected norm; consequently their participation in voting will not increase with age as has been the case in the past (Tarrance, 1978, p. 12). This "negative" trend, clear among

FIGURE 4-2   Voter turnout by race, 1964–1988.

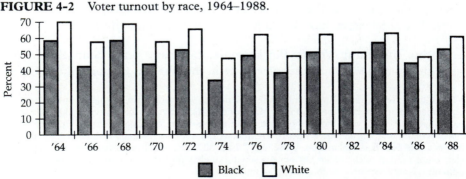

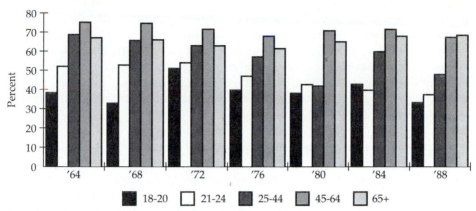

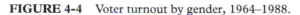

FIGURE 4-3   Voter turnout by age cohort, 1964–1988.

the first two groups of new voters enfranchised under the Twenty-Sixth Amendment, will be watched closely in the years ahead. In fact, recent research attributes the decline in voter turnout to a replacement of the age cohort that first voted before the New Deal, a cohort with consistently high turnout rates but which is disappearing from the electorate because of aging and death, with an age cohort that first voted after the New Deal (after the Great Society administration of Lyndon Johnson), a cohort that constitutes an increasingly large part of the electorate and has a consistently low turnout rate (W. Miller, 1992; Texeira, 1987).

3. **Voting by Women** If blacks and young voters have contributed to the decline in voter turnout, the same cannot be said for women. Turnout among women was quite low in the years immediately after enfranchisement. However, the number of female voters steadily increased until it leveled off at a turnout level only slightly below that of men by 1972 (Figure 4-4). The rejuvenation of political awareness by women qua women in the 1970s led to another increase

FIGURE 4-4   Voter turnout by gender, 1964–1988.

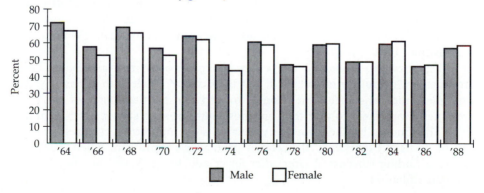

in participation to the point that women now participate in nearly the same proportion as do men. If Gerald Pomper's assertion (1975, p. 88) that women in the south, because of regional and cultural differences, participate less than do women in other regions is correct, the implication is that women in other regions now participate in higher percentages than do men in those areas. Nevertheless, we must go beyond mere demographic characteristics in distinguishing voters from nonvoters.

4. What Distinguishes Voters from Nonvoters? For more than three decades social scientists have been examining the American electorate in some depth. Despite a variety of research techniques, scholars have come to a remarkable consensus on what distinguishes voters from nonvoters. None of these conclusions is surprising, but some of the more important ones should be noted.

First, voting is a function of the "rules of the game." If it is easier to vote, if fewer roadblocks are put in the voter's way, more people vote. Thus, the expansion of the franchise, the easing of registration requirements, and continued efforts to open the door to black voters have increased the number of individuals voting. Those who still face legal roadblocks or racist hassles vote less frequently than do those in areas where voting is easier (A. Campbell et al., 1960; Milbrath & Goel, 1977, chap. 5).

Second, social position distinguishes voters from nonvoters. "Citizens of higher social and economic status participate more in politics. This generalization . . . holds true whether one uses level of education, income, or occupation to measure social status" (Verba & Nie, 1972, p. 125; see also Berelson, Lazarsfeld, & McPhee, 1954; A. Campbell et al., 1960; Dahl, 1961; Lane, 1959; Milbrath & Goel, 1977). Wolfinger and Rosenstone have refined this commonplace notion by isolating the effect of the various components of a voter's socioeconomic status. They conclude that "even after controlling for all other variables, education has a very powerful independent effect on the likelihood of voting" (Wolfinger & Rosenstone, 1980, p. 24). Education has the greatest effect on those with low income or low-status jobs, but it has a continuing effect at all levels. Neither income nor occupation was found to affect voting turnout to the same extent. The obvious importance of this hypothesis is that it helps explain the finding that socioeconomic status affects turnout. Wolfinger and Rosenstone attribute that finding to increased information, to ease of acquiring more information, and to a decline in anxiety because of greater political knowledge more than they do to economic variables that affect wealthier individuals (Wolfinger & Rosenstone, 1980, pp. 18–22).

Third, certain attitudes about politics distinguish voters from nonvoters. These attitudes are obviously interrelated, but they can be dealt with separately. For example, those who feel most strongly toward one political party or the other are much more likely to vote than are those without such strong partisan affiliation. This finding has held for every election since modern survey research began to be used extensively. It becomes particularly significant when combined with the finding (discussed later) that fewer and fewer Americans have strong partisan affiliation.

TABLE 4-2. Percentage of Persons of Differing Partisan Commitments Voting

Year	Strong Partisan, %	Weak Partisan, %	Independent, %	Voting Gap between Strong Partisan and Independent, %
1952	82	73	72	10
1956	80	73	75	5
1960	87	82	65	12
1964	84	77	59	25
1968	83	75	63	20
1972	82	72	51	31
1976	85	68	50	35
1980	85	61	55	30
1984	87	75	66	21
1988	84	68	50	34

Source: SRC/CPS data made available through the Inter University Consortium for Political and Social Research.

Table 4-2 reveals a number of other interesting variations; for example, the voting gap between independents and partisans is not consistent. On the one hand, the gap seems to be widening, again a finding the significance of which magnifies as the number of independent voters grows. On the other hand, peaks and valleys are evident. The fluctuations reflect another factor that distinguishes voters from nonvoters. People who are more interested in politics tend to vote more frequently. Partisans tend to be more interested than nonpartisans and, hence, to vote in higher percentages.

However, certain elections stimulate interest among more voters (Figure 4-5). These tend to be elections that involve dominating personalities (Eisenhower), elections that are important for particular groups (Catholics [or anti-Catholics] in 1960), elections that are perceived to be very close (1960, 1968),

FIGURE 4-5 Voter turnout by degree of interest in campaign, 1956–1988.

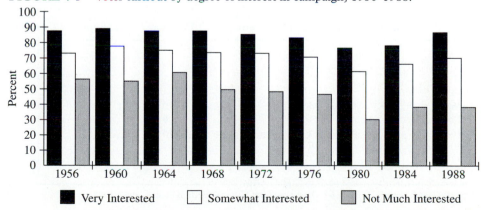

Very Interested   Somewhat Interested   Not Much Interested

or elections that revolve around critical issues and/or where the differences between the candidates are great (1932). Elections that meet none or few of these
criteria (1976) stimulate the least interest and have the lowest turnouts (Berelson et al., 1954; A. Campbell et al., 1960; Hill & Luttbeg, 1980, chap. 3; Milbrath & Goel, 1977, chap. 3; Verba & Nie, 1972).

In addition to partisanship and interest in a campaign, researchers have
found that *voters are distinguished from nonvoters by the number of political stimuli to
which they are exposed.* Again, this finding is not surprising, but it has interesting
implications. We would expect those most interested in politics to receive most
political communication—in fact to seek out such contacts. This expectation is
particularly apt for those highly involved with political parties. And both of
these expectations are supported by a good deal of evidence.

Similarly, those less interested would doubtless not go out of their way to
look for political information. Yet we do not always control the information we
receive, and campaign managers know that those who receive more information
vote more frequently. Therefore, one of their goals is to bombard citizens with
political messages, trying to penetrate the defenses of those who seek to avoid
politics. Why? The more people are reminded about politics, the more they are
reminded of their civic duty to vote, the more they feel guilty about not voting.
Thus, one clear campaign strategy is to work hard to stimulate the participation
of those most likely to support one's cause. If people are not interested in politics because of their own predilection or because of factors related to campaign,
the office seeker must stimulate that interest among his likely supporters, must
appeal to their sense of civic duty, must turn nonvoters into voters. (Almond &
Verba, 1965; Berelson et al., 1954; A. Campbell et al., 1960; Lazarsfeld, Berelson, & Gaudet, 1944; Milbrath & Goel, 1977, chap. 2).

Finally, in a number of different ways scholars have demonstrated that
those who are more knowledgeable about politics participate in greater numbers than those less knowledgeable. Tables 4-3 and 4-4 divide the electorate ac-

TABLE 4-3. Candidate Evaluations among American Voters

Percentage of Respondents Using Various Types of Candidate Evaluations

Year	Ideologue	Issue Oriented	Group Benefit	Partisan	Image	No Content
1952	1	16	5	1	62	15
1956	1	19	6	—	64	10
1960	1	20	5	—	62	12
1964	6	35	5	—	44	9
1968	3	23	5	19	36	15
1972	7	44	5	6	28	10
1976	7	35	9	13	27	9
1980	10	48	3	5	22	12
1984	6	67	5	5	8	10
1988	7	48	5	12	13	16

Source: Gant & Luttbeg, 1991, p. 69. Data taken from National Election Studies, 1952–1988.

TABLE 4-4. Percentage of Different Types of Candidate Evaluators Voting

		Types of Candidate Evaluations				
Year	Ideologue	Issue Oriented	Group Benefit	Partisan	Image	No Content
1952	87	76	63	71	79	48
1956	87	72	73	—	78	42
1960	100	87	84	—	85	50
1964	81	80	69	7	81	51
1968	93	79	64	77	79	54
1972	87	73	79	61	72	43
1976	77	74	70	72	67	33
1980	87	74	60	80	68	53
1984	88	76	73	77	70	45
1988	92	75	75	76	67	35

Source: Gant & Luttbeg, 1991, p. 114. Data taken from National Election Studies, 1952–1988.

cording to how voters evaluate candidates for the presidency. The first table clearly demonstrates a trend toward a more issue-oriented, ideological electorate. Certainly the modern electorate is more knowledgeable than one casting votes based on image or empty rhetoric, and arguably more knowledgeable than one basing evaluations simply on group benefits or partisan appeal. Table 4-4 shows that those who base evaluations on ideology or issues vote in a higher proportion than those relying on image or rhetoric. The clear implication from these data is that frequent voters are becoming more knowledgeable and distinguishing themselves more from nonvoters who are less informed (Gant & Luttbeg, 1991, chap. 2).

C. Summary

Citizen participation is obviously central to the functioning of the American political system. Theorists of democracy know this; social scientists know this; most of all, politicians know this. A politician can be the most brilliant, best informed, most skilled and socially committed citizen in a community, but, as a candidate, that politician is a loser if the votes are not there. Who votes is, therefore, critical.

This review of voter participation has had two rather elementary themes. *First, the eligible electorate has been expanding. Second, the actual electorate has not been growing proportionately.* Legal barriers that have prevented certain groups from voting have been removed, but at least in the case of black and young voters, these changes in law have not always led to mass marches to the polls. Quite the opposite, participation by these groups has not increased as reformers would have liked.

Not only do certain groups fail to participate as fully as the rest of the electorate, but analysts have also postulated other distinctions among voters and nonvoters. One conclusion from these distinctions is that two groups are now in evidence. Among the voters is a broadening group of educated, concerned, issue-oriented or ideological balloters, who often express preferences among candidates based on the considerable store of knowledge that they have obtained and evaluated, not simply because of partisan or image-related appeals.

At the other extreme is a considerable number of nonvoters, individuals who are not interested in politics, who do not associate themselves with either party, who are not informed about political matters. They avoid political stimuli and ignore claims that they have a civic duty to vote.

What does this polarity say about the health of the American polity? Obviously the fact that the voting electorate is informed is a positive sign, though an observer must at least inquire about the implications of the voting patterns of these super-brights for political parties and then determine if one cares what these implications mean. But what about the nonvoters? Does America need "charismatic" candidates, lowest-common-denominator advertising, and divisive issues in order to stimulate participation? Or should anyone care that mobs of Americans stay home and are disinterested? If the state of their lives were unbearable, they would indeed become involved, and so perhaps inactivity is a sign of health. Is there further cause for concern if the nonvoters are in fact a whole new generation of citizens who opt not to participate? One can argue either side of these positions convincingly. To some extent, the answer must depend on what else these individuals do. Thus, before we turn to an examination of individual voting behavior, we will look at varieties of political participation other than voting.

II. PARTICIPATION IN POLITICS IN AMERICA

Social science research into political participation has consistently emphasized voting. The reasons for this concentration are simple. Of all the evidence for political participation, voting can most easily be measured. From official returns we know how many go to the polls; from census data, we know something about the demographic breakdown of the electorate; from survey research we know something about the opinions, attitudes, motivations, backgrounds, affiliations, and other characteristics of voters.[5]

Finding out about other activities involves carefully identifying them, grouping them, and then analyzing them. Few are dichotomous variables. An individual either votes or not. But what about talking about politics? Or trying to tell others how to vote? If a woman casually complained to a friend that George Bush's ads on television offended her, was that discussing politics? How should we measure that activity against a long discussion comparing President Bush's policy on war in the Persian Gulf with that which might have been followed by a President Dukakis? There are other more difficult research questions. Should one group an individual who gives $25 to a friend running for the

---

[5] We also know that there is a problem in distinguishing voters from nonvoters in surveys. Typically survey data overrepresent actual voters by as much as 20 percent. Citizens are not anxious to admit they do not vote. (See Hill & Luttbeg, 1980, pp. 79–80; Sigelman, 1982.)

city school board with another individual who gives $10,000, in $1000 sums, to each of ten congressional candidates, listing both as "those who contribute to campaigns"? What would one learn from such a combination?

Finding out about political "passivists" is also difficult. Probably half of the nonvoters in this country tell survey analysts that they vote. Who are they? Why don't they vote? Why do they lie about it? Scholars do not really know. Thus, it is not easy to ascertain what low voter turnout means for the American system. It is even more difficult to evaluate political behavior that is nonconventional or even illegal. How many urban rioters would discuss their reasons for rioting in response to a scholar's open-ended questions?

Thus, our knowledge about political participation is not as extensive as we would like. On the other hand, we do know a good deal. Two studies, one by Sidney Verba and Norman Nie and their associates (part of a very extensive and expensive multination study) and one by Lester Milbrath and his associates (conducted in Buffalo, New York, but viewed as generally pertinent because of the similarity of its results to the other study's) dominate this field.

These studies find that it is possible to break the American electorate's political behavior down into certain modes of participation. Citizens have been classified as active, passive but supportive, and inactive.

The active group includes those who are identified as party and campaign workers, those who are community activists, those who frequently contact officials about particular problems, and those who are involved in a communica-

Local campaign headquarters, such as this one in New York for Governor Bill Clinton's presidential campaign, are beehives of activity as workers check data on computers and work the telephones to get out their candidate's supporters. (Joe Tabacca /AP/ Wide World Photos)

tions network that discusses political matters (a group identified only by Milbrath). Not many Americans fit into these groups; the numbers cited by Verba and Nie and/or Milbrath range from about 4 percent who contact officials about particular problems, to 20 percent who are community activists, to over 30 percent who engage in some form of campaign activity—such as running a campaign, contributing money, or wearing a button or putting a bumper sticker on the car. These groups are not mutually exclusive, nor is it essential that an American participate in one kind of activity in order to acquire enough sophistication to participate in another. We can identify separate styles of participating in politics. While it is true that most of these "active" individuals also vote, voting as well is a separate style of participation. In fact, the "contact specialists," identified by Verba and Nie, frequently participate in no other form of political activity.

By far the largest group are those identified as passive supporters, individuals who pay taxes, who rise and sing the national anthem at ball games, but whose active involvement in politics is limited to voting. Large numbers of Americans support the system, at least passively—nearly everyone stands for the flag; over 90 percent pay the taxes they owe. More than three in five Americans claim to vote regularly; the number who actually vote is less than that, but voting occasionally is not viewed as an onerous task by most Americans.

The group of citizens defined as inactive or apathetic is the smallest group, constituting less than a quarter of the population. We know little about why they are not involved. We do know that they are uninterested, uninformed, and alienated from the system. It is perhaps important to note, however, that these individuals who engage in no political activity still rally 'round the flag. They are supportive of the system; they are patriotic enough to fly the flag on the Fourth of July; they cheered for star-spangled gymnast Mary Lou Retton and grieved for the crew of the *Challenger.* If these citizens maintain their love of country, even though they do not participate in politics, perhaps their apathy is not, as some fear, wholly dysfunctional for the American polity.

Further support is given this finding by a series of questions in the Milbrath study, absent in Verba and Nie, which identify an additional group of unconventional activists labeled as "protesters." Milbrath (Milbrath & Goel, 1977, pp. 14–19) gathers into this category those who would "protest vigorously if the government does something morally wrong (26%)," "refuse to obey laws (16%)," "attend protest meetings (6%)," "join a public street demonstration (3%)," and "riot if necessary (2%)." These findings should be viewed as tentative because they were derived from one city at a time of considerable urban unrest (1968), but they also reinforce the conclusion drawn above, because protesters, by and large, participate in all forms of political activity. They were not those who withdrew from politics and then "voted with their feet." They were those active in politics who saw protesting as an extension of their activity.[6]

---

[6] Milbrath (Milbrath & Goel, 1977, p. 15) made distinctions among protesters by race and other factors; however, this is not a major part of his finding and might well be peculiar to the situation in Buffalo in the late 1960s.

Is it possible, then, to draw a profile of political participation among Americans? First, most Americans only engage in voting, not in any other political activities. In any given election between 30 and 60 percent of the electorate does not vote, but these nonvoters are not a constant group. Over three-quarters of all American citizens consider themselves to be regular voters.

However, once one gets beyond voting, political participation falls way off. Only one in ten Americans belongs to a political club or organization or contributes money to political campaigns; only a slightly larger number will wear a button or display a sticker; only one in four will try to convince others to vote for specific candidates.

Other modes of behavior have been distinguished from those which some view as in political decline. Nearly a third of all Americans are involved in community activities; many more make certain they are involved in communicating about politics. A much smaller number contact public officials about their personal problems with the government, whether they participate fully or not. Furthermore, some evidence points to the thesis that a small group of people are very actively involved in political life in an unconventional way, people willing to protest (and some even to riot) if necessary to accomplish their political ends. These protesters do not view their activity as illegitimate, but rather as the ultimate expression of their patriotism.

Finally, a small, but not insignificant, number of Americans are inactive and apathetic. They rarely even vote; however, they remain patriotic citizens. It appears that they truly are unconcerned, not turned against the system.

III.   THE POLITICIANS VIEW POLITICAL PARTICIPANTS

The county chairman, along with his friend, walked up the stairs and into the first meeting of the county committee after the state convention. The chairman had been something of a hero at that convention, defending a civil liberties plank against an attack from the far right. This meeting would be a mere formality; he would be reelected, discuss plans for the upcoming election year, and adjourn the meeting in time to catch the last few innings of the Yankee game. As he opened the door into the meeting room, he turned to his friend and said, "We're in for a long evening."

His friend viewed the packed room. "What do you mean? Who are these people?"

"I don't know, but they sure didn't get elected to the county committee to come to vote for me." The about-to-be-ex-county chairman had learned an important political lesson.

For practicing politicians, the most important part of citizens' political participation is predictability. If only 50 percent turn out to vote, no one is bothered, so long as it is always more or less the same 50 percent. If attendance at county committee meetings is sparse, the chairman breathes easy so long as he knows who will be there. If a few people complain when an officeholder

TABLE 4-5. Estimated Turnout in Iowa's Democratic Caucuses, 1968–1988

Year	Turnout
1968	38,000
1972	60,000
1976	38,500
1980	100,000
1984	75,000
1988	126,000

Source: Turnout figures for Iowa precinct caucuses are "soft" at best. These figures are best estimates provided by Des Moines reference librarian Charlene Lakin from newspaper and Democratic party sources. See also Winebrenner, 1985; Abramowitz et al., 1991.

takes a controversial stand, he will not get upset—so long as that reaction was expected.

But the unpredictable reaction—the large turnout, the new faces, the massive protests—those kinds of political participation worry politicians. Worry is too calm a word; unpredictable participation gives politicians nightmares.

The county chairman cited above lost his seat because he took a stand that caused people (who had never been concerned before) to pay attention to him, to take an interest in party politics. He didn't bring his supporters out to help reelect him because he didn't know he was in a contest. When he saw a sea of unfamiliar faces, he knew only too well why they were there. Others cared greatly about his stand at the state convention; they did not view him as a hero. The county chairman was a goat. His opponents took advantage of the meeting to get rid of an unacceptable "radical."

The same scenario is often repeated. Voter turnout, particularly in primary elections, is difficult for politicians to predict accurately. Table 4-5 shows the turnout in Iowa presidential caucuses from 1968 to 1976. A campaign manager looking at the data and planning for the 1980 caucuses would know how many votes his candidate needs to win. Using well-tested and sophisticated techniques for identifying supporters and getting them to the polls, such a manager could judge quite well how his candidate would do on the eve of the caucuses. Then he is faced with the 1980 turnout figures; an estimated 100,000 Democrats voted. He throws out all previous assumptions. Who can judge who these new participants are and how they will react? More nightmares. He tries planning for 1984. How many will turn out? How many supporters does a candidate need to win? To make a good showing?[7]

The same process can be used to examine reactions to governmental policies. History seeks to tell us how people react. But history did not predict the

[7] About 75,000 Democrats did in fact participate in the Iowa caucuses in 1984; in 1988 the number jumped again, to about 126,000. The 1980 and 1984 Iowa turnout estimates are from Winebrenner (1985); the 1988 estimates are from Abramowitz, Rapoport, and Stone (1991).

urban riots of the late 1960s or the campus riots following the Cambodian incursion in 1970. How should politicians react to those events? They do not know. Worse still, our political system has always been based on predictability. Political planning has to follow from what has happened before.

How then have practicing politicians viewed the changes in the electorate presented earlier in this chapter? First and foremost, as unfamiliar terrain they have to cross. When the electorate has expanded, they have dealt with that expansion, making appeals to new voters as they have seen fit. Those who have predicted accurately how the new voters would react, like the southern politicians who have softened their formerly racist rhetoric, have prospered. Those who have guessed wrong—like George McGovern, who assumed that masses of young voters against the war in Vietnam would rush to the polls in 1972—have lost, often badly. Others learn for the next electoral round.

When the electorate is not expanding unpredictably, politicians still proceed with caution. They know more or less what to expect, but they must avoid tearing up the pea patch, arousing opponents who do not normally participate. Politicians always prefer to remain on familiar terrain. Conjointly, their understanding of the electorate has become more and more sophisticated as polling techniques have improved. They know to whom they must appeal to win and how to base that appeal, as do their opponents. Elections, then, turn on the political skill and understanding of both aspirants and officeholders. The discussion in this chapter now turns to the behavior of the electorate which these politicians seek to understand.

IV.   VOTERS IN PRESIDENTIAL ELECTIONS

"I am not a Republican or a Democrat; I vote for the person." How many times have we heard this rationale for how an individual votes? What does it mean?

When we ask our associates whom they favor for a certain office, whether they supported President Bush for reelection, or how they decided to vote for any particular candidate, what do they normally respond? Do they begin elaborate discussions of different candidates' stands on different issues, or do they talk only of one issue that is most important to them, or do they only talk about party, or do they only talk about a candidate's personal characteristics? What is it that makes someone decide how she will exercise her right to vote, once she has decided that she will vote at all?

The individual voter is, after all, the most important actor in the political world. What we really want to know is how each *individual* votes. But we cannot know this about millions, and so we often group individuals together and look at their voting patterns in that way. In this section, we will begin by looking at the individual's voting decision.

A.   Models of Voting Behavior

Too frequently students of political science are aware of what the current professional literature says, but they are ignorant of the earlier writings that laid the groundwork for current studies. Much is lost by failing to look back at what scholars were writing a generation ago. In no case is this loss more in evidence than in the study of voting behavior.

Few books have dominated an area of study in the way that *The American Voter* (A. Campbell et al., 1960) has influenced the study of electoral behavior for a period of more than two decades. Angus Campbell, Philip Converse, Warren Miller, and Donald Stokes, the authors of this classic study, were not the first to study voting behavior in depth. They owed and acknowledged a debt to earlier students of voting behavior in local communities, particularly to Bernard Berelson, Paul Lazarsfeld, and their associates at Columbia University (Berelson et al., 1954; Lazarsfeld et al., 1944), who had earlier hypothesized that social characteristics determine political preference. Campbell et al. drew on some of the findings of these earlier studies and clearly used them as a baseline from which to move.

However, the authors of *The American Voter* and their colleagues at the Survey Research Center at the University of Michigan refined the national survey as a research instrument for social scientists and presented their findings in such a clear and coherent way that their work essentially became the model against which all others compared their results.

Because of the influence of their work, it is important that all students of electoral behavior be aware of its conclusions. The difficulty in presenting the findings of *The American Voter* in a brief summary like this one is that oversimplification will mask the richness of the analysis and the sophistication of the presentation. However, as with many such classics, what people believe Campbell and his associates said is in many ways more important than what they actually did say. It is, after all, this oversimplified view of *The American Voter*—not a detailed, careful analysis—which has determined the influence of this book. Having announced this caveat, we will attempt to summarize the book's conclusions.

Campbell and his associates were engaged in a study of the psychological and sociological determinants of voting behavior. They studied how voters perceived parties, candidates, and issues and why they perceived them as they did. By cumulating their findings about individual voters, they were able to draw conclusions about the American electorate as a whole.

Their first conclusion was that voter perception is a mixture of cognition and evaluation, of perception and affect. How the voter perceives politics is a mixture of what that voter chooses to know and how that voter feels about a political situation. The average voter is concerned about politics, but not all *that* concerned. While the average American does vote, he or she does not think about politics a great deal, does not become involved in many other political acts, does not spend a good deal of time keeping informed about politics.

A number of conclusions follow from this finding. First, the average American has an extremely unsophisticated view of politics. Campbell and his associates make a good deal of the inability of the voter to view politics in abstract terms, to develop a coherent ideology. Rather than making judgments based on a sophisticated view of the issues, voters view candidates as representatives of the two major parties; the parties in turn are viewed as feeling certain ways on issues and toward certain groups in society. Whether or not these views are correct, the voters use their perceptions in making decisions by fitting or ordering their view of politics to the outlines of the perceptions. Because most people do not care much about politics, it is fairly easy to manipulate their views.

According to *The American Voter* model, most Americans have developed a strong, long-term commitment to one or the other of the major political parties, and this commitment is a most significant guide to voting behavior. How is this tie to a political party developed? Campbell and his associates review a good deal of social science literature as well as their own survey findings in order to conclude that the individual's home is the most important source of partisan affiliation. The two most influential factors seem to be the parents' partisanship and their level of political activity. If the parents are both strongly involved with one party, the children are likely to follow the same course. If the parents are split, or if their commitment is not strong, then the likelihood of their children affiliating with one of the parties declines commensurately. In fact, the likelihood of children in those households becoming significantly involved in politics is also low.

Other elements also influence the choice of party, particularly when parental pressure is not strong. Among these influences are other important socializing elements of American society—the school, the work group, the church. Once partisan affiliation is confirmed, it is quite difficult to change; however, factors such as marriage, increased education, changes in job, social status, and/or neighborhood can have an impact. More significantly, cataclysmic events, such as the great depression, can affect the partisan political affiliation of entire generations.

Most important to remember is what this view says about the role that the voter plays in democratic theory. Campbell's is essentially a negative view of the American electorate. Voters are not capable of making decisions based on a rational consideration of issues. In order to cast "issue-oriented" votes, the citizen must have an opinion on an issue ("cognize" the issue, in *The American Voter*'s term), must have knowledge of current governmental policy on the issue, must have some information about competing party stands on the question, and then must feel strongly enough to vote according to the perceived differences between the parties on that issue.

According to Campbell and his associates, voters meet none of these criteria. Rather, partisanship is determined by socializing instruments in society. Voters follow partisan cues for voting. When they stray from these partisan predilections, it is not because of opinions on issues, but because of appeals based on the personality or media image of the particular candidate or because of a particularly compelling short-range issue—such as a scandal or the appeal of a demagogue.

Looking further into *The American Voter*, one reads that independents, those without a strong partisan affiliation, tend to be those least involved in politics, least interested, least committed. Independents are the voters most likely to be swayed by emotional appeals, by charismatic candidates. Given that the Democrats' lead in voter allegiance constituted less than a majority in 1960, at the time this study was done, these least attractive voters—in terms of a democratic model—are often the ones who determine election results.

Not a very optimistic picture. Remember, this summary is an exaggeration of what Campbell and his associates actually wrote. After analyzing the American electorate in great depth, they did not set out to paint such a bleak picture. Rather, they seemed to predicate standards for performance which the electorate, taken as a whole, was unable to meet. Campbell et al. asked for an electorate that was able to order complex political issues, one that was able to make voting decisions based on comparative stands on particular issues, and one that demonstrated qualities such that elections were in fact viewable as mandates for the policies proposed by opposing candidates.

They found instead an uninvolved, unconcerned, unsophisticated electorate, voters making decisions based largely on partisan affiliations, which in turn were handed down from generation to generation. This partisanship was in the first place often based on issues that were perhaps no longer relevant, an oversimplification that led citizens to view the American political dialogue in often unrealistic ways. The element of this electorate which often held the balance of power between the two parties was the group that met the tests of "good" citizens least well, that was most responsive to emotional appeals, that was least well informed, least concerned, and least involved.

1. Critics of *The American Voter* Model Just as it is important for students of political science to know the foundations for current research, so too is it important for them to realize that even basic understandings of significant aspects of American political behavior can and do change over time. The fact that "revealed wisdom" of political analysis is overhauled is not a negative comment on those who have explicated the original model; rather it is a testament to the progressive way in which we learn, drawing on and going further than those who preceded us.

The view presented in *The American Voter* was not been accepted without controversy. Two schools of criticism stand out. The first group of experts, typified by V. O. Key, Jr., maintained that Campbell and his associates had placed too heavy a burden on the American electorate and that the view presented was far more negative than the actual situation warranted. The second group claimed that the heavy reliance on data from the 1950s in *The American Voter* led Campbell et al. to draw certain conclusions about the electorate which would not hold true over longer periods of time. The two schools will be discussed in turn.

V. O. Key, Jr., was perhaps the profession's consummate believer in American democracy. While not refuting the data presented by Campbell and his associates, Key insisted that an expert could reinterpret those data and still arrive at the conclusion that the American electorate was a responsible and trustworthy body. Key dedicated his slim volume, published with the assistance of Milton Cummings after Key's death, to the theme that the ". . . voters are not fools" (Key, 1966, p. 7).

Rather than dividing the population by partisan affiliation, awareness of issues, concern over politics, and ability to conceptualize ideology, Key used survey data to categorize citizens according to how they voted in sets of elections. Looking at presidential elections, Key characterized those who voted for the same political party in two consecutive elections as "standpatters," those who voted for one party in one election and the other party in the subsequent election as "switchers," and those who voted in one election after not having voted in the preceding one as "new voters."

Key then examined the behavior of voters in each of these categories, trying to determine if their behavior could be understood as rational. Most of the voters in any election were standpatters, those who voted the same way in two consecutive elections. However, these voters were rarely numerous enough to determine a winner. The next largest group was the new voters, reaching 30 percent in the election of 1952. These voters tended to side heavily with the winner. Switchers constituted between 13 and 20 percent of the electorate in the time Key studied.

Key's findings about the relative positions of the two parties is important, particularly given *The American Voter*'s conclusion about party affiliation and its determining effect on vote. Key discovered some shifting between elections even though most voters maintained stable party allegiance. Although the maintenance of the relative strength of the two parties between elections leads us to believe that a static situation exists, the supposed immobility is in fact the net result of a dynamic flow.

> A series of maintaining elections occurs only in consequence of a complex process of interaction between government and populace in which old friends are sustained, old enemies are converted into new friends, old friends become even bitter opponents, and new voters are attracted to the cause. (Key, 1966, p. 30)

Key further maintains that membership in certain cultural, economic, and social groups is an important factor in deciding how an American votes, again as Campbell and his associates have maintained, but not in an irrational or predeterministic way. Group pressure or membership becomes important only for issues affecting that particular group. The fact that a voter is a member of a racial or religious group only affects that person's vote if and when that person believes that his or her racial or religious affiliation has an impact on how one distinguishes among candidates. This kind of analysis is significant in viewing the high percentage of blacks who vote Democratic or the switch to Kennedy among Catholic voters in 1960.

Perhaps Key's preeminent conclusion is that the most admirable, most rational voters are the switchers. He maintains that individuals switch because of the way that they perceive the government as treating them in the intervening period between elections. If they are happy with what the incumbent has done, regardless of whether they voted against him in the past, they will support him in the next election. In a parallel way, supporters of an incumbent in one election will turn against him—and importantly against a subsequent nominee of his party—if those voters are unhappy with the effects of policies adopted during the intervening four years.

TABLE 4-6. Composition of Vote for Major-Party Presidential Candidates, According to Voting Record at Preceding Election*

Year	Democratic			Republican		
	Standpatters, %	Switchers, %	New Voters, %	Standpatters, %	Switchers, %	New Voters, %
1940						
Prelection	80	2	18	58	28	14
Postelection	80	3	17	61	25	14
1944						
Preelection	80	4	16	64	22	14
Postelection	79	6	15	74	14	12
1948						
Preelection	73	3	24	58	23	19
Postelection	77	5	18	69	18	13
1952						
Preelection	65	4	31	52	19	29
Postelection	74	5	21	57	23	13
1956						
Preelection	52	17	31	72	4	24
Postelection†	—	—	—	—	—	—
1960						
Preelection	46	24	30	71	6	23
Postelection	56	30	14	78	8	14

* For a description of the data used in this table see Key, 1966, p. 22.

† The Survey Research Center's sample yielded for the data presented by Angus Campbell, "Surge and Decline: A Study of Electoral Change," *Public Opinion Quarterly*, 24 (1960), p. 407.

Source: Key, 1966, p. 27.

Similarly, Key maintains that standpatters are rational voters. Those voters who support the same party in consecutive elections do so either because they like what a winner whom they have supported has done or because they dislike what a winner whom they have opposed has done. "Like" and "dislike" in this context are defined according to how those policies affect the individual in the areas that are of most concern to him.

Key's view of the new voters is not so sanguine. Actually, new voters fall into two categories—first-time voters and "in-and-outers," who vote in one election but not in the next. According to Key, new voters tend to go along with the tide. Those who are infrequent and not consistent participants are similar to the independents described in *The American Voter:* uninformed, unconcerned, uninvolved voters. While this group tends toward trendiness, and while it is a large group, it is not the group that ultimately determines the winner in elections. Key maintains that the switchers play this role in American politics.

Two other conclusions follow from Key's analysis. First, he explicitly rejects the cult of personality. One need not have been a charismatic figure like Franklin Roosevelt in order to convince the Republican voters of 1928 to vote Democratic in 1932. Voters switched because of how they felt about the policies of the Hoover administration. Eisenhower's personality was not the critical element in the presidential race of 1952; the more important factor was that Adlai Stevenson was tied, in the voters' minds, to the policies of Harry Truman, who was perceived to have embroiled America in the Korean war. Truman supposedly had only a certain response to communism. Voters rejected Truman's policies. New voters rejected them in large numbers, but many who voted for Truman in 1948 also rejected them and switched to Eisenhower in 1952.

The other conclusion that follows from Key's analysis has served to structure much of the debate over voting behavior in the last two decades. *Key maintains that voters respond to the past, not to the future* (1966, p. xii). He draws an explicit distinction between prospective (future) and retrospective (past) voting.

Modern scholars, for all that, are quick to criticize Key's methods. His reliance of recall data (voters remembering their past actions) is particularly questionable. However, no one should underestimate his instinctive knowledge of politics and of the important questions to be examined. Key's influence persists three decades after his death.

The American Voter maintains that voters fail to vote prospectively because they are not well-enough informed or concerned. Consequently, they are left to cast their votes irrationally, basing them on party ties; theirs is a retrospective vote, but not an informed one.

Key claims that evaluation is the most important element in rational voting. Key's responsible voters evaluate what has happened in the past four years and make judgments. They are concerned with results only, not with policy promises. They do not give mandates; rather they respond to results of past performance. To vote rationally in this context, one does not need to understand issues thoroughly, nor to recall where the party stands on those issues, nor to know precisely wat the government has been doing. To vote rationally in this context, an American only needs to know if "the shoe is pinching" and, if so, who is causing it to pinch. This is a much easier test for the electorate to meet. According to Key, it is also a perfectly appropriate test.

More recently, scholars have expanded on Key's concept of retrospective voting. Drawing on the theoretical writing of Anthony Downs (1957), Morris Fiorina has developed a carefully crafted conceptual model of individual voting behavior (Fiorina, 1977b, 1981; see also Franklin, 1984; Franklin & Jackson, 1983; J. Jackson, 1975). Fiorina claims that the electorate makes rational choices. Citizens vote retrospectively because doing so is patently more manageable. Human beings simply find it easier to get information about what has gone on in the past than to evaluate what may happen in the future. Retrospective information, in fact, is acquired without effort. Furthermore, it is much more reliable than evaluative projections. Who, as a rational actor, believes politicians' promises today? Who ever did?

In order for retrospective voting to be rational, voting citizens must see some tie between candidates and parties; they must understand that parties are consistent on the issues that most affect them. Thus, a vote against Hubert Humphrey in 1968 was a rational vote, in this context, only if one believes that voters opposed Lyndon Johnson's Vietnam policy and linked Humphrey with that policy. Policy implications determine voting decisions only on a very few instances—those that touch many people, those in which there is a clear link between means and ends, and those that are tied to the parties by the electorate.

Before turning to a discussion of retrospective voting in the context of politics today, we should evaluate the other criticism of *The American Voter,* the one that maintains that even though the study is time-bound, the model of expected behavior is an appropriate one.

Scholars at the Survey Research Center, analyzing the series of National Election Studies (NES) subsequent to the ones on which *The American Voter*

Reprinted with permission of Oliphant/Universal Press Syndicate

'THE ONLY NICE THING ABOUT ELECTIONS ANY MORE IS SEEING THE POLL-TAKERS GETTING HAULED OFF TO THE FUNNY FARM AFTERWARDS.'

was based, noticed a change in voter behavior. They began to look for reasons to explain these changes. Many articles published in the 1970s provided new interpretations of the behavior of the American electorate (Brody & Page, 1972; A. Miller, 1978; A. Miller & Miller, 1977; and A. Miller, Miller, Raine, & Brown, 1976), but it was left to another group of scholars, using National Election Studies data from the 1960s and 1970s, to question some of the basic findings of *The American Voter.*

In *The Changing American Voter,* Norman Nie, Sidney Verba, and John Petrocik explicitly acknowledge their debt to the authors of the earlier classic work. In fact, in the dedication to *The Changing American Voter,* Nie, Verba, and Petrocik acknowledge Campbell, Converse, Miller, and Stokes, "on whose coattails we ride." In calling the paradigm laid out in *The American Voter* into question, the authors of *The Changing American Voter* state that such criticism "does not imply criticism of the paradigm makers" (1979, p. 8). However, they most definitely do call the conclusions into question.

The basic criticism is that the model constructed by the authors of *The American Voter* is based largely on the NES 1956 survey, and according to Nie and his associates, 1956 was hardly a baseline on which to construct a sound hypothesis; that year had some peculiar and problematic characteristics. The task of *The Changing American Voter* is "to separate the timebound from the timeless in political attitudes" (1979, p. 7). If 1956 was too placid a year to use as a baseline, which characteristics of voting behavior are indeed truly timeless, and which are time-bound and therefore in need of reinterpretation? Merely posing that question demonstrates how knowledge accrues.

The major finding of *The Changing American Voter,* one that differs from the conclusions in *The American Voter,* is that the electorate is much less committed to party. This is seen in a rise in the number of independent voters, in a decline in strong partisans, in an increase in ticket splitting. Many more of the respondents to the quadrennial survey of voters express dissatisfaction with the two parties than was the case of the surveys done in the 1950s.

Further, Nie and his associates find that voters use two kinds of measures in presidential voting. The first of these is the personal characteristics of the candidates. The second, and this is the one emphasized, is *issues.*

This group of scholars claims that parties have become increasingly weak in the time since *The American Voter* was published. With Burnham (1970) they argue that this party weakness may well represent a long-term trend. Whatever the length of the trend, its significance is clear. Parties as organizations are feebler; citizens might not oppose parties, but their commitment to parties is wavering; therefore, parties are less relevant to electoral behavior.

The authors of *The Changing American Voter* go further. They also argue that the new independent voters, whom they have identified in increasing numbers, fall into two groups. One group is the same as the independents identified by Campbell and his associates nearly twenty years earlier. The other group, however, is very different. While the original group of independents was the least involved, least concerned, least informed voters, Nie et al. found that the new group is just the opposite. The new independent voter is very well in-

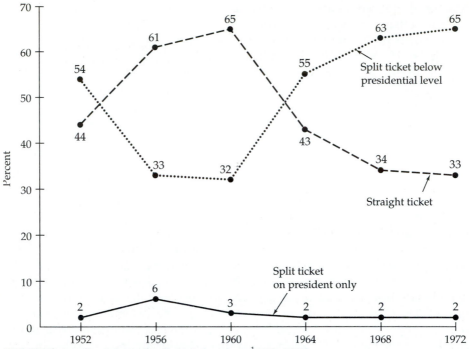

FIGURE 4-6 Straight and split-ticket voting, 1952–1972.

Source: Nie, Verba, & Petrocik, 1979, p. 53.

formed, very concerned about politics, very involved in every way. These voters are people who discuss the two major parties as irrelevant, but for whom politics is very important. They will choose a candidate based on their perception of how that candidate stands on issues. (See also A. Miller & Wattenberg, 1985; Wattenberg, 1984, 1986, 1990b).

What issues? The new and important issues of the day, a new set of issues which distinguish this time from the 1950s. War and peace in Vietnam, lifestyle, race relations were important concerns for the new American electorate of the late 1960s and early 1970s. These are issues on which voters were able to form a coherent political ideology, to distinguish the two parties, and to vote based on issue preference.

Nie, Verba, and Petrocik also show us why these issues have not led to a new realignment. Rejecting retrospective voting, they argue that the parties are so weak and inconsistent in policy that retrospective voting is impossible.

> The individual candidates are more independent of party; they run on the basis of their own characteristics and programs, not as representatives of continuing party institutions. Insofar as this is the case, electoral choice can no longer be retrospective. Voters are less able to vote on the basis of past performance (as V. O. Key and others have argued they did), since the candidate cannot be held responsible for what others in his party have done while in office—unless, of course, the incumbent is the candidate. (Nie, Verba, & Petrocik, 1979, pp. 346–347)

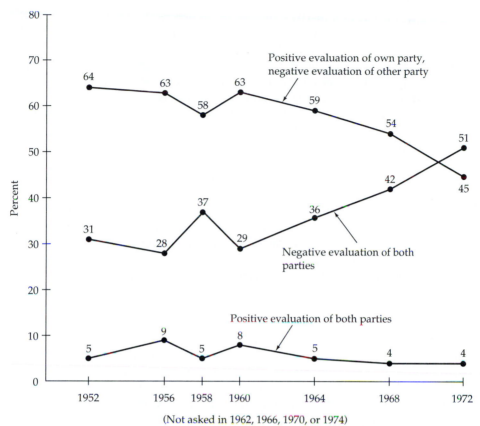

(Not asked in 1962, 1966, 1970, or 1974)

FIGURE 4-7 The decline in positive evaluation of parties, 1952–1972.

Source: Nie, Verba, & Petrocik, 1979.

The Changing American Voter is based on the analysis of the National Election Studies surveys conducted at the time of the 1964, 1968, and 1972 elections. These presidential elections—and this study is only based on presidential voting—might be atypical in terms of being elections determined by highly salient issues just as much 1956 was atypical in terms of being a low-saliency election.

The election of 1964 is the one that best defines the parties in terms of issues, according to Nie, Verba, and Petrocik. This election was perhaps the most ideological of our recent elections. Senator Barry Goldwater, the Republican candidate, was even referred to as "Mr. Conservative" by friend and foe alike.

During the election of 1968, the nation was torn apart by the Vietnamese war. Try as he might, Hubert Humphrey, the Democratic candidate, could not separate himself from Lyndon Johnson, whom he had served with utmost loyalty as vice president. Johnson was generally perceived to be the architect of our military involvement in Vietnam.

Finally, the election of 1972 was the one in which the Democrats chose an extremist candidate, perhaps more in appearance than reality, but certainly in the perception of the voting public. Senator George McGovern (S.D.) was viewed by many as a radical, the candidate of "acid, amnesty, and abortion." The fact that the McGovern election was tainted on the Republican side by Watergate and dirty tricks, and that McGovern was not so far to the left as he was often depicted, does not negate how easy it was for the public to see this election in ideological terms as well.

When the authors of *The Changing American Voter* enlarged their book to include the 1976 election, they began to see a trend that called some of their findings into question. They assumed that an election like 1976, with Carter and Ford, two centrist candidates, would be different. But some of the differences turned out to deserve further analysis. This was particularly true of a tendency away from increased independence of voters and back to allegiance to political parties (see Table 4-7). Again, we are left asking which of the findings are timeless, which time-bound.

At this point it might be worthwhile to go back to Nie, Verba, and Petrocik's rejection of retrospective voting (above). Two phrases stand out. "Insofar as this is the case" and "unless, of course, the incumbent is the candidate." A third phrase might have been necessary: "If the electorate sees that the candidates are rejecting party." The evidence really is not clear on these issues (Wattenberg, 1984). The electorate seems to be linking candidates of the same party together, whether the candidates want that to be the case or not. Even in the 1968 election, on which *The Changing American Voter* is based in part, Hubert Humphrey did all he could to separate himself from Lyndon Johnson. He could not do it. Furthermore, often one of the candidates is the incumbent—or closely tied to the incumbent. That link is all that is necessary for retrospective voting at the presidential level to be possible.

Sometimes political scientists become too involved in their own struggles over methods. The controversy over how one decides if the American public votes prospectively or retrospectively, over how much issues matter, in what circumstances, over whose interpretation of the same data is correct, may well be one such parochial involvement. At times it may well be appropriate to reject the most sophisticated research methodology and go with one's instincts, to use the old Studs Turkel method—sit down in an Irish pub and ask people how they decided. If an analyst did that for the 1980 election, the answer, at least for that election, should be clear. Ronald Reagan had his finger on the pulse of the people. He asked them one question—or rather asked them to ask themselves one question.

> Next Tuesday is election day. Next Tuesday all of you will go to the polls; you'll stand there in the polling place and make a decision. I think when you make that decision, it might be well if you would ask yourself, are you better off than you were 4 years ago? Is it easier for you to go and buy things in the stores than it was 4 years ago? Is there more or less unemployment in the country than there was 4 years ago? Is America as respected throughout the world as it was? Do we feel that our security is as safe, that we're as strong as we were 4 years ago? And if you an-

TABLE 4-7. Party Identification of Americans: 1956–1988

Identification	1956	1960	1964	1968	1972	1976	1980	1984	1988
Strong Dem.	21	20	27	20	15	15	16	18	17
Weak Dem.	23	25	25	25	26	25	23	22	18
Independent Dem.	6	6	9	10	11	12	11	10	12
Independent	9	10	8	11	13	15	12	6	11
Independent Rep.	8	7	6	9	11	10	12	13	13
Weak Rep.	14	14	14	15	13	14	14	15	14
Strong Rep.	15	16	11	10	10	9	10	14	14
Apolitical	4	3	1	1	1	1	2	2	2

Source: *American National Election Studies Data Sourceboo, Sourcebook 1952–1978.* Data for 1980–1988 taken from the NES/ICPSR American Election Studies of those years.

swer all of those questions yes, why then I think your choice is very obvious as to who you'll vote for. If you don't agree, if you don't think that this course that we've been on for the last 4 years is what you would like to see us follow for the next 4, then I could suggest another choice that you have. (Carter, 1982b, p. 2501)

2. Summary Where does this review leave the question of how Americans decide for whom to vote? Certainly the professional social science community is not of one mind. Parts of the model developed by Campbell, Converse, Miller, and Stokes have been rejected; other parts remain intact. Portions of the criticism of Nie, Verba, and Petrocik have been accepted. Other portions might well need reexamination. The theory of retrospective voting, propounded by V. O. Key as a defense of the American electorate against the implied view of *The American Voter,* and amplified by Morris Fiorina and others, has attracted some strong adherents. The concepts involved here are extremely complex. Generations of scholars have devoted their professional lives to studying party identification, with the basic concept being challenged, refined, reexamined, operationalized in various ways, and defended in various forms (see W. Miller, 1991b). The link between party identification and voting—and rationality of voters—has similarly consumed political scientists' attention. No clear consensus has emerged as research controversies abound (see Gant & Luttbeg, 1991, pp. 29–82, for a review of this literature). The necessity of examining the context of each particular election is absolutely clear. On that there can be no question (see A. Miller & Wattenberg, 1985). And in the final analysis, it is important to supplement scientific examinations with common sense, with the knowledge of politics, with a feel for people, not just numbers.

Before turning to an examination of how politicians view electoral behavior, it is necessary to take a step down from the presidential elections. To this point all of the analysis that we have considered has been of presidential voting. Yet only the president and vice president run in elections that have a visibility approaching that discussed in the literature reviewed to this point. What goes on in all the other elections? How do voters decide in cases different from those at the presidential level?

V.   VOTERS IN CONGRESSIONAL AND SENATORIAL ELECTIONS

Almost all the research into American voting behavior has been research into presidential voting. This follows naturally from the fact that scientific survey research is extremely expensive and that the community of scholars have drawn heavily on the data collected by the Survey Research Center and the Center for Political Studies of the Institute for Social Research at the University of Michigan, made available to a large number of scholars through the Inter-University Consortium for Political and Social Research. The Survey Research Center has received a series of substantial grants to study presidential voting. At the same time, studies of voting behavior in nonpresidential elections have been conducted less frequently.

The Survey Research Center did analyze the electorate during the 1958 congressional elections. The most often cited analyses of the data generated by that study describe an electorate not very concerned or knowledgeable about congressional politics (W. Miller & Stokes, 1963; Stokes & Miller, 1962). Nearly half of the respondents replied that they had neither read nor heard anything about *either* candidate. While more than twice as many knew something about the incumbent as they did about the challenger, few had any sense of how their representative stood on issues.

With so little knowledge, voters relied heavily on party affiliation to determine their congressional choice. Those who did not support the party's nominee deserted their party not because they were concerned over issues, but because they had heard of the other party's candidate and not their own. Virtually all the voters who knew anything about their party's nominee supported him. Voting, then, seemed to be the product of blind party loyalty, not of party loyalty as a statement of issue positions. The 1958 respondents knew very little about who organized Congress or how issues distinguished the parties in Congress.

This view of electoral behavior should be recognized as consistent with the *American Voter* model, only more so. The Miller and Stokes analysis reveals an electorate in congressional elections which has virtually none of the characteristics necessary for rational prospective voting or retrospective voting. Rather, voters were almost totally uninformed and voted on the basis of party affiliation and the slightest degree of candidate recognition.

This perception of congressional voting behavior was not seriously reexamined in a systematic way until the Survey Research Center undertook an examination of the electoral behavior in the 1978 congressional elections. This study, tangible evidence of renewed interest by scholars in voting behavior below the presidential level, produced a wealth of literature on congressional elections which reevaluates the Stokes and Miller view (see Abramowitz, 1981; Hinckley, 1981; Jacobson, 1980; Maisel & Cooper, 1981; Mann & Wolfinger, 1980).

The most noticeable change is that most voters have an increased awareness of congressional candidates. Depending on the measure used, voters were able to express an opinion on over 90 percent of the incumbent candidates and nearly half of the challengers. Further, when one examines highly competitive elections, very high percentages of voters were able to evaluate both candidates.

For some years scholars had noted that an extremely high percentage of members of Congress seeking reelection were reelected (see, as examples, Fiorina, 1978; Mayhew, 1974a, 1974b). The 1978 data afforded scholars the opportunity to explore the reasons for this phenomenon. They found that partisanship had been replaced by incumbency as the key voting cue. Further, voters supported incumbents because they knew more positive things about them, resulting in large part from the incumbents' skillful use of the resources available through their offices.

Some of the data are particularly striking. Nearly 90 percent of the respondents reported having had some contact with their congressman; almost a quarter had personally met their congressman; almost three-quarters had received mail from their representative in Washington. These associations, all structured by the incumbent and virtually all positive in content, built a base of a favorable image which was all but impossible to overcome. Typically, challengers were not known at all; voters did not choose between two candidates on equal footing but between one who was well known and positively viewed and another who had to fight to be viewed at all. The electoral success of the incumbents should not be surprising. (See Table 4-8.)

Note that issues were not mentioned as instruments that contribute to an incumbent's popularity. The 1978 data confirm the 1958 findings that citizens know very little about how their congressmen stand on issues. Rather, the congressmen build their reputation through constituent service, frequent communication, and positive publicity on popular causes.

Just as scholars were interested in incumbent advantages in House elections, they were also interested in why incumbent United States senators were frequently defeated. The data from 1978 show that senatorial incumbents did not have the advantages over their challenges that House incumbents had. Senatorial challengers were more well known and contacted voters more frequently. Incumbents also could not "control" all their contacts with constituents as well as congressmen were able to do. Senators were more frequently covered by the news media in situations they could not control; their jobs made them more prominent politicians in most states. Most senators could not build the personal relationships with constituents that congressmen could because of the size of their constituency. The combination—of "balanced" image building, of challengers who start out with better name recognition, and of challengers' ability to spend money to become even more widely known—has significantly reduced the advantage of the incumbent in Senate races. The variation in the number of incumbents defeated revealed in Table 4-9 demonstrates that other factors are clearly at work in these elections.

What of electoral behavior in elections for statewide or local offices? Until very recently, political scientists have not produced systematic studies of elections at these levels (as recent examples see Garand, 1991; Gierzynski & Breaux, 1991; Jewell & Breaux, 1991; and Weber, Tucker, & Brace, 1991). However, some conclusions are inescapable. Races for governor, for instance, probably feature voting behavior parallel to that for senator. Governors are well known, but so are their opponents. Their accomplishments in office are examined in detail in the press. Gubernatorial opponents spend a good deal of money in portraying the negative parts of incumbents' records. Voters decide based on these appeals—on party, image, record. Table 4-10 shows the electoral success of incumbent governors seeking reelection in the last decade. And one would expect a similar pattern for big-city mayors.

State legislators and others running in smaller constituencies face an electoral environment much like congressmen, with one notable exception. Again, few citizens know how a state legislator stands on key issues. In this case, how-

TABLE 4-8. Electoral Success of Incumbent Representatives Seeking Reelection

	1972	1974	1976	1978	1980	1982	1984	1986	1988	1990
Number of incumbents seeking reelection*	390	391	384	382	392	383	408	391	408	406
Number successfully reelected	365	343	368	358	361	354	392	385	402	391
Number losing reelection bid	25	48	16	24	31	29	16	6	6	15

* Does not include persons who died or resigned from office before the election.

Source: *Congressional Quarterly Service* publications.

TABLE 4-9. Electoral Success of Incumbent Senators Seeking Reelection

	1972	1974	1976	1978	1980	1982	1984	1986	1988	1990
Number of incumbents seeking reelection*	27	27	25	25	26	30	29	28	27	32
Number successfully reelected	20	23	16	15	16	28	26	21	23	31
Number losing reelection bid	7	4	9	10	10	2	3	7	4	1

* Does not include persons who died or resigned from office before the election.

Source: *Congressional Quarterly* Service publications.

TABLE 4-10. Electoral Success of Incumbent Governors Seeking Reelection

Year	Number of Incumbent Governors Seeking Reelection	Number Successfully Reelected	Number Losing Reelection Bid
1972	9	7	2
1973	2	1	1
1974	21	16	5
1975	2	2	0
1976	7	5	2
1977	1	1	0
1978	22	17	5
1979	0	—	—
1980	8	6	2
1981	0	—	—
1982	15	14	1
1983	1	1	0
1984	6	4	2
1985	1	1	—
1986	17	16	1
1987	1	—	1
1988	9	8	1
1989	0	0	0
1990	23	17	6
1991	2	0	2*

* Includes Louisiana's Governor Buddy Roemer (R.), who finished third and was thus eliminated in the primary.

Source: *Congress and the Nation*, vol. VII, 1985–1988; *Congressional Quarterly* election issues for 1989 and 1990.

ever—and we note significant variation here from state to state—districts are often small enough that a significant percentage of the voters not only have had personal contact with the official but also know the official on a personal basis. When this is the case, partisanship and issues probably become less important; when the personal relationship does not exist, partisanship and name familiarity again dominate (Garand, 1991; Weber et al., 1991).

VI.   SUMMARY

The picture that emerges of the American electorate in the 1980s is not a clear one. As Table 4-7 shows, most Americans do identify with one major party or the other. The number so identifying themselves declined during the 1960s and early 1970s, but some of that decline seems to have been reversed in recent years. Questions have arisen about the strength of party allegiance—and about the significance of that strength (see Converse & Pierce, 1987, for a discussion of means of measuring partisanship).

Recall the discussion of party systems in Chapter 2. Political scientists concur that the New Deal era ushered in a new party system, the fifth, in which the political line of cleavage dealt with responsibility of the federal government to aid citizens in times of economic crisis. But much less consensus exists concerning what has happened since that realignment.

The research community has been watching elections for signs of a new partisan realignment since 1968. Since 1978 particularly, National Elections Studies' data have shown a decided move toward the Republican party, so that the gap between those considering themselves Democrats and those aligning with the Republicans narrowed to 7 percent by 1988. The major question challenging scholars has been whether we are witnessing a new realignment or a continuing "dealignment," a period in which citizens relate less positively to and are less influenced by political parties. (For a careful review of the recent literature on this debate, see Stanley, Bianco, & Niemi, 1985; see also Niemi & Weisberg, 1976, pp. 357–438; 1984, pp. 391–560.)

The debate continues as political scientists search for meaning in the studies of the recent electorate. Merrill Shanks and Warren Miller (1990) and Miller (W. Miller, 1985a, p. 1) writing alone claim that "the election of 1984 brought the first substantial indications that such a realignment may be occurring along ideological fault lines." Developing the argument further, Miller (1985a) writes:

> The fact that party identification provided somewhat less net support for the Democratic candidate, Mondale, in 1984 was not the consequence of the reduction in its centrality for individual voters' decisions. It was the result of a shift in the partisan balance, the ratio of Democratic to Republican identifications. That shift, in turn, was the product of a large realignment of party identifications which brought party loyalties closer into alignment with voters' ideological perspectives. (p. 14)

Analysis of the 1988 presidential election has tended to confirm the belief that a realignment has occurred. According to Warren Miller (1990, pp. 110–115), this realignment has been a two-stage realignment:

> My analysis of the 1988 elections thus supports the thesis that a significant first phase of the 1980–1988 realignment occurred between 1980 and 1984 among the less experienced and less sophisticated voters who responded to Reagan's personal leadership with an increase in Republicanism. A smaller but perhaps more meaningful second phase then occurred between 1984 and 1988, particularly among the older and better-educated voters who ultimately responded favorably to the Reagan administration's emphasis on conservatism. (Miller, 1990, p. 114; see also Miller, 1991b; Shanks & Miller, 1989, 1990.)

But the conclusions reached by even this most recent scholarship are very tentative. Scholars continue to debate topics such as the extent to which the most recent realignment is regional rather than national in scope (E. Black & Black, 1987), that voters' identification with party is different at the national and state levels (Hadley, 1985; Niemi, Wright, & Powell, 1987), the group composition of the two parties and its significance (Stanley et al., 1986), or the extent to which dealignment is merely a reflection of "unrealized partisanship" (Carmines, McIver, & Stimson, 1987). The research plate stays full, and scholars, fascinated by the interplay of these factors, remain hard at work.

Politicians and political journalists observing the same phenomena are no more certain of their meaning. All these analysts are now relying on an increasing number of sophisticated opinion surveys, those carried out by partisan pollsters and/or those conducted on behalf of major newspapers and television networks. In the aftermath of the 1984 election, much was made of the margin of the "youth" vote for Reagan. Although Shanks and Miller (1990, table 2) and others analyzing the NES data discounted the impact of the youngest age cohort on the shift toward the Republicans in 1984, many politicians and political journalists pointed to this vote as evidence that a major realignment was under way. As an example, Richard Wirthlin, one of the Republicans' leading pollsters, has said, "If we see young people staying the most Republican group in the electorate, if we see first voters registering Republican, . . . then we'll have a good chance to . . . become the majority party of the 1990s" (Broder, 1986, p. 6).

The spectre of the ever-popular Ronald Reagan lingers in the background of all these analyses. Were his elections in 1980 and 1984, and the impact he had on Bush's election in 1988, signals of a realigning electorate or deviations caused by an extremely popular candidate and a unique set of circumstances? How does the fact that the Democrats have held Congress throughout this period relate to the movement of the electorate toward the Republicans at the presidential level?

Thus, how one views the role of party in the electoral decisions reached by voters in the 1980s depends on which theory one espouses. We know that the parties are still important to many, that the major parties are now closer to each other in terms of voters identifying with them, but also that many people will eschew party allegiance, identify with neither party, and vote based on other cues.

What else enters into that decision? When issues seem to play a crucial role in election races, or when the parties clearly differentiate themselves on ideological grounds, issues and ideology can have a large impact on voting behavior. The authors of *The Changing American Voter* explicitly demonstrate that impact in their book.

One could also argue that "issue voting" led to the defeat of a certain number of senatorial incumbents in 1978 and 1980. In those campaigns, the records of liberal senators like Culver and Clark of Iowa, McGovern of South Dakota, and Church of Idaho were systematically attacked, not only by their challengers but also by organized conservative groups who orchestrated campaigns emphasizing key emotional issues (see Chapter 5). Significantly, incumbent congresspeople were winning in these same states in which incumbent senators were losing; voters were splitting their tickets because their votes were based on different criteria.

On the other hand, voters seem often not to care about the details of issues; they appear to be more concerned about their overall well-being and how politicians—in their role as government officials—have contributed to that well-being. Voting based on the evaluation of an incumbent's performance, rather than promises of future action, is the most common explanation of President Reagan's 1980 victory (Pomper, 1981a, p. 97), of his reelection in 1984, and even of the Bush victory in 1988.

But even this retrospective evaluative voting is not always in evidence. Below the presidential—and perhaps senatorial and gubernatorial—levels, citizens know little of incumbents' records or the issues with which they are concerned. While they might blame Congress for the mess the country is in (Fenno, 1972), or might not have much faith in government and politicians generally, they rarely blame *their own* representatives. Voters know these local politicians, view them positively, and frequently reelect the ones who seek reelection. Voters distinguish between the individual they know and trust and the impersonal institution—far removed from their daily lives—causing trouble.

VII.   POLITICIANS VIEW THE VOTERS

Politicians look upon the American electorate as consumers. They, the politicians, are the products that have to be sold. And they are sold in any way appropriate to getting the most people to vote for a candidate.[8]

---

[8] An oft-stated theoretical argument is that politicians seek only a plurality of the votes while making as few commitments and/or concessions as possible in order to guarantee a winning coalition. Nothing so badly misreads politicians as does this argument. Politicians fear losing; they do not fear commitments or concessions. Officeholders never feel secure; they have too much to lose if they are wrong. Consequently, in setting electoral strategy, they seek to generate maximum support, not merely to win. See Jacobson (1980) and Goldenberg and Traugott (1984) on the consequences of failing to win by large margins.

It is also evident to most politicians that an individualized sales approach is the most effective. As one congressman put it, "I love going door-to-door. When I talk to someone in their living room, and when they say they'll support me, I *know* I have their vote. No question about it."

Door-to-door campaigning, that famous one-on-one sale of self, has proved to be successful in campaign after campaign. Eugene McCarthy (D., Minn., 1949–1971), George McGovern, Jimmy Carter, and Gary Hart (D., Colo., 1975–1987) all used that approach successfully in the New Hampshire Democratic presidential primaries. "Walking Dan" Walker, Democratic governor of Illinois (1973–1977), and Lawton Chiles, Democratic senator (1971–1989) and governor (1991–   ) of Florida, spent months walking the length of their respective states to greet voters personally. Many members of Congress have followed a similar strategy, though the publicity that initially accompanied such walks and added to their effectiveness as a campaign technique has lessened considerably as campaign "walks" have become commonplace.

But consider the problems of bringing one's campaigning to individual voters. The average congressional district, for example, has approximately 600,000 citizens. Maybe 400,000 of those are potential voters, who live in 175,000 households. If a candidate spent twenty minutes in each living room, assuming everyone was home and no time was needed in between stops, that candidate would have to have put in nearly 5000 twelve-hour campaign days. Candidates accomplishing one one-hundredth of such a schedule in a two-year cycle feel that they have developed the common touch. Even with surrogates and volunteers, the enormity of "personal" effort becomes apparent. And the effort must be multiplied many times over for senatorial, gubernatorial, or presidential campaigns. Campaigning for individual votes might well work in local elections, and it is used to good effect for some offices in larger districts, but most politicians must use other means to approach the electorate.

Rather than seeing voters as individuals, politicians tend to see them as members of groups to whom appeals can be made. Once the decision has been made to group individuals, a number of options are open, some of which can complement each other. Some others, however, seem to preclude possible strategies.

As an example, look at the strategies followed by the candidates for the 1984 Democratic presidential nomination.[9] Former Vice President Walter Mondale, drawing on connections from his years of public life, sought the support of organized groups—unions, teachers, women's groups—to supplement his ties to Democratic party leaders. Even as he sought to broaden his appeal, he was unable to escape being labeled the candidate of the establishment, of the organizations.

Ohio Senator John Glenn viewed the electorate differently. He felt that his

---

[9] Voting behavior in primary elections is different in important ways from that in general elections. Most significant is the fact that voters do not have the cue of party as an aid in making decisions. However, the example suffices here because it demonstrates the ways in which candidates and campaign strategists view the electorate. In a general election, party members would be one more group to which candidates could appeal.

major opponent would be Vice President Mondale. As Mondale had tied up the organized group support, Glenn tried to appeal to those who perceived the former vice president as too liberal and as a loser because of Mondale's presence on the doomed 1980 Carter ticket. Glenn thus addressed his appeal to voters who supported efforts to build a stronger national defense and who demanded a winner at all costs. Emphasizing his experience in the Marines and as one of the original astronauts allowed Glenn to play to both those groups of voters.

Ernest Hollings of South Carolina and former Governor Reuben Askew of Florida each sought conservative backing and the support of southern voters. Askew particularly staked out his position on such issues as "right-to-life" as being different from the other Democrats' views. He believed that many Democratic voters would follow him on this issue alone. Few did. Although both Askew and Hollings counted heavily on "favorite son" southern support, neither was in the race long enough to contest the first southern primaries.

The Reverend Jesse Jackson was most explicit about the groups whose support he sought. Jackson has long talked of forming a "rainbow coalition" of blacks, Hispanics, women, and others disaffected by American society. His stand on issues was clearly aimed at voters who identified themselves primarily in these ways.

Former South Dakota Senator George McGovern was also clear in identifying those whose support he sought. McGovern reached out to self-identifying liberals, voters who would put principle above practicality. McGovern's campaign, however, had the plaintive ring of nostalgia, calling back those who had supported him in 1972. He sought to appeal to those who still felt they were right, who felt their views had never had a fair chance, who believed that McGovern was a prophet ahead of his time. In the Iowa caucuses he asked voters who agreed with him on issues but felt he had no chance to win to support him anyway; such McGovern loyalists would send a message to the eventual nominee: "Don't compromise your principles." In Massachusetts McGovern reminded voters that they had been with him in 1972—when Massachusetts and the District of Columbia cast the only electoral votes he received—and asked them to send the same message again.

And Gary Hart? The Colorado senator relied on a different kind of nostalgia, a nostalgia for a time when politicians were seen as exciting leaders with the kind of vision necessary to set the country on its future course to peace and prosperity. His looks and his mannerisms reminded voters of John Kennedy, and he evoked that image often. Hart appealed to a new, vaguely antiestablishment generation, to those seeking change and new ideas. His "group" lacked traditional ideological identification as his stand on issues defied ideological definition. He appealed to organized group members over their leaders' heads. Presenting himself as a young alternative, Hart found a receptive audience in many states.

Each candidate thus defined his constituency by grouping the potential electorate in ways that were meaningful to his campaign. Some groupings precluded others; Hart could not establish his theme and then go after organized labor as a group. Other strategies were less limiting; Mondale could still go after

liberals, backing his appeal with his Senate record of support for liberal legislation.

One can also view the system in another way. Two separate theories of
how to campaign in the November presidential election can be analyzed. The
first theory involves the country as a whole. Let's look at the 1988 campaign.
Which groups seemed to favor Vice President Bush? How could he get their
support? He concentrated his campaign remarks on general economic conditions, appealing to people who had benefited from the Reagan years with which
he was so closely associated. Bush reaffirmed his support for the ideological
right, opposing abortion, rekindling the patriotism of the "hard hats" of the
1960s and 1970s by (almost literally on occasion) wrapping himself in the
American flag.

The Democrats countered, casting doubt on the future success of the nation's economy, reminding voters of their hardships under former Republican
presidents. Governor Dukakis claimed that he would be a better manager, that
he could lead the country with a firmer hand.

A second strategic approach groups voters by geographic region. According to this view, the west votes as one bloc, the south as another. The map of

FIGURE 4-8 Republican strength in Electoral College, 1968–1988.

States that GOP has won six times in the last six elections	States that GOP has won five times in the last six elections	States that GOP has won four or fewer times in the last six elections
191 electoral votes	151 electoral votes	196 electoral votes

the nation is drawn in terms of electoral votes. Where can a candidate win the 270 electoral votes needed for election? This strategy uses a different arithmetic; it is based on winning states, not groups of votes. Figure 4-8 demonstrates this calculation. If President Bush can hold the west and the mountain states, he will have nearly half of the electoral votes needed for victory. Where can he get those? He had better concentrate his campaign in those crucial areas.

Note the distinction. Electoral strategies do not normally involve appeals to individuals. Individuals vote, but candidates appeal to them in groups, groups defined by the candidates and their strategists according to their strengths and perceptions of what will work. The larger the constituency, the more this is the case.

Tip O'Neill has been quoted as saying, "In the final analysis, all politics is local." Politicians believe Tip. Many started out as local politicians, and they know the effectiveness of one-on-one campaigns. Their goal, accordingly, is to make national or statewide politics local. They do this by defining smaller groups into which voters fall and then seeking to appeal to these groups. Many techniques are available for these appeals—mass media directed at a certain audience, targeted mailings, speeches to certain groups. But in the end, the political strategy is the same: make an appeal, in any way possible, to the largest number of people, so that it will seem personal to each one. Campaigners sell the product by figuring out what the voters want to buy.

While political scientists can explain voting behavior with some precision, politicians—with the souls of artists, not scientists—try to mold the electorate to the shape they want. The skill of both the scientist and the artist deserves attention.

chapter

5

Organized Groups in the Political Process

The 1988 National Election Study survey from the Survey Research Center at the University of Michigan asked a series of questions about groups. At one point the respondents were asked:

> There's been some talk these days about different social classes. Most people say they belong either to the MIDDLE CLASS or the WORKING CLASS. Do you think of yourself as belonging to one of these classes?

Later the respondents faced this question:

> In addition to being an American, what do you consider your main ethnic group or nationality group?

And still later, the question "How would you rate the following groups?" was followed by the list: labor unions, feminists, civil rights leaders, people on welfare, women, conservatives, poor people, Catholics, big business, blacks, evangelical groups active in politics, the federal government in Washington, liberals.

Obviously, the designers of this question believe that Americans respond to political messages by filtering those messages through reactions that they have as members of a group.

A similar perspective marked the analysis of candidate appeal by journalists during the 1984 Democratic presidential nominating process. Gary Hart supposedly appealed to younger voters and the "new breed of professionals." As the candidate of "new ideas," he sought to build support from a base of voters who sought change.

Walter Mondale was portrayed by his opponents as the candidate of "special interests," as distinguished from the "public interest." Exit polling after the five primaries on March 13, Super Tuesday in the 1984 primary campaign, revealed that Mondale was attracting support from older voters, blacks, and party regulars. Hart, on the other hand, did indeed appeal to younger voters and independents. The "Wednesday morning quarterbacks" asked how each candidate could alter his appeal to gain votes from the others' "social groups."

A careful reading of the preceding paragraphs and our analysis of how

121

politicians appeal to individual voters in Chapter 4 should reveal a conceptual inconsistency. The groups cited in the National Election Study questions were different kinds of groups—social groups, ethnic groups, racial groups, ideological groups, occupational groups, and others. Not only are these groups not mutually exclusive—one could certainly be a black teacher who is a union member—but they are also generically different. The first NES questions seek to know how the respondent perceives himself or herself. The questions allow for more than one answer and then probe for primary self-identification. In analyzing the influence of groups on the electoral process, however, a researcher must distinguish among types of groups and the effect these groups have on politics.

Americans, like citizens of any other nation, divide themselves "automatically" into certain types of groups. The electorate can be divided racially—blacks, whites, Latinos, Orientals, etc.—or religiously—Protestants, Catholics, Jews, etc.—or in terms of age—the elderly, the middle-aged, younger citizens, etc.— or in terms of occupation—farmers, teachers, construction workers, lawyers, etc. Other similar groupings could be added to this list. As mentioned in Chapter 4, politicians often treat the electorate as a collection of such groups, appealing to voters to react through their "group consciousness." In this regard it is important that we know with which groups voters principally self-identify—as the survey asks—and how candidates will appeal to their rivals' "social groups"—as the journalists wondered on the day after the Mondale-Hart primaries in 1984.

However, what commentators for centuries have noted as a distinguishing characteristic of the American populace is not the ability to identify with demographic, occupational, or social groups but rather a long-lived tendency to *join* organized groups.

Until very recent times, analysts, from the authors of the *Federalist* papers through V. O. Key, have focused their attention on the impact of organized groups on the policymaking process, not the electoral process. In the last edition of his classic text, *Politics, Parties, and Pressure Groups,* published in 1964, Key wrote:

> A striking feature of American politics is the extent to which political parties are supplemented by private associations formed to influence public policy. These organizations, commonly called pressure groups, promote their interests by attempting to influence government rather than by nominating candidates and seeking responsibility for the management of government. Such groups, while they may call themselves non-political, are engaged in politics; in the main theirs is a politics of policy. (p. 18)

Although Key acknowledges that "pressure groups may campaign for party candidates and may even become, in fact if not in form, allied with one or the other of the parties" (1964, p. 19), the emphasis in his five chapters on pressure groups is most decidedly on how these organizations seek to effect policy changes *after* elections have been held.

Within a decade of Key's death in 1963, even much less perceptive observers of American politics had come to realize that the role of interest groups (the term "pressure groups" has been all but dropped because of its pejorative connotation) has been drastically altered. *While still playing an important role in all aspects of the policymaking process, organized interest groups—acting as organizations, not merely as associations with which voters identify—now play a central role in the electoral process as well.* (See, as examples, Berry, 1977; the articles in Cigler & Loomis, 1983; Schlozman & Tierney, 1986.) When Walter Mondale was dubbed the "candidate of special interests," the appellation stemmed from his endorsement and support by organizations *as* organizations, not because individual voters who were members of those groups supported him.

This chapter focuses on the role of organized groups in the electoral process. Two aspects of this role will be examined separately: (1) the ways in which these organizations enter into the campaigns of various candidates and (2) the effectiveness of these groups in controlling their members' votes. Before turning to these questions, however, we should come to an explicit understanding of the types of groups to be examined.

I. ORGANIZED GROUPS IN AMERICAN POLITICS

Table 5-1 lists a sampling of organized groups in the United States today. They cover a wide array of interests—from the general to the particular; they come in a variety of sizes—from a few hundred members to tens of millions; they engage in a variety of activities—from sponsoring agricultural fairs to sponsoring presidential candidate debates. Only some of these groups are involved in the political process as groups, though members of virtually every group are involved in politics. Groups involved in electoral politics also can be classified according to the type of association they organize and the impact they have on politics (Schlozman & Tierney, 1986, pp. 38–57).

A. Political and Nonpolitical Associations

Americans form associations for various reasons: camaraderie, education, charitable work, economic advancement (see J. Walker, 1983). Some of these groups have an obvious stake in the political process. For example, the National Federation of Independent Businesses clearly is concerned with legislation affecting small business establishments. Some of these organizations were formed for political purposes, the liberal Americans for Democratic Action standing as one such group. Other groups were formed for purposes unrelated to politics, but they became politically involved as the government began to involve itself in matters relating to that group's purpose. For most of its first hundred years, the American Medical Association tried to stay out of organized politics; for the last forty years or so, the AMA has monitored national legislative action and then frequently lobbied and campaigned to protect its perceived interest. Finally, some groups have stayed above the political fray, despite the expanding role of government. Phi Beta Kappa, the academic honor society formed in the year of

TABLE 5-1. Types of Organizations and Associations Associated with Them

Health and Medical Organizations
International Association for Accidental and Traffic Medicine
Aerospace Medical Association
National Geriatrics Society
American Board of Allergy and Immunology
Society of Behavioral Medicine
March of Dimes Birth Defects Foundation
American Council on Pharmaceutical Education

Religious Organizations
National Association of Church Personnel Administrators
Fellowship of Concerned Churchmen
Society of the Bible in the Hands of Its Creators
International Conference of Police Chaplains
American Zionist Federation
Christian Women's Fellowship

Cultural Organizations
Association of Aviation and Space Museums
Afghanistan Studies Association
Friends of the American Museum in Britain
Drawing Society
Creative Artists Public Service Program
Business Committee for the Arts
Authors' Guild
Virgil Society

Scientific, Engineering, and Technical Organizations
Stonehenge Study Group
American Society of Landscape Architects
Roller Bearing Engineers Committee
Herb Society of America
Musser International Turfgrass Foundation
American Board of Clinical Chemistry

Source: *Encyclopedia of Associations* (Detroit: Gale Research, 1983.)

our Revolution, has never entered the political realm in over two hundred years and remains removed from politics today.

The decision of whether or not to become involved in politics—through either the policymaking process or the electoral process, or both—is a significant one for an organization. As the leaders of an organization see that their group's interest is affected by governmental action, they must decide on the role they wish to play. If they decide to become politically involved, they take on a new status. If they decide to lobby the Congress for legislation, they must register as a lobbying organization. If they decide to support candidates for office, they must form a separate political action committee. In any case, if they had been granted tax-exempt status by the Internal Revenue Service, they will likely forfeit that status. Politicization may make fund-raising more difficult. However, if they stay out of politics, the group's members may decide that the group has become irrelevant to the issues around which it formed; this perception may erode the group's membership and support as well.

At times these decisions are easy for leaders to make; at other times they are not. Environmental groups are an interesting example. The Sierra Club has decided to include lobbying in its arsenal of tactics in support of its cause. The Audubon Society, an organization with a similar perspective, has decided to forgo this approach.

B. Politically Active Groups

Our concern is with those groups, or individuals representing groups, which have decided to become involved politically. The number of such groups is staggering: Over 12,500 individuals were listed in the 1989 directory entitled *Washington Representatives*. Over 2500 political action committees contributed to candidates in the 1980 congressional elections; more than 4000 had registered with the Federal Election Commission by the end of 1984; nearly 4300 by 1988. In the face of these awesome numbers, we should look carefully at the rationale behind the formation of such a farrago of interest groups.

1. Economic or Noneconomic Interest One way to divide interest groups is on the basis of their membership. If the members are motivated *primarily* by economic interests, they can be distinguished from other groups whose members have fewer (or at least less obvious) immediate tangible concerns.

A preponderance of the groups active today exist in order to defend their members' economic interests. Why do people find this economic defense so crucial? As the American economy diversified, our citizens increasingly felt that they needed to band together with people of similar interests to defend themselves against those who seemed to be more powerful. Thus farmers' cooperatives and labor organizing began at various times in the 1800s. As these groups diversified further—and thus developed separate interests—more groups were formed.

The number of economic interest groups also increased rapidly when the federal government became more and more involved in the regulation of the daily life of most Americans. As government took a more and more intrusive role in the regulation of economic matters, larger and larger numbers of Americans came together to advance or defend those interests. Similarly, as the American economy became more and more diversified, the associations became more and more specialized.

Examples of economic interest groups abound. Some are quite well known, such as the United Auto Workers or the National Association of Manufacturers. Others are considerably more obscure, like the Coalition for Common Sense in Government Procurement or the Joint Labor Management Committee of the Retail Food Industry.

Noneconomic groups, sometimes called public interest groups, pursue goals that are viewed by their members as good for the entire society, even if those goals do not serve the economic interest of one particular segment of society. Some people now believe that Ralph Nader invented public interest groups when he founded Public Citizen—and because his name is so closely linked with the term. Some other "Naderite" organizations that are currently active are Congress Watch, Critical Mass, Public Citizen Litigation Group, Tax Reform Research Group, Health Research Group, and various local public interest research groups.

Similarly, others associate public interest groups with Common Cause, the organization of nearly a quarter of a million members formed by former Health, Education, and Welfare Secretary John Gardner in 1970 (McFarland, 1984). Common Cause bills itself as the "citizens' lobby" and concentrates heavily on issues of government reform.

However, many other groups—some older, some younger; some larger, some smaller; some more effective, some less effective—have formed around noneconomic issues and remain active in politics today. These include environmental groups as mentioned earlier, civil rights organizations, ideological groups of the left and the right, religious groups, and many more. Their impact on public policy and on elections is often just as great as the one made by their economic counterparts.

Although the distinction between economic and noneconomic groups is a useful one, it should not be overemphasized. The line can become blurred and change over time. One need only look at organized women's groups formed around the issue of suffrage to see a good example. Suffrage, once achieved, gave way to certain other rights, culminating in the drive for ratification of the Equal Rights Amendment. Along the way, however, women's economic rights were recognized as being as clearly involved as their other rights. One of the important goals of the women's movement became "equal pay for equal work"; the goal was symbolized by the "59 cents" button, signifying that women earned only 59 cents for every dollar a man earned. While "equal-pay" provisions are now mandated by law, "equal pay for comparable work" is a current goal of the women's movement. The economic concerns of organizations like the National Organization for Women (NOW) have spread to include the allegedly discriminatory practices of the insurance industry, compensatory pay for past discrimination, and many other important issues. While NOW is not primarily an economic interest group, it cannot ignore women's economic concerns.

2. **Multipurpose or Single-Purpose Groups** *The discussion of the women's movement raises another possibility for categorizing groups active today. Some groups are organized for a single purpose; others lobby on a whole range of issues of interest to their membership.* The size of each of these divisions depends on how narrowly or widely one defines "single interest." Again, some examples are self-evident; others, however, cannot be so clearly defined.

During the first two decades of this century, the Congressional Committee of the National American Women Suffrage Association was organized for the sole purpose of achieving women's right to vote. Similarly, today's Pro-Life Association and National Abortion Rights Action League (NARAL) are associ-

Reprinted with permission of
Toles/Universal Press Syndicate

ations whose purpose relates to only one issue—the existence or nonexistence of
a woman's right to choose. On the other hand, groups such as NOW, the
League of Women Voters, or the American Association of University Women
are concerned with a whole array of women's issues.

The distinction between single-purpose and multipurpose organizations
has important implications for the effectiveness of these groups. When Kate
Michelman, the leader of NARAL, speaks on the question of abortion, she can
speak authoritatively for the approximately 250,000 dues-paying members of
her group. They joined that group, combining their financial investment often
with a personal investment of time, because they feel a strong commitment to
one side of the issue of abortion. No one can question the firmness of their
stand on this issue.

National Abortion Rights Action League president Kate
Mickelman, here standing before the Supreme Court as it was
hearing a challenge to a woman's right to an abortion, has worked
to make a woman's right to choose a crucial issue in federal, state,
and local campaigns. (Kate Mickelman/AP/Wide World Photos)

On the other hand, if Linda Colvard Dorian, the leader of the Business
and Professional Women's (BPW's) Foundation of America, were to speak on
the same question, despite the fact that she "represents" that group's members
(125,000 members in 3500 individual clubs), her audience could certainly
question the commitment of her members to a strong stand on this particular
issue. BPW's views are not self-evident. The same questions regarding commitment are also important when one tries to determine how important membership in a group is to the member's other political activities. The following dis-

cussion of electoral activities by members of single-issue groups will emphasize just how significant this distinction can be.

3. Federal or National Groups *A distinction like that made above differentiates federal associations from national ones. National organizations are ones in which the members, be they individuals or groups, belong directly to the national organization.* The National Association of Manufacturers is a national organization to which various corporations belong individually. Decisions in these organizations are made directly, with the leaders of the national organization responsible (in ways that are often difficult to define) to their members (see Eismeier & Pollock, 1984).

Federal organizations are ones whose national organization is a conglomeration of state or local organizations, each of which is itself autonomous or semiautonomous. The AFL-CIO is the obvious example of such a group, but it is only one of many which could be given. In organizations of this type, lines of authority are much less distinct. If the various constituent units split on a particular issue, how can the federal leadership speak authoritatively, particularly if the local units are permitted to retain their autonomy? Thus, federal organizations must spend a good deal of time on internal politics, assuring that stands taken in Washington do not cause problems out in Pocatello.

The same distinction between national and federal organizations affects their input into the electoral process. For national organizations, it is clear. If the Grocery Manufacturers of America decide to back a candidate for the United States Senate in Illinois, the organization has spoken. However, before the Americans for Democratic Action decide to take a similar stand, the leadership in Washington has to consult with the local Illinois affiliate. Problems for federal organizations multiply when the autonomous members disagree. And the powers of such a group diminish when politicians perceive that it does not speak for "all."

II. ELECTORAL ACTIVITIES OF ORGANIZED GROUPS

The purpose of drawing the distinctions noted above relates to the varying impact that groups have on the electoral process. First, we should recall why groups became involved in electoral politics in the first place: these organizations became involved in the political arena in order to effect changes in public policy. For many years "interest group" or "pressure group" was used as a synonym for "lobbyist." The primary means used by these groups was lobbying legislators and, to a lesser extent, administrators (Key, 1964; chaps. 2–6). Only *after* the lobbying role was firmly established did organized interest groups become involved in the electoral process in a meaningful way.

Even as their role has expanded, however, it is distinct from the role played by political parties. Parties run candidates for office and seek control in order to organize the governing process. The parties stand for certain principles, but they use these principles chiefly as a means to attract adherents. Interest groups, contrarily, became involved in the electoral arena *only* to forward their policy preferences. Put simply, rather than taking positions to attract followers, they support candidates who support their positions—or oppose candidates who do not favor their positions. This last point is important. Political parties field candidates in order to *win* positions; interest groups at times support one candidate simply to bring about the defeat of another. In the decade of the 1970s, as an example, oil interest groups nationally and particularly in Houston, Texas, supported a whole platoon of opponents of then congressman Bob Eckhardt (D., Tex, 1967–1980), simply because Eckhardt had a long history of supporting environmental concerns over oil interests. The qualities of those candidates were almost completely inconsequential. Political parties, conversely, would not be so concerned with policy positions as they would be with partisan label.

How do interest groups affect the electoral arena? In this section we will examine the activities through which these groups seek to have an impact in the broadly defined political environment. The next section will deal with the impact on the voting behavior of group members. (See Schlozman & Tierney, 1986, pp. 200–220, for a thorough discussion of this entire topic.)

A. Working within the Party

Most interest groups attempt to maintain some degree of bipartisanship because they do not want to alienate, in either party, public officials who favor their policy preferences. However, remaining "above" the partisan battle does not mean removing themselves wholly from the internal operations of both parties. *One technique that interest groups have traditionally used has been to attempt to effect changes in the two party platforms.*

We recall that the suffragists defined platform support for the women's vote as one of their goals earlier in this century. Similarly, those favoring passage of the Equal Rights Amendment fought to have that included in both parties' platforms. The Republicans first expressed support for the ERA when they were seeking to build opposition to four-term President Franklin Roosevelt. One of the most interesting aspects of the 1980 Republican Convention was the successful effort by anti-ERA groups to keep support for that amendment out of the GOP platform. Similarly the Pro-Life Impact Committee was successful in having an antiabortion plank inserted into that platform. In both cases, the debate before the Republican Platform Committee was structured by interest groups (Malbin, 1981, pp. 100–110).

Many other groups were actively involved in the platform-writing process as well. Before most recent conventions, each party has held a series of platform hearings. The stated goal has been to reach out for the opinions of rank-and-file Republicans and Democrats. To a great extent the effect was to reach out for the views of organized groups. The groups sent their leaders to testify, they prepared their own "miniplatforms," and they "lobbied" with the members of the platform committee. The most involved groups have even campaigned, often successfully, to have their followers chosen as members of the platform committees. Although debate continues over the importance of platforms in the policy-making process (see Pomper with Lederman, 1980, chap. 8; Wayne, 1988, pp. 147–151), interest-group leaders unquestionably see the platform as one place where they can have an impact.

While groups try to maintain ties in both parties, no one doubts that some groups are closer to one party than the other. The more feminist-oriented women's groups—NOW, NARAL, ERAmerica—certainly feel more at home in Democratic party circles then they do in Republican circles. The same can generally be said for black organizations. While these groups maintain contact with Republicans and attempt to influence the positions of the Republican party and its candidates, they have been more successful with the Democrats.

The relationship between organized labor and the Democratic party carries this tie to the extreme. While labor has traditionally been close to the Democratic party, labor's loyalty was strained at the 1972 National Convention when the AFL-CIO—as well as many other groups traditionally part of the New Deal coalition—felt excluded. After the overwhelming electoral defeat in 1972, the Democratic party needed once more to appeal especially to labor. Party Chairman Robert Strauss appointed a new Commission on Delegate Selection and Party Structure, to be chaired by United Auto Workers President Leonard Woodcock. Five other prominent labor leaders were appointed to the panel. When Woodcock resigned, claiming he did not have time to devote to the task, the leadership fell to the vice chair, Barbara Mikulski, then a little-known Baltimore city councilwoman. Mikulski, appointed as a representative of ethnics and women, proved to be a feisty and outspoken chair. Labor received less than it wanted from the Mikulski Commission, but a foot was back in the door (Crotty, 1983, pp. 63–74).

Labor has continued its active involvement in the Democratic party. When the Democratic National Committee was elected in 1980, party leaders felt that too few of the members were labor leaders. Consequently, the chair of the DNC used fifteen of his twenty-five at-large appointments to name union officials to the party's ruling body. In addition, four of these union leaders were appointed to the Executive Committee of the DNC, the most important decision-making group.

To cement its ties with the Democratic party further, organized labor formed an advisory committee to help with party fund-raising and strategy-setting immediately before the 1982 elections. The unions represented in the group have contributed substantially to the DNC each year. Finally, in order to "guarantee" an impact on the internal workings of the Democratic party, the AFL-CIO Executive Committee decided that labor leaders would gather in advance of the 1984 presidential primaries to endorse the candidate they felt should be supported as the opponent of President Reagan. They tapped Walter Mondale, and then faced the test of delivering their members' votes in the subsequent primaries and caucuses. The divergence between the opinions of union leaders and their membership is a fairly recent phenomenon that reduces the influence of labor leaders in today's politics.

Regardless of the impact of this endorsement, its intent was clear. Organized labor was saying that the union members' home was in the Democratic party. And one way they intended to effect the public policy changes they desired was through a continuing influence over the internal operations of the party. In 1988 labor leaders backed away from a preprimary endorsement of a presidential candidate, but again many labor leaders were active in candidate organizations. As the 1992 nomination approached, with few Democrats out front looking to be tapped, labor leaders played a more low-key role. However, even early in the process they made it well known that they stood ready as a group to support New York Governor Mario Cuomo should he decide to advance his candidacy.

The extent and openness of organized labor's commitment to the Democrats is unique. At the same time, women and minorities, despite the fact that both groups were also given positions of privilege within the Democratic party, still maintain ties with the Republicans. The National Women's Political Caucus has cochairs of different parties, for instance. Attempting to bring influence to bear on internal party matters is clearly one technique used by interest groups to reach their goals.

B.   Group Ratings

An increasing number of organized groups are "rating" congressmen and senators in terms of the degree to which those legislators support or oppose legislation favored by those groups. These ratings, which usually range from 0 (no support) to 100 (total support), are computed by the groups after they first select the issues most important to them (Fowler, 1982).

Group ratings differ in terms of which issues are chosen (those deemed appropriate to the group's concern), how many votes are chosen (all or only the most important on the selected issues), and how scores are computed (how absentee or proxy votes are counted). However, the ratings are identical in intent: *they identify friends and enemies of the groups for the group members to see and for others interested in the group's opinions to weigh in judging incumbents.*

Some of those ratings are more prominent than others. *The Almanac of American Politics* and *Politics in America,* two widely circulated books that give basic information on every congressman and senator, each list how various groups rate the officeholders. The *Almanac of American Politics* uses ten different group ratings, while *Politics in America* restricts itself to four. Two of the more widely used scores are attempts to rate congressmen and senators ideologically across a range of issues. The Americans for Democratic Action uses a series of votes—on both domestic and foreign policy issues—which it asserts are litmus tests for liberals. In 1990, four senators—Akaka (D., Haw.), Cranston (D., Calif.), Kennedy (D., Mass.), and Lautenberg (D., N.J.)—scored perfect 100s, as did twenty-nine members of the House; the number of members with perfect ADA ratings increased from 1989, which in turn had shown an increase since 1988.

At the other ideological extreme the Americans for Constitutional Action uses a sophisticated system to show how frequently members of Congress vote

". . . for safeguarding the God-given rights of the individual. . . ." (Malbin, 1981, p. 126), that is, to determine how conservative legislators are, according to the ACA's definition. Unsurprisingly, those who score high on the ADA scale frequently score low on the ACA scale, though the two scales are not exact opposites because of different issues chosen and different ways of handling absences. In 1990 the only 100 scores given by the ACA went to Republicans— Senators Helms (N.C.) and Symms (Idaho) and Congressmen Crane (Ill.), Dannemeyer (Calif.), Hancock (Mo.), McEwen (Ohio), and Stump (Ariz.). The number with perfect scores decreased from that which had been recorded in the two previous years.

Similarly, those who do well on the AFL-CIO Committee on Political Education (COPE) rating often do not do well on ratings published by the Chamber of Commerce of the United States. Each of these groups, as well as the more than a dozen others that issue ratings, try to inform voters on how their representatives stand on issues of particular relevance to group members and sympathizers.

The exploding number of ratings can confuse even the most sophisticated political observer. Groups often change their method of computing an incumbent's scores, making comparisons over time difficult. Frequently two groups representing variant elements of the same "constituency" define important issues differently, leading to different ratings of incumbents. This dissimilarity has been the case in recent years with the National Council of Senior Citizens and the National Alliance of Senior Citizens. Even though they are mirror images of each other ideologically, these two groups each produce a rating for senior citizens, leading to some confusion by those using these ratings.

The ratings of incumbents often have direct electoral implications. Although few citizens, and not even most members of the involved groups, monitor these group ratings closely, many interest groups weigh them heavily in determining whom to help financially in upcoming campaigns. In addition, groups take particular care to identify those on the "extreme" as special friends or enemies of whom their members should be aware.

In the 1970s one group, Environmental Action Incorporated, each election year identified the twelve "worst" congressmen according to EAI's rating of environmental concerns. The group dubbed these representatives the "dirty dozen" and targeted them for defeat. Of fifty-two incumbents given the label over the course of the five elections ending with that of 1978, twenty-five were defeated in the same year as they were targeted, giving increased credibility to the power of this group (*Congressional Quarterly Weekly Report*, 1981, p. 510). During the 1980s Environmental Action combined its legislative rating with a compilation of how much money from political action committees (PACs) incumbent candidates accepted from corporate PACs of companies it regarded as the Filthy Five; Environmental Action included senators in its newer rankings. While a lower percentage of the identified incumbents lost in more recent elections, the impact of the group remains impressive; three of the members it targeted were among the losers in 1990 (Friedman, 1990). Besides wishing to avoid being dubbed one of the twelve "worst" legislators on environmental issues, incumbents want to avoid being targeted for defeat by this particular group. Clearly, then, the rating systems perform an important function for the politically involved interest groups.

C. Political Action Committees

Although some politicians complain about the impact of group activity upon the political parties themselves, and many think that the various rating systems portray them unfairly, neither of these approaches has had the influence, nor caused the controversy, of groups participating in the electoral process through political action committees.

A short history is necessary (see Alexander & Haggerty, 1981, chaps. 1–4; E. Epstein, 1980; Magleby & Nelson, 1990; Sorauf, 1988, chap. 2). The critical date in terms of changes in campaign finance laws affecting groups was 1974. Before that time—or, more accurately, before 1971 when the Federal Election Campaign Act was passed, even though that year's provision did not affect groups—the difference between legality and reality was extreme.

The financing of federal elections was governed by a series of outmoded and largely ignored laws—the 1907 Tillman Act, which prohibited corporate contributions; the 1925 Corrupt Practices Campaign Act, which set limits on expenditures in House ($2500 to $5000) and Senate ($10,000 to $25,000) but not presidential campaigns; the 1939 and 1940 Hatch Acts, which put limits on contributions and involvement of federal employees; and the 1944 Smith-Connally and 1947 Taft-Hartley Acts, which prohibited labor unions from contributing directly to campaigns. The most significant aspects of these laws were the ease and impunity with which they were ignored (E. Epstein, 1980; Sorauf, 1988, pp. 28–33).

Candidates set up multiple committees to avoid the campaign spending limits. Corporations were notorious for giving election-year "bonuses," which were then passed on by obedient executives to deserving candidates. According to a *Congressional Quarterly* study of corporate executive giving in 1968, these contributions could well have totaled millions of dollars (*Congressional Quarterly Weekly Report*, 1971, p. 35). Labor unions set up committees on political education (COPE) which were used to solicit "voluntary" contributions from union members, funds which were then used to "educate" the members about the issues of the day, the candidates most deserving of support. The COPE sought to "interest" members in the political process through registration drives, get-out-the-vote drives, and poll watching. COPE activities were also worth millions of dollars, largely to Democrats.

The reality of campaign financing as America entered the decade of the 1970s revealed a picture of significantly increasing expenditures, corporate influence, and union activity, all sidestepping the intent, if not the letter, of the law, and all far removed from public view.

The Federal Election Campaign Act (FECA) of 1971 marked the first step in reforming these practices. The major provisions of this act put a limit on media expenditures, deemed to be the major source of the drastically escalating costs of campaigns. The FECA called for the disclosure of the source of all campaign contributions, identifying sources by occupation and business affiliation as well as by name and address. The theory was that disclosure was the best means of control (see Corrado, 1991a).

The 1974 amendments to the FECA of 1971 have led to a tremendous change in the role played by organized interest groups. The 1974 amendments limited individual contributions to $1000 per campaign but permitted the establishment of political action committees which could contribute up to $5000 in each campaign. The amendments specifically allowed corporations and unions to use money for the "establishment, administration, and solicitation of contributions to a separate, segregated fund" (*Congressional Quarterly Weekly Report*, 1982, p. 43). The weight carried by this action was made all the more clear when, in a 1975 case involving Sun Oil Company, the Federal Election Commission ruled that corporations could use general treasury funds to establish political action committees. This ruling was opposed by organized labor, since the AFL-CIO foresaw the rapid expansion of corporate PACs (E. Epstein, 1980). Table 5-2 shows that the unions' fear had a firm foundation.

Organized labor unions formed PACs shortly after PACs were legalized; the number peaked at 394 in 1984 and has declined somewhat since that time. Similarly, trade, membership, and health associations—the organized groups with which we are concerned—saw the opportunity quickly. While we can list many more PACs in this category than in the labor category, their rate of growth seems to have slowed in recent years. Corporate PACs, to the contrary, are another phenomenon. Since 1975 when the SUNPAC decision was handed down, the number of corporate PACs has expanded more than twentyfold. Although the rate of increase has slowed, many observers predict that the absolute number of corporate PACs will continue to increase, while the number of union PACs has peaked and is declining.

TABLE 5-2. Growth of Political Action Committees, 1974–1990

Year	Total Number of PACs	Corporate	Labor	Trade/ Member- ship/ Health	Non- connected	Other	Contributions to Congressional Candidates (in millions)
1974	608	89	201	318	—	—	$ 12.5
1976	1146	433	224	489	—	—	22.6
1978	1653	784	217	451	165	36	34.1
1980	2551	1204	297	574	378	98	55.2
1982	3371	1467	380	628	746	150	83.1
1984	4009	1682	394	698	1053	182	105.3
1985	3992	1710	388	695	1003	196	
1986	4157	1744	384	745	1077	207	132.7
1987	4165	1775	364	865	957	204	
1988	4268	1816	354	786	1115	197	147.8
1990	4172	1795	346	779	1062	195	149.9

Source: Data are drawn from Ornstein et al., 1992, p. 97.

Why do we discuss corporate PACs in a chapter on organized group activity? The answer should be evident. To a large extent corporate PACs are an extension of trade association PACs. Each PAC is limited in the amount it can contribute to any one campaign. However, corporate members of trade associations can form their own PACs and then give as separate entities, thus becoming the functional equivalents of interest groups (Schlozman & Tierney, 1986, pp. 9–12).

Table 5-3 lists the ten largest PACs in the 1989–1990 election cycle in terms of dollar contributions made to candidates. Six of the ten are labor PACs—the NEA; the United Auto Workers; the Letter Carriers; the State, County, and Municipal Employees; the National Association of Retired Federal Employees Political Action Committee; and the Carpenters. The top three contributors are all membership or trade associations, some of which have their own component units. However, while no individual corporate PACs made the top of the list, taken cumulatively their power seems evident. In the 1989–1990 election cycle, corporate PACs contributed over $54 million to House and Senate candidates, according to Federal Election Commission records. Membership and trade association PACs contributed a total of nearly $40 million. Labor PACs contributed less than $35 million.

The proliferation of PACs and the ever-increasing amounts of money that they contribute have caused many to question the consequences of the campaign finance reforms. One of the key features of these reforms was to be public financing of presidential campaigns. The framers of this reform held that too much "big money" tainted presidential politics. One consequence of public financing of presidential campaigns has been that organized groups are now wielding their considerable financial clout on congressional and senatorial campaigns[1] and on campaigns in the various states. Cynics snicker that we now have the very best Congress that money can buy (Stern, 1988).

Such charges deserve some examination. We should first seek to determine to whom money is being given. The early pattern was for PACs to support incumbent members of Congress on committees that dealt with policies of concern to the association giving the money. The hope was to assure access to these important decision makers. Thus, the American Bankers Association PAC contributed heavily to incumbent members of the banking committee. Contributions seemed to be bipartisan, largely because PAC officers were well aware of the tendency of incumbents to be reelected. Contributors tended to stay away from challengers, contributions to whom were deemed risky investments.

In the early 1980s, however, labor PACs began to contribute more heavily to challengers of incumbents who opposed their views. This strategy followed

---

[1] PAC contributions accounted for about a tenth of those received by House and Senate candidates in 1972, before the public funding of presidential campaigns. By 1978, House candidates were receiving about a quarter of their money from PACs, though the percentage Senate candidates were receiving from these sources had not changed much. In the 1987–1988 election cycle, House candidates received 40 percent of their money from nonparty PACs; Senate candidates received 22 percent (*Congressional Quarterly Almanac*, vol. XXXVI, p. 556; Ornstein, Mann, & Malbin, 1990, table 3-9).

TABLE 5-3. Top Ten PACs in Overall Spending and in Contributions to Federal Candidates, 1989–1990

1   Realtors Political Action Committee
2   American Medical Association Political Action Committee
3   Democratic Republican Independent Voter Education Committee
4   National Education Association Political Action Committee
5   UAW-V-CAP (UAW Voluntary Community Action Program)
6   Committee on Letter Carriers Political Education (Letter Carriers Political Action Fund)
7   American Federation of State, County, and Municipal Employees—PEOPLE, Qualified
8   National Association of Retired Federal Employees Political Action Committee
9   Association of Trial Lawyers of America Political Action Committee
10 Carpenters Legislative Improvement Committee, United Brotherhood of Carpenters and Joiners of AME

Source: Federal Election Commission Press Release, "Political Action Committee Activity Falls in 1990 Elections," Sunday, March 31, 1991.

from recognition of the fact that an incumbent's biggest advantage is often his or her name recognition; with enough money a challenger potentially could offset that advantage. In 1982, for example, 28 percent of the labor PAC money went to challengers. PAC contribution patterns in the most recent election cycles have reverted to the earlier pattern, perhaps reflecting the fact that contributions to challengers did not seem to improve their chances of winning appreciably. Eighty-three percent of PAC contributions in the 1987–1988 election cycle went to incumbents; only 9 percent went to those challenging these incumbents, with the remainder going to candidates in open seats.

Intuitively one would have assumed that the increase in traditionally Republican-oriented corporate PACs would have meant an increase in contributions to GOP candidates in the late 1970s.[2] However, because both houses of Congress were dominated by Democrats at that time, and because PAC strategy emphasized supporting incumbents, the Democratic party got a lion's share of the PAC contributions. In 1978, for example, Democratic candidates received 56.3 percent of PAC contributions while Republican contestants were given 43.7 percent. With the switch in PAC strategy, advantage began to swing toward the Republican party, Republican receipts rising to 48.1 percent of PAC donations to House candidates in 1980. With PACs reverting to the former pattern of supporting incumbents, the Democratic share has risen in recent elections, with Democratic PAC receipts for House candidates nearly doubling that of Republicans in 1988.[3]

[2] This clearly was the perception of House members in 1979 when Republicans voted 29–124 in opposition to the Obey-Railsback amendment which sought to reduce House candidates' acceptances of PAC funds. Democrats supported the measure 188–74. The likelihood of a filibuster thwarted consideration of the bill by the Senate. More recent reform efforts will be discussed in Chapter 9.
[3] Senate figures are more difficult to interpret because only one-third of the Senate is up for reelection each time and because the low absolute number of races (33 or 34 compared with 435 for House races) leads to idiosyncratic results.

One further type of political action committee needs analysis, the so-called independent or nonconnected PAC. These PACs do not grow out of a parent organization; rather they are formed for specifically political purposes. The prototype of this form of organization is the National Conservative Political Action Committee (NCPAC). These PACs can contribute to individual campaigns, but they also take advantage of a provision in the Federal Election Campaign Act which maintains that PACs can make independent political expenditures so long as they are not coordinated with a particular candidate. The Supreme Court in *Buckley v. Valeo*, 424 U.S. 1 (1976), the suit that challenged the constitutionality of the Federal Election Campaign Act, had ruled that limitations on such independent expenditures was an abridgment of the freedom of speech. In 1976 the FECA was amended to correct this constitutional fault.

Using sophisticated direct-mail techniques, independent PACs have subsequently raised a substantial amount of money. For example, in the 1981–1982 election cycle, NCPAC raised over $7 million. How was this money spent? On whose behalf? It was spent as the directors of the fund wished, on behalf of or against any candidates they chose. As John T. Dolan, head of NCPAC said, "I am responsible to absolutely no one." NCPAC ran extensive campaigns *against* particular candidates. NCPAC has even advertised against certain incumbents well before an opponent has surfaced. In 1980 this technique was deemed successful in contributing to the defeats of liberal Senators Birch Bayh (D., Ind.), John Culver (D., Iowa), Frank Church (D., Idaho), and George McGovern (D., S.D.). NCPAC was a feared opponent.

NCPAC's efforts, however, had lost much of their influence by 1982, when likely targets of the group had begun counterattacks on the NCPAC's accuracy and ethics. NCPAC's impact on the 1982 elections was negligible. By 1982 other groups had also formed in response to NCPAC, most notably a liberal countergroup, PROPAC. Independent PACs covered more parts of the political spectrum in targeting 1982 incumbents for defeat than ever before, though the liberal PACs remained much smaller than their conservative counterparts. In the last election cycles, these groups have been much less successful and thus less feared. They have been attacked for their methods; they have been repudiated by the candidates they sought to aid; and, most significantly from their point of view, they have been less successful in raising money needed to carry out their purposes.

The success or failure of specific interest groups does not alter the most important basic question about independent PACs: unlike labor unions, trade associations, or even corporations, these groups represent leaders who are not held accountable in any way to their constituency. There are no members, per se. Individuals are contributors; they can fail to contribute again. But talented fund-raisers will tell you that there is no dearth of small contributors.

This last point raises the key defense for independent PACs and political action committees generally. A salient goal of campaign reform has always been to increase the number of small contributors. The objective is to get "big money" out of politics. PACs do indeed increase the number of small contributors, and PAC leaders argue that these contributors know the causes they are supporting. But do PACs get the big money out of politics? That conclusion is more doubtful. For years Common Cause has waged a vigorous, but so far unsuccessful, campaign against PACs. Common Cause feels that PACs hinder the political process by giving undue influence to powerful groups. PAC defenders argue that they get individuals involved—just as has always been desired. To a large extent where one stands on this debate depends on where one sits. If a person sits in Congress as a recipient of PAC money, that person is not likely to oppose PACs. To the challenger on the outside—or to one who is not likely to receive PAC money—PACs look much more evil. Their impact on the political process can be substantial. The eventual direction is so far indeterminable. (Chapter 10 provides a more detailed discussion on campaign financing.)

III.   INTEREST-GROUP INFLUENCE ON THEIR MEMBERS

As stated above, interest groups try to affect the electoral process in two distinct ways. In addition to attempting to influence the ways in which candidates and parties present themselves, and the ways in which those campaigns are perceived in the electorate at large, interest groups try to influence the voting behavior of their own members.

Leaders of interest groups try to exert this influence for two distinct reasons. The simplest, most direct reason is that they believe their choice of candidates is the best for those sharing their interest; it is logical to try to convince others that Senator X is *their* candidate. A less direct reason is that the influence of interest-group leaders with political figures varies with the extent to which politicians feel that the group leaders have influence with their membership. That influence is demonstrated in two ways—getting members to give money to a campaign and convincing members to support a candidate with their votes.

In this context we should separate interest groups in a way distinct from those already mentioned. Some interest groups—referred to as trade associations above—are actually confederations of other *organizations,* most frequently corporations. The leaders of these parent groups can speak to the leaders of their member groups; they can convince the lesser officials to support candidates with their dollars, but in fact few votes are involved. This type of association is still not unimportant. In fact, the unanimity of corporate PAC support for candidates who are also favored by their trade associations is a testimony to the effectiveness of this kind of network. However, the influence of this partnership is different from that of a union leader who claims to speak for tens of thousands of his members. In the latter case, politicians are increasingly distrustful of the effectiveness of these spokespeople. It is important, therefore, for interest-group leaders to demonstrate that they can distinctly influence their members.

How is this influence achieved? Interest groups use a number of techniques to persuade their members to support the candidates whom their leaders have identified. *One such technique has already been identified: the group rating.* Interest-group leaders make certain that their members know which politician has

These volunteers for the American Association of Retired Persons work hard to convince senior citizens to exercise their clout at the voting booth. (Kenneth Jarecke/Contact Press Images)

supported them and which has not in the past. They make clear to their members who are friends and who are enemies. But few citizens follow politics closely enough to keep up on group ratings. These ratings can be used as evidence for identifying friends and enemies, but persuasion must come about through other means.

A second technique is the use of a newsletter. Various groups use newsletters of different levels of sophistication. The express purpose of communications with group members through a newsletter is educational. The staff of an interest group wants the members to know what and how much they have been doing for the group, how various issues affect the group's interests, and which political officials have been helpful in their efforts to support legislation which is favorable or to oppose that which is harmful. Using this technique, interest-group leaders frequently try to counter the "generalizing" effects of the mass media. The popular media give a general audience a particular view of a political issue and/or a political leader. Through interest-group mailing, interest-group leaders try to show their members in what ways they are a specific segment of the public and how issues and leaders affect them in a *particular* way.

Specialized approaches to a particular audience distinguish other techniques used by group leaders as well. *Many groups use direct-mail and/or telephone campaigns to inform their members about specific pending issues in which they have a stake. Similarly they make certain that their members know when the leaders feel that they have a pressing interest in a particular candidate, when one of their favorites is in trouble, or when they have the opportunity to defeat one of their enemies.*

Groups vary tremendously in terms of their effectiveness in reaching their members. Some groups, like the realtors, have the reputation of reaching their members with persuasive messages in a very short time. Some labor union leaders, on the other hand, seem to be increasingly far removed from the opinions of the rank and file; the leaders are more liberal and more clearly tied to the Democratic party than are their members. In the last few years, more and more groups have concentrated their efforts on educating their members. Labor unions are beginning to use cable television as a means of reaching their constituency. Other groups will soon follow suit, though the cost of new communications technology makes the initial exploration of this area a decided gamble, one beyond the reach of many of those who need it most (see Berry, 1989; Coval, 1984; T. Patterson, 1990, p. 327).

The effectiveness of interest groups in influencing the political opinions of their members has been a frequent subject for political scientists to explore. More than four decades ago, David B. Truman published his seminal interpretation of American politics based largely on group influence (Truman, 1951). *The Governmental Process* dealt with much more than simply the influence of organized groups. However, Truman's explanation of the competition among group influences is as persuasive today as it was when first presented.

Imagine the predicament of a Catholic female union member who is also an active member of *Pax Christi*. She is faced with a choice in a congressional election between a Democrat who is very much a union supporter but also a firm advocate of Star Wars, the Reagan era defense system to guarantee our military superiority, and his Republican opponent who is a female, supported by the local business community for her economic stands and picked by the peace advocates because of her stated desire to forgo new military systems development. Our hypothetical voter is urged by her union leaders to support the Democrat; her economic interest seems to lie in that direction, and, after all, good union members *should* vote for Democrats. But she is torn. Her friends at *Pax Christi* are all for the Republican because of the contrast between that candidate's stand on foreign and military policy and the Democrat's hard-line approach which they view as self-defeating in international politics. She is puzzled, confused, and, quite certainly, not directly represented by the leader of either group with which she is associated.

The issue could be further complicated. Let us suppose that our hypothetical voter is also an ardent feminist. Her deep religious beliefs lead her to oppose abortion. Her feminist beliefs lead her to look at the predicament in which many women, facing unwanted pregnancies, find themselves. She is frankly not certain about her own feelings on the abortion issue. The Democratic candidate is also a Catholic and states quite frankly that he is morally opposed to abortion. She agrees. The Republican candidate says that women often find themselves in untenable situations, that abortion is a terrible alternative, but it is one that many women need. Our hypothetical voter agrees with that assessment as well.

Truman presents exemplary cases of competing group demands, and his book demonstrates that group membership will not always determine a voter's choice on election day. Our own hypothetical voter's dilemma reflects these competing influences. The position in which she finds herself, although exaggerated, is typical of many real situations. Her quandary shows us how difficult it is for group leaders to claim that they can speak for all the members of their association.

One case stands out, however, in which group membership seems to be a determining factor. Let us change the hypothetical situation presented above. Let us assume that our female Catholic union member is also a member of the National Abortion Rights Action League. She has had an unwanted pregnancy and has gone through the painful process of examining her own beliefs. She has emerged from this examination with the firm view that a woman must be able to control her own body, that her religious doctrine must be put aside in this instance, and that it is wrong for others to let their moral convictions dictate her actions. She did not arrive at these decisions lightly. The process that led to her decision was the most difficult she has ever had to undertake. Further, she had to back up her conviction with action, undergoing an abortion, a step she had always been taught was against the law of God. In reaching the decision that an abortion was right for her, she also reached the very strong conclusion that no one should dictate what another could do. After all, anyone who asserted the right to make those decisions for all in society was directly calling into question the very process and the very decision in which she had been so intimately involved.

In this case, for this voter, nothing other than the two candidates' stands on the abortion question mattered. If the Democrat was pro-choice and the Republican was for restricting a woman's right to have an abortion, our hypothetical voter would have cast her vote for the Democrat. If the candidates held the opposite opinions, her vote would have changed accordingly.

The interest-group leaders who are most effective at claiming to represent their members' views and the leaders who are most effective at convincing their members how to vote are the leaders of single-issue groups whose members care more about that one issue than any other. These groups are few and far between. In recent years, in some geographic areas, the groups representing the two sides of the abortion question or the National Rifle Association and those advocating gun control have been in that situation. In close elections, those who vote on the basis of only one issue may in fact determine the result. Certainly it is in the interest of the group leaders to make it appear that they and their members can tip the balance. Single-interest groups seem to be most effective in multicandidate primary fields (Maisel, 1986). However, in closely contested elections, no candidate can ignore the appeal of these groups with impunity.

IV.   POLITICIANS VIEW THE INTEREST GROUPS

The difficulty that politicians have in dealing with interest groups becomes readily apparent when one recalls the prenomination politics in the Democratic party in the winter of 1983–1984.

In the period of time before the first primaries and caucuses, former Vice President Mondale spent much of his time and effort trying to tie up the support of those groups endorsing candidates before nomination. The Mondale camp lined up labor leaders and then pushed to have the AFL-CIO endorse him as early as possible so that none of the other candidates could claim labor's support. Mondale obviously needed organized labor's support; at the same time, labor wanted to be credited with helping crown the eventual winner.

The other candidates made their pitch for labor support. The Glenn camp tried to convince labor leaders to delay their endorsement until after Glenn had had the opportunity to prove the viability of his candidacy. Other candidates followed the same strategy.

In the end, Mondale prevailed. He won the endorsement of organized labor, of the teachers, of the Americans for Democratic Action, of the women's groups, and of just about every group that gave an endorsement. Mondale wanted the support of these groups as part of his effort to sew up the nomination early. He wanted endorsements chiefly in order to discourage the opposition. The endorsing groups played along with this strategy. None of the groups that had decided to endorse before the nomination—to have a say in the nominating process and thus to win the ear of the nominee and be the 1984 equivalent of those who were "with Kennedy before Wisconsin" in 1960—none of them wanted to back a loser, and Mondale had "winner" written all over him in December 1983.

What was the strategy of the other candidates? Obviously to make Mondale seem like the candidate of the special interests. Gary Hart played that tune with a virtuoso's hand. In New Hampshire, Mondale lost support to Hart on just this issue:

> Thirty-one percent of the Hart voters interviewed in an ABC News exit poll listed Mondale as their second choice. . . . Many of them said that the single most important factor in their vote was that Hart "is independent of special interests."
>
> In fact, about one in five of the voters who selected any candidate other than Mondale listed that as the main factor in their vote. (Sussman, 1984, p. 36)

But was labor support—and implicitly the support of other special interests—really bad for Mondale? The same conventional wisdom, supported by exit polling data, which said that being dubbed the candidate of the special interests hurt Mondale in New Hampshire (and Maine, Massachusetts, Rhode Island, and Florida) also said that the union movement delivered Iowa, Alabama, Georgia, and Michigan to Mondale. The question of where one stood once again depended on where one sat.

In this case the factor was often one of effectiveness of union leadership. Many argued that a perceptible anti-Mondale vote by some rank-and-file union members was a reaction to their feeling that their leaders were attempting to dictate to them. If the members had been polled, they might have endorsed Mondale gladly, but they would not be told what to do. On the other hand, when the members were told why they should vote for Mondale, as were the United Auto Workers in Michigan when they were informed of Senator Hart's votes against the Chrysler bailout and domestic content legislation, they followed their leaders' pro-Mondale advice.

Our conclusion must be that interest-group control is viewed as something of a mixed bag by politicians as well. They want the support of groups, but if they do not obtain that support, they devise a strategy to make their opponent who has that support look like a special-interest bad guy. Politics remains more art than science. How successful a candidate is at using group support or at portraying his or her opponent as the pawn of interest groups depends on the skill of the politicians and of the interest-group leaders. If there were an absolutely sure way to play this issue, everyone would be doing so. But "absolutely sure ways" are rare in American politics.

Much the same can be said of the influence of PACs. When Gary Hart barely survived his reelection bid for the Senate from Colorado in 1980, he was undoubtedly thankful for the contributions made to his campaign by dozens of PACs. When he ran for president, he made a big issue of refusing PAC money. Why? Put most cynically, because he was not going to receive very much. Politicians tend not to look a gift horse in the mouth. But when that horse is going to be racing for another stable, they examine its pedigree very carefully. Suddenly the once friendly PACs became the embodiment of the evil "special interests" that control an opponent.

Is there then some conclusion to the dilemma caused by the influence of special interests? One inference is that the appearance of a problem often causes the problem to in fact exist. When *Time* runs a cover story on PACman, when Common Cause complains that we have the best Congress money can buy, when politicians make a campaign issue out of refusing PAC money (as, for instance, former Senator Paul Tsongas [D., Mass.] did almost immediately upon declaring his candidacy for the 1992 presidential nomination), when the public begins to question the influence of PACs, when the credibility of our political institutions is threatened, then, and *only then*, do PACs become a problem in the eyes of politicians.

The tale of two Mitchells is instructive in this regard.

Two Mitchells from Maine

In May of 1980, when President Carter appointed Maine's long-time senior Senator Edmund Muskie (D., 1959–1980) as secretary of state, George Mitchell was appointed to the United States Senate to succeed Muskie. Senator Mitchell faced election for a full term less than two years after he was appointed to the Senate. Mitchell had only run once in a statewide election, losing the gubernatorial election to independent James Longley in 1974. The seat looked ripe for Republican picking. The Republicans united behind popular First District Congressman David Emery as their nominee, and everyone knew that Emery would be able to raise a great deal of money. If Mitchell were to keep his seat, if the Democrats were to save his seat, he would need a great deal of money as well. Where does one go to raise such money? PACs. Mitchell raised and spent more than $950,000;

Emery raised and spent almost the same amount. In each case nearly a half million dollars came from PACs.

Mitchell did what he had to do to win. However, immediately after the election he formed a bipartisan commission to examine the problem of campaign financing, stating that he was "concerned by the high and growing cost associated with modern campaigns. We ought to . . . determine what constructive steps can be taken to reduce the cost and length of campaigns and to lessen the perceived influences of money in the electoral process." Mitchell was concerned about the amount of money that was spent. Some of his commission members were just as concerned about where that money came from. The commission proposed that Mitchell endorse a plan of public financing for Senate elections. Some of the commissioners, while agreeing with that finding, also felt that the problem of PAC money should be attacked separately.

Enter the second Mitchell. In 1984 Maine House Majority Leader Elizabeth Mitchell (no relation) was encouraged to run for the other Maine Senate seat, held by Republican William Cohen, when the state's Governor Joseph Brennan (D., Me., 1987–1991) decided not to challenge the popular incumbent. Because Brennan had been promised a large amount of PAC money, his decision not to challenge Cohen was not based on an inability to raise necessary campaign funds.

When her name began to be seriously mentioned, Majority Leader Mitchell, who had already expressed interest in succeeding Brennan when his gubernatorial term expired in 1986, went to Washington. The presumption was that she was talking to some of the same people who had promised to support Brennan. She returned to Maine determined to run. At her announcement press conference, she surprised nearly all those in attendance by declaring that she would not accept PAC money. Why did she take this stand? One can only guess. Her concerns about the influence of PAC money were no doubt genuine. But her stand did put her in something of an embarrassing position. After all, the popular senator of her own party who had just been reelected had accepted PAC money—lots of it. The governor would have accepted PAC money—all he could get. The Democrats running for other offices had not renounced PACs. Why had this Mitchell?

The logical (and once again cynical) answer is that the money would not have been forthcoming. Consequently, if you cannot raise PAC money, denounce it. Clear evidence exists that the public is leery of PACs, of the influence they wield. But the link has yet to be established between PAC influence on the body politic and the effect it has on one politician's reputation.

Senator Cohen had no fear of taking PAC money. He relied on his own record. And he won handily. In 1988 Senator Mitchell swept to reelection, again accepting PAC money. And in 1990, Senator Cohen was reelected one more time, this time using PAC money to match the nearly $1 million of personal money that his opponent committed to defeating him. Mitchell and Cohen have not been hurt by accepting PAC money, because they have a relationship with their constituents based on a perception of integrity which is unblemished. And that may well be the lesson.

Interest groups, whether by endorsing candidates, convincing their own members to vote for specific candidates, or contributing to campaigns through PACs, are viewed as important by politicians. But that importance is in context. In the context of individual campaigns, candidates must decide how to play the "interest-group card." When looking at the political process of the entire nation, however, public officials have begun to worry about the impact that the perceived influence of groups has on the public's level of confidence in the system. PAC reform is high on the agenda of both political parties. The Senate Election Ethics Act of 1991, passed by the Senate in May of that year, called for the banning of PAC contributions and contained a standby provision for limiting them if the Supreme Court ruled the ban unconstitutional. The future of reform efforts will continue to depend on how politicians view the public's perception of the groups on which they have so heavily depended in the past.

chapter

6

State and Local Nominations

We elect one president of the United States. We elect 50 governors, 100 senators, 435 members of Congress, 1995 state senators, 5466 state representatives, and literally thousands and thousands of mayors, city councillors, county commissioners, judges of probate, clerks of court, water district commissioners, and holders of other elected public offices.

We know a great deal about how presidents receive their parties' nominations. Seemingly for months on end we follow the candidate parade, through the snows of New Hampshire all the way to the national party conventions in late summer. We complain that the process is too long; but when the Democrats did not have an array of candidates on the hustings in the summer of 1991, political pundits wondered whether Democratic politicians were conceding the 1992 election. The process is complex, but much of it is public and open. Anyone who wants to read about the presidential nominations need only look at the front page of any newspaper on almost any day during the year before that nomination is secured. Readers interested in more analytical views can find magazine articles, journal essays, and a large number of books dedicated to the subject (See, as examples, Aldrich, 1980; Buell & Sigelman, 1991; Kessel, 1988, 1992; Lengle & Shafer, 1980; Orren & Polsby, 1987; Wayne, 1988, 1992). The Democratic National Committee has funded blue ribbon commission after blue ribbon commission, the goals of which have been to improve the process. The Republican party, with less publicity and controversy, has also focused on the quality of the presidential nominating process.

Still, what do we know about the ways in which the thousands of other elected public officials are nominated for their offices by their parties? Back in the days of party bosses and dominating political machines, Boss Tweed of Tammany Hall is reported to have claimed, "I don't care who does the electing, just so I do the nominating." When machines dominated American politics, one of the most important aspects of their control was the ability to control political nominations. We know that machines no longer dominate our politics as they once did. But what has replaced them?

Ask yourself! What do you know about how your United States senators were nominated? Your congressman? Your state representative—do you honestly even know who he or she is? What about county commissioners? How do all these people receive the nod of their party for the nomination?

These questions are particularly important when we realize the significance of the decisions that many of these individuals make. They are also important when we remember that many holders of more prestigious positions have used lower offices as stepping-stones for higher, more visible public office. It is to the question of how do state and local officials gain party nomination that the first section of this chapter is devoted.

I.   COMMON VIEWS OF THE NOMINATING PROCESS

What is the conventional wisdom? How are nominations decided? One view is that a couple of guys—almost never women—sit around in a smoke-filled back room and decide who is going to be the nominee. They then anoint that person and dissuade other potential candidates. Who are these people? They are the party leaders, not necessarily in a formal sense, but the people who make the party go. These kingmakers have at least three things in common: party loyalty, intense interest, and money.

Another view is that the nominating process represents the purest form of democracy. Candidates can present themselves to the people, and the people will choose. A person does not have to be tapped by anyone. Potential candidates just declare their availability, and people will choose from among those presenting themselves. No one is in control, and everyone is eligible.

Few hold yet a third view: that the chairman of the local party organization meets with an official committee, and together they decide on the nominees of the party. This view suggests that the process is more open than the smoke-filled room but falls short of the purest democratic ideals. Curiously, all three views are accurate . . . in part.

As with so much in American politics, what one sees depends on where one looks. In the case of nominating politics, the factors that must be examined include the locality and the office sought. How nominations are decided varies from state to state and from locality to locality within a given state. The process is also quite different for the most visible and hotly contested offices—governor, senator, congressman, state legislator in some states but not others, mayor in some cities but not others (one can see the locality variable at work)—than it is for offices that are seemingly less important.

In the sections that follow, we will sort out some of the more important questions about our nominating process. Keeping in mind the differences among localities and offices, we will look at the variety of nominating systems, exploring the question of who participates in the process—as candidates and as voters—and the more general question of how an ideal nominating system for the American political system might be structured.

II.   DEVELOPMENT OF THE DIRECT PRIMARY SYSTEM

The most common means of nomination in American politics today is the *direct primary election*. In a direct primary system, *the citizens of a particular area who are permitted to vote in a party's primary election vote directly to choose the party's nominee*. The direct primary is distinguished from any indirect means of nominating, the most notable example being the presidential nomination, which is decided upon in conventions by delegates—some chosen directly and some indirectly, but delegates in either case.

Direct primaries were not always the most common means used for nominating in the American system. Chapter 2 traced the history of party systems in the United States and made the point that in the second party system the nominating system moved away from a legislative caucus system to a convention system; this move was seen as a democratizing reform. The further movement from the convention system to the direct primary system had two distinct impetuses.

A.   Primaries as a Response to One-Party Domination

At the end of the Reconstruction era, following the Civil War, the Democratic party totally dominated southern politics. The Republican party for all intents and purposes did not exist in the south. In an era of one-party politics, when nominations were determined only by party officials, no mass participatory democracy existed. Citizens were given the opportunity to vote for only one candidate nominated by an elite faction of the dominant party. The primary election was first used, in the Democratic party, as a means to extend some level of democracy into this heavily one-party system.

B.   Primaries as an Item on the Progressive Agenda

For more philosophical and ideological reasons, the members of the Progressive party included the direct primary election as part of their party platform. Shortly after the turn of the century, primaries began to appear as part of the nominating process in states with Progressive party influence. Seen as a response to boss domination of the political process in many northern cities and states, primaries spread rapidly; the direct primary was used to nominate candidates for at least some offices in all but a few states by the end of the second Wilson administration in 1920.

In contrast to the ebb and flow of the use of primaries in the presidential nominating process (see Chapter 8), direct primaries as a means for choosing nominees for state and local office have had a more steady history of development and expansion. Few states that adopted direct primaries as the means for nominating candidates in the early years of this century have taken the nominating process out of the hands of the voter, even for short periods of time; today direct primaries are used as the means for nominating candidates for some offices in all states and for *all* offices in over forty states (Silbey, 1991, pp. 11–14).

It should be noted, however, that nominating conventions have not totally disappeared. A number of southern states give party committees the option of having a primary or of nominating by convention. The Republican party in a number of states has used the convention option, because until recently the party nod was not valued enough to merit a primary contest. In Virginia, both parties have relied heavily on the convention as a means of nominating, often allowing "back-room" politicians to achieve geographically and racially balanced tickets. While nominating conventions are a rarer and rarer phenomenon, they remain among the most interesting aspects of politics for those able to participate in or observe them.[1]

III.   VARIETIES OF PRIMARIES

Stating that the direct primary is the means used for nominating party candidates in most states is not the same as saying that the identical system is used in all states. In some states, state law mandates that a primary will be used and sets very specific rules for that primary. In other states the decision on how to nominate is left to the parties. Therefore, it is not really uncommon for a primary to be used in one party and not in the other; if a primary is used, the rules for that primary are determined by the party, not by state law. As noted previously, in some states the primary is used for all offices; in others it is used for only the more prominent offices (see L. Epstein, 1989, 1991).

A systematic examination of the state and local nominating process is difficult because of the variety of systems in place. The complexity is less troublesome for candidates for statewide office, however, than it is for candidates for the presidency for one very simple reason: whatever particular system is in place in any one state is the only system relevant for state and local candidates. Candidates for the presidency and their strategists have to be aware of fifty separate and often different systems, which are given different weights both in the nominating process and in media coverage of that process (see Chapter 8). On the other hand, candidates for state and local office can plan their strategy to aim at only one event, the primary that will determine whether or not they are the party's nominee. Still, they must be acutely aware of how their state's system works.

States using the direct primary also differ in many other ways. For example, they differ in terms of who is eligible to vote, of whether parties can endorse—in an official way—in advance of the primary, of how such endorsements are made if they are permitted, and of whether a plurality or a majority is necessary to nominate. The variations among primary systems are explored in the sections below. (For further discussion of this material see Jewell, 1984; Jewell & Olson, 1988).

---

[1] I am indebted to Larry Sabato for information on Virginia politics. It should also be noted that a number of states use party conventions either for endorsing purposes (see Section III.A.2 below) or for building solidarity within the party.

A. Who May Run

One would think that the question of who may run in a party's primary would be a simple one to answer. Democrats run in Democratic party primaries; Republicans run in Republican party primaries. If only it were that simple!

1. Party Membership and Petition Requirements The most prevalent rules call for candidates to run in their party's primary if they meet certain fairly simple criteria. *First, the prospective candidate must be a registered member of the political party whose nomination he or she seeks* (or in some other way demonstrate allegiance to that party in states that do not have official party registration).

Second, candidates must meet some sort of "test" to gain access to the ballot. Most often this test involves gathering a certain number of signatures on a petition, but the ease or difficulty candidates have in meeting this requirement is significant.

The number of signatures necessary and who is eligible to sign are important factors. If the number is small and if anyone can sign any number of petitions, then access to the ballot is quite simple. For example, in Tennessee only twenty-five signatures are required for most offices. By contrast, if the number of signatures required is large and if some restrictions apply as to who may sign petitions, then access to the ballot is more restricted. In Maine, candidates must acquire a fairly large number of signatures, only registered party members may sign petitions, and they must sign a petition that only contains the names of party members from their hometown.

In states with easier requirements many more candidates frequently qualify for primaries for the same office. Is this good or bad? "Good," one hears argued, "because anyone can run." But what if one candidate appeals to a relatively small, but extremely dedicated, group of voters whose views are on the fringe of public opinion, and election law requires only a plurality to nominate?[2] Would the extremist nominee represent the voters' opinions in these districts? Is democracy served?

On the other hand, if access to the ballot is relatively restricted, as when a large number of signatures is required or when only certain voters can sign petitions (e.g., statewide office in New York requires signatures by 20,000 enrolled party registrants with at least 100 living in each of seventeen of the state's congressional districts), then fields of candidates tend to be smaller. All the candidates tend to be serious contenders, but groups out of the mainstream have less influence. Moreover, lesser-known individuals are prevented from testing their views in primary campaigns. Is democracy better served?

2. The Role of Political Parties Access to the ballot can be even more restricted in some states than it is in those states that require a large number of

---

[2] When a *majority* is required to win a nomination or an election, the winner must poll one-half plus one of the votes cast. When a *plurality* is required, the winner is that candidate who polls more votes than any *other* candidate, even if that number is considerably less than half. Some systems require that a plurality winner must have received a certain percentage of the total votes cast or a runoff between the top two (or perhaps among the top three) finishers is held to determine the winner. See Section C, "Who Wins," below.

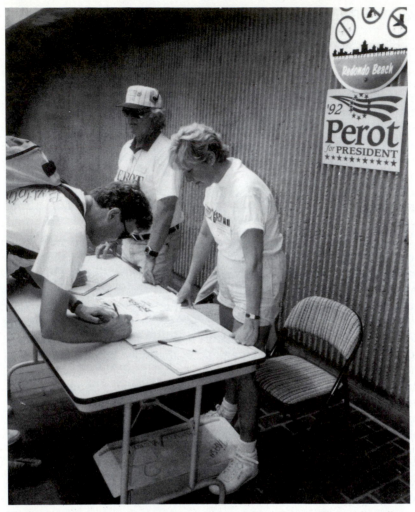

Volunteers supporting independent candidate Ross Perot collected literally millions of signatures in order to place their candidate's name on the presidential ballot. (Tom Prettyman/PhotoEdit)

signatures from a select group of voters. *Eight states*—Colorado, Connecticut, Delaware, New Mexico, New York, North Dakota, Rhode Island, and Utah— *have party conventions that play a significant role in determining access to the primary ballot for at least some offices.* The philosophy behind systems like these is that, while the party voters in the state should have the final say, those most involved with party affairs, i.e., those willing to go through the process of selection as delegate to a convention, should have increased influence.

How do these systems work? In Utah, the top two finishers at the state convention are on the party's statewide primary ballot, unless one candidate wins 70 percent of the convention votes; in that case, he or she is declared the nominee without a primary. In Colorado, New Mexico, and New York anyone who receives a specified percentage of the votes at the state convention has his or her name placed on the primary ballot. In Delaware, North Dakota, and Rhode Island, the person endorsed at the state convention—or by local committees for local offices—automatically appears on the primary ballot, but others must follow the petition route.[3] *Preprimary conventions tend to be used in competitive two-party states with relatively strong party systems.*

Connecticut, which was the last state to adopt a direct primary, implemented a system called a *challenge* primary in 1955. New York State adopted a similar system, for statewide offices only, in 1967. In the challenge primary system, the *convention nominee is automatically the party nominee unless he or she is challenged in a primary after the convention is over.* The assumption that there has to be a primary election is reversed. Losers at the convention with a certain percentage of the delegate votes have an automatic right to challenge, but they have no obligation to do so.

While party endorsement has official status in the eight states mentioned above, and a "semiofficial" status in Massachusetts, in a number of other states—as examples, Illinois, Minnesota, and Wisconsin—*party organization or other party groups endorse candidates and work for their election without that action having any official role in the primary process.*

The quintessential example of this would be Cook County, Illinois, the Greater Chicago area. For many years the vaunted Cook County Democratic party machine was headed by "Hizzonah" the Mayor, Richard J. Daley. Daley's organization stands as the last of the classic urban machines (see Rakove, 1975; Royko, 1971; Tolchin & Tolchin, 1971). When Daley endorsed a candidate, that candidate became a prohibitive favorite. The machine worked the streets. Few challenged the machine because a challenge was fruitless. However, reform clubs did eventually emerge in Chicago (J. Wilson, 1962) to present an alternative to Daley. These clubs served as a base for political activists interested in a different type of politics in Chicago. Again, though they were totally outside of the formal political system, these clubs helped to structure politics in Chicago. They did not play an official role, but their influence was important nonetheless.

Can one generalize about how effective party endorsements have been? As is so often the case, the experience among the states varies widely. The ultimate statement of success is if the endorsed candidate is not challenged in a primary. In Connecticut the assumption has been that a challenge will not be held. Between 1956 and 1990 only 16 of 222 individuals nominated for United States Congress by congressional district conventions were forced to face challenge primaries. Challenges are more common for statewide offices, in both Connecticut and New York, two states with similar systems, but there the similarity ends. In Connecticut, the party endorsement is considered an important advantage, although Democratic candidates try to avoid being labeled as the candi-

---

[3] To demonstrate the variety of state experiences, the Democratic party charter in Massachusetts specifies that a candidate must receive 15 percent of the vote at the convention to appear on the primary ballot; despite the fact that this provision is *not* in state law, the Massachusetts courts have upheld the provision, so that it has the same impact as if it were law. (See Jewell & Olson, 1988, p. 97.)

date of the legendary party bosses. In New York, to the contrary, many candidates view the official party endorsement as the kiss of death.

Malcolm Jewell and David Olson (1988, pp. 96–98) have examined the recent history of party endorsements. Between 1960 and 1986, 57 percent of the endorsees in states with legal endorsement procedures were nominated without opposition; this figure compares with 28 percent in those states with informal endorsement procedures and 20 percent in all elections in northern states during this period. Jewell and Olson (1988, p. 96, table 4-2) note that some state parties are most effective, with endorsees rarely challenged (e.g., Connecticut and Delaware, Democrats and Republicans; Colorado, Democrats; New York, Republicans); other states' endorsees are sometimes challenged but rarely upset (e.g., North Dakota, Republicans; Utah, Democrats); and still other states' endorsees are usually challenged and sometimes upset (e.g., New York, Democrats; Utah, Republicans). The history of the party organizations helps explain this difference, as it does many such discrepancies among states.

3.   Louisiana: An Exception   Early in this section, membership or allegiance to a political party was cited as one criterion for access to the ballot in almost all cases. Even that most basic rule has exceptions. In 1978 the state of Louisiana adopted a system called a *"nonpartisan"* primary, which sounds like a contradiction in terms. A primary, except in cases when party labels are not used, is supposed to determine who a party's nominee will be. How can a "nonpartisan" primary determine a partisan nominee? In fact, Louisiana has changed the entire system around, and Republicans and Democrats appear on the same ballot. *All candidates run on one ballot in the primary election. Each citizen is allowed one vote. If any one candidate receives a majority of the votes cast, that person is declared elected. If no one receives a majority on the first ballot, the general election is held between the top two finishers, regardless of their party affiliation.*

Obviously, party officials do not favor this system. Further, its implications for state politics are not at all clear. When Mississippi tried to adopt a similar system, the changes in the state's election laws were challenged under the provisions of the Voting Rights Act, and the proposed system was disallowed as being disadvantageous to black voters. One problem with assessing the impact of a change as fundamental as this one is that politicians need a certain amount of time to adjust to a new political reality.

In Louisiana the effect of the new system has been to protect incumbents. Of the forty-eight incumbents running for reelection to Congress from the time the system began through the 1990 election, forty-seven have been "reelected" at the primary election, and the remaining incumbent won handily in the general election. Most of the open seats were also uncontested beyond the primary. Party officials are certainly watching the impact of this system closely.

4.   Cross-Filing: Another Exception to Party Allegiance   *Cross-filing* represents another exception to the rule that party nominees must be registered in or hold allegiance to the party whose nomination they seek. In New York State

Supporters of candidates for offices, great and small, blanket prominent street corners with their posters as primary day approaches. (Tony Freeman/PhotoEdit)

a candidate may be the nominee of more than one party if the state party committee of the second party accepts that nominee. New York State has a tradition of strong third, fourth, and even fifth parties. While these parties do not win many offices on their own, they frequently hold the balance of power between the Democrats and Republicans.

One tactic used by the Conservative, Liberal, and Right-to-Life parties in New York is to endorse the candidate of one of the major parties. What is the strategy involved? What are the trade-offs? The minor parties know that they will not win office; however, they are very concerned about certain issues. Similarly, the candidates of the major parties know that minor-party candidates will not win. However, they are concerned that these minor-party candidates might draw votes from them which will swing the election to their opponents. Thus, the major-party candidates are willing to accept certain issue positions of the minor parties in exchange for that party's nomination and another line—literally another listing—on the ballot and some advertising and organizational support from the minor party's followers.

Frequently the trade-offs are not as explicit as the scenario just outlined. However, the implicit understandings are clear. If a major-party candidate in office offends a minor party, then the minor party will run its own candidate in the next election. Officeholders do not like to offend constituents who have that potential. Thus, in congressional elections in New York in 1990, eighteen of the thirty-two Democratic nominees had Liberal party backing; and thirteen of the thirty Republican party candidates also had the Conservative party nomination (and five of these were endorsed by Right-to-Life party).

Because of the way in which the New York State law is written, a candidate may even be nominated by both the Republican and Democratic parties. All that candidates need is the approval of the appropriate party committees to run in their respective primaries. For example, Mayor Koch of New York City ran in the Republican as well as the Democratic party primaries in 1981 and won both parties' nominations by enormous margins. Consequently, he faced only minor-party opposition in the general election. Democratic Congressman Charles Rangel was nominated by the Republicans and the Liberals as well as by the Democrats in 1990, a pattern that has been repeated in almost all his congressional elections since his first in 1970. This kind of situation demonstrates the problems inherent in cross-filing. Popular incumbents can sew up the entire electoral process and eliminate any semblance of a competitive democratic election.

B.   Who May Vote

Just as states and localities differ in who may run in partisan primaries, so too do they differ in who may vote in primary elections.

1.   Closed, Open, and Blanket Primaries   Thirty-eight states use one or another form of *closed primaries. Closed primaries are defined as primary elections in which only those who declare allegiance to a party in advance may vote.* However, the manner in which citizens are required to declare allegiance is not uniform across states.

At one extreme are those states that require citizens to enroll in a political party in a formal sense. Official lists of Democrats and Republicans (and members of minor parties) are maintained by the state. These lists are public information, and thus a registered voter's party affiliation can be found out by others.

States that fall into this category often have specific requirements for changing party affiliation from one party to another or from independent status to party membership. Twelve of these states prohibit voters from changing party identification after the date on which candidates must declare themselves for the upcoming primaries.[4] These and the other states that maintain formal party enrollment lists[5] also differ in the length of time between when a voter must declare party affiliation and when the primary is held, time spans varying from approximately one year in California to primary-day changes in Iowa, Ohio, Wyoming, and other states. Further, we find variations in how state law applies to those previously unenrolled in a party—normally referred to as independents—as opposed to those who want to switch from one party to another.

[4] These states are California, Connecticut, Kentucky, Maine, Maryland, Nebraska, Nevada, New Hampshire, New Jersey, New Mexico, New York, and Oklahoma.
[5] These states are Arizona, Colorado, Delaware, Florida, Iowa, Kansas, Massachusetts, North Carolina, Ohio, Oregon, Pennsylvania, Rhode Island, South Dakota, West Virginia, and Wyoming.

At the other extreme among closed-primary states are those in which citizens openly choose one party or another on primary day, but those choices are not formally recorded by state officials.[6] In some states, for example, Missouri, this choice involves nothing more than public selection of one party's ballot or another, as the voter enters the voting booth. In others, for example, Illinois, it involves a public declaration of intent to support a party's nominees, or of having supported them in the past. Records are not kept of these choices. Only those actually present at the time that the choice was made are aware of the partisan preference of the voter.[7]

A thin line separates closed primaries of this latter type from *open primaries. In open primaries, those voting in the primary elections are not required to choose publicly one party or the other.* Rather, they enter the voting booth and make the choice of party ballot on which they will vote in secret. Obviously, once again, no records are kept of these decisions.[8]

The states of Washington and Alaska have used a unique derivative of the open primary called the *blanket* primary.[9] The blanket-primary ballot carries the theory of the open primary to its logical extreme. *Citizens voting in a blanket primary can cast votes in the Republican primary for one office, the Democratic primary for a second and third office, the Republican primary for a fourth office, and so on.* The only restriction is that they can only vote in one party's primary for each office.

The rules governing state elections are generally specified in state law; those wanting to change the rules of the political game had to work through state legislatures to alter state law. However, in 1984, the Republican party of Connecticut challenged that norm, not for philosophical reasons but for purely political ones. In recent years Connecticut has been a heavily Democratic state; the state has had a closed-primary system. Independents, a large group in Connecticut, have not been permitted to participate in primaries. By allowing them to vote in the Republican primaries, the Republicans hoped to attract the allegiance of independents to Republican nominees. After unsuccessful attempts at changing state law, the state's Republican party challenged the closed-primary law in the courts. In the case of *Tashjian v. Republican Party of Connecticut,* 479 U.S. 208 (1986), the Supreme Court ruled that the Connecticut law failed to meet the First Amendment guarantee of freedom of association because it did

---

[6] These examples show the difficulty and futility in attempting to classify the wide variety of state systems into a small number of categories. Carr and Scott (1984) and Jewell and Olson (1988) classify these states as having open primaries, because of the ease with which one can vote in either party's primary. However, Carr and Scott (but not Jewell and Olson) place Rhode Island in the category of open-primary state, despite the fact that the state maintains party enrollment lists and prospective primary voters must change three months before a primary if they wish to participate in a primary of a party other than the one in which they last voted. This is clearly more restrictive than the rules in some of the other states Carr and Scott classify as closed.

[7] The states that require party selection of this type are Alabama, Arkansas, Georgia, Illinois, Indiana, Mississippi, Missouri, South Carolina, Tennessee, Texas, and Virginia.

[8] The open-primary states are Hawaii, Idaho, Michigan, Minnesota, Montana, North Dakota, Utah, Vermont, and Wisconsin.

[9] The Louisiana primary, in which all candidates' names appear on one ballot, is a variation of the blanket-primary concept. See above.

not permit the Republican party to define its own membership. The law was thus ruled unconstitutional. Connecticut Republicans—and potentially other state parties—were permitted to define their own membership and have an open primary in they decided to do so (L. Epstein, 1989; Maisel, Fowler, Jones, & Stone, 1990). The implications for this change in the ability of parties to define who can participate in their nominating process is not yet clear.

Political scientists use the traditional categories—closed, open, or blanket—to distinguish among primaries. In truth, it is more meaningful to view the variety of primaries as constituting a continuum from those in which party affiliation is the most fixed to those in which it is the least fixed. These distinctions have important consequences, whether they are viewed in terms of the theory of how politics should work or in the most practical political terms as the Connecticut example demonstrates (Carr & Scott, 1984; Finkel & Scarrow, 1985).

2.   Theoretical Arguments Regarding Primary Voter Eligibility The question of who should be eligible to vote in a primary revolves around the theoretical debate over what role political party should play in the electoral process. The more restrictive primary eligibility is, the greater the role that party plays.

If one views the major political parties as distinct, as presenting differing philosophies from among which citizens should choose, then it follows that adherents of those philosophies should make the choice of who will carry their banner into the general election. That means that only those to whom the party is important and truly meaningful should decide the party's nominee.

If, on the other hand, one feels that the parties are really two sides of the same philosophical coin, then the primary is merely a way to pare down the field of eligible candidates. In this case, voters should be able to support the candidate most closely linked with their views.

This assertion is an extension of the argument about who should be able to run. Those who favor stronger parties want more of a role for party organization in determining who can seek a party's nomination; they favor systems that call for preprimary conventions and endorsements of one sort or another. On the other hand, those who view party as an unnecessary intermediary between citizens and their elected servants want anyone to be able to run; they favor no role for party regulars in determining primary contestants.

3.   Pragmatic Considerations Regarding Primary Voter Eligibility If the student of politics looks at the systems in place in various states and then talks to politicians in those states, that observer is led to conclude that politicians generally feel that their states' systems reflect the needs of their constituents quite well. Few call for change. Many, indeed, cannot understand why other states do not do things the way they do.

Two conclusions follow from this observation. Either state politicians have been incredibly astute in creating systems that correctly match the political cultures of their states, or politicians are happy with a system they understand.

Very few politicians in the United States are expert on campaign laws beyond the boundary of the state in which they are working. Why should they be? What they need to know is how to play the game in which they are currently involved. They approve of the rules that are in effect because they know how to play by and win under those rules. Reformers, conversely, tend to be those who are out of power, who have not managed to win with the rules in place. Once again, the efforts by the Connecticut Republicans to open their primary stands as a case in point.

4. Strategic Consequences of Different Primary Rules These comments about the views of working politicians point to the practical consequences of various primary systems. Regardless of how one evaluates a system, the details of that system determine how one will run a campaign.

Imagine the most basic problem facing a candidate in a primary: To whom must I appeal for votes? In a closed-primary state, with recorded party enrollment, the constituency seems easy to determine. Candidates and their campaign managers simply obtain lists of potential voters, i.e., lists of people enrolled in their party and eligible to vote in their party's primary.

In a closed-primary state without permanent enrollment, the only comparably available lists are rosters of those who voted in the party's last primary (if the party had workers collecting such a list at the poll in that last primary). Even where such lists are kept, they tend to be highly inaccurate, ignoring those who think of themselves as members of the party but who did not vote in the last primary. And the lists have no way of accounting for new voters.

But those lists, as flawed as they are, are preferable to the lists that can be obtained in open-primary states. The only official lists that candidates can collect in open-primary states are lists of eligible voters and/or lists of those who did in fact vote in the last primary. Candidates have no way of knowing with certainty which ballot a particular voter marked.

Think of the consequences of these differences for campaign strategy. In the first case direct-mail and/or door-to-door campaigning is possible and efficient. Campaigns can reach those who are eligible to vote. In the second case these techniques of contacting voters are much less efficient, though still possible. In the open-primary scenario, if one does not want to contact all voters, it is necessary to rely on much less accurate methods of deciding on whom to concentrate, e.g., targeting areas in which a high percentage of the voters seemingly favor one's own party.

5. Crossover Voting Politicians are also very concerned about *crossover voting*. Let us assume that a Democratic incumbent is running unopposed for his party's nomination in an open-primary state. We further assume that there is a contested primary in the Republican party. No legal barrier prevents supporters of the Democratic incumbent from crossing over to the Republican primary and voting for the weaker of the two contestants in that primary, in an effort to nominate a weaker opponent for their favorite in the general election.

Hypothetically this scenario could happen easily enough. In practice, however, it is difficult to document instances of this kind of perfidy. First, an orchestrated campaign to nominate the weaker candidate in the other party would require a sophistication unknown to most American political organizations. Raiding the other party's primary could not happen without such orchestration because the American electorate is not sufficiently involved in the nuances of electoral politics to employ such a strategy.

Second, voters who participate in primaries most often are concerned about more than one race. Even if an incumbent lacked a Democratic opponent in one race, still other offices would very likely feature contested Democratic primaries. Democrats crossing over to influence the outcome of a Republican primary would forfeit their rights to vote in these Democratic races, which presumably would be of more interest to them than other Republican primaries (some of which might even be uncontested). The exceptions here are the two blanket-primary states—Alaska and Washington—and the unique situation in Louisiana.

Third, the American voting public believes in fair play. It is very unlikely that enough voters would engage in this type of behavior to have an impact on any particular election. Should a political party openly promote such a strategy, it would run the risk of a moral backlash that would lose it more than manipulation gained.

The fact that behavior of this type is unlikely to happen does not diminish the paranoia of politicians who worry about perfidy. Be that as it may, the true importance of voter eligibility rules relates much more closely to the impact on election strategy than it does to the loyalty of the voters to the party in whose primary they participate.

C. Who Wins

1. Plurality Rule Despite the lip service given to our "basic principle" of majority rule, majority rule is the exception in American politics. *Most elections in America—and certainly most primaries—are determined by plurality rule. That is, the person with the most votes (not necessarily 50 percent plus 1) in the primary wins the nomination.*

Plurality rule has important consequences, particularly in elections with large fields of candidates. For example, in Nebraska's Third Congressional District in 1990, five candidates competed in the Republican primary for the right to be the nominee to succeed the retiring representative, Virginia Smith (R., Neb., 1975–1991). State Senator Bill Barrett won the nomination with under 30 percent of the vote, edging the next two finishers by fewer than 2300 and 4800 votes, respectively, out of almost 83,000 votes cast. Perhaps Barrett was the one whom most Republicans would have supported to succeed Smith in this heavily Republican district, but we will never really know. One might even speculate that plurality-nominee Barrett could command only a maximum of 30 percent of the Republican votes; perhaps those who voted against him would

From *The Wall Street Journal*—Permission, Cartoon Features Syndicate.

"Everyone be prepared to be investigated. I'm running for class treasurer."

have supported any other Republican rather than Barrett. We do know that Barrett beat the Democratic nominee, State Senator Sandra Scofield, in the November election by only 51 percent to 49 percent, a much narrower margin than the 40 percent victory margin typically enjoyed by Virginia Smith.

2. Variations from Plurality Rule: Runoff Primaries Plurality rule is not in effect in every electoral jurisdiction. The major exception to the plurality winner rule is in the south, where *nine states require a majority vote to receive the nomination; if no candidate wins a majority, a runoff or second primary is held.* During his 1984 presidential campaign, the Reverend Jesse Jackson drew a great deal of attention to runoff primaries, claiming that they discriminated against black candidates.

Runoff primaries were instituted in the south shortly after the beginning of this century, during a period of Democratic dominance in the south. Party officials viewed the runoff primary as a means of guaranteeing continued party strength, of assuring that the party was united behind one candidate and could thwart any independent challengers.

Analysts differ over whether racial discrimination was a factor in creating runoff primaries. On the one hand, blacks were denied the right to vote through a whole series of Jim Crow laws and rules at this time; adding still one more discriminatory obstacle to effective black participation would seem to have been superfluous. On the other hand, almost all legislative action dealing with elections at the time was undertaken with the awareness of racial implications. It is difficult to imagine that those involved in establishing runoff primaries were incognizant of the fact that these could have an effect on the chances of blacks seeking office.

But let us put historical arguments aside and examine the effect that runoff primaries have today. Jesse Jackson's attention was directed to this issue

by H. M. "Mickey" Michaux, Jr., a black who lost the Democratic party nomination in North Carolina's Second Congressional District in 1982, after having
captured 44 percent of the vote against two white candidates in the first primary. In the runoff Michaux polled 46 percent and lost to Tim Valentine, who
went on to capture the seat. Using the Michaux contest as an example, some
have claimed that blacks and other minorities would have ten to fifteen more
seats in the Congress if the runoff primary were eliminated.[10]

This claim is based on two premises. First is the assumption that whites
will vote for whites and blacks for blacks in primary elections. Thus, in districts
with large black populations, but without black majorities, blacks can lead in
the first primary but lose when the whites all vote together in the runoff. The
second premise is that voters will stick to party lines in the general election, regardless of the candidates. These two assumptions seem to be at odds with each
other and with recent experience.

If the first assumption is accurate, then runoff primaries are discriminatory against minority groups only in those districts in which they constitute a
large bloc, but not a majority. In districts in which blacks or Hispanics constitute a majority, the runoff primary would seem to work in their favor. In neither
case is it evident that the system is discriminatory, only that one electoral system out of several possible ones has been chosen.

Turning to the second assumption, would it help minority candidates to
get the nomination if they were then to lose in the general election? If voters follow racial lines, wouldn't it be logical for white voters to desert the Democratic
party in the general election and support white Republicans? As the south becomes more and more a two-party region, wouldn't the elimination of the
runoff primary accelerate the growth of the Republicans and lead to victories by
even fewer "progressive" candidates than is now the case (see Bullock & Johnson, 1985; Lamis, 1984; Stanley, 1985)?

Viewing the issue from another perspective, one could argue that plurality
elections are not a good mechanism for guaranteeing popular rule in cases of
factionalized electorates. The states of Iowa and South Dakota each have provisions in their electoral laws which require a primary winner to receive at least 35
percent of the vote in order to be declared the nominee. If no candidate reaches
that threshold, a party convention meets to select a candidate.[11] Thus far, this
chapter has demonstrated that there are many distinctions among primaries. In
the next section the ways in which the various primary systems shape the politics of the nominating process are explored.

---

[10] In 1989, North Carolina amended its runoff primary law to lower the threshold to 40 percent.
Furthermore, the second-place finisher must request a runoff. Not enough elections have been held
since this change to ascertain its impact.

[11] New York City (and a number of other municipalities) has a similar provision, calling for a runoff
election if no nominee polls 40 percent of the primary vote. This provision was struck down by a
federal court which accepted the argument that the runoff provision unfairly discriminated against
minorities and thus violated the Constitution and the Voting Rights Act. However, that decision was
reversed by the circuit court of appeals. Similarly, the Arkansas runoff primary provision was struck
down by a three-judge panel of the court of appeals but reinstated by the entire court sitting *en
banc*. I am indebted to Charles Bullock for these examples.

IV.   THE POLITICS OF NOMINATIONS

A.   Uncontested Nominations

Recall the list of offices at the beginning of this chapter. How much competition is there for clerk of courts? For water district commissioner? Compare the interest in those offices with that for United States senator or governor. Or compare the attractiveness of serving as a state representative in Vermont, where the legislature sits for four to five months a year, where there are 150 state representatives, and where the approximate average annual salary is $6750, with the attractiveness of the same position in California, where serving in the state assembly is a full-time job, where the 80 assemblymen each represent approximately 375,000 people, and where the base annual salary is $40,800.

These kinds of comparisons point to the difficulty in analyzing nominations at the state and local level. The situation varies from office to office and from state to state. Table 6-1 lists the number of contested primaries in five states, chosen to be somewhat illustrative of the diversity of political environments among the states. Obviously, more seats are contested for the more prestigious offices. Nominations for the United States Senate are uncontested much less frequently than nominations for state assembly. Further, state offices in larger states are more likely to attract contested primaries than are similar offices in smaller states.[12] This thesis follows quite naturally from the fact that such offices are more likely to be full-time, highly paid, and prestigious in larger states.

Other conclusions about contested primaries have been found to be similarly predictable. Incumbents win nominatons without the necessity of contesting a primary more often than do challengers. (See Table 6-2.) Contested primaries are more likely to occur for "open" seats, particularly in the party of the retiring incumbent, than for seats in which incumbents are running. Primaries are always more likely to occur in dominant parties than in minority parties. One basic rule seems to apply: *the more valuable the party nomination, the more likely there will be a contested primary.* The value of the party nomination, in turn, relates to two variables—the prestige of the office sought and the likelihood that the party's nomination will result in victory in the general election.

How do candidates get nominated in situations in which there is no contested primary? No systematic research has addressed this question. Thus, most students of politics would answer this question based on their personal experiences. The process is seemingly simple. Each candidate follows whatever procedure is necessary to have his or her name placed on the primary ballot. No one else does so. The nomination then goes by default.

One working assumption is that incumbents normally want to succeed themselves, even for the less prestigious offices. Few people desire or are quali-

---

[12] It should also be noted that there are fewer Republican primaries than Democratic primaries for similar offices in similar states. This phenomenon, which deserves further study, might well reflect the coherence of the Republican party relative to the Democrats.

TABLE 6-1. Contested and Uncontested Primaries in Five States, by Party, 1986, 1988, 1990

Office	Contested Primaries		Uncontested Primaries		No Candidate in Primary	
	Dem.	Rep.	Dem.	Rep.	Dem.	Rep.
Arizona						
1986						
Governor	1	1	0	0	0	0
U.S. senator	0	0	1	1	0	0
U.S. representatives (5)	2	3	2	2	1	0
State senators (30)	4	6	16	18	10	6
State representatives (60)	11	18	32	30	17	12
1988						
Governor	—	—	—	—	—	—
U.S. senator	0	0	1	1	0	0
U.S. representatives (5)	1	1	3	4	1	0
State senators (30)	8	12	16	16	6	2
State representatives (60)	11	28	34	25	15	7
1990						
Governor	1	1	0	0	0	0
U.S. senator	—	—	—	—	—	—
U.S. representatives (5)	1	2	3	3	1	0
State senators (30)	4	11	20	17	6	2
State representatives (60)	3	19	41	31	16	10
Florida						
1986						
Governor	1	1	0	0	0	0
U.S. senator	1	1	0	0	0	0
U.S. representatives (19)	2	3	13	11	4	5
State senators (22)	7	6	12	11	3	5
State representatives (120)	33	27	69	56	18	37
1988						
Governor	—	—	—	—	—	—
U.S. senator	1	1	0	0	0	0
U.S. representatives (19)	5	5	11	9	3	5
State senators (22)	7	5	8	11	7	6
State representatives (120)	24	28	68	52	28	40
1990						
Governor	1	1	0	0	0	0
U.S. senator	—	—	—	—	—	—
U.S. representatives (19)	4	4	10	14	5	1
State senators (20)	5	6	12	12	3	2
State representatives (120)	20	26	79	55	21	39
Massachusetts						
1986						
Governor	0	1	1	0	0	0
U.S. senator	—	—	—	—	—	—
U.S. representatives (11)	5	2	6	2	0	7
State senators (42)	7	1	29	16	6	25
State representatives (160)	37	4	105	53	18	103

TABLE 6-1. Contested and Uncontested Primaries in Five States, by Party, 1986, 1988, 1990 (*cont.*)

Office	Contested Primaries		Uncontested Primaries		No Candidate in Primary	
	Dem.	Rep.	Dem.	Rep.	Dem.	Rep.

Massachusetts

1988

Office	Dem.	Rep.	Dem.	Rep.	Dem.	Rep.
Governor	—	—	—	—	—	—
U.S. senator	0	0	1	1	0	0
U.S. representatives (11)	1	1	10	6	0	4
State senators (42)	13	0	23	23	6	19
State representatives (160)	33	5	111	62	16	93

1990

Governor	1	1	0	0	0	0
U.S. senator	0	1	1	0	0	0
U.S. representatives (11)	1	2	10	4	0	5
State senators (42)	10	6	28	34	4	2
State representatives (160)	50	22	93	99	17	39

Minnesota

1986

Governor	1	1	0	0	0	0
U.S. senator	—	—	—	—	—	—
U.S. representatives (8)	6	2	2	6	0	0
State senators (67)	11	4	56	48	0	5
State representatives (134)	13	13	116	112	5	9

1988

Governor	—	—	—	—	—	—
U.S. senator	1	1	0	0	0	0
U.S. representatives (11)	5	3	3	5	0	0
State senators	—	—	—	—	—	—
State representatives (134)	16	10	114	118	4	6

1990

Governor	1	1	0	0	0	0
U.S. senator	1	1	0	0	0	0
U.S. representatives (8)	1	2	7	6	0	0
State senators (67)	16	7	51	57	0	3
State representatives (134)	20	11	106	110	8	13

Wisconsin

1986

Governor	1	1	0	0	0	0
U.S. senator	1	0	0	1	0	0
U.S. representatives (9)	2	0	6	7	1	2
State senators (17)	2	3	15	13	0	1
State representatives (99)	20	16	63	76	16	7

1988

Governor	—	—	—	—	—	—
U.S. senator	1	1	0	0	0	0
U.S. representatives (9)	4	1	5	7	0	1
State senators (17)	2	4	15	7	0	6
State representatives (99)	16	14	74	66	9	19

TABLE 6-1. Contested and Uncontested Primaries in Five States, by Party, 1986, 1988, 1990 (*cont.*)

Office	Contested Primaries		Uncontested Primaries		No Candidate in Primary	
	Dem.	Rep.	Dem.	Rep.	Dem.	Rep.
Wisconsin						
1990						
Governor	0	1	1	0	0	0
U.S. senator	—	—	—	—	—	—
U.S. representatives (9)	3	1	4	7	2	1
State senators (17)	1	3	13	11	3	3
State representatives (99)	12	14	69	68	18	17

TABLE 6-2. Incumbents' and Challengers' Success in Congressional Primaries, 1978–1990

	1978	1980	1982	1984	1986	1988	1990
Incumbent winners unopposed in both primary and general elections	43	37	35	43	42	44	48
Incumbent winners opposed in the primary but not the general election	15	9	13	16	14	8	4
Incumbent winners unopposed in the primary but opposed in the general election	204	223	207	211	204	253	230
Incumbent winners opposed in both primary and general elections	89	84	85	114	125	97	108
New member beat incumbent in general election after winning primary	14	15	16	7	5	5	9
New member beat incumbent in primary and was unopposed in general election	0	0	0	1	1	1	0
New member beat incumbent in primary and won contested general election	0	0	0	0	1	1	1
New member nominated without primary and beat incumbent in general election	5	11	7	9	1	0	6
Open seat; new member had primary	49	38	49	22	33	21	24
Open seat; new member had no primary	8	10	15	4	9	5	5

Source: Calculated by the author from *Congressional Quarterly Weekly Reports.*

fied to serve as water district commissioner. However, more often than not the individual holding that position is willing to continue to hold it.

If no incumbent is running, or if the incumbent is of the other party, then party officials have the responsibility of finding candidates for office.[13] For prestigious offices this search is not difficult. For less prestigious offices, however, the role of the party official is very different. In these cases officials must identify potential candidates for office and convince them to run. The party organization traditionally controlled access to the ballot. This power was lost for prestigious offices with the advent of the direct primary and with increased popular participation. However, the party's role persists for lesser offices. Some party organizations are quite successful in playing this role; others much less so. In congressional elections during the last decade, one major party or the other did not field a candidate for the United States Congress in about one district in six; eighty-one seats did not see major party competition in 1988; eighty-three in 1990. On the other hand, all eligible gubernatorial and, save a very few, Senate seats were contested by both parties. In 1988, both parties fielded candidates for all gubernatorial and Senate contests; in 1990 all gubernatorial and all, save four (the highest number in more than twenty years), senatorial elections were contested by Democrats and Republicans. Success in structuring the contest for office is one measure of the success of the ways that party organizations do their jobs.

B. Contested Nominations

When most analysts talk about primary elections, they are actually concerned with *contested* primary elections, a subgroup that is a minority of all primaries.[14] Contested primaries are those that receive the most attention because they provide campaign watchers with something to watch. They also play an important role in weeding out contestants for office. Once again it is important to emphasize differences by office and locale as one discusses contested primaries.

1. Incumbent Advantage However, political observers have again been able to make some generalizations about these contested primaries. The first generalization is that incumbents win a high proportion of the primaries in which they are challenged. As Table 6-3 demonstrates, incumbent victories are in-

[13] Party officials—county chairs, state and county committee members, ward and precinct leaders, and the like—are frequently not well known. Why they seek and accept such positions is a most interesting question, the answer to which varies significantly from locale to locale and individual to individual. In any case, one of the responsibilities assumed by these individuals is to see to it that their party is represented on the general election ballot.

[14] One could make the subgroup smaller still. Primary contests could be divided into those involving serious opposition and those in which the opposition is marginal or frivolous. Candidates have a sense of this distinction in advance, but analysts have trouble determining who is serious and who is frivolous until some additional information is added, e.g., how much money a candidate can raise, what kind of organizations or endorsements a candidate can attract, etc. Because these judgments are essentially subjective, this differentiation will not be pursued in this discussion.

**TABLE 6-3. Success Rates of Incumbents Seeking Reelection in
Contested Primaries, 1982–1990**

Year	Number of Incumbents Challenged	Number Successfully Renominated	Number Defeated in Primary
	Governors		
1982	15	14	1
1984	5	5	0
1986	12	11	1
1988	2	1	1
1990	14	13	1*
	U.S. Senators		
1982	15	15	0
1984	13	13	0
1986	10	10	0
1988	11	11	0
1990	13	13	0
	U.S. Representatives		
1982	109	99	10
1984	144	141	3
1986	141	139	2
1988	106	105	1
1990	115	114	1

* In 1991, Louisiana's Republican Governor Buddy Roemer was challenged and finished third and was thus eliminated in the state's unique nonpartisan primary.

Source: Calculated by the author.

creasingly the case for lesser or more local offices. Incumbents have an advantage over opponents in that they have already built up support within the party (Fenno, 1978, p. 18). Unless they have acted so as to undercut their own support, they will rarely be beaten in a primary.

Incumbent losers are so few that analysts can almost always explain each case as idiosyncratic. Congresswoman Katie Hall (D., Ind., 1982–1985) is a case in point. Adam Benjamin (D., Ind., 1977–1982) was viewed as the epitome of a safe incumbent; in his three successful races in the First District he had never polled less than 70 percent. In September 1982 Benjamin died of a heart attack. As the 1982 Indiana primary had already been held, Gary Mayor Richard Hatcher, in his capacity as chairman of the First Congressional District Democratic Committee, had the right to designate a replacement as the party's nominee.[15] Hatcher, a black, chose Hall, a black. This nomination angered

---

[15] Congressional district committees of the two major parties have only one function: to fill vacancies for the nomination should such vacancies occur. Typical of many such party committees, these groups normally do not meet; those who "serve" on these committees are sometimes unaware of their existence.

Robert A. Pastrick, a white, who was chairman of the Lake County Democratic Committee, i.e., head of the local party organization. Pastrick would have preferred the nomination of Benjamin's widow. In November 1982, Hall won *two* elections, the first to fill out Benjamin's unexpired term (until January 1983) and the other to serve the full term that was to commence in January; however, Hall's margin of victory was only 20,000 votes, uncharacteristically small for this predominantly Democratic district.

Not unpredictably, the 1984 primary generated significant interest in the First District contest. Three Democrats, two of whom were eventually to mount very serious campaigns, filed to oppose Hall in the primary. Eleven Republicans, seeing Hall as weak and the Democratic party potentially divided, filed for their party's primary. Lake County prosecutor Jack Crawford, who eventually spent more than $200,000 in the Democratic primary, appeared to have the best chance of beating Hall. However, Peter Visclosky, a former congressional staff member, ran a vigorous grass-roots campaign. For a time it appeared that Crawford and Visclosky would split the Democratic white vote and that Hall, who was backed by Hatcher and his organization and for whom Jesse Jackson campaigned actively, would win a plurality nomination by turning out a heavy black vote in Gary. On primary day, however, the turnout in Gary was only moderate and Visclosky won a narrow victory, edging Hall by 2300 votes and Crawford by 4000, out of over 130,000 cast. The Hall defeat can clearly be explained in terms of racial politics, division within the district, and Hall's inability to build a strong party support system. Analogous explanations frequently apply when incumbents are defeated in primaries.[16] However, the absolute number of defeats is so small that the primary part of the process has become all but meaningless so far as incumbents are concerned.

2. Contests without Incumbents What about races in which incumbents are not running? Conclusions in these cases have proved to be more tentative. Winners tend to be those who best use the resources necessary to win elections.

Although the important resources may vary from race to race, key among them is *name recognition*. If one candidate is much more widely known than his or her opponent(s), that candidate is likely to win. How does one achieve such recognition? Some candidates have it when they enter a race. For instance a state senator who is entering a congressional primary might well have represented many of those who are eligible to vote in the primary, an eventuality likely to happen in large states with sizable state senate districts. Such a candidate would start with an advantage over a political neophyte. Or a candidate might be known for other reasons. When Jack Kemp (R., N.Y., 1971–1989) first sought election to Congress from the suburbs of Buffalo, he was already well known as the quarterback of the NFL Buffalo Bills. Athletes, actors, media personalities, astronauts, and others with similar fame start with a name recog-

---

[16] Visclosky went on to win the general election with some ease. Hall challenged Visclosky in 1986 and again in 1990, polling about 30 percent of the vote in each primary; Visclosky has continued to hold the seat with some ease in general elections.

nition advantage when they enter the political arena (Canon, 1990). They may even become president!

Yet many candidates do not start with these advantages, particularly candidates for local offices. How do they get known? Three key ingredients contribute to successful campaigns—*candidate effort, campaign organization, and money.*

In smaller districts candidates themselves may well be able to "get around," to shake hands with a large portion of the potential electorate. Candidates for sheriff go into high schools and talk about drug and alcohol abuse. Candidates for state representative address the Rotary or the Elks in town after town. All candidates for these offices attend party meetings and picnics, town meetings, PTA meetings, any meeting, in short, at which they can be certain that they will be introduced. They go door-to-door and discuss mutual concerns with voters. Candidate after candidate will attest that there is no better campaign technique than actually talking to a potential voter. If a district is small enough and if a candidate can commit enough time, nothing is more effective.

Many districts (e.g., congressional districts, state senatorial districts) are too large, however, for a candidate to have any chance of meeting even a sizable proporton of the potential electorate. While candidates will still campaign personally to the extent possible, they must rely on an organization to extend their outreach. A candidate's campaign organization uses various techniques to serve as surrogates for personal contact. Workers go door-to-door seeking support for their candidate. They carry literature that describes the candidate's views and qualifications. They telephone potential voters and discuss why they favor the candidate for whom they are working. They put up lawn signs, hand out buttons and bumper stickers, speak on behalf of their candidate at functions she or he cannot attend. An effective organization reaches out for candidates further than they themselves can reach. Such organizations frequently give the appearance of widespread support which itself leads to more recognition and eventually to more support.

Campaign organizations in smaller districts are frequently volunteer organizations. Friends and neighbors of a candidate will offer their assistance. But even these campaigns need some money in order to function effectively. Buttons and bumper stickers, brochures and balloons, all the paraphernalia of a campaign cost money. As the size of the district expands, the cost of the campaign increases. A congressional primary that was won on a budget of $100,000 has recently been cited as evidence that "a congressional seat can still be won without spending a fortune" (*Congressional Quarterly Weekly Report,* 1984, p. 1119). As recently as 1974, when the FEC began keeping these records, only ten congressional campaigns spent $200,000 in the primary and general elections combined, and expenditures of $100,000 in primaries were all but unknown (see Chapter 10).

In many of today's primaries, however, money is important. Media campaigns are expensive and frequently necessary if candidates are to achieve that important name recognition and to reach very large constituencies. While amounts vary significantly from office to office and locale to locale, one can certainly conclude that candidates with substantial financial resources for their campaigns have distinct advantages over those lacking these resources (see Jewell & Olson, 1988, pp. 121–129).

The precise combination of candidate effort, organization, and money which is necessary to win any primary is difficult to ascertain with precision. The ability to arrive at that combination is what separates winners from losers. Still, the imprecision of the calculation is why politics remains more art than science. If one formula worked for every campaign, then every campaign manager and every candidate would do the same thing. Candidates and their campaign managers start with a certain amount of knowledge of how to campaign (most of it gained from experience), with an understanding of their districts, their candidacies, etc., and with a certain amount of resources. Working with these, they devise tactics and strategies. They play on their strengths and try to exploit the weaknesses of their opponents. They play down their weaknesses and try to undercut the strengths of their opponents. Politicians seek to find the formula that will give them the largest number of votes in the primary while doing the least harm to their chances in the general election, ultimately hoping to appear so invincible as not even to be worth challenging (Jacobson, 1983). That, after all, is what the primary campaign is all about (see Maisel, 1982, 1986.)

V. POLITICIANS VIEW THE NOMINATING PROCESS

How do politicians view all of this? The repeated theme recurs—it all depends on their situation. An examination of the recent political history of one congressional district can reveal that the means through which a candidate achieves a party's nomination can either help or hurt that candidate's chances in the general election. And further, the same route to nomination can have differing impacts in different years.

Look at the most recent history of the First Congressional District in Maine (see the accompanying box). Some lessons appear clear. Primaries can be divisive. Kyros in 1974, Barton in 1976, and Kerry in 1982 were definitely hurt by the campaigns they had to wage in order to receive the party nomination. Even if primaries are not divisive, they can hurt a candidate; such was the fate of Quinn in 1978.

On the other hand, winning a nomination without a primary is not always helpful either; Pachios could have used the name exposure an easy primary denied him in 1980; the same held true for Hobbins in 1984. In 1990 Emery might have been reinvigorated if he had had to fight for his party's nomination.

McKernan in 1982 benefited from having a primary contest in which his opponent was not a serious challenger; the press covered McKernan, but no one was making charges against him, and he did not have to spend much of his money. At the same time, he was able to build a successful campaign organization. He had the best of all possible worlds. Andrews's election in 1990 shows that an unexpected primary victory can catapult an underdog into a leader's position.

Politicians generally would like to avoid hotly contested primaries. However, under certain circumstances, such as when a candidate is not well known and/or when a candidate's organization has not been tested, "a little primary can be a good thing." How politicians view primaries depends very much on their political situation. The key question is what impact will the nominating process have on the general election in November. It is to that subject which we now turn.

Maine's First Congressional District, 1972–1990

A Case Study

Maine's First Congressional District has had five different incumbents and has changed party hands twice in the last two decades. One incumbent has been beaten; three times the seat was vacated by incumbents seeking other offices. Primaries have played differing roles in different elections. Thus, this district stands as a good example of how party nominations are achieved and of their impact.

The district was represented by Democrat Peter Kyros for much of the 1960s and into the 1970s. Kyros was a supporter of Lyndon Johnson's Vietnamese war policies; he rubbed many of his constituents the wrong way. In 1972 and again in 1974 he was challenged in the Democratic primary by individuals who opposed his stand on the war in Vietnam and the way in which he represented the district in general. The 1974 primary was particularly bitter, as his opponent was a woman who had worked for Kyros as a district representative for some years.

Despite the fact that Kyros had difficulty with some fellow Democrats, he generally won reelection quite easily. In fact, chances of beating him were viewed as so slim that no Republican wanted to challenge him in 1974. Recall also that 1974 was the year of Watergate, not a particularly auspicious year for a Republican to try to unseat an incumbent Democrat.

The Republican nomination fell by default to David Emery, a very young, practically unknown state representative. Emery raised and spent less than $70,000 in that election. However, Kyros, thinking his election was guaranteed, did not spend heavily and did not campaign hard. Walking much of the district and personally seeing a great many voters, Emery appeared to be earnest and sincere. Legions of voters stayed home in 1974; many Democrats, disheartened with Kyros and angered by his attacks on his former employee during the primary campaign, cast "protest" votes for Emery. On election day, Emery was portrayed as the young David who slew Goliath; his narrow victory was one of only four that Republicans claimed over incumbent Democratic congressmen in 1974.

The lesson was obvious. Emery had won in large part because Kyros, hurt by his stand on the war and his divisive primary, ran a very poor campaign. Thinking that Emery was very beatable, in 1976 six Democrats waged a tough primary campaign seeking their party's nomination. Emery was renominated by the Republicans without opposition. Rick Barton, who survived the Democratic primary, was so wounded by the intraparty fighting that he never had a chance in November. Emery, now the darling of the Republican establishment, raised over $150,000 and increased his margin of victory to over 35,000 votes.

In 1978 four Democrats, including this author, still felt that Emery was vulnerable. We plotted our strategies and set our tactics. We also met as a group and pledged not to attack each other. After all, we had learned the lesson of 1976 and even 1974. The Republicans in California have espoused the so-called eleventh commandment, "Thou shalt not speak ill of another Republican." We vowed to follow that as well. To a large extent we succeeded. The winner of the primary, former State Consumer Advocate John Quinn, ended the primary unscarred by attacks from the rest of us. Why? Because in our brilliance we ignored him. Quinn entered the campaign quite late with little organization and little money. He did not seem to campaign as hard as the rest of us. The other three of us concentrated our tactics on each other, avoiding personal attacks as much as possible, but striving for victory nonetheless. We forgot that one uses hard work, organization, and money in a primary to gain name recognition. John Quinn, as consumer advocate, had published a series of booklets, distributed free throughout the state, helping consumers with such problems as dealing with automobiles deemed to be lemons. Quinn came from a well-known Irish family in Portland, the biggest Democratic stronghold in the state. He was able to cooperate somewhat with the organization of Joe Brennan, who was to win the Democratic nomination for governor. Quinn had advantages none of us thought about. In retrospect his victory should have been predictable.[17] However, those of us in the race and all the state's political journalists were surprised by Quinn's win.

None of us, however, was surprised with the ease with which Emery handled Quinn. Emery, again nominated without opposition, raised and spent over $200,000, nearly three times what Quinn spent. He polled nearly two-thirds of the votes. The primary route was costly for Quinn. He spent a good portion of the money he needed for the general election; he also lost the active support of those Democrats who backed one of his opponents. He gained little because he already had name recognition.

In 1980 the Democrats learned their lesson, right? Wrong. They learned the wrong lesson. Harold Pachios, the Democratic state party chair, was unopposed for the nomination to face Emery, now viewed as a somewhat secure incumbent. Pachios was happy that he would not face a divisive primary. Uncontested primaries cannot hurt a candidacy. Wrong again. No one had heard of Harold Pachios before the primary began, except for active politicians. The same people had heard of him after the primary. Pachios ran a credible general election campaign, but he was outspent by Emery, and, most important, he was outrecognized by Emery. He lost by more than 2 to 1, by more than 100,000 votes.

From here the story can be shortened. In 1982 Emery ran for the Senate. John McKernan won the Republican nomination without major opposition.[18]

---

[17] Maisel (1982, 1986) discusses this campaign in painful detail. That book also goes into much more detail about how primary campaigns for Congress are and are not fought.

[18] The last three times that Republican congressmen have retired in Maine, the individuals succeeding them have received their Republican nomination with relatively little opposition. One might expect this in an area with a strong political party organization. It is all but inexplicable in a state like Maine, in which the Republican party is organizationally very weak. These examples, which certainly deserve further study, illustrate the difficulty one has in generalizing from well-known examples.

John Kerry won the Democratic nomination, but only after a heated campaign in which he alienated a substantial portion of the potential Democratic electorate on the abortion issue. McKernan won in November, in part at least because of the harm done to Kerry in his primary.

In 1984 the pattern of 1980 was repeated. Pachios's successor as Democratic state party chair, State Representative Barry Hobbins, won an easy primary victory over one unknown, underfinanced opponent. Hobbins worked hard, but McKernan had used the advantages of incumbency well for two years. He raised more money than Hobbins and beat him handily.

In 1986, Maine's political leaders "swapped" positions. Democratic Governor Joe Brennan was constitutionally ineligible to succeed himself. Congressman McKernan gave up his relatively safe seat in the House to run for and win the governorship. Brennan, with no primary opposition, won the Democratic nomination for the First Congressional District seat. He won the general election over an unknown but well-financed challenger, H. Rollin Ives, by about 10 percent of the vote. Brennan was reelected handily in 1988. The Republican nomination to oppose him was contested by two political activists, well known within the party but not by the general public, who represented the moderate and conservative wings of the party. The primary was heated and ugly. The moderate winner, Edward S. O'Meara, emerged bruised from the primary battle. In the general election, despite raising and spending over a quarter of a million dollars, he was defeated by Brennan, who himself raised over $450,000, by almost 2 to 1.

Finally, 1990 was the year of the attempted comeback in Maine. Brennan gave up his congressional seat to try to win back the governorship from McKernan. Emery decided to make a bid for his old congressional seat. Each was nominated without opposition—name recognition playing a crucial role. But the Democrats did not concede the seat to Emery. Five Democrats sought their party's nod. The preprimary favorite was Attorney General James Tierney, who had run unsuccessfully for governor in 1986. Again, his name was very well known. But Tierney was upset by State Senator Tom Andrews, who ran an aggressive grass-roots campaign supplemented by enough media exposure to gain recognition. Andrews's victory raised his credibility as a candidate; supporters of his opponents gave him credit for coming from behind and joined his team for the general election. Emery, on the other hand, seemed to have lost interest in campaigning; he appeared to be a warmed-over retread. Andrews won impressively in November and immediately began using the perquisites of his office and his increased visibility throughout the district to build his reputation for future campaigns—either to retain his seat or perhaps to move on to the governorship.

7

State and Local Elections

Compare the experiences of two politicians at the Washington County Fair. Thirty-one states in the union have Washington Counties. These experiences could happen in any of them.

The first politician is a candidate for county board of supervisors. His district encompasses about one-fifteenth of the county. He has been active in county politics and county government for some years.

The second candidate is a member of Congress, running for United States senator. Washington County is one of over sixty counties in the state; she is from the other end of the state and has been to Washington County perhaps twice.

The candidate for board of supervisors has been looking forward to the county fair for months. The fair is one of the most important social events on his annual calendar. Since most of the people in the county attend the fair at least once during fair week, this is also an important political event. Our candidate is in charge of the voter registration booth at the fair, making sure that the decorations are in place and that the booth is always opened. He sees to it that his signs are in evidence. He has set the entire week aside so that he can spend as much time at the fair as is possible. After all, what could be a better way to campaign among likely voters?

The Senate candidate will attend the fair too. She will put in one appearance, for about an hour, at a time that the local people tell her will be quite busy. She is not looking forward to the fair with eagerness. In fact, one day before, she is not even aware that she will be attending. Her staff arranged for the visit. Someone else will be certain that her signs are in place; that she is introduced to the right people; most importantly, that the media know she is there. She probably will not attend every county fair in the state, but it certainly seems to her that she will.

The visit of the Senate candidate to the fair is not only the highlight of the week for the supervisor candidate; it is one of the truly major events of his entire campaign. He is filmed introducing the Senate candidate to some of the local folks; that scene is on television at eleven and everyone sees it. He makes sure that someone takes candid pictures to use in his campaign flyer; maybe the photographer will even get the best one autographed.

The Senate candidate squeezed the visit to the fair into a busy day. She was up at dawn, shaking hands at a factory gate. She flew halfway across the state to have lunch with a union leader whose PAC had promised, but not delivered, financial support. After lunch she did a brief radio interview and stopped in at the local newspaper to talk with the editor. On the flight into Washington County Airport she conferred with her campaign manager and her pollster about the impact of her recent statements on aid to the republics of the former Soviet Union. After the appearance at the fair, she drove a hundred miles to the south for a fund-raising dinner. She did not even see the speech she was to give until an hour before the dinner. She did not know where she was staying that night, but hoped she would have time to make some calls before she went to bed. One of these calls would be to dictate some letters to her secretary; she'd remember to tell her to write a note thanking that guy at the fair—"Can't remember his name or where he's from. Find out from someone."

These two politicians are engaged in the same enterprise, winning the votes of enough people to gain election. To win these votes, they must identify likely supporters and figure out some way to get those supporters to the polls.

Both candidates have to set strategies aimed at accomplishing these goals. They must devise a strategy that involves identifying likely supporters and determining how they can structure a candidacy that will reach these voters. Each candidate must also come up with tactics aimed at carrying out the strategy. What does one do on a day-to-day basis? How does one structure an organization, and what does that organization do? However, as the hypothetical scenario depicted above demonstrates, these two candidates are actually involved in very different enterprises.

I. THE CONVENTIONAL WISDOM: OLD VERSUS NEW POLITICS

This chapter examines campaigning for a wide variety of offices—from governor, senator, or congressman to county supervisor or water district commissioner. One of the chapter's goals is to present and examine the conventional wisdom on this topic. *The conventional wisdom, simply stated, is that a major change has occurred in the last three decades, a change from old to new politics.*

Under the old politics, campaigning was person-to-person and door-to-door; candidates were individuals representing the political parties that structured both the campaigns for office and the institutions of government. Supporters gave allegiance to the parties because they agreed with the parties' stands on issues or because the parties would do certain things for voters if elected. The candidates of the party in control of government, as a group, were held accountable for the performance of the government.

New politics is media- and image-oriented, not person-to-person. It is the politics of television. Political party organization has been replaced by candidate-centered organization. The link between campaigning and governing is difficult to document; institutional accountability has declined as individual candidates win or lose based on the strength of their own efforts, not those of the party (Fiorina, 1990).

The reality of campaigning for office in the last decades of the twentieth century is, like so much else in this text, dependent on context. *New politics has replaced old politics, in some areas, for some offices.* Often the change is more subtle than bold.

Consider again the Washington County Fair. The Senate candidate was running a "new politics," candidate-centered campaign. She was concerned about the perception of *her* position on foreign aid, about raising money for *her* campaign from the union PAC, about the media coverage of *her* appearance at the Washington County Fair.

But the candidate for county supervisor was involved in an "old politics" campaign. The booth at the county fair was a party organization activity; it was part of a voter registration drive run by the party. All the party candidates together put up their posters. He took time out of his normal campaign pattern to "interact" with the senatorial campaign, to "use" it for party and personal publicity, but such events were not part of his overall tactics or strategy. He spent much of the week at the fair because that was where he could greet and talk to the greatest number of people.

Former Philadelphia Mayor Wilson Goode talking with high school students during a campaign. (Frances M. Cox/Stock, Boston)

Old politics and new politics exist hand in hand in America today. New politics gets more attention because that is what it is designed for—getting attention—and because the bigger campaigns, for more visible offices, are often run using state-of-the-art new politics techniques. But that does not mean that all campaigning has changed. In discussing campaigning in the remainder of this chapter, we will show how the two coexist—and how Tip O'Neill's famous adage that "all politics is local" continues to contain a good deal of truth.

II.   POLITICAL CONTEXT AND POLITICIANS' DECISIONS TO RUN

Politicians think in terms of career progression. Is this the time for me to move "up"? How one defines "up" in this context is not absolute, but some definitions are pretty well accepted. For instance, a seat in the House of Representatives is generally considered a step up from a seat in a state legislature. A seat in the United States Senate is a "promotion" from serving as a member of Congress (Schlesinger, 1966).

How do politicians decide if it is time to step up, to take a chance at seeking a higher office? Jacobson and Kernell (1983) have posited an important theory that states that politicians weigh the value of the office for which they strive and the probability of winning against the risk involved in giving up the office they currently hold. Politicians weigh the public climate in determining whether or not they will run. One of the most important sets of decisions made are those made by qualified candidates (who for these purposes are defined as politicians already holding some elective office) about whether or not they will seek a higher office.

That qualified candidates, in the aggregate, decide that the political climate is not right for moving up explains one cause of incumbent reelection success, at least in House elections. When candidates with the greatest likelihood of winning decide not to run, challengers of lesser quality frequently step up to fill the void (Abramowitz, 1981; Hinckley, 1981; Jacobson, 1981; Maisel & Cooper, 1981).

However, it is possible to look more deeply into the reasoning of individual candidates. Jacobson and Kernell review two competing sets of theories that are used to explain electoral results. One body of speculation stresses the impact of economic conditions on electoral outcome (most of this scholarship examines congressional campaigns, because of the availability of data, but the conclusions can be generalized to other offices (see Bloom & Price, 1975; Kramer, 1971; Tufte, 1975, 1978). The other theory uses survey data to explain electoral results in terms of individual voter attitudes (Arsenau & Wolfinger, 1973; Fiorina, 1978, 1981; Kernell, 1977; Kinder & Kiewiet, 1979; Mann & Wolfinger, 1980). In either case the operating assumption is that voters cast their votes for *some* offices based on their overall assessment of the political and economic situation in which they find themselves. Politicians certainly think in these terms, but they also think in terms of separating themselves from such broader issues as Central America and the International Monetary Fund.

In making the decision about whether or not to run for higher office, politicians are very concerned about what else is going on at the time of that election. Potential candidates are aware that voters give most attention to the top of the ballot. If it is a presidential election year, then electoral hopefuls must consider whether the presidential candidate of their party is going to help or hurt them. Will they be able to derive support from a popular candidate? Will they be able to separate themselves from an unpopular candidate? If theirs is an off-year election, one in which no presidential election is being held, what other elections are most likely to capture the voters' interest (e.g., senator, governor)?

How will they be affected by these elections, if at all? Political scientists argue persuasively that party influence on voting has declined, that voters are splitting their tickets much more frequently than they did in the past, that politicians' coattails are shorter than they once were (DeVries & Tarrance, 1972; Ferejohn & Calvert, 1984; Wattenberg, 1990b, 1991). Undoubtedly all these conclusions are true; however, practicing politicians are still very concerned about separating their fates from those of other politicians or taking advantage of remaining coattails.

Recent changes in state election laws demonstrate this trend. In the early 1950s, the governors of nineteen states were elected for two-year terms. As states have changed their two-year terms for governor to four-year terms, virtually every one of them has decided to hold gubernatorial elections in nonpresidential election years, thus insulating the state elections from national politics. As the most recent example, Arkansas switched from a two-year to a four-year term in 1986, with elections held in nonpresidential election years (see Table 7-1).

Candidates for office below governor are aware of this trend as well. In considering a run for the state senate, for instance, a political candidate is confronted with one political environment if the upcoming election year is a presidential election year in which there is also a gubernatorial and senatorial race in his state; that potential candidate faces a very different set of variables if it is a nonpresidential election year in which there is also neither a senatorial nor a gubernatorial election.

Table 7-2 lists the various electoral environments that might confront po-

TABLE 7-1. Electoral Context of Gubernatorial Elections

Years	Four-Year Terms			Two-Year Terms
	Presidential Year	Congressional Year	Odd Year	
1950–1952	10	14	5	19
1988–1990	9	33	3	3

Source: Compiled by the author.

TABLE 7-2. Offices at the Top of the Ballot

Offices	Number of States in:				
	1982	1984	1986	1988	1990
President Governor Senator Representative	X	7	X	10	X
President Governor Representative	X	6	X	2	X
President Senator Representative	X	26	X	23	X
President Representative	X	11	X	15	X
Governor Senator Representative	22	X	26	X	25
Governor Representative	14	X	10	X	11
Senator Representative	10	X	8	X	10
Representative	4	X	6	X	4

Note: Five states hold gubernatorial elections during off-off years, that is, in years ending with odd digits. They are Kentucky, Louisiana, Mississippi, New Jersey, and Virginia. Three states, New Hampshire, Rhode Island, and Vermont, have two-year governorships, with elections in every year ending with even digits.

tential candidates.[1] These combinations are all possible because United States senators serve six-year terms and thus no senatorial seat is contested in any state in one out of three national elections (barring vacancies due to death, resignation, etc.).

These factors were not so important when all politicians for all offices campaigned in the same ways. However, they have become critically important when different types of campaigns are run for different offices. It is in this context that politicians must evaluate how their careers are going to be affected not only by the political climate of the times but also by their ability to campaign using different techniques.

III.   THE NEW POLITICS: CAMPAIGNING IN A MEDIA AGE

Questions of political context are vitally important for politicians in deciding whether or not to "step up" because they go a long way toward answering ques-

[1] Congressional seats are contested every two years in every state. However, in the four states that elect state officials in odd-numbered years—i.e., years with no elections for national offices—only the candidates for state offices appear on the ballot.

tions about how to campaign and how successful various techniques of campaigning are likely to be.

Let us assume that a politician is making a fully rational decision about seeking office.[2] A politician considering stepping up to a larger constituency, a more prestigious office, will seek some information:

1. What voters am I going to need to appeal to?
2. What is the partisan distribution of voters within the new district?
3. What is the normal voting strength for candidates of my party in this district? Conversely, what are the strengths of the opposition candidate and his or her party?
4. What kinds of techniques will work in appealing to the voters whose support I will need?

That list could easily be expanded, but it serves as a starting point for the discussion of so-called new politics. Candidates for all offices ask the same questions about how to get the support of a plurality of all voters. They ask the same questions about their party and/or personal support and that of their opponents.

Based on an analysis of the district (often a very impressionistic analysis of the district), they decide if they can win the election they are considering. Rarely does victory seem certain. If victory were certain, others with similar qualifications would be seeking the office, thereby removing the apparent certainty because of a primary election. If a politician believes that victory in moving up to a higher elective office is indeed certain, the assumptions on which that prediction was made should be reexamined.

If preliminary analysis leads to a conclusion that victory is unlikely, experienced politicians, holding other elective office, generally stay put.[3] It is almost always easier to retain a seat than to move up the ladder (Jacobson & Kernell, 1983, chap. 3).[4] If, however, they feel that victory is possible, that they have a legitimate chance, then they begin to analyze how to get the votes.

At this stage, they must look at *party* strength in detail, at the *potential* for a personal organization, and at the *potential* for a media campaign (see Gibson et al., 1983, 1985). If a candidate is considering a campaign for Congress or for statewide office, or even for state senate in some of the larger states, he must realize that he cannot personally reach all the voters. He must also realize that voters no longer use party affiliation as the only cue in deciding how to vote. What techniques will be successful in convincing voters that they should cast their ballot for this particular candidate?

---

[2] Before we proceed any further, we should recognize that this assumption is, in all likelihood, not supportable. Few politicians really understand the process into which they are entering; even experienced politicians make decisions about campaigns in spite of information that would lead a rational person to another conclusion (Hershey, 1984; Maisel, 1982, 1986).

[3] Exceptions to this generalization include a politician's race for office in order to increase name recognition and visibility for a future race and/or a politician's willingness to run a seemingly futile race in order to assure that a respectable candidate is fielded. The candidate in the latter instance gets many IOUs from the party.

[4] Obviously one key factor is whether one must give up a current office to run. In most cases this is so, but exceptions exist. For example, New Jersey holds state elections in odd-numbered years.

Let us now assume that the candidate, a nonincumbent, has decided to run.[5] Our candidate is either challenging an incumbent or running in an open seat. In either case the tactical problems are the same, though the difficulty of the task may be more exaggerated in the first instance. The candidate has certain resources to utilize and certain tasks to accomplish. The problem is to match resources with tasks in the most effective way.

The first job is to identify likely supporters. The second is to ascertain what other voters are possible converts to the candidate's side. After identifying these two groups, the candidate must set a strategy for reaching both of these groups in a way that will solidify their support and increase the possibility that they will turn out to vote in droves. That might sound simple, but it certainly is not.

The most important resource that any candidate has is personal time (Mann & Wolfinger, 1980). In some races that is all that is necessary. The candidate can identify supporters and potential supporters and go out and talk to them all. Many politicians started in that way for their first campaign. They are used to personal contact and have difficulty realizing that that will not work for all campaigns.

However, "pressing the flesh" of all the voters is not possible when one is campaigning for the United States House of Representatives, in which the average member represents over 650,000 people; nor is it possible when one is campaigning for statewide office, when over forty states have populations exceeding a million. Thus, *the candidate must learn how to use personal time in a new way, not merely contacting individual voters, but maximizing the number of voters on whom that candidate can have an impact.* Surrogates for the candidate are necessary in order to best use the results of time spent, essentially by "expanding" the amount of personal time.

A.   The Role of Political Parties

Many candidates have some experience in using party as a surrogate. Some voters will vote for a candidate because of that candidate's and those voters' party affiliation. For these voters, the candidate need only be certain that party affiliation is well known. Little candidate time is necessary to make this connection. Party is then one resource on which politicians are used to relying.

But political party is not a resource that is equally available to all candidates, nor is it a resource with which all candidates are equally comfortable. Candidates must weigh the impact of party in the new district. Is the organization efficient? Is the degree of partisan affiliation strong among voters? Is the candidate perceived to be in line with most of the others in the party? Or is the candidate an outsider to whom the party people will not automatically flock? Is the candidate's party a majority or not?

---

[5] The candidate is not an incumbent. Incumbents have all faced this problem at some point—when they first sought the office. They are now in the position of a candidate seeking to stay in the same office. By and large, their campaign tactics were dictated by what worked well the last time.

Is party strength spread equally throughout the district, or is it concentrated in some areas? What does the campaign do about the other areas? What is it that party organization can and cannot do in a particular campaign? How important is the campaign for the party organization? Are party activists likely to work hard for this campaign, or are they more concerned about another candidate or another race?

Merely posing these questions demonstrates how complex tactical campaign planning can be. Return for a moment to the question of what other offices are on the ballot. If John Doe is a candidate for Congress, in all likelihood his congressional district does not have the same boundaries as those of districts designed for other elective offices. Most party organizations are structured around the county unit. In rural states, and in rural districts in some of the more urban states, congressional districts tend to encompass a large number of counties. As examples, the First Congressional District in West Virginia includes all or part of ten counties; the First Congressional District in California, in the northeastern corner of the state, includes all or part of thirteen counties. On the other hand, in urban areas many congressional districts fall into single counties. The five counties that compose New York City, as an extreme example, contain all or part of twenty-one congressional districts; Harris County (Houston), Texas, contains all or part of five congressional districts.[6]

For all that, county organizations are notoriously unconcerned about congressional politics. Congressmen, and senators for that matter, deal with issues far away in Washington. Party people care more about issues closer to home, because finally their concern involves those who can more likely be counted on to do something tangible for them.

The local sheriff might well have more immediate impact on these politicians than do their representatives in Washington. Consequently, local polls are more likely to work hard for local candidates. Similarly, they are more likely to work hard for candidates for executive office than they are for candidates for legislative office. All this theorizing assumes, of course, that the party organization exists and is capable of doing effective campaign work at all, an assumption that is far from clear in many areas of the country (Eldersveld, 1982; L. Epstein, 1986; but for a more positive view of the role of county organizations, see Gibson, 1991).

On the other hand, in recent years the national parties, particularly the Republican party, have become more active in local campaigns. Under the leadership of Bill Brock, who became Republican national chairman in 1977, and his successors, the Republicans have built a professional campaign organization at the national level, concentrating their efforts on recruiting good candidates for office—at the congressional level and even at the level of state senator and state representative in some instances—training local candidates and their staffs in basic campaign techniques, and supplying certain technical support services, such as survey research, for their candidates. The Local Elections Division of

---

[6] These examples are illustrative and were chosen before the redistricting that followed the 1990 census.

the Republican National Committee has been active and effective for nearly ten years. The Democrats, while way behind the Republicans in this regard, are beginning to copy their opponents' techniques. Furthermore, both parties, again with the Republicans in the lead, are seeking means to persuade and mobilize voters, on a national or at least regional basis, to back party candidates (see Adamany, 1984, pp. 78–92; Bibby, 1986, 1991; Herrnson, 1988; Reichley, 1985; J. Stewart, 1991; and the discussion in Chapter 3).

With all these caveats, what can one expect from party as a resource? First, in any geographic area some citizens will vote for a candidate because of party label. The number of diehard party loyalists varies from area to area, but candidates should know the history of party loyalty in a district. Similarly, some citizens use party label as a negative voting cue ("I could never vote for a Republican"). A candidate should know the history of antiparty voting as well (Sabato, 1988, chap. 4).

Second, some jobs are better accomplished by party than by any other political organization. Some tasks benefit all candidates who are running under a party label. Thus, candidates frequently call upon party organization to run voter registration drives, especially in areas or among groups that are likely to support candidates of that party. Party organizations can often be counted on to organize get-out-the-vote drives on election day, checking which of their regular supporters have voted and urging those who have not voted to do so. At the very least, the party can be counted on to monitor the polls on election day, to be certain that votes are not lost owing to error or fraud.

In sum, party is a resource that candidates have to be aware of, but they also must beware of. One cannot expect too much from an organization that is probably not strong and that has interests sometimes different from those of a single candidate.

B.   The Role of Organized Groups

Organized groups often work hard in a particular candidate's campaign. Group involvement in political campaigns was discussed in Chapter 5. From a candidate's perspective, questions involving organized groups are like those that must be asked of political parties. Which groups can provide active support? How can they help reach out to supporters, or to potential supporters? How effective are they going to be at that task? How concerned are they going to be about supporting this candidate as opposed to other candidates?

Groups can be very effective surrogates for candidates. We have already seen the techniques that groups use in the political arena (Chapter 5). All those techniques that attempt to influence the voting behavior of group members are important for candidates, because the group replaces the candidate as the prime contact to the voter. Groups attempt to assure that the supporter stays a supporter and actually votes and that the potential supporter comes over to the candidate's side.

However, group support does not come automatically to a candidate. Our hypothetical candidate must expend blocks of time to garner group support and more time to assure that group support stays firm and is mobilized in the most effective way.

Furthermore, candidates must recognize that groups have multiple interests that extend beyond any one campaign, and that, by definition, these groups are engaged in activities other than politics. Thus, group activity can help in a campaign, but it too is a limited resource.[7]

C. Media Politics

The discussion to this point has purposefully avoided *the major surrogate* for personal contact by a candidate, media campaigning. If a candidate cannot reach the voters personally, surely they can be reached through the media. As the twentieth century draws to a close, media campaigning has become a way of life for all of us. Shouldn't that be obvious? Don't all successful candidates use television—and even radio—to reach voters?

Again, reality is not quite what it might appear. Certainly television and politics have blended in familiar ways in recent years. Using the media to carry political messages has become familiar to all viewers; a vast majority of Americans, moreover, receive most of their political information from television. But that does not end the discussion.

A number of different cases suggest themselves. First, look at a candidate for Congress from the Fourth Congressional District in Connecticut in 1988. The voters in the district were concerned about the presidential election (in which George Bush, whose father had been a United States senator from Connecticut and whose brother was a very active Republican politician in the state, was a candidate) and about the senatorial election, in which the incumbent senator was being challenged by the state's attorney general. Most of the voters in the district watch New York television stations; most listen to New York radio; most read the New York newspapers; in fact, many work in New York, as the district is a wealthy bedroom suburb of New York City. How could a Connecticut candidate effectively attract attention in the New York media market? Advertise effectively? Efficiently use the media as a surrogate for person-to-person campaigning or for the other techniques already discussed?

For a second scenario, imagine a candidate running for state senate from a district in San Francisco in 1990. While no presidential election captured the headlines, a gubernatorial race did draw much of the attention. One of the candidates was the former mayor of San Francisco. The other was one of the current United States senators. Both advertised heavily on San Francisco television. The local media blanket the senatorial district, but four out of every five television advertising dollars are wasted in the process of beaming messages to voters in other districts. The same is true of radio and newspaper adver-

---

[7] This discussion does not deal with financial contributions by organized groups. These contributions are often critical for campaigns. However, they are used to pay for campaign techniques that in turn substitute for candidate time or otherwise transmit the candidate's message. These techniques and the entire question of campaign financing have been discussed briefly in Chapter 5 and will be returned to in Chapter 10.

tising. What role, then, should the media play in this state senate campaign?

Contrast these two cases with a third scenario, a campaign for the United States Senate from Arkansas in 1986. The Senate race will top the ballot in Arkansas in 1986; neither a presidential nor a gubernatorial election will compete for voter attention. Moreover, in a state with a population of over 2,250,000, with more than 1,200,000 registered voters, and with approximately 60 percent of the voters living in rural areas, it is impossible for a candidate to reach even a significant proportion of the population personally. Little Rock is centrally located, and that city's media dominate the state. This situation is prime for a media campaign. It does not take a crystal ball to see that Senator Bumpers and his Republican opponent would both use the media, particularly television, heavily as a way to reach voters.

These three examples point to the first conclusion about the role of media in general, and television in particular, in modern campaigns. *Media advertising as a surrogate for personal contact is very important in today's campaigns. However, the electoral context will determine the extent to which media campaigning can replace personal campaigning as a way to reach the voters.*

An increasing amount of money has been spent on television advertising in recent campaigns for the United States Senate and the House of Representatives. However, ample television money is not a resource that is equally available to all candidates. Candidates must determine how much of their financial resources should be spent on media advertising and how much is better spent in other ways. Some districts will be dominated by television campaigns. In other congressional districts television advertising is all but unknown. While media campaigns are more common in statewide races, here too analysts have noted a great variety (Goldenberg & Traugott, 1984).

The second conclusion about the role of media in modern campaigning relates specifically to those districts in which media advertising plays a dominant role. *Only certain kinds of messages can be transmitted through sixty-second or thirty-second commercials.*

These messages can convey impressions and images, but they cannot do a very thorough job of presenting and analyzing issue positions. Nonetheless, such advertisements play a crucial, perhaps even critical, role in many campaigns. Candidates who are virtually unknown become familiar household friends through repeated appearances on television. In those districts and states in which media advertising is an expected part of campaigning, citizens use the television and radio presentations as a prime means of evaluating candidates.

The charge is often made that the media consultant, the political equivalent of a Madison Avenue ad man, makes or breaks a candidate. The implications of this charge for the role of campaigning in the political process are obvious and serious (cf. McGinniss, 1969).

To emphasize this point, one need only look at particular campaigns in which the media surrogates for candidates have played prominent roles. In the North Carolina Senate races between the incumbent Republican Jesse Helms and Democratic Governor James Hunt in 1984 and between Helms and Harvey Gantt, the black mayor of Charlotte, in 1990, the race came down to attack and response in thirty-second or one-minute jibes; injection of the issue of race as well as each candidate's record and performance made these particularly distasteful campaigns. The net result was to discourage many North Carolinians about the qualities of elected leaders.

In each of the last three elections, in race after race, the situation was not improved. In the 1986 Senate campaign in Florida between the first-term Republican incumbent Paula Hawkins and the state's popular Democratic governor, Bob Graham, for instance, each candidate lined up a media guru, Bob Goodman from New York for the Republican and Bob Squier from Washington for the Democrat. The candidates raised vast sums of money so that the media specialists could design pithy spot announcements to convince the populace to support their candidate. Hawkins had won in 1980 with a heavily media-oriented campaign; her emphasis on work for abused children, a reflection of her own background, was used in an attempt to diffuse Graham's attacks on other parts of her record. When Graham originally ran for governor, Squier came up with the idea that the candidate should work one day in each of a long series of jobs, to demonstrate his concern for working Floridians. The 1986 Senate campaign showed the same creative approach, with little emphasis on issues. Perhaps the worst example of media campaigning in 1990 was the campaign of Republican millionaire Clayton Williams against Democratic Treasurer Ann Richards in Texas. Williams's attacks were personal and biting; Richards responded in kind, winning the election, but not the respect of the viewing public.

Example after example can be mustered to amplify this point. In all campaigns for governor and United States senator, and in many campaigns for Congress, mayor, and more local offices where the media environment is appropriate, paid media are thought to be the most important—in some cases the only important—element in a campaign's strategic approach to the voters.

Candidates demonstrate their seriousness by convincing high-priced media consultants to work on their campaigns; those who are considering supporting candidates ask "Who is doing your media?" While all markets do not lend themselves to these kinds of efforts, in those that do, they quickly assume major proportions.

D.   The Candidate's Organization

To this point we have discussed parties, groups, and media as potential surrogates for personal campaigning in races for higher office. The fourth surrogate, the most common one, is the candidate's personal organization. When commentators speak of candidate organizations, they mean a number of different things. At this point, we are concerned with volunteers who go out and campaign on behalf of a candidate. They are figuratively that candidate's eyes, ears, and mouth. While the candidate cannot personally contact every voter, it is possible for others campaigning on the candidate's behalf to do so.

This type of campaigning is done in a number of different ways. Where possible, campaigners go door-to-door, talking to individual voters, asking for

Candidates for state and local office use volunteers to put up
their campaign posters. (Bohdan Hrynewych/Stock, Boston)

their support for a particular candidate. If an organization is sophisticated
enough, these volunteers then compile lists of the voters they have visited, com-
menting on the likelihood that those voters will support the candidate. On election day the likely supporters are called again and urged to go to the polls. The
voters who are likely to vote for another candidate are left alone. Analysis and
follow-up of this sort requires a sophisticated organization with a large number
of trained volunteers.

Other campaigns use volunteers in less complex ways. Some campaigns merely "drop" literature at every door, letting the brochures speak for themselves. Still other campaigns use volunteers, usually young volunteers, to distribute leaflets at shopping centers, malls, ball games, or other locations where large numbers of potential voters are to be found.

Still other campaigns employ telephone banks, phoning perspective voters with messages about the candidate. Telephone campaigns vary tremendously in sophistication, depending on how well-trained the callers are and how organized the entire operation is. At one extreme these campaigns can be as effective as door-to-door campaigning, especially for rural districts; at the other extreme they resemble the scattershot technique of shopping mall leafleting.

One of the keys to establishing a volunteer organization is to have workers who will campaign for just one candidate. In some ways this service is inefficient. If a volunteer is to go door-to-door, why not carry propaganda for a group of candidates? Many volunteers will do this. The marginal difference in effort extended is minimal. However, from a candidate's perspective, the difference is significant.

If a worker carries material or campaigns for more than one candidate, the potential effect of the volunteer contact on the voter is certainly diminished, and it might even be negated. What if the voter has not heard about one candidate but has a negative view of the other candidate, and, using only that opinion, discounts both candidates? The call has been dysfunctional. What if the voter has a negative view about politicians in general but might be persuaded because someone cares enough to go door-to-door on behalf of one very special politician in whom that volunteer truly believes? Again, a positive response would be lost by combining campaign efforts.

While scenarios can be imagined in which combined efforts would help a candidate, if they had their choice, most candidates would want volunteers to work for them and them alone, a far cry from the days when political parties did all of this kind of campaigning on behalf of an entire ticket. Strong individual candidates who are supported by large numbers of dedicated volunteers eschew combined campaign efforts; weaker candidates with fewer supporters are the most eager to have a "team" approach to campaigning.

In the 1988 presidential election, a new twist emerged. Presidential campaigns are publicly financed; that is, the money to run these campaigns comes from a federal fund, and no more money can be spent if the federal grant is accepted (see Chapters 9 and 10). However, presidential campaigns also have the most ability to raise money, because they have had to develop the networks to do so during the primary and because the stakes are highest. The campaign finance laws permit money to be raised at the national level and then spent locally, if it is spent in a coordinated manner on all the party's campaigns. Thus, the Dukakis and the Bush campaigns raised money during the general election phase of the 1988 presidential campaign and organized field campaigns for the entire ticket, as this was the only legal way in which they could raise and spend money on behalf of their candidates. The result was an interesting reversion to the days of party-centered field campaigns. (See Corrado, 1992.)

The ability of candidates to form their own volunteer organization is another factor that varies with what other races are being held at the same time. However, once a winning candidate has a personal organization in place, maintaining it over a period of years is not difficult. Some supporters drop out; new supporters are recruited for each new campaign. But a core of candidate-inspired activists remains as a powerful resource (Fenno, 1978).

E.   The Structure of a Modern Campaign

Volunteer organizations such as the one described above have been an important part of American politics for some time, at least since the spread of direct primaries. In recent years, however, as campaigns have become more expensive and more complex, candidate organizations have taken on a different meaning.

Figure 7-1 depicts a possible organizational chart for a modern general

FIGURE 7-1 Organizational chart of a modern election campaign.

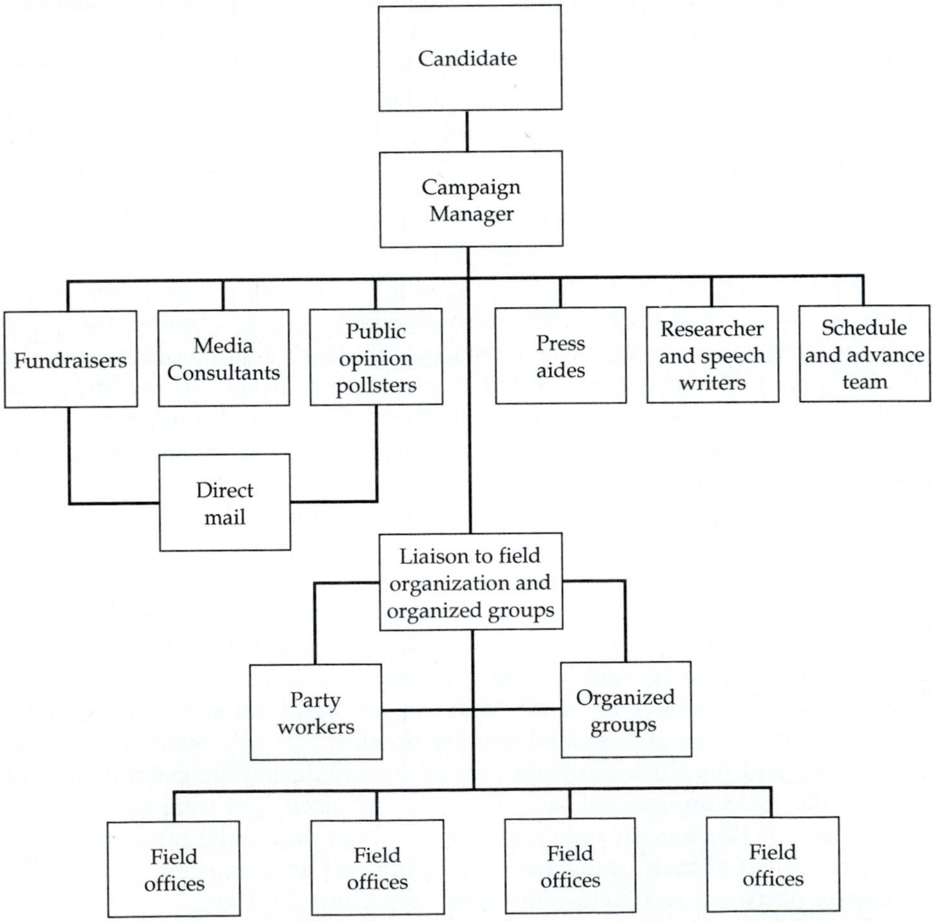

election campaign. The coordination of various means of contacting voters, using traditional and modern techniques, defines the extent to which the new politics has come to dominate campaigns for many offices.

The candidate sits atop the organization. Or at least one hopes the candidate does. Too often campaigns run so efficiently that the candidates seem to be
all but unimportant, merely the product to be packaged. However, in this case,
let us assume that the candidate is in charge, selecting the campaign manager
and coordinating strategy and tactics. (See Agranoff, 1972, 1976; Hershey,
1984; Kayden, 1978; Luntz, 1988; Rothenberg, 1983; Salmore & Salmore,
1985.)

The campaign manager runs the day-to-day campaign. Campaigns for
statewide office routinely require budgets that exceed $1,500,000. This is a ma-
jor enterprise, and one that requires professional management. In the last two
decades a corps of "professional" campaign managers has emerged.

Some work as individual entrepreneurs, working one campaign at a time
and then waiting for the next biennium to begin again. More and more, however, the pattern is for political managers to form companies that take over the
management of a number of campaigns at the same time, handling many of the
tasks from a central headquarters. Political campaign management is indeed a
growth industry these days.

Firms tend to specialize in either Republican or Democratic campaigns.
Different firms have different expertise and!or are willing to handle different aspects of a campaign. In all cases they combine some of the functions described
below with advice on how the campaign should proceed. (See Luntz, 1988;
Sabato, 1981.)

1. Public Opinion Polling Most modern campaigns do not rely on hunches
to determine what the public is thinking nor to evaluate how different approaches to campaigning are working. Public opinion polling has acquired a
prominent role in modern campaigns. In some cases the campaign management
firm handles the public opinion polling; in other cases a polling firm plays a major role in campaign management; in still other cases two firms work together.
Prominent pollsters like Peter Hart, Bill Hamilton, Robert Teeter, Richard
Wirthlin, or Pat Cadell are sought after as key figures in major campaigns. In
any event, pollsters play major roles in ascertaining what issues concern the
public, how the candidate is perceived, how the opponent in perceived, and
what approaches will and will not work.

In more elaborate campaigns, polling goes on continuously throughout
the campaign period. In other campaigns, a pollster will take a first poll, called
a *benchmark* poll, to determine a candidate's position and the views of the public at the beginning of the campaign and then will poll occasionally throughout
the campaign, to measure attitudes and changes in opinions in response to specific events or to determine the impact of specific strategies. Professional pollsters working on major campaigns play a critical and central role in determining
strategy to be followed. They provide and analyze the data. Frequently they interpret what those facts mean in light of other campaigns in which they have

participated (or are currently participating); they draw on their knowledge accumulated from a series of campaigns to devise new approaches based on their interpretations. (See Crespi, 1988, 1989.)

2.   Media Consultants The campaign manager and the pollster also work closely with the media expert on a campaign. Again, various patterns are possible. Some large management firms take care of designing media strategies, making commercials, and buying time for campaigns. Some firms, primarily advertising agencies, specialize in political advertising and take care of other aspects of campaign management as well. Various patterns of interaction with pollsters are possible. Because media expenditures constitute such a high percentage of total campaign expenditures, the role of the media consultant is also central to most campaigns (Goldenberg & Traugott, 1984, chap 6; Pfau & Kenski, 1990).

   If the message of the campaign is to be carried by paid media, then the media consultant has to be involved not only in producing advertisements and commercials and buying time and space, but also in setting strategies, in responding to different campaign situations, and in evaluating how the campaign strategies are or are not working. Goldenberg and Traugott (1984, p. 86) found that congressional candidates in 1978 spent nearly 60 percent of their total campaign budgets on media expenditures and advertising; these expenses included consultant fees and production as well as sheer advertisement purchases. Undoubtedly, similar patterns would be found for campaigns for statewide office. If anything, the percentage of total budgets spent on this category probably increases with the total budget of the campaign and has continued to increase since the 1978 study was completed (see also Diamond & Bates, 1984; Pfau & Kenski, 1990).

3.   Fund-Raisers Polling and media advertising are expensive. Million dollar campaigns were cause for concern in the late 1960s; they are commonplace today. In order to run campaigns of this magnitude, candidates must spend a good deal of time and effort on fund-raising. (The complex topic of campaign financing will be discussed in detail in Chapter 10.) At this point it is sufficient to state that one important part of any campaign organization involves raising the money necessary to conduct the campaign and monitoring how that money is spent. This latter task necessitates complying with increasingly complex federal and state laws regulating the collection, disbursement, and reporting of all campaign finances.

   Many campaigns now hire professionals to handle these tasks. Professional fund-raisers set a strategy for raising money and follow through on that strategy (Herrnson, 1991). They must begin well in advance of the start of actual campaigning for two reasons. First, fund-raising requires a good deal of candidate time. It is difficult to convince a donor to make a major contribution if that donor cannot sit down and actually talk with the candidate. Second, most campaign expenditures require payment in advance. Few of those enterprises used to dealing with campaigns will do so on a credit basis; all too often campaigns end up with unpaid bills.

Therefore, candidates have to raise money in advance in order to start effective campaigning. A number of observers have commented that raising money early can have important strategic consequences for dissuading effective opposition (Goldenberg & Traugott, 1984; Green & Krasno, 1988; Jacobson, 1990b; Jacobson & Kernell, 1983; Sorauf, 1984). This lesson is not lost on politicians.

One important technique for raising money—as well as for communicating campaign messages—is *direct mail*. This is a relatively new technique, first employed on a national level by the Republican party under Chairman Ray

Richard P. Viguerie was one of the first to develop computer-generated direct mail appeals into a successful fundraising tool. (AP/Wide World Photos)

Bliss and perfected by Richard Viguerie, a kind of direct-mail guru who has developed lists and raised money for a series of conservative candidates. Viguerie's success spurred others to copy his techniques, though none quite duplicated his early success in raising large sums of money. Today liberal and conservative candidates, as well as interest groups, use computer-generated lists of potential donors and/or potential voters. They appeal to these voters based on certain known characteristics or preferences. Recent evidence has led observers to question whether Viguerie's success is without bounds. Public reluctance to respond to conservative direct-mail solicitations led to retrenchment by Viguerie's firm (Edsall, 1986), and no direct mailers who base their appeals on inflammatory ideological appeals are as successful as they were early in the 1980s.

As a fund-raising tool, direct mail knows no political boundaries. Mailing firms appeal to potential donors throughout the country as they attempt to convince those who have donated to campaigns in the past that they should do so to similar campaigns now.

As a campaigning tool, direct mail is equally effective. Once lists have been developed, campaigns can direct "personalized" appeals to groups of voters who share certain characteristics. All environmentalists in a state might receive one mailing, stressing the candidate's record on environmental matters; all members of the National Rifle Association might receive a mailing that describes the candidate's opposition to gun control legislation. The environmentalists' mailing will not mention the position on gun control; the NRA members' letter will not mention environmental issues, lest anyone be offended. However, those voters who are on both lists will receive both mailings and will have two reasons to support the candidate.

If a sufficient number of lists can be developed and effective appeals drafted, direct mail can be a most effective way to reach voters with a particular campaign appeal. *Because the letters can be personalized by computer, direct mail can be a perfect surrogate for direct candidate contact.* Direct-mail approaches are so prevalent today that few voters actually believe that the candidate has written directly to them; however, despite this cynicism, voters respond positively to letters from candidates who share their political views.

4.   Scheduling and Advance Work   Other parts of the campaign operation work to coordinate the use of candidate time. For instance, candidates for statewide offices, even in smaller states, frequently have more calls for personal time than they have time available. How to use the limited time of the candidate is not a trivial question. Every major campaign has one person—or even a staff of people—whose job it is to see that the candidate's time is used most effectively. Decisions on the use of candidate time are strategic decisions, not clerical decisions.

The scheduler must determine how much of a candidate's time is spent with what groups, how much in what areas of the district, how much with what kinds of activities. The scheduler must respond to the needs of all the others involved in the campaign, conserving that very scarce resource, the time of the candidate. And this task must be done in a way that both ruffles as few feathers as possible and accounts for the idiosyncrasies of the individual candidate.

Once the scheduler has determined where a candidate will be on a certain day, others in the campaign make sure that the campaign day runs smoothly. In larger campaigns this often involves "advancing" a trip, that is, carefully running through an entire day's schedule, before the candidate makes a trip, to guard against slip-ups (Bruno & Greenfield, 1971).

Candidates like to know who will greet them, what they should avoid discussing, how much time they are expected to spend at each event. Campaign managers want to be certain that the candidate gets as much political mileage out of each campaign stop as possible; the advance team must be concerned with details, such as the size of the room, the composition of the crowd, the accommodations of the press.

Candidates want to be comfortable; they like to know where the microphone will be situated in a room and similar details. Some candidates are very particular about the details of overnight accommodations, travel arrangements, and arrangements for members of their family. It is the responsibility of the advance team to see to it that all of a campaign day's details are arranged properly.

Frequently those who "advance" a trip are with the candidate when the trip takes place. If this is the case, they must have keen political judgment. The advance team is expected to know which people the candidate must be introduced to, must record names of important people whom the candidate meets, must massage the political egos of the people with whom the candidate talks. Those on campaign advance teams often spend as much time with the candidate as anyone in a campaign. They have the responsibility of seeing to it that the candidate benefits as much from a campaign day as possible.

5. Press Relations Another important campaign function involves establishing ongoing relations with the working press. The extent of press coverage varies significantly from campaign to campaign. The key variable in this instance is how important the individual campaign is for the geographic area covered by the various media. Thus, a congressional race in Nevada is important for the print and electronic media in Las Vegas and Reno, because Nevada has only two representatives in Congress. On the other hand, the *New York Times* does not pay much attention to congressional races because more than two dozen congressmen represent the metropolitan area served by the *Times*. The same is true for the electronic media in the New York area.

On the other hand, press aides for Senate or gubernatorial candidates in smaller states need worry about only a small number of media markets and a relatively small number of political reporters. In California, Texas, or other large states, press aides must keep track of literally dozens of radio and television stations, daily newspapers, and weeklies. Candidates in larger states often attract the national as well as local media. Handling the press is an important function, and a complex one as well.

Press aides to candidates in major campaigns do not function alone. Their job is to deal with the press, but they do not do so in a vacuum. Their relationships with the press go a long way toward structuring how the candidate is perceived, indeed in some cases if the candidate is perceived at all. Thus, press re-

Reprinted with permission of Wasserman and *The Boston Globe*.

lations are part of an overall strategy. The press aides work with the scheduler to increase the likelihood that the candidate's campaign day is covered by the media. The press staff works with the advance team to see to it that reporters have ready access to the candidate. They work with the speech writers to be certain that advance releases of the candidate's comments are ready for the press to review. The press aides work with the media consultant and the campaign manager to coordinate the press strategy with the overall strategy of the campaign.

6.   Liaison to Party Organization and Organized Groups   Our understanding of how press aides function demonstrates the need for coordination among those working on a campaign. The same is true of the more traditional parts of the campaign discussed earlier, the work of the political party, the coordination of organized group activity, and the work of the field organization.

In any campaign, the campaign manager and the candidate must determine what effective role political party organization will play. However, even in those areas where political party organization is not strong, someone in a campaign must have the responsibility of coordinating campaign efforts with those of the party leadership. Whatever party officials can do for a campaign to garner the support of their loyal followers is a plus. Whatever extra activities the party can undertake is a plus.

Whatever can be done to avoid alienating party regulars must be done. In some cases these are all important aspects of a campaign organization. Certainly this is the case in Illinois for statewide campaigns for the Democrats; the Cook County organization cannot be ignored, even by those who are not part of the organization. On the other hand, Republicans in Maine do not receive much support from the formal party machinery, but each statewide and congressional campaign keeps in touch with party regulars to benefit from any supportive effort that might be forthcoming.

Another aspect of a large campaign organization coordinates the work of the organized groups that are supporting the candidate. This work involves a number of different problems. In some cases there must be coordination with the fund-raisers; in others, with direct mail; in others, with scheduling. At times it is appropriate to set up separate committees to demonstrate group support— Lawyers for Jones or Teachers for Miller; these efforts might require coordination with the press aide or with the media consultant. If organized groups aid a campaign by providing volunteers, their work should be coordinated with the field organization or with political party machinery. How each resource is used varies from situation to situation according to a number of intangibles, not the least of which is the strength of the candidate and the strategy and tactics that are to be employed.

7. Field Organizations Finally, the field organization plays an essential role in almost any campaign organization. The campaign needs some way to reach out into the geographic area covered by the districts. Campaign managers talk about the need for a physical presence; voters need to know that there are real people behind a campaign. This physical presence takes the form of district offices, of volunteers on the street, of leaflet drops and bumper stickers, of buttons and brochures.

Voters want to know that there are others supporting a candidate before they will do so as well. The field organization gives supporters the feeling of joining an ongoing organization. This is particularly important in statewide campaigns or in campaigns for Congress in geographically large districts. Much of this work is done by volunteers, the type of task that can be completed by those who want to demonstrate support for a candidate, to show the flag.

Some specific campaign tasks are also performed by this organization. Campaign managers like to be able to go door-to-door, to conduct the person-to-person campaign on a large scale which all of them feel is successful on a small scale. This kind of effort must be decentralized. It requires a large number of volunteers, each willing to give a significant amount of time.

Volunteer telephoning often is used as a substitute for door-to-door campaigning in sparsely populated areas, or even in more densely populated areas in which a sufficiently large door-to-door volunteer force cannot be recruited and trained. However, even if a set speech is written for the callers, it is difficult to monitor how many calls are made and what is said by various volunteers, especially since many volunteers prefer phoning from their homes to phoning from a central location. Thus, volunteer telephoning tends to be somewhat unreliable.

As a consequence, many campaigns establish phone banks staffed by trained, paid workers and monitored by a professional staff person. These phone banks are much more easily controlled than are volunteer efforts. Campaign managers can know how many calls are made in an evening, when a certain section of the district or state will be covered, what the response has been to particular appeals. The monitoring staff person can listen in to calls to gauge the effectiveness of the message that is to be delivered or of the appeal of the particular telephone volunteer. Computerized systems are now in use to make these voter calls even more efficient. They represent the ultimate in depersonalizing "personal" contact.

F. Summary

Look back at Figure 7-1. The entire organization is directed toward getting in touch with as many voters as possible in as many effective and efficient ways as possible. Voters are informed about the candidate, through the news media, through paid media, through sessions with the candidate, through mail, or through the campaign efforts of others. An efficient campaign organization will reach each prospective voter a number of times in a number of different ways; most of these appeals will be directed specifically at individual voters. Once voters have been informed about a candidate, they will be asked to support that candidate with their help, with their money, with their votes. They will be asked, again and again, to help in whatever ways are possible. All the efforts of the campaign staff and organization, of the professionals, of the consultants, of the volunteers, are aimed at this goal.

This campaign chart represents "new politics" because of the techniques used. Modern technology has, in fact, replaced older techniques that relied upon person-to-person contact and party allegiance. Now computers, not precinct committeemen, are used to identify and categorize voters, to analyze polling data, to monitor the progress toward reaching certain campaign goals.

Television and radio are used to reach large numbers of voters with messages that were carried by volunteers on foot in an earlier time. Direct mail allows for "personal" contact with significant numbers of voters. Campaign budgets have multiplied to amounts beyond belief even twenty years ago. Professionals are called in to monitor these huge organizations. No candidate can personally manage a major campaign; the two functions (candidacy and management) are separate, and each needs full-time function fillers for a big campaign. However, it is important to keep in mind that the job of the campaign in the modern era is not fundamentally different from what it was in the days before modern techniques changed politics.

IV.   ELECTIONS TO STATE AND LOCAL OFFICE: OLD POLITICS REVISITED

A.   The "Local" Nature of Most Elections

Return still one more time to Figure 7-1; look at the functions that are performed during a campaign. These same functions are performed on campaigns at all levels. But remember the candidate for county supervisor with whom we began this chapter. He staffed the voter registration booth; he put up posters; he scheduled his own time. He was the one shaking the hands of voters at the fair, creating the media event by introducing the Senate candidate, probably with remarks that he himself had labored over. Why was *he* doing all these things himself? Where was *his* organization?

The answer probably is: "He doesn't really have one." How many people can he expect to get excited about working for a candidate for county supervisor? How many people are likely to contribute large sums of money to candidates for county supervisor, clerk of courts, water district commissioner, even city council, school board, state representative, or state senate?

Think about the people who hold these offices in any community. Who are they? What do they do? For such low-visibility offices, do most people really care enough to become involved with active campaigning?

The answer for most of us for most of these offices is a resounding, "Who cares?" When we do care, the reasons are quite obvious. Most often the "organization" of candidates for local offices is made up of friends and neighbors, who are friends and neighbors first and who become involved in politics secondarily.

A personal connection is enough to get someone involved in a campaign. If a neighbor asks for help, a conscientious citizen will probably help in that campaign. Probably she won't become totally engrossed in a campaign; it is unlikely she will make a large financial contribution. But many people will help.

Similarly, these campaigns often involve local issues. If someone is concerned about a particular item on the school board's upcoming agenda, for instance, whether the junior high school should spend more money for football or start a girls' soccer program, he might become involved in a campaign. Often local campaigns are the most intense, because the issues strike closest to home. Issues and personalities are familiar. Neighbors are involved with and against neighbors.

But even when one is involved in these campaigns, the campaign is not of the same scale as a congressional or statewide campaign. With the exception of some of the very largest cities, candidates for city council or school board represent an approachable number of people. The candidate can personally touch those people. Large budgets are not necessary; surrogates are not necessary; complex organizations are not necessary. Furthermore, many of the important campaign functions that help one candidate help all candidates of the same party. Political parties play important roles.

B.   Political Parties: A More Prominent Role

This is not to say that local politics, campaigns for "less" major offices (*all* offices are major to the people seeking them), is a throwback to a time when political parties dominated our political scene. However, *party plays a much more prominent role and the style of campaigning is much more susceptible to party organizational efforts than is the case in larger campaigns.*

Candidates for state and local offices face the same strategic questions that other candidates face. Who are one's likely supporters? Who are those who might be convinced to become supporters? How can these people be convinced? What will draw supporters to the polls? However, these candidates face these questions in an environment, in most cases, in which the public has little awareness or concern about either the candidates or the offices they seek.

Most campaigns for state and local office involve candidates seeking to represent districts that fall within one county, the most common party organizational unit (Eldersveld, 1982). County party activists are familiar with the offices and the candidates; and candidates need only deal with one party committee. Consequently, political party organizations work best in campaigns in districts for which the boundaries coincide with existing party structures.

Furthermore, *party organizations work best at stimulating activity by those who are affiliated with the party.* When candidates are looking for likely supporters, all other things being equal, voters who share party affiliation with them stand out as an obvious target. Thus, candidates are interested in party efforts to register copartisans and to get them out to vote on election day. Those are precisely the kinds of tasks that party organizations still perform quite well.

General election candidates for state and local office rarely have the funds to develop elaborate campaign literature or to purchase expensive media advertising. Party committees often distribute brochures listing all the candidates running under the party label; they are able to organize volunteers who distribute material for a variety of candidates; they will advertise (in a limited way) for all the candidates on the ticket. Again, individual candidates benefit from these activities. If a candidate could do all these things as an individual, that would be preferable. However, joint efforts by the party faithful are better than no efforts at all.

C.   Local Campaigns in the Absence of Party

Campaigns using the party organization work well, if there is a party organization. How does a candidate run when the party organization is nonexistent or inactive, as is the case in many counties throughout the country? Or how does a candidate run if the opposition party is stronger in his or her district, making it necessary to appeal to those in the other party? In these cases it is necessary to return to the original form of "old politics," not party politics, but person-to-person campaigning.

For some candidates, this is what politics is all about, getting to know those who live nearby. In city after city and town after town, evenings and weekends in the autumn see scores of candidates knocking on neighbors' doors. No kind of campaigning is more time-consuming, but none bears greater fruit.

If candidates are willing to devote the time, frequently they can cover an entire district. An early morning breakfast in a country store is more important for a candidate for sheriff than any advertisement the party will take out. Five minutes over coffee in an elderly man's apartment pays more dividends than literature distributed in a shopping center. Politics at these levels is intensely personal.

State and local politics are often low-visibility politics. Citizens vote for someone familiar. If a candidate has taken the time to shake a hand and exchange ideas, that voter will remember. The media, even in small towns, do not give much attention to most local campaigns. Candidates rarely spend more than a few hundred dollars; even in larger areas the thousand dollar race is the exception, not the rule. Most local races are not the campaigns that we think of when we think of politics in America. These campaigns are not the media events, involving politicians who become celebrities, begetting familiar faces on our television screens. But this is what the majority of campaigning in America involves.

Local campaigns with local people are where most politicians start. The roots of most of the politicians who are well known in this country stretch back to local campaigns, to "pressing the flesh," to convincing neighbors that they merit political support. Few politicians forget the early days. Successful campaigners remember the lessons first learned in the quest for some local office. What the local people think remains important to them. As Speaker O'Neill said, "In the final analysis, all politics is local."

V.   DO CAMPAIGNS DETERMINE WHO WIN ELECTIONS?

Earlier in this chapter we discussed conflicting theories about what determines the results of elections. One theory accounted for election results on the basis of aggregate economic conditions in the country. The second theory related electoral results to individual citizens' opinions about conditions in the country. While these theories were developed to explain the results of congressional elections, they should cause anyone reading a chapter on general election campaigns to pause for a moment. Do campaigns—at whatever level—matter?

The answer, simply put, is that they do. Jacobson and Kernell (1983, pp. 29–34) take some pains to demonstrate that the quality of a candidate is an important factor in determining the result of an election. The better candidates, identified as those who have previously achieved electoral success, are more likely to run effectively credible campaigns and, therefore, are more likely to win. (For additional discussions of the importance of candidate quality see Fowler & McClure, 1989; Jacobson, 1987a, 1987b; Maisel, 1989, 1990a.)

In the previous sections we have described how campaign organizations are structured, how campaigns are run, what tasks are performed by whom in a campaign, what strategies and tactics are devised and how they are implemented. In fact, we have been describing how these things are done in well-run campaigns.

For most campaigns, reality does not approximate this ideal. In district after district, in campaign after campaign, in year after year, candidates' names appear on ballots and they are never heard from again. They lose. Most frequently they lose to incumbents.

If no incumbent is running, they lose to the candidate of the dominant party in a particular locale. That they lose is less important than the fact that they never really run a campaign, that the voters are never really given a choice.

Simply put, without competitive campaigning by more than one candidate, the citizens of a district are denied the opportunity to choose. Even if two or more names appear on the ballot, electoral choice is effective only when the citizens are presented with candidates who appear serious to them. If this is not the case, the election goes by default.

For years political scientists have noted that incumbents running for re-election to the Congress have won in large numbers. Many explanations were offered for this phenomenon (Cover, 1977; Ferejohn, 1977; Fiorina, 1977a, 1978; Mayhew, 1974b). In 1978 it was possible, for the first time, to study this phenomenon is some depth, because of the data provided by the National Election Study of that election. The analyses of that election were among the first to demonstrate what Jacobson (1981) has aptly called "the vanishing challengers" (see also Abramowitz, 1981; Hinckley, 1981; Maisel & Cooper, 1981; Mann & Wolfinger, 1980). Whether measured in terms of dollars spent, voter perception, even voter recognition, challengers were basically invisible; incumbents won because no one knew who was running against them.

On the other hand, a similar situation was not identified in Senate campaigns. Incumbent senators were challenged by well-known politicians who ran impressive campaigns. The challengers spent significant amounts of money, were visible throughout the state, were recognized by large percentages of the voters, and were perceived in ways that demonstrated that their campaigns were effective (Abramowitz, 1981; Hinckley, 1981).

While we do not have comparable data to analyze (but see Jewell, 1984), because of the prominence of the office in most states, analysts have speculated that most incumbent governors seeking reelection have also attracted credible challengers. Table 7-3 shows the success rates for gubernatorial challengers in recent elections. Not all incumbent governors are eligible for reelection because of state laws restricting the number of consecutive terms some governors may serve, and so the percentage of incumbents seeking reelection is not so large as it is for senators.

Nonetheless, the data still show that governors seeking reelection do lose more frequently than congressmen, seemingly in numbers more comparable to those for unsuccessful incumbent senators. In fact, the parallel to senators is

TABLE 7-3. Success Rate of Gubernatorial Candidates, 1980–1990

Year	Incumbent Governors Seeking Reelection	Those Successfully Reelected
1980	8	6
1982	15	14
1984	6	4
1986	17	16
1988	9	8
1990	23	17

Source: Compiled by the author.

quite close. At times, elections are quite competitive and many incumbents lose; at other times, this seems less so. The variables at play seem to be particular to one election year and often to one election. Analysts were hard put to explain, for instance, why an anti-incumbent mood in the electorate in 1990 led to the defeat of more incumbent governors than in any other election in two decades while only one incumbent United States senator was defeated and more than 96 percent of the House members seeking reelection were victorious (Idelson, 1990, pp. 3838–3842).

On the other hand, seats in state legislatures do not seem to be so attractive to consistently bring forth large numbers of quality challengers. Table 7-4 shows the number of incumbent state legislators who sought and won reelection in selected states in the period from 1968 through 1986 (Jewell & Breaux, 1988; see Calvert, 1979, for an earlier but similar analysis of a group of twenty-nine states). A large number of these incumbents were reelected without opposition. Recent analysis by Ronald Weber, Harvey Tucker, and Paul Brace (1991) demonstrates that the number of marginal seats and the number of contested seats in a group of twenty states' lower houses declined over the period from 1950 through 1986, though James Garand (1991) warns that a decline in marginality might not necessarily signal a decline in the likelihood of incumbent defeat (see also Jacobson, 1987a).

What can one conclude from these facts? *One obvious interpretation is that what has been happening at the congressional level has been happening at other levels as well. Incumbents are winning because challengers are poor campaigners* (Jewell & Breaux, 1988; Holbrook & Tidmarch, 1991; Weber et al., 1991). When challengers run good campaigns, demonstrated in exceptional case after exceptional case, in state after state, incumbents can lose (Garand, 1991). But good challengers appear too infrequently.

The lack of good challengers and good campaigns insulates incumbent congressmen; in all probability, the same factors insulate those incumbents seeking reelection to other less visible and less attractive offices as well.

Campaigns do matter. The low number of credible campaigns for many offices, and the invulnerability of many incumbents because of the scarcity of these credible campaigns, points to a major flaw in the way in which our electoral system operates.

Is this flaw correctable? What is necessary to run good campaigns? In major elections, the answer that is most often given is money (see, for example, Gierzynski & Breaux, 1990, 1991; Jacobson, 1981, 1985–1986). A good campaign could be run, an incumbent could be seriously challenged, if the opponent's campaign were adequately financed. But this explanation may well beg the question. A challenger's campaign *would* be adequately financed if the challenger were viewed as serious. Serious challengers always appear when the risk of running for office is offset by the attractiveness of the office and the perceived chances of winning.

How can this circle be broken? Two answers seem possible. The 1990 election and the legislative experiences in the 1991–1992 legislative sessions provide hints of one answer. If the electorate becomes dissatisfied with incum-

TABLE 7-4. Incumbents' Reelection Rates in Selected State Legislatures, 1976–1986

State Legislature	% of Incumbents Running for Reelection		% of Incumbents Winning Reelection	
	1968–1976	1978–1986	1968–1976	1978–1986
Connecticut				
Senate	76	82	81	78
House	71	80	82	87
Rhode Island				
Senate	76	74	95	93
House	75	78	92	96
Delaware				
Senate	73	84	92	94
House	62	83	93	89
New York				
Senate	82	88	97	98
House	79	85	90	95
Pennsylvania				
Senate	79	74	89	94
House	81	84	93	97
Michigan				
Senate	74	64	89	99
House	82	79	96	95
Ohio				
Senate	73	81	82	83
House	81	83	94	96
Wisconsin				
Senate	67	75	87	92
House	81	82	90	93
Iowa				
Senate	66	69	77	89
House	67	79	89	92
Missouri				
Senate	67	84	89	99
House	69	84	93	98
Kentucky				
Senate	55	70	79	96
House	67	80	92	96
Colorado				
Senate	60	57	87	96
House	70	70	91	89
Utah				
Senate	70	74	90	81
House	73	72	85	84
California				
Senate	86	81	93	93
House	84	81	95	97

Source: Compiled by the author from data in Jewell & Breaux, 1988.

bents, and this dissatisfaction is widely perceived, then challengers will emerge to give voice to this dissatisfaction. The dissatisfaction was evidenced in the 1990 congressional elections, but it became apparent well after challengers had been selected. Thus, despite the fact that, in House elections, the average incumbent's vote total fell by nearly 5 percent, 96 percent of the incumbents won. Of the twenty-five incumbent representatives whose vote total fell most sharply, over 14 percent in each case, twenty won reelection (R. Cook, 1990). However, the analysts are already looking to the 1992 election to see if the 1990 experience leads to better challengers; the 1992 election will be watched with particular care because it is the first in which members must run in districts that have been reconfigured—in some cases drastically—as a result of population shifts revealed in the 1990 census.

The second answer, clearly related to the first, may well be through a rejuvenation of political parties. Traditionally, as we have seen, political parties controlled access to the ballot. They controlled nominations. When they lost control over nominations, they also lost an important role in the recruiting process. In any case, we know very little about how individuals are recruited to run for office today (Canon, 1990; Cotter et al., 1984; Eldersveld, 1982; Gibson et al., 1985; Maisel, 1991; Maisel et al., 1990; Seligman, 1974; Snowiss, 1966). We do know that many candidates are self-starters, that they themselves determine if and when they will seek office (Maisel, 1986).

However, in the most recent elections, the Republican National Committee has begun to play a more active role in candidate recruitment at all levels (Adamany, 1984; Bibby, 1981, 1991). Jacobson and Kernell (1983) attribute unexpected Republican successes in the 1982 congressional elections to the fact that the Republicans ran a number of very attractive candidates. These candidates did not simply emerge; they were recruited and supported by the national party.

The Republican National Committee is way ahead of its Democratic counterpart in providing services for candidates for office. The Republicans have an advanced fund-raising capability, and they are able to help candidates raise money; in addition, they are able to supply training and services to their candidates which the Democrats cannot match. They even have regional coordinators and field staffs and political operatives assigned to each state to work on elections in those states. This nationalization of congressional politics—an effort that the Democrats are trying to match (Herrnson, 1988)—is an important trend to watch in the future.

But more than that, the successful efforts of the Republican National Committee may set a model not only for the Democrats but also for various state political organizations to mimic (see, e.g., C. Cotter & Bibby, 1980; C. Cotter, Gibson, Bibby, & Huckshorn 1982, 1984; Gibson et al., 1983; Huckshorn et al., 1986).

For some years parties have been looking for a role to play in the era of new politics. Now that role may be emerging. Changes in campaign techniques and in what is expected of candidates, in what is necessary to run for office, have made electoral office less appealing to many prospective qualified candidates and officeholders. The role of the party may well become to recruit these candidates and to support their efforts so that elections in America can become more competitive, so that incumbents will not be guaranteed victory in every election.

As the Republican National Committee staff has moved into fund-raising and polling, into issue research and speech writing, into strategy setting and media advising, other party organizations have seen opportunities to provide services as well. It is becoming more and more clear that parties have an increasing role to play if our electoral system is to become competitive at all levels of government.

VI.   POLITICIANS VIEW THE GENERAL ELECTION

Recall the two candidates with whom we began this chapter. The candidate for county supervisor rearranged other aspects of his life so that he could concentrate on the county fair. For the Senate candidate, the campaign was her life. That defines a critical difference not only between the two individuals, but also between the two jobs.

Think about candidates for different offices. At the more local levels, candidates serve in part-time positions and run quite limited campaigns to get there. Many of these candidates like campaigning. It is a different experience for them. They have the opportunity to meet a variety of interesting people, to observe how people live and what they do for a living, to talk to them about their concerns and about their opinions of government. Even when the campaign is over, they have the opportunity to serve, to work on some of the problems they have learned about, to make their community a better place in which to live. And they also have the opportunity to go back to a more normal kind of existence. They can have dinners with their families, spend weekends in the backyard, shop for groceries without shaking hands. The campaign is what they did for a while to win office; it is not their life's work, certainly not their life itself.

Contrast this normality with the existence—and I have chosen that word carefully—of a member of Congress from a marginal district. Members of Congress in this situation start one campaign the minute the last one ends.

Many of them are at the plant gates the morning after an election, thanking those who voted for them—and hoping that they will remember how much the candidate cared when it came around to voting again. Even those who do not start campaigning for reelection on day one of the new term are constantly campaigning. They come back to the district every weekend, if travel times make it possible. They continue with the same kinds of activities they did in the campaign: speaking to whomever will listen, attending countless suppers, judging at county fairs. During the week they work hard in Congress, but much of their time is spent assuring that their constituents are happy and will vote for them (Cain, Ferejohn, & Fiorina, 1987; Fiorina, 1978; Mayhew, 1974). On weekends and during congressional recesses, they are back in the district. They know that if they work hard, they might be able to squeak out another term. (See Fenno, 1978; Taggart & Durant, 1985.) But what about the rest of their lives—vacations, outings with their children or grandchildren, leisure reading?

Put simply, for many members of Congress, such things do not exist. They rarely see their children or spouses; there is no "rest of their lives." Their only enjoyment is politics. This picture should cause concern. Do we really want to be governed by a group of individuals who are willing to give up their lives to campaign full-time? Even if we are not concerned about the mental health of such individuals,[8] how much can they know about the problems facing their constituents, about the reality of ordinary day-to-day life for the majority of Americans?

Many have expressed concern because members of Congress represent a social and economic elite. Thus, it is argued, they cannot relate to the problems facing middle-class America. The problem may well be more serious than that. Many of today's politicians do not live a real life at all. Not only are they unrepresentative in terms of economic and social indicators; they are even more unrepresentative in terms of their ability to understand the every-day problems Americans face.

Impressionistic evidence indicates that few members of Congress lead "normal" lives, even if normality is defined in as broad a way as is necessary given today's heterogeneous world. Many are single and can imagine no time for a family; the divorce rate on Capitol Hill is very high. Few lead "normal" family lives. Competitive politics at this level has produced a group of officeholders unfamiliar with the daily experiences of most of those they represent.

How do politicians relate to this style of life? A number of responses are possible. Some politicians refuse to enter the arena. Every year political journalists speculate about who are likely candidates for office in a particular region. Every year some refuse to run; some say that they have enough to do where they are now; others are frank in saying that the sacrifices are not worth the honor.

Others immerse themselves in politics totally and then escape. In recent years many have been concerned about the number of members of Congress who are voluntarily retiring, a number that reaches a modern record in 1992 (see, for example, Cooper & West, 1981). Many of these retirees state explicitly that they are leaving because the pressure to campaign is too heavy. Some of the best members of Congress have retired in recent years, often well before the age at which we might normally expect such officeholders to step down. Certainly we could list many reasons for such early retirements besides the exigencies of the two-year election cycle. However, as a matter of public policy, we must be concerned if some of the best officeholders feel that they cannot stay in office and serve because the electoral demands are too costly. Many state legislators, frustrated with the nearly impossible budgetary crises they are faced with in the early 1990s, are making just this decision.

---

[8] One defeated congressional challenger has concluded, "No one can win a congressional seat unless he is willing to campaign full-time twice, knowing that he will lose the first time. Anyone who is willing to do that must be crazy." The reader can draw his or her own conclusion about what that statement says about successful congressional candidates.

A third response is to avoid the pressure of constant election by seeking an office in which one does not face such pressure. In 1992, eleven members of Congress chose not to run for their old seats in order to seek seats in the Senate. One of the reasons for taking this route is that senators face reelection only once every six years, not every other year. Senators campaign very hard in the two years before their term expires, but in the other four years they are much more able to concentrate on the policymaking aspects of their job (Fenno, 1984). In 1990, eight others left the House to seek their state's governorship, again a position with a longer tenure and one that seems to have more likely policy impact.

Not all members of Congress face difficult elections every two years. Some of these members have reached accommodations with their jobs which are not unlike the positions of senators or others who do not feel they must campaign constantly.

When Massachusetts Senator Paul Tsongas decided not to seek reelection in order to spend more time with his family (he was diagnosed as having a serious illness), many speculated that Congressman Barney Frank (D., Mass.) would be among the first in the race for the Senate seat. Frank is one of the more outspoken members of Congress; he won his seat in a hotly contested race when Father Robert Drinan (D., Mass., 1971–1981) was forced not to seek reelection by the papal decree that forbids Catholic clergy from engaging actively in politics. After the 1980 census Frank had to win reelection against Margaret Heckler (R., Mass., 1967–1983) in one of those few races every ten years in which, because of reapportionment in states that have lost seats in Congress, two incumbents must face each other. The Frank-Heckler race in 1982 was the most expensive race in the country. Political journalists conjectured that Frank, fresh from two extremely difficult campaigns, would view the six-year term of a senator as a panacea for all his ills.

Frank saw it differently.

> I've got the best job in the world. Look, I can build up a relationship with this district. I won't have another tough campaign for ten years, when they might fool around with reapportionment again.
>
> I go back to the district every other weekend. I enjoy it. I enjoy what I do there. I can live a normal life here [in Washington]. How many Senators ever live a normal life? They are always in the spotlight. I don't need that.

Frank is satisfied with his life in the House. He, like others who have gained the spotlight in the House of Representatives—men like Thomas Foley (D., Wash., 1965–   ) and his predecessors, such as Tip O'Neill (D., Mass., 1953–1987) or Sam Rayburn (D., Tex., 1913–1961), or congressmen who have dominated particular policy areas, like Carl Vinson (D., 1914–1965) from Georgia or Carl Perkins (D., 1949–1984) from Kentucky, experts on naval matters and education, respectively—have found the House to be a congenial home.

In 1984 Frank had no desire to move on to the Senate. He was making the contributions he wanted in the House. He did not feel that the electoral pressure was burdensome, because he had become comfortable with and to his district. Frank's subsequent electoral experience demonstrates his point. In May of 1987, Frank revealed that he is a homosexual, becoming only the second member of Congress to publicly announce that he is gay. After having won re-election without opposition in 1986, Frank faced a challenger in 1988, but he won with over 70 percent of the vote. In August of 1989 the *Washington Times* revealed that Frank was involved with a male prostitute named Steve Gobie, whom Frank had hired as a household assistant. The House Ethics Committee investigated to determine if Frank had violated any House rules, particularly in response to a charge that Frank had used his influence as a member of Congress to have Gobie's parking tickets fixed. Even after cries for his resignation and weeks of bad publicity, Frank was easily able to weather another serious challenge, winning the 1990 election by nearly 2 to 1. Massachusetts lost a seat in the House as a result of the 1990 census. Frank may well face a difficult race in 1992 in a reconfigured district; but his analysis of the difference between House and Senate seats, at least in his case, seems as prescient as it was nearly a decade ago.

Thus, we see a number of different ways for politicians to respond to general election pressures, from letting politics dominate their entire lives to opting out of the system. How they respond over a period of time is different, however, from how they view general elections in the short run.

The question of how politicians view elections can be approached in two ways. *The first is affectively: what do politicians think about the prospect of campaigning?* As was mentioned earlier in this section, this response varies from individual to individual and may vary as well from office to office and time to time.

Many share the sentiments of an extremely successful politician, who said, "I like lots of it, but not the door-to-door stuff. I feel I am imposing. People are awfully nice, but I feel their home should be their home, not a soapbox for my views." An opposite point of view is represented by Senator William Cohen (R., Me.), who routinely asks people if he can spend the night in their home while campaigning. Cohen figures that people really feel that they know you if they open their home to you and break bread with you in the morning.

Some politicians like talking to big contributors and impressing them with the importance of their election. Others, like the late Senator (1949–1964; 1971–1978) and Vice President (1965–1969) Hubert Humphrey (D., Minn.), found that asking someone for money was the most distasteful part of politics. Some like appearing before large audiences and debating; others are more reticent and seek to have their records speak for themselves.

The list of variations could go on. All that can be said with certainty is that campaigning is a highly personal experience. Some find it totally rewarding in and of itself; others find it a necessary evil withstood in order to attain or hold office.

The second way in which politicians view elections is in a strategic sense: what does this election mean to me? Can I win? What are the costs to me personally? Professionally? From this campaign? What are the costs if I win? What are the costs if I lose? What are the benefits if I win? What are the benefits if I lose?

Were politicians rational men and women in reaching these decisions, they would weigh the costs and benefits carefully and reach judgments based on that evidence. Jacobson and Kernell (1983) lay out this model of electoral decision making and defend it persuasively. On the other hand, Maisel (1982, 1986) demonstrates that politicians do not always behave rationally in reaching decisions about their electoral future. Very often office seekers look at all the facts—as an example the fact that over 90 percent of the incumbent members of Congress seeking reelection are successful—and make decisions assuming, without evidence to sustain the assumption, that they will be among the 10 percent who are exceptions to the rule. Much of their politics comes from the heart, not the mind.

Given this caveat, however, some strategies followed by candidates in the general election reflect their view of this process in the short run. *The objective of the election is not merely to win, but to win by a wide margin.* If a title can be given to this strategy, it would be a "run-scared" strategy. No matter what the evidence says, no matter what one's instincts are, "run scared." Do not appear to be complacent; do not take anything for granted. Build the margin. Assure a big victory; it might frighten away opponents the next time (Goldenberg, Traugott, & Baumgartner, 1986; B. Jackson, 1988; Krasno & Green, 1988; Maisel, 1990b).[9]

Analysts of elections and campaigns describe a rational process. They present a process in which politicians weigh alternatives, reach rational decisions, set appropriate strategies, allocate resources effectively, appeal to the voters persuasively, evaluate their campaigns logically.

The difficulty with this description is that while the entire process viewed as a whole may be rational, individual politicians often act very irrationally. Two seemingly conflicting trends are in evidence. The first is represented by the incumbent member of Congress whose winning percentage has not fallen below 65 percent in ten years, but who is being confronted by one strongly organized group in his district on a particular issue. This politician "runs scared." All evidence from hundreds of campaigns for more than a decade indicates that as an incumbent he is safe. However, for a year he goes home every weekend, spending more time in the district than he has in years. He raises more money than has ever been spent on an election in his district. He employs a professional campaign staff and has it in place before any opposition has surfaced. He campaigns hard throughout the fall, despite the fact that his opponent is unknown and underfinanced.

The second trend could well be represented by his opponent. She believes that the group supporting her has widespread support throughout the district, that that support will carry her to victory. All the evidence about incumbent safety does not deter her. She views this campaign through rose-colored glasses. Objective views of her chances do not mute her optimism. Her efforts are unde-

---

[9] A corollary of this strategy is that if a candidate's chances do not appear strong, she must look for how events could break so that she will have a chance. She seeks the positive interpretation. More votes mean a "symbolic" (if not actual) triumph, and an increase in one's credibility for future campaigns.

terred by the fact that she has little money and is not well known beyond the members of her group. She campaigns hard right up until the election, convinced that the justice of her cause will be sufficient to guarantee victory in the end.

The incumbent wins big. The process is understandable and rational in the overall picture. These two candidates and literally thousands like them campaigning for all sorts of offices all over the country have been acting irrationally. They have been caught up in an amazing exercise in self-deception. Politicians invest so much of themselves in campaigns that they cannot believe that their experiences are not unique.[10]

The November campaigns are a critically important part of politicians' lives. For some, campaigns become too important. These politicians are not willing to put that much of themselves on the line and let others make a judgment about their merit. For others, the election is what their life is all about. Politics is not only a means to an end; it is an end in itself; campaigning becomes not only their life's work, but also their life. For all, it is a deeply personal experience. At whatever level the campaign, the candidate is aware that fellow citizens are making a judgment of him or her. Few can view that process in a detached way, as objective analysts. Most are caught up in the election as one of life's crises, which can only be experienced in the most personal of ways.

Reapportionment and Legislative Redistricting

Article I, Section 2, of the Constitution says, in part:

> Representatives shall be apportioned among the several States which may be included within this Union, according to their respective Numbers. . . .
> The actual Enumeration shall be made within three Years after the First Meeting of the Congress of the United States, and within every subsequent Term of ten Years, in such Manner as they shall by law direct.

Congress has ordered a census every ten years, as the Constitution stipulates. Actually, two processes are involved. Not only is the number of seats that each state is allocated in the House determined by the census (the process of *reapportionment*), but the boundaries of individual districts and of state legislative districts are also redrawn to reflect shifting population patterns (the process of *legislative redistricting*).

During much of the nation's history, the process of reapportionment was made politically painless because Congress continuously voted to expand the size of the House of Representatives. Thus, the House grew from its original 106 members to nearly 400 by 1900. In 1910, however, in part at least because of the size of the chamber, Congress voted to set the size of the House permanently at 435. Since that time this number has only been exceeded for the brief period of time between the admissions of Alaska and Hawaii into the Union and the reap-

---

[10] And, indeed, the few incumbents who lose—and challengers who win—are always the ones that the others recall, not the norm but the aberration.

This famous cartoon, showing redistricting in northeastern Massachusetts, led
to the term "gerrymandering," after its architect Governor Elbridge Gerry, to
describe the practice of drawing district lines in strange shapes to achieve
political goals. (The Bettmann Archive)

portionment following the 1960 census. As a result of the cap on the size of the
House and of shifting population panels, reapportionment has become costly to
some states after every census, with some delegations shrinking to accommodate
growth in others. Since the 1930 reapportionment, a formula has been used which
removes the politics from reapportioning decisions.

The same cannot be said for decisions regarding legislative redistricting
once apportionment is known. Traditionally, district lines have been drawn to accomplish *political* purposes. *Gerrymandering* is a revered part of American political
folklore. Gerrymandering involves drawing districts, often of strange shapes, to
suit the drawer's particular purposes.

In the last fifty years, judicial intervention has led to less blatant gerrymandering when district lines are redrawn. In *Colegrove v. Green*, 328 U.S. 549 (1946), the Supreme Court refused to intervene in a challenge that claimed that congressional districts in Illinois needed to be redrawn because they were of unusual size. The Court held that legislative apportionment was a political question and thus not justiciable. However, in *Baker v. Carr*, 369 U.S. 186 (1962), the Court decided that redistricting was not beyond its purview in all circumstances. The Court was responding to extreme cases of malapportionment; in Tennessee; for instance, state legislative district lines had not been redrawn in sixty years, despite massive population shifts that resulted in some legislators representing 100 times as many citizens as others.

In subsequent rulings (see especially *Gray v. Sanders*, 372 U.S. 368 [1963], and *Wesberry v. Sanders*, 376 U.S. 1 [1964]) the Court established a criterion of "one person–one vote" against which apportionment schemes would be measured (Butler & Cain, 1991; Cain, 1984; Cain & Butler, 1991; Grofman, 1990; Lowenstein, 1991b; Polsby, 1971; Schuck, 1987).

However, judicial regulation does not mean that reapportionment has become apolitical. Political scientists have spent a good deal of time and effort looking at the extent to which redistricting favors incumbents and impacts on subsequent electoral chances (Basehart & Comer, 1991; Born, 1985; Cain, 1985; Gelman & King, 1990; Glazer, Grofman, & Robbins, 1987; King, 1989; Niemi & Jackson, 1991). While the conclusions reached by these scholars lead one to believe that redistricting does not affect one party adversely, nor does it make the ultimate difference in incumbents' reelection bids, there can be no doubt that politicians work very hard to be certain that district boundaries are redrawn so as to meet the judicial criteria but bring as much benefit as possible to those drawing the lines. The Court has moved cautiously into the area of reviewing partisan gerrymandering; in *Davis v. Bandemer*, 478 U.S. 109 (1986), the Court seemed to rule that partisan gerrymandering could be a violation of the equal protection clause of the Constitution, but that the case before the Court did not appear sufficiently egregious to merit judicial intervention (Cain & Butler, 1991, p. 32; Lowenstein, 1991; Schuck, 1987).

Similarly, the Court has stepped gingerly into the area of racial vote dilution by gerrymandering. In these cases the Court was applying the criteria of the Voting Rights Act of 1965 as well as that of the equal protection clause of the Constitution. The Court has wavered between examining whether the *intent* of the redistricting was to dilute racial minorities' power (the standard before the 1982 amendments to the Voting Rights Act) and examining the *effect* of the redistricting, regardless of the intent. Since the Court laid out criteria for examination of unconstitutional dilution of racial minorities' voting power in *Thornburg v. Gingles*, 478 U.S. 30 (1986), state legislatures have looked very carefully at whether the courts might respond that any proposed legislative redistricting plan violated minority rights according to these criteria (Perry, 1991).

The 1990 census seems to have caused particular problems. First, a number of states (and large cities) claimed that the census takers undercounted up to 5 million citizens, most of them minorities living in urban centers. If the Bush administration altered the census count in line with any of the proposed estimates of error, various states stood to gain or lose seats. In fact, the census count was accepted as originally tabulated (though various states have challenged that count in court).

The stakes were so high that lawmakers in state capitols, those charged with redrawing district lines, went about their work very slowly. As late as August of 1991, less than seven months before the first congressional primaries, only seven of the forty-three states with more than one congressional district had drawn their district lines. *Congressional Quarterly*'s commentary on the politics of redistricting used phrases like "both parties have enough power to gum up the redistricting process" in Louisiana or Illinois Democrats "were ready to throw the politically sensitive chore to the courts" (Donovan, 1991, p. 1776).

And the chore was indeed sensitive—and led to some bizarre results. While legislatures are charged with the task of redistricting, sometimes with governors having veto powers and sometimes not,* the actual task of suggesting district lines falls to computer experts who have programmed their machines to draw maps according to certain agreed-upon criteria. Generally the computers have been fed information on racial composition of each voting precinct, on past electoral behavior, and on party registration if that is available. With that information, the computers can draw districts to meet virtually any agreed-upon criteria. In North Carolina in 1991, the criteria included protecting the seat of each incumbent to the extent possible and creating a new black majority seat and a new Republican seat, as well as meeting the court's criteria of populations of each district being as equal as is possible (called for in the case of *Karcher v. Daggett*, 462 U.S. 725 [1983]). The resulting districts surely do not meet the criteria of being "compact and contiguous"; in fact, the Second District looks remarkably like the very district after which gerrymandering was named. (See Figure 7–2.)

All of this is to say that redistricting might well be a more exact art than it once was, that certain democratic principles must be considered, but that in essence the act of redistricting in the 1990s is just as political as it ever was.

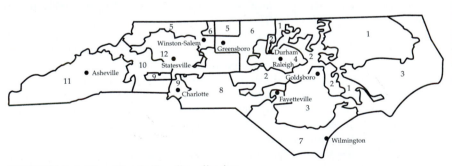

FIGURE 7-2 New North Carolina districts.

Source: *Congressional Quarterly*, July 13, 1991, p. 1917.

_____

* The means of redisricting is set by state law. Some states have special commissions for the purpose. Often the courts are a last resort if the political institutions cannot resolve conflects.

8

Presidential Nominations

The political year 1968 was a watershed in presidential nominating politics. That year, marred by the assassinations of Robert Kennedy and Martin Luther King, Jr., and by the attempted assassination of George Wallace, saw President Lyndon Johnson challenged within his own party and eventually withdrawing from the presidential contest and Vice President Hubert Humphrey, the advocate of the "politics of joy," nominated while the American public watched frustration on the convention floor and violence on the streets of Chicago. Events were set into motion which could not be reversed and which would fundamentally change the ways in which presidential nominees were chosen.

I. THE POST-1968 REFORMS

Democrats competed in fifteen presidential preference primaries in 1968. Senator Robert Kennedy won eleven of the primaries; Senator Eugene McCarthy won the other four. Vice President Hubert Humphrey, the heir apparent after President Johnson withdrew, followed a political strategy in which he avoided confrontation with McCarthy and Kennedy. He did not announce his candidacy until deadlines for filing intentions to run had past in all states. Humphrey backers won just over 2 percent of the primary vote, but votes in primaries did not convert directly to convention votes in 1968. As an example, Senator McCarthy won nearly three-quarters of the votes in the Pennsylvania primary; Vice President Humphrey garnered 80 percent of the Pennsylvania convention votes.

In 1968 primaries were seen as a tool used to influence party officials about electability; they were not a means to "win" a nomination. *The conventional wisdom of party politicians was that the party bosses in the larger states had the power to control the nomination.* They not only believed taht this was true, but also believed that this was as it should be. All of this was to change because of

215

the 1968 Democratic Convention.[1] Needless to say, critics charged that the party was boss-controlled and claimed that the selecton process was undemocratic and unfair.

A.   The McGovern-Fraser Commission

Party leaders responded to this criticism; they saw the frustrations of those who worked within the system. They saw the damage done to the party and the nation by the 1968 nominating process, which so obviously did not reflect the will of those who participated.

Shortly after the 1968 elections, Democratic National Chairman Fred Harris appointed a commission to examine the nominating process. The Commission on Party Structure and Delegate Selection was to be chaired by South Dakota Senator George McGovern, who had taken up the mantle of Senator Kennedy after his assassination. The McGovern Commission (which became known as the McGovern-Fraser Commission after the chairman resigned to run for president and was replaced by Congressman Donald Fraser of Minnesota) began by assessing the situation that existed in 1968. Their general assessment can be summarized succinctly: the "system" was disjointed across geographic lines; the procedures were unfair to many and undemocratic in the broadest

Violence on the streets of Chicago during the 1968 Democratic National Convention symbolized the frustration with the process through which presidential nominees were selected. (Roger Malloch/Magnum)

---

[1] Much of this discussion focuses on the Democratic party because most of the recent reform efforts have been by Democrats. The Republicans have been more satisfied with their procedures but have had to change as well because many of the reforms implemented by the Democrats involved changes in state laws affecting both parties.

sense of that term; the end result did not represent the views of many of those who participated.

Some of the procedures revealed by the McGovern-Fraser Commission seem unbelievable from the perspective of 1993. In two states (Georgia and Louisiana) governors appointed all members of the delegation. State committees appointed all or most of the national convention delegations in eight other states. So disorganized was the situation that no one really knew how the delegations were appointed in many other states. The usual explanation was that party officials met behind closed doors and reached secret accommodations.

None of these revelations was surprising to the professionals in either the Democratic or Republican parties, however, for they made the decisions. From their perspective that was how it should be done.

The McGovern-Fraser Commission's final report, entitled *Mandate for Reform,* specified that nominating procedures must be changed so that the process was *open, timely, and representative.* These goals appeared to be at the heart of a democratic process, but the specific reforms that were suggested, and then accepted as mandatory for state parties for the 1972 nominating process by the Democratic National Committee, rocked the existing system so fundamentally that the ground has yet to settle.

Perhaps the most important guideline promulgated by the McGovern-Fraser Commission was to require that all state parties adopt procedures consistent with the principles it outlined. This requirement with which states had to comply in order to be seated at subsequent national nominating conventions changed the power structure within the Democratic party in a way that has not since been altered.

The eighteen reforms stipulated by the McGovern-Fraser Commission led to the establishment of *one nominating process, with the rules established at the national level by the national Democratic party.* State parties had to adopt and publish written rules that complied with national guidelines.

The McGovern-Fraser guidelines shook party leaders badly. Read with the hindsight of six presidential nominations, they seem to say nothing more than that the procedure should be open, democratic, and representative. Hardly radical notions. However, in 1970, as Democratic state party leaders looked toward the 1972 nomination, many party leaders thought it would be impossible to comply without drastically changing how they operated.

Remember, in 1968 presidential preference primaries had been held in only fifteen states. In some of those states, such as Wisconsin, Oregon, and California, the primaries determined the delegations to the national convention. In many of the other states, such as New Jersey, Pennsylvania, and Illinois, the connection between primaries and convention delegations was less clear. And in thirty-five states, delegates were chosen through some appointive means.

For 1972, two procedures were permissible. States could run *presidential primaries,* under a variety of permissible rules, with the primary result determining at least 90 percent of the state's delegation. Or the states could continue to keep delegate selection a matter for party regulars, selecting delegations through a series of meetings of party members and regulars in a series of local *party caucuses and conventions* organized under the new guidelines.

The differences between primary elections and a caucus/convention system are important and should be made explicit. In a presidential preference primary, party members go to their local polling place and cast a ballot for their preference much as they do in a general election.

In a caucus/convention system, party members go to a meeting; they all must come at the same time and stay for the duration of the meeting. At the meeting or caucus, those in attendance elect representatives to attend another meeting—usually at the county, congressional district, or state level—in proportion to the presidential preferences of those at the caucus. Those at the subsequent meeting (or perhaps a third-level meeting) elect the delegates to the national convention, again in proportion to the presidential preferences of those in attendance.

Does it sound complicated? Party leaders thought so. Many had preferred the caucus/convention system in the past because they could control the results. No public notice; no rules; no stated preferences. But caucuses became more difficult to run under the new guidelines. In many states party leaders felt the procedures were too cumbersome to attempt. Twenty-two states opted to hold presidential preference primaries in 1972; 65 percent of the delegates were chosen in these primaries.

B.   The 1972 Nomination

Imagine that you wrote the rules for a very complicated card game. If hand A were dealt, one set of rules applied; if hand B were dealt, another set of rules came into play; hand C would be played in a different way. Don't you think you would have an advantage the first time you played the game?

George McGovern resigned the chairmanship of the Commission on Party Structure and Delegate Selection after most of the work of that group had been finished. He resigned to run for president—under the new rules, his rules. McGovern chose as his campaign manager and chief strategist a young fellow named Gary Hart, who had been a key staff member of the McGovern Commission. They knew the rules and played them to their advantage.

The key strategy under the new rules was to organize at the grass roots and to compete everywhere. Convention delegates were actually selected in primaries and at caucuses, not by party leaders in secret meetings. The front-runner in 1972 was Maine Senator Edmund S. Muskie, who had impressed the party leaders as Humphrey's vice presidential running mate four years earlier. Muskie followed the old conventional wisdom. He lined up all the party leaders, the opinion leaders in the big states, behind him. Then he proceeded to lose, because they could not deliver. Hubert Humphrey entered the race late, as he had done in 1968, but this time he was too late, for once again party leaders could not deliver. Delegates selected in primaries and caucuses remained loyal to George McGovern, not to local party leaders.

Despite a concerted effort to derail his candidacy, McGovern went on to win the nomination in Miami. The process was not smooth. The openness of the process led to participation by activists interested in discussing controversial issues. The Democratic Convention showed the party for what it was, an amalgamation of differing and competing interests. All the warts were visible to the large national television audience.

When McGovern lost the general electon by a landslide to Richard Nixon, party leaders were quick to blame the new rules. McGovern had been an extremist; he might have been the candidate of women, youth, and minorities, but he was not the candidate of the traditional core of the party. He was not the candidate of the blue-collar, union Democrats. He certainly was not the candidate of the big-city Democrats.

In fact, the rules did not give McGovern the nomination, nor did they cause his defeat. But it was easy to make a logical leap from McGovern rules to McGovern nomination to McGovern debacle. The rules did present something of a conflict between types of representation. As had always been the case, they called for *geographic representation,* now specifying that states break delegations down to more local areas. They also called for *demographic representation,* at least of groups traditionally loyal to and underrepresented in the Democratic party—women, blacks, youth. And they called for representation by candidate preference. Individuals supported presidential candidates based on their views of critical issues; this last type of representation approximated, in the view of many, *ideological representation.*

Critics claimed that the mixing of three kinds of representation, rather than the traditional reliance on geographic representation and domination by party leaders, led to the selection of a new kind of delegate: delegates who were concerned with winning were replaced with issue-oriented delegates who cared more about specific matters of principle than electoral victory. This conclusion has been actively debated (see Kirkpatrick, 1976, 1978; Polsby, 1983; Polsby & Wildavsky, 1988; Ranney, 1975; Sullivan, Nakamura, Weinberg, Arterton, & Pressman, 1977–1978; Sullivan, Pressman, & Arterton, 1976; Sullivan, Pressman, Arterton, Nakamura, & Weinberg, 1977; Wayne, 1988). Regardless of the merits of the debate, party leaders remained concerned about nominating rules, changing them after each subsequent presidential nomination.

C. Continuing Reform of the Process

1. The Mikulski Commission The Mikulski Commission was the first of the "reaction" reform commissions, that is, commissions created by the Democrats as a reaction to the previous year's rules.[2] If the regulars felt they could overturn the McGovern-Fraser reforms with the Mikulski Commission,

---

[2] The post-1972 commission was originally an effort to bring labor back into the fold of the Democratic party. Leonard Woodcock, president of the United Auto Workers, was originally named as the commission chair; Barbara Mikulski, a little-known Baltimore city council member, was named as vice chair. Woodcock resigned, and the leadership role fell to Mikulski. As she has subsequently demonstrated in her congressional career, the fiery Mikulski proved an able and independent leader, not at all what Democratic National Chairman Robert Strauss had in mind when he named her.

they must have been gravely dissatisfied with the results. The commission made a number of concessions to party regulars, but the principles of reform were unchallenged. The major contributions of the Mikulski Commission were *the restriction of participation in the presidential nominating process to Democrats only,* i.e., outlawing the "open" primary, and *the requirement that delegates be allocated proportionally among all contenders receiving at least 15 percent of the votes cast,* i.e., "fair reflection of presidential preference." The legacy of these decisions persists in the nominating process today.

However, while most of the new rules were left intact, state party leaders were given great leeway in interpreting them. The party and the press seemed tired of haggling and fighting over rules, and the 1976 nominating period proceeded without major incident.

2. The 1976 Nomination: Strategies under the New Rules In 1976, thirty states held presidential preference primaries; 76 percent of the delegates to the convention were elected in these primaries. A number of Democrats joined the nominating battle, each eager to demonstrate he had learned the lessons of 1972.

Jimmy Carter, whose term as governor of Georgia expired in 1974, was out campaigning early. He and his chief campaign strategist, Hamilton Jordan, devised a simple, but most effective, strategy. Carter was going to campaign everywhere. Because of proportional representation, he would be guaranteed some delegate support from each state. He would have enough delegate support to be around at the end of the process.

Others strategies were less well thought out. Washington Senator Henry Jackson stayed out of New Hampshire's "first in the nation" primary. This decision allowed Carter to campaign as the only moderate in a sea of liberals in that early test of strength. Positioning himself apart from the pack, Carter "won New Hampshire" with 28 percent of the vote. Jackson's campaign never recovered.

An array of liberals all sought to emulate George McGovern's success of 1972. Morris Udall, congressman from Arizona, was able to separate himself from his fellow liberals but was never able to break through to win a big victory. Udall's campaign was marred by strategic mistakes and unfortunate luck. His losses in Wisconsin and Michigan were each by less than 1 percent of the vote cast and stood as two of his six second-place finishes.

The final challenger to Carter's nomination in 1976 was California Governor Edmund G. (Jerry) Brown, Jr. Brown, like Jackson, entered the race too late. Despite winning the last round of primaries, Brown was too late to stop the Carter march. Despite Carter's losses on the last day of primaries, he still picked up enough delegates to secure the nomination. The convention in New York was a Carter "love-in." The Carter majority was firmly in control of the party machinery.

3. The Winograd Commission In 1976, Democratic Chairman Strauss had appointed Michigan Democratic Chair Morley Winograd as head of a new committee to look at the problem caused by the proliferation of primaries, an unintended consequence of the reforms. The regulars again wanted more control.

The 1976 convention called for another commission, in effect authorizing the extension of the Winograd Commission. However, the new commission was expanded to included representatives of the White House. The not-so-hidden agenda of the commissioners loyal to then President Carter was to assure that the 1980 rules hindered a challenge to the incumbent president.

Despite the fact that Jimmy Carter had been nominated under reform rules, the goal of his supporters was clearly to close the system, to move back from encouraging participation, competition, and an open system. The major contribution of the Winograd Commission was an attempt to shorten the "primary season" by restricting all primaries and first-round caucuses to a three-month period, from early March to early June. This became known as the *"window" concept,* drawing an analogy from the space program which requires a "window" during which launches can be safely attempted. Interestingly, exceptions were allowed for those states that had held caucuses or primaries before the opening of the window in 1976, most notably the early Iowa caucuses and the New Hampshire primary, which had provided the twin launch pads for Jimmy Carter's drive to nomination.

Why restrict the time period? The stated rationale was to shorten the length of campaigns, but it was clear to all that candidates would still start campaigning years in advance of the first official event. The more logical reason was that it would be difficult for a challenger to gain the momentum needed to overcome an incumbent if all the events were closely packed.

Other proposals from the Winograd Commission also represented steps back from reform, designed instead to aid the president's drive for renomination and to increase the power of the party regulars. The principle of "fair reflection of presidential preference" was not repealed, but it was diluted. The threshold of votes necessary in order to receive any representation was raised from 15 to 25 percent, as the campaign progressed.

As another step away from "fair reflection," the Winograd Commission voted to allow "winner-take-all" primaries, if states created single-member districts. The winner-take-all primary at the state level had been eliminated by the McGovern-Fraser Commission. In 1976 various states had run "loophole" primaries, winner-take-all at the congressional district level. That loophole had been closed, over Carter campaign staff objections, by the 1976 convention's adoption of the report of the Rules Committee. The Winograd Commission created a new "loophole," because it appeared that most of the single-member districts to be created would favor Carter. Jimmy Carter tried to take advantage of his incumbency to change the system to his advantage.

4. The 1980 Nomination and the Hunt Commission

The relevant aspect of the 1980 nomination for the purpose of this review of procedural reforms is that Jimmy Carter won renomination despite the fact that by the time the Democratic National Convention ratified his renomination most party officials felt he was bound to lose the general election to Ronald Reagan. The response to this situation was predictable, another "reform" commission. The goals of this new commission, chaired by North Carolina Governor James B. Hunt, Jr., were simply to strengthen the party, to increase the role of party regulars to help the party win elections, and to ensure that the party could govern once in office (Crotty, 1983, p. 88). What could be easier?

One could also argue that this was the "reaction to the Jimmy Carter" commission. Carter had been the outsider who had won control of the party because of the openness of the rules. Once in office he had difficulty governing, in large part because he was an outsider. As the incumbent president, he controlled the party machinery and won renomination, despite the fact that other elected officials doubted he could win.

The Hunt Commission reaffirmed many of the positions taken by previous commissions. *First, it reasserted that the Democratic party nominating process should be open only to Democrats.* The "open primary" was not to be used in any way for selecting delegates to the national convention.[3] Second, it examined the question of minority representation to national conventions, concentrating on the problem of underrepresentation of low-income Democrats. Although encouraging participation by these groups, no mandatory steps were included.

Third, it accepted the window concept, again arguing that a shortened period would shorten the campaign. The commission took this position despite the fact that such a position flew in the face of reality; candidates simply campaign for up to four years in order to be ready for the opening of the window. State after state has devised systems to test strength before the window opens, so candidates fight the battles of the Iowa, Florida, and Maine "straw poll." The Hunt Commission again acquiesced to the desires of Iowa and New Hampshire state party leaders but shortened the "prewindow" exception to two weeks for Iowa and one for New Hampshire.

The Hunt Commission took three positions that changed the 1980 rules for 1984. *First, it unbound the delegates,* returning to a commitment of "good conscience" as the constraint for whether or not delegates could switch from the candidate to whom they had been pledged. This change was more symbolic than real. Given the fact that presidential contenders can approve delegate candidates pledged to them and that delegate candidates are generally among the most committed supporters of the presidential candidates, it is highly unlikely than many would ever switch. This had been demonstrated in delegate support for candidate positions on important rule controversies, including prenomination announcement of vice presidential selection at the 1976 Republican Convention and freeing of "robot delegates" at the 1980 Democratic Convention. Nonetheless some felt this an important issue and the Hunt Commission felt their concern.

---

[3] As a result of this decision, ratified by the Supreme Court in *Democratic Party of the United States v. Wisconsin,* 450 U.S. 107 (1980), Wisconsin and other states hold "beauty contest" open primaries that have no role in determining the composition of the state's delegation to the national convention; the delegations are chosen through a caucus/convention system.

Second, the commission relaxed the rules on proportional representation while maintaining that they were reaffirming the principle of "fair reflection." Their logic was questionable, and the rules they created were more complex than any previously in existence. The result was a reinstitution of "loophole" primaries at the congressional district level in a number of states. This change, a concession to party officials, had a significant impact on the outcome of the 1984 Democratic nomination.

Finally, and most importantly, the Hunt Commission offered a proposal to increase significantly the impact of elected officials at the national convention. The commission reaffirmed the Winograd Commission's "add-on" delegates, but supplemented these with a new category of delegates, quickly dubbed *superdelegates*. These individuals were to be prominent party and/or elected officials, e.g., governors, senators, or congressmen, who had played key roles at conventions before the reforms but whose participation levels had declined. The superdelegates were to come to the convention officially unpledged. The theory was that they would bring practical experience to the convention and help nominate a winning ticket should a situation such as the one that the Democrats faced in 1980 reemerge.

The practice turned out to be quite different. These delegates were selected quite early—in the case of congressional and senatorial delegates—and presidential contenders sought and received their endorsements. If nothing else, however, those most concerned with the elections could no longer claim that they did not have a vote or a stake in the process, and many officials were directly connected with the candidate selected (Mann, 1985).

5. The Fairness Commission and the 1988 Nominating Process Walter Mondale benefited from the rules promulgated by the Hunt Commission. As mentioned, the superdelegates were chosen early and most of them favored Mondale. Moreover, Mondale did very well in those states that held "loophole" primaries, that is, "winner-take-all" or "winner-take-more" primaries. As a result, Mondale had a higher percentage of delegates to the 1984 convention than his voting strength in the primaries or first-round caucuses would have dictated.

The losing candidates at the 1984 convention—Senator Gary Hart and the Reverend Jesse Jackson—were upset by the advantage that the rules gave to Mondale. As a consequence, they called for a new reform commission, a so-called Fairness Commission, to examine what steps could be taken to respond to their complaints. The Mondale forces, magnanimous in victory at the convention, acceded to their request for a new study.

By the time the Fairness Commission began its work, a number of factors had changed. First, Mondale had been badly beaten in the presidential election. Second, Hart and Jackson had lost some of their concern for this particular part of the process. Third, Paul Kirk had become chair of the Democratic National Committee and was intent on strengthening the party. He viewed an increased role for party and elected officials as important in building a strong party.

The Fairness Commission finished its work by November 1985. According to Commission Chairman Donald L. Fowler, a long-time party activist from

South Carolina, "There was a recognition that the 1984 rules worked pretty well and there was no reason to change a lot" (R. Cook, 1986, p. 2158). The commission increased the number of party and elected officials who would be delegates to the 1988 Democratic National Convention, granting superdelegate status to all members of the Democratic National Committee (not just state party chairs and vice chairs as had been the case in 1984) and to 80 percent of the Democratic members of Congress (up from 60 percent in 1984). While the commission did lower the share of the vote that a candidate must receive in order to qualify for delegates to 15 percent from the 20 percent it had been in some states, a move in the direction favored by the Hart and Jackson forces at the 1984 convention, the ability of states to hold winner-take-all or winner-take-more primaries was reaffirmed.

In short, the commission adopted the notion that the name of the game for 1988 was to create a process that would bring more people into line behind the Democratic party candidate. New Hampshire and Iowa were permitted to keep their early dates for their primary and caucus, respectively; Wisconsin Democrats were even permitted to reinstitute their "open" primary, which had been ruled out some years earlier. No party obstacles were to stand in the way of Democrats being happy with the Democratic candidate.

However, while the party rules were not changed as a result of the 1984 nominating process, some states did alter their laws in ways that had a fundamental effect on the 1988 process. In 1984, the second Tuesday in March, so-called Super Tuesday, was the first date on which a large number of delegates were selected. Many viewed the influence of the states holding primaries on that date (or caucuses within that week) as having been significantly increased. Mondale's victories in Georgia and Alabama allowed him to begin the process of turning back the tide that Hart had begun to mount in Iowa and New Hampshire.

Southern politicians hit upon concentrating their delegate selection processes early as a strategy for increasing their influence. They felt that the voice of the south would be heard most loudly if it was all spoken at the same time. Thus, southern state after southern state took the steps necessary to move their delegate selection process up to the second week in March 1988. This effort was led by influential southern governors like Robert Graham of Florida, Richard Riley of South Carolina, Mark White of Texas, and ex-Governor Charles Robb of Virginia. Eventually twenty-one states—including fourteen southern or border states—chose convention delegates during this one-week period; more than a quarter of the delegates to the 1988 Democratic convention and more than 35 percent of those elected to the Republican convention were chosen during this one period.

This change was as significant as any rule changes in recent years. Candidates and their strategists had to rethink how one organized the early stages of the nominating process. As with many "reforms," unintended consequences are often as apparent as intended consequences. For the Democrats, the "winners" of the Super Tuesday sweepstakes were Mike Dukakis and Jesse Jackson as well as Tennessee Senator Al Gore, who took up the mantle of the southern moder-

Reprinted with permission of MacNelly and *The Chicago Tribune.*

ates. Clearly devising a system to help Dukakis and Jackson was not what the southern governors pushing this change had in mind. For the Republicans the clear winner was George Bush, who had more than 60 percent of the delegates needed to be nominated by the end of balloting on Super Tuesday. Again, Bush was not the candidate most reformers thought would have benefited from this change.

However, the reforms can be looked at another way. The 1984 process in the Democratic party had produced a candidate who represented the mainstream of the party. He might have lost badly in November, and he might not have achieved the nomination with the ease desired, but the process had avoided nominating an extremist or nominating an outsider. The election of 1988 was the first in twenty years in which an incumbent president was not eligible for reelection. Each party sought to nominate a candidate who could bring the faithful together to achieve victory in November. And each aptly did that. The process worked as theorists of political parties would want it to work. As Gerald Pomper (1989) has written:

> To achieve victory, they seek politically adept but inoffensive candidates and pursue party unity by conciliating diverse factions, promoting agreement on public policies, and focusing party members' efforts on effective campaigns. . . . In nominating Michael Dukakis and George Bush, they chose two men who were experienced politicians with extensive records of public service, men who, if not stirring, were at least acceptable to tens of millions of their party's voters. (p. 33)

6. Toward 1992 Thus, in 1988 the system worked as it was designed to. Party leaders looked at the results—and while the Democrats might have been dismayed by Dukakis's showing in the general election—they were satisfied with how he was nominated. The only rule changes for the 1992 process involved guaranteeing proportional representation of presidential preference for all states' systems, removing the vestiges of loopholes.

Once again, however, various states, worrying that they did not have enough influence, have sought to move earlier in the process. Because a number of states have moved earlier in the process, and because some southern states have opted out of the early primary, the uniquely southern flavor of Super Tuesday has been diluted. In 1992, candidates for nomination faced a three-week period in March in which twenty-three states chose a total of over 1700 convention delegates, nearly 40 percent of the total.

No one knows whether this front-loaded process will narrow the field and allow for a party consensus to the extent that that happened in 1988.[4] In many ways the concentration of early primaries makes the process resemble a national primary—and the nation has no experience with a national primary. Because of the requirement for proportional representation, it will be more difficult for a clear leader to emerge if the field is composed of equally strong candidates. This could well enhance the role of the superdelegates (Balz, 1991). The result could be confusion as the process emerges, a brokering of delegates, perhaps even a bartered convention. Or, perhaps, a leader will emerge and the process will work as efficiently as it did in 1988.

D. The Reform Movement—An Assessment

Compare the experience of the Democrats with that of the Republicans. We have just discussed four major reform commissions (and one minor one after 1988) in the Democratic party, one for every election since 1968. The Republicans by contrast have been blissfully happy with their system. This is not to suggest that they have not had reform commissions. One was established at the behest of former President Eisenhower after the 1964 Republican Convention appeared on television. A second, the DO (Delegates and Organizations) Committee, established after the 1968 convention, was dominated by members of the Republican National Committee and dealt with no controversial matters. A third, the Rule 20 Committee, chaired by the late William R. Steiger, a moderate Republican congressman from Wisconsin (1967–1978), dealt with disclosing campaign expenditures by Republican candidates and with opening up the party to broader participation.

A number of factors distinguish Republican reform efforts from Democratic. First, *Republicans, even when their nomination has been hotly contested, have not divided their party because of the nominating process.* Each of the last six Republican nominees has had a united party behind him once the convention had reached its decision.

Second, *Republican "reforms" have been suggestions, not mandates.* Philosophically the Republicans do not believe that the national party should dictate

---

[4] The Republicans are not worried this time, as they assume President Bush will be renominated without opposition.

to the states. Certainly they do not believe that a committee of reformers should dictate procedures. The Republican party rules state clearly that the convention is the governing authority. Only the convention can change the rules. Thus any reform would have to be ratified by one convention to take effect in the process four years hence. As it is quite difficult to foresee the impact of some of these reforms, the lack of predictable detrimental political consequences has taken much of the sting out of Republican reform efforts.

However, the Republican process has changed significantly because some of the changes wrought by the Democrats have resulted in changes in state laws which also impact on the Republicans. Look at Table 8-1. In 1968, sixteen states chose delegates to the Republican National Convention through the primary process; 34 percent of the delegates were chosen in that way. By 1988, these numbers had changed to thirty-five states holding primaries and 77 percent of the delegates being chosen in that manner. The Democrats instituted the changes, but the Republicans were forced to follow suit. The Ford nomination battle in 1976, Reagan's in 1980, and Bush's in 1988 were fought and won under rules very different from those in effect when Barry Goldwater captured the hearts of the Republican party in 1964.

The reforms begun in 1968 have fundamentally changed the ways in which the two parties nominate their presidential candidates. The conventional wisdom before 1968 was that party leaders in large states had the most influence over the nominations. The conventional wisdom for 1988 was that the process was open and that demonstrated success in attracting voters was necessary in order to win (R. Cook, 1989; Pomper, 1989b). The delegates to the national conventions are now representatives of those who have participated in the process.

Party leaders and elected officeholders still retain influence, but the change in their role in the last twenty years may provide a perfect example of the difference between influence and power. The strategic premises of presidential contenders in 1960 were not very different from those of 1948 nor for that matter from those of 1928. But since 1968, the situation has been one of continual flux. Winning in 1988 involved mastering the rules, reading the political lay of the land, and learning the right lessons from the most recent contests.

TABLE 8-1. Number of Presidential Primaries and Percentage of Delegates Chosen in Them, 1968–1988

	Democrats		Republicans	
	No. of Primaries	% of Delegates	No. of Primaries	% of Delegates
1968	17	38	16	34
1972	23	61	22	53
1976	29	73	28	68
1980	31	75	35	74
1984	24	61	23	54
1988	34	85	35	77

Source: Data for 1968–1980 are from Wayne (1984) and for 1988 from *Congressional Quarterly* sources.

II.   THE CONTESTS FOR NOMINATIONS

The nomination process is, by its very nature, complex. The goal is to winnow the field of potential presidents down from all those eligible to two, one Democrat and one Republican. What criteria are used? Obviously a principal concern is to find an individual qualified to hold the office, but that concern is for naught if the individual cannot win the general election. Thus, the parties are looking for the individual who will be *the best candidate and the best president*. Those are two separate jobs; different skills are called for in the two. How should those skills be combined?

Perhaps a group of politicos reasoning together could arrive at the perfect mixture of skills and seek the best-qualified individual. But that is not the nature of our political system. The individuals selected are selected through a political process. More accurately, they are chosen through different political processes in each of the fifty states (and the District of Columbia and various other areas). And they are chosen by a large number of participants, each of whom is free to choose based on his or her own conception of how the choice should be made. It is small wonder then that the process is characterized most by complexity.

Presidential contenders must face a complex process, with uncertain dynamics. They do not control the order of events, though they do have some say in the amount of importance they attribute to different events. They do not control others' perceptions of events. To a large extent they proceed by instinct; success or failure is often a function of the acuity of political instincts.

A.   Lessons from the Recent Past

Politicians as a group are firm believers in learning the lessons of the past. Given that, it is somewhat unbelievable how many politicians have learned the wrong lessons from even very recent experiences. A brief listing should be illustrative.

In 1972 Senator Edmund S. Muskie lost the front-runner status by learning the wrong lessons from 1968. He attracted the support of all the big-name politicians he could; he did not realize that the rules had changed and that the 1972 nomination was to be won at the grass-roots level.

In 1976 Congressman Morris Udall (and many others) lost because he tried to follow the McGovern strategy of 1972. He saw the McGovern strategy as capturing the liberal, activist wing of the party. The real McGovern strategy was to have some support everywhere, to win some delegates everywhere, and to differentiate his candidacy from those of the others. Only Jimmy Carter and Hamilton Jordan saw that. They won. (See Pomper, 1977; Schram, 1977; Witcover, 1977).

In 1980 Jimmy Carter's "go everywhere" strategy was emulated by Senator Ted Kennedy in the Democratic primaries and caucuses and by most of the Republican contenders. But the Carter strategy worked in 1976 because he was the only candidate following it. If others had followed that strategy, it would have failed.

Other lessons could have been learned from 1976. Jimmy Carter lost six of the last seven primaries in that year. He was ahead and became the target for others to shoot at. He learned that lesson and, in 1980, did an amazing job of making Senator Kennedy the target, despite the fact that he, Carter, not Kennedy, was the incumbent with an unimpressive four years to explain. Of course, the hostage situation in Iran and Senator Kennedy's own faulty campaign aided the Carter effort. (See Germond & Witcover, 1981; Polsby, 1981; Pomper, 1981b.)

Ronald Reagan also learned the appropriate lessons from 1976. He was the front-runner, but he stayed above the fray in Iowa, not presenting himself as a target. George Bush followed a brilliant strategy in Iowa, learning another lesson from 1976. He emphasized Iowa to the exclusion of almost all other states. The Iowa caucus turned into what Senator Howard Baker has called "the functional equivalent of a primary." The Reagan campaign set a goal for Reagan votes; they exceeded that goal, but still lost.

George Bush had separated himself from the rest of the field. He might have been able to set his sights on the nomination but for a brilliant strategic move by Reagan which turned the tables on Bush. At the famous debate in Nashua, New Hampshire, Reagan's strategy was to make Bush the enemy, the target of all the others. Bush tried to exclude the other candidates; Reagan was willing to be fair to all. Bush faltered.

John Anderson became the darling of the press, winning the moderate wing of the Republican party. But the moderate wing of the Republican party is a minority wing and thus Anderson was no match for Reagan; in Illinois, Anderson's home state, Reagan made Anderson the target. Anderson reeled and eventually fell. By the end Reagan was alone. It was too late for the others to attack him. (See Germond & Witcover, 1981; C. Jones, 1981b; Pomper, 1981b.)

In the political year 1984 only the Democratic contenders had to worry about the lessons of the past. President Reagan was not challenged for the Republican nomination. Again the rules were somewhat changed. As Table 8-2 shows, many states chose to select delegates to the national convention early in the process; the conventional wisdom was that the front-loading of the system helped the front-runner, former Vice President Walter Mondale. Furthermore the superdelegates were something of an unknown. Again, however, the assumption was that they would favor Mondale, a known commodity who had served with many of them.

Mondale did not learn the Reagan lesson of 1980. Because he was apparently alone at the front, he presented himself as a tempting target and never sought to diffuse the attacks as the others took their best shots. Although Mondale captured the endorsements of virtually all groups willing to make endorsements, he was quickly dubbed the candidate of the special interests. He looked old and tired. And he was tied to Jimmy Carter.

The Mondale candidacy showed a new problem in presidential campaigning, the *vice president problem*. Under the old rules, vice presidents made the move to presidential nominee with some regularity. They knew the political leaders and were well known nationally. Vice presidents still gain name recognition under the new rules, but this is a mixed blessing. If the president is unpop-

TABLE 8-2. Presidential Primary Calendar, 1984–1992

Date	Year		
	1984	**1988**	**1992, Democratic dates only**
February 16		New Hampshire	
18			New Hampshire
25			South Dakota
28	New Hampshire		
Total delegates selected to date*	232 (5.9%)	142 (2.1%)	105 (2.5%)
March 1		Vermont (D.)†	
3			
			Colorado
			Maryland
6	Vermont		
7			South Carolina
8		Alabama	
		Arkansas	
		Florida	
		Georgia	
		Kentucky	
		Louisiana	
		Maryland	
		Massachusetts	
		Mississippi	
		Missouri	
		North Carolina	
		Oklahoma	
		Rhode Island	
		Tennessee	
		Texas	
		Virginia (D.)	
10			Florida
			Georgia
			Louisiana
			Massachusetts
			Mississippi
			Oklahoma
			Rhode Island
			Tennessee
			Texas
13	Alabama		
	Florida		
	Georgia		
	Massachusetts		
	Rhode Island		
15		Illinois	
17			Illnois
			Michigan
20	Illinois	Puerto Rico	
24			Connecticut

TABLE 8-2. Presidential Primary Calendar, 1984–1992 (*cont.*)

Date		1984	1988	1992, Democratic dates only
			Year	
	26		Michigan (D.)	
	27	Connecticut		
	29		Connecticut	
Total delegates selected to date		1422 (36.1%)	1818 (43.6%)	2427 (56.7%)
April	3	New York Wisconsin		
	5		Wisconsin	
	7			New York Wisconsin
	10	Pennsylvania		
	19		New York (D.)	
	26		Pennsylvania	
	28			Pennsylvania
Total delegates selected to date		2091 (53.2%)	2729 (65.5%)	3081 (71.9%)
May	1	district of Columbia Tennessee		
	3		District of Columbia Indiana Ohio	
	5	Louisiana		District of Columbia Indiana North Carolina Ohio
	8	Indiana Maryland North Carolina Ohio		
	10		Nevada (D.) Wyoming (D.) Nebraska (R.) West Virginia (R.)	
	12			Nebraska West Virginia
	15	Nebraska Oregon		
	17		Oregon	
	19			Oregon
	24		Idaho (R.)	
	26			Arkansas Kentucky
Total delegates elected to date		3231 (82.2%)	3192 (76.6%)	3604 (84.1%)
June	2			Alabama

TABLE 8-2. Presidential Primary Calendar, 1984–1992 (*cont.*)

| | Year | | |
Date	1984	1988	1992, Democratic dates only
			California
			Montana
			New Jersey
			New Mexico
5	California		
	New Jersey		
	New Mexico		
	South Dakota		
	West Virginia		
7		California	
		Montana	
		New Jersey	
		New Mexico	
12	North Dakota		
Total delegates selected to date	3859 (98.1%)	3814 (91.6%)	4153 (96.4%)

* Total delegates to date represent the number and percentage of delegates to the Democratic National Convention chosen by the end of each month (including those not chosen in primaries).
† Primaries were held in each party unless one is specifically designated.

ular, as Johnson and Carter were when they left office, the vice president is either tied to unpopular programs or susceptible to charges of disloyalty—caught between a political rock and a hard place with no easy way out.[5]

Colorado Senator Gary Hart certainly learned lessons from 1980. He ignored the conventional wisdom that the compressed schedule made Iowa and New Hampshire less important. By making Mondale the target, by successfully distinguishing himself from other contenders as the candidate of a new generation, and by concentrating almost all his resources on these early states, Hart was able to come out of the pack and move into a leading position. These early victories started a movement to Hart which appeared to be unstoppable. No candidate in recent history had been derailed in New Hampshire as had Mondale and been able to come back.

Enter Emma, "Where's the beef?" Never before had a television product commercial taken on such significance in American politics. Mondale's attempt at humor made him appear much more human. And he attacked. He fought for his political life. He struggled back, leaning on all those special interests whose support had cost him earlier, calling in chits from his days as vice president, drawing on old allegiances and loyalties. He won a long, hard struggle. If Jimmy Carter's victory was a marathon run, Fritz Mondale's nomination resulted from

[5] On the other hand, the experience of George Bush in 1988 demonstrates that, if skillfully played, the vice presidency can still prove an advantage. Bush rode into the nomination on the coattails of a popular president, emphasizing whenever he could that he had been loyal to Ronald Reagan.

a fifteen-round heavyweight championship. The winner was the one still standing at the end. (See M. Nelson, 1985; Pomper, 1985; Ranney, 1985.)

Lessons were drawn from 1984, too. Why did Mondale win? How did he recover? What about the endorsements of special interests? Of the superdelegates? What can be learned from Jesse Jackson's success using the free media? (See Barker, 1988; Barker & Walter, 1989; Reed, 1986, chap. 2.) Both major parties had "open" contests in 1988, with no incumbent running and large numbers of candidates running. Kansas Senator Bob Dole learned the lesson of Iowa; win an upset early and that may separate you from the pack. But frontrunner George Bush also had learned. He knew he could not afford to lose New Hampshire after having lost Iowa, and so he pulled all the stops and regained the advantage he had lost in the early caucuses. He also learned the Mondale lesson of raising money and organizing early; he alone of the Republican candidates was capable of contesting the Super Tuesday contests in all twenty-one states. He did so; he did so well; and he sewed up the nomination early.

Democrats too learned the lessons. Mike Dukakis knew he had to make a respectable showing in Iowa in order to hold on to New Hampshire. He did both. But mostly he too learned the lesson of Super Tuesday from Mondale. He used his money wisely and won in a variety of states on Super Tuesday. And like Mondale, he had enough left over to go the long haul, to continue winning when others had to drop out (Black, Blake, Farrell, Oliphant, & Vennochi, 1988). Jesse Jackson also showed that his campaign represented a different kind of politics in 1984—and that that could work again in 1988. He won untraditionally, running an inexpensive campaign, using unpaid media more than paid, assuring that everyone paid attention to him. He competed and won where he was strong. And he was most effective in doing so, establishing himself as a most serious player in the game of nomination politics. The other candidates were less effective in learning from the past, but the question remains whether winning strategies were available to them. (See Buell & Sigelman, 1991; Germond & Witcover, 1989; M. Nelson, 1989; Pomper, 1989b.)

III. STRATEGIC CONSIDERATIONS

In examining the presidential nominating process, any candidate and his supporters try to draw lessons from the past—as demonstrated above—and apply them to new situations. Winners do this well; losers do this poorly. In any case, a number of strategic considerations must be taken into account in any nomination struggle.

A. Momentum

Dandy Don Meredith and Howard Cosell, with their banalities on *Monday Night Football,* have ruined the concept of "momentum" for a generation of Americans. Just because sports commentators have overused and abused the term does not mean it should be trivialized.

Every candidate must know where he or she starts. If a candidate starts behind, the campaign must get going fast enough to show movement, to convince others that gaining ground is possible, to gain media attention, and to raise money. Early strong showings contribute to this. Jimmy Carter in 1976 did this in Iowa and New Hampshire. Gary Hart did the same in 1984. Those who cannot gain momentum are often lost. Senators Fritz Hollings (D., S.C.) and Alan Cranston (D., Calif.) thought they would do well in early states in 1984; they did not, and their campaigns ended early. Jack Kemp and Reverend Pat Robertson each felt that they would benefit from early momentum by winning Michigan, whose Republican delegates were contested under unique caucus rules in January 1988, even before the Iowa caucuses and the New Hampshire primary. They combined to upset Vice President Bush, but neither was able to carry momentum over into those states the media more traditionally viewed as the first tests (Dionne, 1988). Former Arizona Governor Bruce Babbit and Illinois Senator Paul Simon, on the Democratic side, and Delaware Governor Pierre DuPont and former Secretary of State Alexander Haig, on the Republican side, all failed to make significant progress in the early rounds in 1988. They essentially were never factors in the nominating process after the very first rounds (R. Cook, 1989; Germond & Witcover, 1989; Pomper, 1989b).

If one is ahead, one must also maintain momentum. Ted Kennedy started with momentum in 1980; Jimmy Carter was unpopular among the public at large and among activist Democrats. But Kennedy lost his momentum early because he and his campaign organization were not ready for the task at hand. He could not even answer the simple question of why he wanted to be president when Roger Mudd asked him during an interview early in the campaign. Kennedy's campaign could not recover (Polsby, 1981; Pomper, 1981b).

Ronald Reagan was temporarily knocked off track in 1980; he came right back attacking and winning in New Hampshire. Any delay and he might well have lost the nomination (C. Jones, 1981b). The same is true of the Mondale campaign after he lost the New Hampshire primary to Hart. Had Mondale not attacked (and won) in Alabama and Georgia when the next series of primaries were held, he could have packed up his tent very early.

The need to maintain momentum was uppermost in leading contenders' minds in 1988. Vice President Bush knew that he would have difficulty in Iowa, because he was tied to President Reagan's unpopular farm policies. Thus, New Hampshire became critical for him. He had to win in order to take advantage of the organization he had built up and the money he had available for the Super Tuesday states. All of that would have been for naught had he been dubbed a loser after New Hampshire. Thus, he was willing to "go negative" with his advertising on the eve of that state's crucial primary; he was willing to do whatever was necessary to keep his campaign alive.

Similarly, Mike Dukakis faced a difficult situation. He expected to win in New Hampshire, many of whose citizens receive Boston television stations and read Boston newspapers. But Dukakis had to make a credible showing in Iowa so that he did not suffer the fate of others who went into New Hampshire a favorite and emerged in trouble. Again, momentum from New Hampshire was critical to making Dukakis a central player (along with Jesse Jackson and Tennessee Senator Albert Gore, who was pursuing a southern strategy and concentrating solely on the southern Super Tuesday states) on the day in which so many delegates would be selected. In Dukakis's case, some momentum from Iowa, enough to distinguish him from the "field" players, was needed to assure victory in New Hampshire (Black et al., 1988; Germond & Witcover, 1989; Pomper, 1989b).

The analogy between sports and politics is misleading in many ways, but the two places in which the analogy does hold are the necessity to come back right away when one is down and the need to show movement, to expand the lead if one is ahead or to close the gap if one is behind.

B.   Use of Resources

Any serious candidate for president starts the campaign possessing certain resources. Others can be obtained. Still others must be done without. Campaign strategists are often in the business of resource management.

1.   Office The key resource to hold if one wants a presidential nomination seems to be the White House. Eligible incumbent presidents are normally renominated. Renomination may be semiautomatic, resembling coronations, as in the cases of Richard Nixon in 1972 and Ronald Reagan in 1984. Or renomination may require a battle, as was the case with Jimmy Carter in 1980 and Gerald Ford in 1976.

These latter cases are particularly instructive. Carter used the White House to defeat Senator Kennedy. He played a Rose Garden strategy, claiming to be too busy to campaign, for as long as it suited him. At the same time he used the resources of his office—the pulpit from which to speak, cabinet officers to serve as surrogates, federal grants to remind voters of his service—to enhance his campaign. When the situation suited his political purpose, he emerged from the Rose Garden, campaigning with all the trappings of the office to which he had been elected (Germond & Witcover, 1981).

Gerald Ford nearly lost the nomination to Ronald Reagan in 1976. Ford was not very successful at using the office, largely because he had not become used to the office and had not had time to learn from it. Further, Ford had not earned the office through election; thus, he did not have the loyalty of legions of politicians who owed office to him, as does a president elected in his own right. However, it is doubtful Ford ever could have competed with Ronald Reagan if he did not have his incumbency to rely on (Witcover, 1977).

Other offices have also proved useful. We have already discussed the advantages and disadvantages of the vice presidency. The problem faced by former Vice President Mondale had to be overcome. On the other hand Vice President Bush, in 1988, had a tremendous advantage. His only problem was to convince Reagan supporters that he was not only a loyal lieutenant but also a worthy heir.

For some time the Senate was thought to be the incubator of presidential candidates. Twenty-five different senators have run for their party's presidential nomination since 1968 (see Table 8-3). In 1980 Senator Howard Baker of Tennessee tried to parlay his prominence as Senate minority leader into a successful bid for his party's nomination. Senator Robert Dole did the same in 1988. Neither was successful. Dole could not overcome the advantages that a sitting vice president had as heir apparent. Baker found he was too busy in the Senate to campaign as effectively as those freed from day-to-day responsibility.

The Baker case may be most instructive. Senator Baker retired from the Senate, not seeking reelection in 1984, in order to seek the presidency in 1988. The lesson he learned from 1980 was that he needed freedom from office in order to campaign effectively. Senator Gary Hart did not seek reelection in 1986 for the same reason. The experiences of Jimmy Carter, Ronald Reagan, and Walter Mondale, all of whom ran for the presidency while not holding other elective offices, seem to confirm this new wisdom.

On the other hand, both George Bush and Michael Dukakis won nominations in 1988 while holding elected positions. Again, the contrast is instructive. Enough has already been said about Bush as vice president. The demands of the office are not onerous; the opportunities to build political capital are legion. But what of Dukakis? Aren't the responsibilities of a sitting governor too burdensome to allow a race for the presidential nomination? Dukakis considered this question very seriously before deciding to enter the race. One key advantage he had was that Massachusetts is a heavily Democratic state; his party controlled the legislature, and his lieutenant governor was loyal to him. His top staff people could run the state government while he was campaigning (Black et al., 1988). The race would have been much harder for New York Governor

TABLE 8-3. Senators Seeking Their Party's Presidential Nomination, 1968–1992

1968	1984
Robert F. Kennedy	Alan Cranston
Eugene McCarthy	John Glenn
	Gary Hart
1972	Ernest Hollings
Vance Hartke	
Hubert Humphrey	**1988**
Henry Jackson	Joseph Biden
George McGovern	Robert Dole
Edmund S. Muskie	Albert Gore
	Gary Hart
1976	Paul Simon
Birch Bayh	
Lloyd Bentsen	**1992**
Frank Church	Tom Harkin
Fred Harris	Robert Kerrey
Hubert Humphrey	
Henry Jackson	
1980	
Howard Baker	
Robert Dole	
Edward Kennedy	

Mario Cuomo, who was constantly bickering with his state's partisanly divided legislature over state policies. Like Bush, Dukakis could use the office to his advantage, without worrying about constraints, but in today's complex world of governing, this situation may be more the exception than the rule.

2.   Money Running for a presidential nomination actually involves running more than fifty separate campaigns. In 1988 primary elections were held on seventeen different days; first-round caucuses were held on twenty-three days, some of which were also primary days in other states. Candidates had to monitor delegate selection in caucus states and in many primary states as well as many additional facets of the process. An enterprise this vast requires a complex organization, extensive travel by the candidate and staff, sophisticated information gathering and dissemination, and effective advertising. These require money.

Since the 1976 presidential nomination, all contenders for major-party nomination have been eligible for federal matching funds. (See Chapter 10 for a detailed discussion of campaign financing in all elections.) In order to qualify for matching funds, candidates must meet certain minimal criteria, raising at least $5000 in contributions of $250 or less, in each of twenty states. After that, all gifts of $250 or less are matched from the Presidential Election Campaign Fund, provided that the candidate complies with certain overall and state-by-state spending restrictions and does not receive less than 10 percent of the vote in two consecutive presidential primaries in which he or she is running. Since the 1976 election, all candidates for major-party nominations, except former Texas Governor John Connally in 1980, have qualified for public funding and complied with the spending limitation.[6] And as Table 8-4 reveals, they have spent a good deal of money.

Money as a resource for candidates provides opportunities and causes problems. First, in recent years, the ability to qualify for matching funds has become the first test of a serious candidacy. Candidates in 1984 and 1988 tried to have the money needed to qualify for federal funds ready as soon as they announced.

Second, candidates had to raise early money in order to fund extensive campaigns in the early caucus and primary states.[7] Not only have they had to qualify for matching funds, but they have had to raise large amounts quickly.

---

[6] Connally felt that his only chance for success was to outspend and thus outadvertise all his opponents. He felt, correctly, that he could raise a good deal of money from his Texas oil friends and the big-business connections he had cemented during his tenure as secretary of the treasury. He was wrong in believing that he could parlay that money into a successful campaign. When Connally withdrew from the race, he had won only one delegate who, when interviewed on television at the Republican National Convention, was kiddingly referred to as the "$6,000,000 delegate."

[7] Actually many candidates in recent years have campaigned extensively before the time when they announced their candidacy and/or federal funds have became available. The money that some candidates have used has been raised by independent political action committees. These PACs have raised and spent significant amounts of money, giving a platform to the candidate, staffing a nascent organization, preparing for a major campaign. For examples, Walter Mondale's PAC was called The Committee for the Future of America; Ronald Reagan's, Citizens for the Republic; Howard Baker's, The Republican Majority Fund; and Ted Kennedy's, The Fund for a Democratic Majority. See Corrado (1992).

TABLE 8-4. Spending by Candidates for Presidential Nominations, 1976–1988 (in thousands)

Democrats		Republicans	
		1976	
Bayh	$1,200	Ford	$13,600
Bensten	2,200	Reagan	12,600
Brown	1,700		
Carter	11,300		
Church	1,500		
Harris	1,400		
Jackson	6,200		
McCormack	500		
Sanford	600		
Shapp	800		
Shriver	600		
Udall	4,500		
Wallace	7,900		
		1980	
Brown	2,700	Anderson	6,500
Carter	18,500	Baker	7,000
Kennedy	12,300	Bush	16,700
LaRouche	2,200	Connally	12,700
		Crane	5,200
		Dole	1,400
		Fernandez	300
		Reagan	20,700
		Stassen	100
		1984	
Askew	3,353	Reagan	28,687
Cranston	8,213		
Glenn	14,408		
Hart	24,284		
Hollings	2,796		
Jackson	10,095		
LaRouche	4,970		
McGovern	1,848		
Mondale	37,772		
Others	504		
		1988	
Babbitt	4,349	Bush	33,911
Biden	3,981	Dole	28,307
Dukakis	31,237	du Pont	9,153
Gore	14,958	Haig	2,633
Hart	3,553	Kemp	20,576
Jackson	26,644	Robertson	41,029
LaRouche	3,983		
Simon	13,346		

Source: Data for 1976 are from Wayne, 1981; for 1980 from Malbin, 1984b; for 1984 from FEC "Presidential Pre-Nomination Campaigns" Final Report, April, 1986; for 1988, FEC Press Release, "FEC Releases Final Report on 1988 Presidential Primary Campaign," August 25, 1989

Beyond that, candidates have had to plan how to spend their money strategically because of the limitations to which they acquiesce when they accept public financing. Malbin (1985) has demonstrated that candidates spend a good deal of money before the year of the presidential nomination and that they spend a much higher percentage of the permitted limit in the early states than they do in later states. But as Walter Mondale nearly found out in 1984, too much money spent too early may leave too little to spend later when it is needed (Corrado & Maisel, 1988; Maisel, 1988).

In an earlier era, wealthy candidates could spend their own money to finance their own campaigns. Today the amounts needed make that all but impossible, even if candidates who accepted public financing were not limited to spending $50,000 of their own money.[8]

In today's political world, money is a strategic resource that must be raised and then spent wisely. Candidate strategists must decide how to spend money, when to spend it, and where to spend it in order to assure that it is used more effectively. The ultimate goal is to win a majority of delegates to the national convention. Too much too early may not leave enough money to spend later. Or saving money for the end may result in poor showings early which cannot be overcome. It is a small wonder that candidates and their managers spend much of their early time planning budgetary allocations.

3. **The Media** In many ways the press makes the presidential nominating process work. How many average citizens are thinking about presidential politics over a year before an election, when the contenders are courting delegate candidates in Florida, Iowa, and Maine? Has the public begun to focus on the next election when scores of candidates and their staffs are trooping through the snows of New Hampshire? The answer is a resounding no! But the working press is gearing up.

Initially one or two reporters will accompany a candidate on a campaign swing. If a candidate is lucky or if a press secretary is extremely good, a television crew may cover part of a campaign trip. Particularly at the beginning of the primary process, free publicity is the key. Odd as it seems, presidential contenders are not necessarily well known to the general public. Table 8-5 shows the preferences that voters identified among Democratic presidential contenders early in the 1984 selection process and early in the 1988 process. Look first at 1984. One obvious conclusion is that some of the large gap between candidates Mondale and Glenn, on the one hand, and Hart, on the other, is a reflection of the number of voters who had heard of Senator Hart. However, with his good showing in the Iowa caucuses and win in the New Hampshire primary, each of which was accompanied by significant publicity, both his name recogni-

---

[8] In 1991, first mentions of the potential candidacy of West Virginia's Democratic Senator John D. Rockefeller IV was almost always accompanied by speculation that he would fund his own campaign; perhaps the Rockefeller wealth would have been the exception that proved the rule, but most observers felt that if he did finance his own campaign effort, his wealth and not his experience or position on issues would have been the most frequent topic of discussion.

TABLE 8-5. Early Poll Standings of Presidential Contenders

1984*		1988†	
Candidate	**%**	**Candidate**	**Mean%**
Democrats		Democrats	
Walter Mondale	40	Bruce Babbitt	2
John Glenn	21	Michael Dukakis	13
Jesse Jackson	10	Richard Gephardt	5
George McGovern	8	Albert Gore	7
Alan Cranston	6	Gary Hart	‡
Gary Hart	3	Jesse Jackson	19
Reuben Askew	1	Paul Simon	7
Ernest Hollings	1		
		Republicans	
		George Bush	42
		Robert Dole	20
		Pierre du Pont	2
		Alexander Haig	5
		Jack Kemp	8
		Pat Robertson	6

* From Gallup poll of November 3, 1983.
† From four Gallup polls between June and October 1987.
‡ Hart had about 20% in the very early polls but then withdrew from the race; there are no poll results from the brief time he was back in the race.

tion and the number of voters selecting him as their choice for the nomination rose substantially.

Now look at 1988. None of the candidates was really well known in the Democratic party, with Jesse Jackson the leader, again largely reflecting name recognition. Senator Hart was not included in the Gallup poll ratings, because he was out of the race at that time. However, in earlier counting by the ABC/*Washington Post* poll, Senator Hart stood around 40 percent, reflecting the recognition he had garnered from his race four years earlier (Buell & Davis, 1991, p. 18). In the Republican party, the lead of Vice President Bush over Senator Dole again reflects the difference in how many people had any impression of them at all. As with the cases discussed earlier, these numbers changed drastically after the first caucuses and primaries and the media exposures wrought by those events.[9]

The goal in the early stages of a campaign is to be mentioned. Television advertising cannot be effective without the public focusing on the campaign, and so candidates court press attention. They play to local media wherever they go; more important, they seek mention in the national press, some positive reference as a real contender.

[9] Early poll results also have an impact on the ability to raise money. When Michael Dukakis approached his principal fund-raiser, Robert Farmer, to ask if enough money could be raised to wage a viable campaign, Farmer first assured the governor that it could be done—he added the caveat that he had never raised money for someone who stood at 1 percent in the polls before (Black et al., 1988).

These efforts can be spectacular successes or abysmal failures. At times a candidate's relationship with the press may make the candidate feel like a yo-yo on the end of a string. As an example, look at the John Anderson Republican effort in 1980. Anderson was one of those congressmen who was widely respected in Washington but virtually unknown to the nation when he decided to forgo a difficult reelection campaign in Illinois in order to seek the presidency. Anderson was photogenic, articulate, and much too liberal for most of the activists in the Republican party. Most of all, he was good press. He understood that advocating gun control before the National Rifle Association would be regarded as newsworthy by the press (Robinson & Sheehan, 1983).

In the early states in 1980 the media covered John Anderson like a glove. Reagan was not yet campaigning full-time; he never really did. The other Republicans were exciting neither the voters nor the media. Anderson was good copy. But after some early good showings, Anderson had to produce a victory. The press soon came to the hard truth. Anderson could not run successfully in the Republican party. That statement became the press line by the time of the Illinois primary in March. John Anderson could not win among Republicans; his chances for the nomination were downplayed in the press as much as they had been exaggerated earlier.

Anderson's roller coaster with the press at least gave him some national attention, the early exposure helping his eventual third-party campaign. Compare that experience to Reuben Askew's, the ex-governor of Florida who sought the Democratic nomination in 1984. Askew never became more than an asterisk in the polls. He tried to base an early appeal on his conservative stands on social issues, hoping that certain dedicated followers would support him and that would distinguish him from the other candidates. What distinguished him was a brief trip to Maine and New Hampshire. The national political correspondent for a major newspaper decided to catch up with Askew, to see how he was doing. The reporter tried to call the local Askew headquarters; there was none. He called the national headquarters in Florida and asked for a local contact; there was none. He asked his Florida contact how to get in touch with the candidate; the contact didn't know. He asked where Askew was; his headquarters hadn't heard from him in days. The case of the missing candidate made news, but not the kind of news Askew counted on. His campaign was held up to a kind of ridicule from which it never recovered.

A third experience, that of Bruce Babbit from Arizona in the 1988 primaries, falls somewhere between these two. Babbit was not a main contender. He never made a real impact on the voting public. But he was impressing the media who were following the candidates. In one of the New Hampshire debates, he called for everyone who believed that taxes needed to be raised to stand up. None of the other candidates did. They knew Babbit was right, but they would not take a politically unpopular "stand." The press loved it—and Babbit benefited from a couple of weeks' worth of good coverage. However, like Anderson, he failed because he could not transform that into votes in a primary—still the sine qua non for electoral success.

Recent experience leads one to the conclusion that a key to gaining early press at-

tention is to do better than is expected. In this regard the Iowa caucuses and the New Hampshire primary have been very important (Orren & Polsby, 1987). In 1972 George McGovern lost New Hampshire to Ed Muskie; but New Hampshire was the state next to Muskie's Maine, and Muskie should have won bigger than he did. The press wrote the story as if Muskie had lost, and McGovern was on his way (Crouse, 1973; White, 1973).

In 1976 Jimmy Carter "won" New Hampshire with 28 percent of the vote. Because he had come out on top, and because this result was unexpected, Carter was pictured as a big winner; all the others were losers. His picture graced the covers of *Time* and *Newsweek;* he was on his way. That same year President Ford edged Ronald Reagan in New Hampshire. Reagan had been expected to do very well in this conservative state; his campaign did not recover until the North Carolina primary, months later (Orren & Polsby, 1987; T. Patterson, 1980; Witcover, 1977).

In 1980 George Bush took his turn at exceeding expectations. His "win" in Iowa, although again with much less than a majority, broke him out of a pack of Republicans chasing Ronald Reagan. It was Ted Kennedy who did not meet expectations. His poor showings in Iowa and especially in New Hampshire, billed as his neighboring state and not as the more conservative bastion it in fact is, all but nailed the lid on the coffin of a campaign that faltered from the start.

Gary Hart, who had engineered George McGovern's "upset" of Ed Muskie in New Hampshire in 1972, returned to familiar territory in 1984. His strong showing in the Iowa caucuses served notice that his campaign was on the move. Despite internal campaign staff information that he would do very well in the New Hampshire primary, Hart played down his chances for success. When he won, again exceeding the press's predictions, more attention and cover stories followed.

In 1984 the Reverend Jesse Jackson demonstrated that the press could prove to be a crucial resource in another way. Jackson was newsworthy. He ran an entire campaign based on free media exposure. The press did not dare to ignore him because he was a serious black contender for a major-party nomination—that was news. He was articulate and controversial, and he was drawing large numbers of blacks to the polls—again, news. When he challenged his opponents, when he slept in the ghettos, when he traveled to Syria, when he did not disavow the support of the controversial Reverend Farrakhan, when he won in the south, Jesse Jackson was news. He knew how to use the media. His rhetoric was made for television; his dynamism demanded action photos; his place in history commanded attention. Despite his total inability to draw white support, despite the fact that his Rainbow Coalition never really materialized, Jesse Jackson stayed on page one. He stayed on the nightly news. Mondale, Hart, and Jackson. Hart, Mondale, and Jackson. But always Jackson, demonstrating the power of the press as a candidate resource (Barker & Walter, 1989).

In 1988, Jackson's campaign took off from the spot at which his 1984 campaign had ended. Not only was he a serious candidate; he was a serious contender. He did not do well in the early rounds, though his strength in Maine surprised many. However, on Super Tuesday, he was clearly one of the winners.

Reverend Jesse Jackson campaigned hard for the 1984 and 1988 Democratic presidential nominations and was an important factor in the 1992 race, even though he himself was not a candidate. (Donna Binder/Impact Visuals)

Again, Jackson built a campaign without a great deal of money, gaining attention from free media because of the symbolism of his campaign and its successes. Jackson won where the intensity of his supporters turned into electoral success. Thus, he did better in caucus states than in primaries. His most noteworthy success was in the restricted primary in Michigan, a primary that functioned more like a caucus. But the press was notably unanalytical in examining the Jackson successes; Jackson was succeeding beyond everyone's expectation. Dukakis, Gephardt (D., Miss.), and Jackson. Dukakis, Gore, and Jackson. Dukakis and Jackson. Always Jackson (Black et al., 1988; Pomper, 1989b; Runkel, 1989).

Of course, the obverse of doing better than expectations is not to do worse than expectations. In 1988, as has been discussed above, both Dukakis's and Bush's managers worried about expectations. Dukakis had to prove that he was a national candidate in Iowa and then win in New Hampshire. His Super Tuesday strategy was based on demonstrating successes—even though he succeeded only in the carefully selected areas in which he chose to compete (Black et al. 1988). Bush had to recover in New Hampshire to cement the Super Tuesday landslide he had so carefully planned for. Once he met those expectations, the game was over for the other contenders (Runkel, 1989).

The role of the press in the nominating process has received a great deal of critical attention. That attention has been deserved because the national media, print and electronic journalists alike, have not done a very good job of defining their role in this process. The nominating process itself has come under scrutiny because it is so easily manipulated by the press. (See Grassmuck, 1985; Orren & Polsby, 1987; Traugott, 1985.) But reform is not the immediate province of candidates for party nominations. They are concerned with winning. In reaching for that goal, the press is a resource they must learn to use. Free media attention has made and broken many presidential campaigns.

While most of the attention has been given to the role of free media in the nominating process (Arterton, 1984; Graber, 1984a; Matthews, 1978; T. Patterson, 1980; Traugott, 1985, as examples), relatively little attention has been paid to the role of media advertising at this stage of an election. In 1988, campaign managers had to plan carefully for Super Tuesday. The Gore campaign, as one example, tried to save most of its resources for the southern states on Super Tuesday, ignoring the early rounds in Iowa and New Hampshire.[10] The Gephardt campaign hoped that a win in Iowa would stimulate enough momentum to carry its candidate through New Hampshire—and that that victory would lead to the infusion of enough money to advertise widely on Super Tuesday. That did not happen. Bob Dole's strategy paralleled Gephardt's; and it might well have worked had he not failed to respond to Bush's last minute attack on him in New Hampshire.

Dukakis and Bush planned all along for heavy media campaigns in the Super Tuesday states. Bush had organizational strength everywhere and enough money to overwhelm the others. Dukakis planned strategically, organizing in areas in which he could win—the northern and western states that were competing for press attention with the south on Super Tuesday and specific areas within the south in which his advisers thought he could do well—suburban areas with northern transplants, Hispanic areas, etc. Dukakis and his advisers concentrated their efforts on specific congressional districts and media markets, knowing that they could not blanket the region and that they would lose to either Gore or Jackson in many areas. That advertising strategy was crucial to the degree of success that Dukakis enjoyed on Super Tuesday, a success that was duly reported in the free mass media (Black et al., 1988; R. Cook, 1989; Runkel, 1989; Pomper, 1989b).

C. Use of Influential Leaders

When Ed Muskie's presidential drive fizzled in 1972, many felt the lesson of the campaign was that the support of influential leaders was no longer necessary in presidential nominating politics. The success of Jimmy Carter in 1976 reaffirmed that view to even more political observers. One should not jump to conclusions such as that so quickly. Support by public officeholders and party officials can still be very important.

[10] There is some evidence that the Gore campaign unsuccessfully attempted a most sophisticated "exceed expectations" strategy. While claiming that he had pulled out of Iowa and New Hampshire to concentrate on southern states, Gore in fact spent some time and expended a good deal of organizational and financial resources in New Hampshire. Apparently he was hoping for a better than anticipated New Hampshire finish with consequent press attention benefiting his Super Tuesday campaign in the south.

Look first at the Republican party. Ronald Reagan was renominated without opposition in 1984; that was because all the party leaders supported him. In 1972, Richard Nixon virtually ignored his two Republican challengers. He was confident he would be renominated because of support within his party's leadership circles.[11]

Delegates to Republican conventions from caucuses are not chosen through a procedure so complicated, nor so cumbersome or constraining, as are Democratic delegates. Frequently caucus and convention delegates go to Republican National Conventions without stating their presidential preferences. Some of the party leaders have a good deal of influence over those delegates. At close conventions, as the Republicans held in 1976, these leaders can hold the balance of power. That potential should not be ignored.

Even in the Democratic party influential leaders can be a key resource for presidential contenders. Under the Hunt Commission rules, officeholders and party leaders held 15 percent of the delegate seats as uncommitted superdelegates. In 1988 there were 645 superdelegates. A vast majority of them voted for Dukakis, who was clearly more acceptable to mainstream Democratic politicians than was Jesse Jackson. In 1992, the number of superdelegates rose to 766—and given the requirements of proportional representation in allocation of state delegations, this bloc of delegates could have played a critical role. The Hunt Commission, following dissatisfaction with the lack of peer review of potential nominees by practicing politicians, explicitly attempted to increase the influence of these individuals. Recent experience has demonstrated the success of this effort.

In addition, some elected and party officials can still be very significant back in their states. But contenders for the nomination must be careful to pick the "right" influentials. Ted Kennedy was not helped when he was booed along with Chicago Mayor Jane Byrne in 1980. On the other hand, the support of Senator Christopher Dodd (D., Conn.) undoubtedly helped Gary Hart in Connecticut in 1984. George Bush was aided by the support of party leaders throughout the nation in the 1988 nominating contest.

Perhaps no campaign has epitomized the postreform "insider" strategy more than the Mondale prenomination campaign in 1984. Mondale lined up the support of almost every elected official, labor leader, party leader, or other influential individual he could convince to support him. At the same time, he set up an efficient campaign organization at the grass roots. He went after group support and individual support. He nearly monopolized the "superdelegations," but he did not ignore local caucuses. In the end the breadth of his support brought him the nomination.

Out of necessity, Gary Hart chose the other route. Few leaders backed him, and so he ran as the antiestablishment candidate. He pressed the "old establishment" label on Mondale, depicting himself as the loner, the outsider, and

---

[11] Patrick Buchanan's challenge of George Bush in 1992 demonstrated the president's unpopularity with the conservative wing of his party and caused some concern in the White House, but the overall effect on the president's renomination bid was negligible.

the candidate with new ideas. The strategy almost worked. Jimmy Carter in 1976 and Ronald Reagan in 1980 had played similar tunes right into nominations.

The strategic consideration in the use of influential leaders is quite simple. If you have them, use them. If you do not have their support, turn that into a virtue. In neither case is it effective to pretend that everyone is equal in the political process. Those who have spent lifetimes in politics, who have followers and influence, can parlay their support into support from others. That political fact of life is not lost on presidential contenders.

D. Use of the Rules

The rules of the game are never neutral. George McGovern showed that in 1972; Jimmy Carter showed it in 1976; the efforts of the White House representatives on the Winograd Commission demonstrated an explicit recognition of the fact. But never was it more in evidence than in the Democratic nominating process in 1984.

The Hunt Commission rules were designed to increase the chances that the party would unite behind one contender early in the process and that that contender would be able to concentrate his efforts toward defeating President Reagan. Most observers felt that Walter Mondale would be that nominee; he had a head start in organization, he was well known, and his campaign was well funded. Democratic party leaders hoped that Mondale would win the early primaries; sew up the nomination with impressive wins on Super Tuesday, the first day on which a large number of primaries were held; and use the rest of the prenomination period to unite the party behind him. They felt that the front-loading of the schedule (recall Table 8-2) would prevent any insurgent candidate from gaining momentum from one early victory and nipping away at Mondale's lead from there.

Saying that the rules are not neutral is not the same as saying that their impact is always predictable. Hart did upset the Mondale bandwagon in early primaries. In contrast to what was predicted, Hart did gain momentum and Mondale, staggered by early blows, almost did not have time to recover. The front-loading of the delegate-rich early primaries nearly proved to be Mondale's downfall.

But in the final analysis the rules did help Mondale and hurt Hart (and Jackson). Hart's strategy called for major efforts in Iowa and New Hampshire, to defuse Mondale and to gain momentum. In order to mount these efforts, his organization did not spread itself across the nation. Hart delegate slates were not formed and filed in time to meet deadlines in many states. Thus, while Hart won the Florida primary, Mondale won more delegates in Florida. The front-loading had made it impossible for a weakly organized candidate to compete effectively in all the early primaries. Hart did not have time to capitalize on his early victory.

Further, the Hunt Commission rules allowed states to reinstitute "loophole" primaries, primaries in which the leading candidate won all the delegates from an area. "Loophole" states turned out to be states in which Mondale, supported by party leaders, did quite well. (See Table 8-6.) Mondale concentrated his efforts in these states, picking up large numbers of delegates, while not losing so badly in the delegate race in other states that used proportional representation. The rules clearly benefited Mondale in this instance.

Finally, remember the superdelegates. Most of the uncommitted superdelegates cast their votes for Mondale. Again the "insider" candidate benefited from a rule designed specifically to benefit the "insiders." Mondale and his strategists helped design these rules; they knew the rules well and played them for all they were worth. Knowledge of the rules is the key; so too is having rules designed to favor a certain type of candidacy.

In 1988 as well, the rules worked to the advantage of the eventual winners. Even though the post-1968 rules seemed to benefit ideologically extreme candidates or political outsiders, in 1988 the rules played to the advantage of mainstream party moderates. These candidates used the rules to their advantage, as has been discussed above. It should be noted, however, that the political environments, the contexts in which these campaigns were run, the particular mix of candidates seeking the nomination, played into the hands of the moderate candidates as well (Pomper, 1989b, pp. 33–37).

E.   Summary

Nominating campaigns are difficult to assess. Viewed with 20–20 hindsight, one can easily see that the Muskie strategy was flawed, that the Carter strategy was brilliant, and so on. The evidence again points strongly to the conclusion that politics is more art than science.

TABLE 8-6. Democratic Presidential Contenders' Support

By Type of Primary, 1984			
Type of Primary	**Mondale**	**Hart**	**Jackson**	**Others**
---	---	---	---	---
Loophole primaries, %	40	36	19	5
Bonus systems, %	41	32	21	6
Proportional representation, %	32	39	17	12
Nonbinding primaries, %	37	49	9	5

In States Using Dual Systems, 1988					
State	**Date**	**Turnout**	**Dukakis**	**Jackson**	**Uncommitted**
Idaho					
Caucus	March 8	4,633	38%	19%	29%
Primary	May 24	51,242	73%	16%	—
Texas					
Caucus	March 8	100,000	38%	40%	10%
Primary	March 8	1,766,904	33%	25%	—
Vermont					
Caucus	April 19	6,000	45%	46%	—
Primary	March 1	50,791	56%	26%	—

Some of the most effective members of Congress—Wilbur Mills of Arkansas, Fritz Hollings of South Carolina, Ed Muskie of Maine, Bob Dole of Kansas—proved to be poor presidential candidates. Skills are not always transferable. The corps of national campaign experts is very small, and these "experts" frequently learn the wrong lessons from their previous experience. New faces often have the clearest sense of how to attack the system—Hart as McGovern's strategist in 1972, Jordan for Carter in 1976, Jim Baker for George Bush in a losing effort in 1980, John Sasso for Michael Dukakis in 1988.

All candidates show their strengths and weaknesses as they announce their candidacy. All understand the need for money, for an effective press strategy, for influential followers, for gaining and maintaining momentum, but few are successful in doing all these things. The political terrain is difficult to read. The process is so interesting precisely because those of us who are political analysts and members of the interested public can sit back and watch the contenders compete and test their strategies. Monday morning quarterbacks have no better process to kibitz.

IV.   THE CONVENTIONS

The excitement was electric at the 1976 Republican Convention in the Kemper Arena in Kansas City. Betty Ford came in from one end and the band struck up the University of Michigan fight song, "Hail to the Victors." Nancy Reagan en-

The national conventions cap the nominating process and give the party faithful a chance to come together behind their nominees. (Paul Conklin/Monkmeyer)

tered from the other end; the band responded with "California, Here I Come!" The crowds cheered loudly as Ford and Reagan supporters tried to drown each other out. Television commentators tried to gauge support for the two candidates by the intensity of the cheering. The convention was as thrilling as any college football game one can imagine.

But the broader question to be addressed is whether or not national nominating conventions decide anything at all any more. Table 8-7 lists the ballots on which successful nominees were chosen at Republican and Democratic National Conventions in this century. In the early part of the century the delegates to the conventions chose the presidential nominees. In recent decades, and particularly since the democratizing reforms of the 1970s, the conventions seem to have become rubber stamps. The delegate selection process has worked in such a way that one candidate has a guaranteed first-ballot majority by the time the convention opens.

Many observers felt that the Democratic rules change that calls for "fair reflection of presidential preference" would return decision-making power to the conventions. The argument went that many candidates going through a system that called for proportional representation of their popular support on delegate support would guarantee a situation in which no one candidate achieved a

TABLE 8-7. Number of Ballots Needed to Choose Presidential Nominees, 1900–1992

Year	Democrats	Republicans
1900	1	1
1904	1	1
1908	1	1
1912	46	1
1916	1	3
1920	43	10
1924	103	1
1928	1	1
1932	4	1
1936	Acclamation	1
1940	1	6
1944	1	1
1948	1	3
1952	3	1
1956	1	1
1960	1	1
1964	Acclamation	1
1968	1	1
1972	1	1
1976	1	1
1980	1	1
1984	1	1
1988	1	1
1992	1	1

Source: *Congressional Quarterly Guide to U.S. Elections.*

majority. In 1976, Jimmy Carter disproved this theory by outdistancing all his opponents combined. The very tight Republican race that year was between only two candidates. Thus, the winner would, by definition, be a majority winner.

The Hunt Commission strove to increase the possibility that the leading candidate would achieve a majority and be able to solidify the party before the convention, goals thought important to aid the candidate in the November election. Walter Mondale's inability to do just that points out once again how difficult it is to anticipate the impact of reforms. In 1988 George Bush emerged from Super Tuesday as the clear winner in the Republican nominating contest; Michael Dukakis guaranteed himself a first-ballot nomination by the time the primaries had ended. In 1992 both President Bush and Arkansas Governor Bill Clinton seemed assured of first-ballot nominations months before their respective conventions met.

As much of the nation's attention focuses on the nominating conventions every fourth summer, it is appropriate for us to examine whether this attention is warranted. Certainly recent history leads to the conclusion that the conventions do not decide the nominee. What about the other decisions made in these political arenas? (See Davis, 1983; Parris, 1972; Shafer, 1988; Sullivan et al., 1976; Wayne, 1984, chap. 5.)

National nominating conventions make four different kinds of decisions. In addition to deciding on the nominees, they rule on credentials disputes, changes in the party rules, and platform language.

A. Credentials Challenges

Credentials disputes are the most easily understood. In party rules and in the call to the convention, each party establishes the procedures through which delegates are to be chosen. In most cases no one challenges the delegates presenting themselves as representing a certain state. However, the procedures are not always simple. The political situations are not always unbiased, and challenges result. Each party appoints a Credentials Committee that hears challenges to proposed delegations and rules on the disputes. The report of the Credentials Committee is the first order of official business before the nominating convention.

While most credentials challenges are disposed of without major controversy, those that do attract attention are often critically important. Among the most noteworthy challenges was that of the Mississippi Freedom Democratic party in 1964 (see White, 1965). The appeal by the Mississippi black Democrats, led by Aaron Henry, was instrumental in desegregating Democratic politics in the south.

The credentials battles at the 1972 Democratic Convention in Miami were more closely related to the impending presidential nominations. Recall that the 1972 nomination was the first conducted under the "reformed" rules. Many irregularities were in evidence. The results of a series of credentials challenges were to determine whether George McGovern, the clear front-runner, was going to be able to secure a first-ballot nomination or if the ABM forces (anyone but McGovern) could derail his candidacy at the last moment.

The three most significant challenges dealt with South Carolina (where feminists felt too few women had been selected), Illinois (where McGovern forces charged that the Cook County organization of Mayor Richard Daley had not followed procedures for opening and publicizing caucuses), and California (where a winner-take-all primary had been given an exemption from the rules by the National Committee). On close votes, aided by an important procedural ruling from Convention Chair Lawrence O'Brien, McGovern delegates were allowed to replace anti-McGovern, Daley delegates in Illinois and to hold all the delegates won in California. The result was that McGovern forces controlled enough votes to secure the first-ballot victory (White, 1973).

B. Rules Disputes

The National Convention of each party is the ultimate rule-making authority for the national party.[12] Each party appoints a Rules Committee that examines proposed changes in party rules. In most cases party rules are sufficiently obscure and esoteric that few notice the workings of the Rules Committee. Often the real impact of rules changes will not be felt for four years; in the heat of an ongoing campaign, few are looking that far ahead.

On occasion, however, the work of the convention Rules Committee is seen as having immediate impact. In 1976, candidate Ronald Reagan tried a desperate ploy to wrest the nomination from President Gerald Ford. In an unprecedented move, Reagan announced, in advance of the convention, that he would choose Pennsylvania Senator Richard Schweiker as his running mate were he nominated for the presidency. Reagan's bold move was a reaching out toward the liberal wing of his party, toward those who felt he was too conservative. The battle was very close. Reagan hoped the needed few delegates would swing to his side; few budged.

As a second step in his strategy, Reagan sought a change on Rule 5 of the Republican Party Rules, requiring that prospective presidential candidates designate their choice for running mate in advance. Reagan hoped that this rule change would force President Ford into a choice that would cost him support from the followers of the hopefuls who were not chosen and give the nomination to Reagan. The ploy failed; the rule was not changed, although the vote on it was very close, and Ford secured the nomination (Pomper, 1977, pp. 18–27; Wayne, 1988, chap. 5; Witcover, 1977).

The 1980 Democratic National Convention saw Senator Edward Kennedy attempt a similar tactic. The Democratic rules at that time bound delegates to the candidate to whom they had pledged support for one ballot. (Some state rules extended that commitment even further.) Though a majority

---

[12] By any definition this is true in the Republican party. As mentioned earlier, in recent years the Democrats have permitted the National Committee and/or specially appointed commissions to change rules between national conventions. Whether these commissions in the DNC ran overrule specific votes at a national convention is still in question.

of the delegates were pledged to President Carter, Kennedy felt that some might swing to him if they were unbound, because Carter's popularity had fallen to an all-time low. The binding rule had been part of an effort to guarantee that convention delegations reflected the views of the citizens who had chosen them. Kennedy ignored this rationale and attacked them as "robot delegates," seeking a rule change to allow them to "vote their consciences." The Kennedy effort failed, and of course, Carter was nominated (Shafer, 1988, pp. 193–196; Wayne, 1988, chap. 5).

National political journalists have focused on the disputes described above as pivotal events in each of the cited conventions. In some senses they were, but in a more realistic sense they were very predictable. Delegates to conventions are the type of people who choose early which candidate they will support and work hard for that candidate. They are seeking two goals. Their principal goal is to help their candidate secure the nomination. Their secondary goal is to be a delegate for that candidate, to share in the candidate's success.

These individuals are not fooled by the intricacies of credentials or rules fights. The questions may be worded differently, but delegates know that the real question is which candidate for the presidency you favor. Female McGovern delegates in 1972 voted against the challenge by South Carolina women because it would have hurt McGovern's chances (see Weil, 1973; White, 1973). *The most important factor to note in convention votes on credentials or rules fights is how close the votes in these battles are to the first-ballot votes for the presidential nomination.* Though roll calls by individual delegates are not available, delegates are very aware of the impact these votes have on their favorite candidate's chances for nomination and vote accordingly. Put simply, the Carter delegates in 1980 were not robots; they were dedicated supporters of Jimmy Carter voting their consciences (Pomper, 1981b, pp. 25–32).

C.   Party Platforms

The party platforms are statements of the direction in which the two parties want our country to go. Their significance is frequently disputed, though Gerald Pomper (1982) demonstrated that they show real differences between our parties and that much of them are implemented and not forgotten. It is clear that they receive a lot of press attention at the time they are adopted.

The Democrats use the platform-writing process as a means to reach out to grass-roots activists around the country. In many years, their platform committee, the composition of which reflects candidates' strengths, has turned into a traveling road show, seeking advice from Democrats around the country. The Republican Platform Committee, on the other hand, normally only meets in the convention city on the weekend before the convention itself. It is not a road show, but perhaps a sideshow before the main event.

Platforms serve different purposes for different individuals. For activists and ideologues it is often a means to gain a foothold into party dogma. For interest groups, it is one way to gain support for particular views. For candidates, the platform process has served as a way to reach out to those in the party who did not support them.

Each candidate at a national convention has an extensive organization. Since the 1960 nomination of John F. Kennedy in Los Angeles (White, 1961), each convention has seen increasingly sophisticated communication networks so that candidate organizations can reach their supporters on the floor. Each candidate sets up a "whip" organization so that delegates are instantly informed how they must vote on critical matters.

Credentials and rules disputes, which can determine who wins and loses, are seen as critical matters. The whips inform the delegates; the delegates fall in line. At times the same is true of platform disputes. Thus, in 1988, the Dukakis campaign operatives allowed votes on the platform planks dealing with increasing taxes on upper-income families and pledging to forgo the first use of nuclear weapons, but they also assured that their candidate would not be saddled with a platform with which he was not comfortable (Pomper, 1989b, pp. 49–65). On the other hand, platform disputes are seen as matters of conscience more frequently than is the case of credentials or rules disputes. The delegates often are freed to vote as they choose. At times, as was the case with Jimmy Carter in 1980 and Walter Mondale in 1984, winning candidates concede platform disputes to their vanquished foes so that the losers have some pride with which to return home and so they retain some enthusiasm for the party.

That is not to say that the platform-writing and -adopting processes are not important. However, winning nominees do not want to win minor battles only to lose the bigger war. The platforms, which do distinguish the two parties, can still be used by skilled politicians as a means of uniting the party for the November showdown.

D. Summary

The national television networks have cut way back on their television coverage of the recent nominating conventions. They did this because the excitement was gone—because the ratings were not there. Obviously, they have every right to make that judgment.

But they are wrong. Conventions are important events. They are times for partisans to share and to celebrate. That is newsworthy. They are "comings together," which is what "convention" really means. Republicans and Democrats around the country can share this via television, if they are permitted to do so.

Television journalists define news as controversy. Surely the 1984, 1988 and 1992 conventions lacked that. But the rhetoric of Mario Cuomo and Jesse Jackson, the emotions caused by the nomination of Geraldine Ferraro, the depth of the feelings for Gary Hart and Fritz Mondale, the humanness of photographer and outgoing Senate leader Howard Baker, the degree of unanimity behind and pride in Ronald Reagan and George Bush, these too were important news events in 1984. And so too were their 1988 and 1992 counterparts—the return of Jesse Jackson, Mike Dukakis's and Bill Clinton's rising to the rhetorical occasion by giving the best speeches of their lives in accepting their party's nomination, the choice of Senator Dan Quayle and Al Gore and the delegates' reactions to those, the emotional appeal of the American flag and the

National Anthem. Television misses a major opportunity by focusing on journalists' interviewing journalists when the public really wants to experience the
thrill of a convention vicariously.

Conventions have not been forums for decision making in recent years.
That is not to say they will not again become so. The delegates will continue to
be pledged and bound (by conviction) to their favorite candidates. If one candidate has gained majority support before the opening gavel, the "competition"
will be a charade. But if this does not eventuate, we may once again see real decisions made by conventions.

Many scenarios could be painted of how that would work. The frank answer is that we do not know. Could candidates control their delegates? Would
demographic representation—of women, blacks, Hispanics—become more important? Would interest groups come to the fore? Would impressive rhetoric win
the day? We just do not know. The old keys—domination by a few bosses—no
longer fit, but it is unclear if anyone has yet crafted the new ones.

During the 1984 Republican National Convention, Walter Cronkite nos-
talgically recalled conventions of another era, when the crowds and the demon-
strations were important, when emotions swept the floor, when spontaneous excitement ruled the day. Conventions still have that potential. They are an
important element of American politics and continue to deserve attention as
potentially significant events, not as dinosaurs from another era. (See Polsby &
Wildavsky, 1988, chap. 3; Shafer, 1988; Wayne, 1988, chap. 5.)

V.   POLITICIANS VIEW THE NOMINATING PROCESS

Frequently how one views a certain situation depends on whether or not one
benefits from that situation. Junior members of congressional committees liked
the seniority system less than did senior members. Five-foot-eight-inch point
guards favor a wider lane under the basket than do seven-foot centers. Such is
human nature.

At one extreme perhaps is the Walter Mondale of 1976. After testing the
presidential waters for a number of months, Mondale withdrew. The reason: "I
simply do not want it enough. I cannot face a whole year of nights in Holiday
Inns." The process was dehumanizing. It was too long and too boring, and, in
Mondale's case that year, offered too little hope for success.

Others have echoed Mondale's criticism in other ways. After his own unsuccessful bid for the 1976 Democratic nomination, Arizona Congressman
Morris Udall became one of the staunchest congressional advocates of reform.
Udall wanted the process to be shortened and made more rational. He favored
a series of regional primaries, with states in one region all to hold their primaries on one day. Thus, candidates would not have to travel all around the
country to compete in a series of elections scheduled at random. To reduce the
advantage of candidates with support in the region polling first, Udall would
have had the region whose primary is held first determined by lot (or in another
proposal rotated in different presidential years).

Still others would carry the process further, calling for a national primary. This idea has been discussed at length but never received serious attention. Political scientist Tom Cronin and others, responding to criticisms that a national primary might well prove indecisive, have called for preprimary conventions to determine who the candidates in the national primary should be. Another alternative would be to have postprimary conventions to decide among the top finishers. (See Grassmuck, 1985.)

The 1984 Democratic National Convention called for a Fairness Commission to reexamine, yet again, the rules used by the Democrats. The complaint that led to this commission was that Jesse Jackson did not receive delegates in proportion to the votes he received in primaries. Big surprise! The rules were written for just that purpose. And both the call for a new reform commission and the fact that no major changes were proposed by that commission illustrate the problem. Essentially the same process followed the 1988 Democratic nomination. A call for reform by those who lost, but only minor changes when the reformers examined the process.

What's progressive reform to some is unfair to others. Politicians' ultimate view of the nominating system—other than complaints about how arduous it is—relates to whether they are helped or hurt. Jackson was hurt so he cried for reform. The rules about which he complained were written by supporters of Walter Mondale in order to aid his candidacy. The Mondale forces, controlling the convention, allowed the call for a Fairness Commission in 1984 because they no longer cared. Their candidate would not be involved in a nomination fight in 1988. The stakes that had been high during the Hunt Commission had become low.

The nominating process will always be controversial. Politicians are vying for the highest office in our land. Those even considering the nomination are already successful politicians at some level. But the national arena is different. The breadth of this country, the diversity of our people, the accidents of history that have led to varying political traditions, the magnitude of the office sought, and the expectations that citizens have of presidential candidates, on the one hand, and presidents, on the other, combine to make the design of the perfect nominating system a pipe dream.

The process will always be long. It will always be complex. It will always seem to favor some candidates over others. Candidates will always be dissatisfied. But the system can be viewed as successful if the citizens feel that the candidates have been tested fairly, in a variety of ways, under rules that were designed to be as even as possible for all contenders. The system gives legitimacy to the nominees. The concessions of losing candidates confirm that legitimacy, and the process moves on from there.

9

Presidential Elections

The seemingly well-oiled Mondale political organization could hardly have performed more poorly as the Democratic nominee launched his 1984 general election campaign. The former vice president's fortunes seemed to peak at the San Francisco convention. During the next month, as the bloom of the Ferraro (D., N.Y., 1978–1984) flower was wilting under the lights of investigations into her husband's finances and her failure to list his income on her financial disclosure forms, as Mondale's own leadership capabilities were called into question by his handling of staffing problems, and generally as the spotlight shifted from those praising Mondale to those criticizing him, the lead that President Reagan enjoyed over his challenger widened.

The Mondale campaign's difficulties were apparent for all to see on Labor Day, 1984, as the Democratic presidential and vice presidential nominees paraded down empty streets in New York, marching in a Labor Day Parade before the expected crowd of Democratic boosters had arrived. A nonfunctioning microphone at a California rally was the final blow in a terrible day. This example would not be so appropriate were it not often repeated. In a similar way, the 1988 Dukakis general election campaign, in terms of strategy and execution, paled in comparison to the battle for the nomination.

I.   FROM THE CONVENTION TO THE GENERAL ELECTION

Why should these problems have plagued such experienced, seasoned campaign organizations? Why do candidates typically have problems as they begin general election campaigns which one would think should have been solved during primary contests? After all, many more things are known about the general election than are known about the contests for a party's nomination. At the most rudimentary level, strategy can target voters who can use party affiliation as a cue to evaluating candidates; the plan of action can be formulated with a single opponent in mind. Why aren't there fewer problems instead of more problems?

Politicians at the national level spend a good deal of time complaining about the length of presidential campaigns. What they are really concerned with is the length of the campaign for nomination. For successful contenders for the two parties' nominations, and for the advisers most closely involved with their campaigns, the break between the convention and the general election is almost meaningless. They continue to campaign hard, to work on the same issues, to work at the same pace, with the same goal in mind. There is little time for relaxation or reflection.

What is lost in their fatigue is the realization that the general election is separate from the campaign for nomination. The opponent is different, the rules are different, the strategies are different, and the length of time one is campaigning is different. General election campaigns are in fact quite short. The two parties' conventions are held in mid- or late summer. The general election is held on the first Tuesday after the first Monday in November. The general election campaign begins and is over in about three months.

In this short period of time, the candidates and their staffs must run a truly national campaign. The battle for the nomination was complicated by the facts that separate campaigns had to be fought in each state, that different states had different rules, that the political calendar spreads over five months. The general election campaign is different on all accounts. One of the most significant of these is that the campaign must reach its peak in every state throughout the entire nation on the same date. Whereas during the preconvention period it was possible to run separate campaigns in each state and to reuse human resources by switching staff from one state in which the primary or caucus had been held to another state in which the contest was upcoming, in the general election campaign the organization must cover the entire expanse of the nation at one time. The logistics of an operation of this scale are beyond anything with which first-time campaign organizations and staff have had to deal.

Furthermore, the rules of the election contest make strategic planning intricate. The point in the general election is not simply to win a plurality of the votes. While vote maximization is desirable, in our presidential elections the winner is that candidate who is supported by a majority of the electoral college. Therefore, each state is, in some ways, a separate contest. Campaign strategists must determine into which states they should put how much effort. Because all states (except Maine and Nebraska) award the winner of the popular contest in a state all of that state's electoral votes, strategists not only focus on large states but also have to determine which states are lost (and therefore not worth additional effort), which other states are safe (and therefore further effort is superfluous), and which states are competitive (and therefore worthy of increased effort).[1] These estimates must be evaluated and reevaluated as the campaign progresses.

Candidates for the presidency are interested first in winning, but they are also interested in winning with a large mandate. Therefore, even apparent winners cannot coast. They must be aware of the strategies of their opponents and

---

[1] In Maine the winner of the First Congressional District's popular vote receives one electoral vote, the winner of the Second Congressional District's popular vote receives one electoral vote, and the winner of the entire state receives two electoral votes. Since this provision has been in effect (1976), Maine has delivered all of its electoral votes to the same candidate every time. Nebraska switched to a similar system for 1992.

must effectively counter them. They must take into account the mix of voters throughout the nation as they respond to the events of the day. They are uniquely aware of the complexity and the magnitude of the job that they are seeking. They have reached the point at which they are not just among those considered for the presidency, but are one of two individuals who will hold that job. They must be certain that the conduct of their campaign does not make governing more difficult.

In the remainder of this chapter, we will look at the campaigns for the presidency, from after the conventions to the November election. We will begin by examining campaign organization and planning and proceed to look at the strategies and tactics used in these most important contests. (On presidential elections generally, see Kessel, 1988, 1992; Wayne, 1988, 1992; on specific campaigns see, as examples, C. Black & Oliphant, 1989; Drew, 1981; Germond & Witcover, 1985, 1989; P. Goldman & Fuller, 1985; May & Fraser, 1973; Moore, 1981; Moore & Fraser, 1977; Runkel, 1989; Schram, 1977; White, 1965, 1969, 1973, 1982; Witcover, 1977.)

II. ORGANIZING FOR THE GENERAL ELECTION

The campaign organization for the general election must be much more extensive than that for the series of primaries and caucuses that lead up to a presidential nomination. A presidential campaign must be run in each state at the same time. Some aspects of the campaign are controlled in a centralized manner, but others are decentralized. Further, the magnitude of the tasks that can be handled centrally call for significant and sophisticated staffing.

A. Structuring the Campaign Organization

1. **The Campaign Headquarters** A number of questions must be faced when a nominee and his closest advisers reassess their campaign organization after having been victorious at their national convention. A very basic question involves the location of the *campaign headquarters*. Should there be one national headquarters for the campaign? Probably yes. Where should it be located? Washington is the logical choice, but it is not the only choice. In 1976, for example, candidate Jimmy Carter decided that his national headquarters would remain in Atlanta, Georgia. For Carter this was a strategic choice. He wanted to emphasize that he was not part of the old Washington crowd. While many "regular" Democrats and politicians who were old hands at presidential campaigns decried this decision, Carter stuck by it throughout that winning campaign. Similarly, Michael Dukakis, who ran his nominating campaign out of a Boston headquarters, decided not to move his central staff to Washington in 1988. In this case the decision seemed to be more one of convenience than strategy.

Most candidates have chosen Washington as their national headquarters. This decision is dictated, in part at least, because Washington is the seat of government and also the home of the Democratic and Republican National Committees. But merely mentioning these committees raises another set of questions.

2. The National Committee What should be the relationship between the candidate's personal organization and the staff of the national committee? This is not an easy relationship to work out. Obviously the national committee staff is a resource that a candidate should use. While the national committees remain officially neutral in the prenomination phase of the election, once the nominee has been chosen, the national committees are dedicated to helping their candidate win.

A number of patterns have become apparent. When an incumbent president has been renominated, the national committee staff was often pretty much under his control before the nomination was secure. Thus, the Democratic National Committee in 1980, while officially neutral in the nominating contest, was in fact staffed largely with Carter loyalists who were anxious to help in his reelection effort. In 1984, the Republican National Committee, its chair, and its staff made no secret of the fact that they were helping President Reagan in his reelection bid.

But what about the other cases, when no incumbent president has a nomination in hand or when an out-party nominee begins to organize for the general election? The tradition has been for the nominee to name his own people as officers of the national committee and for the national committee to get to work on the campaign. In 1972, for example, George McGovern named Jean Westwood, a loyal supporter from the state of Utah, as DNC chair; and she headed that organization during his unsuccessful effort to unseat Richard Nixon. But the tradition requires reexamination.

First, the two national committees are no longer the same. The Republican National Committee is an extremely professional, well-financed, well-staffed organization that is capable of helping a number of candidates in very important ways. The RNC works for the presidential candidates, but it also helps Republican candidates for Congress, the Senate, and other offices as well. (See Chapter 10, Tables 10-13 and 10-14.)

On the other hand, the Democratic National Committee is a quasi-professional, underfinanced, understaffed organization. Since assuming the 1968 campaign debts of Robert Kennedy and Hubert Humphrey, the DNC has been struggling to reverse these debts and to catch up with the expertise, in all aspects of campaign work, demonstrated by its Republican counterpart. Much progress was made under the party leadership of Chuck Manatt, and so the DNC now functions much more like the RNC, but still the main function of the DNC has been to serve as a communication mechanism for Democrats throughout the nation.

Other factors further complicate the relationship between the national committee and the candidate. The Federal Election Campaign Act of 1971 mandated that each candidate have a separate central campaign committee that is responsible for all spending during the campaign. (This is discussed at length in Chapter 10.) Thus, in 1972 the Nixon campaign set up the Committee to Re-elect the President as a separate entity, a pattern that has been followed ever since. The roles played by the national committees have had to be pointedly separate from those played by candidates' central campaign committees.

One result in recent elections has been multiple campaign headquarters, a candidate's national headquarters and the national committee headquarters. The two national committees work for the presidential candidates' campaigns, but they also work for their entire ticket. However, in 1984 and 1988 both parties' presidential campaigns have taken advantage of a loophole in the campaign finance legislation. Money raised by the national committees and spent on behalf of the entire ticket can be used in addition to the grants given the presidential campaigns from public financing. As presidential campaigns have extensive fund-raising operations in place during the primaries, they are better able than the national committees to continue raising money during the fall. Thus, in each of the last two presidential elections, the nominees have essentially transferred their fund-raising operations to the national committees after the conventions, thus allowing the national committees to raise and spend more money on the fall campaign than they otherwise would have been able to do (see Chapter 10 and Alexander, 1986; Alexander & Bauer, 1991; Center for Responsive Politics, 1985, 1989).[2]

Traditionally, every presidential nominee has assumed that naming the national committee chair was his prerogative in order to ensure cooperation between the national committee and the presidential campaign. However, the interdependence between the presidential campaign and the national committees has not always been routine. For example, in 1984, Walter Mondale, assured of the Democratic nomination, sought to name Bert Lance, the chair of the Georgia State Democratic Committee, one of Mondale's most important supporters in the south, and Jimmy Carter's friend, confidante, and first budget director (until he was forced to resign), as chair of the Democratic National Committee. But the Democratic National Committee had taken on a life of its own. DNC chair Chuck Manatt had worked hard at retiring the Democrats' debt, at increasing the professionalism of the DNC staff, at closing the gap between the Democrats' fund-raising abilities and those of the Republicans, and at restoring some luster to the badly tarnished DNC image. Manatt's success had earned him the admiration, loyalty, and support of the DNC members throughout the nation. Many members of the DNC were not willing to see Manatt unceremoniously dumped in favor of a political crony whose ethical standards had been publicly called into question. Vehement in their opposition to Lance, they forced Mondale to back down and announce that Manatt would stay on. Not only did one of the first attempts to structure the campaign fail, but while the DNC did work with the Mondale campaign, the DNC also remained, in fact as well as in theory, an independent organization.

---

[2] The amounts raised and spent in this manner were estimated at $22 million for the Republicans and $23 million for the Democrats in 1988 (Alexander & Bauer, 1991, p. 37).

Campaign headquarters are places where decisions are made. Multiple headquarters makes some sense because different kinds of decisions can be made by national party committees, which are concerned with all candidates throughout the nation, and candidate organizations, which are only concerned about one office. Combining these offices made more sense when the only concern of the national committees was the presidential campaign. However, because of changes in federal law and committee expertise, this is no longer the case.

3.   The Mobile Headquarters But if the definition of campaign headquarters is where important decisions are made, then one must also consider the mobile nature of presidential campaigns in this era of crisscrossing the nation in a matter of hours. In a very real sense, the campaign headquarters is where the candidate is. Presidential campaigns travel in an airplane that is outfitted for the candidate's comfort and his staff's needs. In essence, the candidate's plane is a traveling office (see Kessel, 1984, p. 354; 1988, p. 131; 1992, pp. 123–124). Those traveling with the candidate (not those in the permanent campaign headquarters) make many of the important strategic decisions, because often decisions must be made quickly. Thus, candidates often insist that their most trusted advisers travel with them. However, those on the plane can lose sight of the fact that many important decisions are not instantaneous, but rather require planning and staff work, and must be made back in the more permanent headquarters.

Campaign managers face a dilemma. They know that managing a national campaign with a multimillion dollar budget represents a major administrative challenge. To handle this task requires time for planning, staff assistance, a complete organization. On the other hand, they need access to the candidate, and he needs their counsel on the road. Most managers divide their time between the permanent headquarters and the plane, the traveling headquarters of the campaign.

4.   Division and Integration of Authority and Responsibility Since a tremendous amount of work must be done on a presidential campaign, a large number of people, all of whom are quite powerful politically, are involved in organization and management. Authority is divided among the chair of the national committee, the campaign manager, the chair of the candidate's campaign committee, and perhaps others with similar titles. Each of these has access to the candidate; each came to the campaign with a certain power base; each hopes to leave with more power. Each definitely has a personal stake not only in the outcome of the campaign but in his or her own role in reaching that outcome.

In addition, various individuals assume authority over functional aspects of the campaign. They carve out their own space and either apply existing expertise or quickly develop expertise, so that they know the area in which they are working better than anyone else. In short, they make themselves indispensable. These individuals must be made to fit into the campaign organization. On the one hand they are important cogs in a wheel that needs to be complete in order to function efficiently. On the other hand, they demand (and often require) a certain amount of autonomy. The juggling act is often difficult.

One test of a campaign organization is how well it all works together. With the stakes so high, for the candidate and for the individuals involved, with the time period so short, with the task so formidable, it is possible that integration of the campaign organization is never accomplished. A fragmented campaign often is the result of frustration when strategies are not working; that kind of fragmentation only compounds the problems that created it. Many who watched the 1984 Mondale campaign felt that problems such as those just mentioned plagued that effort until the very last weeks. On the other hand, observers of the Dukakis campaign in 1988 felt that many of his problems came from an inability to listen to what his advisers said (C. Black & Oliphant, 1989).

The 1984 Reagan and the 1988 Bush campaigns each gave the appearance of a unified organization, a group working together for a common goal. Staff rivalries and jealousies were put on the back burner. Again, this seems to be a more common occurrence with winning campaigns than with campaigns in trouble. If things are going well, there is enough glory to share and enough spoils so that everyone can be rewarded. When things are going badly, the problems inherent in campaign organizations are exacerbated as everyone looks for someone else to blame for the deteriorating situation.

B.   Functions of a Presidential Campaign Organization

In simplest terms, the function of a presidential campaign organization is to carry the candidate's campaign for the presidency the length and breadth of the country. The structures adopted by various campaigns over the years to achieve this goal have had a number of similarities.

1.   Grass-roots Politics The media lead observers to believe that candidates and their top aides take some time to rest after securing a presidential nomination. In fact, nothing could be further from the truth. They simply are engaged in a different type of activity, less visible, involving less travel and fewer speeches, but not less importance. They are engaged in the task of building and cementing an organization that spans the nation, that draws in as many different types of people from different locales as is possible, and that is ready to jump into action, to perform the tasks necessary to campaign nationally, as soon as it is called upon.

These tasks involve the grass-roots approach to politics. Friends and neighbors must be convinced to support the candidate. A campaign must be visible in area after area. There must be a feeling that it is right to support a candidate actively, because there are lots of others doing so. When the candidate or his running mate appears in an area, enthusiastic crowds must be in evidence. This enthusiasm breeds more enthusiasm, but the initial response does not occur spontaneously; it results from continuous activity on the part of those most actively on board.

Geographic Organization Basic to any presidential campaign organization is a national campaign committee that stands at the pinnacle of a pyramid of more local geographically defined committees. That is, below the national level a campaign will set up regional committees, below that level state committees, and below that level local committees. One test of the strength of an organization is its ability to find individuals willing to lead and serve on all these committees. During the prenomination phase of the campaign, it is not at all uncommon for a campaign to have spotty coverage, to have some areas where no coterie of supporters emerges to run the campaign for a candidate. After the nomination, the task is to fill these gaps and to augment previously existing committees with important individuals who may have previously supported other candidates. Thus, a state chair in a pivotal state may have to be wooed and courted to join the campaign; such negotiations take time, often the scarce time of the candidate himself. But this is a nontrivial task requiring organizational skills and tact. It is one of the first important tests for an organization after the nomination has been secured.

In establishing a national organization, a candidate and his campaign manager must remember a number of important factors. First, they must be cognizant of the role of party and of the relationship of the candidate's supporters to local party officials in various areas. In some cases the local committee for a presidential campaign will be the same as the local party committee. In other areas, such an arrangement would be counterproductive. Detailed political knowledge is the only way such decisions can be made. Thus, one can see the importance of having state and regional advisers who are attuned to the nuances of local politics. In the 1984 and 1988 elections, the ability of the presidential campaigns to offer local committees financial assistance—from soft money channeled through the national committees—has been an important incentive for state and local party organizations to work for the presidential ticket.

Demographic Organization Further, campaign organizers must beware of the trap of thinking only in geographic terms. An activist woman from Pittsburgh might well relate more closely to women's groups supporting a candidate than to the Pittsburgh party organization. Consequently, campaign organizers frequently set up a series of committees based on demographic characteristics which are parallel to those based on geographic location.

For these committees to work, a number of conditions must be met. Group members must have a sense of unity and a sense that there is a reason for them as a group, not just as individuals, to back one candidate. Second, a key leader of the group must be willing to take a visible position, heading that group's efforts on behalf of the candidate. The leader must be aware of the internal politics within the group and of the ways to unify that group behind one candidate. Finally, the communications network between the campaign organization and the group organization must be extremely sensitive.

Whenever parallel organizations are established with overlapping responsibilities, there is the possibility of conflict. Every woman, every black, every Hispanic, every Jew, every member of every group lives somewhere. Most of these individuals are members of more than one demographic group. Many are members of other self-defined groups, e.g., labor unions, teachers, clergy. Their loyalty is often divided. They are undoubtedly part of a group for reasons other than electoral politics; members share a common interest but not necessarily a common political orientation. Group leaders in each group appeal for their support. These efforts, while all well-intentioned, can work at cross-purposes. Gaining the benefits of group efforts without losing support because of intergroup conflict, or conflict between group organizations and geographically defined committees, defines another test of the strength of a candidate's overall campaign organization (see Kessel, 1984, p. 363; 1988, pp. 131–136; 1992, pp. 125–133).

Grass-roots politics at the presidential level might seem to be a contradiction in terms, but that type of campaigning remains crucial. Building enthusiasm for a candidate at the grass roots is the most important function performed by many of those working on that candidate's behalf. Without that effort, the work of the rest of the organization, to which we now turn, would be fruitless.

2. Staffing the Candidate's Plane As mentioned earlier, one of the key decisions faced early in a campaign concerns who should travel with the candidate. In many ways, the candidate's plane does become a surrogate campaign headquarters. Many of the functions that are performed at a campaign headquarters for a local campaign are in fact service functions for the candidate. It only seems logical that those performing these tasks need to be near the candidate wherever he happens to be campaigning.

Thus, *press aides* must accompany a candidate. The press is traveling with him. Those charged with massaging the press so as to polish the candidate's image need to be along as well.

Similarly, the candidate needs to have *speech writers* in his traveling entourage. For some time journalists have been aware that every candidate for national office develops a set speech that is given at virtually every campaign stop along the way. "The speech" is an important part of a candidate's campaign arsenal, but it is not the only public address given during a campaign.

"The speech" is modified in two ways. First, it is shaped and molded and improved along the way. Speech writers come up with new lines for the candidate to try. If they work, if they receive a positive response, they are incorporated into the speech for future presentations. Less successful phrases or topics, or those that have lost their time value, are dropped. On the other hand, if the new parts of the speech do not receive the anticipated audience reaction, they are dropped as quickly as they are tried. Some candidates work hard at the details of their set speech. Most leave that to the wordsmiths, those traveling with the candidate who are responsible for his spoken word.

"The speech" reflects the basic themes of a presidential campaign. However, almost every day a candidate must speak to a specialized audience or on a detailed or technical topic. The set speech will not do for these occasions. Again, the craft of the speech writer is called for. Many have marveled at the ability of candidates for national office to speak authoritatively on a wide range of subjects. Their real skill is to present the words of others as if they were their own.

When a speech to a group with a particular interest is called for, or when a new policy statement must be outlined, the candidate and his top advisers go over the general topic, refining the positions to be taken. The speech writers then take over, converting some vaguely stated ideas into smooth-flowing prose that echoes the cadences and images thought to be unique to their candidate. If the speech is of particular significance, the candidate and top staff might review draft after draft, suggesting changes, calling for the amplification of some points, the downplaying of others. The candidate might even practice speeches that will be seen by large or influential audiences. However, just as frequently, the candidate will give a speech he has seen but once. The true test for a candidate comes when he is asked to clarify points he has made in a speech he has hardly had time to read, let alone to study.[3]

To make certain that a candidate's day runs smoothly, the plane also carries logistical staff. Campaigns employ teams of *advance men and women,* whose job it is to go into an area ahead of a candidate, plan all the logistics of the visit, and then remain for the candidate's visit in order to ensure that all goes as planned. Advance work has become an art, the art of knowing where a candidate should appear when, the art of knowing which politicians should be consulted and which can be given less attention, the art of knowing how to bring out the biggest crowd, or the crowd that appears the biggest, the art of assuring good visuals for the nightly news. (See Bruno & Greenfield, 1971, for a description of advance work by one of the acknowledged experts.)

The work of the press aides becomes easier if the speech writers and those concerned with the logistics of a presidential campaign are doing their job well. When they are not, however, decisions must be made about how a campaign can be turned around. In order to do this, most candidates want a group of their top advisers with them at all times. Access to the candidate means influence, and so those who view themselves as important often want to be traveling with the candidate at all times.

Thus, yet another element of the campaign plane involves *key political advisers.* Everyone with important responsibilities on a campaign must decide whether those responsibilities can best be carried out on the road with the candidate or from the national headquarters. The senior campaign advisers, in consultation with the candidate, must determine who should have instant access to the candidate and on whose counsel the candidate wants to be most dependent. These decisions often change as a campaign progresses. However these decisions are made, it is clear that the staff on the campaign plane nearly parallels that in campaign headquarters, and it is imperative that there is constant communication between the two loci of decision making.

---

[3] "The speech" is as much a part of the arsenal of candidates when they are seeking the nomination as it is after they are nominated. In January 1988, the *New York Times* ran a series in which the set speeches of those seeking the nomination were reprinted.

3. Staffing the Campaign Headquarters Certain functions must be performed in every presidential campaign. While the individuals involved vary and the precise definition of responsibilities varies from campaign to campaign, these functions remain virtually the same.

Research Speech writers, as mentioned earlier, perform one type of research necessary for a campaign to function smoothly. But more is expected of a presidential candidate than the ability to turn a quick phrase. Speech writers draw on the research performed by an array of issues specialists.

Some of these people are paid staff, professionals who are working on detailed presentations of a candidate's views. Others are supporters of the candidate, or of his party, drawn into the campaign for a particular purpose. Recent campaigns have used task forces of experts, drawn from universities, research "think tanks," and the private sector to work on a candidate's position in a certain area. For instance, candidate Michael Dukakis often tapped his former colleagues at the John F. Kennedy School of Government at Harvard for expert advice. Most often a staff member coordinates the work of these groups and presents the material in a coherent way, ready for review by the candidate and his top staff and for eventual presentation to the public.

The general public is not very concerned about the details of the wide range of proposals presented by presidential candidates. However, one of the means that the press uses to assess the effectiveness of a campaign and the quality of a candidate is to evaluate the specific proposals floated by that candidate to handle the nation's problems. The press (and the most interested parts of the public) is also concerned about the quality of the individuals who are working for a candidate. Who a candidate is advised by during a campaign gives some indication of who will staff an administration should that candidate be elected. The press and the attentive public view these matters seriously. Their evaluation of the individuals who advise a candidate on issues does play an important role as the public arrives at an overall evaluation of that candidate. For all these reasons, presidential campaign organizations spend a good deal of time developing a corps of issue advisers to serve throughout the fall campaign.

Public opinion pollsters do an entirely different kind of research for presidential campaigns. Though the tasks and the methods are different from those researching specific policy issues, the results are put to surprisingly similar use.

Public opinion polling has played an important role in presidential campaign politics at least since John Kennedy's campaign in 1960. However, as pollsters have become more sophisticated and as campaigns have become more sophisticated, that role has been changing.

Today every major-party candidate for the presidency employs a professional public opinion pollster full-time throughout the campaign. In 1984, both President Reagan and Walter Mondale employed teams of pollsters, coordinated by respected professionals who have made a career of polling for candidates of one particular party. In 1988 Robert Teeter headed polling for the Bush campaign; Tubby Harrison was the lead pollster for Governor Dukakis, but his efforts were coordinated with those of Tom Kiley, a respected pollster who was working closely with the campaign management team on media strategy. Whereas once pollsters sampled public opinion a couple of times during a campaign, today that opinion is constantly under scrutiny. The latest polling technique involves a *rolling sample;* the pollsters are continuously testing public opinion. They arrive at their latest judgments by replacing responses that are a couple of days old with ones coming in over night, rolling over a third or a fourth of the sample each day. Thus the pollsters feel they can tell, on a day-to-day basis, how a campaign is moving, what appeals are working with what groups, what ideas should be dropped. In addition, public opinion experts are now relying on *focus groups* to supplement their polling data. Focus groups are smaller groups of citizens taken to be roughly representative of some subpopulation, whose views on a particular subject are probed in depth by a public opinion analyst. Focus groups are typically employed to see how people are likely to react to a new campaign initiative or to a proposed commercial.

The pollster of today is, almost by definition, a major adviser to a candidate.[4] The pollster tests the political waters on new ideas, gauges how the public will respond to new issue positions or to the candidate's response to an emerging crisis, and advises how a campaign can present the best image to the public. Major-party candidates for the presidency are too well known, and their positions are too well known, for any candidate to change his views according to the latest polling results. But that is not to say that these candidates are not capable of molding their views, shaping their position papers, and determining where to place their emphasis according to their pollsters' latest reading of the public's will.

Pollsters are still used for the traditional task of determining how a campaign is doing. It was Pat Caddell who told President Carter that he was about to be badly defeated as he finished his 1980 campaign. Similarly, shortly after his final debate with President Reagan, Walter Mondale was told by Peter Hart, his chief pollster, that he could not possibly win the presidential election. And it was President Reagan's chief pollster, Richard Wirthlin, who told the president that he had the chance to carry all fifty states.

But in the final analysis, knowing whether one is winning or losing is not very important unless one can do something about it. The increased sophistication of modern polling techniques has allowed pollsters to play a key role in political decision making precisely because they are the ones who can give the best indication of what is necessary to maintain or improve the fortunes of a campaign in progress.

---

[4] The example of Tom Kiley in the Dukakis campaign is instructive here. For many years Kiley and his partner John Martilla have run one of the most successful "general-purpose" campaign management firms, specializing in polling and media. Martilla worked in the Biden campaign for the presidential nomination. Kiley was considered as one of the possible candidates to replace John Sasso, when Sasso had to resign as campaign manager for having leaked information on Biden's past to the news media and then denying that fact (C. Black & Oliphant, 1989, pp. 59–70). Kiley was not hired, in part at least because of his partner's association with Biden. However, when Susan Estrich became Dukakis's campaign manager, she did hire Kiley, to help both with polling and generally with media strategy. Although he did not do most of the polling for the campaign, his input was clear throughout (C. Black & Oliphant, 1989, pp. 75–76).

Public Relations Similarly, the press aides who travel with the candidate are not the only ones on a campaign concerned with public relations. Press aides traveling with the candidate are only part of a larger public relations team. The *public relations team* works on many different levels. The press aides are concerned with the working press that covers the candidate on a day-to-day basis. This group includes the traveling press corps and the local media in the areas the candidate visits. (See Adams, 1982; T. Patterson, 1980; T. Patterson & McClure, 1976; Robinson & Sheehan, 1983; Wayne, 1988, 1992, chap. 7.)

At the same time, others are concerned with how the candidate is perceived by the press throughout the nation. The candidate on the road stimulates coverage in most of the nation's newspapers. The campaign headquarters staff concerned with press relations monitors this coverage and seeks means to assure that the campaign is perceived in the best light. Thus, staff members send out appropriate "press packages" to local newspapers; they talk with editors and publishers; they work to enhance the campaign's image by giving members of the press whatever will help them know the candidate better. Campaign managers are very concerned about the image a candidate portrays in the daily newspapers, on the nightly news shows on television, and in the weekly newsmagazines. Thus, a good deal of effort goes into working with those responsible for the media. (See Adams, 1982; Crouse, 1973; Robinson & Sheehan, 1983.)

However, to an uncomfortable extent, how a candidate and a campaign are portrayed in the press is beyond the control of the campaign staff. Hard as they may work, the final decisions are made by those observing their actions and interpreting them, not by campaign staff. On the other hand, the campaign organization has direct control over paid media. A crucial part of the public relations effort revolves around producing paid commercials for television and advertising for other media.

Ever since the Eisenhower campaigns of 1952 and 1956, advertising firms have played a key role in presidential campaigns. Many were scandalized that General Eisenhower was a "Madison Avenue" candidate. The extent to which he relied on commercial advertising to create a favorable image seems paltry compared with today's standards.

In modern presidential campaigns, the advertising executive is, again almost by definition, one of the key political advisers. While this appeared to be the case in the 1950s and early 1960s, it became apparent for everyone to see in the 1968 campaign. Richard Nixon was presented to the public in a carefully packaged manner, and this packaging was chronicled in Joe McGinniss's popular book, *The Selling of the President 1968* (1969). McGinniss presented a picture of a presidential candidate who was sold to the American people in much the same manner as any commercial product is marketed. Just as with commercial marketing, the bad sides of the product were hidden from public view. Only the most favorable images, carefully screened, were ever seen by the buying (or rather, voting) public.

While the McGinniss book is clearly critical of the Nixon experience, more recent accounts have merely accepted the preeminence of media specialists as campaign advisers. Gerald Rafshoon carried this role to one logical extreme by accompanying Jimmy Carter to the White House in order to create the correct image for a president just as he had for a presidential candidate. The transformation from media adviser for a candidate, creating paid commercials to garner necessary support, to media consultant for a president, staging walks down Pennsylvania Avenue on inauguration day or fireside chats in cardigan sweaters, seemed almost imperceptible as Rafshoon moved from a campaign payroll to a White House job.

David Garth, working for John Anderson (R., Ill., 1961–1981) in 1980, carried the role of media consultant to the other extreme. When it became apparent that the Anderson campaign could not build the kind of national organization necessary to run a full-fledged campaign throughout the nation, Garth assumed overall campaign direction. Essentially the Anderson campaign became a mass media campaign. Garth devised a media strategy that was aimed at creating a candidate image, raising money, convincing voters, and, in the most fundamental way, remaining viable.

Criticism of the media packaging of candidates was renewed in 1988. Roger Ailes, the media adviser for the Bush campaign, structured a hard-hitting campaign that critics felt was short on substance and unduly negative. In order to picture Governor Dukakis as someone soft on crime, Ailes created a commercial that showed criminals in a revolving door, leaving incarceration unattended. The ad was a not too subtly veiled reference to the record of Willie Horton, a man convicted of murder in Massachusetts, who raped a woman while out on furlough under a program passed during the Dukakis administration. The ad seemed to go out of its way to provoke racial antagonism. While the ad did not mention Horton directly, Bush's campaign operatives highlighted the Horton episode at every opportunity.

Other advertisements wrapped candidate Bush in the American flag and seemed to question the strength of Governor Dukakis's patriotism. Political analysts and media critics cried "Foul!" but the Bush campaign operatives defended their strategy as an appropriate way to highlight weaknesses in Dukakis's record (Germond & Witcover, 1989). Perhaps more to the point, the Dukakis campaign let these commercials air unanswered throughout the first months of the campaign. While the methods of the Bush campaign advertising staff were questioned, the inability of Dukakis's counterparts to mount a counteroffensive has been raised as one of the main failings of that campaign. According to Christine Black and Thomas Oliphant, *Boston Globe* reporters who followed the Democratic campaign closely:

> The advertising failure was colossal, stupendous, dramatic, intricate, but also at times side-splitting, thigh-slapping, head-scratching. It was a failure that needed long and complex roots because it was far too gigantic to have been produced by one lone bumbler. To produce a failure this sweeping took scores of people, meetings, committees, plans, proposals, outlines. . . . [I]nternal rivalry, a balky candidate, and some fatally flawed judgments kept it tearing at the increasingly tattered fabric that was Michael Dukakis's presidential candidacy (1989, pp. 234–235; see also pp. 235–259).

The public relations aspect of a campaign cannot be devised in a vacuum. What the candidate is saying on the road, what issues the candidate chooses to emphasize, how the candidate is perceived in the press, and the themes of paid media commercials all must fit together into one harmonious package. Thus, in 1988, the Bush campaign as a whole was seen as negative, with emphasis on the symbols of patriotism but without substance. It was, however, a winning campaign; the contrasting images portrayed permitted Bush to come from far back in the summer public opinion polls into a commanding lead by the time of the general election. Thus, the Bush team portrayed a coordinated and an effective message; the Dukakis team did not. Unless the public reacts negatively to the way in which a message is presented, it is that job of coordination, of management, which defines the success or failure of these campaign enterprises, not the evaluations of critics of democracy (see Buchanan, 1991).

C.   Directing the Campaign Organization

1.   **The Inner Core** In every modern presidential campaign, some one individual has had the title of campaign manager or perhaps campaign director; in some campaigns there have been both. What is essential to realize is that the enterprise of running a national presidential campaign in such a short period of time is so monumental that no one person can have overall responsibility. *In virtually every recent campaign the major-party nominees have surrounded themselves with an inner core of dedicated and trusted advisers who collectively have made the major decisions for the campaign.*

Who are the individuals who constitute this core group? Typically they are the advisers who have served the candidate throughout his political career, his personal friends, his most trusted confidantes. Thus, for candidate Ronald Reagan in 1980, this group included Edwin Meese, who had served Reagan throughout his California governship; Richard Wirthlin, who had polled for Reagan throughout his political career; William Casey, who had been a friend and adviser to Reagan for the better part of three decades; William Timmons, a Republican strategist who had been with Reagan since 1968; Stuart Spencer, a long-time California political consultant; and Michael Deaver, the aide who was personally closest to the Reagans.

President Carter's strategy group in that 1980 campaign was composed mainly of the same group of Georgians who had advised candidate Carter in 1976. The names are familiar. Hamilton Jordan, the White House chief of staff and campaign manager in both 1976 and 1980, and Jody Powell, the president's press secretary, had both been with Carter since his days as Georgia's governor. Charles Kirbo, a prominent Atlanta attorney, had been Carter's senior adviser throughout his career. Robert Lipshutz, issues coordinator Stuart Eizenstat, pollster Pat Caddell, and media consultant Gerald Rafshoon all continued to retain their positions of influence.

In 1988, the Bush inner core was headed by his long-time friend James Baker. Baker had run Bush's unsuccessful campaign for the Republican nomination in 1980. He served in the Reagan administration as White House chief of staff and then secretary of the treasury. But he left the administration to help orchestrate the general election campaign of his Texas neighbor. Bush and Baker worked closely together throughout their careers; it was Baker whose instincts the candidate trusted most. But the team had others—seasoned professionals whose political instincts were tested and proven: Robert Teeter, the pollster; Roger Ailes, the media guru; Lee Atwater, the strategist; and Robert Mosbacher, the fund-raiser. All had experience in national campaigns; all were close to George Bush and committed to his success.

Michael Dukakis had never run a national campaign before 1988. His inner core were those who were close to him in Massachusetts. His campaign suffered from the loss of John Sasso, his long-time political confidante who resigned during the primary campaign because of his role in releasing to the media some tapes of one of Senator Biden's speeches in which he adopted the words and even life history of British Labour party leader Neil Kinnoch as his own, without attribution, and his denying that role (C. Black & Oliphant, 1989, pp. 59–70). But in some ways it is a testimony to the strength of Dukakis's inner core that his campaign survived the loss of his right-hand man. Dukakis relied on the advice of his old friend and neighbor, attorney Paul Brountas; his fund-raiser, Robert Farmer; Susan Estrich, the Harvard law professor who succeeded Sasso; and Sasso himself, who returned to the general election campaign in a less public but equally important role.

The pattern of deriving a core group in this manner has been broken only once in recent campaign history. That exception proves the rule. In the 1976 Ford campaign, the inner circle comprised individuals with important campaign responsibilities, but, on the whole, not people who were personally close to the president. The group was made up of five individuals whose goal was to retain the White House for the Republican party. Their loyalty was to that goal much more than to the individual whose campaign they were running.[5]

Why did Ford not rely on long-time political advisers? Quite simply because Ford had not been a national politician for very long. He had had a very successful career in the House of Representatives. But congressional politics is local politics. He quickly discovered that his political cronies were out of their league in the national arena. His strategy then was to form a team of professionals to run the best campaign that experience could produce.

The function of this core group, in any case, is to set the overall strategy and to coordinate all the aspects of the campaign in order to carry out that strategy. Typically the members of this group who have specific areas of responsibility choose their own subordinates to monitor those areas. These individuals in turn choose their own subordinates, and a network of campaign workers grows.

---

[5] I am indebted to Anthony Corrado, who has correctly pointed out to me that one advantage Republicans have had in recent presidential campaigns is that they have been able to rely on campaign professionals experienced in presidential campaigns. No group parallel to that assembled to run the Ford campaign—many of whom were active before and would be active again, for Reagan and Bush—has emerged within the Democratic party. Rather, each Democratic campaign seems to bring in new campaign consultants who must relearn the lessons of the past.

2.   Expanding the Core Expanding the campaign organization is a time-consuming task. Work in this area begins immediately after a nomination has been secured. Efforts are made to draw in party regulars who have worked for other candidates or who have remained neutral in the prenomination phase of the process. The party organization's role is defined, with an appropriate (but often second-level) loyalist in charge of that operation.

Once the vice presidential candidate has been named, his or her campaign staff must be melded with that of the presidential candidate. In some cases, as when Ronald Reagan chose George Bush in 1980, this entailed working the existing Bush staff into the Reagan organization. The vice presidential candidate came to the fall campaign with an experienced and proven staff ready to work.

On the other hand, when Walter Mondale chose Geraldine Ferraro as his running mate in 1984, she did not have an experienced staff ready to aid in the general election campaign. Ferraro's most recent political experience had all been in the House of Representatives; her staff was not ready to undertake a national campaign. Consequently, the Mondale organization had to dilute its resources to serve the vice presidential candidate and then had to recruit new individuals to fill gaps that had been created.

The contrast in 1988 on this score is instructive. When Governor Dukakis chose Texas Senator Lloyd Bentsen, he was choosing an experienced and mature politician. To be sure, Bentsen had not run a national campaign, but he had seasoned staff members and contacts throughout the nation. The Dukakis staff coordinated with the Bentsen staff (Tad Devine, a key Dukakis aide who had been delegate selection coordinator during the prenomination phase of the campaign, moved over to run the Bentsen effort), but the Dukakis staff did not have to rely solely on its own staff members to take over total management of Bentsen's time.

On the other hand, when George Bush chose Indiana Senator J. Danforth Quayle, he was selecting a junior, inexperienced politician. In addition to spending hour upon hour defending the choice, the Bush management team had to supply a complete staff for Quayle, not just to coordinate his efforts with the presidential candidate's, but to assure that he did not have a negative impact on the campaign.

3.   Co-opting the Losers Finally, in working to establish a smoothly functioning organization for the general election campaign, the strategists must come up with some way of bringing into line the key supporters of those who were defeated for the nomination. The ritualistic display of unity on the platform at the national convention must be converted into a situation in which those who supported losing candidates not only vote for the winning nominee but also work for that nominee. This is not an easy task.

In recent years the Republicans have been much more successful at doing this than have the Democrats. Contrast the lack of support for Hubert Humphrey by supporters of Eugene McCarthy or Robert Kennedy in 1968, or the lack of support for Jimmy Carter by the supporters of Mo Udall in 1976 or Edward Kennedy in 1980, or of that by supporters of Jesse Jackson for Mondale in 1984 and Dukakis in 1988, with the more unified front presented by the Republican party for President Ford in 1976, despite a very narrow victory over Ronald Reagan at the Kansas City convention, or for Ronald Reagan in 1980, when his chief opponent for the nomination accepted the vice presidential nod, or for George Bush himself in 1988, when none of his opponents presented an obstacle to his unifying the party. These differences reflect some of the differences between the parties discussed earlier as well as differences in the personalities involved. However, whatever the cause, *the ability or inability of an organization to unite all factions of a party behind the nominee has important consequences for the functioning of the general election campaign.*

While building an organization is not glamorous work, some of that work is public in nature. That is, as the organization takes shape, one of the jobs of the press aides to a candidate is to let the political world know who will be working for the candidate and what they will be doing. If these events are given the correct kind of press treatment, the act of building an organization can also be a demonstration of strength and competence. If leaders of vanquished opponents' campaigns join a candidate's ranks, that demonstrates that the candidate has been successful in bringing the party together.

D. Setting a Campaign Strategy

The enormity of the postconvention work cannot be overestimated. Certainly much of the organization was in place during the nomination battle. The key advisers were all known. But the game has changed, the organization has to be expanded, the prenomination opposition must be absorbed, and, most importantly, the new opposition has to be assessed.

Not only is setting a campaign strategy not glamorous work, but also it is not done in public. While candidates appear to be resting after gaining the nomination, frequently they and their advisers are hard at work, devising a plan that will maximize the chances of victory in November. The public does not know of these plans; their effectiveness would be limited if they were made public.

Chroniclers of recent campaigns have had access to some of these plans after the campaigns have ended. (See, as examples, Caddell, 1981; Drew, 1981; Wirthlin, 1981.) Some are quite elaborate. The plan for Ronald Reagan's 1980 campaign filled two full volumes. Others have been little more than one-page outlines of what had to be accomplished. *The sophistication of these plans says a good deal about the sophistication of the campaign organization, for it is at this time that the basic themes of the campaign are debated, that decisions are made about where and when to campaign, and that strategies for conveying a winning image in the first weeks of campaigning are set.*

Campaigns for the presidency traditionally open around Labor Day, with a major speech and a national swing by the candidate and his running mate. The success of this opening gambit is a reflection of the work that has gone before. It is also frequently a precursor of events to come.

III.   STRATEGIES FOR THE GENERAL ELECTION

A.   Geographic Determinations

The basic goal of a presidential campaign is deceptively simple: garner 270 electoral college votes. The key question then is where one should go to get those votes.

Different campaigns have used different techniques to determine which states are secure (won), which are hopeless (lost), and which are marginal (possible). Increasingly the techniques used to devise campaign strategies are more and more sophisticated, but sophisticated scientific precision is not a substitute for political judgment. As has been oft-repeated, politics remains more art than science. Strategies must reflect changing political times, multiple perceptions of the stakes involved, and the chemistry of certain candidacies as well as the more stark realities of political analysis.

The last four presidential campaigns reflect these differences. Hamilton Jordan made a systematic assessment of the chances of the Carter-Mondale ticket winning various states in both 1976 and 1980. In 1976, the Jordan strategy was laid out in a long memorandum in which the importance of each state was determined by a formula using its size (electoral college votes), the potential of a Democrat carrying that state (based on certain strategic premises, survey data, and the Carter experience during the primaries), and the importance of that state to Carter's winning the election. After the "value" of each state was determined, the human resources of the campaign were allocated accordingly, giving so much weight to an appearance by Carter, so much to Mondale, right down to an estimate of the importance of visits by members of the Carter family (Schram, 1977, pp. 239 ff.).

By 1980, Jordan used a more sophisticated mathematical formula to arrive at a similar breakdown. Using regression analysis of presidential voting data from 1956 through 1976, he predicted how large the turnout would be in each state, what the Democratic strength was in each state, and whether or not the voters in that state were persuadable. After these calculations, Jordan determined that four states were safe, seventeen were lost, and the remaining states were marginal, though some of these were leaning one way or the other. Using his political instincts, Jordan shifted some states around, because of the Anderson campaign or because of particular strengths or weaknesses in the Carter candidacy. Once these judgments were made, the Carter-Mondale team devoted virtually no resources to states deemed either safe or lost and relatively less to those leaning one way or the other, concentrating virtually all of their efforts on the twenty-four states thought to be truly marginal (Drew, 1981; Jordan, 1982, pp. 305–309; Moore, 1981).

The Republican strategies in these two years were similar in outcome but arrived at quite differently. In 1976, the Ford advisers started with the premises that their candidate was far behind, that this was caused by some perceptions of both candidates which needed to be altered, and that the likelihood of doing this before November varied from state to state. One traditional strategy says that a candidate should start from his base, work into swing states, and only then attack the other candidate's base. The Ford advisers started with this basic view but altered it because they felt that their base was very small. Thus, they followed a national strategy of changing how the two candidates (Ford and Carter) were viewed by the voting public at large, hoping that they could swing voters in a large number of states in this way (Schram, 1977, pp. 251 ff.; Witcover, 1977).

The Reagan strategy in 1980 started with the assumption that whatever base Jimmy Carter had built up in 1976 had eroded because of his performance. Members of the Reagan team further posited that Reagan had no base, because he had never run a national campaign and because he was viewed as very conservative by a large portion of the population. Consequently they felt that he would have to move toward the center and appeal to voters in states where many voters were independent and moderate.

When the Reagan strategists started looking for states that would contribute to the necessary 270 electoral college votes, they felt that their greatest strength lay in the west and the Plains states, areas that had helped the most recent Republican candidates. By adding states that they felt were going toward their candidate because of his conservative views—Indiana, Virginia, Texas, Florida, Kentucky, and Iowa—they were over 200 electoral votes. They needed to target additional states to reach 270. Their first target states were the Great Lakes states of Illinois, Michigan, Ohio, and Pennsylvania, states in which they viewed the Democratic coalition as vulnerable. Their secondary targets were Mississippi, Connecticut, and New Jersey. Converting these judgments into action, they concentrated heaviest resources on the Great Lakes target states, and then slightly less heavy resources on states they felt more secure in—Texas, Florida, Missouri, Kentucky, and Virginia—and progressively less and less on states in which they felt more and more certain. Quite obviously, the strategy worked (Drew, 1981; Moore, 1981; White, 1982).

In 1984, the strategies of the two candidates were somewhat different. Walter Mondale's strategists started with the premise that he was trailing a popular incumbent by a wide margin. In a sense, they felt they were in a desperate situation. Two possible strategies presented themselves. Using the more conservative strategy, Mondale could solidify the traditional Democratic base and then move out from there. That was the safe strategy, maximize the electoral votes that could be won. However, the estimation in the Mondale camp was that not enough votes could be won in that manner to reach the needed 270. Therefore, Mondale and his strategists turned to a more radical strategy. Ignoring his supposed base, Mondale began by attacking in states that seemed secure for Reagan but that had to be won if Mondale were to achieve victory. The apparent strategy was to gain momentum by making inroads in states where inroads seemed unlikely. The hope was that a turnaround in these states would lead to success elsewhere.

The Reagan campaign saw the Mondale strategy as an opportunity. Rather than working on states that they viewed as safe, the Reagan advisers decided to move quickly into states that the Democrats normally carried. Because

Mondale was not working those states, the president had a golden opportunity. He took it. The result was that the president put Mondale on the defensive in the very states Mondale needed to carry to have any chance of winning. Mondale responded, but it was too late. Reagan eventually carried every state (traditional Democratic and Republican strongholds alike), with the single exception of Mondale's home state of Minnesota (and the District of Columbia).

The general assessment of these campaigns by political pundits is that Mondale strategists made a fatal mistake, costing their candidate any chance he had to do at all well. An alternative interpretation is that Mondale might have done slightly better with another strategy, but, short of a miracle, he could not have won. The strategy he followed was one of high risk, high payoff; he had some chance of a major upset, but risked a devastating defeat if the strategy failed. As it did.

By 1988 the concept of an electoral college "lock" was part of the everyday parlance of political analysts. The "lock" referred to those states that seemed to be safe for Republican presidential candidates in recent elections. Twenty-three states (with over 200 electoral votes) have voted for the Republican candidate in every presidential election since 1968. If one added the states that supported only Jimmy Carter among the Democratic hopefuls in this period, considering them as aberrations because of his southern candidacy, the safe Republican states contained more electoral votes than the number needed for victory—the Republicans had a lock on the election.

The Bush strategy in 1988 was to secure that Republican base and then to expand from there. The Bush campaign strategy was a close copy of the Reagan geographic strategy—win the southern and western states, including Texas; then be certain to add New Jersey and Ohio and the total would exceed 270. As the campaign evolved, Bush strategists felt comfortable in the base; in the final weeks of the campaign Bush spent over half of his time in just six states—Ohio, New Jersey, California, Illinois, Michigan, and Missouri (Germond & Witcover, 1989; Runkel, 1989).

For Democrats examining the electoral college "lock," devising a winning geographic strategy is difficult. Dukakis himself insisted that he would follow a "fifty-state" strategy, conceding nothing. Part of his reasoning was that if he could win the popular vote, the electoral college votes would somehow fall in line. Others on his staff carefully looked for state-by-state targets of opportunity. They decided that there were places Dukakis had to win to have any opportunity—the District of Columbia, Hawaii, Maryland, Massachusetts, Minnesota, New York, Rhode Island, and West Virginia. Sixteen states fell into a "should win" category—California, Connecticut, Illinois, Iowa, Michigan, Montana, New Jersey, New Mexico, North Dakota, Ohio, Oregon, Pennsylvania, South Dakota, Vermont, Washington, and Wisconsin. Together these states had a total of 303 electoral votes, enough to win. Ten other states (with 196 electoral votes) were in a "could win" category.

As the campaign evolved, the list of states in each category shifted. Polling data on a state-by-state basis made the likely seem only probable, the probable

Disneyland's Magic Kingdom provided the backdrop for this
appearance by candidate George Bush during the 1988
campaign. (AP/Wide World Photos)

only possible, and the possible beyond reach. "New math" took over; how
could the candidate reach 270? Dukakis spent fully three-quarters of his time in
the closing weeks of the campaign in just eight states—California, Illinois,
Michigan, Texas, New York, Ohio, Pennsylvania, and Missouri, states with a
combined total of 225 electoral votes. Even as defeat became apparent, he
looked for ways to maintain respectability. (See C. Black & Oliphant, 1989, pp.
148–150, 309–310; Germond & Witcover, 1989, pp. 414–418; Runkel, 1989.)
Geographic strategies are always part of decisions involving the allocation of
scarce resources, candidate time, and campaign dollars.

B.   Coalitional Strategies

While the election is contested in the states, campaign strategists realize that voters do not see themselves merely as citizens of states, nor do they only receive campaign stimuli as citizens of states. Thus, another approach that campaign advisers use is to look at voters as members of groups that logically may be expected to be either for or against a certain candidate. While strategies with this premise are not so explicit as are those based on geography, they are nonetheless important in campaign planning.

For instance, as mentioned earlier, Ronald Reagan's strategists knew they had the conservative vote assuredly in their column in 1980. No other candidate could "outconservative" the record that the former California governor had established. On the other hand, Reagan was vulnerable from the center, with John Anderson and Jimmy Carter both appealing to the moderate element in the voting public.

The Reagan response to this perception was to mute some of his more conservative views and to appeal explicitly to the moderates and independents. He did this by denying some of the more outrageous charges against him, by concentrating on issues around which a consensus could be built, and by placing emphasis on moderate stands with which he was comfortable.

In 1980 President Carter knew that he needed to capture the center away from Ronald Reagan and that he needed to cement the traditional New Deal coalition, much of which was leaving his camp for Reagan. The strategy was to base specific appeals to union members, to Jews, to Catholics, to blacks, and to women. He also planned to emphasize the differences between his views and those of Governor Reagan on foreign policy, hoping to depict Reagan as a dangerous reactionary who might lead us into an unthinkable war. The strategy was

Reprinted with courtesy Meyer and *The San Francisco Chronicle*.

a wise one, but he was less successful in painting a frightening picture of Reagan than Reagan was in painting Carter as an incompetent.

Polling data can tell strategists how they are perceived by groups of voters. Historical data also reveal how candidates from the two parties have done with various groups in previous elections. Just as it is possible to set targets for states by analyzing election returns, so too is it possible to set targets for groups by analyzing polling data. *It is also possible to base some parts of a candidate's appeal on group loyalties.* However, with few exceptions, group members do not live in concentrated geographic areas. Most of the appeals in a campaign are through the mass media, which is, by and large, geographically based. Therefore, appealing to group loyalties as separate from geographic location is a difficult task for a campaign to undertake.

During 1988, Bush defined his group as those who agreed with his *values.* His clear message was that the values of the "liberal" Michael Dukakis, the values of someone who allowed criminals out of jail, who refused to mandate leading the Pledge of Allegiance, who was a "card-carrying" member of the American Civil Liberties Union, were different from the values of the average voting American. Allowing the audience to define themselves into his group, Bush never was clear in stating what the values he was espousing were.

The Dukakis strategists, on the other hand, tried to convince their candidate that an appeal based on economic class would be a winning one. They wanted Dukakis to stress that Reagan-Bush policies hurt the common man. However, only in the final days of the campaign did Dukakis find a medium for his message, the phrase "I'm on *your* side." By using that phrase, he too allowed the audience to define themselves into his group.

C. Timing of Strategic Considerations

1. The Opening Gambit Remember again that a presidential general election campaign is run in a two- to three-month period. Before the opening of the campaign a good deal of time and effort is expended in setting the appropriate strategy. Everything should be in place before the first round of campaign appearances takes place.

That first round is always well thought out. How is the campaign strategy, so carefully planned out and so fully accepted by the senior advisers, to be implemented? It is to be implemented with a set speech that talks about certain themes, with visits to predetermined states and cities and even neighborhoods, with television and supporting advertisements stressing the appropriate messages, and with a coordinated effort at the grass roots to carry the most convincing message to the largest number of people. All is in readiness before the campaign rolls. Then momentum takes over.

2. Changes in Strategy But what if it is not working? Campaign strategies are not static; they are not set in cement. Situations change and the candidate must react. Pollsters, journalists, strategists, and the candidate himself all make assessments about "how it is going." All these observers see what is working and what is not. They know when it is time for a change, when it is time for a "strategic adjustment" (Kessel, 1984, p. 314; 1992, pp. 75–76).

Changes in basic strategy are not easy to make. First, it takes some time to realize that all is not going as planned. With modern polling, and with candidates sensitive to the "pulse of the people," feedback is constant. Still it takes some time to realize that a pattern of failure is appearing, that the campaign is not having its desired impact. Second, those who have made the initial decision about strategy, by and large, are the same ones who are assessing this new information. The team consensus about what should work was not easily arrived at. Consequently, it is not easily disrupted either.

Perhaps the most noteworthy example of a recent change in strategy was not in a general election, but in the 1980 Republican primaries. Ronald Reagan was upset in the Iowa caucuses; he had followed a pre-Iowa strategy of remaining above the fray and not campaigning. As the campaign moved from the Iowa caucuses to the first primary in New Hampshire, he changed his strategy altogether. He began active campaigning, presented himself to the Republican party as a partisan combatant, and changed campaign staff and leadership as well.

The dramatic impact of the defeat in Iowa and the fact that a significant amount of time remained before the nominating process would be complete made a change of this magnitude possible. However, once again we are seeing an exception that proves the rule.

Similar changes in general election campaigns are much more difficult for a number of reasons. No events in a general election campaign are as decisive as a caucus or primary defeat to signal the need for change. The campaign team has experienced too much success together for the candidate to consider a change in senior advisers. Too little time remains before the November election to plot a whole new strategy and to implement it. Finally, the advisers on board have given the situation the benefit of their best analysis, and thus it is unlikely they will come up with anything different.

As a result of these factors, despite the fact that campaigns are not static events, major strategic adjustments are most difficult to make. More frequently, concerns are expressed and minor adjustments are made. Some states are emphasized; others are written off. Tactical decisions, not strategic decisions, are the order of the day.

The Dukakis campaign in 1988 epitomizes all these problems—and one more. Dukakis strategists had proposed an effective, coordinated campaign plan even before he was nominated. They anticipated Bush's attacks on the governor's record; they proposed responses. But they never received the candidate's authorization to implement their strategy. The line between a "robot" candidate, handled by his managers without input into his own campaign, and an overly intrusive candidate, who does not let his campaign strategists set strategy, who controls details as well as broad themes, is a difficult one to draw. Most evaluations of the Dukakis defeat place a good deal of blame on the candidate himself; a strategy was in place which could have emphasized his strengths and his principles while still responding to Bush attacks; the candidate would not allow the strategy to be implemented (Black & Oliphant, 1989, especially chaps. 7 and 8).

3. The Calendar Moves On And while these assessments and adjustments are being made, the days slip by. Soon it is time for the final push to election day. And by that time, as political scientist John Kessel has so aptly put it, "time's up" (Kessel, 1984, p. 316; 1992, p. 76). Minor adjustments can be made, but, by and large, these are changes at the margin. The push to election day might be very important in a close election, but what one does in those last days cannot represent a major change in the strategies that have been set out in advance.

What can happen during the course of the campaign is a series of tactical adjustments. Before turning to an examination of tactics used to implement campaign strategies, we will first look at two specific strategic situations, the case of incumbents and the case of third-party candidates.

D.   The Strategic Use of Incumbency

One would think that incumbents would have enormous advantages in seeking reelection. First, an incumbent president has the power and prestige of the office at his beck and call. No one speaks for the nation as does the president. Even the most cynical political observer realizes that "Hail to the Chief" quickens the heartbeat of many Americans. When the president travels, he travels in *Air Force One,* with "United States of America" proudly emblazoned on its side. When he speaks, the presidential seal adorns the podium. And presidents play their role to the hilt. The basic premise is that the incumbent is "our" president, and anyone else is a pretender to the throne.

Other advantages follow from this one. *Whatever the president says or does is news.* Thus an incumbent president is guaranteed front page stories in all the nation's press every day. More than that, his views are considered important and legitimate merely because they are the views of the president. Few are willing to put presidential statements under the same scrutiny as those of a mere challenger to office.

As well, *presidential action shapes events.* When a president travels overseas, he is the United States government negotiating with another power. When a challenger travels, he is gaining experience in foreign affairs. When a president signs a bill into law, the law goes on the books. When he vetoes legislation, Congress must deal with his veto. When a challenger says what he would do, there are no consequences. When a president says he will not close an Air Force base, or that a public works project will be pushed, the base remains open or the bridge is built. Citizens know too well the difference between wielding actual power and promising what might be done. Presidents for some time have used the advantages of their office to time grants, appointments, legislation, and travel for strategic political purposes.

Presidents do not have to prove that they are capable of handling the office, that they have the background and experience that is appropriate; they have held the job for four years. What is better experience for being president than having been president?

Finally, *incumbent presidents have a political organization in place.* In most cases this is an organization that has already run and won a national election. But even in the cases of those incumbents who have succeeded to the presidency, the White House staff serves the president for political purposes as well as governmental purposes. Their job is to keep the president in a strong enough political position so that he can achieve his policy objectives (Neustadt, 1976); one consequence of this job is to enhance his chances for reelection.

With all these advantages, one would think that incumbent presidents seeking reelection would be invulnerable; these are some of the reasons that Democratic challengers to George Bush were so difficult to find during 1991. But remember Gerald Ford and Jimmy Carter. The record is strong in favor of incumbent presidents winning reelection, but it is not unblemished.

Earlier in this century, Presidents Taft and Hoover lost bids for reelection, but these defeats are easily explained. Taft lost because former President Theodore Roosevelt ran as a third-party candidate, as the candidate of his famous Bull Moose party, and split the Republican vote, allowing Woodrow Wilson to win with less than a majority. Hoover lost because he was president at the time of the great depression and was blamed for the economic situation by the voting public. Each of these cases was before the time when the electronic media multiplied the advantages of incumbency.

Further, Truman won with great difficulty in 1948; and Truman in 1952 and Johnson in 1968 each decided not to seek their party's nomination, in part at least because it seemed they would succeed in doing so only at great political cost. But only Ford and Carter have lost in recent years. How can their cases be distinguished from the two Roosevelts, Wilson, Eisenhower, Johnson (1964), Nixon, and Reagan? It is a fact that all these presidents did seek renomination and did win reelection, all with relative ease.

Ford is an exception that can be explained because he was never elected to a national ticket, having been appointed to the vice presidency when Spiro Agnew resigned that position, and succeeding to the presidency after Nixon stepped down under threat of impeachment. His short period in office was marked by continuing controversy over the Watergate scandal, his pardon of former President Nixon, and a recession in 1975. He did not have the opportunity to use the prestige of the office to build up his own reputation.

However, there are commonalities in the Ford and Carter cases, with parallels in the cases of Truman (1952) and Johnson (1968), which are more revealing. For all the advantages of incumbency, one important consequence serves as a countervailing force. *Incumbents are held accountable for what happens while they are in office, even if they are not the cause of those events.* Truman and Johnson were president during unpopular wars (and the narrowness of Truman's earlier victory was caused by economic difficulties at home for which Truman was blamed). Ford was the president who presided over the end of the Watergate debacle and probably will be most vividly remembered as the individual who pardoned Richard Nixon. (Recall the discussion of Chapter 4.)

President Carter's problems also were caused by difficulties that arose during his presidency. The prestige of the nation was compromised, as night after night the news programs emphasized that "America was held hostage" by a band of terrorists in Iran. The economy was floundering so that challenger Reagan could ask citizens to examine whether they were better off than they had been four years earlier. The answer for most Americans was no, and they evaluated President Carter accordingly.

The lessons for incumbents seeking reelection appear to be clear. *The incumbency is a tremendous advantage in running for the White House if the first term has been a successful one.* Only an incumbent can point to leadership ability, experience, and accomplishments in precisely the appropriate context. Only an incumbent can say to the American voting public, "Let's not rock the boat. Things are going well because of me. Why change?" The themes of "Let Us Continue," or "Re-elect the President," or "Four More Years" can be complemented by a strategy of emphasizing the presidential character of the incumbent, by running a Rose Garden campaign in which the candidate is always seen as the president, not as a campaigner.

However, if the accomplishments are not there, if the country does not have a positive view of the way in which the incumbent has run the country, if the four years since the last election have been troubled ones, then the president is likely to be blamed. If the difficulties outweigh the accomplishments, the election is just as likely to be a referendum on the last four years and the outcome is not so likely to be a happy one for the man in the Oval Office.

E. Strategies for Third-Party Candidates

The American party system has been described as a strong two-party system. Yet in three of the last eleven presidential elections more than two parties have fielded candidates who have had a significant impact on the strategies of the major-party nominees (and perhaps on the outcome of the elections themselves).[6]

In 1948 the Democratic party was split from the left (by former Vice President Henry Wallace) and from the right (by the Dixiecrat walkout and the candidacy of Strom Thurmond). Wallace ran a national campaign that attracted over a million popular votes but no electoral college votes. Thurmond ran a regional campaign that attracted slightly fewer voters to his cause but, because they were regionally concentrated, garnered thirty-nine electoral votes. Both of these candidacies were thought to hurt the Truman campaign and help his Republican opponent, New York Governor Thomas Dewey. However, Truman

---

[6] In addition a series of minor-party candidates have qualified for the ballot in some states in virtually every modern presidential election. While the role of minor-party candidates in American politics is an interesting one, particularly in historical perspective, these candidates do not have significant impact on either the strategies of the major-party candidates or the outcome of the general election. For those reasons only, they are not dealt with in greater length in this text. (See Mazmanian, 1974.)

In 1968 third-party candidate George Wallace campaigned hard for votes, especially in his native South. (AP/Wide World Photos)

still managed to win both the popular vote and a majority of the electoral college.

The 1968 campaign of Alabama Governor George Wallace and the 1980 campaign of Illinois Congressman John Anderson provide more recent examples of the potential impact of third-party efforts. Wallace left the Democratic party because he felt that the party was too liberal for his views and those of his followers. He attracted a disenchanted Democratic following. Originally political analysts thought that he would only appeal to racist southerners who remembered Wallace's defiance of Kennedy administration civil rights policies. However, during the course of the campaign it became clear that his appeal was to the more conservative elements of the Democratic party throughout the nation. In that way, he was drawing votes away from the Humphrey candidacy. On the other hand, because Hubert Humphrey was so unpopular in the south, the Wallace appeal in that segment of the country seemed to be drawing votes away from Richard Nixon; many white southern Democrats would have voted for Nixon before voting for a liberal pro-civil rights Democrat.

Each of the major candidates had to adopt a strategy for dealing with Wallace. They had to assess whether he was taking votes away from them or their opponent; they had to determine how they could minimize the impact on their voters. For Humphrey this meant an appeal to party loyalty in the north. For Nixon, it meant stressing his appeal to southern conservatives as a potential president who shared their views. The Wallace strategists had to find a way to stay viable in all areas of the country, to convince followers that a vote for Wallace was not a wasted vote.

In 1980 the "Anderson difference" sought to set candidate John Anderson apart from the Democratic incumbent and his Republican challenger by finding a middle ground between the two major-party candidates. Anderson had done well among a certain segment of Republicans in the primaries, but he could never capture the heart of the Republican party because he was viewed as too liberal on social issues. In running an independent campaign in the general election, Anderson wanted to attract voters who combined the orthodox Republican party view on economic matters with the Democratic party view on social issues. He carved a nice niche and exploited his personal strengths—intelligence, charisma, and rhetorical skills—and policy positions to maximize his support among those who disliked each of the other two candidates.

The Carter campaign viewed Anderson as more of a threat than did the Reagan campaign. The strategy of Carter's staff members against Anderson was clear. They belittled his campaign effort. First, they sought to ignore him and to convince the media to ignore him as well. They rejected any debate format that included Anderson, saying he was not really a factor in the campaign.

However, after Reagan agreed to debate Anderson and both received national attention for that debate, the Carter strategists decided to attack Anderson head on. They did not attack John Anderson the man or his ideas. Rather, they attacked the idea of a third-party candidacy. Their approach was to say, in essence, "John Anderson is a fine man with good ideas, but he is not going to win. If you really favor his ideas, vote for Carter, because his views are much closer to yours than are Reagan's."

Third-party candidates in American presidential elections frequently suffer a loss of support as election day approaches. Candidates win electoral votes only if they lead a state's ballot on election day, not if they do better than expected. Many voters realize that a protest vote for a third-party candidate is, in fact, a wasted vote, because that candidate will not win enough votes in their state to capture any electoral votes. Thus, they are convinced that it serves their interest better to vote for whichever major-party candidate more closely reflects their views. It is difficult to know the extent to which the Carter strategy of dealing with the Anderson candidacy worked. It is clear, however, that Anderson's vote total on election day was much less than the percentages he was drawing in the polls a month earlier in the campaign.

The Anderson campaign demonstrates the problem faced by third-party candidacies. Without the base of political party support, a nonmajor-party candidate has a difficult task demonstrating viability. To be viable, the candidate must remain visible throughout the campaign. The candidate must not fall too far behind in the polls. Television (both paid commercials and news broadcasts) must keep the candidate's name before the public, on a footing as nearly equal to those of the major-party candidates as is possible. Such a campaign requires a good deal of money. The major-party candidates do not have to worry about having a critical mass of money with which to run their general election campaign. Their campaigns are funded out of the federal Treasury. But minor-party candidates must raise their own money (which will be repaid from the Treasury if they poll a certain percentage of votes). The financial burden is a heavy one. It may well be too heavy for any minor-party candidate to overcome except in the case of a grave national crisis. The exception, of course, would be a fabulously wealthy individual who could fund his own campaign, as billionaire Ross Perot claimed he would do in 1992.

IV.   TACTICS FOR THE GENERAL ELECTION

The distinction between strategies and tactics is often a subtle one. The *strategy* that a campaign adopts is its overall plan to convince voters controlling a majority of the electoral college that a candidate deserves support. The *tactics* are the day-to-day means used to implement that strategy. As an example, a strategic decision involves which areas of the country should be emphasized; a tactical decision would be how to carry the message to the specified areas. A strategy might dictate that a certain percentage of resources will be used to win over a certain ethnic group. The tactical decisions convert that strategy into action, laying out which resources will be used in which ways. This section will review four specific tactical considerations to which all campaigns must give attention—scheduling of the candidate and other campaign principles, the message that will be used in the paid media, the issues that will be emphasized, and the decisions concerning possible candidate debates.

A.   Tactical Considerations of Where to Go

The most scarce resource during a presidential campaign, as with a campaign for state or local office, is the time of the candidate. Strategic decisions about what areas of the country to stress dictate some tactical decisions about where the candidate should campaign.

But other factors must be taken into account as well. As an example, the Mondale campaign in 1984 decided that Mondale and vice presidential nominee Ferraro should campaign together for much of the early campaign. They wanted to appear as a team, so that Mondale could draw on what some saw as Ferraro's charismatic appeal. This meant that the two of them could cover only half as many media markets in a day as would have been the case if they had traveled separately.

Similarly, the campaign had to decide where Mrs. Mondale should campaign, when she should be with her husband and when on her own; the same questions had to be asked and answered about the other members of both candidates' families and about other surrogates for the candidate such as Senators Hart and Kennedy. Who would be best for which areas? Or who would suffice in less important areas? These tactical questions were aimed at implementing a strategy that determined where the candidate would have to do well in order to win.

These are decisions that can be changed over time. As some states become more marginal, as some campaigners gain in appeal or effectiveness, as specific situations warrant reconsideration, these tactical decisions can be reviewed. It is difficult to make broad strategic adjustments, but it is much less difficult to refine the strategies by changing tactics. Candidate and surrogate schedules require some advanced planning. However, they do not require the lead time, nor the fundamental rethinking, that changes in strategy do. Thus, recall the discussion above about the amount of time Bush and Dukakis spent in a very small number of states in the closing days of the 1988 campaign. Similarly, many have noted that the Republican vice presidential candidate, Dan Quayle, was used in small towns with limited media markets, and almost never in the company of George Bush, particularly after his disastrous showing in the vice presidential debate. By contrast, because of his increasing appeal, Democratic running mate Lloyd Bentsen was highlighted and frequently seen with Dukakis, particularly in the south.

B. Tactical Considerations of Media Use

Today it is a given in planning a presidential campaign that a large percentage of a campaign's budget will be spent on paid media. For example, in 1988, George Bush spent $31.5 million and Michael Dukakis spent $23.5 million of the $46.1 million allocated to their campaigns by the Federal Election Commission on paid media advertising.[7] However, important decisions about how this money will be spent need to be made.

The general strategy of a campaign lays out how one will appeal to the voters, how a candidate will be distinguished from his opponent. The tactical considerations include what specific messages will be emphasized on the media campaign at what times. Of particular importance is the opening message, for this sets the theme for a campaign. The 1980 election demonstrates the relationship between these messages and campaign strategy.

In 1980 President Carter's strategists knew that they would be in trouble if their strategy called for emphasizing the four-year Carter record. At the same time, they could not ignore the fact that he was the president, and they did not want to lose the benefits that still accrued from incumbency. The result was a series of television advertisements that emphasized the complexity of the job and the fact that President Carter was experienced and growing in that job—a tactic appropriate to the strategy.

The 1980 Reagan campaign was faced with a strategic problem of convincing the public that Ronald Reagan was "up" to the job, that he could handle the same complexities that Carter was emphasizing. The tactical response was an opening series of ads that discussed the Reagan experience as governor of California, "the second toughest job in America." Again, the media tactics were appropriate for the strategic needs.

---

[7] Republicans traditionally spend more than Democrats on paid media. This difference is a consequence of at least two factors. First, the Republican party organization can raise more money at the state level than can the Democrats; consequently the Democrats need to spend more on "ground" operations than do the Republicans. Second, Republicans feel they are safely ahead in some states and therefore spend little on organization in those states, again leaving more for media. Finally, in 1988 George Bush wrapped up his nomination much earlier than did Michael Dukakis. Much of the "prenomination" money spent by the Bush campaign in the late spring and summer of 1988 was actually money invested in the general election campaign.

Just as a candidate's schedule can be altered, so too can the way in which the media message is transmitted be corrected in midcourse. The two 1976 campaigns serve to demonstrate this point.

The strategy that Hamilton Jordan outlined for the 1976 Carter campaign assumed that the south was a base out from which Carter's support could spread. In the middle of the campaign, this base seemed to be eroding. As a result, in a tactical adjustment, media consultant Gerald Rafshoon designed and filmed a series of television ads, to run only in southern markets, which emphasized the southern roots of the Democratic candidate. The tactics had been altered to increase the likelihood that the strategy would succeed.

President Ford had an image problem in that same campaign. As discussed earlier, he had not been in office long enough, nor had he been successful enough, to project a presidential image of strength. To the contrary, he was viewed as a bumbler, perhaps an incompetent, certainly someone whose ability to handle the job of president was in doubt. How could this image be altered?

The first tactic was to emphasize the presidency, to appear presidential, to stay close to the White House. This tactic was not having the desired effect. In midcourse the tactic was changed. The altered effort was to show Ford as a common man in a difficult job, one who removed the pomp and ceremony from the White House but still handled the job, a president to whom the people could relate. One of the most successful tools in changing the Ford image was to emphasize his athletic achievements. In city after city he appeared with well-known football coaches. He went on television with Joe Garagiola, a former baseball player who had become a popular television personality, as the interviewer. The public did not know Garagiola's politics, but he was an "all right" guy. The tactic seemed to be working; the image was changing from a negative one to a positive one. Votes were swinging toward Ford, not enough to change the result of the election as it turned out, but more than seemed likely before this final tactical adjustment.

The 1984 Mondale campaign also shows the potential for an adjustment in media tactics. The Mondale strategy was a desperate one; somehow he had to convince the American public that an incumbent president, who appeared to most voters to have been enormously successful, was in fact not worthy of reelection. Mondale tried to build his own image and that of his running mate in the early television campaign, but that kind of positive campaign, calling on Americans to look to their potential and the future, was not succeeding. As a tactical maneuver, Mondale strategists produced a new series of ads, emphasizing foreign and defense issues. The most memorable ad was one that called on Americans to end the nuclear arms race, to "draw a line at the heavens." Reagan responded with an ad that questioned how one could combat a threatening bear (symbolic of the Soviet Union) without sufficient arms. Many thought the Mondale ad effective and the Reagan ad too sophisticated. But these observers forgot that the artistic value of the ads was not the question; the only question was the impact. Mondale's tactical shift did not result in any significant change in voter attitudes away from the president; it represented an unsuccessful tactical shift.

In 1988 the Bush strategy was brilliantly conceived and executed, even if controversial. The Dukakis campaign was unable to make a tactical adjustment until much too late. Governor Dukakis did not want to go negative, but he was seemingly incapable of responding to Bush's attack on his character. Only in the waning days of the campaign did he finally cut an ad in which he charged that Bush was inappropriately portraying his record. This tactical shift might have been successful had it come earlier, but when it came, most voters' impressions of the two candidates were already formed.

C.   Tactical Considerations of Which Issues to Discuss

The questions of what issues a candidate should discuss and what the emphasis of television ads should be are obviously closely related. For example, the Mondale shift to the nuclear issue for his television campaign was paralleled by a change in his basic speech. In fact, his television commercials showed clips from his speeches on the stump.

Right from the start, the content of the speech repeated at each stop by a candidate is a tactical expression of his basic strategy. Perhaps the 1980 Reagan campaign shows this most clearly. Reagan's strategy in 1980 called for disabusing voters of the notion that he was a radical. His early speeches emphasized his willingness to change, that his views were not set in ideological stone. When President Carter was unsuccessful in his attempt to convince Americans that they had to be afraid of a Reagan presidency, the Reagan strategists knew that their tactic had worked. Poll results confirmed this assessment.

At that point, the Reagan tactics changed. His image was secure, so he could begin to attack the Carter image. He could begin talking about the Carter four-year record. The tactical decision was that of switching to those issues that reflected badly on Carter once Reagan's own image was secure in the minds of the voters. The final weeks of the campaign saw Reagan repeatedly asking one question, "Are you better off now than you were four years ago?" The tactic was to change the focus of the debate from Reagan's image to Carter's record. It was a most successful switch.

In 1984 the issues emphasized by each camp reflected tactical efforts to apply a basic strategy. Mondale knew that the American people were basically better off in 1984 than they had been four years earlier. Therefore, he had to ask them to look to the future. He stressed the budget deficit, the escalation of the nuclear arms race, and the America we would leave for future generations. That tactic, while not successful, was the only one available given the strategic situation in which the Democratic candidate found himself.

On the other hand, President Reagan could emphasize what he had done in office. He talked of the present, not the future. He pointed to indicators of an improved economy, to the increased prestige with which America was held abroad, to the fact that as citizens we could "feel good about America again." These issues were clearly chosen to implement the strategy of stressing the success of Reagan's presidency. They achieved their desired end.

Again the experience in 1988 proves this point. The Bush strategy was to make Michael Dukakis the issue. Bush wanted to raise questions about Dukakis's competence. Thus what he talked about was the "liberal" Dukakis; he talked about Dukakis as soft on crime; he talked about Dukakis as less than totally patriotic. His issues were not the positive accomplishments of the Reagan-Bush administration; his issues were the negatives in Governor Dukakis's administration.

Dukakis wanted to stress the positive. However, the Bush campaign had a head start on the Dukakis campaign; the Bush strategists started attacking Governor Dukakis before the Democratic candidate had a positive image in the voters' minds. As a result, Dukakis was not successful when he discussed the issues with which he was comfortable. Only very late in the election campaign did he make the tactical switch to other issues, issues that drew distinctions between those who were helped by a Reagan-Bush domestic policy and those who would be helped by a Dukakis domestic policy, emphasizing the importance of the distinction on those issues with his "I'm on your side" slogan. Again, however, by the time these changes were made, most voters' decisions had also been made.

D.   The Tactics of Presidential Debates

Debates between (or among) presidential candidates have become a familiar part of the election process, but it was not always so. Until 1960 the television networks felt that they were restricted from presenting debates between the Republican and Democratic candidates for the presidency because of the equal time provision, which specified that if any candidate for an office was given free time on television, all candidates should be given equal time. The networks were concerned about how this applied to minor-party candidates. In 1960 Congress suspended the equal time provision to allow for the famous Kennedy-Nixon debates (Kraus, 1962; see also Ranney, 1979). These set one agenda for campaign tacticians for the future. Should a candidate seek (or accept) a series of debates with his opponent(s)?

The legal questions about the viability of debates have been ironed out. The pattern of having debates sponsored by a nonpartisan third party, a role played by the League of Women Voters until it was taken over in 1988 by the Commission on Presidential Debates, set up by the two major parties, has been accepted. But every four years the candidates must decide if they will debate and, if so, who will debate and how often.

In 1976 both candidates saw that debates were to their advantage. For Jimmy Carter the debates gave him an opportunity to appear on the same platform with the president of the United States and to demonstrate his intellectual acuity. For President Ford the debates were a chance to appear presidential and to convince the public that he could handle the difficult issues. As those debates turned out, President Ford was hurt by one gaffe, in which he proclaimed eastern Europe to be free from Soviet domination; but in fact he was hurt less by that mistake than by his refusal for some days afterward to admit his error and by the media's focus on the situation.

In 1980, the debates were most important to the articulate and photogenic John Anderson. Participation in the debates, which the League of Women Voters assured if he remained above 15 percent in the public opinion polls, gave legitimacy to his candidacy. On the other hand, Jimmy Carter, who felt threatened by the Anderson candidacy, did not want to participate if Anderson were involved. His advisers felt that a presidential appearance with Anderson would only enhance Anderson's status. Ronald Reagan remained above the fray, seeming almost presidential in his disdain for the other candidates' haggling, and gracefully agreed to debate both Anderson and Carter.

After the initial Reagan-Anderson debate, in which the absent Jimmy Carter was the common target, the Carter tactics changed. His campaign was going badly, and he believed he needed a joint appearance with Reagan in order to paint the image of Reagan as someone frightening to the American people. Carter was supremely confident of his ability to "win" any debate with Reagan. He confused intellectual superiority with the ability to communicate through the electronic media. Reagan understood these differences and accepted the debate because he, too, was confident of victory. In the debate Reagan not only did not frighten the American people, but seemed totally responsible, almost fatherly. On the other hand, Carter seemed uptight and frustrated. Reagan's closing statement, which turned out to be a knockout punch, was the first in which he asked Americans to compare their position now with what it had been four years earlier. As people pondered that question, any uncertainty about the election result was resolved.

In 1984, a different situation obtained. President Reagan, now firmly entrenched and leading, had no need to debate Walter Mondale. Reagan had everything to lose and nothing to gain. However, avoiding debates has become a possible issue because the public now expects them to occur. Mondale, on the other hand, wanted as many debates as possible on as many subjects as possible. Reagan controlled the agenda, as having no debate would have been just fine with him. He made concessions because of his sense of fair play and his confidence in his own abilities. After long negotiations by the two campaign committees, two debates between the presidential contenders and one between the vice presidential candidates were scheduled.

In the first debate, Reagan appeared old, tired, and confused. For a brief moment, the tactic of debating seemed to have been a serious Reagan error, his first major error of the campaign. Mondale subtly raised the question of Reagan's age and ability to hold the office for four more years. But any doubt was removed in the second debate. In this debate Reagan raised the age issue, with a deft joke about not emphasizing his opponent's youth and lack of experience. Thus ended the age issue and Mondale's brief comeback.

Michael Dukakis felt that there was no way he could lose in debating George Bush in 1988. For a number of years Dukakis had hosted the PBS television show *The Advocates*. He felt totally comfortable on television and totally comfortable in the debate format.[8] The Democrats wanted as many debates as

---

[8] All the presidential contenders in 1988 became debate veterans. During the primary campaign season some or all of the candidates of the two parties participated in more than forty debates, with the Democrats involved in many more than the Republicans.

possible; the Republicans as few. The Democrats also wanted to assure that the vice presidential candidates debated.

The presidential candidates debated twice in 1988; the vice presidential candidates, once. The presidential debates were another lost opportunity for Dukakis. He was given plenty of material by his staff; he never went after George Bush. Dukakis looked like the well-prepared, well-briefed technocrat; Bush looked human and funny. Dukakis won the debating points; Bush the hearts of the listeners. The most poignant moment came at the start of the second debate when Bernard Shaw of CNN asked Governor Dukakis, who opposed the death penalty, how he would respond if his wife Kitty were raped and killed. Dukakis responded mechanically, answering the question but never revealing any emotion. If Dukakis's goal was to connect with his audience, Shaw had flipped him a gopher ball, and he swung and missed. The debate came at a time when the Democratic campaign desperately needed a boost; instead it fell flat (C. Black & Oliphant, 1989, pp. 262–272, 282–296; Germond & Witcover, 1989, pp. 219, 251–254, 425–447).

On the other hand, the vice presidential debates aided the Democrats and hurt the Republicans. Those who were preparing Senator Bentsen for this debate had noted that Dan Quayle frequently compared his background to President Kennedy's before he took office. When Quayle used the line in the debate, Bentsen pounced: "Senator, I served with Jack Kennedy. I knew Jack Kennedy. Jack Kennedy was a friend of mine. Senator, you're no Jack Kennedy." The lines were delivered so perfectly, so slowly, with such a measured rhythm that no one who heard them—least of all Dan Quayle—will ever forget them. Bentsen was the statesman who exuded confidence; Quayle was like a wounded puppy. The debate caused a momentary bump in the Dukakis-Bentsen polling numbers, but it had no lasting effect on the presidential election. It did, however, leave an indelible mark on Dan Quayle's reputation.

The debates have become an accepted part of presidential campaigning. That does not mean that there will be debates every four years, but whether or not to debate will remain one of the tactical questions all campaigns must address as they view the ways to implement their strategies. And debates will have an impact, not necessarily a decisive impact, but surely one about which every campaign manager must be concerned.

V. POLITICIANS VIEW THE CAMPAIGNS

From a candidate's perspective, the key aspect of a presidential campaign is that it is totally consuming. If one is the incumbent president, certainly other duties must be performed. But the emphasis is on winning reelection. The duties of the presidency are wound around the exigencies of the campaign. If one is the challenger, or if no incumbent is running, then the campaign is everything. The race for the White House is the peak of any candidate's political career. There is no higher prize in the American system, no higher stakes exist.

Once the strategy is set and the active phase of the fall campaign begins, the two presidential candidates and their chief surrogates are on the road constantly. If the campaign is going well, then they continue what they are doing. If it is not going well, then they must figure out what to do with the feeling that they are not accomplishing their goals. But they cannot sit down and think about a new strategy. They must leave that to someone else. They simply do not have time. The candidate and his entourage can have input, but their fate is in the hands of the organization they have carefully molded over an extended period of time.

No campaign could demonstrate all these points more than the 1984 Mondale campaign. Mondale had campaigned for four years for the Democratic nomination. After the nomination he and his wife and their children and Congresswoman Ferraro and her family gave all their efforts to the campaign.

After the second debate between the presidential contenders, the Mondale strategists knew that their campaign was not going to stop the Reagan bandwagon. What was the reaction of Mondale and Ferraro? To campaign harder. Many saw Mondale's finest hours as those of his last two weeks. He knew he was going to lose, but he decided that he would lose being himself, showing Americans the kind of individual they could have had as president. He never slackened his pace; he never seemed discouraged. The campaign ended with his best efforts.

And how did Mondale respond to his devastating defeat? He made a very quick assessment of his political career and said that it had gone as far as it was going to go. Walter Mondale had stood before the American people for four years, seeking their mandate for leadership. His appeal had been rejected. He accepted that verdict and chose to move on to other pursuits.

Much the same can be said of the losing campaign of Michael Dukakis, but in this case the biggest price was paid by his wife, Kitty. His best friend, his constant companion, his most loyal supporter, Kitty Dukakis was more sensitive than was her husband to the criticisms from George Bush and to the judgments of the people. The campaign took a heavy toll on her mental health, one that took many months to overcome. The Dukakis family weighed the personal costs of a campaign heavily before they embarked on what the governor frequently described as a "marathon." But it seems that they were unable to imagine what those personal costs really would be.

The glare of public light was too much for Gary Hart and Joe Biden in the 1988 primaries; the emotional roller coaster was too much for Kitty Dukakis. As the 1992 election approached, prospective candidate after prospective candidate was looking not only at political questions, but also at personal questions. Was the prize worth the costs to himself and those he loved?

One has to look with amazement at a Thomas Dewey or an Adlai Stevenson or a Richard Nixon or a Hubert Humphrey. How these men could see the verdict of a nation regarding their candidacy and then come back to run again is difficult to comprehend. Each must have had a great sense of his own worth, of his ability to convince the nation that its decision had been in error, or of the inability of his strategists to convey the correct image and message. Nixon went on to victory, then to disgrace, and eventually, some feel, to resurrection as a wise man (others disagree). Humphrey died as the Happy Warrior, seemingly always ready to have another go at the nation's highest office.

For most, however, one unsuccessful campaign for the presidency is enough. A number of candidates have tried in the prenomination phase more than once, but few have come back from a losing general election campaign to try again. Why? Because of the effort involved, because of the finality of the decision, because once one has campaigned throughout the entire nation, once one has presented his best effort to the electorate, and once one has been rejected, that verdict is enough.

On the other hand, victorious presidential candidates want that same experience again. George Bush's health has not deterred him; Ronald Reagan's age did not deter him from seeking reelection; Jimmy Carter's unpopularity did not deter him. In the last fifty years, only Lyndon Johnson, saddled with an unpopular war and dissent within his own party, and Harry Truman, in much the same situation, did not run for reelection when they were eligible (and each of these had served more than one full term, having first succeeded to the presidency). Victory in a national election seems to have nearly aphrodisiac qualities. "If the public loved me once, they will love me again. And I owe it to them to give them the chance." That very personal reaction is the essence of a candidate's evaluation of a presidential campaign.

10

Campaign Financing

When Richard Nixon's reelection campaign spent over $60 million, more than twice the amount spent on his 1968 campaign, analysts began to focus on the fact that the costs of campaigns were escalating out of sight.

Table 10-1 depicts the rise in political spending for all campaigns in presidential years over the last three decades. The amounts seem staggering; the escalation is obvious. The costs of all elections in America have grown nearly twentyfold since 1952; even if one computes these figures in constant dollars, the rise is startling. When one also considers that the number of votes cast has risen by only about 25 percent in this time, or when one looks at the amounts spent on some individual campaigns for the House or Senate or governorships, such as the $20 million Helms-Gantt Senate campaign in North Carolina or the Wilson-Feinstein gubernatorial election in California in 1990, the concern grows.

Two very real questions arise. First, does the rising cost of campaigns distort election outcomes in the direction of the moneyed interests? Second, does undue influence accrue to those who give large sums of money to successful politicians' campaigns? That is, how do the escalation in campaign costs and the politicians' search for sources of money affect the government?

Politicians who have come of age in the last two decades might feel that these problems are of recent origin, brought on by the age of television and the consequent exponential rise in the cost of campaigns for major offices. But some historical perspective is in order. Neil O. Staebler's political career has spanned half a century, during which time he has served Michigan as a member of the state committee and its chair, as a national committeeman, and as a member of Congress (D., 1963–1965); he also served as a member of the Federal Election Commission. In short, his credentials as an observer of campaign financing practices are impeccable. According to Staebler,

> Money corruption has been present in politics for 170 or 180 years. We've been actively working at it since Teddy Roosevelt started back in 1907. But for sixty years practically nothing useful was done. A few acts were passed—cosmetic in nature—and many of us in politics reached the point of despair. . . . Politics was

TABLE 10-1. Total Political Spending in Presidential Election Years

Year	Actual Expenditures (in millions)
1952	$ 140
1956	155
1960	175
1964	200
1968	300
1972	425
1976	500
1980	1203
1984	1750
1988	2728

Source: The 1952 and 1956 data are from Heard (1960); the data from 1960 to 1988 are from the quadrennial studies of campaign financing compiled by Herbert Alexander and the Citizens' Research Foundation (Alexander, 1971, 1976a, 1983; Alexander & Bauer, 1991; Alexander & Haggerty, 1987).

very much the art of figuring out what you could get away with. (Alexander & Haggerty, 1981, p. 13)[1]

I. THE CLIMATE FOR REFORM

However, it is apparent that certain types of excesses, dramatized for the entire nation by television, provided the impetus for overcoming the inertia and despair of which Staebler complained. Concern over the cost of campaigns and the impact of media advertising reached a crescendo after the gubernatorial elections of 1966. Two of those elections stand out.

In Pennsylvania, millionaire Milton Shapp, an ambitious man with no previous political experience, decided that he wanted to be governor. He hired

[1] For nearly three decades the research into campaign finance practices and reform has been dominated by a small group of political scientists. Alexander Heard of Vanderbilt University set the agenda for much of the work in this area (see Heard, 1960). Since 1960 Herbert Alexander, director of the Citizens' Research Foundation, has gathered and analyzed more data on the financing of federal elections than anyone would have thought possible (see Alexander 1971, 1976, 1979a, 1979b, 1980, 1983, 1991; Alexander & Bauer, 1991; Alexander & Haggerty, 1987). This quotation is taken from the report of one of the conferences on campaign finance reform which have been sponsored by CRF and directed by Alexander. Since the Federal Election Commission has been gathering data, more political scientists have begun to look systematically at the ways in which American elections are financed (see particularly Jacobson, 1980, 1991, and elsewhere; Magleby & Nelson, 1990; Malbin, 1984b; Mutch, 1988; Sabato, 1989; Sorauf, 1988). Relatively little work has been done on elections at the state or local level, largely because the experiences differ so widely from state to state and data are difficult to gather (but see Gierzynski & Breaux, 1991; Jones, 1984, 1991).

media consultant Joseph Napolitan to design an advertising campaign to sell "Shapp for governor" to the Pennsylvania voters. Napolitan spent millions of dollars to help Shapp win the Democratic nomination, though he lost the general election that year (Agranoff, 1976, p. 9). In the next election, Shapp, again spending his own money quite heavily, became Pennsylvania's chief executive.

In neighboring New York State, incumbent Governor Nelson Rockefeller was thought to be out of favor with his constituents as the 1966 election approached. He mounted a multimillion dollar campaign, relying heavily on paid media to transform the Rockefeller image and the public perception of his tenure as governor. Governor Rockefeller's record was sold to the New York voters in the same way as Madison Avenue sold soap products.

Other examples abound. Politics seemed to be leaving the realm of political parties and entering the suites of advertising executives. Those who had the money to afford extravagant media campaigns won the privilege of governing us. In the 1968 presidential election, Richard Nixon outspent Hubert Humphrey by 2 to 1, and the nation was presented with a "new" Nixon, carefully packaged to rectify an unfavorable image that had emerged from the former vice president's first two decades in public life. Joe McGinniss's chronicle of that election paraphrased the well-known series of books by author Theodore White (1961, 1965) with its title *The Selling of the President 1968* (1969). Reformers found a more favorable climate for renewed attention to problems of campaign financing. The concern was for the amounts of money being spent, the sources of those funds, and the campaign techniques purchased with those funds. In a basic way reformers were questioning if a truly representative government could be chosen through a system characterized by inequity among the contesting parties and openness only to those with access to huge sums of money.

Despite dissatisfaction with the system in existence, reform did not come easily. In the first place, those interested in changing the system had to be clear about what aspects they found objectionable and how these should be changed. Next they had to convince those with power, the very people who had reached office using the system that was being criticized, that change should occur. As has been oft-stated, the rules of the game are not neutral. This truism is particularly apt for campaign financing rules. The lawmakers examining proposed changes have been most cognizant of the impact of potential reforms on their own careers.

In the remaining sections of this chapter, we will look at the reforms in campaign financing during the decade of the 1970s. The examination of the evolution of the current campaign finance legislation will identify the problems that reformers sought to correct. Some of those problems seem very much in the public eye today, twenty years after the passage of the first of the major reform bills. The total costs of campaigns, the sources of campaign money and the incentives for giving that money, and the impact of the ways in which money is raised and spent will be examined as a backdrop for an analysis of current reform proposals.

II. CAMPAIGN FINANCE REFORMS OF THE 1970S

A. Historical Background

A brief legislative history is in order. Before the 1970s, campaign financing for elections to federal office was regulated by a series of acts, none of which was rigorously enforced. President Theodore Roosevelt's efforts, referred to by Neil Staebler, were a response to the success Republican boss Mark Hanna had in soliciting campaign money directly from corporations. The 1907 Tillman Act forbade corporate contributions to federal election campaigns. However, corporations remained active in financing political activity through indirect means, most notably election year "bonuses" to executives which often then found their way quickly to the appropriate campaign coffers and through visible and generous contributions by well-known corporate presidents and chief executive officers.

The Federal Corrupt Practices Act of 1925 was the principle means for regulating campaign financing before 1972. The 1925 act called for disclosure of receipts and expenditures by candidates for the House and the Senate and by political committees that sought to influence federal elections in more than one state. The law was silent about campaign activities by presidential and vice presidential candidates. By establishing a large number of committees supporting a particular candidate, it was possible to circumvent the act. The multiple committees also made it nearly impossible to find out who was giving how much to a candidate and/or how much was being spent on behalf of a candidacy.

The 1940 Hatch Act prohibited political activities by certain federal employees and set a limit on the amount an individual could donate to a candidate. The limit was meaningless, however, because the law was interpreted so as to allow contributions to a number of different committees all supporting the same candidate. According to James H. Duffy, for two decades the counsel to the Senate Subcommittee on Privileges and Elections, "Money flowed through channels which were recognized as legal avoidance of existing acts" (Alexander & Haggerty, 1981, p. 15).

The first major impetus for reform once campaigning entered the television age came from President Kennedy. Sensitized to the issue by claims that his father had "bought" the Democratic nomination, Kennedy appointed a bipartisan Commission on Campaign Costs, which was charged with examining ways to reduce the costs of presidential campaigns and to finance those costs that were necessary. The commission's recommendations, which were endorsed by Kennedy and his two immediate predecessors, Presidents Truman and Eisenhower, set the agenda for future reformers, though few of the recommendations were immediately enacted (President's Commission on Campaign Costs, 1962). (For histories of campaign finance and reform efforts before 1970, see Heard, 1960; Mutch, 1988, chaps. 1 and 2; Overacker, 1932; Sorauf, 1988, pp. 16–34; for a more journalistic account, see Thayer, 1973.)

B. Federal Election Campaign Act of 1971

The first congressional response to pressure to reform campaign finance laws was the passage of an act regulating political broadcasts; however, this bill, which passed Congress in 1970, was vetoed by President Nixon.

In 1971, Congress regrouped and passed two significant pieces of legislation. The more comprehensive piece of legislation, the *Federal Election Campaign Act of 1971* (FECA), attacked three perceived problems. It dealt with the problem of extremely wealthy candidates "buying" their own elections by limiting the amount of money a candidate and/or his or her family could spend to win federal office. It dealt with the "Madison Avenue approach" to politics by placing a limit on media expenditures. And it dealt with the sources and uses of campaign funds by tightening the requirements for disclosure of receipts and expenditures by candidates for federal office (Corrado, 1991a; Sorauf, 1988).[2]

Some of the provisions of this act were amended by Congress after only the briefest experience. Other provisions were declared unconstitutional by the Supreme Court in *Buckley v. Valeo* (see below). But the first important steps had been taken. Congress had identified some of the areas in need of attention—meaningful disclosure of campaign expenditures and receipts, the impact of media advertising, and the influence of personal wealth. These items were to remain on the agenda throughout the period of reform.[3]

The second piece of reform legislation passed in 1971 was the Revenue Act of that year. This law encouraged small contributions to political campaigns by allowing a tax credit or (alternatively) a tax deduction for limited contributions to campaigns. In addition, the Revenue Act provided for a tax checkoff to subsidize future presidential campaigns. The first of these provisions has remained in law to this day; and the amounts of creditable contributions have been raised. The second provision brought into existence the Presidential Campaign Fund, which has been used to finance presidential campaigns since 1976.

C. The 1974 Amendments to the FECA

The first election regulated under the provisions of the FECA of 1971 was the 1972 election, as key provisions of that law became effective in April 1972.[4]

---

[2] The congressional response dealt only with candidates for federal office—and thus would not have impacted on the Shapp or Rockefeller campaign discussed above—because of perceived limitations of congressional jurisdiction. Various states responded in different ways at different times (Alexander, 1976a; R. Jones, 1984, 1991).

[3] It should also be noted that this law did have a significant impact on campaign finance practice. Despite the fact that the Government Accounting Office, which was assigned enforcement responsibilities for the presidential campaigns' compliance with this law, had very little time to gear up for its new role, the Government Accounting Office did investigate and prosecute some major violations of the law, including the "laundering" of campaign funds by President Nixon's Committee to Re-elect the President during the 1972 campaign.

[4] It should be noted that the public financing of presidential elections, called for in the 1971 act, was not to go into effect until the 1976 election; this provision was part of the agreement necessary to prevent a veto of the legislation by Richard Nixon, who was, of course, a candidate for reelection in 1972.

With considerable understatement one can conclude that the 1972 experience was not one that would convince reformers that all was in order. The unethical and illegal practices of the Committee to Re-elect the President (and to a lesser degree of some of the Democratic campaigns in 1972) have been well documented, not only by the General Accounting Office (GAO), but also by two special prosecutors (Archibald Cox and Leon Jaworski), by the Senate Select Committee on Presidential Campaign Activities (the Ervin Committee), by the House Committee on the Judiciary as it considered impeachment proceedings in the summer of 1974, and by journalists and scholars too numerous to list.

The amendments of 1974 were in response to the first experience under the FECA and to the increased urgency that many felt after the 1972 experience and Watergate. The 1974 act totally revised the 1971 FECA, fundamentally changing the ways in which campaigns in this country are funded (Corrado, 1991b; Sorauf, 1988).

The 1974 FECA amendments dealt with all federal elections. Presidential elections (including the prenomination phase) were to be publicly financed, at least in part. If candidates accepted public financing, they also had to accept a cap on total spending, and so the runaway inflation on the cost of running for president was halted. While the cap on media spending for congressional elections, imposed in 1971, was lifted, much stricter limits were placed on individual ($1000 to any campaign—primary, runoff, or general—in a single election, with a total cap of $25,000 to all campaigns in any one year) and political action committee (PAC) ($5000 to any campaign in a single election but with no cumulative limitation) contributions; additionally, reporting and disclosure requirements were improved. Even the amount that an individual could spend on electoral activities independent of an organized campaign was limited. Finally, an independent, bipartisan Federal Election Commission was established to oversee the reporting and enforcement requirements of this act.

D. *Buckley v. Valeo*

Shortly after the 1974 amendments became effective, a curious coalition of liberals and conservatives joined in a lawsuit challenging the constitutionality of the FECA. *The law was attacked because it allegedly limited free speech and discriminated against presidential candidates of minor parties.* The judicial branch of the government was asked to define the line between the guaranteed rights to free speech and free association, on the one hand, and the obligation of the polity to protect the integrity of elections, on the other.

In the case of *Buckley v. Valeo*, 424 U.S. 1 (1976), the Supreme Court ruled that some aspects of the 1974 act were unconstitutional, while other provisions, deemed separable, were permitted to stand. With regard to the question of free speech, the Court held that limits on campaign expenditures, on independent expenditures, and on the amounts individuals could spend on their own campaigns restrained the interchange of ideas necessary to bring about social change and were therefore unconstitutional. The Court also struck down the way in which the Federal Election Commission was appointed, requiring that all appointments be by the president with the advice and consent of the Senate.

At the same time, the Court allowed other provisions of the law to stand if public funding was accepted: the limitations on the total amount to be spent on a campaign and the limitations on individual and group contributions (Gottlieb, 1985, 1991; Lowenstein, 1991a).

Buckley v. Valeo was handed down in the middle of the 1976 campaigns. The decision effectively closed down the Federal Election Commission and left many aspects of the funding of the 1976 presidential election in doubt. Those doubts were most serious for the candidates for the major parties' presidential nominations, as they had been counting on matching funds to finance their campaigns. Congressional and senatorial candidates also had to alter their financial planning.

E. The 1976 FECA Amendments

Despite the urgency felt by many of those involved, Congress took nearly four months to revise the FECA to comply with the Court's ruling. A number of controversial issues not dealt with in the challenge to the 1974 amendments were included in that debate, including the difficult question of public financing of congressional elections.

When the FECA was eventually revised in May 1976, the provisions for public funding of congressional elections were not included; however, other significant changes did become part of the campaign finance legislation. The 1976 amendments reconstituted the Federal Election Commission; they set limitations on the amounts individuals could give to PACs and to the national political parties; they restricted the proliferation of PACs established by one organization and the fund-raising abilities of PACs; and they limited the spending by candidates for the presidency and the vice presidency if the candidates accepted public financing of their campaigns. A series of other changes that affected the reporting and disclosing of obligations of campaigns and the powers of the FEC were also included.

Again in 1979 Congress amended the FECA. However, recent amendments are mainly perfecting amendments, involving marginal changes as a response to experiences with the recent laws. As one example, state and local party committees have been allowed to contribute volunteer time to campaigns so that the grass-roots approach to politics was not lost in the rush to reform. (See Adamany, 1984; Aoki & Rom, 1985, and Jacobson, 1985–1986, among others, on the role of campaign finance legislation in the revival of political parties.)

F. Summary

As a consequence of these laws, a number of issues have been settled. *Disclosure is accepted as a key element of campaign finance reform.* Whatever is done must be opened to public scrutiny. *Large contributions to individuals' campaigns are suspect and therefore restricted.* Gone are the days when a wealthy contributor can contribute $250,000 to one campaign. On the other hand, *individual candidates can spend what they want on their own campaigns,* provided that they do not accept public funds for those campaigns. The right to express one's political beliefs includes the right to spend money to do so; this same logic extends to independent expenditures for political reasons, provided those expenditures are not coordinated with the efforts of a particular campaign. Similarly, *the concept of public financing has been accepted, at least by the Democrats; it has been applied to presidential elections and tied with a restriction on the amount of money to be spent in those elections.*

Still, some old issues are not settled and some new ones have appeared. No means have been found to control the amount of money spent on campaigns not funded by public money. Seemingly the Court ruled that any such restriction must be tied to the acceptance of public funds. Many are still concerned about the sources of campaign funds for federal offices below the presidential level, particularly about the influence of political action committees. Others are concerned about the impact of finance regulations and of PACs on political parties. The issue of how finance regulation influences challengers' opportunities to unseat incumbents is never far from the minds of those concerned with further reform. It is to these and related issues that we turn in the remainder of this chapter.

III.   THE COSTS OF DEMOCRACY

Recall Table 10-1. Just how concerned should we be with the amount of money being spent by political campaigns? What does it mean to say that Americans spent $2.7 billion on political elections in 1988? Is that too much or too little? Relative to what? In 1988 Philip Morris spent over $2.05 billion on advertising within the United States (*Advertising Age,* 1989, p. 1), and much of that was to convince the American people to buy products that the surgeon general of the United States has found to be hazardous to their health. No one complained very loudly. That is free enterprise. The top 100 advertisers in 1988 spent a total of over $32.2 billion; no one complained. If no one complains about the advertising budgets of the tobacco industry (or of the $1.51 billion spent by Procter & Gamble, the $1.29 billion by General Motors, the $1.05 billion by Sears, Roebuck, or the comparably staggering amounts by over 100 other corporations which each spend over $100 million annually on advertising, more than was spent on the two presidential campaigns combined [*Advertising Age,* 1989, p. 1]), why should we complain about the costs to maintain a democracy?

The simple answer seems to be that Americans feel that the escalation in campaign costs has been caused by increased use of electronic media to sell political candidates and that we should not package our political candidates like cigarettes or soap products, or like automobiles or ketchup. The increases in the costs of campaigns do not mean that we know more about our candidates (Buchanan, 1991; but cf. T. Patterson, 1980). The increased costs merely mean that the campaigns are telling us what they want us to know more frequently and in different ways.

A. Presidential Elections

The concern about the rising costs of campaigns first focused at the presidential level, particularly after the elections of 1968 and 1972. Table 10-2 shows the rapid rise in the costs of running for president and the disparity that existed between the two major parties before 1976, the first election in which costs were contained because public funds were used.[5]

A common assumption was that all of the increase in money was due to television advertising. This assumption was wrong, though the percentage of funds spent on radio and television advertising jumped from approximately 33 percent in 1952 to 50 percent in 1968 (Alexander, 1976a, p. 28). In 1972, partly as a response to criticism of the 1968 campaign, the Nixon strategy called for spending far less on television and more on other forms of campaigning. The radio and television budget of the Nixon reelection campaign in 1972 was only $4.3 million, compared with the more than $12 million spent on electronic media during his 1968 effort. Nixon as president used free media very expertly, emphasizing his service in office; this permitted a strategy of campaigning by other means, direct mail as an example.

Perception can dictate policy as much as reality does. One of the responses to the 1972 campaign was the passage of public financing for the 1976 presidential election. The figures shown in Table 10-2 for 1976, 1980, 1984,

TABLE 10-2. Costs of Presidential General Elections* (in millions)

Year	Total	Republican	Democrat
1952	$11.6	$ 6.6	$ 5.0
1956	12.9	7.8	5.1
1960	19.9	10.1	9.8
1964	24.8	16.0	8.8
1968	37.0	25.4	11.6
1972	91.4	61.4	30.0
1976	43.6	21.8	21.8
1980	58.8	29.4	29.4
1984	80.8	40.4	40.4
1988	92.1	46.1	46.1

* Major-party candidates only; other candidates' spending was relatively small except for George Wallace's $9 million in 1968 and John Anderson's $14.4 million in 1980.

Source: Data for 1952–1972 are from Alexander (1976a); data for 1976–1988 are the amounts of the federal grants to the various campaigns from the Federal Election Commission.

[5] These data should be interpreted with some caution because it is frequently unclear what expenditures are and are not reported in "official" reports.

and 1988 reflect the amounts allocated to the presidential campaigns under the provisions of the FECA of 1974.

These figures underestimate the cost of electing a president in three important ways. First, they do not take into account the prenomination expenses of various candidates. Obviously the total amount of these expenses varies according to how many candidates are contesting for their parties' nominations and how long these candidates remain active. In 1980, the total amount spent by all candidates during the prenomination phase of the election was over $106 million. In 1984, the amount rose to $110 million; the Reagan campaign spent $19 million in this phase of the election campaign, despite the fact that the president's renomination was unchallenged. In 1988, with intense competition for both parties' nominations, the cost of the preconvention phase of the presidential election was $233.5 million.

The second reason that the amounts in Table 10-2 underestimate the cost of electing a president is that they do not reflect the expenditure of so-called soft money. Soft money is money spent through a loophole created in the 1979 amendments to the Federal Election Campaign Act. The loophole allows for the raising of money, outside the federal limits, if it is to be spent on behalf of party tickets, not just individual candidates for federal office. Such expenditures are regulated by any state campaign finance laws that apply. As has so often been the case, the Republicans took advantage of this loophole before the Democrats recognized it. In each of the two Reagan campaigns, the Republi-

Gala political fundraisers such as this one raise hundreds of thousands of dollars for candidates throughout the nation. (Stock, Boston)

cans spent about $125 million in soft money; the Democrats spent about $10 million between the two. In 1988, however, both parties understood the importance of soft money and geared up the presidential candidates' prenomination fund-raising teams to raise soft money for the presidential campaigns and the party tickets (recall Chapter 9). The Democrats ended up raising and spending $23 million, despite Finance Chair Robert Farmer's boast that he could raise $50 million. The Republicans, whose effort was spearheaded by Robert Mosbacker, raised and spent about $1 million less (Alexander & Bauer, 1991, pp. 37–43).

Finally, the reported figures do not include unauthorized independent expenditures on behalf of or in opposition to one of the candidates in the general election. In 1980 these expenses amounted to over $12 million for the Reagan-Bush campaign and $1.7 million for Carter-Mondale. In 1984, over $17 million in unauthorized independent expenditures was spent on the presidential campaign, again the lion's share in support of the Republican ticket (Sabato, 1985, p. 190). In 1988, for the first time, the amount of independent expenditures decreased, with about $9.4 million spent for the Bush-Quayle campaign (or against Dukakis-Bentsen) and about $630,000 spent favoring the Democratic ticket or opposing the Republicans (Alexander & Bauer, 1991, pp. 82–85).[6] Not only do these expenditures raise the total amount spent for presidential elections, through a means that the Court has held to be beyond regulation by campaign finance law, but they also lead to a disparity in the amounts spent on behalf of the two parties' nominees, despite efforts to end these disparities through public financing.[7]

B.   Senatorial and Congressional Elections

While some experts were concerned about spending in senatorial and congressional elections before 1972, reporting procedures were so lax that it was difficult to identify just how much was being contributed or spent by whom. The perception was that some campaigns spent a great deal of money, excesses that were troubling. But little was known about overall spending patterns. Two events changed the financing of congressional elections in fundamental ways.

First, the Federal Election Commission began to collect data on and publicize the costs of running campaigns for Congress. From 1974 on, detailed data on the costs of running for the House and the Senate and on the variations in those elections are available.

Second, the FECA of 1974 implemented the public financing of presidential campaigns. Suddenly those who had contributed heavily to presidential

---

[6] While the amount spent in this way decreased, the significance of it did not necessarily lessen. In fact, the most devastating anti-Dukakis ad during the general election campaign—the so-called Willie Horton ad—was run by an independent organization. Thus, the Bush campaign could claim no responsibility when the ad was criticized (C. Black & Oliphant, 1989, chap. 8).

[7] These numbers also do not include prenomination expenditures. In 1988 independent organizations spent about $4 million dollars before the conventions, about 80 percent of it favoring one candidate or another, with the other 20 percent as negative ads aimed at one candidate or another.

campaigns in the past had to look elsewhere to spend their money in order to influence the political process. One of the results of this reallocation of political resources was the pattern of congressional and senatorial spending revealed in Table 10-3.

No matter how one reads these data, the same pattern is clear: increasingly large sums are being spent to finance campaigns. In 1974, the mean expenditure for all candidates for the House of Representatives was $53,384; in 1990, it was $284,256. For incumbents the mean expenditure rose from $56,539 to $399,309 during that period; for challengers to incumbents, from $40,015 to $109,377; thus the gap between incumbents and challengers has widened. For open seats, the mean expenditure rose from $90,426 to $483,728. And increases have continued in recent years in all categories, with the notable exception that challengers' expenditures have decreased slightly in each of the last two election cycles. This decrease reflects an awareness of the hopeless electoral situation in which challengers find themselves. In fact, only thirty-four House challengers spent more than the *average* spent by incumbents in 1990.[8]

In the Senate, the mean expenditure for all candidates went from $437,482 in 1974 to $2,574,868 in 1990. For incumbents the mean expenditure surpassed $3.54 million in 1990; for challengers the mean was about half that amount, still a daunting $1.7 million. Only three seats were open in 1990; the mean expenditure in these was $1.6 million, down from recent years. Of course, because only one-third of the Senate is up for reelection in every election year, comparisons can be misleading—especially in cases like this one in which the seats that were open were not in the same states as in 1988. However, if one looks in Table 10-3 at the percentage increase from 1984 to 1990, when the same seats were contested (though recognizing that different seats were open), one quickly sees the extent to which campaign expenditures have continued to rise, with overall expenditures nearly doubling between those two elections.[9]

In 1974, only ten candidates for the House of Representatives spent over $250,000 on their campaigns, and none spent over $500,000. In 1990, the average incumbent spent nearly $400,000, and forty spent over three-quarters of a million dollars each. The million dollar campaign for the Senate was the exception in 1974; that amount was only spent in very expensive campaigns in very large states. By 1982 candidates in a state as small and as conservative in terms of spending as Maine contemplated million dollar expenditures. By 1990,

---

[8] These data do not deflate the averages by including uncontested seats. The data used in this discussion are drawn from FEC reports on the elections over this period. These data, for the period from 1974 to 1990, have been summarized in various sources including Malbin (1984b) and Ornstein et al. (1990).

[9] It should be noted that the total spending for Senate campaigns in 1990 was less than that in 1988, a drop of just over 10 percent. The comparison is difficult, because different states hold elections in different years, but the drop in Senate campaign expenditures, when combined with a smaller rise in House campaign expenditures, meant the first drop ever in the total congressional campaign expenditures since the Federal Election Commission has been publishing these data (Federal Election Commission, 1991a).

TABLE 10-3. Mean Congressional Campaign Expenditures, 1974 and 1984–1990

	1974	1984	1986	1988	1990	Percentage Increase, 1974–1990	Percentage Increase, 1984–1990
House							
Expenditures	$ 53,384	$ 191,610	$ 259,544	$ 273,811	$ 284,256	432	48
Incumbents	56,539	276,019	334,386	378,316	399,309	606	45
Challengers	40,015	119,121	124,815	118,877	109,377	173	–8
Open-seat candidates	90,426	194,767	431,213	480,685	483,728	435	148
Democrats	53,993	191,552	264,558	287,560	316,457	486	65
Republicans	54,835	197,629	253,954	258,441	250,503	357	27
Senate							
Expenditures	$437,482	$1,385,365	$2,789,360	$2,802,118	$2,574,868	489	86
Incumbents	555,714	2,486,207	3,307,430	3,988,821	3,547,193	538	43
Challengers	332,579	631,666	1,976,286	1,816,113	1,703,504	412	170
Open-seat candidates	401,484	2,003,333	3,358,295	2,886,383	1,600,722	299	–20
Democrats	487,775	1,368,333	2,377,390	2,934,817	2,464,191	679	80
Republicans	382,343	1,410,169	3,201,329	2,669,420	2,688,899	601	91

Note: Includes primary and general election expenditures for general election candidates only.

Source: Data have been compiled from Federal Election Commission sources; data up to 1988 are also reported in Ornstein et al. (1990, tables 3-1 and 3-4).

twenty-seven of the thirty-two incumbents seeking reelection spent at least a million dollars. By every possible means candidates were raising and spending money. Politicians and the public expressed a good deal of concern about what it meant to spend these huge sums for attaining public office. Regardless of where the money came from, concern was expressed about the amounts being spent.

C.   State and Local Elections

Campaign expenditure data are much less readily available for state and local elections than they are for elections at the federal level. Consequently, few analysts have examined financing of state elections. This paucity of analysis is caused by the magnitude of the task of gathering information on a variety of offices in the fifty states and is complicated because the data that can be gathered are often not comparable. Most states now require candidates to report campaign contributions and expenditures in some systematic way. However, few states have the resources to do the kinds of analyses that the FEC has done for federal elections.

Despite the limitations of the data available, some analyses have been undertaken. *The conclusion of those studying state and local elections is that the same escalation of the costs of campaigns seen at the federal level is present at the state and local levels.*

Looking at aggregate data, Herbert Alexander of the Citizens' Research Foundation has concluded that the cost of state and local elections now constitutes nearly 45 percent of the total amount spent on elections in the United States (Alexander & Bauer, 1991, p. 3).[10] That percentage is higher now than it was a decade ago. In 1980, Alexander estimated that $265 million was spent on state elections and $200 million on local elections (Alexander, 1984, p. 104). It should be remembered that more state and local elections are held in nonpresidential years than in presidential elections years and, further, that some of these elections (e.g., New Jersey's or Virginia's) are held in odd-numbered years.

Ruth S. Jones has examined costs of state legislative campaigns in a sample of states which do analyses of candidate reports. Her conclusions demonstrate that the pattern for campaigns for the House and Senate identified above is indeed repeated for state legislative races (R. Jones, 1984, pp. 174–180). In each of the states examined, the cost of the average legislative race has increased significantly over the four campaigns studied; Jones's data also show that the percentage of this increase varies from state to state, a pattern not unexpected given the differing nature of politics among the American states. Anthony Gierzynski and David Breaux, in examining the impact of money on state legislative races, gathered data from a different sample of states more recently. Their findings are similar; both are summarized in Table 10-4.

---

[10] Ruth Jones, an expert on the cost of state and local campaigns, feels that Alexander's estimate is low; on this topic scholars must speculate because of the lack of systematic data. For instance, Alexander estimates that $540 million was spent on state races and $365 on local races, but election officials in a majority of states do not publish aggregate figures on receipts and expenditures for those offices (Sorauf, 1988, p. 288).

TABLE 10-4. Average Cost of State House Races, Selected States, Selected Years

State	1974	1976	1978	1980	1986
Alaska	$15,241	$35,844	$32,319	$60,778	
California			93,572		$229,031
Colorado	5,385	8,219	12,280	17,403	25,920
Minnesota	8,256	9,694	11,813	15,882	
Nebraska			7,365		30,013
Oregon	10,413	17,765	27,133	31,773	42,953

Source: 1974, 1976, and 1980 data for all the states listed and 1978 data for Alaska, Colorado, Minnesota, and Oregon from R. Jones (1984, p. 175); 1986 data for all the states listed and 1978 data for California and Nebraska from Gierzynski and Breaux (1991, p. 207).

Jones also looked at sources of campaign funds. She found that most of the increase in recent years is from nonparty political organizations (1984, pp. 186–187). While PAC activity at the state level has lagged behind that at the federal level, it has not been far behind. States are now beginning to look at the implication of this infusion of PAC money into the political process at the state level and at its obvious implications for the increased escalation of the costs of running for state (and local) offices.

IV. SOURCES OF CAMPAIGN FUNDS

While some people have a vaguely uneasy sense that campaigns in America cost too much, *many more people are concerned about where the money for campaigns comes from and what strings, if any, are attached to political contributions.* This type of concern led to the laws that prohibit individuals from contributing large sums of money to specific campaigns. The presumption is that these individuals do not act in a charitable manner but rather contribute huge sums in reward for past action and in hope of some later benefit. Although little empirical evidence supports the assumption of a link between contribution and "payoff," the general perception—if not the reality—is that few people give something for nothing.

Because both politicians and voters are still concerned about the sources of campaign funds, a good deal is known about the sources of funds for campaigns for federal office. In the sections that follow we will examine the five primary sources of money and the questions that accompany each funding base.

A. Sources of Campaign Contributions

The Federal Election Commission has changed the ways in which it categorizes the sources of campaign contributions over the years; thus, comparison is not always possible. Generally, campaign funds come from the following sources: the candidate himself or herself, other individuals (some of whom give larger and some smaller amounts), political action committees, political parties, and public financing (which is only available to presidential candidates). While the

ways in which these categories are analyzed have varied over the years, it is possible to discuss relative contributions with some historical perspective.

Gary Jacobson (1984) has studied what proportion of congressional candidates' contributions come from each of the identified sources. As is shown in
Table 10-5, the *majority of contributions to both House and Senate candidates comes
from individual contributors.* The amount that candidates contribute themselves
was not reported between 1978 and 1986. For House candidates the amount
contributed by candidates themselves tended to be just under 10 percent in the
earlier period and much less than that more recently. There is wide variation,
however, with some candidates financing much of their own campaigns while
others contribute relatively little (Wilcox, 1988). The same variations hold for
Senate candidates, but because so few Senate elections are held in each election
year, no pattern emerges; for instance, when John Heinz (R., 1973–1991) spent
a large amount of his own money to win the Pennsylvania Senate seat in 1976,
his expenditure raised the average for all Senate races in that year. When one
estimates the amount that individuals donate to their own campaigns, it is clear
that well over half of the money spent in congressional campaigns comes from
contributions from other individuals, the amounts of which have been limited
by the FECA since 1974.

One conclusion that could be drawn from Table 10-5 is that restricting
and disclosing contributions by individuals has solved most of the problem
about the source of campaign funds. However, if one looks further into these
data, that relatively optimistic view becomes clouded. Two patterns have
emerged since 1974. The clearest pattern is that the role of PACs has increased
at a rapid pace. (Refer to Chapter 5.) Jacobson (1984, p. 40) has determined
that the increase in PAC contributions from 1980 to 1982 was over 200 percent
for both House and Senate races. By 1988 and 1990, PACs were contributing
just under 40 percent of the money given to House campaigns, though the rate
of growth has slowed significantly. More interesting, perhaps, is the fact the
PACs contributed half of the money raised by incumbent House Democrats
(Federal Election Commission, 1991b). Thus, the fact that individuals contribute more than do PACs does not allay the fears of those concerned about
group influence.

In addition, the role of political party organizations has changed drastically over recent years. (Recall Chapter 3.) The data in Table 10-5 only consider party contributions made directly to candidate campaigns. In 1982 and
again in 1984, the Republican party spent a significant amount of money on behalf of congressional candidates independent of their campaign committees. In
1982 the Republican National Committee spent more than $200,000 on behalf
of sixteen different Senate candidates; the Democrats spent that much for only
one candidate. Table 10-6 shows that, while direct contributions by the parties
to candidates have not been rising rapidly in recent years, direct spending on
behalf of those candidates, particularly by the Republican party, but also by the
Democrats, has increased.

Federal Election Commission reports also make it possible to analyze contributions to presidential campaigns. Whereas the congressional data presented

TABLE 10-5. Sources of Contributions to Congressional Campaigns, 1974–1990

	1974	1976	1978	1980	1982	1984	1986	1988	1990
House Elections									
Average raised	$61,084	$79,421	$111,232	$148,268	$222,620	$240,722	$280,260	$282,949	$308,269
Percentage from:									
Individuals	73	59	61	67*	63*	51	52	49	45
Parties†	4	8	5	4	6	3	2	2	7¶
PACs	17	23	25	29	31	39	39	43	42
Candidates‡	6	9	9	—	—	6	7	6	6
Senate Elections									
Average raised	$445,515	$624,094	$951,390	$1,079,346	$1,771,167	$2,273,635	$2,721,793	$2,649,492	$2,661,559
Percentage from:									
Individuals	76	69	76	78*	81*	68	69	68	65
Parties†	6	4	2	2	1	1	1	1	—
PACs	11	15	14	21	18	20	25	26	23
Candidates‡	1	12	8	—	—	11	6	6	5
Unknown sources	6	—	—	—	—	—	—	—	7¶

* Includes candidates' contributions to their own campaigns, loans, transfers, and other items.
† Does not include party expenditures in behalf of candidates.
‡ Includes candidates' loans unrepaid at time of filing.
¶ Includes contributions from unknown sources as party contributions.
Source: Jacobson (1992, p. 65), based on Federal Election Commission sources.

TABLE 10-6. Party Contributions and Spending, Congressional Elections, 1978–1990 (in thousands)

Year		Democrats	Republicans
	House		
1978	Direct contributions	$1,262	$3,621
	Spending for candidate	73	1,297
	Total	1,335	4,918
1980	Direct contributions	1,026	3,498
	Spending for candidate	256	2,203
	Total	1,282	5,701
1982	Direct contributions	1,052	4,721
	Spending for candidate	694	5,293
	Total	1,746	10,014
1984	Direct contributions	1,281	4,060
	Spending for candidate	1,774	6,190
	Total	3,055	10,250
1986	Direct contributions	969	2,520
	Spending for candidate	1,836	4,111
	Total	2,805	6,631
1988	Direct contributions	1,198	2,650
	Spending for candidates	2,800	4,163
	Total	3,998	6,813
1990	Direct contributions	941	2,027
	Spending for candidates	3,267	3,001
	Total	4,208	5,028
	Senate		
1978	Direct contributions	$ 467	$ 703
	Spending for candidate	229	2,724
	Total	696	3,427
1980	Direct contributions	480	677
	Spending for candidate	1,133	5,435
	Total	1,613	6,112
1982	Direct contributions	579	600
	Spending for candidate	2,265	8,715
	Total	2,844	9,315
1984	Direct contributions	441	591
	Spending for candidate	3,948	6,518
	Total	4,389	7,109
1986	Direct contributions	621	730
	Spending for candidate	6,656	10,078
	Total	7,277	10,808
1988	Direct contributions	489	721
	Spending for candidate	6,592	10,261
	Total	7,081	10,982
1990	Direct contributions	510	859
	Spending for candidates	5,193	7,721
	Total	5,703	8,580

Source: Jacobson (1984, p. 49). Data from 1984 through 1990 compiled by the author from FEC end-of-campaign reports.

312

above totaled primary and general election contributions (for those candidates who competed in the general election), for presidential candidates the sources of funds for the prenomination and general election periods are reported separately because they are quite different.

In the prenomination phase of the presidential election, contributions come from three sources—individual contributions, PAC contributions, and federal matching funds. As Table 10-7 shows, for the major-party candidates in 1980, 1984, and 1988, PAC contributions play a more minor role in presidential nominating politics than they do in congressional elections. No candidate received even 10 percent of his contributions from PACs. The most recent FEC statistics combine political action committee money with other committee contributions. Much of the money listed in this category, and accumulated in these statistics, is in fact money transferred from other political committees, e.g., to the Dukakis 1988 presidential campaign from the surplus in the successful 1986 Dukakis gubernatorial campaign. Of course, political parties do not contribute to campaigns for nominations, so these sources of contributions are absent. In short, the sources of funds for the presidential primaries are basically individual contributions and public matching funds.

The prevailing myth is that public financing of the presidential general election erased the problems that caused the concern about sources of campaign contributions for that contest. That myth is not based in fact. Independent spending on behalf of the Reagan-Bush and Carter-Mondale campaigns

" THE BOSS WOULDN'T GIVE ME A RAISE...BUT HE
GAVE ME A $10 POLITICAL CONTRIBUTION AND
SUGGESTED I RUN FOR CONGRESS! "

Reprinted with permission Stayskal and *The Tampa Tribune.*

TABLE 10-7. 1980, 1984, and 1988 Prenomination Campaign Receipts, by Source, for Major-Party Candidates Raising More Than $1 Million (in millions)

	Total	Individual	PAC	Federal Match
1980				
Democrats				
Brown	$ 2.65	$ 1.71	$0.04	$0.89
Carter	18.55	12.93	0.46	5.05
Kennedy	12.29	7.75	0.23	3.86
LaRouche*	2.14	1.55	0.01	0.53
Republicans				
Anderson	$ 6.63	$ 3.91	$0.02	$2.68
Baker	7.14	4.20	0.13	2.64
Bush	16.71	10.87	0.13	5.72
Connally	12.72	11.64	0.21	0.00
Crane	5.24	3.47	0.00	1.75
Dole	1.43	.90	0.05	0.45
Reagan	21.39	13.76	0.29	7.29
1984				
Democrats				
Askew	$ 3.20	$ 1.63	$0.00	$0.90
Cranston	7.43	3.25	0.29	1.78
Glenn	13.59	6.36	0.35	3.00
Hart	21.59	7.78	0.01	4.20
Hollings	2.76	1.35	0.24	0.82
Jackson	6.85	3.59	0.01	1.90
LaRouche	3.81	1.52	0.00	0.45
McGovern	1.53	.73	0.01	0.51
Mondale	31.53	15.00	0.00	7.25
Republicans				
Reagan	$27.05	$16.16	$0.12	$10.10
1988				
Democrats				
Babbitt	$ 4.34	$ 2.25	$0.01	$1.08
Biden	3.98	3.71	0.03	0.00
Dukakis	31.2	19.3	0.27	9.04
Gephardt	13.30	6.27	1.04	2.89
Gore	14.96	7.87	0.54	3.85
Hart	3.55	2.29	0.00	1.08
Jackson	26.64	12.26	0.09	7.70
LaRouche	3.98	3.02	0.01	0.83
Simon	13.35	6.08	0.33	3.60
Republicans				
Bush	$33.91	$22.32	$0.69	$8.39
Dole	28.30	16.91	2.00	7.62
Du Pont	9.15	5.42	0.00	2.55
Haig	2.63	1.37	0.02	0.54
Kemp	20.58	10.18	0.62	5.88
Robertson	41.03	20.58	0.00	9.69

* Lyndon LaRouche ran as a Democrat in Democratic primaries before becoming the U.S. Labor party candidate.

Source: Data compiled by the author from FEC reports.

played a major role in 1980. The Federal Election Campaign Act was designed to "level the playing field" in presidential elections; each campaign was supposed to spend the same amount of money. Each candidate received the same federal grant; each national committee was allowed to spend the same amount of money directly on each campaign. Still, the total amounts spent varied considerably. One source of this variation is the so-called soft money expenditures discussed above. However, the major source of this variation is *independent expenditures*. Nearly $13 million was spent on behalf of the Reagan-Bush campaign (or against the Carter-Mondale campaign) and only $1.7 million on behalf of Carter-Mondale in independent expenditures. In 1984 the total spent by independent groups exceeded $17 million, again the bulk of it spent on behalf of the Reagan-Bush ticket. When the Supreme Court, in *Federal Election Commission (FEC) v. National Conservative Political Action Committee (NCPAC)*, 470 U.S. 480 (1985), ruled that these expenditures could not be limited, it formalized a new, unregulated source of funding for the two major-party candidates' presidential campaigns. However, despite fears that the sums spent independently could skyrocket—and that they would cause an imbalance between the campaigns—the amount actually spent in 1988 declined, to about $10 million, though the Republicans did hold a 3 to 1 advantage (Alexander & Bauer, 1991, pp. 82–85).

B. Individual Contributions

While much of the early concern expressed by reformers dealt with large contributions by individuals to campaigns, that concern has been tempered in the last decade. *If the campaign finance reforms of the 1970s have been successful in any one area, it has been in curbing the very large contributions by wealthy individuals and thus limiting the alleged abuse caused by huge contributions.*

Before the reforms the stories about extremely large contributions were legion. Most dealt with contributions to presidential campaigns, because the costs of congressional and senatorial campaigns were less and because data on the sources of funds for these campaigns were difficult to obtain.

However, the mere recitations of a few numbers underscore the anxieties of the reformers. In 1972 Stewart R. Mott contributed nearly half a million dollars to various Democratic presidential candidates in the prenomination phase of the campaign; he contributed over $800,000 to all campaigns in that year. In that same year, fifty-one multimillionaires contributed a total of over $6 million to political campaigns, more than $5.5 million to Republican candidates. While the number of Americans who contributed to political campaigns was nearly 12 million in 1972, nearly half of all money contributed to political campaigns in that year came in individual contributions of more than $500 (Alexander, 1976a, chap. 4). Most of the 12 million gave contributions considerably smaller than that.

With the advent of the campaign finance reforms, the amounts that individuals could give to a single campaign and the total amounts that they could contribute were restricted (with the exceptions of contributions to their own campaigns and independent expenditures). The clear result of this change has been that large individual contributions play a smaller role in politics and smaller contributions play a larger role.

These results are demonstrated in Table 10-8. The FEC analysis does not isolate contributions under $500 or candidate contributions, since these have not been the cause for recent concern. Thus, the amounts in these categories are lumped with "Other," that amount left over after PACs, parties, and individual contributions of $500 or more have been accounted for.

TABLE 10-8. Funding Sources for Congressional Candidates, 1974–1990

	Amount Raised by Candidates and Party Expenditures on Behalf of Candidates (in millions)[a]	Percentage Distribution			
		Non-party PACs	Party	Individual Contributions, $500+	Other (Individual to $500, Candidate to Self, Unrepaid Loans)[b]
		House			
1974[c]					
All candidates	$ 45.7	17	4	15	64
Democrats	23.9	22	1	16	61
Republicans	21.7	10	7	15	68
1976					
All candidates[d]	66.1	22	8	11	59
Democrats	35.1	27	4	11	58
Republicans	30.5	17	13	11	59
1978[e]					
All candidates[d]	93.6	24	7	12	57
Democrats	48.7	27	3	13	57
Republicans	44.2	22	11	12	55
1980[e]					
All candidates[d]	127.1	28	6	15	51
Democrats	61.4	32	2	17	49
Republicans	64.6	25	9	13	53
1982[e]					
All candidates[d]	189.8	31	6	15	48
Democrats	94.3	34	2	15	49
Republicans	95.4	27	10	16	47
1984[e]					
All candidates[f]	223.6	34	6		60
Democrats	122.2	38	2		60
Republicans	100.8	29	10		60
1986					
All candidates	235.1	36	4		60
Democrats	129.4	42	2		56
Republicans	108.7	29	6		65
1988					
All candidates	248.9	40	4		56
Democrats	140.0	46	3		51
Republicans	108.9	31	6		63

TABLE 10-8. Funding Sources for Congressional Candidates, 1974–1990 (*cont.*)

	Amount Raised by Candidates and Party Expenditures on Behalf of Candidates (in millions)[a]	Percentage Distribution			
		Non-party PACs	Party	Individual Contributions, $500+	Other (Individual to $500, Candidate to Self, Unrepaid Loans)[b]
House					
1990					
All candidates	248.7	42	6		52
Democrats	142.8	48	6		46
Republicans	105.9	33	7		60
Senate					
1974[c]					
All candidates	28.2	11	6	27	56
Democrats	16.2	13	2	27	58
Republicans	11.6	7	13	28	52
1976					
All candidates[d]	39.2	15	4	27	54
Democrats	19.5	19	2	32	47
Republicans	18.8	11	6	22	61
1978[e]					
All candidates[d]	68.9	13	6	21	60
Democrats	27.8	14	3	27	56
Republicans	40.6	12	8	17	63
1980[e]					
All candidates[d]	83.5	19	9	24	48
Democrats	42.0	18	4	27	51
Republicans	41.2	21	15	21	43
1982[e]					
All candidates[d]	127.0	17	10	24	49
Democrats	64.0	17	4	26	53
Republicans	62.7	17	15	22	46
1984[e]					
All candidates[f]	174.9	17	7		76
Democrats	84.3	17	5		78
Republicans	90.4	17	8		75
1986					
All candidates	208.7	21	9		70
Democrats	90.2	22	8		70
Republicans	118.5	21	9		70
1988					
All candidates	199.5	22	9		69
Democrats	103.1	23	7		70
Republicans	96.4	22	11		67

TABLE 10-8. Funding Sources for Congressional Candidates, 1974–1990 (*cont.*)

Amount Raised by Candidates and Party Expenditures on Behalf of Candidates (in millions)[a]	Percentage Distribution			
	Non-party PACs	Party	Individual Contributions, $500+	Other (Individual to $500, Candidate to Self, Unrepaid Loans)[b]
Senate				
1990				
All candidates	178.3	23	7	70
Democrats	85.7	24	4	72
Republicans	92.6	22	9	69

[a] The "Amount Raised" column includes the sum of what general election candidates raised from January 1 of the odd-numbered year preceding an election through December 21 of the election year.

[b] "Other" includes contributions from individuals of less than $500, contributions from the candidate to himself or herself, unrepaid loans, and, for the 1974 Senate races, some funds whose sources were not identified. Because of confusion over unrepaid loans, the FEC says that it cannot specify loan amounts or candidate self-financing and that its numbers from 1976 and 1978 are unreliable. This also affects the data for small individual contributions, many of which need not be reported individually because those figures had been derived by subtracting all other categories from the total.

[c] The figures for 1974 are only for candidates who are opposed in the general election.

[d] Includes minor-party candidates.

[e] Louisiana instituted a two-step election process in 1978 in which candidates of all parties run against one another in a September primary. If no candidate wins 50 percent or more of the vote at that time, the top two candidates run against each other in November. In these data, candidates in a September Louisiana primary are considered "general election candidates" when the September balloting produces a clear winner with more than half the total vote.

[f] In 1984, the FEC began lumping all individual contributions together regardless of size. The numbers for 1984 represent all individual contributions and loans, combining the last two columns. In the House, loans made up 12% of total funds (D.—15%, R.—8%). In the Senate, loans made up 13% of funding (D.—20%, R.—8%).

Source: Data for 1974–1988 are taken from Ornstein et al. (1990, table 3-9). Data for 1990 compiled by author from FEC press release dated February 22, 1991.

A number of implications follow from these data. First, as was intended in the reforms, large contributions are not the dominant means of raising campaign funds as they once were. (Although this cannot be seen in the most recent years, because the data are not reported in this fashion, the limit on the size of contributions has remained in place and thus the percentages from large contributors in the more recent elections should not be very different from that reported earlier.) Second, as a result of the limits on large contributions, candidates must work at developing a large base of smaller contributors in order to fill their campaign coffers. Candidates have had to develop new techniques for raising money. The Goldwater campaign of 1964 and the George Wallace campaign of 1968 demonstrated the power of direct mail as a tool for raising large amounts of money (and for cementing the allegiance of large numbers of voters). The techniques used in those campaigns have been emulated and improved upon by politicians throughout the land. Richard Viguerie, who was first to gain prominence as an expert in raising money through direct mail, has become an important political figure in his own right. His skills and foresight have given conservative candidates a head start that liberals are still fighting to overcome.[11] One clear impact of the efforts of Viguerie and those who emulate his techniques has been to broaden the base of political donors in much the way the reformers desired.

C. Political Action Committees

If large contributions from individuals are not so threatening as they were thought to be before the reforms of the 1970s, contributions from political action committees are more so. In fact, it can be argued that the "evils of PACs," for those who see such evils, are a direct consequence of the reform movement. And as a consequence of recent experience, PAC reform has been highest on the agenda of campaign finance reformers.

Much has been written about PACs; it is important to understand clearly exactly what is meant by a political action committee (recall Chapter 5). As is not atypical when one scrutinizes commonly used terms, one finds that the term "political action committee" does not appear in the statutes of the federal government. However, the statutes do refer to *"political committees"* which are distinct from either party committees or candidate committees. A political committee, according to the U.S. Code (26 U.S.C. 9001 [9]) is:

> any committee, association, or organization (whether or not incorporated) which accepts contributions or makes expenditures for the purpose of influencing, or attempting to influence, the nomination or election of one or more individuals to Federal, State, or local elective public office.

The U.S. Code further defines *"multicandidate political committees,"* a distinction that is important because it is these groups that can contribute up to $5000 to an individual campaign, not the $1000 limit that applies to individuals. A "multicandidate political committee" is:

> a political committee which has been registered . . . for a period of not less than 6 months, which has received contributions from more than 50 persons, and, except for any State political party organization, has made contributions to 5 or more candidates for Federal office. (4 U.S.C. 441 [a])

Finally, *political action committees, as we normally think of them, are separate from their parent or sponsoring organization (if there is one).* Campaign finance legislation has long prohibited direct political contributions by labor unions or corporations; however, provisions have been made for establishing a "separate segregated fund" for political purposes. The law specifies how money for this fund may and may not be raised. Political action committees with parent organiza-

---

[11] However, as early as 1986 Tom Edsall (1986) and others raised questions about the ongoing success of Viguerie and other conservative fund-raisers. In most recent elections they have been much less successful, as have all small-contributor–direct-mail fund-raising operations.

tions then are the committees set up to administer these "separate segregated funds" (Sorauf, 1984a, chap. 1; 1991). The term PAC is thus commonly used to refer to a nonparty, noncandidate committee that funds more than one candidate and may or may not be affiliated with an established corporation, union, or interest group (Sabato, 1985).

The Federal Election Commission identifies four major types of political action committees: labor, corporation, trade/membership/health, and nonconnected.[12] The first three types identified can be defined as multicandidate political committees which are administering campaign funds that have been raised from, but kept separate and segregated from, some parent organization, be that a labor union, a corporation, or a trade, membership, or health organization (such as the American Bankers Association or the American Medical Association). The nonconnected PACs tend to be ideological multicandidate political committees that have come together for specific political purposes and that do not draw on an established parent organization.

While their prominence is a recent phenomenon, political committees have been on the American political scene for some time. From the 1940s until its merger with the American Federation of Labor (AFL) in 1955, the Congress of Industrial Organizations (CIO) operated a separate fund to receive and dispense voluntary contributions from labor unionists to political campaigns. The AFL-CIO Committee on Political Education (COPE), established after the 1955 merger, has been described as "the model for virtually all political action committees" (E. Epstein, 1980, p. 100). In the late 1950s and early 1960s some of the larger membership and trade professional organizations, like the American Realtors and the American Medical Association, formed political committees (Alexander, 1979b, pp. 559–566; Sorauf, 1984a, p. 33).

However, the recent growth of PACs, an increase in the number of PACs as well as an increase in the size of the role they play (as measured in the dollars they contribute), and the pattern of that growth are the phenomena that have caused most concern. The FECA amendments of 1974 put a more stringent limit on individual contributions than on contributions by multicandidate political committees. This followed naturally from the fact that reformers were more concerned about huge contributions by individuals than they were about group contributions. The 1974 amendments also lifted the restriction that had prohibited government contractors from setting up separated segregated political committees. The public financing of presidential elections, effective for the 1976 election, led PACs to switch their emphasis from presidential to congressional campaigns. But the viability of PACs under the FECA was initially unclear; there was only cautious movement toward establishing new PACs. This situation changed in 1975 when the FEC, in response to an inquiry from the Sun Oil Company, issued an advisory opinion in which it informed Sun Oil that the corporation could legally establish a separated segregated fund for the purpose

---

[12] It also lists cooperative PACs and PACs for corporations without stock, but these two categories together constitute fewer than 5 percent of all political action committees, in terms of number of committees and/or amounts contributed.

Arkansas Governor Bill Clinton sought the support of organized labor during the Democratic presidential primary in Pennsylvania in 1992. (AP/Wide World Photos)

of contributing to political campaigns and that it could solicit voluntary contributions from its employees to support that fund. As a result of all these actions, political action committees as a major force in funding congressional elections became a most visible aspect of electoral politics, and hundreds of other corporations followed Sun Oil's lead (E. Epstein, 1980).

Look back at Table 5-2 which depicts the rapid growth of political action committees in the last decade. The total number of PACs has grown from slightly over 600 in 1974 to well over 4200 in 1988. The expenditures of the PACs during that period have grown proportionally, from $12.5 million in 1974 to $151.3 million in 1988. It should be noted further that this growth has not been constant among the various types of PACs. Labor was very quick to see that PACs could increase their influence. Nearly all major labor unions immediately organized political action committees. However, the number of labor PACs did not even double between 1974 and 1988. On the other hand, corporations were quite slow in realizing the potential influence they could wield through PACs. Corporate PACs have continued to increase, with a major jump coming after the 1974 law changes and the 1975 SUNPAC opinion, but with substantial growth continuing ever since. (See Eismeier & Pollock, 1985a, 1985b; Malbin, 1984a.) As can be seen in the table, the largest growth in recent years has been in the nonconnected PACs, as more "political entrepreneurs" see this as a viable way to increase political influence.

TABLE 10-9. Growth of PAC Influence on Congressional Elections

Year	PAC Contributions (in millions)	Average Percent of House Receipts from PACs	Average Percent of Senate Receipts from PACs
1974	$ 12.5	17	11
1976	22.6	22	15
1978	35.2	24	13
1980	55.2	28	19
1982	83.6	31	17
1984	105.3	36	18
1986	139.4	36	21
1988	151.3	40	22
1990	150.6	38	22

Source: Data from 1974–1988 from Ornstein et al. (1990, table 3-9); data from 1990 from Federal Election Commission press release, dated February 22, 1991.

The growth in the number of PACs and the amounts they are contributing to political candidates, more specifically to congressional candidates, has led to a number of concerns. While it is possible to classify these concerns in a number of different ways, we will deal with four specific areas: the necessity of PAC support to secure electoral victory, the link between PAC support and legislative behavior, the ideological imbalance of present and future PACs, and the responsibility of PAC leaders to contributors.

1. The Influence of PACs on Electoral Outcomes Some things are clear. If one looks at recent elections for the United States Congress, by and large winners spend more money than do losers. While it is appropriate to be concerned about who gets money from each source, attention has been focused on PACs because PACs contribute an increasingly large amount of money.

Table 10-9 shows PAC activity in recent House and Senate elections. Both the amount and the proportion of money contributed by PACs have been rising faster than the total amount spent on elections or the proportion coming from any other source.[13] This is particularly clear for House elections, in which PAC contributions now represent nearly 40 percent of total expenditures. It is also clear from these data that virtually all successful candidates must raise a significant amount of money from political action committees. Incumbents are able to do this more easily than challengers. While PACs flirted with supporting more challengers in the early 1980s (see Eismeier & Pollock, 1985b, 1986; Jacobson, 1985–1986; Sabato, 1985; J. Wright, 1985), in the last elections they have reverted to the pattern of giving most of their contributions to incumbents. In 1988, 74.2 percent of PAC contributions to congressional candidates went to incumbents; in 1990 the percentage rose to 79.1 percent (Federal Election Commission, 1991b). Ironically, money is more significant for challengers than

[13] The one apparent exception is in 1990, but the total spending went down slightly because of the particular mix of Senate seats contested in that year, as compared with those in 1988.

it is for incumbents (Jacobson, 1980, chap. 5). The key is whether challengers can attract enough money, including PAC money, to mount enough of a campaign to have a chance of victory. More and more they do not seem to be able to do so.

2. The Influence of PACs on Legislative Decision Making Many political action committees are connected to specific groups that have a direct interest in legislative decision making. The funds may be separate and segregated, but the connection is there in the minds of all involved. One does not have to stretch one's imagination too far to see that the directors of the Amoco political action committee have certain views on issues affecting the oil industry or that those deciding on the allocation of funds from the Machinists Non-Partisan Political League care greatly about the level of governmental support for the aerospace industry.

The PAC leaders know this, and the candidates know this. Former Congresswoman Millicent Fenwick (R., N.J., 1975–1983) put it most succinctly:

> That these groups influence voting is undeniable. "I took $58,000. They want it," was the explanation one colleague gave for his vote, bought by a number of donations from a number of groups of similar orientation. (Quoted in Sorauf, 1984a, p. 90)

Note the figure $58,000. PACs are limited to contributions of $5000 in a single campaign. The sum of $5000 will not buy a great deal of influence in a campaign with a budget of $250,000. *But if ten groups with similar interests (e.g., oil or medical policy) all make maximum contributions, then the total impact might be significant. And that defines the concern.* Many feel that PAC money does not directly buy influence; however, contributions do buy access, and access can lead indirectly to influence.

On the one hand, PACs contribute to individuals likely to support their cause in any case; individual PAC contributions are not significant considering the total amounts spent on campaigns; incumbents have tremendous electoral advantages regardless of PAC actions or intentions, and incumbents face a wide array of pressures so that they cannot only listen to PAC leaders.

On the other hand, congressmen do accept large amounts of money from groups of individuals with a direct stake in legislation; the total contributed by like-minded groups might well represent a sizable percentage of a candidate's campaign funds; and interest-group representatives are often quite overt in exercising pressure when key decisions are pending. There is, in the Supreme Court's words, "the appearance of impropriety" which might well be as detrimental to the system as the reality.

Alleged PAC influence on legislation tarnishes the reputation of political action committees (Common Cause, 1986; Drew, 1983; B. Jackson, 1988; Stern, 1988). PAC supporters argue persuasively that citizens should have a right to associate with others of similar views in order to maximize the strength with which their views are heard. PAC detractors point to the number of cases in which large PAC contributions have been funneled to incumbents facing no challengers as evidence that PACs are polluting the system by setting up an assumption that legislative behavior is for sale to the highest bidder. Political scientists have searched for evidence of PAC influence on legislative behavior, but their conclusion is that hard evidence of the corrupting influence of PACs is all but absent (Evans, 1986; Frendeis & Waterman, 1985; Grenzke, 1989, 1990; Schroedel, 1986; J. Wright, 1985). In a very real sense, this debate has been the focus of reform efforts for more than a decade.

3.   The Ideological Imbalance of Present and Future PACs Labor leaders were among those most interested in writing legislation allowing for the formation of PACs in the early years of the 1970 reform movement. They saw tremendous advantages as they tried to exert influence over the electoral process.

However, these labor leaders were shortsighted, as the most recent trends in the increases in PACs show. Labor PACs are organized and about as effective as they are likely to be. However, corporate PACs continue to form at a rapid rate; the number that may form in the years ahead is difficult to calculate. Now labor leaders, Democrats, and other liberals in this country worry that PAC influence will increasingly become conservative, business, and Republican influence.

This argument can be dealt with on two levels. First, Table 10-10 shows that in recent years PACs have not given significantly more to Republicans than to Democrats. To the contrary, Democrats have received more than have Republicans. Of course, to a certain extent this can be explained because PACs have tended to support incumbents. (See Table 10-11.) The Democrats have controlled the House (and the Senate except for the period between 1980 and 1986), and since incumbents have received more PAC support, the Democrats have benefited. Were the Republicans to gain control of the House, one might expect their PAC receipts to increase accordingly. Some evidence of this trend was found in the 1984 and 1986 Senate elections, in which the majority of incumbents defending their seats were Republicans. In each of those elections PACs gave substantially more to Republican candidates than they did to Democrats (Magleby & Nelson, 1990, p. 82, table 5-3).

At a more theoretical level, questions of the locus of power in the United States have long been debated. PAC influence is only one more manifestation of this question. Literally hundreds of PACs contribute to the most expensive campaigns for the House and Senate. Scholars would have to look long and hard to find the conspiracy that linked these contributions. Size alone does not dictate specific kinds of influence. Our polity functioned under a system through which a few very wealthy individuals gave great sums to political campaigns in virtual anonymity. It is difficult to conclude that it cannot survive even a significant influx of PAC contributions made in the light of day.

4.   The Lack of Accountability for PAC Decision Making Even those who are not troubled by the supposed influence of political action committees have some concern over how decisions are made by PACs. Until very recently very

TABLE 10-10. PAC Contributions to Congressional Candidates by Party, 1980–1990

	Republican	Democratic	Other
1980			
Corporate	64.1%	35.8%	0.1%
Labor	6.3	93.6	0.1
Trade/membership/health	55.9	43.9	0.2
Nonconnected	69.6	29.5	0.9
Other	38.8	61.2	
Total	47.4%	52.3%	0.2%
1982			
Corporate	65.7%	34.3%	
Labor	5.4	94.6	
Trade/membership/health	57.3	42.6	
Nonconnected	49.0	50.9	0.1
Other	38.6	61.4	
Total	45.7%	54.3%	
1984			
Corporate	61.7%	38.1%	0.1%
Labor	5.6	94.3	0.1
Trade/membership/health	50.8	49.1	0.1
Nonconnected	47.5	52.4	
Other	39.4	60.4	
Total	43.2%	56.7%	0.1%
1986			
Corporate	61.1%	38.9%	
Labor	7.5	92.5	
Trade/membership/health	51.1	48.9	
Nonconnected	42.3	57.6	
Other	46.4	53.6	
Total	43.6%	56.4%	0.0%
1988			
Corporate	52.9%	47.1%	
Labor	7.7	92.3	
Trade/membership/health	44.8	55.2	
Nonconnected	36.7	63.3	
Other	39.9	60.0	
Total	38.2%	61.8%	0.0%
1990			
Corporate	52.6%	47.4%	
Labor	6.9	93.0	0.2
Trade/membership/health	44.9	55.1	
Nonconnected	35.7	64.2	0.1
Other	37.0	63.0	
Total	36.9%	63.1%	0.05%

Source: Reports of the FEC.

little was known about how PACs function (but this is changing; see Sabato, 1985; Sorauf, 1984a, 1984b). The general assumption has been that, with the possible exception of labor union PACs, members have very little influence over PAC decision making.

TABLE 10-11. PAC Contributions to Congressional Candidates, by Candidate Status and Party Affiliation, 1980–1990

	Incumbents		Challengers		Open Seat	
	Rep.	Dem.	Rep.	Dem.	Rep.	Dem.
1980						
Corporate	24.6%	32.0%	29.6%	1.6%	10.2%	2.2%
Labor	5.5	65.5	0.5	16.1	0.3	12.0
Trade/membership/health	26.7	37.5	20.2	2.8	9.0	3.7
Nonconnected	10.8	20.8	44.2	4.7	14.6	4.0
Other	22.6	54.7	8.4	2.1	7.7	4.4
Total	19.3	41.4	20.4	5.7	7.8	5.2
1982						
Corporate	42.6%	29.9%	11.7%	1.6%	11.4%	2.8%
Labor	4.5	52.4	0.1	27.5	0.8	14.7
Trade/membership/health	39.6	34.2	8.6	4.5	9.1	4.0
Nonconnected	18.7	26.9	19.3	15.5	10.9	8.5
Other	30.6	50.9	2.2	5.4	5.9	5.1
Total	29.0	36.9	8.7	10.6	8.0	6.8
1984						
Corporate	43.6%	34.4%	9.1%	1.3%	9.0%	2.6%
Labor	4.7	59.4	0.3	22.8	0.4	12.5
Trade/membership/health	37.7	41.0	6.5	4.4	6.1	4.0
Nonconnected	18.9	14.9	18.6	14.9	9.3	6.7
Other	32.1	53.6	2.9	4.0	3.1	4.3
Total	29.1	42.2	7.4	9.1	6.1	5.9
1986						
Corporate	44.9%	31.6%	4.3%	3.5%	12.8%	3.2%
Labor	7.2	50.9	0.08	24.8	0.0	16.2
Trade/membership/health	39.2	38.2	2.9	5.9	9.3	5.2
Nonconnected	23.1	26.8	7.4	17.9	10.8	13.6
Other	38.0	41.9	3.9	9.9	9.6	7.5
Total	31.7	37.0	3.3	11.4	26.5	24.4
1988						
Corporate	40.5%	30.7%	5.6%	1.2%	7.4%	3.9%
Labor	6.8	58.4	0.0	21.5	0.4	13.0
Trade/membership/health	35.7	45.4	3.3	3.5	6.9	4.8
Nonconnected	21.0	38.5	6.8	15.0	7.8	10.4
Other	31.3	51.5	3.1	3.2	5.8	4.3
Total	28.1	45.9	3.5	8.5	5.8	6.9
1990						
Corporate	38.3%	43.6%	8.1%	1.0%	7.1%	1.9%
Labor	6.4	71.3	0.2	15.4	0.0	15.6
Trade/membership/health	33.7	48.4	4.8	2.5	6.7	4.1
Nonconnected	22.2	46.4	7.2	8.0	7.2	9.6
Other	27.6	57.7	4.4	1.9	4.8	2.9
Total	27.4	50.4	5.0	4.8	5.6	6.4

Note: Figures may not add up to 100% due to rounding and contributions to other parties.
Source: Data from reports of the FEC.

Iowa Republican Congressman Jim Leach has argued:

> Groups seldom reflect the same collective judgment as all their members. More importantly, decisions for organizations frequently occur at the top not the bottom. . . . Individuals who control other people's money become power brokers in an elitist society. Their views, not the small contributors to their associations, become the views that carry influence. (Quoted in Sorauf, 1984a, p. 96)

This concern is especially troublesome for nonconnected PACs, organizations that are often built around the reputation of one or two individuals and a mailing list. Nonconnected PACs have been on the increase in recent years. They have been most active in influencing the electoral process through independent expenditures on behalf of, or in opposition to, a candidate. However, as has been noted often, only a few of these PACs spend significantly, and their influence seems to be waning (Alexander & Bauer, 1991, pp. 84–86; C. Nelson, 1990).

Those who support the activity of political action groups most often argue that PAC activity is nothing more than constructive collective activity. If this is so, then collective decision making is a logical correlate. The lack of accountability of PAC leaders to their "followings" will be a pressing reform issue for the agenda of the future.

5. PAC Influence: A Summary The consequences of reform are often not immediately apparent to the reformers. Few involved in the campaign finance reforms of the early 1970s could have foreseen the rise in influence of political action committees. With two decades of experience, the same reformers are beginning to look at what their work has wrought. While the discourse often breaks down on partisan lines, the entire question seems to be one on which reasonable men and women can differ and the "prevailing view" is in flux.

Led by Common Cause and Congressman David Obey (D., Wisc.), reformers have kept proposals for the limitation of PAC influence on the legislative agenda for a number of years. They have been countered by the position frequently articulated by Congressman Bill Frenzel (R., Minn.), who champions the cause of political action committees. As of the 102nd Congress, though PAC reform has passed one house or the other in various forms on a number of occasions, no campaign finance reform bill dealing with this problem has become law.

The growth of PACs and their apparent influence has given rise to a good deal of uncertainty. Many feel that PAC growth is a force in escalating the total costs of campaigns. But the experience with the 1970s reforms leads to caution. How will PAC influence shake down? What other factors and changes are likely to come into play?

In 1983 the Twentieth Century Fund convened a distinguished, bipartisan Task Force on Political Action Committees, under the leadership of former senator and secretary of state Edmund S. Muskie. The task force concluded that the integrity of the system necessitated reforms, including a limitation on the amounts that candidates could receive from PACs, efforts to preclude collusion between those running campaigns and those making "independent expenditures," partial voluntary public funding, a strengthening of the roles of political parties in campaign finance, and an increase in the amount individuals could contribute to campaigns (Twentieth Century Fund, 1984). What might be most significant about this report was that only six of the thirteen members of the task force agreed with the final conclusions without significant reservations. Three separate statements of views were filed, one by a well-known Democrat, one by a well-known Republican, and one by a noted academician. A problem is perceived, but no consensus exists on the solution. Significant reform requires a climate for action. To date such a climate has not existed.

D. Political Parties

If the controversial item on the campaign finance agenda in the mid-1980s was PAC money, perhaps the most underrated item was the change in the role that the major political parties played in financing campaigns (Sorauf, 1988, chap. 5).

   The conventional wisdom in the 1970s was that parties did not play a major role in campaign finance. The Nixon campaigns of 1968 and 1972 raised substantial amounts of money independent of the Republican National Committee. The major financial effort on behalf of the Democrats was to retire the debts incurred by the Humphrey and Kennedy campaigns of 1968. The Democratic National Committee expended most of its fund-raising efforts in paying off debts, not in aiding candidates.

   Congressional and senatorial campaigns did not cost the large amounts that are in evidence today. The national parties were not active in raising large sums for these campaigns; the state and local parties did not have sufficient resources to make significant differences.

   However, as Gary Jacobson (1984, p. 49; 1985–1986), Frank Sorauf (1988, pp. 127–149), and others have shown, the biggest change in campaign financing in the 1980s was the significant role played by the political parties, particularly the Republican party, on behalf of congressional and senatorial candidates and the efforts the Democrats made to match Republican efforts (B. Jackson, 1988). (Recall Table 10-6; see also Arterton, 1982.)

   The difference between Republican and Democratic party efforts has become most troublesome for Democrats over the last decade. As Tables 10-12 and 10-13 show, the Republicans have had much more money to spend on campaign functions than have the Democrats. This difference has become apparent at all electoral levels. The Republican National Committee has spent money to provide in-kind services for candidates at reduced costs. They have provided funding so that, at the state and local level, Republican organizations are stronger and better financed than the Democrats.

   The last decade has seen the emergence of the Republican Senatorial and Congressional Campaign Committees as important forces in congressional politics. At each of these levels, the Republicans have been more active than their Democratic counterparts and more successful. Most discouraging for

TABLE 10-12. Annual Budgets of State Political Parties

	Republicans ($n = 40$)	Democrats ($n = 30$)
Less than $250,000	26%	63%
$250,000–750,000	39%	20%
Over $750,000	34%	17%

Source: American Council on Intergovernmental Affairs Survey of State Chairs, 1983–1984, reported in Conlan et al. (1984, p. 8).

Democrats is that, despite Herculean efforts in recent years, the gap does not seem to be contracting. Senator George Mitchell and Congressman Tony Coelho (D., Calif., 1979–1989), who headed the Democratic Senatorial and Congressional Campaign Committees, respectively, in the mid-1980s, played important roles in their party's future as they attempted to bring these committees to the point at which they can compete effectively with their Republican counterparts. Each used the campaign committee experience as a takeoff point for a position in their party's formal congressional hierarchy.[14] Their successors as well see the importance of their roles, both for their party's electoral chances and for their own political futures.

The implications of these data are not all totally obvious. No one needs to point out that Republican candidates have a significant advantage over their Democratic counterparts. But one more subtle implication is that Democratic congressmen, who receive a good deal of PAC money because of their incumbency, are very leery about restricting the activities of political action committees if the resulting system will increase the advantage that the Republicans have because of the strength of their political party organizations (Gibson et al., 1983, 1985).

Frequently those who examine the various sources of campaign funds view their impacts in isolation. Candidates for office look at all sources as a whole. Any reform that affects one will have a concomitant effect on the total available. Democratic candidates, who know that their party organization is much weaker than the Republican party, are unwilling to change the system in any way that will force them to rely more on political parties to fund their campaigns. Republicans, who sense a growing advantage in PAC growth, may be equally unwilling to limit PAC growth downward and certainly realize the potential advantage created by an enhanced funding role for political parties.

E. The Debate over Public Financing

The reformers of the 1970s proposed public financing as the way to take the taint of money out of politics. If political campaigns were funded by the mass public, politicians would not have to deal with those seeking to buy influence.

---

[14] Coelho eventually resigned his seat in Congress, in part, at least, because of implications of impropriety in the connections he made while raising money for his party.

TABLE 10-13. Party Committee Adjusted Disbursements, 1987–1988*

	Adjusted Receipts	Adjusted Disbursements	Contributions to Presidential, Senate, and House Candidates	Expenditures for Presidential, Senate, and House Candidates
Democratic				
National Committee	$ 52,295,783	$ 47,036,799	$ 137,998	$ 8,107,044
Senatorial	16,297,386	16,289,589	420,579	6,206,137
Congressional	12,469,354	12,481,532	666,637	2,425,603
Conventions, other national	19,164,401	19,152,131	0	0
State/local	27,696,663	26,967,036	507,092	1,177,205
Total Democratic	127,923,587	121,927,087	1,732,306	17,915,989
Republican				
National Committee	$ 90,980,761	$ 89,893,536	$ 325,440	$ 8,291,273
Senatorial	65,896,691	63,350,247	760,488	10,250,638
Congressional	34,483,260	33,569,320	1,583,503	4,107,689
Conventions, other national	9,646,685	9,610,085	0	0
State/local	62,249,430	60,532,621	718,487	64,853
Total Republican	263,256,827	256,956,304	3,387,918	22,714,353

* Figures are net, not adjusted.

Source: Data for 1988 compiled from Federal Election Commission, "FEC Summarizes 1988 Political Party Activity," press release, March 27, 1989.

Since 1976, public financing has been an important part of presidential campaigns. During the prenomination phase of the presidential election, after reaching a qualifying plateau, candidates for the two parties' nominations receive matching funds for all contributions of $250 or less received from individuals. As Table 10-14 shows, over $67 million was paid out of the Presidential Election Campaign Fund during this phase of the 1988 election.

Each of the major parties is granted public funds to run its nominating convention. The nominee of each major party is granted public funds for running a general election campaign; other candidates for the presidency qualify for public funding according to the success they achieve. As seen in Table 10-15, the total cost to the public of running the 1988 presidential election was almost $176 million.

Reformers also feel that public financing should be applied to congressional elections. In 1977 a public financing bill was high on President Carter's initial legislative agenda. However, that bill, given the symbolic designation of H.R. 1, never emerged from the House Administration Committee.

The debate over public financing of congressional and senatorial elections is a heated one. Proponents say that public financing has worked for presidential elections and will do so at the congressional level as well. They hold that using public funds to finance elections is fairer, less susceptible to corruption,

TABLE 10-14. Prenomination Public Contributions to Major Party Candidates, 1988 (in thousands of dollars)

Candidate	Federal Matching Funds	Percentage of Total Receipts
Democrats		
Bruce Babbit	$ 1,079	24.8%
Joseph Biden, Jr.	—	—
Michael Dukakis	9,040	28.9
Richard Gephardt	2,896	21.8
Albert Gore, Jr.	3,853	26.8
Gary Hart	1,084	30.5
Jesse Jackson	7,608	28.6
Lyndon LaRouche	826	20.7
Paul Simon	3,603	27.0
Subtotal	29,989	26.0
Republicans		
George Bush	8,393	24.8
Robert Dole	7,618	26.9
Pete du Pont	2,550	27.9
Alexander Haig, Jr.	539	20.5
Jack Kemp	5,877	28.6
Pat Robertson	9,691	23.6
Subtotal	34,670	25.6
Total	$64,659	25.8%

Source: Federal Election Commission, "Reports on Financial Activity, 1987–1988: Presidential Pre-Nomination Campaigns," (August 1989), pp. 1–5; percentages calculated by author.

**TABLE 10-15. Cost of Public Financing
of the 1988 Presidential Election**

Prenomination phase	
Democrats	$ 29,989,000
Republicans	34,670,000
New Alliance party	939,000
Subtotal	65,598,000
Conventions	
Democrats	9,220,000
Republicans	9,220,000
Subtotal	18,440,000
General Election	
Dukakis-Bentsen	46,100,000
Bush-Quayle	46,100,000
Subtotal	92,200,000
Total	$176,238,000

Source: Federal Election Commission sources.

and, in the long run, the only way to reduce the costs of elections, especially given the Supreme Court ruling that only those who accept public financing can be restricted in the amounts they spend.

Opponents of public financing argue from a number of different points. Some argue that any public financing bill would automatically protect all incumbents, because challengers must spend huge sums of money to overcome the advantages of incumbency. This argument is especially important for House Republicans, who are in the minority.

Others argue that public financing would be impossible to implement for congressional and/or senatorial elections because the congressional districts (and even states) are so different that amounts of money needed to campaign effectively in different districts would vary by large amounts. They are further concerned about candidates who receive public funds when no serious challenger exists.

Still others argue that public funding would create opposition to popular incumbents where none now exists. Some incumbents are forthright enough to state that they will not support public financing because it is against their best interest. Others hedge this argument, stating that it is not in the interest of the nation to force people to pay for unwanted campaigns. Challengers and those eager to support competitive elections see this as an advantage of public financing because it encourages competition.

One could go on to list additional points made on each side. Should people be forced to pay for campaigns for candidates they oppose? Can fair competition ever be imposed through law? Is there anything wrong with the current situation, and if not, why change it?

In the final analysis, public financing has not been passed for congressional and senatorial elections for much the same reason that PAC contributions have not been limited. While there is some consensus on a definition of the problem, there is none on a solution. The climate is not ripe for reform. Too many of those in office are happy with the current system; there is very little pressure on them to change it. Any change that would benefit one party over the other faces an impossible hurdle in achieving passage in a Democratically controlled Congress without facing a veto from a Republican president. If a scandal of Watergate proportions were to be revealed once again, action might follow. The scandal involving the Keating Five and the incredibly high incumbent return rates have improved the climate for reform, but the question remains whether it is balmy enough. Until that time, however, fundamental reform is far from likely.

It should also be noted that eighteen states have some form of public financing for some state offices (Alexander & Eberts, 1986; R. Jones, 1980, 1984; Noragon, 1981; Sorauf, 1988, p. 286). In some states the funds are allocated to the political parties. In other states, the public funds are allocated directly to candidates for office. The states' experiences vary widely in the amounts of money involved, in the ways in which the funds are dispensed, and in the assessment of the ways in which public financing has worked. The eighteen different public financing programs have provided interesting laboratories for those interested in public policy formation.[15]

This area of reform is still of interest to those concerned about the costs of running for office and the influence of those supporting candidates. How quickly action is taken (and in fact if it is taken) in a particular state varies with the political climate experienced by decision makers in that state.

V.   POLITICIANS VIEW CAMPAIGN FINANCING

Congressmen Al Swift (D., Wash.) and Bill Thomas (R., Calif.) both addressed a recent conference sponsored by the Citizens' Research Foundation. While they disagreed on many particular aspects of what is desirable, both congressmen reached the same conclusion about the likelihood of campaign finance reform.

According to Swift:

> The issues of campaign finance reform inherently affect partisan politics. There will be winners and losers. These issues are particularly difficult when one house is controlled by one party with Priorities X, and the other house is controlled by the other party with List Y.

---

[15] The states with some form of public financing are Alabama, California, Florida, Hawaii, Idaho, Iowa, Kentucky, Maine, Massachusetts, Michigan, Minnesota, Montana, New Jersey, North Carolina, Rhode Island, Utah, Virginia, and Wisconsin. In addition, Alaska and Maryland are special cases to examine; and Oklahoma and Oregon had systems in place which are no longer operative. It should also be noted that many western democracies have strong systems of public financing of elections. These too have been a source of information from experience for those interested in changing the American system.

Thomas's conclusion about the motivations of those seeking reform was similar:

> What's motivating people who are opposed to PACs is something that is basic and totally American—politics. All they are concerned about is who gets what? When? And how?

And those are precisely the issues. Politicians view campaign finance reform from the position of winners and losers, of where they stand now. Politicians are not generally in the business of creating the perfect world; they want to create the best world within the very practical limits that they see. Again, Congressman Swift summarized this view:

> I think that public financing would be a good solution to much of the problem that we see, but I also happen to believe that we have enough to do in the Congress and that chasing chimeras is not very productive. . . . . No legislation can emerge from our subcommittee which will pass the full House and which would pass the Senate. So, seeing no use in spinning our wheels, we move on to other topics.

Campaign finance reform falls into the realm of political reality. Incumbents tend to win under the current system; they have a tremendous advantage in raising money and in maintaining visibility. They will vote to retain any system that continues to benefit them. If a scandal were to erupt, then the current system would not benefit them, because it would bring the integrity of the entire process into doubt. Barring such a scandal, however, incumbents—those who write the laws—benefit by any system that continues to let them campaign in the same way as their challenger does.

When asked about the evils of PAC money, Barney Frank was noncommittal. PAC money in the abstract was of no interest. But "If my opponent takes no PAC money, I'll take no PAC money. Heck, if he makes no speeches, I'll make no speeches." The point is clear. Incumbents win most of the time unless they give their opponent some advantage. They are not likely to change the system to their own disadvantage. No nonincumbents would favor changing the system to incumbents' further advantage, and so the system remains as is.

That is not the same as saying that all politicians like the current system of campaign finance. Far from it. Most feel as the late Hubert Humphrey felt, that having to ask for money is the most demeaning part of politics. Many feel that too much money is spent in the wrong ways on politics. Many also feel that independent expenditures, particularly negative campaigning done in this way, hurts the entire system.

After his 1982 election to the Senate, George Mitchell convened a bipartisan Task Force on Campaign Finance. The conclusion of that group, which included Republican as well as Democratic politicians, academicians, and representatives of the media, was that fundamental changes were necessary to right the perceived wrongs in the system, but that most of the changes either were beyond the reach of the legislative process because of the Supreme Court's ruling in *Buckley v. Valeo* or were politically infeasible. Senator Mitchell joined the list of politicians who entered a bill into the campaign finance reform hopper;

the Mitchell bill met the fate of most of its predecessors. It was never heard from again.

Now, of course, Mitchell is the Senate majority leader—and campaign finance reform remains high on his agenda. However, politicians will continue to fret about the system. They will continue to tinker at the fringes. Some will continue to propose grandiose solutions. But the problems will remain, and the basic system will remain, until a major force overcomes the inertia that is strongly in favor of the status quo.

chapter

11

The Party in Government

Remember the story at the very beginning of Chapter 1: Texas Congressman Phil Gramm resigned from Congress, switched his party affiliation from Democratic to Republican, and easily won a special election to succeed himself. This story was designed to make the point that party itself did not mean that much to the voters, that they supported the candidate they knew and liked. Voters will elect the candidate who can raise enough money to run a credible campaign.

Now think about Phil Gramm from another point of view. The Democratic party in Congress "punished" Gramm for disloyalty to party positions on key issues. Party leaders removed Gramm from his seat on the important Budget Committee, a position crucial to his policy influence. They were clearly expressing the view that party affiliation still mattered in the House of Representatives.

One significant goal of political parties is to elect officeholders. At the national level virtually every major elected official is either a Democrat or a Republican.[1] The same is true in most states, though Nebraska operates with a nonpartisan legislature, and Connecticut in 1990 elected an independent governor, Lowell Weicker, a former Republican United States senator from the state. Even more to the point, the two political parties organize Congress and all the state legislatures save that in Nebraska. This partisan control of the structure of legislative politics in the United States and the fact that virtually all chief executives are elected under partisan labels is the context for the discussion of party in government that follows. Much of this material deals with the national government; the assumption is that many of the same points will hold for state legislatures and the relationships between governors and state legislators, but adequate data are not available to provide similarly detailed analysis.

---

[1] Congressman Bernard Sanders (I., Vt.) is the only member of the 102d Congress who was not elected as the candidate of one or the other of the major parties. Independents and third-party candidates have been so rare in the modern Congress that most "political junkies" can name them all.

I. THE CONCEPT OF PARTY IN GOVERNMENT

In his classic text *Politics, Parties, and Pressure Groups* (1964), V. O. Key, Jr., his generation's most prominent analyst of American politics, divided his discussion of party into the party organization, the party in the electorate, and the party in government. The basis for that division was the classic notion that partisans, once elected to office, should be able to implement the programs on which they ran. That notion is an old and revered one in the study of the American polity.

When Woodrow Wilson wrote *Congressional Government* in 1885, his notion was that parties should be strong enough to govern. His well-known complaint about committee government was in essence Wilson's way of lamenting the lack of strong parties controlling Congress. He was distressed by the absence of strong party leaders in the Congress he analyzed (1885, p. 76). His solution: "The great need is, not to get rid of parties, but to find and use some expedient by which they can be managed and made amenable from day to day to public opinion" (1885, pp. 79–80). Woodrow Wilson, the political observer and analyst, Wilson the scholar, was a "small d" democrat; his view was that strong parties were the best mechanism through which a democracy could convert public opinion into policy alternatives.

Sixty-five years later, the Committee on Political Parties of the American Political Science Association prescribed stronger parties in its influential report "Toward a More Responsible Two-Party System" (1950). Again the complaint was familiar. American parties were too weak to form a link between the electorate and the elected. Parties did not stand firmly on issues; candidates did not feel bound to implement party programs once in office. Essentially the norm that was espoused was a parliamentary system—programmatic parties, strong leaders, compliant followers, party-dominated legislative decision making. And American parties were found lacking.

Political analysts of the contemporary Congress have tended not to view parties as critically important to understanding the national legislature. In fact, a recent study by Melissa Collie (1986) reveals that political scientists publishing in the leading scholarly journals have all but ignored parties as significant to understanding the legislative process. The conventional wisdom holds that changes in electoral politics and the congressional reforms of the 1970s have stripped parties of (1) their ability to influence the behavior of legislators and thus (2) their ability to shape policy. In short, the conventional wisdom seems to be that the party in government deserves little attention.

But that "fact" has not always been a fact, and the conventional wisdom may well need reassessment as we examine the 1990s. In a seminal article on congressional leadership, Joseph Cooper and David Brady (1981) noted the importance of context in examining the ways in which Speakers of the House have led their body; they focused particularly on the rules of the House and on the role of political parties—and on changes in each of those and the interplay between them. Brady, writing alone and with a series of coauthors, has spent a number of years studying party behavior in the House. His astute analysis of the historical importance of party voting and of the variables that have influenced the strength of partisanship in Congress has been critical to our understanding of when party is most important in the legislative context. (See, as examples, Brady, 1988, 1990; Brady, Cooper, & Hurley, 1979; Brady & Ettling, 1984; Brady & Sinclair, 1984; Collie & Brady, 1985; Cooper, Brady, & Hurley, 1977). Most recently, David W. Rohde (1991), drawing on the theory developed earlier, has also called into question the conventional wisdom that parties are insignificant to understanding the workings of Congress. Rohde demonstrates that political parties made a significant comeback in recent sessions of the House of Representatives; he also analyzes the context and contrasts the House with the Senate (see also Sinclair, 1989, 1990).

Much of this analysis of party in government has dealt with partisanship in the House of Representatives, the more party-sensitive of the two houses of Congress. Other analysts have looked at the partisan role that the president plays, though frequently their studies have dealt mainly with the president as a leader of Congress, as an agenda-setter, and as a leader of his copartisans in Congress (Bond & Fleisher, 1990; Edwards, 1980; Edwards & Wayne, 1990; Wayne, 1978). And there has also been a start in analyzing the partisanship of recent presidents in making policy-level appointments (Mackenzie, 1990).

The model implicit in studies that stress the importance of party in government is essentially a parliamentary model, i.e., a government structured in such a way that the individual who leads a party in the election is the same person who leads that party in government. In a parliamentary system such as the one in Great Britain, of course, the party leader is a member of the legislature as well as the prime minister. Our political system, with its legislative and executive powers separated, is quite different. Legislators' electoral bases are distinct from that of the president—though presidential elections are held on the same day as House and Senate elections (only one-third of the Senate, however, is up for election in any one year). And, of course, neither the president nor any of his top administrative officers are members of the legislature.

Most of the pre-1950 discussion of party in government assumed that most citizens cast votes for candidates of either one party or the other; as a consequence, Congress and the White House would be controlled by the same party. Such control was in fact the norm for much of the nation's history. However, for a variety of reasons (see Chapters 4 and 7 and Jacobson, 1990c), the presumption that the president's party will control Congress has been reversed in the last forty years. In fact from 1952 to 1992, the same party controlled the presidency and both houses of Congress for only fourteen years, roughly one-third of the time. Divided government has become the norm. With divided government has come a clearer realization that party members in the legislature might not always share the views of their copartisan in the White House (Rohde, 1991, pp. 138–151). Thus, party in government is something of an evolving concept. The remaining sections of this chapter will deal with the structural organization of the parties in government and with the impact of party as an organizing element of the national government.

II. PARTY AS THE ORGANIZING ELEMENT OF THE U.S. CONGRESS

Today congressional observers take for granted that the major political parties are quite elaborately organized to coordinate their work in Congress. In fact, however, the development of party structures in Congress is a rather recent phenomenon. Article I, Section 2, of the Constitution mandates that the House of Representatives elect its own Speaker, and from the earliest days of the Republic, Speakers have always been partisan leaders of that body (Peters, 1990). But no other congressional or party officers are mentioned in the Constitution. From its first session the Senate has chosen a president pro tempore to serve in the chair in the absence of the vice president (whom the Constitution designates as the president of the Senate); twenty-four senators served as president pro tem in the first ten Congresses, and the position was viewed as more honorific than powerful. The roles of majority and minority leader (and majority and minority whip, their assistants) did not appear until late in the nineteenth century in the House and after the first decade of the twentieth century in the Senate. Institutional development of the organizational support for these leaders followed slowly (Sinclair, 1983).

A. The Democrats in the House of Representatives

The Democrats have been the majority party in the House of Representatives continuously since 1954. Thus, discussion of majority-party leadership in the House is discussion of how the Democrats organize as the *majority* party; discussion of *minority*-party structure is, therefore, discussion of Republican organization. When the partisan roles were reversed is temporally too far removed to be relevant.

The leader of the majority party in the House is the Speaker. Officially an officer of the entire House, Speakers have been party leaders virtually since the inception of the role. Speakers are elected by the entire House. However, the vote for Speaker, the first vote in each new Congress, turns out to be a strictly party-line vote. Each party's caucus—i.e., a meeting of all members of that party—nominates a candidate for Speaker. All the Democrats vote for their candidate; all the Republicans for their candidate. Because the Democrats have been in the majority for nearly four decades, nomination by the Democratic Caucus has been tantamount to election since 1954.[2]

But more than that can be said. The modern Speaker is always a "man of the House," an individual who has chosen the House of Representatives as his

---

[2] The losing candidate for Speaker becomes the minority leader. The last two times that party control switched hands—when the Republicans took control for the Eighty-Third Congress, after the 1952 election, and then the Democrats regained control for the Eighty-Fourth and subsequent Congresses, after the 1954 election—the two party leaders, Sam Rayburn (D., Tex., 1913–1961; Speaker, 1940–1947, 1949–1953, 1955–1961) and Joseph W. Martin, Jr. (R., Mass., 1925–1967; Speaker, 1947–1949, 1953–1955), merely switched positions.

career. Progressive ambition to a future Speaker of the House is progression within the party hierarchy in Congress, not "rising" from the House to some other office (Schlesinger, 1966). The current Speaker, Thomas S. Foley (Wash.), had served in the House for a quarter century before his election as Speaker in 1989; he had served as chair of the Agriculture Committee (1975–1981), majority whip (1981–1987),[3] and majority leader (1987–1989). His immediate predecessors, Jim Wright (Tex., 1954–1989) and Thomas P. (Tip) O'Neill, Jr. (Mass., 1952–1987), had served thirty-three and twenty-five years, respectively, before their elections as Speaker. Each of these men—and their immediate predecessors as well—had served as majority leader before ascending to the Speakership; the path through the majority whip position has been common but not always followed. Within the Democratic party at least, succession to the Speakership has become routine. While the party has staged heated contests for election to other leadership posts, recent Speakers have routinely been nominated and renominated by the Democratic Caucus without opposition (Peabody, 1976).

The Speaker has two rather distinct jobs. As an officer of the entire House, he not only presides over debates, but also serves as the chief administrator (Obey Commission, 1977). His administrative role has certain political implications, but much of it involves rather routine matters, such as supervising the Capitol Police Force, and is often delegated to staff (to whom some influence then accrues). These roles were not deemed very significant until the House Bank and House Post Office scandals of 1992.

For present purposes, the more important role is as party leader. His position is the linchpin for policy determination and strategy sessions. He is the visible leader of the party. The Speaker also chairs the important Democratic Steering and Policy Committee (discussed below) and personally appoints nine of its members. He also appoints (with caucus approval) the chair and the Democratic members of the powerful Rules Committee. In recent years the Speaker has been given the power to refer bills to more than one committee, either simultaneously or sequentially, and other controls over the flow of legislation (Bach & Smith, 1988; Collie & Cooper, 1989). Thus, the Speaker is the party leader, and party and House rules give him the potential to exercise leadership powers in an effective way.

The majority leader is the Speaker's chief lieutenant and heir apparent. For many years the Democratic party leadership was composed of one representative from the southwest and one from the northeast, the so-called Austin-Boston connection.[4] The leaders represented the geographic and often the ideo-

---

[3] When Foley became whip after the Democrats' electoral debacle of 1980, an election that cost his predecessor John Brademas (D., Ind., 1959–1981) his seat in Congress, the whip was appointed by the Speaker and majority leader. A party rule change now calls for whips to be elected by the Democratic Caucus, a practice used in the selection of Foley's successors, William H. Gray III (D., Pa., 1978–1991) and David E. Bonior (D., Mich.).

[4] The name was most in vogue when Texan Sam Rayburn was the Speaker and John W. McCormack (D., Mass., 1928–1971; Speaker, 1962–1971) was majority leader. When McCormack succeeded to the Speakership, Carl Albert (D., Okla., 1947–1977; Speaker, 1971–1977) moved up

logical bases of the party. However, succession to majority leader has not always been routine.

Jim Wright's election as majority leader stands as a perfect example of intraparty conflict. When Carl Albert retired from Congress and the Speakership, no Democrat challenged Majority Leader Tip O'Neill's succession to the party leadership. But four Democrats sought to succeed O'Neill (and thus to be next in line to become Speaker). John J. McFall (D., Calif., 1957–1979), the appointed majority whip, sought to move up the leadership ladder. He was challenged by Richard Bolling (D., Mo., 1949–1983), a leading ally of Speaker Rayburn and a well-known party reformer; by Philip Burton (D., Calif., 1964–1983), a leader of the liberal Democratic Study Group and an outspoken critic of old-style politics; and by Wright, who was billed as a somewhat flamboyant but politically centrist southerner. The party rules call for successive secret ballots, with the candidate receiving the lowest total dropped after each ballot. McFall, whose reputation had been tainted by the "Koreagate" scandal, trailed on the first ballot and was dropped. Wright edged Bolling by two votes on the second ballot and Burton by one on the third. Thus the nonreformer became the second-ranking Democrat in a very reform-minded party in the late 1970s. Personality and region as well as ideology and political acumen apparently contributed to Wright's victory, but such are often the vagaries of intraparty warfare.

The majority leader's role is a delicate one. He is clearly second in the party hierarchy, but he is often the party's spokesperson on the floor of the House. He must master the nuances of parliamentary procedure in the House, to aid the Speaker as they monitor the flow of legislation through a very complex legislative labyrinth. He must be alert to the actions of other congressmen, often those with different stakes or views of the policymaking process, assuring that the leadership is not taken by surprise and not unprepared for unwanted legislative initiatives. He must do all these things while maintaining his base of support in his own district, building his own stature as a national politician, and forming alliances and accumulating debts that will result in his subsequent elevation to the Speakership.

The third person in the Democratic hierarchy is the majority whip. We have seen that in 1980 Tom Foley was the last Democratic whip appointed by the Speaker and majority leader. As part of the reform efforts to democratize the House, the majority whip is now elected by the caucus. Foley's successor, and thus the first elected whip, was Tony Coehlo (D., Calif., 1978–1989). Coehlo's election says a good deal about the connection between party organization and

---

from whip to majority leader. When Albert became Speaker, for one Congress the majority leader was Hale Boggs (D., La., 1941–1943, 1947–1973); thus the southwest-northeast axis was broken. However, after Boggs's untimely death (in a plane accident while campaigning in Alaska), Tip O'Neill became majority leader and the connection was reestablished. The pattern remained in place while O'Neill was Speaker and Jim Wright majority leader. In the most recent Congresses, however, with northwesterner Tom Foley securing a leadership position and with none of the current leaders from either the northeast or the southwest, the once solid tradition seems permanently broken.

party in the electorate. Coehlo had sought and received appointment as chairman of the Democratic Congressional Campaign Committee in 1980. The DCCC had never been a base of power in the House; indeed it seemed only a poor imitation of its Republican counterpart. But Coehlo saw potential and grabbed it. He raised unprecedented sums of money by emulating the methods of the National Republican Congressional Committee and reminding political action committees of which party controlled the House. He won himself a position in the House leadership hierarchy by virtue of the increased importance that the DCCC played in maintaining majority status. While he could not match the NRCC's dollar totals, he built a first-class operation and won the admiration of (and accumulated political IOUs from) those whose campaigns he supported (B. Jackson, 1988). When the whip's seat opened, with Wright's and then Foley's ascent on the leadership ladder. Coehlo was ready. He drew on his reputation, called in his chits, and won the election.[5]

The Democratic whip in the House now heads an extensive supporting organization. (This section draws heavily on Rohde, 1991, pp. 82–93, and on Ripley, 1964, 1967, and Sinclair, 1983.) The whip organizations in Congress developed out of the intense partisan conflict in the late nineteenth century. By the time of the New Deal, however, the sectional and ideological conflicts within the Democratic party also required attention. Under Speaker Rayburn, the majority whip was assisted by a phalanx of regional whips. Rayburn's leadership style was so personal, however, that he rarely relied on the whip system. While the regional whips could potentially gather information, their capability to perform this function and to have it as an important part of leadership's role was never developed.

Regional whips were either appointed by senior Democrats in a region or elected by the members from that region; they did not owe loyalty to the party leader. In fact, they were never included in the leadership structure; and at least during the Kennedy and Johnson administrations (when New Frontier and Great Society programs split the party on ideological and regional grounds), they often did not support the party leader's policy preferences.

Much of this rebellious individualism changed during the Nixon administration, when the majority Democrats saw the need to organize in opposition to Republican policy initiatives. First, the whip organization was enlarged, with the creation of the position of chief deputy whip and with the addition of three deputy whips and the first at-large whips, representing the Women's Caucus, the Black Caucus, and the class of newly elected members. Then the visibility of the office was enhanced when the whip and the chief deputy whip were given ex officio seats on the Steering and Policy Committee. The whip organization began to play the role of persuading members to support the party as well as that of informing House members of the leadership's intentions and desires and informing the leadership of the members' reactions to those positions.

[5] Coehlo became whip at the remarkably young age of forty-three. He seemed destined for a rapid rise up the leadership ladder—and a long career atop that ladder—until he was forced to resign from Congress in 1989 because of allegations that he had used his office and influence inappropriately.

The most significant changes in the whip organization have occurred in the period since Foley took over as the whip. An additional deputy whip was added, and the number of at-large whips was increased to fifteen. By the time Foley left the whip office, he was supported by seven deputy whips and thirty-two at-large whips. The whip organization had come to include one-fourth of the Democratic membership of Congress. By the time Coehlo resigned, *his* organization included a chief deputy whip, fifteen deputy whips, sixty-five at-large whips, four task force chairs (who had the same status as deputy whips), and fifteen assistant whips elected by zone; the whip organization included 40 percent of the members of the caucus. It was involved heavily in disseminating and gathering information, conducting frequent whip polls; it was also involved more and more in persuading members to follow the position of the leadership, a task made somewhat easier by the initiation of so many members into the leadership and by the now nearly regularized position of standing in opposition to the views of a president of the other party.

The chain of command below the whip is less clear-cut. Recent succession struggles make that apparent. During the 101st Congress, Speaker Wright and Majority Whip Coehlo each resigned under taint of scandal. Majority Leader Foley moved into the Speakership without a challenge. Richard Gephardt (Mo.), who had recently completed two terms as *Democratic Caucus chair* and who had been a presidential candidate with the support of many of his House colleagues in 1988, easily defeated conservative Georgian Ed Jenkins to succeed Foley. The race to succeed Coehlo involved three serious candidates, who had followed three different routes up the leadership ladder. The winner, William H. Gray, Jr., had been elected as head of the "Class of 1978" when he entered Congress. In rapid succession he had won a seat on the Appropriations Committee, a seat on the Budget Committee, the chairmanship of the Budget Committee, and, at the start of the 101st Congress in 1989, a role in the leadership hierarchy as caucus chair. As such, he became the highest-ranking black man in the history of Congress. In the contest for majority whip, Gray beat David Bonior, who ran from his position as *chief deputy whip,* an office to which he had been appointed by Wright (with Foley's and Coehlo's concurrence) and in which he was serving with distinction. Gray also beat Beryl Anthony (Ark.), who had succeeded Coehlo as *chair of the Democratic Congressional Campaign Committee,* again serving with great success.

Speaker Foley prevailed upon both Bonior and Anthony to remain in their leadership positions. Steny H. Hoyer (Md.) was elected to succeed Gray as caucus chair. When Gray himself unexpectedly resigned from Congress (and thus as majority whip) to head the United Negro College Fund, in the middle of the 102d Congress, Bonior edged Hoyer in the race to succeed Gray. Thus at least three positions—below the top three party leadership slots, whose incumbents are elected by the caucus—are apparently viewed as logical steppingstones in potential leaders' careers.

However, merely identifying these positions does not suffice to describe leadership in the majority party. Any close observer of the modern Congress would list Dan Rostenkowski (Ill.) as one of the top Democrats, as the individual most likely to challenge for the Speakership should Foley resign, as one of the most powerful men in Congress. Yet Rostenkowski does not hold any of the positions mentioned thus far. Rather, he is chair of the powerful Ways and Means Committee in the House, the committee that writes all tax bills and handles other important legislation, including revisions of the Social Security System. Committee leaders are important party leaders as well.

Until the implementation of congressional reforms in the last two decades, committee chairs were often referred to as "committee barons"—and each ran his own little fiefdom. Speaker Rayburn and his immediate successors clearly shared power with the strongest of these chairmen. The reform movement took power away from the committee chairs and spread it more evenly among the members. The reform era marked the reinvigoration of the caucus, the empowerment of rank-and-file (and thus junior) members of Congress, and the decentralization of power to subcommittees and their leaders (Oleszek, 1989; Ornstein, 1975; Rohde, 1974, 1991, chap. 2; Sheppard, 1985; S. Smith & Deering, 1990).[6]

Part of the reform effort aimed at reinvigorating centralized party leadership involved giving more power to the *Democratic Steering and Policy Committee,* concomitantly giving the Speaker more control over that committee. Thus Steering and Policy is the committee that recommends committee assignments for all House Democrats and subcommittee chairmanships for the important Appropriations Committee. It is the committee that examines party priorities and helps to set strategy.

The committee's membership is important. Steering and Policy is very much the Speaker's committee; he is the chair. The majority leader is the vice chair; the caucus chair the second vice chair. Other party leaders have seats on this committee because of the offices they hold—the whip and his chief deputy, the chair of the DCCC, the vice chair of the caucus. Twelve "rank-and-file" members are elected to the committee by fellow Democrats, based on region of the country. The Speaker himself appoints nine additional members; these members, along with the members of his leadership team, assure the Speaker dominance over the committee. But equally important to note is that the chairs of the four most powerful committees in the House—Appropriations, Budget, Rules, and Ways and Means—are also members of the committee. These ex officio memberships are clear recognition of the continuing importance and power of committee chairs in the modern Congress.

Changes in the structure of the Democratic party leadership in the House have reflected changes in the role of the party in the government. Once Speakers had to rely heavily on their relationships with powerful and independent committee chairs—men who owed their positions to the safety of their seats and to their seniority on their committees, not to the party or to the Speaker—to

---

[6] Conventional wisdom held that one of the unintended consequences of these reforms was the disaggregation of power to so many junior members (many of them subcommittee chairs) to the extent that it was impossible to lead the House. For reasons that Rohde (1991, chaps. 4 and 6) astutely points out, the party leaders were also given new powers, but they did not effectively exercise their new powers for some time.

pass legislation. Then for a time power was seemingly fragmented and no one appeared to be able to formulate a party position in the House. Today, however, the Speaker stands atop a party hierarchy that has the potential to present party positions effectively and to induce allegiance from rank-and-file members. Before examining the extent to which this happens, we will turn to a (somewhat briefer) examination of the structures of the Republican party in the House and of the two parties in the Senate.

B.   The Republicans in the House of Representatives

Just as the Democrats' continuous majority-party status—and the fact that often the president has been a Republican while they have held the majority in the House—has affected the functioning of the Democratic party in Congress, so too has the fact that the Republicans have continuously been in the minority and have often tried to pass programs promulgated by a president of their own party affected the Republican party in the House (C. Jones, 1970; Ripley, 1967).

One obvious impact has been in the careers of a succession of *minority leaders*. After the Republican party did poorly in the 1958 midterm elections, minority leader Joseph Martin, who had been his party's leader in the House since before World War II, was challenged and defeated by Charles A. Halleck (R., Ind., 1935–1969), who claimed that the party needed new, more forceful leadership and a new image if it was to achieve majority status. Six years later, after another Republican electoral debacle in 1964, Halleck was challenged and replaced by Gerald Ford, who represented Grand Rapids, Michigan, in the House from 1949 until he was named to succeed Spiro Agnew as vice president in 1973. Like Halleck before him, Ford claimed that new leadership was necessary if the Republicans were ever to overcome their position as the minority in the House.

Ford in turn was succeeded by John J. Rhodes (Ariz., 1953–1983). The minority status of the Republicans continued. Rhodes's leadership style, like that of Ford and also of Martin, was to attack the Democrats publicly on occasion but to work with Democratic leaders in Congress cooperatively in private. This style rankled a group of younger, more ideologically conservative Republicans at the time when Ronald Reagan assumed the presidency. Rhodes eventually decided to retire rather than to manage the conflict within his own party. His successor, Robert Michel (Ill.), has been a most effective minority leader, castigating the vociferous Speaker Wright for overt partisanship but working more closely with Speaker Foley when the new Speaker toned down the level of partisan debate.

For thirty years, through the leaderships of Martin, Halleck, and Ford, the second-ranking Republican in the House was Leslie Arends (Ill., 1935–1974). However, as *minority whip*, Arends was not a dominating figure in the Republican hierarchy. He was a loyal supporter of the leader, even that succession of leaders who overthrew their predecessors. The Republican whip's job was largely routinized; for most of this period the party was not split, and thus the whip organization did not have to concern itself much with persuading members to do what they would have done in any partisan case.

Arends was succeeded by Michel, who used the job as a springboard to party leadership by building ties with both Rhodes's supporters and the more conservative junior Republicans. The minority whip's job has become more important and clearly is now seen as a possible launching pad for advancement. When Michel became minority leader in 1983, Trent Lott (Miss.) won election as whip. Lott had headed the caucus of Republicans, called the *Republican Conference*, and was the first of the new breed of southern conservative Republicans to step into a party leadership position. But Lott did not plan for his career to be in the House; he gave up a safe seat and his leadership role to run successfully for the Senate in 1988.

Lott was succeeded briefly by Richard Cheney (Wyo., 1979–1989). Cheney, who had served as chief of staff in the Ford White House, switched to the legislative branch and was rising rapidly in the party's leadership hierarchy. He was viewed by many as "the future" of the House Republican party, perhaps as a future Republican Speaker. But just as suddenly as he had switched from service in the Ford White House to running for Congress, in 1989 he switched branches again, resigning his seat and leadership position to accept President Bush's nomination to serve as secretary of defense. Michel endorsed the candidacy of his friend and Illinois neighbor Edward Madigan (Ill., 1973–1991) to succeed Cheney. The membership, however, had other ideas. Despite Michel's popularity as leader, they chose the acerbic Newt Gingrich (Ga.), an outspoken conservative and the leading critic and accuser of deposed Speaker Jim Wright, as minority whip.[7]

The organization that Gingrich heads is less extensive than the one run by Bonior for the Democrats. The Republicans have two chief deputy whips, five deputy whips, three assistant deputy whips, and four assistant whips for geographic zones. While some division exists within the party, few see the need for an inclusive organization of the magnitude organized by the Democrats.

The remaining positions in the Republican leadership organization are well-defined; unlike their Democratic counterparts, Republican leaders are all elected (by the full Republican Conference). As with the election of Gingrich, these races frequently reflect divisions within the party. Thus, those chosen are less tools of the minority leader and more powers in their own right.

The reelections of Jerry Lewis (Calif.) and Guy Vander Jagt (Mich.) as *Republican Conference chairman* and *National Republican Congressional Committee chairman*, respectively, are cases in point. Lewis's career is typical of a moderate Republican accommodationist who has worked his way up, serving the party as chairman of the Research Committee and the Policy Committee before his election as conference chairman in 1988. He sees himself as a future leader. He believes that his party should work closely with the White House and with con-

---

[7] In 1991, Madigan resigned from the House to accept Bush's invitation to serve as secretary of agriculture, avoiding a difficult choice in 1992 when his district might well be collapsed with Michel's as a result of the decennial reapportionment and redrawing of district lines.

President Bush is seen meeting in the White House to establish party strategy on
pending legislation with Republican leaders of the House of Representatives: Minority
Whip Newt Gingrich of Georgia (left) and Minority Leader Bob Michel of Illinois
(center). (AP/Wide World Photos)

servative Democrats when that is necessary. Lewis was challenged by Carl
Pursell of Michigan. Pursell was backed by Minority Whip Gingrich, who views
Lewis as an obstacle in his own bid to succeed Michel as party leader. But
Pursell differs mainly from Lewis over style. He believes that the minority party
in the House should be an independent force, not reliant on the White House
for policy leadership. In the final vote, members of the Republican Conference
reelected Lewis in a vote generally interpreted to be a reaffirmation of his accommodationist style and a setback to confrontational Gingrich (Hook, 1990).

Similarly, Vander Jagt was challenged by Don Sundquist of Tennessee.
Vander Jagt, who took over as chair of the NRCC after the Watergate fiasco,
built that organization into a wealthy and effective aid to Republican candidates. Still the Republicans have remained in the minority in the House. In
1990 he was challenged by Sundquist, largely over the issue of how the NRCC
spent its money—it had raised nearly four times as much as the DCCC but
given only about a million dollars more to candidates than had the Democrats.
But the challenge also reflected internal party differences. Sundquist is an old
friend of John Sununu, who at the time was White House chief of staff, and
who had clashed openly with the NRCC's executive director, Ed Rollins. Vander Jagt turned back Sundquist's challenge, perhaps in part because of the
anger of his House colleagues over meddling by the executive branch. In any

case, if the Republicans do not fare better in the 1992 elections, Vander Jagt may face another challenge to his slot on the Republican leadership team (Alston, 1990).

Republican assignments to committees are made by a twenty-one-member Committee on Committees. Under a unique arrangement adopted in 1988, the minority leader, who chairs this committee, has twelve votes; the minority whip has six; and each of the other members, who are chosen by region, have as many votes as there are Republican members in the state delegations they represent. The minority leader also has been given the power to name Republican members of the Rules Committee. Each of these changes is an institutional response that gives Republican leadership more tools with which to lead their party colleagues.

Republicans in the House also have two other committees that aid the leadership. The Policy Committee, chaired since 1988 by Mickey Edwards (Okla.) is a thirty-six-member group that assists the minority leadership in setting policy direction for the party. The Research Committee, a twenty-three-member body chaired by Duncan Hunter (Calif.), is in fact a staff-holding operation, giving the Republicans the capability to conduct thorough research on pending issues and on the consequences of policy alternatives.

While Republican party members have split in recent years as they have viewed questions of policy and tactics, their splits are still narrow compared with the ones among their Democratic counterparts. Their leadership structure reflects the more homogeneous composition of the Republican party and the fact that much of their recent history has been that of a minority party backing the programs proposed by a president they support.

C.   Party Leadership in the Senate

For very good reasons, party as an organizing element is more important in the House than it is in the Senate. First, the Senate is a smaller body. Senators know most other senators, not just members of their state delegation, or of their committees, or of their parties. Senate staff members know other staff members. A body of 100 people is manageable; one of 435 is not.

Second, senators tend to see themselves as powerful individuals, able to attract media attention, to be listened to for their special expertise, and to be deferred to because of their prominence. Senators are less likely to follow party line because it is party line. They are less likely to defer to others because of institutional prerogatives, more likely to build alliances with like-minded people whom they know and with whom they have worked. As was mentioned in Chapter 8, the Senate is now seen as the incubator of presidential candidates. At any time as many as 10 percent of the senators are, either actively or with a few confidantes, exploring their options of running for the White House. In the Senate they want to be seen and heard; they want to make a difference; they are not interested in toeing the party line. While the House is structured in such a way as to permit majorities to work their will in almost all circumstances, individual incentives and institutional differences make clear that this is not the case in the Senate (Rohde, 1992).

In addition, or perhaps because of these reasons, the Senate is a less partisan body than is the House. The aisle that separates Democrats from Republicans in the House of Representatives is a true gulf. Few cross it, and those who do are viewed with suspicion. The same simply is not true in the Senate. Leaders work more closely together; senators work closely with members of the other party. Friendships and alliances cross party lines. (For an analysis of the differences between the House and Senate in terms of the size of the two bodies, the electoral environments, the prominence of the members, and the partisan contexts, see Baker, 1989a.)

The differences between the two houses of the national legislature lead to very real differences in the roles played by the parties in the two houses. In many ways, the differences between the parties in the House and the parties in the Senate are more significant than party differences between the Democrats and Republicans in the Senate itself.

1. The Senate Democrats George Mitchell (Me.) is only the fourth Democratic party leader in the Senate in the last forty years. Lyndon Johnson served from 1953 until he became vice president in 1961. Mike Mansfield (Mont.) led the Democrats as the majority leader from 1961 until he retired in 1977. Robert C. Byrd (W.V.) succeeded Mansfield and served as the party leader—in majority and minority—until he decided not to continue as leader (though remaining in the Senate as president pro tempore and chair of the Appropriation Committee) after the 1988 elections.

Byrd was eased toward retirement as leader because of dissatisfaction among the Democratic senators about the image he portrayed. Byrd, though never a member of the old Senate establishment, is clearly a child of "old-style" politics. He became leader because of his ability to work hard, to serve the members, to exploit the intricacies of Senate procedure. But he never was capable of—or interested in—developing a media personality with which his colleagues were comfortable.

The Democrats lost their majority in the Senate in a Republican landslide in 1980. They regained majority status in 1986; Mitchell had served as chair of the Democratic Senatorial Campaign Committee for that election. In addition, Mitchell had proved to his colleagues during the televised Iran-Contra hearings that he could use the media to convey their message to the public. Many of the newer members were, moreover, not so deeply enamored of life in the Senate as was Byrd. They wanted to be able to lead personal and political lives apart from the Senate, and Byrd showed no inclination to accommodate them.

Mitchell's election was viewed as an upset by most media analysts. He beat two more senior and well-established Democrats, Bennett Johnston (La.) and Daniel Inouye (Haw.). He won by proving to members that he could be the kind of leader they wanted, one capable of combating the Republican in the White House, concerned about the legitimate demands of the members, and dedicated to including more Democrats on his leadership team.

In the Johnson, Mansfield, and Byrd days, the leadership of the Democratic party in the Senate was centrally controlled. The leader chaired all party committees and kept most decisions close to his vest. Mitchell's first move as majority leader was to expand the powers of the Policy Committee and to name Thomas A. Daschle (S.D.), a member of the class of 1986 that Mitchell had aided in their election, as cochair. Four other senators were named vice chairs on this committee of twenty. The new majority leader asked Inouye, the popular senior member he had defeated, to chair the party's Steering Committee, which makes Democratic appointments to the legislative committees. He also named Wyche Fowler (Ga.) as assistant floor leader. The majority whip, Alan Cranston (Calif.), remained in office for Mitchell's first Congress, but when he was embroiled in the Keating Five scandal, he resigned as whip, to be replaced by Wendell Ford (Ky.); Ford's organization includes a chief deputy whip and eight other senators, chosen by region, who serve as either deputy or assistant deputy whips. Finally, Charles Robb (Va.) chairs the Democratic Senatorial Campaign Committee. The pattern is quite clear. Mitchell wants his party leadership group to be inclusive, not exclusive. Virtually every Democratic senator serves on one party committee or another; many serve on more than one. He works hard to include all relevant actors in each political discussion.

Mitchell has received very high marks for his first years as leader. He has been criticized at times for not taking on the Republican White House strongly enough, but at other times he has responded to initiatives from President Bush vigorously. He has built an organization that allows him to lead his party cohesively on those issues clearly separating Democrats from Republicans, though the narrowness of his less-than-two-thirds majority does not allow him the luxury either of overriding presidential vetoes or even of breaking filibusters without Republican assistance.

2. The Senate Republicans The structure for the Senate Republicans is similar to, though slightly different from, that of the Senate Democrats. Bob Dole (Kan.) has been Republican leader since 1985, for one Congress as majority leader and since as *minority leader*. Dole, like his predecessor Howard H. Baker, Jr. (Tenn.), once made a run for president. Both found it difficult to carry on the tasks of Senate leader while actively campaigning. Baker in fact decided not to run for reelection to the Senate, presumably to begin another presidential campaign, though he eventually served as White House chief of staff and did not again seek his party's presidential nomination.

Dole, who also ran unsuccessfully as Republican candidate for vice president in 1976, has faced the difficult task of carrying forward the program of George Bush, the man who beat him for the presidential nomination in 1988. However, the somewhat bitter feelings that appeared during the nomination campaign seem to have been smoothed over. The senator's wife, Elizabeth Dole, served for a time as Bush's secretary of labor; and Dole has been a firm loyalist in representing the president and his program in the Senate.

The second-ranking Republican, who performs the function of whip, is the *assistant minority leader,* in the 102d Congress, Alan Simpson of Wyoming. Simpson's organization consists of seven deputy whips. The Republican leadership also includes the *conference chair* (Thad Cochran [Miss.]), a position that the majority leader himself holds for the Democrats. Republican Committee assignments are made by a three-member *Committee on Committees,* chaired by Trent Lott (Miss.). Finally, Phil Gramm of Texas chairs the *Republican Senatorial Campaign Committee.*

While traditionally the Democrats have been more deeply divided than the Republicans, recent elections have brought to the Senate a new breed of acerbic conservatives anxious to make stands of principle, even if such ideological assertiveness requires taking on members of their own party. No one would ever accuse Dole or Simpson of being flaming liberals, but frequently they have clashed with their own copartisans—for instance, Gramm or Jesse Helms (N.C.)—on some of the volatile issues of the day. Dole has tried hard to work with Mitchell and the Democrats on some issues, e.g., campaign finance reform, further alienating some of his fellow Republicans.

However, the Senate is a small place, and the minority party is a small group. Obviously, the Republicans have a vested interest in maintaining unity against the Democrats on key issues. Therefore, on issue after issue they have stood together with their president, sustaining vetoes that the Democrats have sought to override or threatening to filibuster bills that they have not wanted passed. Ironically, the strength of the Republican unity in the Senate is probably as much a function of their minority status and the advantages that Senate rules give to a heartfelt minority as it is to the organization and skills of the party leaders.

3. The Muted Role of Party Leaders This rather brief discussion of Senate party leaders leads back to the question of why partisanship—and particularly partisanship in the roles of party leaders—is less prominent in the Senate than in the House. To a great extent this difference follows directly from the rules of the two bodies.

While it is true that the parties "organize" the Senate—e.g., they make committee assignments—the leaders are not given the powers and resources that House leaders hold. The majority leader has the responsibility to schedule floor debate and to provide leadership for his party's positions, but he is not given the tools to do so without significant cooperation from his colleagues.

In fact, the only advantage the party leaders have over other senators is that they will be recognized first when a number of senators are seeking recognition. Beyond that, the norms and the rules of the Senate give resources and power to individual senators, not to institutional officers. Senators have multiple committee assignments and are rarely discouraged from speaking on areas outside of their committees' jurisdictions. Individual senators can hold the floor indefinitely, exercising their right to filibuster a bill. As the Senate does not have a powerful Rules Committee to schedule floor debate, the flow of legislation onto the floor is arranged through unanimous consent decrees, which the party leadership negotiates in consultation with committee leaders and other concerned senators. Any senator can upset scheduling agreements arranged by party leaders by objecting to these unanimous consent decrees.

Rules such as these mean that the job of the majority leader is really that of a negotiator. He must constantly confer with his own allies, to be certain they are all on board. He must work closely with the minority leader, to be certain that the other party will not disrupt agreed-upon arrangements. Individual egos must be stroked; individual personalities taken into account; individual agendas accommodated. (On these aspects of the role of the majority leader, see Sinclair, 1990.)

George Mitchell's job as majority leader has been to reach for a new definition of the role of the Democratic majority in the Senate. He has accomplished this goal by drawing more senators into the leadership clique, by expanding the powers of the Policy Committee, by assuming the dual role of media spokesperson for the party and consummate inside player in Senate politics. His success has led to the somewhat ironic situation in which the role of the party leader does not seem to have been enhanced, but the role of the party has been—because of the work of the leader.

Robert Dole's role has been similar. He has had to define the Republican party's role as a minority in the Senate, many of whose members also do not agree with at least some of a Republican president's proposals. Dole then has had to work with Mitchell and with Bush and his allies. He too has had to walk a tightrope. And he too has done so successfully, enhancing his own prestige as a leader and statesman, muting conflict within his own party, confronting Mitchell when necessary and working with him when possible.

III. THE IMPACT OF PARTY ON CONGRESSIONAL BEHAVIOR

This discussion of the organization of the two parties in the national legislature and some of the politics involved in that organization may be interesting, but the more vital questions about party in government relate to whether the parties structure the behavior of their copartisans in the legislature. Remember that the model employed as a "goal" is a parliamentary model, a system in which party discipline is enforced by strong party leaders. Throughout this text we have given many reasons why the American electoral system differs from a parliamentary system, most notably the decentralized nature of political parties, the independence of the nominating system, and the personalization of campaigning and appeals to the voter. In this section we turn briefly to how the federal legislators elected through this system respond to the legislative choices with which they are confronted.

Political scientists use three different measures of party voting. First, *party unity votes* are those votes in which a majority of the Democrats voting cast their votes on one side of an issue and the majority of Republicans on the other side.[8]

---

[8] These votes are distinguished from *nonparty unity* votes and *consensual* votes. Consensual votes are those in which over 90 percent of those present vote for or against a particular issue (Rohde, 1991, p. 51); see also Collie (1986) for a slightly different definition of *universalistic* votes. Nonparty unity votes are the rest.

Party unity scores are the percentage of times that an individual legislator votes with his or her party on party unity votes.[9] *Party cohesion scores* are the absolute difference between the percentage of a party voting for an issue and the percentage voting against it. Thus, if every Democrat voted "aye" on a particular vote while 75 percent of the Republicans voted "nay" and 25 percent voted "aye," that would be a party unity vote (a majority of Democrats voting on one side and a majority of Republicans on the other), that vote would be included in a computation of the legislators' party unity score, and the party cohesion score for the Democrats on that vote would be 100 points (100 – 0) and for the Republicans 50 points (75 – 25). Systems in which party structures legislative decisions tend to have more party unity votes, higher party cohesion scores, and higher party unity scores.

Table 11-1 lists the number of party unity votes in the House and Senate for the last forty years. Even from these very rudimentary data, a number of conclusions follow. First, the number of party unity votes did fall during the middle years of this period, but just as significantly, partisan voting has made a comeback in more recent years. In fact, the percentage of party unity votes has been at or near a majority of all votes in both houses of Congress since the beginning of the second Reagan term, with the sole exception of the Senate in 1989.[10]

Tables 11-2 and 11-3 reveal the truly remarkable extent to which party voting has again become an important factor in Congress and give some clues to the reasons. First, claiming that party voting is not important is difficult when the average party unity scores of Democrats and Republicans in both houses of Congress have been above 75 percent for the last decade. The Republican party, always assumed to be the more ideologically homogeneous, has shown remarkable unity throughout the period under study. Democratic party scores declined in the mid-1960s and into the 1970s, particularly in the House of Representatives; then they rebounded—to really astoundingly high levels— during the Reagan administration. However, David Rohde (1991, pp. 50–58) has demonstrated that much of the decline in the Democratic party scores was in fact a decline in the party unity scores of southern Democrats. The average scores of northern Democrats never fell below 80 percent during this entire period. Rohde also demonstrates that the mean Democratic cohesion fell dramatically during the Johnson administration and remained quite low through the Nixon and Ford administrations. However, Democrats voted much more cohesively in the Reagan years—and their voting has shown only slightly less cohesion in the first years of George Bush's presidency.

---

[9] *Party opposition scores*, a concept not employed in this discussion, are the percentage of times an individual legislator votes against his or her party on party unity votes. This score is not the residual of party unity scores only because of differences caused by absences.

[10] Some caution must be used in evaluating these figures. Perhaps the Senate figures in 1989 reflected a go-slow attitude of the new majority leader, George Mitchell. But it is just as logical to speculate, as has political scientist Tom Mann, that the 1990 increase in partisanship is a reflection of the relatively large number of divisive roll call votes cast on two particular issues—clean-air legislation and the civil rights bill (Zuckman, 1990).

TABLE 11-1. Party Unity Votes in Congress, 1953–1990 (percentage of all votes)

Year	House, %	Senate, %
1953	52	n.a.
1954	38	47
1955	41	30
1956	44	53
1957	59	36
1958	40	44
1959	55	48
1960	53	37
1961	50	62
1962	46	41
1963	49	47
1964	55	36
1965	52	42
1966	41	50
1967	36	35
1968	35	32
1969	31	36
1970	27	35
1971	38	42
1972	27	36
1973	42	40
1974	29	44
1975	48	48
1976	36	37
1977	42	42
1978	33	45
1979	47	47
1980	38	46
1981	37	48
1982	36	43
1983	56	44
1984	47	40
1985	61	50
1986	57	52
1987	64	41
1988	47	42
1989	55	35
1990	49	54

n.a. = not available.
Note: Data indicate the percentage of all recorded votes on which a majority of voting Democrats opposed a majority of voting Republicans.
Source: *Congressional Quarterly Almanac,* various years; *Congressional Quarterly Weekly Report,* December 30, 1989; December 22, 1990.

Note that this discussion of party in government in Congress has related party unity and party cohesion to presidential administrations. The concept of party in government implies a unified government. As has been mentioned many times, the norm for the American polity in recent decades has been di-

TABLE 11-2. Party Unity Scores in House Voting, 1954–1990

Year	All Democrats, %	Southern Democrats, %	Republicans, %
1954	80	n.a.	84
1955	84	68	78
1956	80	79	78
1957	79	71	75
1958	77	67	73
1959	85	77	85
1960	75	62	77
1961	n.a.	n.a.	n.a.
1962	81	n.a.	80
1963	85	n.a.	84
1964	82	n.a.	81
1965	80	55	81
1966	78	55	82
1967	77	53	82
1968	73	46	76
1969	71	47	71
1970	71	52	72
1971	72	46	76
1972	70	44	76
1973	75	55	74
1974	72	51	71
1975	75	53	78
1976	75	52	75
1977	74	55	77
1978	71	53	77
1979	75	60	79
1980	76	64	79
1981	75	57	80
1982	77	62	76
1983	82	67	80
1984	81	68	77
1985	86	76	80
1986	86	76	76
1987	88	78	79
1988	88	81	80
1989	81	68	72
1990	81	73	74

n.a. = not available.

Note: Data show percentage of members voting with a majority of their party on party unity votes. Party unity votes are those roll calls on which a majority of a party votes on one side of the issue and a majority of the other party votes on the other side. The percentages are normalized to eliminate the effects of absences as follows: party unity + (unity)/(unity + opposition).

Source: *Congressional Quarterly Almanac,* various years; *Congressional Quarterly Weekly Report,* December 30, 1989, December 22, 1990.

vided government. The question then becomes: With whose party in government are we to be concerned—that of the legislative leaders or the president's? And how do they relate?

What is clear from this analysis, and from any study of policymaking in the United States, is that the two are clearly interrelated, despite the separation of powers and their separate electoral bases. Political analysts are virtually

TABLE 11-3. Party Unity Scores in Senate Voting, 1954–1990

Year	All Democrats, %	Southern Democrats, %	Republicans, %
1954	77	n.a.	89
1955	82	78	82
1956	80	75	80
1957	79	81	81
1958	82	76	74
1959	76	63	80
1960	73	60	74
1961	n.a.	n.a.	n.a.
1962	80	n.a.	81
1963	79	n.a.	79
1964	73	n.a.	75
1965	75	55	78
1966	73	52	78
1967	75	59	73
1968	71	57	74
1969	74	53	72
1970	71	49	71
1971	74	56	75
1972	72	43	73
1973	79	52	74
1974	72	41	68
1975	76	48	71
1976	74	46	72
1977	72	48	75
1978	75	54	66
1979	76	62	73
1980	76	64	74
1981	77	64	85
1982	76	62	80
1983	76	70	79
1984	75	61	83
1985	79	68	81
1986	74	59	80
1987	85	80	78
1988	85	78	74
1989	78	73	78
1990	80	74	75

n.a. = not available.

Note: Data show percentage of members voting with a majority of their party on party unity votes. Party unity votes are those roll calls on which a majority of a party votes on one side of the issue and a majority of the other party votes on the other side. The percentages are normalized to eliminate the effects of absences as follows: party unity + (unity)/(unity + opposition).

Sources: *Congressional Quarterly Almanac*, various years; *Congressional Quarterly Weekly Report*, December 30, 1989, December 22, 1990.

unanimous in agreeing that presidents play the primary role in setting the congressional agenda (Fishel, 1985; C. Jones, 1988b, 1988c; Kingdon, 1984; Light, 1983). Analysts of congressional behavior have explained how the parties function relative to the president's program. *Congressional Quarterly* computes presidential support and presidential opposition scores annually. It also notes how often the president succeeds and how often he fails on key votes. Party performance is analyzed in terms of legislators' support for a president of their own party or opposition to a president of the other party, clearly implying that the president defines the issues on which the parties might or might not divide.

The analysis in this section, drawing on the contextual theory argued most forcefully by Cooper and Brady (1981) and Rohde (1991), implies that an analysis of party in the legislature is more complex than that.

> Thus, analysts saw, united government increased partisanship, while divided government reduced it. Yet there are other possibilities. . . . Rather, the impact of party control on the two branches is . . . conditional. *If,* under united government, the president's proposals reflect the views of the dominant faction in the majority party, and *if* the majority party is relatively homogeneous on major issues and the minority party doesn't have incentives to go along, then the result will be a fairly partisan pattern of support. . . . In the case of divided government, *if* parties are internally divided, and *if* the president does not push radical departures from the status quo, and *if* the administration's inclination is to compromise a significant share of the differences with congressional Democrats, . . . then partisanship should be muted. (Rohde, 1991, p. 140)

In addition, this analysis demonstrates that congressional parties in the 1990s are stronger than they were twenty years ago. Rohde (1991) is right in his analysis that the reforms of the 1970s have rejuvenated the parties and their leaders, even if that reaction was somewhat delayed. But it is also clear that party leadership—and as a consequence the extent of partisanship in Congress—is a function of personality as well as context and rules. Nothing could reveal this personality quotient more dramatically than the transfer of power from the highly partisan Speaker Jim Wright to the more accommodating Tom Foley (Sinclair, 1990). And finally, looking at both Democratic and Republican congressional leaders, we can simply comment that leaders only lead as far and as fast as their followers want them to. Leadership has its privileges to be sure, but the rank-and-file members still exert those independent judgments that constrain leadership prerogatives.

IV. THE PRESIDENT AS A LEADER OF PARTY IN GOVERNMENT

Much of the previous discussion has dealt with the president as a force in determining the direction taken by his party's members in Congress. The president is the most visible symbol of his party in the government. It is the *president's* program that is presented to Congress. It is the *president's* budget that Congress responds to. The members of the *president's* cabinet defend the *president's* proposals in hearings on Capitol Hill. In the current context no one talks about the Republican policy agenda; it is the Bush policy agenda. Commentators do not discuss the Republicans' response to a civil rights bill; they discuss President Bush's response. Thus, the first way that the president serves as a leader of his party in government is in defining issues—and this action goes a good way toward defining his relationship with Congress.

But the agenda-setting role is not the only one played by presidents. Leadership involves convincing supporters to follow as well. Thus, part of the role of the president is to convince his copartisans in Congress to follow his lead. Presidents can do this through *persuasion,* that is, convincing legislators to vote as the president wants, or through *conversion,* that is, by convincing them to want the same things the president wants (if they did not want these things before). An additional role played by presidents is as leader of an administration, an administration he largely staffs. This section will explore first the role the president plays in leading Congress, following on the discussion of the party in Congress above, and then the partisan role the president plays in leading his administration.

A.   The President as Leader of His Party in Congress

The key to understanding the importance of the president's role in setting the congressional agenda is to note differences in how that role is played. When President Kennedy was elected in 1960, for instance, he won by a very narrow margin. His party had delicate majorities in Congress, and the conservative branch of his party controlled many of the key posts in Congress. Consequently, despite his call for a New Frontier, he went very slowly in proposing major changes to Congress.

By way of contrast, after his landslide election in 1964, an election in which his party also made huge gains in congressional majorities, Lyndon Johnson proposed sweeping reforms in his Great Society legislation. Those proposals energized the Democrats, particularly the liberal Democrats, and most particularly the newly elected liberal Democrats, many of whom believed that they had ridden into office on Johnson's coattails. Similarly, the scope of Johnson's legislative initiatives stimulated reaction from the Republicans, enhancing the role of party for them as well.

When Jimmy Carter became president in 1977, his agenda was tied closely to the role for government that he had developed as a governor in Georgia. He wanted to streamline government; he wanted to cut costs. Carter's "ideology" was difficult to pin down. He was a liberal idealist on some issues, advancing the cause of human rights and halting nuclear proliferation to name two, but he was something of a conservative on others. He had not been the presidential candidate of the liberals in Congress—many of them had backed Mo Udall—and his program invoked neither strong united support from the Democrats nor strong united opposition from the Republicans. (See C. Jones, 1988c.)

Again, the contrast with Carter's successor is illustrative. Ronald Reagan won a landslide victory with a campaign in which he espoused a series of extremely conservative policy alternatives.[11] He advocated a conservative agenda

[11] The question of whether his landslide represented the voters' mandate for his policy views—a proposition that is highly dubious in light of public opinion surveys both on how voters decided and on how they stood on the issues—is irrelevant. What is relevant is that Reagan perceived the election as a mandate to go forward with at least some of these programs. Furthermore, Speaker O'Neill and many southern Democrats initially agreed with the president's view of the election and did not oppose his programs in his first two years.

Reprinted with permission Schorr and *The Kansas City Star*.

in his first Congress, particularly on fiscal matters. Reagan's party supported him on many of these matters. The liberal Democrats opposed him often, but many of the more conservative, mostly southern, Democrats, a group who came to be known as the Boll Weevils, signed on with the Reagan alternatives. Rohde (1991, pp. 138–144; see also C. Jones, 1988b) and others have demonstrated that a president's agenda has a direct impact on partisanship in Congress, but that his ability to lead his own party—and either to win support in the other party or to coalesce opposition—changes over the course of an administration, as the president's power waxes and wanes.

Not surprisingly, the president's ability to serve as party leader for his co-partisans in Congress is in part a function of how well he works with Congress. The first organized efforts at congressional liaison are generally traced to the Eisenhower administration, though some would say that the role really goes back at least as far as Thomas Jefferson (Young, 1966). Lawrence F. O'Brien, who built a congressional liaison staff in the Kennedy years, is often given credit for institutionalizing this staff function within the White House staff. But the sheer existence of an office and the effective functioning of that office are two different things.

Never was this difference clearer than during the Carter administration. Carter was elected to the presidency as an outsider. He campaigned as an outsider; the voters liked the fact that he was an outsider; he refused to "play the Washington game." But working with Congress is inherently "playing the Washington game." Carter's chief of staff, Hamilton Jordan, often seemed to go out of his way to insult the new Speaker of the House, Tip O'Neill. The presidential assistant in charge of liaison with Congress was Frank Moore, a Carter loyalist from Georgia who had few contacts on Capitol Hill and little knowledge of how the system worked. The result was a disaster. Carter and his party's

leaders in Congress seemed almost at war. Given this background, that Democratic party unity scores did not soar when a Democrat recaptured the White
House is unremarkable. The ability of a president to muster support for his programs from his own party's members of Congress is a function of both the program and his efforts to work with Congress—and the latter seems to be as much
a function of personality as it is of policy.

Three decades ago—and in subsequent editions of his classic book—
Richard Neustadt (1976) wrote that a president's power is "the power to persuade." This now-famous aphorism seems especially appropriate for a discussion of the president's ability to lead his party in Congress. And presidents can
persuade in a number of ways. They can persuade by the power of the argument, by their logic, by their expertise, by the quality of the programs put forward, and by the skills of those they appoint.

But they can also persuade by exploiting their own popularity. After
Ronald Reagan's tremendous 1980 election victory, he garnered support for his
economic programs in Congress not because those who once dubbed his proposals "voodoo economics" were convinced by the merits of his arguments but
because politicians who viewed themselves as potentially vulnerable in future
elections judged that Reagan had caught the temper of the times. If he was popular with the people and he was espousing trickle-down economics, many rea-
soned, opposing trickle-down economics would be politically detrimental. Also
noteworthy, however, is the fact that this kind of power is ephemeral. When
presidents become less popular with the people, as Reagan did after the Iran-
Contra affair near the end of his second term, or even if the president's power
fades as it inevitably will as his administration ends, fewer and fewer members
of his party are likely to be converted to his side of controversial issues on the
basis of his perceived popularity with the people alone. Other factors would
have to come into play.

In the final analysis, the president's ability to lead his party in Congress is
a function of politics and personality. America's is *not* a parliamentary system.
We do not elect presidents and give them a mandate to push their policy alter-
natives through Congress. Congress is a separate branch of the government;
Representatives and senators have separate electoral bases from the president.
Divided government has become almost a norm, certainly not an exception.
Therefore, the ability of the president to lead his party in Congress will depend
on his popularity, the majority or minority status of his party in Congress, the
fit between his views and those of the majority of the members of his party in
Congress, the perceived need or desire to compromise on the part of all concerned, and the mix of the personalities involved. A president can be a party
leader, but nothing in our system guarantees that he will play that role, much
less that he will play it effectively.

B. Party in the President's Administration

The final aspect of party in government that requires explication is the role of
the party in staffing a president's administration. Partisan control of presidential

appointments is often discussed in terms of the *spoils system,* which reached its height during the Jacksonian party system: "To the victor goes the spoils." When a party captured the White House, its followers received jobs, and followers of the losing party lost jobs. The spoils system was deeply embedded in American politics. It was, for example, the glue that held traditional political machines in place.

However, in terms of federal employment, the spoils system was undercut by the civil service system. Before the passage of the Pendleton Act, which created the civil service system in 1883, none of the roughly 100,000 civilian employees of the federal government were covered by a merit system. By 1920, roughly four-fifths of the civilian employee force for the federal government were so covered—and that number has not changed dramatically since (Mackenzie, 1990, p. 273). However, the expansion of the functions of the federal government left a great many patronage jobs. Contrary to popular belief, most of those jobs were not in Washington. Rather they were out in the states, in post offices, in court houses, and they were appointments controlled by local party leaders, not by national party leaders.

Presidents still did have a number of positions to fill. Throughout the first half of the twentieth century, presidents, lacking alternative means, relied heavily on the party machinery to suggest people to fill these positions. The Eisenhower administration marked a turning point in this process.[12] Eisenhower had few ties to the Republican party; in fact he had never even voted before his own presidential election in 1952. His appointees had few ties to the party. For the first time a centralized personnel function was established in the White House, with the creation of a special assistant for personnel management. This position was continued in the Kennedy and Johnson administrations. The object was to make certain that congressional and party leaders did not oppose a nominee for an appointive position, but the recruitment process was separated from the party. As Dan H. Fenn, Jr., who assisted the Kennedy administration on personnel matters, concluded: "The kind of people we were looking for weren't the kind of people who were active in party activities" (quoted in Mackenzie, 1990, p. 280).

In recent years the centralization of the personnel function in the White House Office has become institutionalized with the establishment of the Presidential Personnel Office. The key component of this operation, developed in the Nixon administration and expanded ever since, has been the implementation of a recruitment function. Recent presidents have set up an organization to staff and to maintain their administrations. They have not relied on other existing organizations to find people to serve in appointive positions. The key elements have become the ability to do the job, and ideological and personal loyalty to the president.

At the same time, as recent presidents have increasingly exercised personal control over the appointment process, more positions in public employment are

---

[12] Much of what follows draws heavily on the work of my colleague G. Calvin Mackenzie, especially "Partisan Presidential Leadership: The President's Appointees" (1990).

being protected from partisan politics. Thus, the role of party is doubly diminished: the president has fewer positions to fill, and the party has a diminished role in advising the president on how those that do exist should be filled. What does this tell us about the role of the president as the leader of his party in this sense? Interestingly, it probably reveals very little. When more appointments were available, and when they were made by party, party leaders rarely suggested a potential appointee based on his views on issues and ability to serve the president in that way. Indeed, appointments were offered to those who had served the party in an electoral sense. The president may have benefited from this activity indirectly, but the appointee's political activity was usually at the state or local level, not the national level.

In recent years, with personalized campaigning, presidents have developed their own following, loyalists who have worked with the president earlier in his career or on his campaign, men and women who share policy views and visions with the president. In this sense the president is the leader of his administration, but the party plays a greatly diminished role (Mackenzie, 1990, pp. 286–288).

V.   POLITICIANS VIEW THE PARTY IN GOVERNMENT

Much of the discussion to this point says a great deal about how politicians view the party in government. Generally speaking, if the party is saying and doing what the politicians want to be said and done, if backing the party seems to be in their own interest, then they are all for the party in the government. If the party leaders are not taking those views, then opposition mounts.

Perhaps the best proof of this hypothesis is seen in the Republican party in the 102d Congress. As discussed earlier, Republican Conference Chairman Jerry Lewis was challenged by Carl Pursell. At every level the issue concerned how the party should be led. On the surface, questions were raised about loyalty. Lewis felt that the Republican party in the House should back its president: "If we are not going to support the president when that office gives us an opportunity to affect policy, . . . the entire leadership of the minority party needs to be reviewed" (Hook, 1990, pp. 3997).

Pursell felt that the Republican leader in the House should listen to his membership—and if the members are more conservative than the president or want to go in a different direction, so be it. As one of Pursell's followers said, "If you are elected by the Conference, your loyalty is to the Conference" (Hook, 1990, p. 3998).

At another level, the Lewis-Pursell contest drew clear distinctions between the styles of Minority Leader Bob Michel and Minority Whip Newt Gingrich. Gingrich is the leader of the Conservative Opportunity Society. He made his reputation in the House by attacking Democrats, especially Speaker Jim Wright, with a confrontational and combative style. Michel's style is quieter, more accommodationist. He competes with the Democrats, fights hard when he thinks partisanship is dominating a discussion, but also understands that compromise is necessary to achieve results. Gingrich has attacked President

Bush when he felt the president has strayed from conservative policies. Michel would be much more likely to criticize the president in private but support him in public. Gingrich would like to succeed Michel as Republican leader. So would Lewis, whose style as well as philosophy is more like Michel's.

Lewis beat Pursell easily, but Gingrich was not even challenged in his bid for reelection as whip. So the debate between politicians who see their role as confronting ideologues and those who see their role as working within the party goes on. And as with so much else in this chapter, that debate is unlikely to be resolved in a permanent way, but rather movement toward one side or the other will be affected by political context and personalities involved.

12

Conclusions: The Electoral Process at the Century's End

To this point we have examined the historical development of the electoral process and the present context in which elections are contested from an empirical point of view. That is, we have analyzed how elections have been decided, what the process looks like; we have looked at the implications of some of the aspects of that process.

In this final chapter we will move from empirical analysis to evaluation. Specifically we will be concerned with how well the electoral process performs the role it is assigned in our system of government. We will look into recent trends in order to see what these portend. We will look ahead to changes that might impact on American politics as we approach the twenty-first century. Finally, we will look at implications of the electoral process for governing the United States.

I.   THE ROLE OF ELECTIONS

Recall Professor Finer's (1949) definition of the role that elections must play if a democracy is to function effectively:

> The real question . . . is not whether the government designs to take notice of popular criticisms and votes, but whether it can be voted out of office or forced by some machinery or procedures to change its policy, above all against its own will. (p. 219)

In the most theoretical terms, the answer to Professor Finer's question with regard to the American system is that the government can be forced to change its policies against its own will; the government can be voted out of office. But in an empirical sense, is that what elections mean in the United States? Do elections today give the citizenry a chance to decide on the course of action that their government will take? This question is more easily posed than answered.

364

A. The Context of Federalism

It should come as no surprise at this point that the answer to the basic question will vary depending upon whether one is analyzing federal, state, or local elections. Once again we must be alert not to generalize about the electoral process in the United States, when the process at the federal level is different from that at the state level (and states differ significantly from each other) and the processes in the various states are different from those in localities throughout the country.

1. Presidential Elections Presidential elections come closest to meeting the criterion set forth above. The American public has shown that it is willing and able to remove presidents when the policies of the government have consequences that displease the citizenry. A number of linkages are implied in that conclusion.

First, we assume that the policies of the president and those of the government are the same. We know this assumption to be false in part—because of separation of powers nearly all policies are the result of compromise. But we also know that the public makes this linkage even if it is not in fact accurate.

Second, we assume that the consequences of governmental policies were those that were desired or at least foreseen when those policies were implemented. Again, we know that this linkage is partial at best. For example, the success or failure of an administration's agricultural policies is dependent on the weather, advances in technology, and the actions of other nations as well as on the wisdom of the policies put forth. Again, however, we know that the public holds the president accountable for the consequences of his actions, not for the intentions of those actions, and so the assumed linkage has the effect hypothesized.

Third, we assume that all the citizens view all the policies in the same way and vote accordingly. Again, we know that this linkage is not complete. From the time of Madison, American politicians have recognized and dealt with the diversity of interests throughout this land. Even in landslide presidential elections approximately two out of every five voters support the losing candidate. Those voting for either candidate in such elections do not all do so for the same reasons. But, once again, a perfect linkage is not necessary. What is necessary is for a critical mass of citizens to express dissatisfaction with the policies (either general or specific) of an administration and to translate those feelings into support for another candidate.

Given the standard stipulated above, a number of presidential elections in this century meet the criterion for serving as the appropriate connection between the views of the citizens and the actions of their government. The election of 1932, in which the Republican policies of Herbert Hoover were blamed for the great depression, stands as a prominent example. Franklin Delano Roosevelt was elected—in simplest terms—because he proposed to change what the government was doing and the citizens wanted a change. The election of 1932 was a "critical election" and might therefore be viewed as an exception to the linkage we are seeking, not as an appropriate example (Brady et al., 1988).

But other elections, which have not involved massive shifts in allegiance to the two political parties, are also in evidence. The elections of 1976 and 1980, in which incumbent presidents were defeated, demonstrate this point. In 1976, the public said, again in vastly oversimplified terms, that the policies of President Ford, in dealing with inflation, in pardoning President Nixon, and in continuing with the same type of government that had been in place before, were not acceptable. The election of Jimmy Carter, running as an outsider, sent a message that the voting public wanted things done differently. And Carter as president attempted to fulfill some of the promises he had made. (See C. Jones, 1988c; A. Miller, 1978; Wayne, 1984, chap. 8.)

However, President Jimmy Carter was less appealing to the public than candidate Jimmy Carter. By 1980 the voters were again ready for a change. Carter wanted to continue his policies, but the public wanted other policies, promulgated by other individuals. Ronald Reagan's overwhelming victory has been subject to many interpretations (see as examples Abramson, Aldrich, & Rohde, 1982; Kessel, 1984; Pomper, 1981a; Price, 1984; Schneider, 1981; Wayne, 1984), but virtually all interpretations involve some indications that the public wanted things done differently between 1981 and 1985 from the ways they had been done in the previous four years.

Other presidential elections prove the same point in other ways. In 1952 and again in 1968 incumbent presidents saw public dissatisfaction with their policies and opted not to seek reelection. President Eisenhower won in 1952 with promises to reverse the policies of the Truman administration, particularly with regard to the Korean war. Again in 1968 an administration's war policy, the Johnson policy in Vietnam from which Democratic candidate Humphrey could not dissociate himself, was repudiated by a challenger in the other party. President Nixon campaigned on the theme that he had a secret plan to end the war within a year. While many factors contributed to his election, the public's desire to change the course of events in southeast Asia was surely one of them.

In 1964, 1972, and 1984 the voters opted not to change course, saying in effect that they preferred the policies that were being enacted to the rather radical changes proposed by those challenging incumbents in those years. (See Converse, Clausen, & Miller, 1965; A. Miller et al., 1976; Shanks & Miller, 1990; Wayne, 1984, chap. 8.)

Finally, in 1988 the voters elected a president of the same party as a retiring incumbent. This election was generally interpreted as a reaffirmation of the Reagan legacy, though definitions of that legacy varied. Even with that caveat accepted, the election of George Bush, Ronald Reagan's vice president and designated heir, as Reagan's successor reinforces the point that presidential elections can serve as an effective means to allow the citizens to express their views of the policies of the day (Jones, 1988a; Pomper, 1989a; Shanks & Miller, 1991).

2. Congressional Elections Presidential elections are particularly salient. What about the impact of other elections to federal offices—to the Senate and the House of Representatives? In these cases, the findings are mixed. In Chapters 6 and 7 we presented a good deal of evidence demonstrating incumbent advantages in House elections. Senate incumbents have fewer advantages—and challengers have greater assets—but recent Senate elections lead one to believe that incumbents in those races are not without strengths. (Recall Tables 4-9 and 6-3.) Do these elections serve to link the views of the public with the policies of the government? Or are incumbents so protected as to erase the connection between elections and outcomes which Professor Finer defines as necessary? Or is voter satisfaction with incumbent representatives for whatever reason sufficient cause to evaluate the electoral process positively?

If one is looking at elections in individual districts and/or states, it is difficult to find the proscribed connection. One can point to cases in which key issues have led to the defeat of an incumbent; but that defeat does not lead directly to changes in policy. More frequently, incumbent defeats are related to personal scandal, not policy preferences. Furthermore, only rarely are individual congresspeople or senators so influential that their presence or absence in office determines governmental policy.

However, the case can still be made in a number of less direct ways. First, certain groups with particular stands on specific issues have been very involved in political campaigns, singling out candidates who are well-placed in the Congress and whose views on the issues at question are well-defined and widely known. Typically these groups have used negative campaigns against those who oppose their views. The environmentalists and those on both sides of the abortion question are obvious examples. The success of some of the campaigns waged by these groups has drawn widespread attention. Individuals have been

Reprinted with permission Stayskal and *The Tampa Tribune.*

removed from the legislature and replaced by others with totally opposite points of view. Moreover, others in similar situations have seen the impact of these campaigns. Direct evidence does not exist, but one would certainly suspect that the views of those who have seen themselves as vulnerable have been altered because of these efforts. The policy movement in the direction the environmentalists favored in the late 1960s and early 1970s, toward restrictions on women's rights to abortions in the last decade, and back in the pro-choice direction in most recent years can be traced at least in part to the electoral efforts of those supporting those positions.

At the macro level, that is, looking at all elections in one year as a whole, *considerable evidence exists to support the claim that the elections reflect the policy preferences of the voters, at least on the major economic issues of the day* (Jacobson & Kernell, 1983; Tufte, 1975, 1978). While other theories question this impact (see Chapter 7), certainly at times of massive public discontent with governmental policies, the impact of an election on the shape of the legislature is sufficient to lead to changes in those policies (Brady et al., 1988). The congressional elections of 1964 and 1966 stand as obvious examples in the not too distant past. That is perhaps the minimum level of evidence necessary to sustain the argument that elections do effectively link the opinions of the citizens to the policies of the government in the case of federal legislative elections.

3. State and Local Elections However, the case is much more difficult to sustain at the state and local levels. While some states are becoming more and more competitive, as was demonstrated in Chapter 1 (see also Bibby et al., 1983; Jewell & Olson, 1982, 1988), one party or the other has a decided advantage in statewide elections in many states and in certain districts in virtually every state (Crotty, 1985, chap. 8). How can citizens effect policy change if the result of the election will have virtually no impact on who governs?

Local elections have the same types of problems as do state elections, only more so. On the one hand, many localities are now and have been for some time dominated by one political party or the other. We read often about the strength of the Democratic party organization in Cook County, Illinois, the area including and surrounding Chicago. In the city of Chicago, Democratic party nomination is all but tantamount to election. While other organizations are not so strong as that in Cook County, one-party rule in local elections remains very common (see Gibson et al., 1985; Schlesinger, 1985).

4. Nonpartisan Politics Even more common than one-party rule is nonpartisan government. This text has dealt only with partisan elections, because those are the elections that see the most competition in the American system. While we have not examined nonpartisan elections, we cannot fail to comment on them.

Nearly two-thirds of the cities in the United States with populations of over 5000 hold nonpartisan elections to determine who will hold local offices (Crotty, 1985, p. 105). The movement toward nonpartisan governments was

Environmental activists plead their case on the State House steps in Boston. (Stock, Boston)

part of the progressive era reforms; advocates of nonpartisan local government feel that running a local government should be more like administering a business than like playing partisan politics. Frequently they cite the corruption and the inefficiency of partisan politics. "There is no Republican and no Democratic way to clean a street."

On the other hand, those concerned with democratic control over the means of governing have not been overly impressed with the experience of nonpartisan elections. Critics contend that nonpartisan elections tend to draw fewer voters, because citizens do not care who wins these elections and because elections without the cue of party often confuse voters. The voters are less informed about the issues than is the case in partisan elections. Fewer races are competitive in the sense of close elections; in fact, in many races only one candidate runs. The advantages of incumbency are increased over those in even heavily one-party areas with partisan elections, because the opposition is deprived of its chance to organize.

The end result is less serious, less issue-oriented campaigning, more domination by those with well-recognized names, an increase in domination by single-issue groups that have the ability to mobilize their supporters, and generally less representative and less accountable government.

If the goal of reformers was to establish a system in which democracy functioned more effectively, and if one defines democracy for this purpose as a system in which the views of the voters on policy matters are converted into government policy, then non-partisan elections represent a regressive step. Only if one believes that all that local government is involved in is administration and that there are no policy implications of decisions made at the local level—a belief that is difficult to sustain with empirical examples—or perhaps if one can document that nonpartisan governments are less corrupt—can one claim that the movement to nonpartisan elections stands as an improvement in the representative nature of our electoral process. (For criticism of nonpartisan elections see Adrian & Williams, 1959; Crotty, 1985; Greenstein, 1970; Hawley, 1973.)

We conclude, therefore, that the sought-after linkage is frequently not present for elections at the local level. Nonpartisan elections may have served some purposes of reformers, but they did not enhance the ability of citizens to convert their policy preferences into governmental action through the electoral process. On the other hand, partisan elections at the local level do not move us very far toward that goal either, because the level of competition between the two parties is often minimal.

If one is examining the effectiveness of the American electoral system, one must be careful to look at the question in the context of American federalism. Elections in the United States seem to work best at translating the will of the electorate into public policies—or at least of having the potential to do that—at the federal level and specifically in presidential elections. As one moves to legislative elections for the United States Congress, to statewide elections and elections to state legislatures, and to local elections, the ideal of an electoral system guaranteeing representative government seems to be less and less well served.

Political observers are concerned that too many polling places show the inactivity of this one in the gym of Brooklyn's PS 282 as voter turnout continues to decline. (Robert Fox/Impact Visuals)

B. Citizen Participation

Those concerned with democratic government in the United States point with alarm to the decline in voter turnout in American elections (Chapter 4). Turnout in presidential elections has never exceeded the 63 percent in 1960 and recently has hovered at just over half of the eligible electorate. The congressional elections held at the same time as presidential elections see a "fall-off" of about 4 percent. Congressional elections held in nonpresidential years have seen turnouts between 10 and 20 percent below that of presidential years, with substantial differences among the states. Turnouts in local partisan elections are lower than those; turnouts in nonpartisan elections are even lower yet.

One political scientist, Thomas Cavanagh, estimated that, while the size of the eligible electorate increased by about 40 million between 1968 and 1976, the total number voting increased by less than 7 million and the number of "core voters," which he defines as those who vote consistently, went up by only 4 million. The number of "core nonvoters" doubled during that period, while the total number not participating increased by over 20 million to nearly 60 million. Cavanagh's conclusion is that this pattern reflects a basic change in traditional political behavior, from a norm of voting toward a norm of nonvoting (Cavanagh, 1979; Crotty, 1985, pp. 11–15; see also W. Miller, 1992).

To compound this matter, the movement toward nonvoting has been exaggerated in some specific groups. Various political scientists, using a variety of techniques, have all reached the conclusion that certain groups are underrepresented in the American electorate, particularly those at the lowest end of the socioeconomic scale, members of certain minority groups—blacks, Latinos—the young, the very old, the unemployed, and those with least education. Nonvoting among those least well represented at the current time is increasing at a rate greater than that of groups currently overrepresented. (See, as examples, Abramson & Aldrich, 1982; Cavanagh, 1981; Crotty & Jacobson, 1980; Wolfinger & Rosenstone, 1980.)

If elections are to serve as the means through which dissatisfied citizens express their dissatisfaction and act to correct their situation, then the decline in voter turnout and the exaggeration in that decline among groups in this country generally perceived to be disadvantaged are cause for concern. That is, if those elected represent the views of those who chose them, underrepresentation in the electorate can convert into less satisfaction with governmental policies on the part of those generally least advantaged in our society.

Theorists examining the phenomenon of low turnout among those seemingly most in need of an active government pursuing policies in their favor have reached two conflicting conclusions. Some, following Schattschneider (1960), conclude that nonvoting is a form of "implied consent" and that those who choose not to participate are generally satisfied with the system and their place in it. The view at the other extreme holds that those who do not vote have become so dissatisfied with the system, so frustrated with their lack of progress, that they refuse to participate and are susceptible to calls for more radical action. (Recall the discussion in Chapter 4.)

Whichever of these theories one holds, it is impossible to ignore the fact that the opinions of these groups—and of an increasing number of citizens—cannot be converted into governmental policies through the electoral process in which they refuse to participate. While one can question whether or not this is a threat to our political system, one is forced to conclude that the electoral process does not serve its purpose very well in this regard.

C.   Voters and Elections

In evaluating the effectiveness of elections, not only is it important to note the differences in the ways elections are decided in different localities and the differences in turnout rates for different elections, between more recent elections and those a decade or so ago and among different groups of people, but *it is also important to look at how voters are deciding for whom they will vote.*

The American Voter model stipulated that most voters used political party as a cue in determining their electoral choices during the decade of the 1950s. *The Changing American Voter* analysis revealed that issue orientation was more important in determining vote than had been the case when the earlier study was undertaken. But more needs to be known than that party or issue orientation is the most important cue for voting. Specifically, we are concerned with how voters gain the information that helps them to determine how they will vote.

In the 1950s—and for some time before—we believe that voters cast their votes largely on the cue of party and that party affiliation was determined by influences such as parental partisanship and group pressures. If party is a less important cue today, how do citizens learn what candidates stand for?

1.   Television as a Source of Political Information For more than two decades approximately two-thirds of those responding to the National Election Studies surveys conducted by the Center for Political Studies of the Survey Research Center at the University of Michigan have responded that television is their most important source for political information. Nearly 90 percent rely on television to some extent. While newspapers are listed as one source by approximately three-quarters of the respondents, only about 20 percent consider newspapers as their primary source. (See, as examples, Adams, 1982; T. Patterson, 1980; Ranney, 1990; Robinson & Sheehan, 1983.)

What are the implications of this reliance on television? Television is a visual medium and emphasizes stories that can be presented visually. In Chapters 8 and 9 we discussed the media's emphasis on campaign-oriented stories: Who is gaining? Who is falling? What are the various strategies, and how are they working?

Doris Graber has studied television coverage of presidential elections for some years. Her conclusions support the commonly held view that television presents the news and covers campaigns in a simplified manner. In every election that she studied, save that of 1968, the media in general and the television journalists in particular presented stories on campaign events more than analyses of domestic politics, foreign affairs, economic policy, or social problems (Graber, 1980, 1982, 1984a, 1984b, 1989, 1990; see also Buchanan, 1991; Crouse, 1973; T. Patterson, 1980; Robinson & Sheehan, 1983).

During the election of 1968 the war in Vietnam as a news event and as an issue received more coverage than did campaign events. However, this may well be the exception that proves the rule. Vietnam was a news issue that could be covered visually. That was the first war that was telecast live into America's living rooms. As a news story, it had the ability to capture the attention of the viewing audience.

But compare the coverage of the war in Vietnam with television coverage of the major economic policy crises that have dominated the governmental agenda in recent years. How many times can the network news anchors show bar graphs that describe the growth of the federal deficit? How many times can they depict the federal budget with pie charts? These economic issues—and the important issues of domestic politics, foreign affairs, and social problems—are complex problems that do not translate easily into two-minute spots on the network news (Graber, 1980; see also Buchanan, 1991; H. Gans, 1979). Yet these are undoubtedly the important issues of the day. And television, which cannot and does not cover these issues very well, is the medium most relied on by the voting public for its political information. The necessary conclusion is that voters are deciding based on a grossly oversimplified view of the important issues of the day.

2. Television as a Source for Information about State and Local Issues The above discussion has dealt with national news events and presidential elections, because that is the only context that has been studied in depth by social scientists. It does not take much intuition, however, to extend this discussion to the state and local contexts. Think for a moment about the quality of news coverage in local newspapers and on local television news broadcasts. Let us assume for the moment that most citizens gain their political information about events at the state and local level from television, just as they do for events at the national level.[1]

The average local news program spends nearly as much time on weather and sports as it does on all news. The news segment frequently carries one story about national news and at least one human interest story. Then, of course, there is the obligatory story about the latest local disaster—fire, murder, automobile accident. But how often is there in-depth coverage of a state house hearing on workers' compensation, of a city council debate on zoning ordinances, of a school board discussion on resource allocation? When state and local elections are held, how often are the candidates seen on local television?

---

[1] The reason we are taking this as an assumption is that we have no data on citizens' sources of local news.

Example after example could be mounted, but the point would remain the same. It should be emphasized, however, that all the blame does not rest with the television journalists (nor with newspaper reporters, for much the same argument would apply to most local papers). In point of fact, they are faced with a nearly impossible task. Local journalists for all media have very few resources with which to cover a vast amount of material. They do not have large staffs or large budgets; they have limited space or time; they have many localities and issues to cover.

They are under tremendous pressure to draw an audience. It is difficult to imagine how one could cover most issues that face state and local governments—or most issues that distinguish candidates for state and local offices—in a way that would excite the public. Yet if newspapers do not sell and television broadcasts do not achieve high ratings, the business end of these enterprises fails, and the public is even less well served (Berkman & Kitch, 1986; H. Gans, 1979). As a consequence, local journalists do what they can to cover state and local government and politics; in most instances what they can do is very little. And again, very little is what the public is left to rely on in making its decisions!

D. Summary

The purpose of this section has been to evaluate the electoral process we have described as a means of selecting representative governments in the United States. What we have found is that the American voting public represents barely a majority of American citizens and that those who do vote are not representative of the country as a whole. Each of these conclusions is exaggerated as we progress from the presidential election through the federal system down to local elections.

Furthermore we have found that most Americans rely heavily on television for providing them with information about political events; we have concluded that television is not a very apt medium for supplying in-depth information and analysis. Once again, this is even more true for local elections than it is for more visible national elections.

The process that we have discussed at some length throughout this book advantages some and disadvantages others. In electoral terms, the advantage clearly lies with incumbents, with those whose names are well known, and with those who have or have access to large amounts of money. For those trying to influence policy through the electoral process, money seems to be the most relevant resource. Those with fewer resources, those challenging the status quo, those less advantaged in American society, are those least advantaged by the electoral system.

In an earlier era, parties served to offset this balance somewhat. Decrying the decline of political parties, Walter Dean Burnham (1970) characterized them as "the only devices thus far invented by the wit of Western man which with some effectiveness can generate countervailing collective power on behalf of the individually powerless against the relatively few who are individually— and organizationally—powerful" (p. 133). Burnham's point was that political parties serve many functions in the American system, not the least of which is to help new and less advantaged groups "make it" in American society.

But parties seem to have lost much of their influence over the electoral process. They have been replaced by candidate-centered campaigns, by media messages, by low voter turnout, by increased apathy, and, it could be argued, by a governing elite more concerned with maintaining power, and with using office to maintain power, than with using the offices to which they have been elected in order to benefit the greater number in American society. Polls show a cynicism among the public which reflects this view.

II. THE REJUVENATION OF POLITICAL PARTIES

If the picture painted to this point is not a sanguine one, are there no positive signs? Analysts writing during the decade of the 1970s saw little to be optimistic about. Walter Dean Burnham wrote of the "onward march of party decomposition" (1970, chap. 5). *Washington Post* journalist David Broder wrote a book that he called *The Party's Over,* as he put it, "not in prophecy, but in alarm" (1971, p. xvi). William Crotty and Gary Jacobson entitled their 1980 book *American Parties in Decline.* The list could go on. The general picture that was being painted was one of political parties as dying institutions, no longer commanding the allegiance of loyalists in the electorate, organizationally weak, financially bankrupt. The only questions remaining to be answered were those concerning the consequences of party decline.

But while these obituaries of parties were being written, all the evidence did not point in one direction. Some scholars claimed that voters were not negative toward political parties, but only neutral (Wattenberg, 1981, 1984, 1990b, 1991). Others pointed to the functions that were being performed by county and local party organizations (Gibson et al., 1983). And politicians themselves began the work of rejuvenating the parties.

A. Republican Efforts

In this context the work of Bill Brock, the former senator from Tennessee who became chair of the Republican National Committee in 1977, stands out and merits reemphasis. The national committees had traditionally been viewed as the weakest link in party organization (Cotter & Hennessey, 1964). However, Brock saw the potential for using the Republican National Committee to rebuild a party devastated by Watergate and electoral defeats in 1974 and 1976.

Brock's tenure as party chair was highlighted by efforts to make the RNC a useful part of the campaign apparatus available to all Republican candidates. The Republican national headquarters in Washington built resources on which state and local Republican organizations and Republican candidates could draw. In that way, the national party became a relevant part of the electoral process.

Brock's effort took many directions. First, he set up an extraordinarily successful direct-mail, small-donor fund-raising program. The success of this program allowed the RNC to provide services—campaign schools and workshops, technical assistance with surveys and data processing, research, and the like—to Republican candidates and to aid others with contributions. In addition, the party appointed regional political directors and finance directors to aid state party development and to coordinate state party efforts with those of the national party and the National Republican Congressional and Senatorial Committees. The party began an active program of candidate recruitment and even began to advertise on its own behalf, seeking to portray the Republicans as the "party of new ideas."

All these projects did not begin at once; some developed over a period of time. However, by the time of the 1980 election, the cumulative impact was apparent. "A new Republican organization has emerged—a multimillion-dollar bureaucracy in Washington that employs 350 and plays an increasingly important role in all aspects of Republican campaigning and party policy" (Malbin, 1980, p. 85; see also Bibby, 1981; Crotty, 1983; Crotty & Jacobson, 1980). The Republicans viewed their effort as steps toward creating a new majority party.

B. Democratic Responses

And this impact was apparent to the Democrats as well. While the Republican party had been increasing its efforts to serve state and local party organizations and candidates, the Democratic party at the national level had been extending its control over state and local operations through rule changes (see Chapter 8). But these had little impact on the kind of politics that was of most concern to those working at the local level and, in the view of many, served mainly to weaken the party further.

And they were of little consequence to those concerned with winning elections. In fact, many felt that these efforts were counterproductive (Ceaser, 1982; Kirkpatrick, 1976; Polsby, 1983; Ranney, 1975). The earlier reforms in the Democratic party were aimed at democratizing party processes and were headed in a totally different direction from that of the Republican party.

But Democratic politicians saw the direction that the Republicans were taking and were envious. Their party was not aiding them in the way in which their opponents were being aided. The complaints were heard at the Democratic National Committee, and after the 1980 election, steps were taken to emulate the Republicans. While the Democrats are far behind their partisan opponents in these efforts, and the massive defeat in the 1984 presidential campaign put their fledgling effort back several steps, at the national level they too have begun to raise money through direct mail and to use the proceeds from those solicitations to help Democratic candidates, through both direct contributions and candidate services.

In moving in this direction, the Democrats were acting most pragmatically. The earlier reforms in the presidential nominating process had been based on a theory of government, one that says that the party's decision-making bodies should be representative of the party. The results of those reforms were not always positive from an electoral point of view. As a consequence, some retrenchment has taken place, e.g., elected officials play more of a role in the nominating process, and steps have been taken in other directions, increasing the services to candidates running under the party label.

C.   The Current Role of Political Parties in the Electoral Process

Where does all this leave the electoral process? Certainly the "rejuvenation" of parties as important actors in the electoral process—particularly if recent trends continue and accelerate—is a change. But is it an improvement? The answer to that is not clear. One observer of this process, political scientist Christopher Arterton, sees the emerging role of political parties as little more than as super PACs (1982, p. 135). Is that the appropriate role for party to play in the electoral process? Where does that leave the voters, who have somewhat neutral views toward parties at best?

These are questions that must still be answered, but one is hard-pressed to find signs that the recent trends will have a profound impact on the problems with the electoral process which we noted earlier. The political parties seem to be acting in a manner that will guarantee their survival and a role in the process, a direction not unexpected for any group whose value was so widely questioned. But what does this new role do for the electoral process? That the change can be in a positive direction is not immediately apparent.

There have been two directions in party reform. While they are different, they are not mutually exclusive. The direction that the Republicans have chosen and that the Democrats are emulating is appealing because there are fast payoffs for the party. But the direction in which the Democrats started in 1968, and which has been criticized because it does not immediately lead to electoral advantages, can be a positive direction as well.

Critics claim that the so-called democratizing reforms are "democratic" only in the most cosmetic sense, that they do not encourage participation but rather reward participation by the socioeconomic elite minority that participates extensively already, the better educated, affluent, and liberal wing of the party, not the unemployed or underemployed, largely minority, undereducated followers of the party. But the merit of this criticism is a function of the ways in which participatory reforms are implemented.

Far down that latter road could lie an expended participatory citizenry more involved with the political process, more informed about what is going on, more convinced that participation leads to effective input. Down that road could lie a voting public confident that its views on policy questions will be heard by those in government. But these citizens must be encouraged to participate in partisan politics at all levels, including the local level. Remember again Speaker O'Neill's aphorism that "all politics is local."

If political parties are to play a role in improving the electoral process so that it is more responsive to popular views, so that citizen dissatisfaction can be expressed and acted upon, then the parties must be revitalized at the local level as well as at the national level. And this revitalization must take the form of increased involvement by an increasingly large number of people who see parties as a way to impact on the government that they elect, not just as a means to fund political campaigns.

This analysis leads directly to a call for citizen action and for political party rejuvenation at the local level. If that sounds like a nostalgic call for a return to political machines, it is not. Mayor Daley's greatest disservice to the American public had nothing to do with the way he governed nor with the way in which he ran the Cook County machine. His disservice was in giving strong local party organizations a bad name (Price, 1984). Political parties serve many functions and have done so for many years. One of the most important and often overlooked of those functions is that of involving citizens with their government. As the role of parties has diminished in recent decades, that function has not been picked up by other governmental institutions. The reason is that political parties, particularly local political parties, play that role best.

However, citizens will only become involved in political parties if they see that there is some reason for their involvement (Tolchin & Tolchin, 1971). What motivates citizens? A number of factors have been cited over the years, factors perhaps best summarized as material, purposive, and solidary incentives (J. Wilson, 1962). Some people do and others do not get a good feeling from the kind of camaraderie that surrounds political organizations. The changes that can be made to improve solidary incentives seem to be marginal at best.

However, the political parties and our governing structures very definitely control the other two types of incentives. The direction that the Republican party has taken is to increase the material incentives for those most involved in partisan politics, candidates and party officials. That is all to the good, and it is fine that the Democrats are emulating those directions.

The Democratic party reforms in the presidential nominating process represented an attempt to draw people to the party for purposive rewards at the level of national politics. That is, people were encouraged to participate in the presidential nominating process in order to change national policies. One of the positive unpredicted consequences of those reforms was an increase in local activism, because one of the means through which individuals were encouraged to act was participation in local caucuses (Maisel, 1975, pp. 193–220). That is a benefit that should not be lost sight of.

Citizens can also be drawn to the party because of concern for state and local issues and state and local policies, if they see a connection between their activism and eventual governmental action. Most often these incentives would be purposive, that is, a desire to change state or local laws. But certainly some of the attraction would still be material, at least in the sense of gaining a feeling that some slight personal benefits might accrue because of political involvement. If the cost of increased citizen involvement is slight preferential treatment for those who are so involved, that seems a small price to pay for more responsive government. Clearly, however, a balancing act is called for. An effort to reinvolve citizens in partisan politics is not the same as reinstituting the odious elements of political machines. But the demise of these machines does not necessitate eliminating their beneficial aspects. (On the rejuvenation of parties see also Sabato, 1988.)

III.   REFORMING THE ELECTORAL PROCESS

No matter when an author decided to write a textbook on political parties and the electoral process, one topic for consideration would have to be ongoing efforts to reform the ways in which Americans choose their elected officials. And the present context is no exception. When Americans are dissatisfied with the job their government is doing, they seek solutions in the way in which that government is chosen.

But before we begin a brief examination of pending reforms, a warning should be issued. Institutional and political reform is not an easy process. Those satisfied with the status quo have an advantage, because it is always easier to resist change than to implement it. Furthermore, those seeking change are normally more certain about the problems they see than they are about the consequences of their intended reforms. You need only remember that political action committees were not considered a serious problem—in fact, they did not exist in their current configuration—before the passage of the Federal Election Campaign Act and its amendments, legislation designed to rid campaigns of the influence of big money. With that caveat noted, it does seem appropriate to provide a brief list of pending electoral reforms and to speculate on their consequences for parties and the electoral process.

A.   National Voter Registration

As the 101st Congress drew to a close on the eve of the 1990 election, a House-passed bill that would have implemented a national voter registration program fell to a Republican filibuster in the Senate. The proposed voter registration program would have been tied to citizens' applications for, renewal of, or changes of address on a license to drive a car. President Bush threatened to veto the bill, claiming it would increase the chance of voter fraud and raise the cost of election administration in the states. All Senate Republicans except two voted together to defeat the cloture motion, thus ending any chance the bill had because so much business had to be accomplished before the end of the session. Similar legislation is on the Senate agenda in the 102d Congress, with House supporters awaiting Senate action before they begin another push.

So-called motor vehicle registration is an attempt to "solve the turnout problem" in American politics. Many Americans do not vote because they are not registered to vote. Registration in this country is much more difficult than in most western democracies, many of which have virtually automatic registration. Those who want to increase turnout have not gone so far as to propose penalties for not voting, but they do want to ease voting as much as is possible. Those who oppose these measures cite cost and possible fraud, but they are also concerned about the political consequences. The partisan split in Congress on this measure is a reflection of the Republicans' view that those voters attracted to the polls by a measure such as this one would likely support Democratic candidates—a view with which Democrats, who by and large support the measure, concur.

The political judgments made by party leaders are based largely on intuitive senses of who is not registered to vote and why. While empirical evidence on the voting intentions of nonregistered citizens is all but impossible to obtain, those studies that do exist lead one to question the accuracy of these stereotypical views of nonregistrants (W. Miller, 1990, 1991b, 1991c; Ranney, 1968; Ranney & Epstein, 1966). The conclusion one might draw is that decisions on matters such as this should be based on a philosophical discussion of the role of voting. Is it a right? Is it a privilege? Is it an obligation? Rarely does congressional debate address such questions.

B. National Political Primary

Relatively few citizens understand the complex means used to nominate presidential candidates, described in Chapter 8. The one common opinion held by those who do understand the process is that it should be changed. But there the agreement ends. No consensus exists on how the process should be changed. The result has been constant tinkering—marginal changes every four years, changes of dates here, changes of rules there.

The most radical change that has been proposed calls for the implementation of one national primary to select the parties' presidential candidates. Various national primary proposals deal with details in differing ways. For example, some call for a runoff if no candidate receives a majority (or in other proposals a specified percentage necessary for nomination); others call for a convention to choose among or between the leading contenders. The common element is that party members (again defined differently in different proposals) throughout the nation would vote on one day to select their parties' presidential candidate.

The most obvious advantage of a proposal such as this one is that it is simple. Everyone could understand what was happening. The television networks would turn the primary into a major media event. Public attention would be focused on the selection of the nominees in a way that is far different from the current practice. Americans seem to get excited about national elections. This would be another national election. Other advantages are also mentioned. Some say the process would be shorter, because the focus would be on one primary, not a series of primaries and caucuses spread over many months. Others say that the process would be less costly, again because candidates would be running one national campaign, not fifty separate state campaigns. Still others say that the process would be more democratic; more people would vote because of the attention focused on the primary and because of the elimination of nominating caucuses that attract relatively small turnouts.

For every advantage that is raised, others would point to disadvantages. The process would not be shorter or less expensive, because candidates would have to start very early to gear up a full national campaign and such an effort would require huge amounts of money. The cost of simplifying the process would be the elimination of dark horse candidates, qualified politicians (frequently from smaller states) who have not had the media exposure of some of their colleagues. Democratization takes the element of peer review out of the process. More people may vote, but they know the prospective candidates and their qualifications less well than do those who currently have a major role in the process.

Two consequences seem certain. First, a change of this nature would hinder the revitalization of political party organizations. The greater the role that parties play in the process, the better the process is for parties as organizations. Potential candidates, elected officials for all offices, and activists have more of a stake in party qua organization when the role of the organization is enhanced and conversely less stake when the role of party is diminished. Second, different types of candidates would emerge. Candidates could not use the early contests to achieve name recognition and to build momentum. Thus lesser known candidates like Barry Goldwater, Eugene McCarthy, George McGovern, Jimmy Carter—and virtually every Democrat who surfaced as a potential nominee only nine months before the 1992 convention—would be disadvantaged. Challenging incumbent presidents would be virtually impossible. Candidates using the nominating process to raise significant issues would be eliminated from contention. Some may favor those consequences, and some may oppose them. At this point what should be noted is that few discuss them.[2]

C. Campaign Finance Reform

The passage of the Federal Election Campaign Act of 1971 spawned a virtual growth industry for those interested in continuing reform in the way American elections are financed. (Refer to the various works published by Herbert E. Alexander and those by Anthony J. Corrado cited in the References.) A number of analysts feel that the principle of public financing which is applied to presidential campaigns is appropriate but that some additional changes are still necessary. They cite anomalies in the use of soft money and/or of political action committees sponsored by potential presidential candidates (Alexander, 1986; Corrado, 1992).

However, most of the recent debate has centered on the financing of congressional elections (and in some states, on financing state elections). Concern

---

[2] Another point rarely raised in the discussion of implementing a national primary is the mechanism through which such a change could be accomplished. A series of Supreme Court decisions make it clear that the political parties have a good deal of freedom in specifying their own rules. Could Congress impose a national primary on the parties against their will—or in the absence of their expressed will? No sure answer to that question can be given, but it is certain that the parties would challenge such a preemptive strike on the very essence of their role in American electoral politics. (See L. Epstein, 1989, 1991.)

has been voiced over the overall costs of campaigns, over the advantages incumbents have in raising money, over the role of political action committees, over the type of television advertising used in campaigns, over the role of political parties and party committees. In the 101st Congress each house passed significant campaign finance legislation. However, the two bills differed so significantly—and were passed so late in the session—that no conference was ever convened to seek a compromise.

In 1991 the Senate passed legislation that imposed state-by-state spending limits on Senate campaigns. In order to convince candidates to comply with these limits, thus avoiding the constitutional limitations spelled out in *Buckley v. Valeo*, the legislation offers incentive to those who comply, including discounts on political broadcasts and public financing to candidates whose opponents exceed the limits. The Senate bill also prohibits federal candidates from accepting political action committee contributions.

The House leaders on campaign finance reform have different ideas. Sam Gejdenson (D., Conn.), who chairs the House task force on campaign finance reform, believes that it might make most sense for the two houses to have separate rules—to pass one piece of legislation which specifies the rules for funding elections for each house (Alston, 1991). A number of issues make campaign finance reform very difficult.

First, the candidates running for the House and Senate face very different problems. The average senator winning in 1990 spent approximately ten times as much money as did the average representative. House members rely much more heavily on PAC contributions than do senators. On the other hand, senators receive a higher percentage of their money—and much more money in absolute terms—from individuals donating large sums of money (say, over $500 each). Finally, because they run every two years and because they represent smaller districts (except for those from states with only one representative), House members tend to be much more closely allied with other candidates of their party.

Second, party differences are not insignificant. The Republican party as an organization is much more capable of supporting individual candidates, through coordinated expenditures and agency agreements as well as direct contributions, than is the Democratic party. The Democrats rely much more heavily on political action committees centered in Washington for raising funds for candidates throughout the nation than do the Republicans. Democrats are in the majority—and while they give lip service to wanting fair and competitive campaigns, few Democrats want to write their own political obituaries, nor those of their copartisans. While Republicans are in the minority and want to help those candidates challenging Democrats, they do not want to do so in such a way as to jeopardize their own reelection efforts. The list could mount.

Again, the rhetoric often stresses philosophical differences. President Bush says he is opposed to all political action committee funding, but that he also opposes public financing because it will cost the Treasury dearly and because individuals will be "forced" to contribute to candidates they oppose. While these

points are not irrelevant, critics often point to the coincidence that the philosophical positions taken by candidates of both parties just happen to correlate
directly with the pragmatic political considerations they face in raising money.

The point is not to say that campaign finance reform is not important, nor
to claim that some meaningful reform will not pass. However, observers should
note the practical consequences of every proposed reform. Who benefits? Who
loses? The real search is for a formula that appeals to the public's sense of fairness but that does not disadvantage either incumbents or one party over the
other unduly.

D.   Electoral College Reform

No listing of proposed reforms would be complete without at least passing reference to the near continuous criticism of the electoral college system. Reformers point out the problems with the electoral college system: the candidate who
receives fewer votes could win; a third-party candidate could throw the election
to the House of Representatives and confuse succession; votes cast in different
states are given different weights because of the way in which the electoral college is composed; the "winner-take-all" system in place in every state except
Maine essentially disenfranchises those whose candidate does not carry a plurality in their state; so-called faithless electors can cast their votes for candidates
other than those to whom they have been pledged. It really does seem like a terrible system.

And every election year someone comes out with the "what if" scenario. If
candidate X had won merely 5000 more votes in these particular states, the
election would have gone to the "wrong" candidate or been thrown into the
House of Representatives. A constitutional crisis would have ensued. I do not
mean to belittle these critics. The scenarios they pose are possible; we could
again face a situation in which a minority candidate wins the presidency or in
which the House is asked to decide.

Reformers in the Congress have pushed for various changes. The most
popular measure calls for direct election of the president by popular vote. It
seems highly unlikely, however, that any reform will pass without a crisis to
bring it to the fore. Too few politicians see the need to change a system which—
despite its confusion and evident flaws—has worked for so long. No election in
this century has resulted in any of the scenarios the reformers fear. And again,
few examine the consequences of changing systems. Would different kinds of
candidates emerge? Perhaps not. Would candidates campaign in different ways?
Probably. Would the impact of minorities and other groups be altered? Undoubtedly. But few can predict how these changes would impact on the power
of these groups. Would the relationship between the president and Congress
change? Certainly that is worth exploring. As with other reforms, what is apparent is often not real, and politicians are not anxious to change a known system
for an unknown one, even one with an appeal as evident as "one person–one
vote."

E. Term Limitations

Certainly the "hottest" reform proposal of the early 1990s has been the effort to restrict the number of terms that a legislator is permitted to serve. The Twenty-Second Amendment to the U.S. Constitution restricts the president to two terms, and many gubernatorial terms are similarly limited. However, no restriction exists on the tenure of representatives or senators; and, until recently, none existed for state legislators. However, with incumbents increasingly safe in their bids for reelection (recall Chapter 7), with citizens often dissatisfied with the performance of the legislatures (though apparently not their individual legislators), three states have passed restrictions on the number of terms a legislator may serve.

In part the term limitation reforms are aimed at the perceived problem of "divided government." During the period from 1952 to 1992, the same party controlled both houses of Congress and the presidency for only fourteen years—the first two years of the Eisenhower administration, the eight years of the Kennedy and Johnson administrations, and the four years of the Carter administration. In recent years, state governments have been "divided" almost to the same extent that the federal government has been (Fiorina, 1992). After the 1990 election, as an example, the Republicans controlled both houses of the legislature and the governorship in only three states; the Democrats, eighteen states. Twenty-eight states were ruled by "divided" governments.[3]

The argument goes that divided government is inefficient and does not promote governmental responsibility (Sundquist, 1988; see also Cox & Kernell, 1991; Thurber, 1991). Reformers argue that one cause of divided government is the fact that the Democrats have a "lock" on Congress because of their majority status and the invulnerability of incumbents.[4] Therefore, they argue, the way to end divided government is to limit the terms of legislators. They buttress this argument by claiming that legislators have become a class of professional politicians and that the original intent of the founders was to have citizen legislatures.

Again, the point here is not to comment on the specific reform proposals, nor, in this case, on the questionable constitutionality of some of the proposals. Rather, the intent is to raise questions that reformers seem to ignore. To whom would power fall if legislators rotate in office so frequently that they could not match executive branch expertise? What would the impact be on the performance of legislators who knew that their tenure was limited? Would it not be logical to assume that they would always be looking for the next office to run for? Or for a way to better themselves in the private sector after leaving office? What would the impact be on the political parties?

---

[3] Nebraska is not included in these totals because of its unique unicameral, nonpartisan legislature.

[4] A number of careful observers have pointed out that this argument fails the most basic empirical tests. For instance, over 90 percent of all House seats have come vacant at least once during the recent period of divided government, and yet the Republicans have not made significant gains. Furthermore, the Republicans have won fewer open seats than have the Democrats. Finally, the Senate switched hands twice in the last decade. (See Fiorina, 1992; Jacobson, 1990a, 1990c.)

Morris Fiorina's (1992) detailed study of divided government raises these and other questions. He analyzes the causes of divided government in great detail, concluding that Republican failure to field competitive candidates is the variable that must be explained. Would term limitations help Republicans to do so? That is, Fiorina believes the question is not the ability of good Republican candidates to win but rather the ability of the Republican party organization to field good candidates. Infrequently is the debate on term limitations or the debate on divided government one that centers on the role of party organization; but the recruitment function of the parties, a role that was limited by the earlier reform of instituting the direct primary election, seems to play a central role in both incumbent success rates (at the state level as well as at the national level) and the recurring phenomenon of divided governments.

IV.   CONCLUDING REMARKS

It is of more than passing interest to some that the political scientists who are the more vocal advocates for stronger political party organizations are also among those who have themselves been active in politics (Bill Crotty, David Price, Tom Cronin, Bob Huckshorn, John Bibby, Kay Lawson, Larry Longley, and this author to name a few). That link is not coincidental. When one is involved in the political process, one becomes acutely aware that many citizens simply do not care. But one is also concerned that the policies that government officials pass often have direct and immediate impact on those citizens. And further, one sees that it is difficult to know how the people feel on lots of issues, certainly in advance of the time at which decisions must be made. One hears from those most concerned, but not from a wide variety of citizens.

So the search begins for a mechanism to involve more people in the political process, particularly in the electoral process because it is the vital link between the citizens and their government. And the institution of party readily stands out; for, with all its imperfections, so vividly described by political analysts and journalists of all types, party remains the vital linking institution. When parties are weak, the linkage role of the electoral process is not played well. When they are strong, a possibility exists that representation and accountability will follow. Other institutions—the media, interest groups—have tried to pick up the slack, but they have done so without notable success. And thus we are led back to the conclusion that if political parties did not exist, someone would have to invent them. Since ours already exist, we should get on with the work of making them function more productively.

References

Abramowitz, Alan I. (1980). "A Comparison of Voting for U.S. Senator and Representative in 1978." *American Political Science Review, 74,* 633.

Abramowitz, Alan I. (1981). "Party and Individual Accountability in the 1978 Congressional Election." In L. Sandy Maisel & Joseph Cooper, eds., *Congressional Elections.* Beverly Hills, Calif.: Sage.

Abramowitz, Alan I., & Kenneth J. Cribbs. (1989). "Don't Worry, Be Happy: Evaluations of Senate and House Incumbents in 1988." Paper presented at the Annual Meeting of the American Political Science Association, Atlanta, Ga.

Abramowitz, Alan I., Ronald B. Rapoport, & Walter J. Stone. (1991). "Up Close and Personal: The 1988 Iowa Caucuses and Presidential Politics." In Emmett H. Buell, Jr., & Lee Sigelman, eds., *Nominating the President.* Knoxville: University of Tennessee Press.

Abramowitz, Alan I., & Jeffrey Segal. (1991). "Throwing the Bums Back in: The 1990 Congressional Elections." Paper presented at the Annual Meeting of the Midwest Political Science Association, Chicago.

Abramson, Paul R., & John H. Aldrich. (1982). "The Decline of Electoral Participation in America." *American Political Science Review, 76,* 502.

Abramson, Paul R., John H. Aldrich, & David W. Rohde. (1982). *Change and Continuity in the 1980 Elections.* Washington, D.C.: Congressional Quarterly Press.

Achen, Christopher H. (1989). "Prospective Voting and the Theory of Party Identification." Paper presented at the Annual Meeting of the American Political Science Association, Atlanta, Ga.

Adamany, David. (1984). "Political Parties in the 1980s." In Michael J. Malbin, ed., *Money and Politics in the United States.* Washington, D.C.: American Enterprise Institute and Chatham House.

Adamany, David, & George E. Agree. (1975). *Political Money.* Baltimore, Md.: Johns Hopkins University Press.

Adams, William C. (1982). "Media Power in Presidential Elections: An Exploratory Analysis, 1960–1980." In Doris A. Graber, ed., *The President and the Public.* Philadelphia: Institute for the Study of Human Issues.

Adler, Bill, ed. (1964). *The Kennedy Wit.* New York: Citadel Press.

Adrian, Charles, & Oliver Williams. (1959). "The Insulation of Local Politics under the Nonpartisan Ballot." *American Political Science Review, 53,* 1052.

Agranoff, Robert. (1972). *The Management of Election Campaigns.* Boston: Holbrook Press.

Agranoff, Robert. (1976). *The New Style in Election Campaigns.* Boston: Holbrook Press.

Aldrich, John H. (1980). *Before the Convention: Strategies and Choices in Presidential Nomination Campaigns.* Chicago: University of Chicago Press.

Aldrich, John, & Richard G. Niemi. (1990). "The Sixth American Party System: The 1960s Realignment and Candidate-Centered Parties." Unpublished manuscript, University of Rochester, New York.

Alexander, Herbert E. (1971). *Financing the 1968 Election.* Lexington, Mass.: Lexington Books.

Alexander, Herbert E. (1972). *Money in Politics.* Washington, D.C.: Public Affairs Press.

Alexander, Herbert E. (1976a). *Financing Politics: Money, Elections, and Political Reform.* Washington, D.C.: Congressional Quarterly Press.

Alexander, Herbert E. (1976b). *Financing the 1972 Election.* Lexington, Mass.: Lexington Books.

Alexander, Herbert E. (1979a). *Financing the 1976 Election.* Washington, D.C.: Congressional Quarterly Press.

Alexander, Herbert E. (1979b). *Political Finance.* Beverly Hills, Calif.: Sage.

Alexander, Herbert E. (1980). "The Impact of the Federal Election Campaign Act on the 1976 Presidential Campaign: The Complexities of Compliance." *Emory Law Review, 29,* 315.

Alexander, Herbert E. (1983). *Financing the 1980 Election.* Lexington, Mass.: D. C. Heath.

Alexander, Herbert E. (1984). "Making Sense about Dollars in the 1980 Presidential Campaigns." In Michael J. Malbin, ed., *Money and Politics in the United States: Financing Elections in the 1980s.* Washington, D.C.: American Enterprise Institute and Chatham House.

Alexander, Herbert E. (1986). *"Soft Money" and Campaign Financing.* Washington, D.C.: Public Affairs Council.

Alexander, Herbert E. (1991). "Financing Presidential Campaigns." In L. Sandy Maisel, ed., *Political Parties and Elections in the United States: An Encyclopedia.* New York: Garland Press.

Alexander, Herbert E., & Monica Bauer. (1991). *Financing the 1988 Election.* Boulder, Colo.: Westview Press.

Alexander, Herbert E., & Mike Eberts. (1986). *Public Financing of State Elections: A Data Book on Tax-Assisted Funding of Political Parties and Candidates in Twenty States.* Los Angeles: Citizens' Research Foundation.

Alexander, Herbert E., & Brian A. Haggerty. (1981). *The Federal Election Campaign Act: After a Decade of Political Reform.* Washington, D.C.: Citizens' Research Foundation.

Alexander, Herbert E., & Brian A. Haggerty. (1987). *Financing the 1984 Election.* Lexington, Mass.: Lexington Books.

Allsop, Dee, & Herbert F. Weisberg (1988). "Measuring Change in Party Identification in an Election Campaign." *American Journal of Political Science, 32,* 996.

Almond, Gabriel A., & Sidney Verba. (1965). *The Civic Culture.* Boston: Little, Brown.

Alston, Chuck. (1990). "Contest Raises Hard Questions about How NRCC Uses Funds." *Congressional Quarterly Weekly Report, 48,* 4000.

Alston, Chuck. (1991). "One Chamber's View of Reform Is Anathema in the Other." *Congressional Quarterly Weekly Report, 49,* 1727.

American Political Science Association, Committee on Political Parties. (1950). "Toward a More Responsible Two-Party System." *American Political Science Review, 64.*

Andes, Gary J. (1985). "Business Involvement in Campaign Finance: Factors Influencing the Decision to Form a Corporate PAC." *PS, 18,* 213.

Anthony, Susan B., & Ida Husted Harper, eds. (1902). *The History of Woman Suffrage* (vol. IV). Indianapolis: Hollenbeck Press.

Aoki, Andrew L., & Mark Rom. (1985). "Financing a Comeback: Campaign Finance Laws and Prospects for Political Party Resurgence." Paper presented at the Annual Meeting of the American Political Science Association, New Orleans, La.

Arsenau, Robert B., & Raymond E. Wolfinger. (1973). "Voting Behavior in Congressional Elections." Paper presented at the Annual Meeting of the American Political Science Association, New Orleans, La.

Arterton, F. Christopher. (1978a). "Campaign Organizations Confront the Media-Political Environment." In James David Barber, ed., *Race for the Presidency*. Englewood Cliffs, N.J.: Prentice-Hall.

Arterton, F. Christopher. (1978b). "The Media Politics of Presidential Campaigns: A Study of the Carter Nomination Drive." In James David Barber, ed., *Race for the Presidency*. Englewood Cliffs, N.J.: Prentice-Hall.

Arterton, F. Christopher. (1980). *Media Politics: The News Strategies of Presidential Campaigns*. Lexington, Mass.: Heath.

Arterton, F. Christopher. (1982). "Political Money and Party Strength." In Joel L. Fleishman, ed., *The Future of American Political Parties*. Englewood Cliffs, N.J.: Prentice-Hall.

Arterton, F. Christopher. (1984). "Campaign Organizations Confront the Media-Political Environment." In Doris A. Graber, ed., *Media Power and Politics*. Washington, D.C.: Congressional Quarterly Press.

Asher, Herbert B. (1980). *Presidential Elections and American Politics: Voters, Candidates, and Campaigns since 1952*, rev. ed. Homewood, Ill.: Dorsey.

Austin, Erik W., Jerome M. Clubb, William H. Flanigan, Peter Granda, & Nancy H. Zingale. (1991). "Electoral Participation in the United States, 1968–86." *Legislative Studies Quarterly, 16*, 145.

Axelrod, Robert. (1972). "Where the Votes Come from: An Analysis of Electoral Coalitions, 1952–1968." *American Political Science Review, 66*, 11.

Bach, Stanley, & Steven S. Smith. (1988). *Managing Uncertainty in the House of Representatives: Adaption and Innovation in Special Rules*. Washington, D.C.: The Brookings Institution.

Baker, Ross. K. (1989a). *House and Senate*. New York: Norton.

Baker, Ross K. (1989b). *The New Fat Cats: Members of Congress as Political Benefactors*. New York: Priority Press Publications, The Twentieth Century Fund.

Balz, Dan. (1991). "The Democrats' 50-State Dash to Nomination." *Washington Post National Weekly Edition*, June 10–16, p. 11.

Banfield, Edward C., & James Q. Wilson. (1963). *City Politics*. Cambridge, Mass.: Harvard University Press.

Barber, James David, ed. (1978). *Race for the Presidency: The Media and the Nomination Process*. Englewood Cliffs, N.J.: Prentice-Hall.

Barker, Lucius J. (1988). *Our Time Has Come: A Delegate's Diary of Jesse Jackson's 1984 Presidential Campaign*. Urbana: University of Illinois Press.

Barker, Lucius J., & Ronald Walter, eds. (1989). *Jesse Jackson and the 1984 Presidential Campaign*. Urbana: University of Illinois Press.

Barone, Michael, & Grant Ujifusa. (1981). *The Almanac of American Politics*. Washington, D.C.: Barone and Company.

Barone, Michael, & Grant Ujifusa. (1983). *The Almanac of American Politics*. Washington, D.C.: Barone and Company.

Barone, Michael, & Grant Ujifusa. (1985). *The Almanac of American Politics*. Washington, D.C.: National Journal.

Barone, Michael, Grant Ujifusa, & Douglas Matthews. (1972). *The Almanac of American Politics*. New York: Dutton.

Barone, Michael, Grant Ujifusa, & Douglas Matthews. (1973). *The Almanac of American Politics*. New York: Dutton.

Barone, Michael, Grant Ujifusa, & Douglas Matthews. (1975). *The Almanac of American Politics*. New York: Dutton.

Barone, Michael, Grant Ujifusa, & Douglas Matthews. (1977). *The Almanac of American Politics*. New York: Dutton.

Barone, Michael, Grant Ujifusa, & Douglas Matthews. (1979). *The Almanac of American Politics.* New York: Dutton.

Bartels, Larry M. (1985). "Expectations and Preferences in Presidential Nominating Campaigns." *American Political Science Review, 79,* 804.

Bartels, Larry M. (1988). *Presidential Primaries and the Dynamics of Public Choice.* Princeton, N.J.: Princeton University Press.

Basehart, Harry, & John Comer. (1991). "Partisan and Incumbent Effects in State Legislative Redistricting." *Legislative Studies Quarterly, 16,* 65.

Baumer, Donald C. (1990). "Senate Democratic Leadership in the 101st Congress." Paper presented at the Annual Meeting of the American Political Science Association, San Francisco.

Beeman, Richard R. (1991). "Republicanism in the First Party System." In L. Sandy Maisel, ed., *The Encyclopedia of American Political Parties and Elections.* New York: Garland.

Bennett, Stephen E. (1990). "The Uses and Abuses of Registration and Turnout Data." *PS, 23,* 166.

Bennett, Stephen E., & David Resnick. (1990). "The Implication of Nonvoting for Democracy in the United States." *American Journal of Political Science, 34.*

Berelson, Bernard, Paul F. Lazarsfeld, & William N. McPhee. (1954). *Voting.* Chicago: University of Chicago Press.

Berkman, Ronald, & Laura Kitch. (1986). *Politics in the Media Age.* New York: McGraw-Hill.

Berry, Jeffrey M. (1977). *Lobbying for the People.* Princeton, N.J.: Princeton University Press.

Berry, Jeffrey M. (1989). *The Interest Group Society.* Glenview, Ill.: Scott, Foresman.

Beyle, Thad L. (1983). "Governors." In Virginia Gray, Herbert Jacob, & Kenneth N. Vines, eds., *Politics in the American States,* 4th ed. Boston: Little, Brown.

Bibby, John F. (1981). "Party Renewal in the National Republican Party." In Gerald Pomper, ed., *Party Renewal in America.* New York: Praeger.

Bibby, John F. (1986). "Party Trends in 1985: Constrained Advance of the National Party." *Publius, 16,* 79.

Bibby, John F. (1990). "Party Organization at the State Level." In L. Sandy Maisel, ed., *The Parties Respond: Changes in the American Party System.* Boulder, Colo.: Westview Press.

Bibby, John F. (1991). "Republican National Committee." In L. Sandy Maisel, ed., *Political Parties and Elections in the United States: An Encyclopedia.* New York: Garland.

Bibby, John F., Cornelius P. Cotter, James L. Gibson, & Robert J. Huckshorn. (1983). "Political Parties." In Virginia Gray, Herbert Jacob, & Kenneth N. Vines, eds., *Politics in the American States,* 4th ed. Boston: Little, Brown.

Binkley, Wilfred. (1963). *American Political Parties,* 4th ed. New York: Knopf.

Black, Christine, Andrew Blake, John Aloysius Farrell, Thomas Oliphant, & Joan Vennochi. (1988). "The Road to Nomination." *The Boston Globe,* May 8, 9, 10, and 11, page 1.

Black, Christine M., & Thomas Oliphant. (1989). *All by Myself: The Unmaking of a Presidential Campaign.* Chester, Conn.: Globe Pequot Press.

Black, Earl, & Merle Black. (1987). *Politics and Society in the South.* Cambridge, Mass.: Harvard University Press.

Bloom, Howard S., & H. Douglas Price. (1975). "Voter Response to Short-Run Economic Conditions: The Asymmetric Effect of Prosperity and Recession." *American Political Science Review, 69,* 1240.

Bolingbroke, Lord. (1976). *The Works of Lord Bolingbroke* (Philadelphia: Carey and Hart, 1841). Cited in Giovanni Sartori, *Parties and Party Systems: A Framework for Analysis.* New York: Cambridge University Press.

Bond, Jon R., Cary Covington, & Richard Fleisher. (1985). "Explaining Challenger Quality in Congressional Elections." *Journal of Politics, 47,* 510.

Bond, Jon R., & Richard Fleisher. (1990a). "Assessing Presidential Support in the House II—Lessons from George Bush." Paper presented at the Annual Meeting of the American Political Science Association, San Francisco.

Bond, Jon R., & Richard Fleisher. (1990b). *The President in the Legislative Arena.* Chicago: University of Chicago Press.

Bone, Hugh A., & Austin Ranney. (1976). *Politics and Voters,* 4th ed. New York: Mc-Graw-Hill.

Born, Richard. (1985). "Partisan Intentions and Election Day Realities in the Congressional Redistricting Process." *American Political Science Review, 79,* 305.

Boyd, Richard W. (1981). "Decline in U.S. Voter Turnout: Structural Explanations." *American Politics Quarterly, 9,* 133.

Brady, David W. (1988). *Critical Elections and Congressional Policymaking.* Stanford, Calif.: Stanford University Press.

Brady, David W. (1990). "Coalitions in the U.S. Congress." In L. Sandy Maisel, ed., *The Parties Respond: Changes in the American Party System.* Boulder, Colo.: Westview Press.

Brady, David W., Charles S. Bullock III, & L. Sandy Maisel. (1988). "The Electoral Antecedents of Policy Innovations: A Comparative Analysis." *Comparative Political Studies, 20,* 395.

Brady, David W., Joseph Cooper, & Patricia A. Hurley. (1979). "The Decline of Party in the U.S. House of Representatives, 1887–1968." *Legislative Studies Quarterly, 4,* 381.

Brady, David W., & John Ettling. (1984). "The Electoral Connection and the Decline of Partisanship in the Twentieth Century House of Representatives." *Congress and the Presidency, 11,* 19.

Brady, David W., & Joseph Stewart, Jr. (1986). "When Elections Really Matter: Realignment and Changes in Public Policy." In Benjamin Ginsberg & Alan Stone, eds., *Do Elections Matter?* Armonk, N.Y.: Sharpe.

Brady, David W., & Barbara Sinclair. (1984). "Building Majorities for Policy Change in the House of Representatives." *Journal of Politics, 46,* 1033.

Bridges, Amy. (1984). *A City in the Republic: Antebellum New York and the Origins of Machine Politics.* Cambridge: Cambridge University Press.

Broder, David S. (1971). *The Party's Over.* New York: Harper & Row.

Broder, David S. (1986). "Campaign Time: Away We Go." *Washington Post National Weekly Edition.*

Brody, Richard A., & Benjamin I. Page. (1972). "Policy Voting and the Electoral Process: The Vietnam War Issue." *American Political Science Review, 66,* 979.

Bruno, Jerry, & Jeff Greenfield. (1971). *The Advance Man.* New York: Morrow.

Buchanan, Bruce. (1991). *Electing a President: The Markle Commission Research on Campaign '88.* Austin: University of Texas Press.

Buell, Emmett H., Jr., & James W. Davis. (1991). "Win Early and Often: Candidates and the Strategic Environment of 1988." In Emmett H. Buell, Jr., & Lee Sigelman, *Nominating the President.* Knoxville: University of Tennessee Press.

Buell, Emmett H., Jr., & Lee Sigelman. (1991). *Nominating the President*. Knoxville: University of Tennessee Press.

Bullock, Charles S. III. (1977). "Explaining Congressional Elections: Differences in Perceptions of Opposing Candidates." *Legislative Studies Quarterly, 2*, 295.

Bullock, Charles S. III, & Loch K. Johnson. (1985). "Runoff Elections in Georgia." *Journal of Politics, 47*, 937.

Burke, Edmund. (1976). "Thoughts on the Cause of the Present Discontents" (in *The Works of Edmund Burke*, vol. 3. Boston: Little, Brown, 1839). Cited in Giovanni Sartori, ed., *Parties and Party Systems: A Framework for Analysis*. New York: Cambridge University Press.

Burnham, Walter Dean. (1970). *Critical Elections and the Mainsprings of American Politics*. New York: Norton.

Burnham, Walter Dean. (1975). "American Parties in the 1970s: Beyond Party?" In L. Sandy Maisel & Paul M. Sacks, eds., *The Future of Political Parties*. Beverly Hills, Calif.: Sage.

Burnham, Walter Dean. (1982). "Shifting Patterns of Congressional Voting Participation." In W. D. Burnham, ed., *The Current Crisis in American Politics*. New York: Oxford University Press.

Butler, David, & Bruce E. Cain. (1991). *Congressional Redistricting: Comparative and Theoretical Perspectives*. New York: Macmillan.

Caddell, Patrick H. (1981). "The Democratic Strategy and Its Electoral Consequences." In Seymour Martin Lipset, ed., *Party Coalitions in the 1980s*. San Francisco: Institute for Contemporary Studies.

Cain, Bruce E. (1984). *The Reapportionment Puzzle*. Berkeley: University of California Press.

Cain, Bruce E. (1985). "Assessing the Partisan Effects of Redistricting." *American Political Science Review, 79*, 320.

Cain, Bruce E., & David Butler. (1991, July/August). "Redrawing District Lines: What's Going On and What's at Stake." *The American Enterprise, 2*(4), 28.

Cain, Bruce E., John Ferejohn, & Morris Fiorina. (1987). *The Personal Vote: Constituency Service and Electoral Independence*. Cambridge, Mass.: Harvard University Press.

Cain, Bruce E., D. Roderick Kiewiet, & Carole J. Uhlaner. (1991). "The Acquisition of Partisanship by Latinos and Asian Americans." *American Journal of Political Science, 35*, 390.

Calderia, Gregory A., & Samuel C. Patterson. (1982). "Contextual Influences on Participation in U.S. State Legislative Elections." *Legislative Studies Quarterly, 7*, 359.

Calderia, Gregory A., Samuel C. Patterson, & Gregory A. Markko. (1985). "The Mobilization of Voters in Congressional Elections." *Journal of Politics, 47*, 490.

Calvert, Jerry W. (1979). "Revolving Doors: Volunteerism in State Legislatures." *State Government, 52*, 174.

Campbell, Angus. (1960). "Surge and Decline: A Study of Electoral Change." *Public Opinion Quarterly, 24*, 397.

Campbell, Angus, Philip E. Converse, Warren E. Miller, & Donald E. Stokes. (1960). *The American Voter*. New York: Wiley.

Campbell, James. (1989). "The Cross-Pressured Partisan." Paper presented at the Annual Meeting of the American Political Science Association, Atlanta, Ga.

Canon, David T. (1990). *Actors, Athletes, and Astronauts: Political Amateurs in the United States Congress*. Chicago: University of Chicago Press.

Canon, David T., R. Michael Alvarez, & Patrick J. Sellers. (1990). "Contesting Senate

Primary Elections: 1972–1988." Paper presented at the Annual Meeting of the Midwest Political Science Association, Chicago.

Carmines, Edward G., John P. McIver, & James A. Stimson. (1987). "Unrealized Partisanship: A Theory of Dealignment." *Journal of Politics, 49,* 376.

Carmines, Edward G., & James A. Stimson. (1989). *Issue Evolution.* Princeton, N.J.: Princeton University Press.

Carr, Craig L., & Gary L. Scott. (1984). "The Logic of State Primary Classification Schemes." *American Politics Quarterly, 12,* 465.

Carter, Jimmy. (1982a). *Keeping Faith: Memoirs of a President.* New York: Bantam Books.

Carter, Jimmy. (1982b). *Public Papers of the President.* Washington, D.C.: U.S. Government Printing Office.

Cassel, Carol A., & Robert C. Luskin. (1988). "Simple Explanations of Voter Turnout." *American Political Science Review, 82,* 1321.

Catt, Carrie C., & Nettie R. Shuler. (1969). *Woman Suffrage and Politics.* Seattle: University of Washington Press.

Cavanagh, Thomas E. (1979). "Changes in American Electoral Turnout, 1964–1976." Paper delivered at the Annual Meeting of the Midwest Political Science Association, Chicago.

Cavanagh, Thomas E. (1981). "Research on American Voter Turnout: The State of Evidence." Paper prepared for the Conference on Voter Participation, Washington, D.C.

Ceaser, James W. (1982). *Reforming the Reforms.* Cambridge, Mass.: Ballinger.

Center for Responsive Politics. (1985). *Soft Money—A Loophole for the '80s.* Washington, D.C.: Center for Responsive Politics.

Center for Responsive Politics. (1989). *Soft Money '88.* Washington, D.C.: Center for Responsive Politics.

Chambers, William N. (1963). *Political Parties in a New Nation: The American Experience 1776–1809.* New York: Oxford University Press.

Chambers, William N. (1975). "Party Development in the American Mainstream." In William N. Chambers & Walter D. Burnham, eds., *The American Party Systems: Stages of Political Development,* 2d ed. New York: Oxford University Press.

Chambers, William N., & Walter D. Burnham, eds. (1967). *The American Party Systems: Stages of Political Development.* New York: Oxford University Press.

Chambers, William N., & Walter D. Burnham, eds. (1975). *The American Party Systems: Stages of Political Development,* 2d ed. New York: Oxford University Press.

Charles, Joseph. (1956). *The Origins of the American Party System.* Williamsburg, Va.: Institute of Early American History and Culture.

Cigler, Alan J., & Burdett A. Loomis, eds. (1983). *Interest Group Politics.* Washington, D.C.: Congressional Quarterly Press.

Clark, Peter, & Susan Evans. (1983). *Covering Campaigns: Journalism in Congressional Elections.* Stanford, Calif.: Stanford University Press.

Clem, Alan L. (1976). "The Case of the Upstart Republican: The First District of South Dakota." In Alan L. Clem, ed., *The Making of Congressmen: Seven Campaigns of 1974.* North Scituate, Mass.: Duxbury.

Cohen, Jeffrey E., Michael A. Krassa, & John Hamman. (1991). "The Impact of Presidential Campaigning on Midterm U.S. Senate Elections." *American Political Science Review, 85,* 165.

Cohen, Richard E. (1984). "Many Are Skeptical about Jackson's Dual Primary Argument." *National Journal,* 922.

Collie, Melissa. (1986). "New Directions in Congressional Research." *Legislative Studies Section Newsletter, 110,* 90.

Collie, Melissa P., & David W. Brady. (1985). "The Decline of Partisan Voting Coalitions in the House of Representatives." In Lawrence C. Dodd & Bruce I. Oppenheimer, eds., *Congress Reconsidered,* 3d ed. Washington, D.C.: Congressional Quarterly Press.

Collie, Melissa P., & Joseph Cooper. (1989). "Multiple Referral and the 'New' Committee System in the House of Representatives." In Lawrence C. Dodd & Bruce I. Oppenheimer, eds., *Congress Reconsidered,* 4th ed. Washington, D.C.: Congressional Quarterly Press.

Commission on Party Structure and Delegate Selection. (1970). *Mandate for Reform.* Washington, D.C.: Democratic National Committee.

Committee on Political Parties of the American Political Science Association. (1950). *Toward a More Responsible Two-Party System.* New York: Rinehart.

Common Cause. (1986). *Financing the Finance Committee.* Washington, D.C.: Common Cause.

Congress and the Nation. (1981). Washington, D.C.: Congressional Quarterly, Inc.

Congressional Quarterly Almanac. (1971–1984). Washington, D.C.: Congressional Quarterly, Inc.

Conlan, Timothy, Ann Martino, & Robert Dilger. (1984). "State Parties in the 1980s: Adaption, Resurgence, and Continuing Constraints." *Intergovernmental Affairs, 10,* 6.

Converse, Philip E., Angus Campbell, Warren E. Miller, & Donald E. Stokes. (1961). "Stability and Change in 1960: A Reinstating Election." *American Political Science Review, 55,* 269.

Converse, Philip E., Aage R. Clausen, & Warren E. Miller. (1965). "Electoral Myth and Reality: The 1964 Election." *American Political Science Review, 59,* 321.

Converse, Philip E., & Warren E. Miller. (1969). "Continuity and Change in American Politics: Parties and Issues in the 1968 Election." *American Political Science Review, 63,* 1083.

Converse, Philip E., & Richard G. Niemi. (1971). "Nonvoting among Young Adults in the United States." In William J. Crotty, Donald M. Freeman, & Douglas S. Gatlin, eds., *Political Parties and Political Behavior,* 2d ed. Boston: Allyn and Bacon.

Converse, Philip E., & Roy Pierce. (1987). "Measuring Partisanship." *Political Methodology, 11,* 143.

Cook, Rhodes. (1986). "Democrats Alter Rules Slightly in Effort to Broaden Party Base." *Congressional Quarterly, 44,* 2158.

Cook, Rhodes. (1989). "The Nominating Process." In Michael Nelson, ed., *The Elections of 1988.* Washington, D.C.: Congressional Quarterly Press.

Cook, Rhodes. (1990, November 10). "Most House Members Survive, But Many Margins Narrow." *Congressional Quarterly Weekly Report,* 48(45), 3798–3800.

Cook, Timothy E. (1990). "Thinking of the News Media as Political Institutions." Paper presented at the Annual Meeting of the American Political Science Association, San Francisco.

Cooper, Joseph, & David W. Brady. (1981). "Institutional Context and Leadership Style: The House from Cannon to Rayburn." *American Political Science Review, 75,* 411.

Cooper, Joseph, David W. Brady, & Patricia A. Hurley. (1977). "The Electoral Basis of Party Voting: Patterns and Trends in the U.S. House of Representatives,

1887–1969." In Louis Maisel & Joseph Cooper, eds., *The Impact of the Electoral Process*. Beverly Hills, Calif.: Sage Publications.

Cooper, Joseph, & William West. (1981). "The Congressional Career in the '70's." In Lawrence Dodd & Bruce Oppenheimer, eds., *Congress Reconsidered*, 2d ed. Washington, D.C.: Congressional Quarterly Press.

Copeland, Gary W. (1983). "Activating Voters in Congressional Elections." *Political Behavior, 5,* 391.

Corrado, Anthony J. (1991a). "Federal Election Campaign Act of 1971." In L. Sandy Maisel, ed., *Political Parties and Elections in the United States: An Encyclopedia*. New York: Garland.

Corrado, Anthony J. (1991b). "Federal Election Campaign Act Amendments of 1974." In L. Sandy Maisel, ed., *Political Parties and Elections in the United States: An Encyclopedia*. New York: Garland.

Corrado, Anthony J. (1992). *Creative Campaigning: PACs and the Presidential Selection Process*. Boulder, Colo.: Westview Press.

Corrado, Anthony J., & L. Sandy Maisel. (1988). "Campaigning for Presidential Nominations: The Experience with State Spending Ceilings, 1976–1984." Paper presented at the Annual Meeting of the Western Political Science Association, San Francisco; Occasional Paper no. 88-4, Center for American Political Studies, Harvard University, Cambridge, Mass.

Costikyan, Edward N. (1980). *How to Win Votes: The Politics of 1980*. New York: Harcourt Brace Jovanovich.

Cotter, Cornelius P., & John F. Bibby. (1980). "Institutional Developments of Parties and the Thesis of Party Decline." *Political Science Quarterly, 1,* 95.

Cotter, Cornelius P., James L. Gibson, John F. Bibby, & Robert J. Huckshorn. (1982). "Party-Government Linkages in the States." Paper delivered at the Annual Meeting of the American Political Science Association.

Cotter, Cornelius P., James L. Gibson, John F. Bibby, & Robert J. Huckshorn. (1984). *Party Organization in American Politics*. New York: Praeger.

Cotter, Cornelius P., James L. Gibson, John F. Bibby, & Robert J. Huckshorn. (1989). *Party Organization in American Politics*. New York: Praeger.

Cotter, Cornelius P., & Bernard C. Hennessy. (1964). *Politics without Power: The National Party Committees*. New York: Atherton.

Coval, Michael. (1984). "The Impact of the 1980 Election on Liberal Political Organization." Honors project presented at Colby College, Waterville, Me.

Cover, Albert D. (1977). "One Good Term Deserves Another: The Advantages of Incumbency in Congressional Elections." *American Journal of Political Science, 21,* 523.

Covington, Cary, Richard Fleisher, & Jon R. Bond. (1985). "Explaining Challenger Quality in Congressional Elections." Paper presented at the Annual Meeting of the Midwest Political Science Association, Chicago.

Cox, Gary, & Samuel Kernell, eds. (1991). *The Politics of Divided Government*. Boulder, Colo.: Westview Press.

Crespi, Irving. (1988). *Pre-election Polling: Sources of Accuracy and Error*. New York: Russell Sage Foundation.

Crespi, Irving. (1989). *Public Opinion, Polls, and Democracy*. Boulder, Colo.: Westview Press.

Crotty, William J. (1968). "The Party Organization and Its Activities." In William J. Crotty, ed., *Approaches to the Study of Party Organization*. Boston: Allyn and Bacon.

Crotty, William J. (1978). *Decision for the Democrats: Reforming the Party Structure.* Balti-more, Md.: Johns Hopkins University Press.

Crotty, William J. (1983). *Party Reform.* New York: Longman.

Crotty, William J. (1985). *The Party Game.* New York: Freeman.

Crotty, William J. (1986). *Political Parties in Local Areas.* Knoxville: University of Ten-nessee Press.

Crotty, William J., & John S. Jackson III. (1985). *Presidential Primaries and Nominations.* Washington, D.C.: Congressional Quarterly Press.

Crotty, William J., & Gary C. Jacobson. (1980). *American Parties in Decline.* Boston: Lit-tle, Brown.

Crouse, Timothy. (1973). *The Boys on the Bus.* New York: Ballantine.

Cunningham, Noble E. (1957). *The Jeffersonian Republicans.* Chapel Hill, N.C.: Univer-sity of North Carolina Press.

Cunningham, Noble E. (1965). *The Making of the American Party System, 1789 to 1809.* Englewood Cliffs, N.J.: Prentice-Hall.

Dahl, Robert. (1961). *Who Governs? Democracy and Power in an American City.* New Haven, Conn.: Yale University Press.

Darcy, R., & Sarah Slavin Schramm. (1977). "When Women Run against Men." *Public Opinion Quarterly, 41,* 1.

Davidson, Roger H. (1989). "The Impact of Agenda on the Post-Reform Congress." Paper presented at the Annual Meeting of the American Political Science Associa-tion, Atlanta, Ga.

Davidson, Roger H., ed. (1992). *The Postreform Congress.* New York: St. Martin's.

Davis, James W. (1983). *National Conventions in an Age of Party Reform.* Westport, Conn.: Greenwood Press.

Dawson, Richard E., & James A. Robinson. (1963). "Inter-Party Competition, Eco-nomic Variables, and Welfare Policies in the American States." *Journal of Politics, 25,* 265.

Dennis, Jack. (1966). "Support for the Party System by the Mass Public." *American Po-litical Science Review, 60,* 600.

Dennis, Jack. (1978). "Trends in Public Support for the American Party System." In Jeff Fishel, ed., *Parties and Elections in an Anti-Party Age.* Bloomington, Ind.: Indi-ana University Press.

DeVries, Walter, & Lance Tarrance, Jr. (1972). *The Ticket-Splitter: A New Force in Amer-ican Politics.* Grand Rapids, Mich.: Eerdmans.

Diamond, Edwin, & Stephen Bates. (1984). *The Spot: The Rise of Political Advertising on Television.* Cambridge, Mass.: MIT Press.

Dionne, E. J., Jr. (1988, January 15). "Michigan G.O.P. Snarled in Uncertainty." *The New York Times,* p. B4.

Dodd, Lawrence C., and Sean Q. Kelly. (1990). "The Electoral Consequences of Pre-sentational Style." Paper presented at the Annual Meeting of the American Politi-cal Science Association, San Francisco.

Donovan, Beth. (1991). "Deadlines Not Always Met When Stakes Are High." *Congres-sional Quarterly Weekly Report, 49,* 1776.

Downs, Anthony. (1957). *An Economic Theory of Democracy.* New York: Harper & Row.

Drew, Elizabeth. (1979a). *American Journal: The Events of 1976.* New York: Random House.

Drew, Elizabeth. (1979b). *Senator.* New York: Simon and Schuster.

Drew, Elizabeth. (1981). *Portrait of an Election: The 1980 Presidential Campaign.* New York: Simon and Schuster.

Drew, Elizabeth. (1983). *Politics and Money: The New Road to Corruption.* New York: Macmillan.

Duverger, Maurice. (1951). *Political Parties.* New York: Wiley.

Edsall, Thomas B. (1986). "Conservative Fund-Raisers Hit Hard Times." *Washington Post.*

Edsall, Thomas B. (1988). "The Reagan Legacy." In Sidney Blumenthal & Thomas Byrne Edsall, eds., *The Republican Legacy.* New York: Pantheon.

Edwards, George C. III. (1980). *Presidential Influence in Congress.* San Francisco: W. H. Freeman.

Edwards, George C. III. (1989). *At the Margin: Presidential Leadership of Congress.* New Haven: Yale University Press.

Edwards, George C. III., & Stephen J. Wayne. (1990). *Presidential Leadership: Politics and Policy Making,* 2d ed. New York: St. Martin's Press.

Ehrenhalt, Alan, ed. (1984). *Politics in America: Members of Congress in Washington and at Home.* Washington, D.C.: Congressional Quarterly Press.

Ehrenhalt, Alan. (1991). *The United States of Ambition: Politicians, Power and the Pursuit of Office.* New York: Times Books.

Eisenstein, James. (1991). "Pennsylvania's 1990 Legislative Elections: From Virtually No Competition to Low Competition." *Comparative State Politics, 12,* 36.

Eismeier, Theodore J. (1985). "The Microeconomy of PACs." Paper presented at the Annual Meeting of the American Political Science Association, New Orleans, La.

Eismeier, Theodore J., & Philip H. Pollock III. (1984). "Political Action Committees: Varieties of Organization and Strategy." In Michael J. Malbin, ed., *Money and Politics in the United States.* Washington, D.C.: American Enterprise Institute and Chatham House.

Eismeier, Theodore J., & Philip H. Pollock III. (1985a). "The Microeconomy of PACs." Paper delivered at the Annual Meeting of the American Political Science Association.

Eismeier, Theodore J., & Philip H. Pollock III. (1985b). "An Organizational Analysis of Political Action Committees." *Political Behavior, 7,* 192.

Eismeier, Theodore J., & Philip H. Pollock III. (1986). "Strategy and Choice in Congressional Elections: The Role of Political Action Committees." *American Journal of Political Science, 30,* 197.

Eldersveld, Samuel J. (1964). *Political Parties: A Behavioral Analysis.* Chicago: Rand McNally.

Eldersveld, Samuel J. (1982). *Political Parties in American Society.* New York: Basic Books.

Entman, Robert M. (1989). *Democracy without Citizens: Media and the Decay of American Politics.* New York: Oxford University Press.

Epstein, Edwin M. (1980). "Business and Labor under the Federal Election Campaign Act of 1971." In Michael J. Malbin, ed., *Parties, Interest Groups and Campaign Finance Laws.* Washington, D.C.: American Enterprise Institute for Public Policy Research.

Epstein, Leon D. (1967). *Political Parties in Western Democracies.* New York: Praeger.

Epstein, Leon D. (1986). *Political Parties in the American Mold.* Madison: University of Wisconsin Press.

Epstein, Leon D. (1989). "Will American Political Parties Be Privatized?" *Journal of Law and Politics, 5,* 239.

Epstein, Leon D. (1991). "The Regulation of State Political Parties." In L. Sandy

Maisel, ed., *Political Parties and Elections in the United States: An Encyclopedia.* New York: Garland.

Erie, Steven. (1988). *Rainbow's End: Irish-Americans and the Dilemmas of Urban Machine Politics, 1840–1985.* Berkeley: University of California Press.

Erikson, Robert S. (1981). "Why Do People Vote? Because They Are Registered." *American Politics Quarterly, 9,* 259.

Erikson, Robert S., Thomas D. Lancaster, & David W. Romero. (1989). "Group Components of the Presidential Vote, 1952–1984." *Journal of Politics, 51,* 337.

Evans, Diana. (1986). "PAC Contributions and Roll-Call Voting." In Allan Cigler & Burdett A. Loomis, eds., *Interest Groups and Politics.* Washington, D.C.: Congressional Quarterly Books.

Federal Election Commission. (1991a). "1990 Congressional Election Spending Drops to Low Point." Press Release, February 22, 1991.

Federal Election Commission. (1991b). "PAC Activity Falls in 1990 Elections." Press Release, March 31, 1991.

Feigert, Frank B., and Pippa Norris. (1989). "Candidate Recruitment and Government Popularity in Special and By-Elections: The United States, Canada, Britain, and Australia." Paper presented at the Annual Meeting of the American Political Science Association, Atlanta, Ga.

Fenno, Richard F. (1972). "If, as Ralph Nader Says, Congress Is 'the Broken Branch,' How Come We Love Our Congressmen So Much?" Presented for discussion at the Harvard Club, Boston.

Fenno, Richard F. (1978). *Home Style: House Members in Their Own Districts.* Boston: Little, Brown.

Fenno, Richard F. (1984). *The United States Senate: A Bicameral Perspective.* Washington, D.C.: American Enterprise Institute for Public Policy Research.

Fenno, Richard F., Jr. (1990). *The Presidential Odyssey of John Glenn.* Washington, D.C.: Congressional Quarterly Press.

Ferejohn, John A. (1977). "On the Decline of Competition in Congressional Elections." *American Political Science Review, 71,* 525.

Ferejohn John A., & Randall Calvert. (1984). "Presidential Coattails in Historical Perspective." *American Journal of Political Science, 28,* 127.

Ferejohn, John A., & Morris P. Fiorina. (1974). "The Paradox of Not Voting: A Decision Theoretic Analysis." *American Political Science Review, 68,* 525.

Finer, Herman. (1949). *The Theory and Practice of Modern Government.* New York: Holt.

Finkel, Steven E., & Howard A. Scarrow. (1985). "Party Identification and Party Enrollment: The Difference and the Consequence." *Journal of Politics, 47,* 620.

Fiorina, Morris P. (1973). "Electoral Margins, Constituency Influence, and Policy Moderation: A Critical Assessment." *American Politics Quarterly, 1,* 479.

Fiorina, Morris P. (1977a). "The Case of the Vanishing Marginals: The Bureaucracy Did It." *American Political Science Review, 71,* 166.

Fiorina, Morris P. (1977b). "An Outline for a Model of Party Choice." *American Journal of Political Science, 21,* 618.

Fiorina, Morris P. (1978). *Congress: Keystone of the Washington Establishment,* 4th ed. New Haven, Conn.: Yale University Press.

Fiorina, Morris P. (1981). *Retrospective Voting in American National Elections.* New Haven, Conn.: Yale University Press.

Fiorina, Morris P. (1990). "An Era of Divided Government." In Bruce Cain & Gillian Peele, eds., *Developments in American Politics.* London: Macmillan.

Fiorina, Morris P. (1992). *Divided Government.* New York: Macmillan.

Fishel, Jeff. (1973). *Party and Opposition: Congressional Challengers in American Politics.* New York: David McKay.

Fishel, Jeff. (1977). "Agenda Building in Presidential Campaigns: The Case of Jimmy Carter." Paper presented at the Annual Meeting of the American Political Science Association. Washington, D.C.

Fishel, Jeff. (1985). *Presidents and Promises.* Washington, D.C.: Congressional Quarterly Press.

Flanigan, William, & Nancy Zingale. (1983). *Political Behavior of the American Electorate,* 5th ed. Boston: Allyn and Bacon.

Foner, Eric. (1988). *Reconstruction: America's Unfinished Revolution, 1863–1877.* New York: Harper & Row.

Formisano, Ronald P. (1974). "Deferential-Participant Politics: The Early Republic's Political Culture, 1789–1890." *American Political Science Review, 68,* 473.

Fowler, Linda L. (1979). "The Electoral Lottery: Decisions to Run for Congress." *Public Choice, 34,* 399.

Fowler, Linda L. (1980). "Candidate Perceptions of Electoral Coalitions: Limits and Possibilities." Paper presented at the Conference on Congressional Elections, Houston, Tex.

Fowler, Linda L. (1982). "How Interest Groups Select Issues for Rating Voting Records of Members of the U.S. Congress." *Legislative Studies Quarterly, 7,* 403.

Fowler, Linda L. (1989). "Candidate Recruitment and the Study of Congress: A Review Essay." Paper presented at the Conference on Elective Politicians, Institute of Politics, Kennedy School of Government, Harvard University, Boston.

Fowler, Linda L., & Robert McClure. (1989). *Political Ambition: Who Decides to Run for Congress.* New Haven, Conn.: Yale University Press.

Franklin, Charles H. (1984). "Issues, Preferences, Socialization, and the Evolution of Party Identification." *American Journal of Political Science, 28,* 459.

Franklin, Charles H., & John E. Jackson. (1983). "The Dynamics of Party Identification." *American Political Science Review, 77,* 957.

Fraser, Steve, & Gary Gerstle, eds. (1989). *The Rise and Fall of the New Deal Order, 1930–1980.* Princeton, N.J.: Princeton University Press.

Freed, Bruce F. (1978). "Political Money and Campaign Finance Reform, 1971–1976." In Jeff Fishel, ed., *Parties and Elections in an Anti-Party Age.* Bloomington, Ind.: Indiana University Press.

Frendeis, John P., James L. Gibson, & Laura L. Vertz. (1990). "The Electoral Relevance of Local Party Organization." *American Political Science Review, 84,* 226.

Frendeis, John P., & Richard Waterman. (1985). "PAC Contributions and Legislative Behavior: Senate Voting on Trucking Deregulation." *Social Science Quarterly, 66,* 401.

Friedman, Paul A. (1990). "Environmental Action's Dirty Dozen of 1990." *Environmental Action Magazine, 22* (2), 16.

Gais, Thomas L., Mark A. Peterson, & Jack L. Walker. (1984). "Interest Groups, Iron Triangles, and Representative Institutions in American National Government." *British Journal of Political Science, 14,* 161.

Gans, Curtis B. (1990). "A Rejoinder to Piven and Cloward." *PS, 23,* 175.

Gans, Herbert J. (1979). *Deciding What's News.* New York: Random House.

Gant, Michael M., & Norman L. Luttbeg. (1991). *American Electoral Behavior.* Itasca, Ill.: F. E. Peacock.

Garand, James C. (1991). "Electoral Marginality in State Legislative Elections, 1968–86." *Legislative Studies Quarterly, 16,* 7.

Geer, John G. (1989). *Nominating Presidents: An Evaluation of Voters and Primaries.* Westport, Conn.: Greenwood.

Geer, John G. (1991). "Critical Realignments and the Public Opinion Poll." *Journal of Politics, 53,* 434.

Gelman, Andrew, & Gary King. (1990). "Estimating the Electoral Consequences of Legislative Redistricting." *Journal of the American Statistical Association, 85,* 274.

Germond, Jack W., & Jules Witcover. (1981). *Blue Smoke and Mirrors: How Reagan Won and Why Carter Lost the Election of 1980.* New York: Viking.

Germond, Jack W., & Jules Witcover. (1985). *Wake Us When It's Over: Presidential Politics of 1984.* New York: Macmillan.

Germond, Jack W., & Jules Witcover. (1989). *Whose Broad Stripes and Bright Stars? The Trivial Pursuit of the Presidency, 1988.* New York: Warner Books.

Gibson, James L. (1991). "County Party Organizations." In L. Sandy Maisel, ed., *Political Parties and Elections in the United States: An Encyclopedia.* New York: Garland.

Gibson, James L., Cornelius P. Cotter, John F. Bibby, & Robert J. Huckshorn. (1983). "Assessing Party Organizational Strength." *American Journal of Political Science, 27,* 193.

Gibson, James L., Cornelius P. Cotter, John F. Bibby, & Robert J. Huckshorn. (1985). "Whither the Local Parties?: A Cross-Sectional Analysis and Longitudinal Analysis of the Strength of Party Organizations." *American Journal of Political Science, 29,* 139.

Gibson, James L., John P. Frendreis, & Laura L. Vertz. (1989). "Party Dynamics in the 1980s: Change in County Party Organizational Strength, 1980–1984." *American Journal of Political Science, 67.*

Gienapp, William E. (1987). *The Origins of the Republican Party, 1852–1856.* New York: Oxford University Press.

Gienapp, William E. (1991). "The Formation of the Republican Party." In L. Sandy Maisel, ed., *The Encyclopedia of American Political Parties and Elections.* New York: Garland.

Gierzynski, Anthony, & David Breaux. (1990). "It's Money That Matters': The Role of Campaign Expenditures in State Legislative Primaries." Paper presented at the Annual Meeting of the American Political Science Association, San Francisco.

Gierzynski, Anthony, & David Breaux. (1991). "Money and Votes in State Legislative Elections." *Legislative Studies Quarterly, 16,* 203.

Ginsberg, Benjamin, & Martin Shefter. (1985). "A Critical Realignment? The New Politics, the Reconstituted Right, and the Election of 1984." In Michael Nelson, ed., *The Elections of 1984.* Washington, D.C.: Congressional Quarterly Press.

Ginsberg, Benjamin, & Alan Stone, eds. (1986). *Do Elections Matter?* Armonk, N.Y.: Sharpe.

Glazer, Amihai, Bernard Grofman, & Marc Robbins. (1987). "Partisan and Incumbency Effects of the 1970s Congressional Redistricting." *American Journal of Political Science, 30,* 680.

Goldenberg, Edie N., & Michael W. Traugott. (1980). "Campaign Effects on Voting Behavior in the 1978 Congressional Elections." Paper presented at the Annual Meeting of the American Political Science Association, Washington, D.C.

Goldenberg, Edie N., & Michael W. Traugott. (1984). *Campaigning for Congress.* Washington, D.C.: Congressional Quarterly Press.

Goldenberg, Edie N., Michael W. Traugott, & Frank R. Baumgartner. (1986). "Preemptive and Reactive Spending in U.S. House Races." *Political Behavior, 8,* 3.

Goldman, Peter, & Tony Fuller. (1985). *The Quest for the Presidency, 1984.* New York: Bantam Books.

Goldman, Ralph M. (1990). *The National Party Chairmen and Committees: Factionalism at the Top.* Armonk, N.Y.: M. E. Sharpe.

Gosnell, Harold. (1939). *Machine Politics: Chicago Model.* Chicago: University of Chicago Press.

Gottlieb, Stephen E. (1985). "Fleshing Out the Right of Association: The Problem of the Contribution Limits of the Federal Election Campaign Act." *Albany Law Review, 49,* 825.

Gottlieb, Stephen E. (1991). *"Buckley v. Valeo."* In L. Sandy Maisel, ed., *Political Parties and Elections in the United States: An Encyclopedia.* New York: Garland.

Graber, Doris A. (1980). *Mass Media in American Politics.* Washington, D.C.: Congressional Quarterly Press.

Graber, Doris A. (1982). *The President and the Public.* Philadelphia: Institute for the Study of Human Issues.

Graber, Doris A. (1984a). *Mass Media and American Elections.* Washington, D.C.: Congressional Quarterly Press.

Graber, Doris A. (1984b). *Media Power in Politics.* Washington, D.C.: Congressional Quarterly Press.

Graber, Doris A. (1989). *Mass Media in American Politics,* 3d ed. Washington, D.C.: Congressional Quarterly Press.

Graber, Doris A. (1990). *Media Power in Politics,* 2d ed. Washington, D.C.: Congressional Quarterly Press.

Grassmuck, George, ed. (1985). *Before Nomination: Our Primary Problem.* Washington, D.C.: American Enterprise Institute for Public Policy Research.

Gray, Virginia, Herbert Jacob, & Robert B. Albritton. (1990). *Politics in the American States: A Comparative Analysis,* 5th ed. Glenview, Ill.: Scott, Foresman/Little, Brown.

Green, Donald, & Jonathan Krasno. (1988). "Salvation for the Spendthrift Incumbent: Reestimating the Effects of Campaign Spending in House Elections." *American Journal of Political Science, 32,* 884.

Greenstein, Fred I. (1970). *The American Party System and the American People,* 2d ed. Englewood Cliffs, N.J.: Prentice-Hall.

Greenstein, Fred I., & Frank B. Feigert. (1985). *The American Party System and the American People,* 3d ed. Englewood Cliffs, N.J.: Prentice-Hall.

Grenzke, Janet. (1989). "PACs in the Congressional Supermarket: The Currency Is Complex." *American Journal of Political Science, 33,* 1.

Grenzke, Janet. (1990). "Money and Congressional Behavior." In Margaret Latus Nugent & John R. Johannes, eds., *Money, Elections, and Democracy: Reforming Congressional Campaign Finance.* Boulder, Colo.: Westview Press.

Grofman, Bernard, ed. (1990). *Political Gerrymandering and the Courts.* New York: Agathon.

Hadley, Charles D. (1985). "Dual Partisan Identification in the South." *Journal of Politics, 47,* 254.

Hamilton, Alexander, John Jay, & James Madison. (1981). *The Federalist.* New York: New American Library.

Hargrove, Erwin C., & Michael Nelson. (1985). "The Presidency: Reagan and the Cycle of Politics and Policy." In Michael Nelson, ed., *The Elections of 1984.* Washington, D.C.: Congressional Quarterly Press.

Hawley, Willis D. (1973). *Nonpartisan Elections and the Case of Party Politics.* New York: Wiley.

Heard, Alexander. (1960). *The Costs of Democracy.* Chapel Hill, N.C.: University of North Carolina Press.

Herrnson, Paul S. (1988). *Party Campaigning in the 1980s.* Cambridge, Mass.: Harvard University Press.

Herrnson, Paul S. (1989). "National Party Decision-Making, Strategies, and Resource Distribution in Congressional Elections." *Western Political Quarterly, 42,* 301.

Herrnson, Paul S. (1990a). "Campaign Professionalism and Fundraising in Congressional Elections." Paper presented at the Annual Meeting of the American Political Science Association, San Francisco.

Herrnson, Paul S. (1990b). "Reemergent National Party Organizations." In L. Sandy Maisel, ed., *The Parties Respond: Changes in the American Party System.* Boulder, Colo.: Westview Press.

Herrnson, Paul. (1991). "Campaign Professionalism and Fundraising in Congressional Elections." Unpublished manuscript, University of Maryland.

Hershey, Marjorie R. (1974). *The Making of Campaign Strategy.* Lexington, Mass.: D. C. Heath.

Hershey, Marjorie R. (1984). *Running for Office: The Political Education of Campaigners.* Chatham, N.J.: Chatham House Publishers.

Hershey, Marjorie R., & Darrell M. West. (1983). "Single Issue Politics: Pro-Life Groups and Senate Campaigning in 1980." In Allan Cigler & Burdett A. Loomis, eds., *The Changing Nature of Interest Group Politics.* Washington, D.C.: Congressional Quarterly Press.

Hess, Stephen, & Michael Nelson. (1985). "Foreign Policy: Dominance and Decisiveness in Presidential Elections." In Michael Nelson, ed., *The Elections of 1984.* Washington, D.C.: Congressional Quarterly Press.

Hill, David B., & Norman R. Luttbeg. (1980). *Trends in American Electoral Behavior.* Itasca, Ill.: F. E. Peacock.

Hill, David B., & Norman R. Luttbeg. (1983). *Trends in American Electoral Behavior,* 2d ed. Itasca, Ill.: F. E. Peacock.

Hinckley, Barbara. (1980a). "The American Voter in Congressional Elections." *American Political Science Review, 74,* 641.

Hinckley, Barbara. (1980b). "House Reelections and Senate Defeats: The Role of the Challenger." *British Journal of Political Science, 10,* 441.

Hinckley, Barbara. (1981). *Congressional Elections.* Washington, D.C.: Congressional Quarterly Press.

Hofstadter, Richard. (1969). *The Idea of a Party System.* Berkeley, Calif.: University of California Press.

Holbrook, Thomas M., & Charles M. Tidmarch. (1991). "Sophomore Surge in State Legislative Elections, 1968–86." *Legislative Studies Quarterly, 16,* 49.

Hook, Janet. (1990). "Republican Contests Reflect Election Woes, Party Rift." *Congressional Quarterly Weekly Report, 48,* 3997.

House, Ernest R. (1988). *Jesse Jackson and the Politics of Charisma: The Rise and Fall of the PUSH/Excel Program.* Boulder, Colo.: Westview Press.

Hrebenar, Ronald J., & Ruth K. Scott. (1990). *Interest Group Politics in America.* Englewood Cliffs, N.J.: Prentice-Hall.

Huckshorn, Robert J. (1976). *Party Leadership in the States.* Amherst: University of Massachusetts Press.

Huckshorn, Robert J. (1985). "Who Gives It? Who Got It? The Enforcement of Campaign Finance Laws in the States." *Journal of Politics, 47,* 773.

Huckshorn, Robert J. (1991). "State Party Leaders." In L. Sandy Maisel, ed., *Political Parties and Elections in the United States: An Encyclopedia.* New York: Garland.

Huckshorn, Robert J., James L. Gibson, Cornelius P. Cotter, & John F. Bibby. (1986). "Party Integration and Party Organizational Strength." *Journal of Politics, 48,* 977.

Huckshorn, Robert J., & Robert C. Spencer. (1971). *The Politics of Defeat: Campaigning for Congress.* Amherst: University of Massachusetts Press.

Hume, David. (1976). "The Philosophical Works of David Hume." In Giovanni Sartori, ed., *Parties and Party Systems: A Framework for Analysis.* New York: Cambridge University Press.

Hurley, Patricia A. (1989). "The Senate, Representation, and Recruitment to the Presidency." Paper presented at the Annual Meeting of the American Political Science Association, Atlanta, Ga.

Idelson, Holly. (1990, November 10). "Governors Find Re-Election a Trickier Proposition." *Congressional Quarterly Weekly Report, 48,* (45).

Inglehart, Ronald, & Avram Hochstein. (1972). "Alignment and Dealignment of the Electorate in France and the United States." *Comparative Political Studies, 5,* 343.

Jackman, Robert W. (1987). "Political Institutions and Voter Turnout in Industrial Democracies." *American Political Science Review, 81,* 405.

Jackson, Brooks. (1988). *Honest Graft.* New York: Alfred Knopf.

Jackson, Brooks. (1990). *Broken Promises: Why the Federal Election Commission Failed.* New York: Priority Press Publications, The Twentieth Century Fund.

Jackson, John E. (1975). "Issues, Party Choices, and Presidential Votes." *American Journal of Political Science, 19,* 161.

Jackson, John S., Barbara Leavitt Brown, & David Bositis. (1982). "Herbert McClosky and Friends Revisited: 1980 Democratic and Republican Party Elites Compared to the Mass Public." *American Politics Quarterly, 10,* 158.

Jacob, Herbert, & Kenneth Vines, ed. (1971). *Politics in the American States: A Comparative Analysis.* Boston: Little, Brown.

Jacob, Herbert, & Kenneth Vines, eds. (1976). *Politics in the American States: A Comparative Analysis,* 2d ed. Boston: Little, Brown.

Jacobson, Gary C. (1980). *Money in Congressional Elections.* New Haven, Conn.: Yale University Press.

Jacobson, Gary C. (1981). "Congressional Elections, 1978: The Case of the Vanishing Challengers." In L. Sandy Maisel & Joseph Cooper, eds., *Congressional Elections.* Beverly Hills, Calif.: Sage.

Jacobson, Gary C. (1983). *The Politics of Congressional Elections.* Boston: Little, Brown.

Jacobson, Gary C. (1985a). "Congress: Politics after a Landslide without Coattails." In Michael Nelson, ed., *The Elections of 1984.* Washington, D.C.: Congressional Quarterly Press.

Jacobson, Gary C. (1985b). "Parties and PACs in Congressional Elections." In Lawrence D. Dodd & Bruce I. Oppenheimer, eds., *Congress Reconsidered,* 3d ed. Washington, D.C.: Congressional Quarterly Press.

Jacobson, Gary C. (1985–1986). "Party Organization and Distribution of Campaign Resources, Republicans and Democrats in 1982." *Political Science Quarterly 100,* 603.

Jacobson, Gary C. (1987a). "The Marginals Never Vanished: Incumbency and Competition in Elections to the U.S. House of Representatives, 1952–1982." *American Journal of Political Science, 31,* 126.

Jacobson, Gary C. (1987b). *The Politics of Congressional Elections*, 2d ed. Boston: Little, Brown.

Jacobson, Gary C. (1989). "Strategic Politicians and the Dynamic of House Elections, 1946–1986." *American Political Science Review, 83,* 773.

Jacobson, Gary C. (1990a). "Divided Government, Strategic Politicians, and the 1990 Congressional Elections." Paper presented at the Annual Meeting of the Midwest Political Science Association, Chicago.

Jacobson, Gary C. (1990b). "The Effects of Campaign Spending in House Elections: New Evidence for Old Arguments." *American Journal of Political Science, 34,* 334.

Jacobson, Gary C. (1990c). *The Electoral Origins of Divided Government: Competition in U.S. House Elections, 1946–1988.* Boulder, Colo.: Westview Press.

Jacobson, Gary C. (1991). "Financing Congressional Campaigns." In L. Sandy Maisel, ed., *Political Parties and Elections in the United States: An Encyclopedia.* New York: Garland.

Jacobson, Gary C. (1992). *The Politics of Congressional Elections*, 3d ed. Boston: Little, Brown.

Jacobson, Gary C., & Samuel Kernell. (1983). *Strategy and Choice in Congressional Elections.* New Haven, Conn.: Yale University Press.

Jewell, Malcolm E. (1984). *Parties and Primaries.* New York: Praeger.

Jewell, Malcolm E., & David Breaux. (1988). "The Effect of Incumbency on State Legislative Elections." *Legislative Studies Quarterly, 13,* 495.

Jewell, Malcolm E., & David Breaux. (1991). "Southern Primary and Electoral Competition and Incumbent Success." *Legislative Studies Quarterly, 16,* 129.

Jewell, Malcolm E., & David M. Olson. (1982). *American State Political Parties and Elections.* Homewood, Ill.: Dorsey.

Jewell, Malcolm E., & David M. Olson. (1988). *Political Parties and Elections in American States,* 3d ed. Chicago: Dorsey Press.

Jones, Charles O. (1970). *The Minority Party in Congress.* Boston: Little, Brown.

Jones, Charles O. (1981a). "The New, New Senate." In Ellis Sandoz & Cecil C. Crabb, Jr., eds., *A Tide of Discontent: The Elections of 1980 and Their Meaning.* Washington, D.C.: Congressional Quarterly Press.

Jones, Charles O. (1981b). "Nominating Carter's 'Favorite Opponent': The Republicans in 1980." In Austin Ranney, ed., *The American Elections of 1980.* Washington, D.C.: American Enterprise Institute.

Jones, Charles O., ed. (1988a). *The Reagan Legacy.* Chatham, N.J.: Chatham House.

Jones, Charles O. (1988b). "Ronald Reagan and the U.S. Congress: Visible-Hand Politics." In Charles O. Jones, ed., *The Reagan Legacy.* Chatham, N.J.: Chatham House.

Jones, Charles O. (1988c). *The Trusteeship Presidency: Jimmy Carter and the United States Congress.* Baton Rouge: Louisiana State University Press.

Jones, Charles O. (1989). "Presidents and Agenda Politics: Sustaining the Power of Office." Paper presented at the Annual Meeting of the American Political Science Association, Atlanta, Ga.

Jones, Ruth S. (1980). "State Public Financing and the State Parties." In Michael J. Malbin, ed., *Parties, Interest Groups, and Campaign Finance Laws.* Washington, D.C.: American Enterprise Institute for Public Policy Research.

Jones, Ruth S. (1984). "Financing State Elections." In Michael J. Malbin, ed., *Money and Politics in the United States: Financing Elections in the 1980s.* Washington, D.C.: American Enterprise Institute for Public Policy Research.

Jones, Ruth S. (1991). "Financing State Campaigns." In L. Sandy Maisel, ed., *Political Parties and Elections in the United States: An Encyclopedia.* New York: Garland.

Jordan, Hamilton. (1982). *Crisis: The Last Year of Carter's Presidency.* New York: Putnam.

Just, Marion R., W. Russell Neuman, & Ann N. Crigler. (1989). "Who Learns What from the News: Attentive Publics versus a Cognitive Elite." Paper presented at the Annual Meeting of the American Political Science Association, Atlanta, Ga.

Kayden, Xandra. (1978). *Campaign Organization.* Lexington, Mass.: Heath.

Kayden, Xandra, & Eddie Maye, Jr. (1985). *The Party Goes On.* New York: Basic Books.

Kazee, Thomas A. (1979). "The Decision to Run for Congress: Challenger Attitudes in the 1970s." Paper presented at the Annual Meeting of the Midwest Political Science Association, Chicago.

Kernell, Samuel. (1977). "Presidential Popularity and Negative Voting: An Alternative Explanation of Midterm Congressional Decline of the President's Party." *American Political Science Review, 71,* 44.

Kessel, John H. (1968). *The Goldwater Coalition: Republican Strategies in 1964.* Indianapolis: Bobbs-Merrill.

Kessel, John H. (1972). "The Issue in Issue Voting." *American Political Science Review, 66,* 459.

Kessel, John H. (1980). *Presidential Campaign Politics: Coalition Strategies and Citizen Response.* Homewood, Ill.: Dorsey.

Kessel, John H. (1984). *Presidential Campaign Politics: Coalition Strategies and Citizen Response,* 2d ed. Homewood, Ill.: Dorsey.

Kessel, John H. (1988). *Presidential Campaign Politics: Coalition Strategies and Citizen Response,* 3d ed. Homewood, Ill.: Dorsey.

Kessel, John H. (1992). *Presidential Campaign Politics: Coalition Strategies and Citizen Response,* 4th ed. Homewood, Ill.: Dorsey.

Kessel, John H., John M. Bruce, & John A. Clark. (1990). "Advocacy Parties: A Stable Feature of American Politics." Paper presented at the Annual Meeting of the American Political Science Association, San Francisco.

Kessel, John H., John A. Clark, John M. Bruce, & William G. Jacoby. (1989). "I'd Rather Switch Than Fight: Lifelong Democrats and Converts to Republicanism among Campaign Activists." Paper presented at the Annual Meeting of the American Political Science Association, Atlanta, Ga.

Key, V. O. Jr. (1955). "A Theory of Critical Elections." *Journal of Politics, 17,* 3.

Key, V. O. Jr. (1956). *American State Politics.* New York: Knopf.

Key, V. O. Jr. (1959). "Secular Realignment and the Party System." *Journal of Politics, 21,* 198.

Key, V. O. Jr. (1964). *Politics, Parties, and Pressure Groups.* New York: Crowell.

Key, V. O. Jr. (1966). *The Responsible Electorate.* Cambridge, Mass.: Harvard University Press.

Kinder, Donald R., & P. Roderick Kiewiet. (1979). "Economic Discontent and Political Behavior: The Role of Personal Grievances and Collective Economic Judgments in Congressional Voting." *Journal of Political Science, 23,* 495.

King, Anthony, ed. (1990). *The New American Political System,* 2d ed. Washington, D.C.: American Enterprise Institute Press.

King, Gary. (1989). "Representation through Legislative Redistricting: A Stochastic Model." *American Journal of Political Science, 33,* 787.

Kingdon, John W. (1984). *Agendas, Alternatives, and Public Policies.* Boston: Little, Brown.

Kirkpatrick, Jeane Jordan. (1976). *The New Presidential Elite: Men and Women in National Politics.* New York: Russell Sage Foundation.

Kirkpatrick, Jeane Jordan. (1978). *Dismantling the Parties.* Washington, D.C.: American Enterprise Institute for Public Policy Research.

Kirschten, Dick. (1985). "An Uncertain Transition." *National Journal.*

Kramer, Gerald L. (1971). "Short-Term Fluctuations in U.S. Voting Behavior. 1896–1964." *American Political Science Review, 65,* 131.

Krasno, Jonathon S., & Donald Philip Green. (1988). "Pre-empting Quality Challengers in House Elections." *Journal of Politics, 50,* 920.

Kraus, Sidney. (1962). *The Great Debates: Kennedy vs. Nixon, 1960.* Bloomington: Indiana University Press.

Ladd, Everett Carll, Jr. (1978). "The Shifting Party Coalitions—1932–1976." In Seymour M. Lipset, ed., *Emerging Coalitions in American Politics.* San Francisco: Institute for Contemporary Studies.

Ladd, Everett Carll, Jr. (1982). *Where Have All the Voters Gone? The Fracturing of America's Political Parties,* 2d ed. New York: Norton.

Ladd, Everett Carll, Jr., & Charles D. Hadley. (1975). *Transformations of the American Party System,* rev. ed. New York: Norton.

Lamb, Karl A., & Paul A. Smith. (1968). *Campaign Decision-Making: The Presidential Election of 1964.* Belmont, Calif.: Wadsworth.

Lamis, Alexander. (1984). "The Runoff Primary Controversy: Implications for Southern Politics." *PS, 17,* 782.

Lane, Robert E. (1959). *Political Life.* New York: Free Press.

Laver, Michael, & Kenneth A. Shepsle. (1990). "Divided Government: America Is Not 'Exceptional.' " Cambridge, Mass.: Center for American Political Studies, Harvard University.

Lawson, Kay. (1976). *The Comparative Study of Political Parties.* New York: St. Martin's Press.

Lazarsfeld, Paul F., Barnard Berelson, & Hazel Gaudet. (1944). *The People's Choice: How the Voter Makes Up His Mind in a Presidential Campaign.* New York: Columbia University Press.

Lemann, Nicholas. (1985). "Implications: What Americans Wanted." In Michael Nelson, ed., *The Elections of 1984.* Washington, D.C.: Congressional Quarterly Press.

Lengle, James I. (1981). *Representation of Presidential Primaries: The Democratic Party and the Post-Reform Era.* Westport, Conn.: Greenwood Press.

Lengle, James I., & Byron E. Shafer. (1980). *Presidential Politics.* New York: St. Martin's Press.

Leuthold, David A. (1968). *Electioneering in a Democracy: Campaigns for Congress.* New York: Wiley.

Light, Paul C. (1983). *The President's Agenda.* Baltimore, Md.: Johns Hopkins University Press.

Light, Paul C., & Celinda Lake. (1985). "The Election: Candidates, Strategies, and Decisions." In Michael Nelson, ed., *The Elections of 1984.* Washington, D.C.: Congressional Quarterly Press.

Longley, Lawrence D. (1989). "Changing the System: Anticipated versus Actual Results in Electoral and Legislative Reform." Paper presented at the Annual Meeting of the American Political Science Association, Atlanta, Ga.

Lowenstein, Daniel Hays. (1991a). "Campaign Finance and the Constitution." In L. Sandy Maisel, ed., *Political Parties and Elections in the United States: An Encyclopedia.* New York: Garland.

Lowenstein, Daniel Hays. (1991b). "Legislative Districting." In L. Sandy Maisel, ed., *Political Parties and Elections in the United States: An Encyclopedia*. New York: Garland.

Lowi, Theodore J. (1985). "An Aligning Election, a Presidential Plebiscite." In Michael Nelson, ed., *The Elections of 1984*. Washington, D.C.: Congressional Quarterly Press.

Luntz, Frank I. (1988). *Candidates, Consultants, and Campaigns*. Oxford: Blackwell.

Mackenzie, G. Calvin. (1991). "Partisan Presidential Leadership: The President's Appointees." In L. Sandy Maisel, ed., *The Parties Respond: Changes in the American Party System*. Boulder, Colo.: Westview Press.

MacKuen, Michael, Robert S. Erikson, & James A. Stimson. (1989). "Macropartisanship." *American Political Science Review, 77*, 957.

MacNeil, Neil. (1981). "The Struggle for the House of Representatives." In Ellis Sandoz & Cecil C. Crabb, Jr., eds., *A Tide of Discontent: The 1980 Elections and Their Meaning*. Washington, D.C.: Congressional Quarterly Press.

Magleby, David B., & Candice J. Nelson. (1990). *The Money Chase*. Washington, D.C.: Brookings.

Maisel, L. Sandy. (1982). *From Obscurity to Oblivion: Running in the Congressional Primary*. Knoxville, Tenn.: University of Tennessee Press.

Maisel, L. Sandy. (1986). *From Obscurity to Oblivion: Running in the Congressional Primary*, 2d ed. Knoxville, Tenn.: University of Tennessee Press.

Maisel, L. Sandy. (1988). "Spending Patterns in Presidential Nominating Campaigns, 1976–1988." Paper presented at the Annual Meeting of the American Political Science Association, Washington; Occasional Paper no. 88-6, Center for American Political Studies, Harvard University, Cambridge, Mass.

Maisel, L. Sandy. (1989). "Challenger Quality and the Outcome of the 1988 Congressional Elections." Paper presented at the Annual Meeting of the Midwest Political Science Association, Chicago.

Maisel, L. Sandy. (1990a). "Congressional Elections: Quality Candidates in House and Senate Elections, 1982–1988." Paper presented at the "Back to the Future: The United States Congress at the Bicentennial" Conference at the Carl Albert Congressional Research and Studies Center, the University of Oklahoma, Norman.

Maisel, L. Sandy. (1990b). "The Incumbency Advantage." In Margaret Latus Nugent & John R. Johannes, eds., *Money, Elections, and Democracy: Reforming Congressional Campaign Finance*. Boulder, Colo.: Westview Press.

Maisel, L. Sandy, ed. (1990c). *The Parties Respond: Changes in the American Party System*. Boulder, Colo.: Westview Press.

Maisel, L. Sandy, ed. (1991). *Political Parties and Elections in the United States: An Encyclopedia*. New York: Garland.

Maisel, L. Sandy, & Joseph Cooper. (1981). *Congressional Elections*. Beverly Hills, Calif.: Sage.

Maisel, L. Sandy, Linda L. Fowler, Ruth S. Jones, & Walter J. Stone. (1990). "The Naming of Candidates: Recruitment or Emergence." In L. Sandy Maisel, ed., *The Parties Respond: Changes in the American Party System*. Boulder, Colo.: Westview Press.

Maisel, Louis. (1975). "Party Reform and Political Participation: The Democrats in Maine." In Louis Maisel & Paul M. Sacks, eds., *The Future of Political Parties*. Beverly Hills, Calif.: Sage.

Maisel, Louis, & Joseph Cooper, eds. (1977). *The Impact of the Electoral Process*. Beverly Hills, Calif.: Sage.

Maisel, Louis, & Paul M. Sacks, eds. (1975). *The Future of Political Parties*. Beverly Hills, Calif.: Sage.

Malbin, Michael J. (1980). *Parties, Interest Groups and Campaign Finance Laws*. Washington, D.C.: American Enterprise Institute for Public Policy Research.

Malbin, Michael J. (1981). "The Conventions, Platforms, and Issue Activists." In Austin Ranney, ed., *The American Elections of 1980*. Washington, D.C.: American Enterprise Institute for Public Policy Research.

Malbin, Michael J. (1984a). "Looking Back at the Future of Campaign Finance Reform: Interest Groups and American Elections." In Michael J. Malbin, ed., *Money and Politics in the United States: Financing Elections in the 1980s*. Washington, D.C.: American Enterprise Institute for Public Policy Research.

Malbin, Michael J., ed. (1984b). *Money and Politics in the United States: Financing Elections in the 1980's*. Washington, D.C.: American Enterprise Institute for Public Policy Research.

Malbin, Michael J. (1985). "You Get What You Pay For, but Is That What You Want?" In George Grassmuck, ed., *Before Nomination: Our Primary Problem*. Washington, D.C.: American Enterprise Institute for Public Policy Research.

Mann, Thomas E. (1985). "Elected Officials and the Politics of Presidential Selection." In Austin Ranney, ed., *The American Elections of 1984*. Durham, N.C.: Duke University Press.

Mann, Thomas E., & Norman J. Ornstein. (1981). "The Republican Surge in Congress." In Austin Ranney, ed., *The American Elections of 1980*. Washington, D.C.: American Enterprise Institute for Public Policy Research.

Mann, Thomas E., & Raymond E. Wolfinger. (1980). "Candidates and Parties in Congressional Elections." *American Political Science Review, 74*, 617.

Marchant-Shapiro, Theresa, & Christopher H. Achen. (1990). "Do Party Elites Pick Better Presidential Candidates Than Primary Voters?" Paper presented at the Annual Meeting of the American Political Science Association, San Francisco.

Masters, Marick F., & Gerald D. Keim. (1985). "Determinants of PAC Participation among Large Corporations." *Journal of Politics, 47*, 1158.

Mattei, Franco, & Richard G. Niemi. (1991). "Unrealized Partisans, Realized Independents, and the Intergenerational Transmission of Partisan Identification." *Journal of Politics, 53*, 161.

Matthews, Donald. (1978). "Winnowing: The News Media and the 1976 Presidential Nominations." In James D. Barber, ed., *Race for the Presidency*. Englewood Cliffs, N.J.: Prentice-Hall.

May, Ernest R., & Janet Fraser. (1973). *Campaign '72: The Managers Speak*. Cambridge, Mass.: Harvard University Press.

Mayhew, David R. (1974a). *Congress: The Electoral Connection*. New Haven, Conn.: Yale University Press.

Mayhew, David R. (1974b). "Congressional Elections: The Case of the Vanishing Marginals." *Polity, 6*, 295.

Mayhew, David R. (1986). *Placing Parties in American Politics*. Princeton, N.J.: Princeton University Press.

Mazmanian, Daniel A. (1974). *Third Parties in Presidential Elections*. Washington, D.C.: Brookings Institution.

McFarland, Andrew S. (1984). *Common Cause*. Chatham, N.J.: Chatham House.

McGinniss, Joe. (1969). *The Selling of the President 1968*. New York: Trident Press.

Mendelsohn, Harold, & Irving Crespi. (1970). *Polls, Television, and the New Politics*. Scranton, Pa.: Chandler, 1970.

Mezey, Michael L. (1989). "Congress within the United States Presidential System." Paper presented at the Annual Meeting of the American Political Science Association, Atlanta, Ga.

Milbrath, Lester W. (1963). *The Washington Lobbyists*. Chicago: Rand McNally.

Milbrath, Lester W., & M. L. Goel. (1977). *Political Participation: How and Why Do People Get Involved in Politics?* Chicago: Rand McNally.

Mileur, Jerome. (1991). "Party Renewal." In L. Sandy Maisel, ed., *Political Parties and Elections in the United States: An Encyclopedia*. New York: Garland.

Miller, Arthur H. (1978). "The Majority Party Reunited? A Comparison of the 1972 and 1976 Elections." In Jeff Fishel, ed., *Parties and Elections in an Anti-Party Age*. Bloomington, Ind.: Indiana University Press.

Miller, Arthur H., & Warren E. Miller. (1977). "Partisanship and Performance: 'Rational' Choice in the 1976 Presidential Elections." Paper presented at the Annual Meeting of the American Political Science Association, Washington, D.C.

Miller, Arthur H., Warren E. Miller, Aldern S. Raine, & Thad E. Brown. (1976). "A Majority Party in Disarray: Policy Polarization in the 1972 Election." *American Political Science Review, 70,* 753.

Miller, Arthur H., & Martin P. Wattenberg. (1985). "Throwing the Rascals Out: Policy and Performance Evaluations of Presidential Candidates, 1952–1980." *American Political Science Review, 79,* 359.

Miller, Warren E. (1985a). "The Election of 1984 and the Future of American Politics." Paper presented at the Thomas P. O'Neill, Jr., Symposium on Elections in America, Boston College, Chestnut Hill, Mass.

Miller, Warren E. (1985b). "Participants in the Nominating Process: The Voters, the Political Activists." In George Grassmuck, ed., *Before Nomination: Our Primary Problem*. Washington, D.C.: American Enterprise Institute for Public Policy Research.

Miller, Warren E. (1990). "The Electorate's View of the Parties." In L. Sandy Maisel, ed., *The Parties Respond: Changes in the American Party System*. Boulder, Colo.: Westview Press.

Miller, Warren E. (1991a). "Party Identification." In L. Sandy Maisel, ed., *Political Parties and Elections in the United States: An Encyclopedia*. New York: Garland.

Miller, Warren E. (1991b). "Party Identification, Realignment, and Party Voting: Back to Basics." *American Political Science Review, 85,* 557.

Miller, Warren E. (1992). "The Puzzle Transformed: Explaining Declining Turnout." *Political Behavior, 14.*

Miller, Warren E., & Teresa E. Levitin. (1976). *Leadership and Change: Presidential Elections from 1952 to 1976*. Cambridge, Mass.: Winthrop.

Miller, Warren E., Arthur H. Miller, & Edward J. Schneider. (1980). *American National Election Studies Data Sourcebook, 1952–1978*. Cambridge, Mass.: Harvard University Press.

Miller, Warren E., & Merrill Shanks. (1982). "Policy Directions and Presidential Leadership: Alternative Interpretations of the 1980 Presidential Elections." *British Journal of Political Science, 12,* 266.

Miller, Warren E., & Donald S. Stokes. (1963). "Constituency Influence in Congress." *American Political Science Review, 57,* 45.

Miroff, Bruce. (1980). "Presidential Campaigns: Candidates, Managers and Reporters." *Polity, 12,* 667.

Moncrief, Gary F. (1990). "The Increase in Campaign Expenditures in State Legislative

Elections: A Comparison of Four Northwestern States." Paper presented at the Annual Meeting of the American Political Science Association, San Francisco.

Moore, Jonathan. (1981). *The Campaign for President: 1980 in Retrospect.* Cambridge, Mass.: Ballinger.

Moore, Jonathan, & Janet Fraser, eds. (1977). *Campaign for President: The Managers Look at 1976.* Cambridge, Mass.: Ballinger.

Morehouse, Sarah McCally. (1980). "The Effect of Preprimary Endorsements on State Party Strength." Paper presented at the Annual Meeting of the American Political Science Association, Washington, D.C.

Mutch, Robert E. (1988). *Campaigns, Congress, and Courts: The Making of Federal Campaign Finance Law.* New York: Praeger.

Napolitan, Joseph. (1972). *The Election Game and How to Win It.* Garden City, N.Y.: Doubleday.

Nelson, Candice J. (1990). "Loose Cannons: Independent Expenditures." In Margaret Latus Nugent & John R. Johannes, eds., *Money, Elections, and Democracy: Reforming Congressional Campaign Finance.* Boulder, Colo.: Westview Press.

Nelson, Michael, ed. (1985). *The Elections of 1984.* Washington, D.C.: Congressional Quarterly Press.

Nelson, Michael, ed. (1989). *The Elections of 1988.* Washington, D.C.: Congressional Quarterly Press.

Neumann, Sigmund, ed. (1956). *Modern Political Parties: Approaches to Comparative Politics.* Chicago: University of Chicago Press.

Neustadt, Richard E. (1976). *Presidential Power: The Politics of Leadership with Reflections on Johnson and Nixon.* New York: Wiley.

Nie, Norman H., Sidney Verba, & John R. Petrocik. (1976). *The Changing American Voter.* Cambridge, Mass.: Harvard University Press.

Nie, Norman H., Sidney Verba, & John R. Petrocik. (1979). *The Changing American Voter,* enlarged ed. Cambridge, Mass.: Harvard University Press.

Niemi, Richard G., & Larry M. Bartels. (1985). "The Efficacy of Registration Drives." *Journal of Politics, 4,* 1212.

Niemi, Richard G., & Simon Jackson. (1991). "Bias and Responsiveness in State Legislative Districting." *Legislative Studies Quarterly, 16,* 183.

Niemi, Richard G., Simon Jackson, & Laura R. Winsky. (1991). "Candidacies and Competitiveness in Multimember Districts." *Legislative Studies Quarterly, 16,* 91.

Niemi, Richard G., & M. Kent Jennings. (1991). "Issues and Inheritance in the Formation of Party Identification." *American Journal of Political Science,* forthcoming.

Niemi, Richard G., & Herbert F. Weisberg, eds. (1976). *Controversies in American Voting Behavior.* San Francisco: Freeman.

Niemi, Richard G., & Herbert F. Weisberg, eds. (1984). *Controversies in American Voting Behavior,* 2d ed. Washington, D.C.: Congressional Quarterly Press.

Niemi, Richard G., Stephen Wright, & Linda W. Powell. (1987). "Multiple Party Identifiers and the Measurement of Party Identification." *Journal of Politics, 49,* 1093.

Noragon, Jack L. (1981). "Political Finance and Political Reform: The Experience with State Income Tax Checkoffs." *American Political Science Review, 75,* 667.

Norpoth, Helmut. (1987). "Under Way and Here to Stay: Party Realignment in the 1980s?" *Public Opinion Quarterly, 51,* 376.

Nugent, Margaret Latus, & John R. Johannes, eds. (1990). *Money, Elections, and Democracy: Reforming Congressional Finance.* Boulder, Colo.: Westview Press.

Obey Commission (1977). *Final Report of the Commission on Administrative Review,* United States House of Representatives, David R. Obey, Chairman, 95th

Congress, 1st Session. Washington, D.C.: United States Government Printing Office.

Oleszek, Walter J. (1989). *Congressional Procedures and the Policy Process*, 3d ed. Washington, D.C.: Congressional Quarterly Press.

One Hundred Leading National Advertisers. (1984). *Advertising Age.*

Oppenheimer, Bruce I., James A. Stimson, & Richard W. Waterman. (1986). "Interpreting U.S. Congressional Elections: The Exposure Theory." *Legislative Studies Quarterly, 11,* 227.

Ornstein, Norman J. (1975). "Causes and Consequences of Congressional Change: Subcommittee Reforms in the House of Representatives." In Norman J. Ornstein, ed., *Congress in Change.* New York: Praeger.

Ornstein, Norman J., Thomas E. Mann, & Michael J. Malbin. (1990). *Vital Statistics on Congress, 1989–1990.* Washington, D.C.: Congressional Quarterly.

Ornstein, Norman J., Thomas E. Mann, & Michael J. Malbin. (1992). *Vital Statistics on Congress, 1991–1992.* Washington, D.C.: Congressional Quarterly.

Ornstein, Norman J., Thomas E. Mann, Michael J. Malbin, Allen Schick, & John F. Bibby. (1985). *Vital Statistics on Congress, 1984–1985 Edition.* Washington, D.C.: American Enterprise Institute for Public Policy Research.

Ornstein, Norman J., & David W. Rohde. (1978). "Political Parties and Congressional Reform." In Jeff Fishel, ed., *Parties and Elections in an Anti-Party Age.* Bloomington, Ind.: Indiana University Press.

Orren, Gary R. (1985). "The Nomination Process: Vicissitudes of Candidate Selection." In Michael Nelson, ed., *The Elections of 1984.* Washington, D.C.: Congressional Quarterly Press.

Orren, Gary R., & Nelson W. Polsby. (1987). *Media and Momentum: The New Hampshire Primary and Nomination Politics.* Chatham, N.J.: Chatham House.

Overacker, Louise. (1932). *Money in Elections.* New York: Macmillan.

Page, Benjamin I. (1978). *Choices and Echoes in Presidential Elections: Rational Man and Electoral Democracy.* Chicago: University of Chicago Press.

Parker, Glenn R., & Suzanne L. Parker. (1989). "Why Do We Trust Our Congressman and Does It Matter?" Paper presented at the Annual Meeting of the American Political Science Association, Atlanta, Ga.

Parris, Judith. (1972). *The Convention Problem.* Washington, D.C.: Brookings Institution.

Patterson, Samuel C. (1984). "The Etiology of Party Competition." *American Political Science Review, 78,* 691.

Patterson, Samuel C., & Gregory A. Caldeira. (1983). "Getting Out the Vote: Participation in Gubernatorial Elections." *American Political Science Review, 77,* 495.

Patterson, Thomas E. (1980). *The Mass Media Election: How Americans Choose Their President.* New York: Praeger.

Patterson, Thomas E. (1990). *The American Democracy.* New York: McGraw-Hill.

Patterson, Thomas E., & Richard Davis. (1985). "The Media Campaign: Struggle for the Agenda." In Michael Nelson, ed., *The Elections of 1984.* Washington, D.C.: Congressional Quarterly Press.

Patterson, Thomas E., & Robert D. McClure. (1976). *The Unseeing Eye: The Myth of Television Power in National Politics.* New York: Putnam.

Peabody, Robert L. (1976). *Leadership in Congress: Stability, Succession, and Change.* Boston: Little, Brown.

Perry, H. W., Jr. (1991). "Racial Vote Dilution Cases." In L. Sandy Maisel, ed., *Political Parties and Elections in the United States: An Encyclopedia.* New York: Garland.

Peters, Ronald M., Jr. (1990). *The American Speakership: The Office in Historical Perspective.* Baltimore, Md.: Johns Hopkins University Press.

Petracca, Mark P., & Pamela A. Smith. (1989). "Please Don't Bring Back My Party to Me." Paper presented at the Annual Meeting of the American Political Science Association, Atlanta, Ga.

Petrocik, John R. (1987). "Realignment: New Party Coalitions and the Nationalization of the South." *Journal of Politics, 49,* 347.

Petrocik, John R. (1989). "Issues and Agendas: Electoral Coalitions in the 1988 Election." Paper presented at the Annual Meeting of the American Political Science Association, Atlanta, Ga.

Petrocik, John R., & Frederick T. Steeper. (1987). "The Political Landscape in 1988." *Public Opinion, 10,* 41.

Pfau, Michael, & Henry C. Kenski. (1990). *Attack Politics: Strategy and Defense.* New York: Praeger.

Pitney, John J., Jr. (1990). "Republican Party Leadership in the U.S. House." Paper prepared for the Annual Meeting of the American Political Science Association, San Francisco.

Piven, Frances Fox, & Richard A. Cloward. (1988). *Why Americans Don't Vote.* New York: Pantheon.

Piven, Frances Fox, & Richard A. Cloward. (1989). Governmental Statistics and Conflicting Explanations of Nonvoting." *PS, 22,* 580.

Piven, Frances Fox, & Richard A. Cloward. (1990). "A Reply to Bennett." *PS, 23,* 172.

Polsby, Nelson W., ed. (1971). *Reapportionment in the 1970s.* Berkeley: University of California Press.

Polsby, Nelson W. (1981). "The Democratic Nomination." In Austin Ranney, ed., *The American Elections of 1980.* Washington, D.C.: American Enterprise Institute for Public Policy Research.

Polsby, Nelson W. (1983). *Consequences of Party Reform.* New York: Oxford University Press.

Polsby, Nelson W., & Aaron Wildavsky. (1984). *Presidential Elections,* 6th ed. New York: Scribner.

Polsby, Nelson W., & Aaron Wildavsky. (1988). *Presidential Elections,* 7th ed. New York: Scribner.

Polsby, Nelson W., & Aaron Wildavsky. (1991). *Presidential Elections,* 8th ed. New York: Scribner.

Pomper, Gerald M. (1972). "From Confusion to Clarity: Issues and American Voters, 1952–1968." *American Political Science Review, 66,* 415.

Pomper, Gerald M. (1973). *Elections in America.* New York: Dodd, Mead, and Company.

Pomper, Gerald M. (1975). *Voter's Choice: Varieties of American Electoral Behavior.* New York: Dodd, Mead, and Company.

Pomper, Gerald M. (1977). "The Nominating Contests and Conventions." In Gerald M. Pomper, ed., *The Election of 1976: Reports and Interpretations.* New York: David McKay Company.

Pomper, Gerald M. (1980). *Party Renewal in America.* New York: Praeger.

Pomper, Gerald M. (1981a). *The Election of 1980: Reports and Interpretations.* Chatham, N.J.: Chatham House Publishers.

Pomper, Gerald M. (1981b). "The Nominating Contests." In Gerald M. Pomper, ed., *The Election of 1980: Reports and Interpretations.* Chatham, N.J.: Chatham House.

Pomper, Gerald M. (1985). *The Election of 1984: Reports and Interpretations.* Chatham, N.J.: Chatham House.

Pomper, Gerald M., ed. (1989a). *The Election of 1988: Reports and Interpretations.* Chatham, N.J.: Chatham House.

Pomper, Gerald M. (1989b). "The Presidential Nominations." In Gerald M. Pomper, ed., *The Election of 1988: Reports and Interpretations.* Chatham, N.J.: Chatham House.

Pomper, Gerald M., with Susan S. Lederman. (1980). *Elections in America,* 2d ed. New York: Longman.

Poole, Keith T., & R. Steven Daniels. (1985). "Ideology, Party, and Voting in the U.S. Congress, 1959–1980." *American Political Science Review, 79,* 373.

Porter, K. H. (1918). *A History of Suffrage in the United States.* Chicago: University of Chicago Press.

Powell, G. Bingham. (1986). "American Voter Turnout in Comparative Perspective." *American Political Science Review, 80,* 17.

President's Commission on Campaign Costs. (1962). *Financing Presidential Campaigns.* Washington, D.C.

Price, David E. (1984). *Bringing back the Parties.* Washington, D.C.: Congressional Quarterly Press.

Prysby, Charles. (1989). "Congressional Elections in the American South." Paper presented at the Annual Meeting of the American Political Science Association, Atlanta, Ga.

Quirk, Paul J. (1985). "The Economy: Economists, Electoral Politics, and Reagan Economics." In Michael Nelson, ed., *The Elections of 1984.* Washington, D.C.: Congressional Quarterly Press.

Rakove, Milton L. (1975). *Don't Make No Waves . . . Don't Back No Losers.* Bloomington: Indiana University Press.

Ranney, Austin. (1962). *The Doctrine of Responsible Party Government: Its Origins and Present State.* Urbana: University of Illinois Press.

Ranney, Austin, & Leon D. Epstein. (1966). "The Two Electorates: Voters and Nonvoters in a Wisconsin Primary." *Journal of Politics, 28,* 598.

Ranney, Austin. (1968). "The Representativeness of Primary Electorates." *Midwest Journal of Political Science, 12,* 224.

Ranney, Austin. (1975). *Curing the Mischiefs of Faction: Party Reform in America.* Berkeley: University of California Press.

Ranney, Austin. (1979). *The Past and Future of Presidential Debates.* Washington, D.C.: American Enterprise Institute for Public Policy Research.

Ranney, Austin, ed. (1981). *The American Elections of 1980.* Washington, D.C.: American Enterprise Institute for Public Policy Research.

Ranney, Austin. (1983). *Channels of Power.* New York: Basic Books.

Ranney, Austin, ed. (1985). *The American Elections of 1984.* Durham, N.C.: Duke University Press.

Ranney, Austin. (1990). "Broadcasting, Narrowcasting, and Politics." In Anthony King, ed., *The New American Political System,* 2d ed. Washington, D.C.: American Enterprise Institute Press.

Rapoport, Ronald B., Walter J. Stone, & Alan I. Abramowitz. (1991). "Do Endorsements Matter? Group Influence in the 1984 Democratic Caucuses." *American Political Science Review, 5,* 193.

Reed, Adolph L., Jr. (1986). *The Jesse Jackson Phenomenon.* New Haven, Conn.: Yale University Press.

Reichley, A. James. (1985). "The Rise of the National Parties." In John E. Clubb & Paul E. Peterson, eds., *The New Directions in American Politics*. Washington, D.C.: Brookings.

Reiter, Howard L. (1985). *Selecting the President: The Nominating Process in Transition*. Philadelphia: University of Pennsylvania Press.

Riordan, William L., ed. (1963). *Plunkitt of Tammany Hall*. New York: Dutton.

Ripley, Randall B. (1964). "The Whip Organizations in the United States House of Representatives." *American Political Science Review, 58,* 561.

Ripley, Randall B. (1967). *Party Leaders in the House of Representatives*. Washington, D.C.: Brookings Institution.

Ripley, Randall B. (1990). "Congress and the President: Stability and Change." Paper presented at the Annual Meeting of the American Political Science Association, San Francisco.

Robinson, Michael, & Margaret Sheehan. (1983). *Over the Wire and on TV*. New York: Russell Sage Foundation.

Roche, John P. (1961). "The Founding Fathers: A Reform Caucus in Action." *American Political Science Review, 55.*

Rohde, David W. (1974). "Committee Reform in the House of Representatives and the 'Subcommittee Bill of Rights.' " *Annals, 411,* 39.

Rohde, David W. (1989). "Democratic Party Leadership, Agenda Control and the Resurgence of Partisanship in the House." Paper presented at the Annual Meeting of the American Political Science Association, Atlanta, Ga.

Rohde, David W. (1991). *Parties and Leaders in the Post-Reform House*. Chicago: University of Chicago Press.

Rohde, David W. (1992). "Electoral Forces, Political Agendas, and Partisanship in the House and Senate." In Roger H. Davidson, ed., *The Postreform Congress*. New York: St. Martin's.

Roll, Charles W., Jr., & Albert H. Cantril. (1972). *Polls: Their Use and Misuse in Politics*. New York: Basic Books.

Rosenstone, Steven J., & Raymond E. Wolfinger. (1978). "The Effect of Registration Laws on Voter Turnout." *American Political Science Review, 72,* 27.

Rothenberg, Stuart. (1983). *Winners and Losers: Campaigns, Candidates, and Congressional Elections*. Washington, D.C.: Free Congress Research and Education Foundation.

Royko, Mike. (1971). *Boss: Richard J. Daley of Chicago*. New York: Dutton.

Runkel, David B., ed. (1989). *Campaign for President: The Managers Look at '88*. Dover, Mass.: Auburn House.

Sabato, Larry J. (1981). *The Rise of Political Consultants*. New York: Basic Books.

Sabato, Larry J. (1985). *PAC Power: Inside the World of Political Action Committees*. New York: Norton.

Sabato, Larry J. (1988). *The Party's Just Begun: Shaping Political Parties for America's Future*. Glenview, Ill.: Scott, Foresman.

Sabato, Larry J. (1989). *Paying for Elections: The Campaign Finance Thicket*. New York: Priority Press Publications, The Twentieth Century Fund.

Salmore, Stephen A., & Barbara G. Salmore. (1985). *Candidates, Parties, and Campaigns*. Washington, D.C.: Congressional Quarterly Press.

Sartori, Giovanni. (1976). *Parties and Party Systems: A Framework for Analysis*. Cambridge: Cambridge University Press.

Schattschneider, E. E. (1942). *Party Government*. New York: Holt, Rinehart, and Winston.

Schattschneider, E. E. (1960). *The Semisovereign People*. Hinsdale, Ill.: Dryden.

Schlesinger, Joseph A. (1966). *Ambition and Politics: Political Careers in the United States*. Chicago: Rand McNally.

Schlesinger, Joseph A. (1985). "The New American Political Party." *American Political Science Review, 79*, 1152.

Schlozman, Kay L., & John T. Tierney. (1986). *Organized Interests and American Democracy*. New York: Harper & Row.

Schneider, William. (1981). "The November 4th Vote for President: What Did It Mean." In Austin Ranney, ed., *The American Elections of 1980*. Washington, D.C.: American Enterprise Institute for Public Policy Research.

Schneider, William. (1988). "The Political Legacy of the Reagan Years." In Sidney Blumenthal & Thomas Byrne Edsall, eds., *The Republican Legacy*. New York: Pantheon.

Schram, Martin. (1977). *Running for President, 1976: The Carter Campaign*. New York: Stein and Day.

Schroedel, Jean Reith. (1986). "Campaign Contributions and Legislative Outcomes." *Western Political Quarterly, 39*, 371.

Schuck, Peter H. (1987). "The Thickest Thicket: Partisan Gerrymandering and Judicial Regulation of Politics." *Columbia Law Review, 87*, 1325.

Seligman, Lester. (1974). *Patterns of Recruitment: A State Chooses Its Law-Makers*. Chicago: Rand McNally.

Shafer, Byron E. (1983). *Quiet Revolution: The Struggle for the Democratic Party and the Shaping of Post-Reform Politics*. New York: Russell Sage Foundation.

Shafer, Byron E. (1988). *Bifurcated Politics: Evolution and Reform in the National Nominating Convention*. Cambridge, Mass.: Harvard University Press.

Shaffer, Stephen D., & George A. Chressanthis. (1990). "Accountability in U.S. Senate Elections: Implications for Governance." Paper presented at the Annual Meeting of the American Political Science Association, San Francisco.

Shanks, J. Merrill, & Warren E. Miller. (1989). "Alternative Interpretations of the 1988 Election: Policy Direction, Current Conditions, Presidential Performance, and Candidate Traits." Paper presented at the Annual Meeting of the American Political Science Association, Atlanta, Ga.

Shanks, J. Merrill, & Warren E. Miller. (1990). "Policy Direction and Performance Evaluation: Contemporary Explanations of the Reagan Elections." *British Journal of Political Science, 20*, 143.

Shanks, J. Merrill, & Warren E. Miller. (1991). "Partisanship, Policy, and Performance: The Reagan Legacy in the 1988 Election." *British Journal of Political Science, 21*, 129.

Sheppard, Burton D. (1985). *Rethinking Congressional Reform*. Cambridge, Mass.: Schenkman.

Sigelman, Lee. (1982). "The Nonvoting Voter in Voting Research." *American Journal Political Science, 26*, 47.

Sigelman, Lee, Philip W. Roeder, Malcolm E. Jewell, & Michael A. Baer. (1985). "Voting and Nonvoting: A Multi-Election Perspective." *American Journal Political Science, 29*, 749.

Silbey, Joel H. (1990). "The Rise and Fall of American Political Parties." In L. Sandy Maisel, ed., *The Parties Respond: Changes in the American Party System*. Boulder, Colo.: Westview Press.

Silbey, Joel H. (1991). *The American Political Nation, 1838–1893*. Stanford, Calif.: Stanford University Press.

Sinclair, Barbara. (1983). *Majority Party Leadership in the U.S. House.* Baltimore, Md.: Johns Hopkins University Press.

Sinclair, Barbara. (1989). *The Transformation of the U.S. Senate.* Baltimore, Md.: Johns Hopkins University Press.

Sinclair, Barbara. (1990). "The Congressional Party: Evolving Organizational, Agenda-Setting, and Policy Roles." In L. Sandy Maisel, ed., *The Parties Respond: Changes in the American Party System.* Boulder, Colo.: Westview Press.

Smith, Gregg W. (1990). "Party Organizations and Voter Turnout: The 1988 Elections." Paper presented at the Annual Meeting of the American Political Science Association, San Francisco.

Smith, Steven S., & Christopher J. Deering. (1990). *Committees in Congress,* 2d ed. Washington, D.C.: Congressional Quarterly Press.

Snowiss, Leo M. (1966). "Congressional Recruitment and Representation." *American Political Science Review, 60,* 627.

Sonenshein, Raphael J. (1990). "Can Black Candidates Win Statewide Elections?" *Political Science Quarterly, 105,* 219.

Sorauf, Frank J. (1980). *Party Politics in America.* Boston: Little, Brown.

Sorauf, Frank J. (1984a). "Political Action Committees in American Politics: An Overview." In Twentieth Century Fund, *What Price PACs?* New York: Twentieth Century Fund.

Sorauf, Frank J. (1984b). "Who's in Charge? Accountability in Political Action Committees." *Political Science Quarterly, 99,* 591.

Sorauf, Frank J. (1988). *Money in American Elections.* Glenview, Ill.: Scott, Foresman.

Sorauf, Frank J. (1990). "Political Organizations: Concepts and Categories." Paper presented at the Annual Meeting of the American Political Science Association, San Francisco.

Sorauf, Frank J. (1991). "Political Action Committees." In L. Sandy Maisel, ed., *Political Parties and Elections in the United States: An Encyclopedia.* New York: Garland.

Sorauf, Frank J., & Paul A. Beck. (1988). *Party Politics in America,* 6th ed. Glenview, Ill.: Scott, Foresman.

Sparks, Jared, ed. (1840). *The Writings of George Washington.* Boston: F. Andrews.

Spitzer, Robert J. (1987). *The Right to Life Movement and Third Party Politics.* Westport, Conn.: Greenwood.

Squire, Peverill, Raymond E. Wolfinger, & David P. Glass. (1985). "Residential Mobility and Voter Turnout." Paper presented at the Annual Meeting of the American Political Science Association, New Orleans, La.

Squire, Peverill, Raymond E. Wolfinger, & David P. Glass. (1987). "Residential Mobility and Voter Turnout." *American Political Science Review, 81,* 45.

Stanley, Harold W. (1985). "The Runoff: The Case for Retention." *PS, 18,* 231.

Stanley, Harold W., William T. Bianco, & Richard G. Niemi. (1985). "A New Perspective on Partisanship and Group Support over Time." Paper presented at the Annual Meeting of the American Political Science Association, New Orleans, La.

Stanley, Harold W., William T. Bianco, & Richard G. Niemi. (1986). "Partisanship and Group Support over Time: A Multivariate Analysis." *American Political Science Review, 80,* 969.

Stanley, Harold W., & Richard G. Niemi. (1989). "Partisanship and Group Support." Paper presented at the Annual Meeting of the American Political Science Association, Atlanta, Ga.

Stanley, Harold W., & Richard G. Niemi. (1990). *Vital Statistics on American Politics,* 2d ed. Washington, D.C.: Congressional Quarterly.

Steinberg, Alfred. (1972). *The Bosses*. New York: Macmillan.

Stern, Philip M. (1988). *The Best Congress Money Can Buy*. New York: Pantheon Books.

Stewart, Charles III. (1990). "Responsiveness in the Upper Chamber: The Constitution and Institutional Development in the Senate." Paper presented at the Annual Meeting of the Midwest Political Science Association, Chicago.

Stewart, John G. (1991). "Democratic National Committee." In L. Sandy Maisel, ed., *Political Parties and Elections in the United States: An Encyclopedia*. New York: Garland.

Stokes, Donald E., & Warren E. Miller. (1962). "Party Government and the Saliency of Congress." *Public Opinion Quarterly, 26,* 531.

Stone, Walter J., Ronald B. Rapoport, & Alan I. Abramowitz. (1989). "The Reagan Revolution and Party Polarization in the 1980s." Paper presented at the Annual Meeting of the American Political Science Association, Atlanta, Ga.

Stone, Walter J., Ronald B. Rapoport, & Alan I. Abramowitz. (1990). "Candidate Perception among Nomination Activists: A New Look at the Moderation Hypothesis." Paper presented at the American Political Science Annual Meeting, San Francisco.

Sullivan, Denis G., Robert T. Nakamura, Martha Wagner Weinberg, F. Christopher Arterton, & Jeffrey L. Pressman. (1977–1978). "Exploring the 1976 Republican Convention." *Political Science Quarterly, 92,* 531.

Sullivan, Denis G., Jeffrey L. Pressman, & F. Christopher Arterton. (1976). *Explorations in Convention Decision Making: The Democratic Party in the 1970s*. San Francisco: Freeman.

Sullivan, Denis G., Jeffrey L. Pressman, F. Christopher Arterton, Robert T. Nakamura, & Martha Wagner Weinberg. (1977). "Candidates, Caucuses, and Issues: The Democratic Convention, 1976." In Louis Maisel & Joseph Cooper, eds., *The Impact of the Electoral Process*. Beverly Hills, Calif.: Sage Publications.

Sullivan, Denis G., Jeffrey L. Pressman, Benjamin I. Page, & John J. Lyons. (1974). *The Politics of Representation: The Democratic Convention 1972*. New York: St. Martin's Press.

Sundquist, James L. (1983). *Dynamics of the Party System: Alignment and Realignment of Political Parties in the United States*, rev. ed. Washington, D.C.: Brookings Institution.

Sundquist, James L. (1988). "Needed: A Political Theory for the New Era of Coalition Government in the United States." *Political Science Quarterly, 103,* 613.

Sussman, Barry. (1984). "How Can Labor Ties Hurt Mondale if Americans Cherish Unions?" *Washington Post National Weekly Edition, 1* (20).

Taggart, William A., & Robert F. Durant. (1985). "Home Style of a U.S. Senator: A Longitudinal Study." *Legislative Studies Quarterly, 10,* 489.

Tarrance, V. Lance. (1978). "Suffrage and Voter Turnout in the United States: The Vanishing Voter." In Jeff Fishel, ed., *Parties and Elections in an Anti-Party Age*. Bloomington, Ind.: Indiana University Press.

Texeira, Ruy. (1987). *Why Americans Don't Vote*. New York: Greenwood.

Thayer, George. (1973). *Who Shakes the Money Tree?* New York: Simon and Schuster.

Thurber, James A. (1991). *Divided Government*. Washington, D.C.: Congressional Quarterly Press.

Tolchin, Martin, & Susan Tolchin. (1971). *To the Victor . . . Political Patronage from the Clubhouse to the White House*. New York: Vintage Books.

Traugott, Michael W. (1985). "The Media and the Nominating Process." In George Grassmuck, ed., *Before Nomination: Our Primary Problem*. Washington, D.C.: American Enterprise Institute for Public Policy Research.

Truman, David B. (1951). *The Governmental Process.* New York: Knopf.

Tufte, Edward E. (1975). "Determinants of the Outcomes of Midterm Congressional Elections." *American Political Science Review, 69,* 312.

Tufte, Edward E. (1978). *Political Control of the Economy.* Princeton, N.J.: Princeton University Press.

Twentieth Century Fund. (1984). *What Price PAC?* New York: Twentieth Century Fund.

Uslaner, Eric. (1981). "'Ain't Misbehavin': The Logic of Defensive Issue Voting Strategies in Congressional Elections." *American Politics Quarterly, 9,* 3.

Verba, Sidney, & Norman H. Nie. (1972). *Participation in America: Political Democracy and Social Equality.* New York: Harper & Row.

Walker, Jack L. (1983). "The Origins and Maintenance of Interest Groups in America." *American Political Science Review, 77,* 390.

Walters, Ronald W. (1988). *Black Presidential Politics in America: A Strategic Approach.* Albany: State University of New York Press.

Waterman, Richard W., Bruce I. Oppenheimer, & James A. Stimson. (1991). "Sequence and Equilibrium in Congressional Election: An Integrated Approach." *Journal of Politics, 53,* 372.

Wattenberg, Martin P. (1981). "The Decline of Political Partisanship in the United States: Negativity or Neutrality?" *American Political Science Review, 75,* 941.

Wattenberg, Martin P. (1984). *The Decline of American Political Parties, 1952–1980.* Cambridge, Mass.: Harvard University Press.

Wattenberg, Martin P. (1986). *The Decline of American Political Parties, 1952–1984.* Cambridge, Mass.: Harvard University Press.

Wattenberg, Martin P. (1989). "The Hollow Realignment Continues: Partisan Change in 1988." Paper presented at the Annual Meeting of the American Political Science Association, Atlanta, Ga.

Wattenberg, Martin P. (1990a). "And Quayle Too: Examining the Electoral Effect of Vice Presidential Candidates." Paper presented at the Annual Meeting of the American Political Science Association, San Francisco.

Wattenberg, Martin P. (1990b). *The Decline of American Political Parties, 1952–1988.* Cambridge, Mass.: Harvard University Press.

Wattenberg, Martin P. (1991). "Dealignment in the American Electorate." In L. Sandy Maisel, ed., *The Encyclopedia of American Political Parties and Elections.* New York: Garland.

Wayne, Stephen J. (1978). *The Legislative Presidency.* New York: Harper & Row.

Wayne, Stephen J. (1981). *The Road to the White House: The Politics of Presidential Elections.* New York: St. Martin's Press.

Wayne, Stephen J. (1984). *The Road to the White House: The Politics of Presidential Elections,* 2d ed. New York: St. Martin's Press.

Wayne, Stephen J. (1988). *The Road to the White House: The Politics of Presidential Elections,* 3d ed. New York: St. Martin's Press.

Wayne, Stephen J. (1992). *The Road to the White House: The Politics of Presidential Elections,* 4th ed. New York: St. Martin's Press.

Weber, Ronald E., Harvey J. Tucker, & Paul Brace. (1991). "Vanishing Marginals in State Legislative Elections." *Legislative Studies Quarterly, 16,* 29.

Weil, Gordon L. (1973). *The Long Shot.* New York: Norton.

Wekkin, Gary D. (1984). "National-State Party Relations: The Democrats." *Political Science Quarterly, 99,* 45.

West, Darrell M. (1990). "Television Advertising in Nomination Politics." Paper prepared for the Annual Meeting of the American Political Science Association, San Francisco.

White, Theodore H. (1961). *The Making of the President, 1960.* New York: Atheneum.

White, Theodore H. (1965). *The Making of the President, 1964.* New York: Atheneum.

White, Theodore H. (1969). *The Making of the President, 1968.* New York: Atheneum.

White, Theodore H. (1973). *The Making of the President, 1972.* New York: Atheneum.

White, Theodore H. (1982). *America in Search of Itself: The Making of the President, 1956–1980.* New York: Harper & Row.

Wilcox, Clyde. (1988). "I Owe It All to Me: Candidates' Investments in Their Own Campaigns." *American Politics Quarterly, 16,* 266.

Williams, T. Harry. (1969). *Huey Long.* New York: Alfred A. Knopf.

Wilson, James Q. (1962). *The Amateur Democrat.* Chicago: University of Chicago Press.

Wilson, James Q. (1973). *Political Organizations.* New York: Basic Books.

Wilson, Woodrow. (1885). *Congressional Government.* Boston: Houghton Mifflin.

Winebrenner, Hugh. (1983). "The Evolution of the Iowa Precinct Caucuses," *Annals of Iowa, 46,* 618.

Winebrenner, Hugh. (1985). "The Iowa Precinct Caucuses: The Making of a Media Event." *Southeastern Political Review.*

Wirthlin, Richard B. (1981). "The Republican Strategy and Its Electoral Consequences." In Seymour Martin Lipset, ed., *Party Coalitions in the 1980s.* San Francisco: Institute for Contemporary Studies.

Witcover, James. (1977). *Marathon: The Pursuit of the Presidency 1972–1976.* New York: Viking.

Wolfinger, Raymond E., & Steven J. Rosenstone. (1980). *Who Votes?* New Haven, Conn.: Yale University Press.

Wright, Gerald C., Robert S. Erikson, & John P. McIver. (1985). "Measuring State Partisanship and Ideology with Survey Data." *Journal of Politics, 47,* 469.

Wright, John R. (1985). "PACs, Contributions, and Roll Calls: An Organizational Perspective." *American Political Science Review, 79,* 400.

Young, James. (1966). *The Washington Community.* New York: Harcourt, Brace and World.

Zuckman, Jill. (1990). "Thirty-Year High in Partisanship Marked 1990 Senate Votes." *Congressional Quarterly Weekly Report, 48,* 4188.

Index